# HOCKEY GUIDE

## 1989-90 EDITION

*Editor/Hockey Guide*
**LARRY WIGGE**

*Compiled by*
**FRANK POLNASZEK**

*Contributing Editor/Hockey Guide*
**BARRY SIEGEL**

*President-Chief Executive Officer*
**RICHARD WATERS**

*Book Publisher*
**GREGORY WILEY**

*Director of Books and Periodicals*
**RON SMITH**

Published by

### The Sporting News

1212 North Lindbergh Boulevard
P.O. Box 56 — St. Louis, MO 63166

Copyright © 1989
The Sporting News Publishing Company

A Times Mirror
Company

**IMPORTANT NOTICE**

The Hockey Guide is protected by copyright. All information, in the form presented here, except playing statistics, was compiled by the publishers and proof is available.
Information from the Hockey Guide must not be used elsewhere without special written permission, and then only with full credit to the Hockey Guide, published by THE SPORTING NEWS, St. Louis, Missouri.

ISBN 0-89204-329-6          ISSN 0278-4955

# TABLE OF CONTENTS

1988-89 NHL Season in Review .................................................................. 3-13
NHL Office Directory ................................................................................ 14
NHL Divisional Alignment ......................................................................... 15
NHL Team Directories and Rosters ......................................................... 16-57
THE SPORTING NEWS 1988-89 NHL All-Star Team ................................. 58
National Hockey League Summary and Statistics, 1988-89 ................. 61-89
NHL Miscellaneous Achievements in 1988-89 ...................................... 90-100
NHL Departmental Leaders .................................................................. 101-103
Stanley Cup Playoffs, 1989 ................................................................... 104-112
Year-by-Year NHL Standings ................................................................ 113-123
Stanley Cup Winners ............................................................................... 124
Stanley Cup Records ............................................................................... 125
NHL Awards and Leaders .................................................................... 126-132
NHL Entry Draft ................................................................................... 133-136
All-Time Individual Records (National Hockey League, World Hockey
    Association, Central Hockey League, American Hockey League,
    International Hockey League) ......................................................... 137-139
American Hockey League ......................................................................... 140
International Hockey League .................................................................... 157
East Coast Hockey League ....................................................................... 170
Memorial Cup Winners ............................................................................. 175
Ontario Hockey League ............................................................................ 176
Western Hockey League ........................................................................... 190
Quebec Major Junior Hockey League ....................................................... 203
American College Hockey ........................................................................ 212
National Hockey League Schedule for 1989-90 ...................................... 236

ON THE COVER: Al MacInnis, who became the first defenseman in the history of the National Hockey League to lead in playoff scoring, was chosen winner of the Conn Smythe Trophy while leading the Calgary Flames to their first-ever Stanley Cup title.

Photo by Paul Bereswill

# Lemieux, Gretzky Battle, But Calgary Bags Title

**By JIM MATHESON**

Jacques Demers once dressed up in a Santa Claus suit and put a Bob Probert jersey under the tree for his boy. Chances are, the Detroit Red Wings' coach would just as soon pull a No. 99 or 66 sweater out of his gift bag today.

Those jersey numbers belong to Wayne Gretzky and Mario Lemieux, who remained the marquee National Hockey League names in 1988-89. Probert, a once-popular winger on Demers' Detroit team, was arrested on drug charges and handed a lifetime suspension by NHL President John Ziegler.

The Probert story was the saddest of an otherwise enjoyable NHL season. Gretzky wrote a wonderful script for the proceedings, first taking his act to Los Angeles in a stunning off-season trade, then leading the lowly Kings to the fourth-best point total in the league while winning his ninth Hart Trophy, given annually to the league's most valuable player. Lemieux captured his second straight Art Ross Trophy (the NHL's top regular-season scorer) with 199 points, compared to Gretzky's 168.

Gretzky and Lemieux were the headliners for a season that included:

•The Calgary Flames winning their first-ever Stanley Cup title and doing it the hard way—beating the Montreal Canadiens at the Forum, where the Habs had never lost a Cup final-ending game.

•The Kings jumping from 68 to 91 points while playing before 24 sellout crowds, and then defeating Gretzky's old teammates, the defending NHL-champion Edmonton Oilers, in a thrilling seven-game Smythe Division semifinal playoff series.

•Guy Lafleur defying the calendar by coming back at age 37 after a four-year retirement to score 45 points for the New York Rangers.

•Detroit captain Steve Yzerman becoming Stevie Wonder with a 155-point performance.

•The Kings' Bernie Nicholls, with a little help from Gretzky, becoming only the fifth player in NHL history to score 70 goals in a season.

The not-so-highlights included:

•Buffalo goalie Clint Malarchuk suffering a partially severed jugular vein during a violent goalmouth collision. "As my heart would beat, it would squirt blood. I

Wayne Gretzky took his amazing talents to Los Angeles and helped the 1988-89 Kings to the NHL's fourth-best point total while winning his ninth Hart Trophy, given annually to the league's most valuable player.

thought I was dying," he said.

• Marcel Dionne, the third-leading point producer (1,771) of all time, being sent to Denver (International Hockey League) by the New York Rangers. "There's no animosity. I'm not bitter. If I stay in New York fine; if I don't fine," said Dionne, who returned and stayed for the last month of the season.

• Philadelphia goalie Ron Hextall getting a 12-game suspension for assaulting Montreal's Chris Chelios during the Wales Conference final playoff series; Rangers defenseman David Shaw, normally a pacifist, getting a 12-game penalty for smacking Lemieux in the chest with his stick; center Stephane Richer (Montreal) and wingers Rick Tocchet (Philadelphia), John Kordic (Montreal) and Miroslav Frycer (Toronto) getting 10-game suspensions for various fighting and stick infractions.

• Boston Coach Terry O'Reilly getting a four-game suspension for punching New Jersey winger Jim Korn after a game.

Gretzky and Lemieux continued their private battle to determine which is Hertz and which is Avis. It appears that the 24-year-old Lemieux slowly is gaining the upper hand in point production.

Over 80 games, the Penguins star scored 85 goals, second only to Gretzky's 92 in 1981-82 and 87 in 1983-84. He fought a nagging wrist injury for a three-week period that might have kept him from challenging Gretzky's one-season record of 215 points (1985-86). As it was, he still outdistanced Gretzky in the scoring race by 31 points and enjoyed several one-game performances that underline his vast talents. And, most importantly, Lemieux helped the Penguins earn their first playoff berth since 1982.

First, Lemieux scored two goals and added six assists for eight points in an October game against St. Louis. Then he enjoyed a five-goal, three-assist New Year's Eve explosion against New Jersey. In the game against the Devils, Lemieux scored one of his record 13 shorthanded goals, he connected off the power play, he scored once at even strength, he scored off a penalty shot and he capped the night by scoring into an empty net.

"I think we all saw Mario's gift, maybe a little late, for Christmas," said Pittsburgh Coach Gene Ubriaco, "But it was a gift for me and all the fans."

"They're going to have to put this one on video for kids to buy and watch," said Rob Brown, Lemieux's linemate. "Even when he wasn't scoring goals, he was putting the puck through legs, making twirls.... It was a classic example of the best hockey player in the world teaching us how to play."

Most observers are not quite ready to concede that title to the 6-foot-4 center. But many, including Gretzky himself, concede that it might just be a matter of time before the scoring records begin to fall.

"New people come along and break your records," Gretzky said. "I did it to guys like Bryan Trottier and Guy Lafleur, and some day Mario will find out how it feels, too. But in the meantime, if he scores 93 goals and has 216 points, I'll be the first one in line to shake his hand."

Lemieux and more than a few of his supporters were shocked when Gretzky was awarded the Hart Trophy. Gretzky was even a little taken aback by the honor.

"This means more to me than ever before," he said. "I didn't really expect to win so I don't want to gloat. I remember leaning over to my wife at the awards ceremony and saying, 'I never really sat anywhere and didn't win. How do you react?' I had a lot of things going through my mind."

About a week before the awards, Gretzky told writers, "Whoever wins, there's going to be controversy."

He was right on. Lemieux, the 1987-88 Hart winner, reacted to the loss like he'd been hit in the head with a lead pipe. He obviously was dazed and hurt.

"In the past they've given the Hart to the best player or the top scorer," he said. "I don't know why it changed. Nothing in this league makes sense."

Nothing made sense about the trade of No. 99 to Los Angeles, either. Gretzky was one of Canada's greatest national resources, its golden boy. But on that infamous August day when Kings Owner Bruce McNall introduced his new prize to the Los Angeles media, the course of West Coast hockey took a dramatic turn.

Nobody expected that even Gretzky could spark such a major turnaround for a mediocre franchise, but then the Great One always has weaved a special brand of magic. When the 80-game season ended, the Kings had averaged 14,875 fans, more than 2,000 higher than their all-time high (in 1974-75). At the paywindow, McNall realized $7-10 million more in revenue.

While Gretzky was leading the Kings to new heights, the Detroit Red Wings were struggling through an 80-point season, 13 below their 1987-88 effort. Part of their problem was the distraction created by the Probert nightmare.

Probert, a 62-point producer in 1987-88, had been battling an alcohol problem for

**Pittsburgh's Mario Lemieux captured his second straight scoring title, outdistancing Wayne Gretzky, 199-168.**

three years. His demise came in March, when he tried to cross the Canadian border between Windsor and Detroit with cocaine hidden in his underwear. A strip search resulted in his arrest and Ziegler quickly banned the veteran winger for life.

"It is a special privilege to play in the National Hockey League, and if you choose to be involved with illegal drugs, you will lose that privilege," Ziegler said in his statement announcing the ban. "If it (drug use) is your choice, we want you out of our business."

"The book is closed on Bob Probert now," Demers said. "His problems just got out of hand."

The Probert distraction did not seem to bother Yzerman, who scored 65 goals and added 90 assists in a superb season. The 24-year-old center was the reason that the Red Wings were able to win their second straight Norris Division title, finishing two points ahead of St. Louis.

"He's the best mortal forward in the world," said a Philadelphia paper, an obvious supporter of the notion that Gretzky and Lemieux are talents from another world.

Nicholls, who'd never scored more than 46 goals in one season, came close to scoring 50 in his first 50 games. His 70-goal, 150-point season included a two-goal, six-assist outburst against Toronto on December 1.

In all, nine players reached the 100-point plateau. Joining Lemieux, Gretzky, Yzerman and Nicholls were Pittsburgh's Rob Brown (115) and Paul Coffey (113), Calgary's Joe Mullen (110) and Edmonton's Jari Kurri (102) and Jimmy Carson (100).

Mullen broke Carson's record for points by an American-born player, while Lemieux, Gretzky (54), Yzerman, Nicholls, Mullen (51) and Calgary's Joe Nieuwendyk (51) all hit the magic 50-goal figure. Nicholls compiled the longest goal-scoring streak (10 games), one more than Yzerman and Tocchet. Nieuwendyk scored five goals against Winnipeg on January 11, tying Lemieux for the biggest one-game outburst.

The back-to-back 50-goal seasons by Nieuwendyk allowed the second-year Calgary center to accomplish a feat achieved only by former New York Islanders star Mike Bossy in his first two NHL seasons (1977-78 and '78-79).

Gretzky scored 54 goals and 114 assists in 1988-89 and did a superb job of improving the Kings, but his chase of Gordie Howe's all-time scoring record (1,850 points) fell 13 points short.

The Great One also returned to Edmonton to score one goal and two assists and lead the Campbell Conference to a 9-5 victory over the Wales Conference in the NHL's All-Star Game in February.

However, the most heart-warming story was Lafleur. The Hall of Famer bucked the odds by returning to the ice and actually played fairly well, scoring 18 goals and adding 27 assists. He rewarded a standing-room crowd at Montreal's Forum by scoring two goals in a 7-5 loss February 4. Many of those fans had paid scalper's prices to get a look at their old hero and to give him a well-deserved, spine-tingling ovation.

"He's our idol," Montreal's Stephane Richer said. "All the young guys in the dressing room were saying, 'The Flower's back.' I know I grew up wanting to be Lafleur, all the French kids in Quebec did."

The season was not without its usual run of coaching changes.

Terry Simpson (New York Islanders), John Brophy (Toronto), Dan Maloney (Winnipeg), Michel Bergeron (New York Rangers), Ted Sator (Buffalo), Robbie Ftorek (Los Angeles) and Larry Pleau (Hartford) all were members of the casualty list. Bergeron's was the cruelest blow. He was let go with two games remaining in the season by General Manager Phil Esposito, who later was purged himself in a Ranger front-office reshuffling.

The Quebec Nordiques replaced Ron Lapointe with Jean Perron when Lapointe had a cancerous kidney removed. Then Perron stepped aside to let Bergeron take over the Quebec coaching duties. In Edmonton, Glen Sather, the sixth winningest coach in NHL history (442), gave up the dual role of coach and general manager after 10 seasons, co-Coach John Muckler taking over bench duties.

"It's time to step away," Sather said, "it's time to rebuild."

Boston's Terry O'Reilly, who took the Bruins to the Stanley Cup finals against Sather's Oilers in 1988, resigned after Boston was able to win only one playoff round in 1989. He was replaced by former Bruins defenseman Mike Milbury.

Filling the other coaching vacancies were Rick Dudley (Buffalo), Bob Murdoch (Winnipeg), Rick Ley (Hartford) and Tom Webster (Los Angeles). Interim coaches Al Arbour (Islanders) and George Armstrong (Toronto) were asked to remain on the job for the 1989-90 season.

The year's biggest trades besides the Gretzky shocker involved goaltenders Kelly Hrudey and Tom Barrasso.

The New York Islanders sent Hrudey to the Kings for defenseman Wayne

**Detroit winger Bob Probert, shown leaving a Detroit courtroom after his arraignment on drug charges, was handed a lifetime suspension by NHL President John Ziegler.**

McBean, goalie Mark Fitzpatrick and a future consideration, which turned out to be veteran defenseman Doug Crossman.

Many felt the Kings had mortgaged their future, but Gretzky merely shrugged.

"If you ask me, the future is way overrated," he said. "People in L.A. won't wait four or five years. They want to win now and don't care what it costs."

Buffalo's Barrasso, the highest-picked goalie in the history of the NHL draft (fifth in 1983), went to Pittsburgh for Doug Bodger and Darrin Shannon, the Penguins' No. 1 draft choice in 1988. Barrasso, who had been shoved aside by Daren Puppa in Buffalo, helped the Penguins reach the Patrick Division playoff final, where they lost to Philadelphia.

In other big deals, the St. Louis Blues dealt center Doug Gilmour and right wing Mark Hunter to Calgary for center Mike Bullard and left wing Craig Coxe. Just over a month into the season, the Blues then sent Bullard to Philadelphia for Peter Zezel. Montreal sent Kordic to Toronto in a deal for center Russ Courtnall.

The Washington Capitals sent winger Mike Gartner to the Minnesota North Stars for winger Dino Ciccarelli, and Malarchuk to Buffalo for defenseman Calle Johansson; the Toronto Maple Leafs peddled goalie Ken Wregget to Philadelphia for two No. 1 draft picks, and the Chicago Black Hawks traded winger Rick Vaive to Buffalo for center Adam Creighton. The Black Hawks also traded a fifth-round draft pick to Winnipeg for goalie Alain Chevrier, who rewarded them by leading them into the Campbell Conference finals.

For the second straight year, the NHL's final playoff berth was earned on the last night of the season at Chicago Stadium. In 1987, New Jersey defeated the Black Hawks on an overtime goal by John MacLean to capture the final spot in the Patrick Division. This time, the Hawks got a goal 48 seconds into sudden death by Troy Murray to defeat Toronto, 4-3, and squeak past the Maple Leafs for the final playoff spot in the Norris Division.

While others were angling for playoff berths, Calgary and Montreal waged a season-long battle for the President's Tro-

**Detroit captain Steve Yzerman enjoyed a superb season, scoring 65 goals and dishing out 90 assists for 155 points.**

phy, awarded to the team that collects the most points during the regular season. The Flames eeked out a 117-115 victory, with Washington finishing a distant third (92 points) and Los Angeles fourth. New Jersey, which advanced to within one win of the Stanley Cup finals in 1988, tumbled to 66 points and failed to make the playoffs.

The Kings ended Edmonton's hopes for a fifth Cup victory in the 1980s by rallying from a 3-1 series deficit to beat the Oilers, 6-3, in Game 7. With the next day's headline proclaiming, 'The kings are dead; long live the Kings!' Gretzky couldn't help but feel compassion for his former teammates.

"Right now I have a lot of mixed emotions," he said. "I really didn't enjoy playing the series. I was very happy we won, but I was disappointed for their players.

"I wanted to talk to them when we shook hands when it was over, but I didn't want to bother them. No one takes losing harder than Mark Messier or Kevin Lowe. I feel most sorry for them. But for the people of L.A., I couldn't be happier."

Gretzky collected 13 points in the series and unsung Chris Kontos, who spent the season in Switzerland before he was signed in March, scored eight goals.

The Kings' joy was shortlived. They were unceremoniously swept from the playoffs in the next round by the charging Flames.

The Flames had barely escaped their first-round series against unheralded Vancouver. The Canucks, who finished 43 points behind Calgary in the regular season, gave the talented Flames everything they could handle throughout the series and it all came down to a Game 7 overtime goal by Calgary's Joel Otto. The Flames were saved, literally, by goaltender Mike Vernon, who made numerous remarkable saves throughout the series to keep them alive.

"Vernon gave us a stay of execution," said Calgary General Manager Cliff Fletcher.

But there was no stopping the Flames after that close call. They wheeled past the Kings in four games and the Black Hawks in five. Meanwhile, Montreal dispatched Hartford in four games, Boston in five and Philadelphia in six to set up a much-anticipated clash with Calgary in the finals.

"This is what everybody expected, wasn't it?" asked Calgary winger Hakan Loob. Indeed, the season had come down to a head-to-head battle between the league's two best regular-season teams. It was also a rematch of the 1986 finals, when the Flames won the opener, but then watched the Canadiens win the next four games for their 23rd Stanley Cup title.

The Flames drew first blood when little Theoren Fleury ripped a shot past Montreal goalie Patrick Roy in the second period to give them a 3-2 victory. For the 5-5, 155-pound Fleury, this was the stuff of which dreams are made. He had grown up in a small Manitoba town as a rabid Canadiens fan. Now, here he was, living out a real-life fantasy.

"This one was for my mum, Mother's Day," he said.

"He's like an Indian rubber ball. You throw him against a wall, and he keeps bouncing back," said Flames Coach Terry Crisp. "He's a little guy who plays like a big man. He's a pest."

While Fleury was buzzing, teammate Al MacInnis was stinging. In the opener, the Calgary defenseman scored two goals and

**One of the season's most heartwarming stories was the comeback of former Montreal great Guy Lafleur, who returned to the ice after a four-year retirement and scored 45 points for the New York Rangers.**

**One of the major reasons behind Calgary's 1988-89 success was Joe Mullen, who compiled 110 points during the season and then enjoyed a big playoff.**

took his first step toward winning the Conn Smythe Trophy as playoff MVP. He had the Montreal faithful shaking their heads.

"On his first goal (a 40-footer), they could have put a piece of plexiglass in front of the goal and it wouldn't have made a difference," said Canadiens Coach Pat Burns. "Patrick wasn't going to stop it."

Montreal came back in Game 2 to tie the series with a 4-2 victory at Calgary's Saddledome. The hero for the Canadiens was Chris Chelios, the Norris Trophy winner as the league's top defenseman. He hammered a shot past Vernon eight minutes into the third period and Montreal never lost its lead.

"He's the complete player. He can shoot, maybe not like MacInnis, but when there's adversity and a lot of stuff written, Chris and our team seem to rise to the occasion," said fellow Montreal defenseman Craig Ludwig. "And if Chris is the villain, it doesn't bother him."

Chelios, who has carried a reputation as a scrapper and an off-ice troublemaker, was booed roundly by the Calgary crowd, but took it all in stride.

"He may not be the most popular player because if you give him a shot he'll give it back. But that's the way he is," said Burns, who asked Chelios to say a few words to his teammates after the Canadiens were outshot, 16-4, and outscored, 2-0, in the a bad second period in which the Flames had tied the score.

"I think he's proven beyond a doubt that he's a professional and his heart's in the right place."

Game 3 in Montreal began on Friday night and turned into Saturday Morning Live. Ryan Walter put an end to the second-longest Cup final game in history when he put a short shot past Vernon with 1:52 remaining in the second overtime. It was 12:20 a.m. when Walter gave Montreal its 4-3 victory, a win that seemed improbable with only 41 seconds to play in the third period. That's when Mats Naslund whipped a 40-footer past Vernon to tie the score.

"You begin to wonder if it will ever end," said Walter. "I didn't do much on the goal... it was all Stephane (Richer). It looked like he was going to go behind the net and he threw it back to me. Next thing I know, the puck's in the net and Larry (Robinson) is grabbing me and punching my helmet into my face. I could hardly breathe."

It looked like Montreal was on its last breath until Naslund gulped once or twice and sent his Hail Mary shot sailing past

**Calgary defenseman Al MacInnis, who possesses one of the hardest shots in the league, enjoyed an excellent playoff run and walked away with the Conn Smythe Trophy, given annually to the playoff MVP.**

Vernon. That came after he pounced on an errant clearing pass by Calgary's best defenseman, Brad McCrimmon.

"Of course we dodged a bullet. But you pull the goalie... and all you do is hope," Burns said.

"No sense being depressed," Crisp said. "Why should we feel sorry, nobody else is for us. I hope we're angry."

They certainly appeared to be as they came out and controlled Game 4 while recording a 4-2 victory. The importance of the series-tying win was not lost on the Flames.

"Biggest win in the franchise," said Vernon.

"I guess we've reached a different plateau now," said Fletcher. "We only won the one game from Montreal when we played them in 1986. We knew that if we'd lost to go down 3-1... well I didn't like our chances."

Mullen keyed the victory with a pair of goals, his 14th and 15th of the playoffs. MacInnis also blew a 20-footer past Roy late in the third period, and Vernon robbed Naslund on a key shot to keep the momentum from shifting.

"Having a day between games helped to get the anger out of our system," Vernon said. "It really devastated us to lose like we did (in Game 3). But once we stepped back and thought it over, we realized in our minds we'd been outplaying them. We just needed more fire."

MacInnis scored another game-winner in Game 5, as the Flames built a 3-1 cushion and held on for a 3-2 triumph over Montreal. The goal ran MacInnis' consecutive point streak to 16 playoff games.

"What can you do?" shrugged Roy.

"He's got the type of shot where you have no idea where it's going to go," said Flames' backup Rick Wamsley. "There's no anticipation, so you start spreading out and hope it hits you."

Mullen doesn't have MacInnis' cannon, but he got his 16th playoff goal to help the cause. His play was inspirational to at least one person in the Saddledome.

"I'd like to adopt the guy," said Crisp. "He's a throwback to Gordie Howe and Glenn Hall. No hoopla, no banners. Just put the jersey on him and stand back and watch him play."

In the final game, the ghosts of Cups past finally left the haunted Forum after 61 years of perfect attendance. The Flames defied history by becoming the first visiting team to end a Stanley Cup final series at the Forum since 1928. At that time, it was the Rangers beating the Montreal Maroons.

"I was only a rookie then... I didn't play in the game," kidded Lanny McDonald, who finished out a 16-year career with a goal to break a 1-1 tie early in the second period of the Flames' 4-2 Cup-clinching victory. It was the first time in 12 tries since 1928 that anybody other than the Canadiens had embraced the silver mug at the Forum.

"Screw the ghosts," said Nieuwendyk early in the six-game series.

"I was out there looking for them in the morning, but then they only come out at night, right?" laughed Crisp.

Back in Edmonton, Sather didn't appear upset over the prospect of the Cup going to the arch-rival Flames.

"They were the best team all year," he said. "I don't dislike anybody down there. I've done TV commercials with Lanny (McDonald) and (assistant general manager) Doug Risebrough is a good friend."

But didn't it burn him that he'd be seeing a Stanley Cup banner at the Saddledome.

"Not really," he said. "We've got four of them."

Crisp didn't argue the point.

"This was no message to Edmonton," he said. "We're still three behind them with a long way to go. Really, the biggest thing that happened to our club was getting swept four straight in '88. It was a very long summer."

But it wouldn't be this time around.

"You know I scored my first NHL goal at the Forum. So it's a heck of a way to...." McDonald said, not wanting to say retire after more than 500 career goals and 1,000 points. "Who knows, maybe I'll drop back and play defense for another five or six years. Winning the Cup was the most peaceful feeling in the world."

MacInnis, who got assists on goals by Colin Patterson and Gilmour in the final game to run his point streak to 17 games (only Bryan Trottier's streak of 18 was longer), finished the playoffs with 31 points. In the process, he became the first defenseman ever to lead the NHL in playoff scoring.

"I guess I couldn't have picked a better time to get hot. The coaches kept saying shoot, fire it," he said.

"He doesn't have the hardest shot in the league for nothing," Nieuwendyk said. "We kept working it around to get him open."

"I guess when I look back over the summer, when I'm having a few ginger ales, it'll sink in," joked MacInnis.

So will winning the Cup for the Flames, who have been cursed to play in the same division as the Oilers all these years.

"Now I know how Glen (Sather) and Bill (Islander General Manager Torrey) felt," said Fletcher, who never griped that Calgary's time hadn't come. "There's no divine right in sports. You have to earn it."

Certainly the Canadiens know that.

"I don't feel we have to apologize to the Richard brothers or (Jean) Beliveau. We gave it all we had," said Bobby Smith.

"It was a lot like the regular season," Burns added. "We came up short then and a little short in the playoffs."

**Lanny McDonald capped his 16-year NHL career by triumphantly hoisting the Stanley Cup.**

# National Hockey League

Organized November 22, 1917

## NHL Offices

**John A. Ziegler, Jr.**

Sun Life Building
1155 Metcalfe Street, Suite 960
Montreal, Que., Canada H3B 2W2
Phone—(514) 871-9220

Central Scouting & Officiating
Suite 200, 1 Greensboro Drive
Rexdale, Ont. M9W 1C8
Phone—(416) 245-2926

650 Fifth Avenue
33rd Floor
New York, NY 10019
Phone—(212) 398-1100

| | |
|---|---|
| Chairman of the Board | WILLIAM W. WIRTZ |
| President | JOHN A. ZIEGLER, JR. |
| Vice-Chairman | RONALD COREY |
| | |
| Secretary | ROBERT O. SWADOS |
| Executive Vice-President | BRIAN F. O'NEILL |
| Vice-President and General Counsel | GILBERT STEIN |
| Vice-President, Finance | KENNETH G. SAWYER |
| Vice-President, Hockey Operations | JIM GREGORY |
| Vice-President, Project Development | IAN "SCOTTY" MORRISON |
| Vice-President, Broadcasting | JOEL NIXON |
| Vice-President, Marketing-Public Relations | STEVE RYAN |
|    Director of Central Registry | Garry Lovegrove |
|    Director of Officiating | Bryan Lewis |
|    Assistant Director of Officiating | Wally Harris |
|    Director of Public Relations | Gerry Helper (New York) |
|    Executive Director of Communications | Gary Meagher (Montreal) |
|    Director of Broadcasting and Publishing | Stu Hackel |
|    Supervisors of Officials | John Ashley, Matt Pavelich, Jim Christison, John D'Amico |
|    Coordinator of Development | Will Norris |
|    Director of Administration | Phil Scheuer |
|    Director of Security | Frank Torpey |
|    Assistant Director of Security | Al Wiseman |

# National Hockey League

## 1989-90

### Campbell Conference

#### Smythe Division
Calgary Flames
Edmonton Oilers
Los Angeles Kings
Vancouver Canucks
Winnipeg Jets

#### Norris Division
Chicago Black Hawks
Detroit Red Wings
Minnesota North Stars
St. Louis Blues
Toronto Maple Leafs

### Prince Of Wales Conference

#### Patrick Division
New Jersey Devils
New York Islanders
New York Rangers
Philadelphia Flyers
Pittsburgh Penguins
Washington Capitals

#### Adams Division
Boston Bruins
Buffalo Sabres
Hartford Whalers
Montreal Canadiens
Quebec Nordiques

## Board of Governors

| | |
|---|---|
| Jeremy M. Jacobs ................................ Boston | John O. Pickett, Jr. ................................ N. Y. Islanders |
| Seymour H. Knox, III ........................... Buffalo | Richard H. Evans ...................... N. Y. Rangers |
| Cliff Fletcher ....................................... Calgary | Jay T. Snider ................................ Philadelphia |
| William W. Wirtz ................................ Chicago | Marie Denise DeBartolo York ........................ Pittsburgh |
| Michael Ilitch ..................................... Detroit | Marcel Aubut ..................................... Quebec |
| Peter Pocklington ........................... Edmonton | Michael F. Shanahan ........................ St. Louis |
| Richard H. Gordon ........................... Hartford | Harold E. Ballard ............................... Toronto |
| Bruce McNall ...................... Los Angeles | Frank A. Griffiths ............................ Vancouver |
| George Gund III .............................. Minnesota | Abe Pollin .......................... Washington |
| Ronald Corey ...................... Montreal | Barry L. Shenkarow ........................ Winnipeg |
| John J. McMullen ........................... New Jersey | |

# Boston Bruins
## Adams Division

| | |
|---|---|
| Owner and Governor | Jeremy M. Jacobs |
| Chief Operating Officer | Louis Reif |
| Alternative Governor | Louis Jacobs |
| Alternate Governor, President and General Manager | Harry Sinden |
| Vice President | Tom Johnson |
| Assistant to the President | Nate Greenberg |
| Director of Administration | Dale Hamilton |
| Assistant General Manager and Coach | Mike Milbury |
| Assistant Coaches | Gordie Clark, Ted Sator |
| Goaltending Coach | Joe Bertagna |
| Coordinator of Minor League Player Personnel/Scouting | Bob Tindall |
| Director of Player Evaluation | Bart Bradley |
| Scouting Staff | Jim Morrison, Andre Lachapelle, Joe Lyons, Don Saatzer, Lars Waldner, Marcel Pelletier, Jean Ratelle |
| Controller | John J. Dionne |
| Trainer | Jim Narrigan |
| Equipment Manager | Bob Crocker, Jr. |
| Director of Media Relations | Heidi Holland |
| Home Ice | Boston Garden |
| Address | 150 Causeway Street, Boston, Mass. 02114 |
| Seating Capacity | 14,448 |
| Club colors | Gold, Black and White |
| Phone | (617) 227-3206 |

**Harry Sinden**

**Tom Johnson**

**Mike Milbury**

# Boston Bruins 1989-90 Roster

## FORWARDS

| Name | Hgt. | Wgt. | Place of Birth | Date | 1988-89 Club | G. | A. | Pts. |
|---|---|---|---|---|---|---|---|---|
| Benic, Geoff | 6:03 | 210 | Toronto, Ont. | 9-1-68 | Indianapolis | 1 | 0 | 1 |
| Beraldo, Paul | 5:11 | 175 | Hamilton, Ont. | 10-5-67 | Maine-Boston | 25 | 28 | 53 |
| Brickley, Paul | 5:11 | 200 | Melrose, Mass. | 8-9-61 | Boston | 13 | 22 | 35 |
| Buda, Dave | 6:04 | 190 | Mississauga, Ont. | 3-14-66 | Northeastern Univ.-Maine | 26 | 24 | 50 |
| Burridge, Randy | 5:09 | 180 | Fort Erie, Ont. | 1-7-66 | Boston | 31 | 30 | 61 |
| Byers, Lyndon | 6:01 | 200 | Nipawin, Sask. | 2-29-64 | Boston-Maine | 1 | 7 | 8 |
| Carpenter, Bobby | 6:00 | 190 | Beverly, Mass. | 7-13-63 | Los Angeles-Boston | 16 | 24 | 40 |
| Carter, John | 5:10 | 175 | Winchester, Mass. | 5-3-63 | Boston-Maine | 25 | 16 | 41 |
| Cimetta, Rob | 6:00 | 190 | Toronto, Ont. | 2-15-70 | Toronto Jrs.-Boston | 57 | 47 | 104 |
| Crawford, Lou | 6:00 | 185 | Belleville, Ont. | 11-5-62 | Adirondack | 23 | 23 | 46 |
| Cruickshank, Gord | 5:11 | 185 | Mississauga, Ont. | 4-4-65 | Did not play | .. | .. | .. |
| Douris, Peter | 6:01 | 195 | Toronto, Ont. | 2-19-66 | Peoria | 28 | 41 | 69 |
| Hall, Dean | 6:01 | 175 | Winnipeg, Man. | 1-14-68 | Seattle-Northern Michigan U. | 18 | 19 | 37 |
| Harlow, Scott | 6:01 | 185 | E. Bridgewater, Mass. | 10-11-63 | Peoria-Maine | 32 | 44 | 76 |
| Janney, Craig | 6:01 | 190 | Hartford, Ct. | 9-26-67 | Boston | 16 | 46 | 62 |
| Jensen, David | 6:01 | 195 | Newton, Mass. | 8-19-65 | Maine | 12 | 8 | 20 |
| Johnston, Greg | 6:01 | 190 | Barrie, Ont. | 1-14-65 | Boston-Maine | 16 | 16 | 32 |
| Joyce, Bob | 6:01 | 195 | St. John, N.B. | 7-11-66 | Boston | 18 | 31 | 49 |
| Kekalainen, Jarmo | 6:00 | 190 | Kuopio, Finland | 7-3-66 | Clarkson Univ. | 19 | 25 | 44 |
| Lalonde, Todd | 6:00 | 190 | Sudbury, Ont. | 8-4-69 | Sudbury | 32 | 44 | 76 |
| Linseman, Ken | 5:11 | 180 | Kingston, Ont. | 8-11-58 | Boston | 27 | 45 | 72 |
| Markwart, Nevin | 5:10 | 180 | Toronto, Ont. | 12-9-64 | Maine | 0 | 1 | 1 |
| Montanari, Mark | 5:09 | 185 | Toronto, Ont. | 6-3-69 | Kitchener | 33 | 69 | 102 |
| Neely, Cam | 6:01 | 210 | Comox, B.C. | 6-6-65 | Boston | 37 | 38 | 75 |
| Neufeld, Ray | 6:03 | 210 | St. Boniface, Man. | 4-15-59 | Winnipeg-Boston | 6 | 5 | 11 |
| O'Dwyer, Billy | 6:00 | 190 | S. Boston, Mass. | 1-25-60 | Boston | 1 | 2 | 3 |
| Penney, Jackson | 5:10 | 180 | Edmonton, Alta. | 2-5-69 | Victoria | 41 | 49 | 90 |
| Stevenson, Shayne | 6:01 | 190 | London, Ont. | 10-26-70 | Kitchener | 25 | 50 | 75 |
| Sweeney, Bob | 6:03 | 200 | Concord, Mass. | 1-25-64 | Boston | 14 | 14 | 28 |
| Townshend, Graeme | 6:02 | 225 | Kingston, Jamaica | 10-23-65 | RPI-Maine | 8 | 17 | 25 |
| Turcotte, Alfie | 5:09 | 170 | Gary, Ind. | 6-5-65 | Moncton | 27 | 39 | 66 |
| Walz, Wes | 5:10 | 180 | Calgary, Alta. | 5-15-70 | Lethbridge | 29 | 75 | 104 |

## DEFENSEMEN

| Name | Hgt. | Wgt. | Place of Birth | Date | 1988-89 Club | G. | A. | Pts. |
|---|---|---|---|---|---|---|---|---|
| Allain, Rick | 6:00 | 190 | Guelph, Ont. | 5-20-69 | Kitchener | 2 | 16 | 18 |
| Beers, Bob | 6:02 | 200 | Cheektowaga, N.Y. | 5-20-67 | Univ. of Maine | 10 | 27 | 37 |
| Blum, John | 6:03 | 205 | Detroit, Mich. | 10-8-59 | Adirondack-Detroit | 1 | 19 | 20 |
| Bourque, Ray | 5:11 | 210 | Montreal, Que. | 12-28-60 | Boston | 18 | 43 | 61 |
| Cote, Alain | 6:00 | 200 | Montmagny, Que. | 4-14-67 | Maine-Boston | 7 | 19 | 26 |
| Galley, Garry | 6:00 | 190 | Montreal, Que. | 4-16-63 | Boston | 8 | 22 | 30 |
| Hawgood, Greg | 5:08 | 175 | Edmonton, Alta. | 8-10-68 | Boston-Maine | 18 | 33 | 51 |
| Kluzak, Gord | 6:04 | 215 | Climax, Sask. | 3-4-64 | Boston | 0 | 1 | 1 |
| Moore, Steve | 6:02 | 185 | Toronto, Ont. | 1-21-67 | RPI | 2 | 10 | 12 |
| Pedersen, Allen | 6:03 | 210 | Ft. Saskatchewan, Alta. | 1-13-65 | Boston | 0 | 6 | 6 |
| Quintal, Stephane | 6:03 | 215 | Boucherville, Que. | 10-22-68 | Maine-Boston | 4 | 11 | 15 |
| Schulman, Jeff | 6:03 | 210 | Buffalo, N.Y. | 2-15-67 | Univ. of Vermont | 3 | 4 | 7 |
| Shoebottom, Bruce | 6:02 | 200 | Windsor, Ont. | 8-20-65 | Maine-Boston | 1 | 11 | 12 |
| Sirkka, Jeff | 6:01 | 200 | Sudbury, Ont. | 6-17-68 | North Bay-Toronto Jrs. | 0 | 11 | 11 |
| Sweeney, Don | 5:11 | 170 | St. Stephen, N.B. | 8-17-66 | Maine-Boston | 11 | 22 | 33 |
| Thelven, Michael | 5:11 | 185 | Stockholm, Sweden | 1-7-61 | Boston | 3 | 18 | 21 |
| Wesley, Glen | 6:01 | 195 | Red Deer, Alta. | 10-2-68 | Boston | 19 | 35 | 54 |
| Wiemer, Jim | 6:04 | 210 | Sudbury, Ont. | 1-9-61 | Cape Breton-Los Ang.-N. Haven | 15 | 33 | 48 |

## GOALTENDERS

| Name | Hgt. | Wgt. | Place of Birth | Date | 1988-89 Club | Mins. | GA. | SO. |
|---|---|---|---|---|---|---|---|---|
| Caprice, Frank | 5:09 | 165 | Hamilton, Ont. | 5-2-62 | Milwaukee | 2204 | 143 | 2 |
| Foster, Norm | 5:09 | 175 | Vancouver, B.C. | 2-10-65 | Maine | 2411 | 156 | 1 |
| Jeffrey, Mike | 6:03 | 195 | Kamloops, B.C. | 4-6-65 | Maine | 2368 | 148 | 1 |
| Lemelin, Reggie | 5:11 | 170 | Quebec City, Que. | 11-19-54 | Boston | 2396 | 120 | 0 |
| Moog, Andy | 5:08 | 170 | Penticton, B.C. | 2-18-60 | Boston | 2486 | 133 | 1 |
| Parson, Mike | 6:00 | 170 | Listowell, Ont. | 3-12-70 | Guelph | 3047 | 194 | 0 |

# Buffalo Sabres
### Adams Division

| | |
|---|---|
| Chairman of the Board and President | Seymour H. Knox III |
| Vice-Chairman of the Board and Counsel | Robert O. Swados |
| Vice-Chairman of the Board | Robert E. Rich, Jr. |
| Treasurer | Joseph T. J. Stewart |
| Assistant to the President | Seymour H. Knox IV |
| Senior Vice-President, Administration | Mitchell Owen |
| Senior Vice-President, Finance | Robert W. Pickel |
| General Manager | Gerry Meehan |
| Coach | Rick Dudley |
| Assistant Coaches | Don Lever, John Tortorella |
| Director of Professional Evaluation and Development | Craig Ramsay |
| Director of Amateur Evaluation and Development | Don Luce |
| Director of Scouting | Rudy Migay |
| Coordinator of Minor League Professional Development | Joe Crozier |
| Scouting Staff | Don Barrie, Jack Bowman, Larry Carriere, Frank Deegan, Dennis McIvor, Paul Merritt, Mike Racicot, Frank Zywiec |
| Director of Communications | Paul Wieland |
| Director of Public Relations | John Gurtler |
| Director of Information | Budd Bailey |
| Trainer | Jim Pizzutelli |
| Assistant Trainer | Rip Simonick |
| Equipment Supervisor | John Heidinger |
| Home Ice | Memorial Auditorium |
| Address | Memorial Auditorium, Buffalo, N.Y. 14202 |
| Seating Capacity | 16,433 (including standees) |
| Club Colors | Blue, White and Gold |
| Phone | (716) 856-7300 or (800) 333-7825 |

Seymour Knox III

Gerry Meehan

Rick Dudley

# Buffalo Sabres 1989-90 Roster

## FORWARDS

| Name | Hgt. | Wgt. | Place of Birth | Date | 1988-89 Club | G. | A. | Pts. |
|---|---|---|---|---|---|---|---|---|
| Andersson, Mikael | 5:11 | 183 | Malmo, Sweden | 5-10-66 | Buffalo-Rochester | 18 | 34 | 52 |
| Andreychuk, Dave | 6:03 | 214 | Hamilton, Ont. | 9-29-63 | Buffalo | 28 | 24 | 52 |
| Arniel, Scott | 6:01 | 188 | Kingston, Ont. | 7-17-62 | Buffalo | 18 | 23 | 41 |
| Audette, Donald | 5:08 | 182 | Laval, Que. | 9-23-69 | Laval | 76 | 85 | 161 |
| Boyce, Ian | 5:08 | 177 | St. Laurent, Que. | 1-24-68 | Univ. of Vermont | 15 | 27 | 42 |
| Brydges, Paul | 5:11 | 180 | Guelph, Ont. | 6-21-65 | Rochester | 8 | 3 | 11 |
| Corkum, Bob | 6:02 | 195 | Salisbury, Mass. | 12-18-67 | Univ. of Maine | 17 | 31 | 48 |
| deCarle, Mike | 6:00 | 180 | Covina, Calif. | 8-20-66 | Lake Superior State | 20 | 24 | 44 |
| Donnelly, Mike | 5:11 | 185 | Detroit, Mich. | 10-10-63 | Rochester-Buffalo | 36 | 43 | 79 |
| Foligno, Mike | 6:02 | 195 | Sudbury, Ont. | 1-29-59 | Buffalo | 27 | 22 | 49 |
| Gage, Jody | 6:00 | 188 | Toronto, Ont. | 11-29-59 | Rochester | 31 | 38 | 69 |
| Guay, Francois | 6:00 | 186 | Gatineau, Que. | 6-8-68 | Rochester | 6 | 20 | 26 |
| Hartman, Mike | 6:00 | 183 | Detroit, Mich. | 2-7-67 | Buffalo | 8 | 9 | 17 |
| Hogue, Benoit | 5:10 | 177 | Repentigny, Que. | 10-28-66 | Buffalo | 14 | 30 | 44 |
| Jackson, Jim | 5:08 | 190 | Oshawa, Ont. | 2-1-60 | Rochester | 19 | 50 | 69 |
| Kerr, Kevin | 5:10 | 170 | North Bay, Ont. | 9-18-67 | Rochester | 20 | 18 | 38 |
| Loewen, Darcy | 5:10 | 182 | Calgary, Alta. | 2-26-69 | Spokane | 31 | 27 | 58 |
| MacVicar, Andrew | 6:01 | 195 | Dartmouth, N.S. | 3-12-69 | Peterborough | 25 | 29 | 54 |
| Maguire, Kevin | 6:02 | 200 | Trenton, Ont. | 1-5-63 | Buffalo | 8 | 10 | 18 |
| Martin, Grant | 5:10 | 190 | Smooth Rock F'lls, Ont. | 3-13-62 | Rochester | 7 | 5 | 12 |
| McCrory, Scott | 5:10 | 175 | Sudbury, Ont. | 2-27-67 | Baltimore | 38 | 51 | 89 |
| Metcalfe, Scott | 6:00 | 195 | Toronto, Ont. | 1-6-67 | Rochester-Buffalo | 21 | 32 | 53 |
| Mogilny, Alexander | 5:11 | 186 | Khabarovski, USSR | 2-18-69 | Central Red Army | 11 | 11 | 22 |
| Napier, Mark | 5:10 | 183 | Toronto, Ont. | 1-28-57 | Buffalo | 11 | 17 | 28 |
| Nelson, John | 5:10 | 174 | Scarborough, Ont. | 7-9-69 | Toronto Jrs. | 39 | 60 | 99 |
| Parker, Jeff | 6:03 | 194 | St. Paul, Minn. | 9-7-64 | Rochester-Buffalo | 11 | 13 | 24 |
| Priestlay, Ken | 5:10 | 187 | Vancouver, B.C. | 8-24-67 | Rochester-Buffalo | 58 | 37 | 95 |
| Ray, Robert | 6:00 | 203 | Stirling, Ont. | 6-8-68 | Rochester | 11 | 18 | 29 |
| Ruuttu, Christian | 5:11 | 190 | Laappen, Finland | 2-20-64 | Buffalo | 14 | 46 | 60 |
| Savage, Joel | 5:11 | 195 | Surrey, B.C. | 12-25-69 | Victoria | 37 | 32 | 69 |
| Shannon, Darrin | 6:02 | 190 | Barrie, Ont. | 12-8-69 | Windsor | 33 | 48 | 81 |
| Sheppard, Ray | 6:01 | 186 | Pembroke, Ont. | 5-27-66 | Buffalo | 22 | 21 | 43 |
| Tkachuk, Grant | 5:10 | 180 | L. LaBiche, Alta. | 9-24-68 | Rochester | 12 | 13 | 25 |
| Tucker, John | 6:00 | 200 | Windsor, Ont. | 9-29-64 | Buffalo | 13 | 31 | 44 |
| Turgeon, Pierre | 6:01 | 203 | Rouyn, Que. | 8-29-69 | Buffalo | 34 | 54 | 88 |
| Vaive, Rick | 6:01 | 192 | Ottawa, Ont. | 5-14-59 | Chicago-Buffalo | 31 | 26 | 57 |

## DEFENSEMEN

| Name | Hgt. | Wgt. | Place of Birth | Date | 1988-89 Club | G. | A. | Pts. |
|---|---|---|---|---|---|---|---|---|
| Anderson, Shawn | 6:01 | 196 | Montreal, Que. | 2-7-68 | Buffalo-Rochester | 7 | 24 | 31 |
| Baseggio, Dave | 6:03 | 210 | Niagara Falls, Ont. | 10-28-67 | Yale Univ. | 10 | 23 | 33 |
| Bodger, Doug | 6:02 | 200 | Chemainus, B.C. | 6-18-66 | Pittsburgh-Buffalo | 8 | 44 | 52 |
| Dunn, Richie | 6:00 | 200 | Boston, Mass. | 5-12-57 | Rochester-Buffalo | 9 | 35 | 44 |
| Halkidis, Bob | 5:11 | 200 | Toronto, Ont. | 3-5-66 | Buffalo-Rochester | 0 | 7 | 7 |
| Haller, Kevin | 6:02 | 182 | Trochu, Alta. | 12-5-70 | Regina | 10 | 31 | 41 |
| Hofford, Jim | 6:00 | 195 | Sudbury, Ont. | 10-4-64 | Rochester | 1 | 9 | 10 |
| Housley, Phil | 5:10 | 179 | St. Paul, Minn. | 3-9-64 | Buffalo | 26 | 44 | 70 |
| Krupp, Uwe | 6:06 | 230 | Cologne, W. Germany | 6-24-65 | Buffalo | 5 | 13 | 18 |
| Ledyard, Grant | 6:02 | 190 | Winnipeg, Man. | 11-19-61 | Washington-Buffalo | 4 | 16 | 20 |
| McSween, Don | 5:11 | 194 | Detroit, Mich. | 6-9-64 | Rochester | 7 | 22 | 29 |
| Miller, Brad | 6:04 | 200 | Edmonton, Alta. | 7-23-69 | Regina | 8 | 18 | 26 |
| Playfair, Larry | 6:04 | 225 | Ft. St. James, B.C. | 6-23-58 | Los Angeles-Buffalo | 0 | 6 | 6 |
| Ramsey, Mike | 6:03 | 187 | Minneapolis, Minn. | 12-3-60 | Buffalo | 2 | 14 | 16 |
| Smith, Steve | 5:09 | 195 | Trenton, Ont. | 4-4-63 | Rochester-Buffalo | 2 | 12 | 14 |
| Sutton, Ken | 6:00 | 184 | Edmonton, Alta. | 5-11-69 | Saskatoon | 22 | 31 | 53 |
| Whitham, Shawn | 5:11 | 175 | Verdun, Que. | 3-13-67 | Rochester | 4 | 15 | 19 |

## GOALTENDERS

| Name | Hgt. | Wgt. | Place of Birth | Date | 1988-89 Club | Mins. | GA. | SO. |
|---|---|---|---|---|---|---|---|---|
| Cloutier, Jacques | 5:07 | 167 | Noranda, Que. | 1-3-60 | Buffalo-Rochester | 2313 | 149 | 0 |
| Eliot, Darren | 6:01 | 175 | Hamilton, Ont. | 11-26-61 | Rochester-Buffalo | 1036 | 66 | 0 |
| Ford, Brian | 5:10 | 170 | Edmonton, Alta. | 9-22-61 | Rochester | 1075 | 60 | 2 |
| Malarchuk, Clint | 6:00 | 190 | Grande, Alta. | 5-1-61 | Washington-Buffalo | 2764 | 154 | 2 |
| Puppa, Daren | 6:03 | 197 | Kirkland Lake, Ont. | 3-23-65 | Buffalo | 1908 | 107 | 1 |
| Wakaluk, Darcy | 5:11 | 176 | Pincher Creek, Alta. | 3-14-66 | Rochester-Buffalo | 1780 | 112 | 1 |

# Calgary Flames
## Smythe Division

| | |
|---|---|
| Owners | Norman N. Green, Harley N. Hotchkiss, Norman L. Kwong, Mrs. Sonia Scurfield, Byron J. Seaman, Daryl K. Seaman |
| President, General Manager and Governor | Cliff Fletcher |
| Vice-President, Business and Finance | Clare Rhyasen |
| Vice-President, Hockey Operations | Al MacNeil |
| Vice-President, Sales and Broadcasting | Leo Ornest |
| Assistant to the President | Al Coates |
| Assistant General Manager | Doug Risebrough |
| Coach | Terry Crisp |
| Assistant Coaches | Tom Watt, Paul Baxter |
| Goaltending Consultant | Glenn Hall |
| Director of Public Relations | Rick Skaggs |
| Assistant Public Relations Director | Mike Burke |
| Chief Scout | Gerry Blair |
| Coordinator of Scouting | Ian McKenzie |
| Area Scouts | Al Godfrey, Larry Popein, Ray Clearwater, Lou Reycroft |
| Scouting Staff | Ben Hays, Garth Malarchuk, David Mayville, Gerry McNamara, Lars Norrman, Tom Thompson, Bill White |
| Controller | Lynne Tosh |
| Trainer | Jim "Bearcat" Murray |
| Equipment Manager | Bobby Stewart |
| Home Ice | The Olympic Saddledome |
| Address | P.O. Box 1540, Station M, Calgary, Alta. T2P 3B9 |
| Seating Capacity | 20,002 |
| Club colors | Red, White and Gold |
| Phone | (403) 261-0475 |

Cliff Fletcher

Al MacNeil

Doug Risebrough

Terry Crisp

# Calgary Flames 1989-90 Roster

| FORWARDS | Hgt. | Wgt. | Place of Birth | Date | 1988-89 Club | G. | A. | Pts. |
|---|---|---|---|---|---|---|---|---|
| Barkovich, Rick | 5:09 | 185 | Kirkland Lake, Ont. | 4-25-64 | Indianapolis | 32 | 35 | 67 |
| Bergqvist, Jonas | 5:11 | 185 | Sweden | 9-26-62 | Leksand | .. | .. | .. |
| Bucyk, Randy | 5:11 | 180 | Edmonton, Alta. | 11- 9-62 | Salt Lake | 28 | 59 | 87 |
| Bureau, Marc | 6:00 | 190 | Trois Rivieres, Que. | 5-19-66 | Salt Lake | 28 | 36 | 64 |
| Chernomaz, Rich | 5:08 | 185 | Selkirk, Man. | 9- 1-63 | Salt Lake-Calgary | 33 | 68 | 101 |
| Deasley, Bryan | 6:03 | 205 | Toronto, Ont. | 11-26-68 | Team Canada | 19 | 19 | 38 |
| Fleury, Theoren | 5:06 | 160 | Oxbow, Sask. | 6-29-68 | Salt Lake-Calgary | 51 | 57 | 108 |
| Gilmour, Doug | 5:11 | 170 | Kingston, Ont. | 6-25-63 | Calgary | 26 | 59 | 85 |
| Grimson, Stu | 6:05 | 220 | Kamloops, B.C. | 5-20-65 | Salt Lake | 9 | 18 | 27 |
| Hayward, Rick | 6:00 | 180 | Toledo, O. | 2-25-66 | Salt Lake | 4 | 20 | 24 |
| Holmes, Mark | 6:02 | 200 | Kingston, Jamaica | 6- 7-64 | Salt Lake | 6 | 12 | 18 |
| Hrdina, Jiri | 6:00 | 195 | Prague, Czech. | 1- 5-58 | Calgary | 22 | 32 | 54 |
| Hunter, Mark | 6:00 | 200 | Petrolia, Ont. | 11-12-62 | Calgary | 22 | 8 | 30 |
| Hunter, Tim | 6:02 | 202 | Calgary, Alta. | 9-10-60 | Calgary | 3 | 9 | 12 |
| Lappin, Peter | 5:11 | 185 | St. Charles, Ill. | 12-31-65 | Salt Lake | 48 | 42 | 90 |
| MacLellan, Brian | 6:03 | 215 | Guelph, Ont. | 10-27-58 | Minnesota-Calgary | 18 | 26 | 44 |
| Mahoney, Scott | 5:10 | 190 | Peterborough, Ont. | 4-19-69 | Oshawa | 14 | 22 | 36 |
| Makarov, Sergei | 5:11 | 185 | Chelyabinsk, USSR | 6-19-58 | Central Red Army | 21 | 33 | 54 |
| Matteau, Stephane | 6:03 | 190 | Rouyn, Que. | 9- 2-69 | Hull | 44 | 45 | 89 |
| McDonald, Lanny | 6:00 | 194 | Hanna, Alta. | 2-16-53 | Calgary | 11 | 7 | 18 |
| Mullen, Joe | 5:09 | 180 | New York, N.Y. | 2-26-57 | Calgary | 51 | 59 | 110 |
| Nieuwendyk, Joe | 6:01 | 194 | Oshawa, Ont. | 9-10-66 | Calgary | 51 | 31 | 82 |
| Otto, Joel | 6:04 | 220 | Elk River, Minn. | 10-29-61 | Calgary | 23 | 30 | 53 |
| Patterson, Colin | 6:02 | 195 | Rexdale, Ont. | 5-11-60 | Calgary | 14 | 24 | 38 |
| Peplinski, Jim | 6:03 | 209 | Renfrew, Ont. | 10-24-60 | Calgary | 13 | 25 | 38 |
| Pickell, Doug | 5:11 | 190 | Sherwood Park, Alta. | 5- 7-68 | Salt Lake | 7 | 6 | 13 |
| Priakin, Sergei | 6:03 | 210 | Moscow, USSR | 12- 7-63 | Soviet Wings-Calgary | .. | .. | .. |
| Ranheim, Paul | 6:00 | 195 | St. Louis, Mo. | 1-25-66 | Salt Lake-Calgary | 68 | 29 | 97 |
| Roberts, Gary | 6:01 | 190 | North York, Ont. | 5-23-66 | Calgary | 22 | 16 | 38 |
| Simard, Martin | 6:03 | 215 | Montreal, Que. | 6-25-66 | Salt Lake | 13 | 15 | 28 |
| Sweeney, Tim | 5:11 | 180 | Boston, Mass. | 4-12-67 | Boston College | 29 | 44 | 73 |
| Wenaas, Jeff | 6:00 | 200 | Eastend, Sask. | 9- 1-67 | Team Canada-Salt Lake | .. | .. | .. |

| DEFENSEMEN | Hgt. | Wgt. | Place of Birth | Date | 1988-89 Club | G. | A. | Pts. |
|---|---|---|---|---|---|---|---|---|
| Biotti, Chris | 6:01 | 200 | Waltham, Mass. | 4-22-67 | Salt Lake | 6 | 14 | 20 |
| Glynn, Brian | 6:04 | 215 | Iserlohn, W. Germany | 11-23-67 | Salt Lake-Calgary | 3 | 11 | 14 |
| Grant, Kevin | 6:03 | 210 | Toronto, Ont. | 1- 9-69 | Sudbury-Salt Lake | 9 | 42 | 51 |
| Johansson, Roger | 6:01 | 185 | Ljungby, Sweden | 4-17-67 | Farjestads | 5 | 15 | 20 |
| Leavins, Jim | 5:11 | 185 | Dinsmore, Sask. | 7-28-60 | Salt Lake | 8 | 13 | 21 |
| Lessard, Rick | 6:02 | 200 | Timmins, Ont. | 1- 9-68 | Salt Lake-Calgary | 10 | 43 | 53 |
| MacInnis, Al | 6:02 | 196 | Inverness, N.S. | 7-11-63 | Calgary | 16 | 58 | 74 |
| Macoun, Jamie | 6:02 | 197 | Newmarket, Ont. | 8-17-61 | Calgary | 8 | 19 | 27 |
| McCrimmon, Brad | 5:11 | 197 | Dodsland, Sask. | 3-29-59 | Calgary | 5 | 17 | 22 |
| Murzyn, Dana | 6:02 | 200 | Calgary, Alta. | 12- 9-66 | Calgary | 3 | 19 | 22 |
| Nattress, Ric | 6:02 | 210 | Hamilton, Ont. | 5-25-62 | Calgary | 1 | 8 | 9 |
| Olsen, Darryl | 6:00 | 180 | Calgary, Alta. | 10- 7-66 | Northern Michigan Univ. | 16 | 26 | 42 |
| Sabourin, Ken | 6:03 | 205 | Scarborough, Ont. | 4-28-66 | Salt Lake-Calgary | 2 | 19 | 21 |
| Suter, Gary | 6:00 | 190 | Madison, Wis. | 6-24-64 | Calgary | 13 | 49 | 62 |
| Tarrant, Jerry | 6:02 | 190 | Burlington, Vt. | 4- 3-66 | Univ. of Vermont | 3 | 19 | 22 |

| GOALTENDERS | Hgt. | Wgt. | Place of Birth | Date | 1988-89 Club | Mins. | GA. | SO. |
|---|---|---|---|---|---|---|---|---|
| Cowley, Wayne | 6:00 | 185 | Scarborough, Ont. | 12- 4-64 | Salt Lake | 1423 | 94 | 0 |
| Guenette, Steve | 5:10 | 175 | Gloucester, Ont. | 11-13-65 | Pittsburgh-Muskegon-S. Lake | 3050 | 162 | 2 |
| Vernon, Mike | 5:09 | 170 | Calgary, Alta. | 2-24-63 | Calgary | 2938 | 130 | 0 |
| Wamsley, Rick | 5:11 | 185 | Simcoe, Ont. | 5-25-59 | Calgary | 1927 | 95 | 2 |

# Chicago Black Hawks
## Norris Division

| | |
|---|---|
| President | William W. Wirtz |
| Vice-President | Arthur M. Wirtz, Jr. |
| Vice-President and Assistant to the President | Thomas N. Ivan |
| General Manager | Bob Pulford |
| Assistant General Manager and Director of Player Personnel | Jack Davison |
| Head Coach | Mike Keenan |
| Assistant Coaches | Jacques Martin, E. J. McGuire |
| Scouts | Jimmy Walker, Don Smith, Dave Lucas, Kerry Davison, Michel Dumas, Jim Pappin, Jan Spieczny |
| Public Relations | Jim DeMaria |
| Trainers | Mike Gapski, Lou Varga, Randy Lacey |
| Home Ice | Chicago Stadium |
| Address | 1800 W. Madison Street, Chicago, Illinois 60612 |
| Seating Capacity | 17,317 |
| Club colors | Red, Black and White |
| Phone | (312) 733-5300 |

William W. Wirtz

Bob Pulford

Jack Davison

Mike Keenan

# Chicago Black Hawks 1989-90 Roster

## FORWARDS

| Name | Hgt. | Wgt. | Place of Birth | Date | 1988-89 Club | G. | A. | Pts. |
|---|---|---|---|---|---|---|---|---|
| Arabski, Rob | 5:10 | 178 | Brantford, Ont. | 7-17-68 | Guelph | 18 | 51 | 69 |
| Bassen, Bob | 5:10 | 180 | Calgary, Alta. | 5-6-65 | N.Y. Islanders-Chicago | 5 | 16 | 21 |
| Black, Andy | 6:02 | 190 | Oshawa, Ont. | 10-28-65 | Ferris State | 10 | 9 | 19 |
| Braccia, Rick | 6:00 | 195 | Revere, Mass. | 9-5-67 | Boston College | 3 | 7 | 10 |
| Creighton, Adam | 6:05 | 214 | Burlington, Ont. | 6-2-65 | Buffalo-Chicago | 22 | 24 | 46 |
| Dam, Trevor | 5:10 | 208 | Scarborough, Ont. | 4-20-70 | London | 33 | 59 | 92 |
| Eagles, Mike | 5:10 | 180 | Sussex, N.B. | 3-7-63 | Chicago | 5 | 11 | 16 |
| Egeland, Tracy | 6:01 | 180 | Lethbridge, Alta. | 8-20-70 | Prince Albert | 28 | 22 | 50 |
| Elvenas, Stefan | 6:01 | 183 | Lund, Sweden | 3-30-70 | Rogle | .. | .. | .. |
| Eriksson, Tom | 5:11 | 183 | Umea, Sweden | 5-3-66 | Djurgarden | 0 | 0 | 0 |
| Gilbert, Greg | 6:01 | 192 | Mississauga, Ont. | 1-22-62 | N.Y. Islanders-Chicago | 8 | 13 | 21 |
| Graham, Dirk | 5:11 | 190 | Regina, Sask. | 7-29-59 | Chicago | 33 | 45 | 78 |
| Greyerbiehl, Jason | 6:00 | 176 | Bramalea, Ont. | 3-24-70 | Colgate Univ. | 6 | 9 | 15 |
| Hudson, Mike | 6:01 | 185 | Guelph, Ont. | 2-6-67 | Saginaw-Chicago | 22 | 33 | 55 |
| Johansson, Jim | 6:02 | 200 | Rochester, Minn. | 3-10-64 | Salt Lake | 35 | 40 | 75 |
| Kozak, Mike | 6:02 | 195 | Toronto, Ont. | 3-14-69 | Clarkson Univ. | 10 | 9 | 19 |
| Lacouture, Bill | 6:02 | 192 | Framingham, Mass. | 5-28-68 | Univ. of New Hampshire | 1 | 0 | 1 |
| Lafayette, Justin | 6:06 | 200 | Vancouver, B.C. | 1-23-70 | Ferris State | 3 | 4 | 7 |
| Lappin, Mike | 5:10 | 175 | Chicago, Ill. | 1-1-69 | Boston Univ. | 11 | 16 | 27 |
| Larmer, Steve | 5:10 | 189 | Peterborough, Ont. | 6-16-61 | Chicago | 43 | 44 | 87 |
| Loach, Lonnie | 5:10 | 181 | New Liskeard, Ont. | 4-14-68 | Flint-Saginaw | 29 | 32 | 61 |
| Ludzik, Steve | 5:11 | 186 | Toronto, Ont. | 4-3-62 | Saginaw-Chicago | 22 | 57 | 79 |
| Mackey, David | 6:03 | 190 | New Westminster, B.C. | 7-24-66 | Saginaw-Chicago | 23 | 25 | 48 |
| McCormick, Mike | 6:02 | 220 | St. Boniface, B.C. | 5-14-68 | Univ. of North Dakota | 1 | 4 | 5 |
| Murray, Troy | 6:01 | 195 | Calgary, Alta. | 7-31-62 | Chicago | 21 | 30 | 51 |
| Nanne, Marty | 6:00 | 180 | Edina, Minn. | 7-21-67 | Saginaw | 4 | 10 | 14 |
| Noonan, Brian | 6:01 | 180 | Boston, Mass. | 5-29-65 | Chicago-Saginaw | 22 | 25 | 47 |
| Persson, Joakim | 5:08 | 163 | Gavle, Sweden | 5-15-66 | Brynas | 7 | 10 | 17 |
| Phillips, Guy | 6:00 | 178 | Brooks, Alta. | 2-13-66 | Saginaw | 20 | 17 | 37 |
| Presley, Wayne | 5:11 | 172 | Detroit, Mich. | 3-23-65 | Chicago | 21 | 19 | 40 |
| Roenick, Jeremy | 5:11 | 170 | Boston, Mass. | 1-17-70 | Hull-Chicago | 43 | 45 | 88 |
| Rucinski, Mike | 5:11 | 190 | Chicago, Ill. | 12-12-63 | Saginaw-Chicago | 35 | 72 | 107 |
| Rychel, Warren | 6:00 | 190 | Tecumseh, Ont. | 5-12-67 | Saginaw-Chicago | 15 | 14 | 29 |
| Sanders, Matt | 6:00 | 180 | Ottawa, Ont. | 7-17-70 | Northeastern Univ. | 8 | 9 | 17 |
| Sandstrom, Ulf | 5:10 | 180 | Fagerstad, Sweden | 4-24-67 | Modo | 19 | 14 | 33 |
| Sanipass, Everett | 6:01 | 192 | Big Cove, N.B. | 2-13-68 | Chicago-Saginaw | 15 | 21 | 36 |
| Savard, Denis | 5:10 | 167 | Pt. Gatineau, Que. | 2-4-61 | Chicago | 23 | 59 | 82 |
| Secord, Al | 6:01 | 210 | Sudbury, Ont | 3-3-58 | Toronto-Philadelphia | 6 | 10 | 16 |
| Suk, Joe | 5:11 | 190 | Chicago, Ill. | 2-26-70 | Hull | 35 | 54 | 89 |
| Sutter, Duane | 6:01 | 185 | Viking, Alta. | 3-16-60 | Chicago | 7 | 9 | 16 |
| Thomas, Steve | 5:10 | 185 | Stockport, England | 7-15-63 | Chicago | 21 | 19 | 40 |
| Torkki, Jari | 6:00 | 163 | Finland | 8-11-65 | Saginaw-Chicago | 31 | 42 | 73 |
| Van Dorp, Wayne | 6:04 | 225 | Vancouver, B.C. | 5-19-61 | Rochester-Saginaw-Chicago | 7 | 9 | 16 |
| Vincelette, Dan | 6:01 | 202 | Verdun, Que. | 8-1-67 | Chicago-Saginaw | 11 | 4 | 15 |
| Watson, Bill | 6:01 | 190 | Pine Falls, Man. | 3-30-64 | Saginaw-Chicago | 26 | 25 | 51 |
| Willams, Sean | 6:01 | 182 | Oshawa, Ont. | 1-28-68 | Saginaw | 32 | 27 | 59 |
| Woodcroft, Craig | 6:01 | 185 | Toronto, Ont. | 12-3-69 | Colgate Univ. | 20 | 29 | 49 |

## DEFENSEMEN

| Name | Hgt. | Wgt. | Place of Birth | Date | 1988-89 Club | G. | A. | Pts. |
|---|---|---|---|---|---|---|---|---|
| Bennett, Adam | 6:04 | 206 | Georgetown, Ont. | 3-30-71 | Sudbury | 7 | 22 | 29 |
| Brown, Keith | 6:01 | 191 | Cornerbrook, Nfld. | 5-6-60 | Chicago | 2 | 16 | 18 |
| Cassidy, Bruce | 5:11 | 176 | Ottawa, Ont. | 5-20-65 | Saginaw-Chicago | 16 | 66 | 82 |
| Cleary, Joe | 5:11 | 186 | Buffalo, N.Y. | 1-17-70 | Boston College | 5 | 7 | 12 |
| Dagenais, Mike | 6:03 | 198 | Gloucester, Ont. | 7-22-69 | Peterborough | 14 | 23 | 37 |
| Doyon, Mario | 6:00 | 174 | Quebec, Que. | 8-27-68 | Saginaw-Chicago | 17 | 33 | 50 |
| Hamilton, Brad | 6:00 | 175 | Calgary, Alta. | 3-30-67 | Michigan State | 9 | 20 | 29 |
| Hayton, Brian | 6:01 | 201 | Peterborough, Ont. | 1-22-68 | Peterborough | 6 | 30 | 36 |
| Heed, Jonas | 6:00 | 174 | Sodertalje, Sweden | 1-3-67 | Sodertalje | 4 | 9 | 13 |
| Konroyd, Steve | 6:01 | 195 | Scarborough, Ont. | 2-10-61 | N.Y. Islanders-Chicago | 6 | 12 | 18 |
| Kurzawski, Mark | 6:03 | 199 | Chicago, Ill. | 2-25-68 | Saginaw | 2 | 11 | 13 |
| Manson, Dave | 6:02 | 190 | Prince Albert, Sask. | 1-27-67 | Chicago | 18 | 36 | 54 |
| McGill, Bob | 6:01 | 190 | Edmonton, Alta. | 4-27-62 | Chicago | 0 | 4 | 4 |
| Moscaluk, Gary | 6:00 | 195 | Waskatenau, Alta. | 5-23-67 | Saginaw | 0 | 12 | 12 |
| Murray, Bob | 5:10 | 186 | Kingston, Ont. | 11-26-54 | Saginaw-Chicago | 5 | 11 | 16 |
| Playfair, Jim | 6:04 | 200 | Ft. St. James, B.C. | 5-22-64 | Saginaw-Chicago | 3 | 6 | 9 |
| Russell, Cam | 6:04 | 175 | Halifax, N.S. | 1-12-69 | Hull | 8 | 32 | 40 |
| Speer, Michael | 6:02 | 202 | Toronto, Ont. | 3-26-71 | Guelph | 9 | 31 | 40 |
| Wilson, Doug | 6:01 | 187 | Ottawa, Ont. | 7-5-57 | Chicago | 15 | 47 | 62 |
| Wolf, Todd | 6:02 | 214 | E. Aurora, N.Y. | 11-5-67 | Colgate Univ. | 1 | 13 | 14 |
| Yawney, Trent | 6:03 | 183 | Hudson Bay, Sask. | 9-29-65 | Chicago | 5 | 19 | 24 |

## GOALTENDERS

| Name | Hgt. | Wgt. | Place of Birth | Date | 1988-89 Club | Mins. | GA. | SO. |
|---|---|---|---|---|---|---|---|---|
| Doneghey, Michael | 6:00 | 165 | Boston, Mass. | 7-28-70 | Catholic Memorial H.S. | 1080 | 30 | 9 |
| Belfour, Ed | 5:11 | 170 | Carman, Man. | 4-21-65 | Saginaw-Chicago | 2908 | 166 | 0 |
| Chevrier, Alain | 5:08 | 180 | Cornwall, Ont. | 4-23-64 | Winnipeg-Chicago | 2665 | 170 | 1 |
| LeBlanc, Ray | 5:10 | 170 | Fitchburg, Mass. | 10-24-64 | Saginaw-Flint | 2507 | 166 | 0 |
| Pang, Darren | 5:05 | 155 | Meaford, Ont. | 2-17-64 | Chicago-Saginaw | 1733 | 126 | 0 |
| Waite, Jimmy | 6:00 | 163 | Sherbrooke, Que. | 4-15-69 | Chicago-Saginaw | 798 | 53 | 0 |

# Detroit Red Wings
## Norris Division

| | |
|---|---|
| Owner and President | Michael Ilitch |
| Executive Vice-President | James Lites |
| Secretary/Treasurer | Marian Ilitch |
| General Counsel | Denise Ilitch-Lites |
| Vice-President and General Manager | Jim Devellano |
| Vice-President/Marketing/Advertising Sales | Rosanne Kozerski-Brown |
| Assistant General Manager | Nick Polano |
| Head Coach | Jacques Demers |
| Assistant Coaches | Colin Campbell, Dave Lewis, Phil Myre |
| Assistant Coach/Goaltenders | Dave Dryden |
| Pro Scout | Dan Belisle |
| USA College/High School Scout | Billy Dea |
| Eastern USA Scout | Jerry Moschella |
| Western Canada Scout | Ken Holland |
| Scouts | Chris Coury, Frank Michalek, Dave Polano, Christer Rockstrom, Mike Daski |
| Director of Public Relations | Bill Jamieson |
| Director of Advertising Sales/Promotions | Terry Murphy |
| Physical Therapist | Kirk Vickers |
| Trainer | Mark Brennan |
| Assistant Trainer | Larry Wasylon |
| Home Ice | Joe Louis Sports Arena |
| Address | 600 Civic Center Drive, Detroit, Mich. 48226 |
| Seating Capacity | 19,275 |
| Club colors | Red and White |
| Phone | (313) 567-7333 |

Michael Ilitch

Jim Devellano

Nick Polano

Jacques Demers

# Detroit Red Wings 1989-90 Roster

## FORWARDS

| Name | Hgt. | Wgt. | Place of Birth | Date | 1988-89 Club | G. | A. | Pts. |
|---|---|---|---|---|---|---|---|---|
| Barr, Dave | 6:01 | 190 | Toronto, Ont. | 11-30-60 | Detroit | 27 | 32 | 59 |
| Burr, Shawn | 6:01 | 195 | Sarnia, Ont. | 7-1-66 | Detroit | 19 | 27 | 46 |
| Chabot, John | 6:02 | 200 | Summerside, P.E.I. | 5-18-62 | Detroit-Adirondack | 5 | 12 | 17 |
| Colbourne, Darren | 5:11 | 190 | Cornerbrook, Nfld. | 1-5-68 | Cornwall | 51 | 46 | 97 |
| Eaves, Murray | 5:10 | 185 | Calgary, Alta. | 5-10-60 | Adirondack | 46 | 72 | 118 |
| Federko, Bernie | 6:00 | 180 | Foam Lake, Sask. | 5-12-56 | St. Louis | 22 | 45 | 67 |
| Fedyk, Brent | 6:00 | 195 | Yorkton, Sask. | 3-8-67 | Adirondack-Detroit | 42 | 28 | 70 |
| Gallant, Gerard | 5:10 | 185 | Summerside, P.E.I. | 9-2-63 | Detroit | 39 | 54 | 93 |
| Gober, Mike | 6:00 | 192 | St. Louis, Mo. | 4-10-67 | Adirondack | 15 | 7 | 22 |
| Goodall, Glen | 5:08 | 170 | Fort Nelson, B.C. | 1-22-70 | Seattle-Flint | 57 | 66 | 123 |
| Graves, Adam | 5:11 | 185 | Toronto, Ont. | 4-12-68 | Detroit-Adirondack | 17 | 16 | 33 |
| Habscheid, Marc | 6:00 | 185 | Swift Current, Sask. | 3-1-63 | Minnesota | 23 | 31 | 54 |
| Holland, Dennis | 5:10 | 165 | Vernon, B.C. | 1-30-69 | Portland | 82 | 85 | 167 |
| Kennedy, Sheldon | 5:10 | 170 | Brandon, Man. | 6-15-69 | Swift Current | 58 | 48 | 106 |
| King, Kris | 6:00 | 193 | Bracebridge, Ont. | 2-18-66 | Detroit | 2 | 3 | 5 |
| Klima, Petr | 6:00 | 190 | Chaomutov, Czech. | 12-23-64 | Detroit-Adirondack | 30 | 17 | 47 |
| Kocur, Joe | 6:00 | 195 | Calgary, Alta. | 12-21-64 | Detroit | 9 | 9 | 18 |
| Kocur, Kory | 5:11 | 188 | Kelvington, Sask. | 3-6-69 | Saskatoon | 45 | 57 | 102 |
| Krentz, Dale | 5:11 | 190 | Steinbach, Man. | 12-19-61 | Adirondack-Detroit | 24 | 23 | 47 |
| McCosh, Shawn | 6:00 | 188 | Oshawa, Ont. | 6-5-69 | Niagara Falls | 41 | 62 | 103 |
| McKay, Randy | 6:01 | 185 | Montreal, Que. | 1-25-67 | Adirondack-Detroit | 29 | 34 | 63 |
| McKegney, Tony | 6:01 | 200 | Montreal, Que. | 2-15-58 | St. Louis | 25 | 17 | 42 |
| Merkosky, Glenn | 5:10 | 175 | Edmonton, Alta. | 4-8-59 | Adirondack | 31 | 46 | 77 |
| Murphy, Joe | 6:01 | 190 | London, Ont. | 10-16-67 | Adirondack-Detroit | 32 | 42 | 74 |
| Nill, Jim | 6:00 | 185 | Hanna, Alta. | 4-11-58 | Detroit | 8 | 7 | 15 |
| Robertson, Torrie | 5:11 | 200 | Victoria, B.C. | 8-2-61 | Hartford-Detroit | 4 | 6 | 10 |
| Shank, Daniel | 5:10 | 190 | Montreal, Que. | 5-12-67 | Adirondack | 5 | 20 | 25 |
| Sillinger, Mike | 5:10 | 190 | Regina, Sask. | 6-29-71 | Regina | 53 | 78 | 131 |
| Yzerman, Steve | 5:11 | 185 | Cranbrook, B.C. | 5-9-65 | Detroit | 65 | 90 | 155 |

## DEFENSEMEN

| Name | Hgt. | Wgt. | Place of Birth | Date | 1988-89 Club | G. | A. | Pts. |
|---|---|---|---|---|---|---|---|---|
| Anglehart, Serge | 6:02 | 189 | Hull, Que. | 4-18-70 | Drummondville | 6 | 15 | 21 |
| Bignell, Greg | 6:00 | 188 | Kitchener, Ont. | 5-9-69 | Belleville | 6 | 27 | 33 |
| Boughner, Bob | 5:11 | 201 | Windsor, Ont. | 3-8-71 | Sault Ste. Marie | 6 | 15 | 21 |
| Chiasson, Steve | 6:01 | 205 | Barrie, Ont. | 4-14-67 | Detroit | 12 | 35 | 47 |
| Doyle, Rob | 5:11 | 185 | Lindsay, Ont. | 2-10-64 | Adirondack | 24 | 52 | 76 |
| Dupuis, Guy | 6:02 | 199 | Moncton, N.B. | 5-10-70 | Hull | 15 | 56 | 71 |
| Houda, Doug | 6:02 | 200 | Blairmore, Alta. | 6-3-66 | Detroit-Adirondack | 2 | 14 | 16 |
| Jones, Bob | 5:11 | 196 | Sault Ste. Marie, Ont. | 1-13-69 | Sault Ste. Marie | 13 | 21 | 34 |
| Kotsopoulos, Chris | 6:03 | 215 | Scarborough, Ont. | 11-27-58 | Toronto | 1 | 14 | 15 |
| Kruppke, Gord | 6:01 | 200 | Slave Lake, Alta. | 4-2-69 | Prince Albert | 6 | 26 | 32 |
| LaMoine, Mike | 6:00 | 188 | Grand Forks, N.D. | 12-1-66 | Univ. of North Dakota | 3 | 12 | 15 |
| Luongo, Chris | 6:00 | 180 | Detroit, Mich. | 3-17-67 | Michigan State | 4 | 21 | 25 |
| Mayer, Derek | 6:00 | 185 | Rossland, B.C. | 5-21-67 | Canadian Nat. Team | 3 | 13 | 16 |
| Mokosak, John | 5:11 | 200 | Edmonton, Alta. | 9-7-63 | Adirondack-Detroit | 4 | 32 | 36 |
| Morton, Dean | 6:01 | 196 | Peterborough, Ont. | 2-27-68 | Oshawa | 2 | 15 | 17 |
| Norwood, Lee | 6:01 | 198 | Oakland, Calif. | 2-2-60 | Detroit | 10 | 32 | 42 |
| O'Connell, Mike | 5:09 | 180 | Chicago, Ill. | 11-25-55 | Detroit | 1 | 15 | 16 |
| Praznik, Jody | 6:01 | 180 | Winnipeg, Man. | 6-28-69 | Saskatoon | 2 | 9 | 11 |
| Racine, Yves | 6:00 | 185 | Matane, Que. | 2-7-69 | Victoriaville | 23 | 85 | 108 |
| Salming, Borje | 6:01 | 185 | Kiruna, Sweden | 4-17-51 | Toronto | 3 | 17 | 20 |
| Schena, Rob | 6:01 | 190 | Saugess, Mass. | 2-5-67 | RPI-Adirondack | 8 | 6 | 14 |
| Sharples, Jeff | 6:01 | 195 | Terrace, B.C. | 7-28-67 | Detroit-Adirondack | 4 | 13 | 17 |
| Stark, Jay | 6:00 | 190 | Vernon, B.C. | 2-29-68 | Seattle-Flint | 3 | 12 | 15 |
| Wilkie, Bob | 6:02 | 200 | Calgary, Alta. | 2-11-69 | Swift Current | 18 | 67 | 85 |
| Zombo, Rick | 6:01 | 195 | Des Plaines, Ill. | 5-8-63 | Detroit | 1 | 20 | 21 |

## GOALTENDERS

| Name | Hgt. | Wgt. | Place of Birth | Date | 1988-89 Club | Mins. | GA. | SO. |
|---|---|---|---|---|---|---|---|---|
| Cheveldae, Tim | 5:10 | 175 | Melville, Sask. | 2-15-68 | Adirondack-Detroit | 1817 | 97 | 1 |
| Glickman, Jason | 5:09 | 179 | Chicago, Ill. | 3-25-69 | Hull | 2116 | 131 | 1 |
| Hanlon, Glen | 6:00 | 185 | Brandon, Man. | 2-20-57 | Detroit | 2092 | 124 | 1 |
| Hansch, Randy | 5:10 | 165 | Edmonton, Alta. | 2-8-66 | Canadian Nat. Team | 1489 | 96 | 0 |
| Reimer, Mark | 5:11 | 170 | Calgary, Alta. | 3-23-67 | Flint-Adirondack | 1922 | 147 | 0 |
| St. Laurent, Sam | 5:10 | 190 | Arvida, Que. | 2-16-59 | Adirondack-Detroit | 2195 | 122 | 2 |
| Stefan, Greg | 5:11 | 180 | Brantford, Ont. | 2-11-61 | Detroit | 2499 | 167 | 0 |

# Edmonton Oilers
## Smythe Division

| | |
|---|---|
| Owner/Governor | Peter Pocklington |
| Alternate Governor | Glen Sather |
| General Counsels | Bob Lloyd, Gary Frohlich |
| President/General Manager | Glen Sather |
| Coach | John Muckler |
| Co-Coach | Ted Green |
| Assistant Coach | Ron Low |
| Assistant General Manager | Bruce MacGregor |
| Director of Player Personnel/Chief Scout | Barry Fraser |
| Scouting Staff | Lorne Davis, Ace Bailey, Ed Chadwick, Matti Vaisanen, Harry Howell |
| Controller | Werner Baum |
| Executive Secretary | Lana Alexander |
| Director of Public Relations | Bill Tuele |
| Assistant Public Relations Director | Steve Knowles |
| Trainer | Barrie Stafford |
| Assistant Trainer | Lyle Kulchisky |
| Athletic Therapist | Ken Lowe |
| Team Physician | Dr. Gordon Cameron |
| Home Ice | Northlands Coliseum |
| Address | Edmonton, Alta. T5B 4M9 |
| Seating Capacity | 17,503 (Standing 190) |
| Club colors | Blue, Orange and White |
| Phone | (403) 474-8561 |

Peter Pocklington

Glen Sather

John Muckler

Ted Green

# Edmonton Oilers 1989-90 Roster

## FORWARDS

| Name | Hgt. | Wgt. | Place of Birth | Date | 1988-89 Club | G. | A. | Pts. |
|---|---|---|---|---|---|---|---|---|
| Anderson, Glenn | 6:01 | 190 | Vancouver, B.C. | 10-2-60 | Edmonton | 16 | 48 | 64 |
| Beaulieu, Nicolas | 6:02 | 200 | Rimouski, Que. | 8-19-68 | Cape Breton | 10 | 13 | 23 |
| Brown, Dave | 6:05 | 205 | Saskatoon, Sask. | 11-12-62 | Philadelphia-Edmonton | 0 | 5 | 5 |
| Buchberger, Kelly | 6:02 | 205 | Langenburg, Sask. | 12-2-66 | Edmonton | 5 | 9 | 14 |
| Carson, Jimmy | 6:01 | 200 | Southfield, Mich. | 7-20-68 | Edmonton | 49 | 51 | 100 |
| Currie, Dan | 6:02 | 195 | Burlington, Ont. | 3-15-68 | Cape Breton | 29 | 36 | 65 |
| Drulia, Stan | 5:11 | 188 | Elmira, N.Y. | 1-5-68 | Niagara Falls | 52 | 93 | 145 |
| Eriksson, Peter | 6:04 | 224 | Kramfors, Sweden | 7-12-65 | HV 71 | .. | .. | .. |
| Gelinas, Martin | 5:11 | 195 | Shawinigan, Que. | 6-5-70 | Hull-Edmonton | 39 | 41 | 80 |
| Glover, Mike | 5:11 | 200 | Ottawa, Ont. | 7-23-68 | Cape Breton | 9 | 11 | 20 |
| Haas, David | 6:02 | 196 | Toronto, Ont. | 6-23-68 | Cape Breton | 9 | 9 | 18 |
| Hunter, Dave | 5:11 | 195 | Petrolia, Ont. | 1-1-58 | Winnipeg-Edmonton | 6 | 6 | 12 |
| Issel, Kim | 6:04 | 196 | Regina, Sask. | 9-25-67 | Cape Breton-Edmonton | 34 | 28 | 62 |
| Joseph, Fabian | 5:08 | 170 | Sydney, N.S. | 12-5-65 | Cape Breton | 32 | 34 | 66 |
| Kurri, Jari | 6:01 | 195 | Helsinki, Finland | 5-18-60 | Edmonton | 44 | 58 | 102 |
| Lacombe, Normand | 6:00 | 205 | Pierrefonds, Que. | 10-18-64 | Edmonton | 17 | 11 | 28 |
| Lamb, Mark | 5:09 | 180 | Ponteix, Sask. | 8-3-64 | Cape Breton-Edmonton | 35 | 57 | 92 |
| LeBlanc, John | 6:01 | 190 | Campbellton, N.B. | 1-21-64 | Milw.-Cape Breton-Edmonton | 44 | 31 | 75 |
| Lehmann, Tommy | 6:01 | 185 | Solna, Sweden | 2-3-64 | Maine-Boston | 5 | 15 | 20 |
| MacTavish, Craig | 6:01 | 195 | London, Ont. | 8-15-58 | Edmonton | 21 | 31 | 52 |
| Martin, Don | 6:00 | 200 | London, Ont. | 3-29-68 | Cape Breton | 0 | 0 | 0 |
| Matulik, Ivan | 6:01 | 200 | Nitra, Czech. | 6-17-68 | Cape Breton | 0 | 0 | 0 |
| McClelland, Kevin | 6:02 | 205 | Oshawa, Ont. | 7-4-62 | Edmonton | 6 | 14 | 20 |
| Messier, Mark | 6:01 | 210 | Edmonton, Alta. | 1-18-61 | Edmonton | 33 | 61 | 94 |
| Simpson, Craig | 6:02 | 195 | London, Ont. | 2-15-67 | Edmonton | 35 | 41 | 76 |
| Soberlak, Peter | 6:02 | 195 | Kamloops, B.C. | 5-12-69 | Swift Current | 25 | 33 | 58 |
| Tikkanen, Esa | 6:01 | 200 | Helsinki, Finland | 1-25-65 | Edmonton | 31 | 47 | 78 |
| Tisdale, Tim | 6:01 | 186 | Swift Current, Sask. | 5-28-68 | Swift Current | 57 | 82 | 139 |
| Van Allen, Shaun | 6:01 | 200 | Shaunavon, Sask. | 8-29-67 | Cape Breton | 32 | 42 | 74 |
| Ware, Mike | 6:05 | 208 | York, Ont. | 3-22-67 | Cape Breton-Edmonton | 1 | 12 | 13 |
| Wilks, Brian | 5:11 | 180 | North York, Ont. | 2-27-66 | N. Haven-Los Ang.-C. Breton | 19 | 31 | 50 |

## DEFENSEMEN

| Name | Hgt. | Wgt. | Place of Birth | Date | 1988-89 Club | G. | A. | Pts. |
|---|---|---|---|---|---|---|---|---|
| Barbe, Mario | 6:00 | 204 | Cadillac, Que. | 3-17-67 | Cape Breton | 1 | 11 | 12 |
| Beukeboom, Jeff | 6:04 | 215 | Ajax, Ont. | 3-28-65 | Edmonton-Cape Breton | 0 | 9 | 9 |
| Charlesworth, Todd | 6:01 | 190 | Calgary, Alta. | 3-22-65 | Muskegon | 10 | 53 | 63 |
| English, Jim | 6:02 | 190 | Toronto, Ont. | 5-3-66 | New Haven-Cape Breton | 5 | 22 | 27 |
| Ennis, Jim | 6:00 | 198 | Sherwood Park, Alta. | 7-10-67 | Cape Breton | 3 | 15 | 18 |
| Foster, Corey | 6:03 | 200 | Ottawa, Ont. | 10-27-69 | Peterborough-New Jersey | 14 | 42 | 56 |
| Gregg, Randy | 6:04 | 215 | Edmonton, Alta. | 2-19-56 | Edmonton | 3 | 15 | 18 |
| Huddy, Charlie | 6:00 | 210 | Oshawa, Ont. | 6-2-59 | Edmonton | 11 | 33 | 44 |
| Joseph, Chris | 6:02 | 210 | Burnaby, B.C. | 9-10-69 | Edmonton-Cape Breton | 5 | 6 | 11 |
| Lowe, Kevin | 6:02 | 195 | Lachute, Que. | 4-15-59 | Edmonton | 7 | 18 | 25 |
| Muni, Craig | 6:03 | 200 | Toronto, Ont. | 7-19-62 | Edmonton | 5 | 13 | 18 |
| Odelein, Selmar | 6:00 | 205 | Quill Lake, Sask. | 4-11-66 | Cape Breton-Edmonton | 8 | 21 | 29 |
| Smith, Geoff | 6:02 | 190 | Edmonton, Alta. | 3-7-69 | Kamloops | 4 | 31 | 35 |
| Smith, Steve | 6:04 | 215 | Glasgow, Scotland | 4-30-63 | Edmonton | 3 | 19 | 22 |

## GOALTENDERS

| Name | Hgt. | Wgt. | Place of Birth | Date | 1988-89 Club | Mins. | GA. | SO. |
|---|---|---|---|---|---|---|---|---|
| Beals, Darren | 6:00 | 200 | Dartmouth, N.S. | 8-28-68 | Cape Breton | 738 | 65 | 0 |
| Fuhr, Grant | 5:10 | 186 | Spruce Grove, Alta. | 9-28-62 | Edmonton | 3341 | 213 | 1 |
| Greenlay, Mike | 6:03 | 200 | Vitoria, Brazil | 9-15-68 | Lake Superior St.-Saskatoon | 1203 | 102 | 0 |
| Ranford, Bill | 5:10 | 170 | Brandon, Man. | 12-14-66 | Edmonton | 1509 | 88 | 1 |
| Roach, David | 5:10 | 175 | Burnaby, B.C. | 1-10-65 | Cape Breton | 1810 | 130 | 1 |

# Hartford Whalers
### Adams Division

| | |
|---|---|
| Managing General Partner and Governor | Richard H. Gordon |
| General Partner and Alternate Governor | Benjamin J. Sisti |
| Partner and Alternate Governor | Donald G. Conrad |
| President and Alternate Governor | Emile Francis |
| Vice-President and General Manager | Ed Johnston |
| Assistant General Manager | Robert Crocker |
| Special Assistant to the Managing General Partner | Gordie Howe |
| Coach | Rick Ley |
| Assistant Coaches | Jay Leach, Brent Peterson |
| Director of Player Personnel and Scouting | Ken Schinkel |
| Scouts | Leo Boivin, Steve Brklacich, Claude Larose, Bruce Haralson, Fred Gore, Jiri Chra |
| Trainer | Tommy Woodcock |
| Equipment Manager | Skip Cunningham |
| Strength and Conditioning Coach | Doug McKenney |
| Executive Vice-President for Administration and Finance | W. David Andrews |
| Vice-President, Marketing and Public Relations | William E. Barnes |
| Treasurer | Michael J. Amendola |
| Director of Public Relations | Phil Langan |
| Assistant Director of Public Relations | Mark Willand |
| Chief Statistician | Frank Polnaszek |
| Director of Advertising Sales | Rick Francis |
| Home Ice | Hartford Civic Center |
| Address | One Civic Center Plaza, Hartford, CT 06103 |
| Seating Capacity | 15,580 |
| Club colors | Blue, Green and White |
| Phone | (203) 728-3366 |

**Richard H. Gordon**

**Ed Johnston**

**Emile Francis**

**Rick Ley**

# Hartford Whalers 1989-90 Roster

## FORWARDS

| Name | Hgt. | Wgt. | Place of Birth | Date | 1988-89 Club | G. | A. | Pts. |
|---|---|---|---|---|---|---|---|---|
| Anderson, John | 5:11 | 200 | Toronto, Ont. | 3-28-57 | Hartford | 16 | 24 | 40 |
| Atcheynum, Blair | 6:02 | 190 | Estevan, Sask. | 4-20-69 | Moose Jaw | 70 | 68 | 138 |
| Bechard, Jerome | 5:11 | 185 | Regina, Sask. | 3-30-69 | Moose Jaw | 29 | 52 | 81 |
| Black, James | 5:11 | 185 | Regina, Sask. | 8-15-69 | Portland | 45 | 51 | 96 |
| Bodak, Bob | 6:02 | 200 | Thunder Bay, Ont. | 5-28-61 | Binghamton-Salt Lake | 15 | 25 | 40 |
| Brant, Chris | 6:01 | 190 | Belleville, Ont. | 8-26-65 | Binghamton | 28 | 28 | 56 |
| Buchanan, Trevor | 6:00 | 176 | Thompson, Man. | 6- 7-69 | Kamloops | 13 | 21 | 34 |
| Bucsis, Wayde | 6:01 | 185 | Prince Albert, Alta. | 1-18-68 | Prince Albert | 40 | 44 | 84 |
| Callaghan, Gary | 5:11 | 175 | Oshawa, Ont. | 8-12-67 | Binghamton | 23 | 17 | 40 |
| Daniels, Scott | 6:02 | 225 | Prince Albert, B.C. | 9-19-69 | Regina | 21 | 26 | 47 |
| Dineen, Kevin | 5:11 | 190 | Quebec City, Que. | 10-28-63 | Hartford | 45 | 44 | 89 |
| Evason, Dean | 5:10 | 180 | Flin Flon, Man. | 8-22-64 | Hartford | 11 | 17 | 28 |
| Ferraro, Ray | 5:10 | 185 | Trail, B.C. | 8-23-64 | Hartford | 41 | 35 | 76 |
| Francis, Ron | 6:02 | 200 | Sault Ste. Marie, Ont. | 3- 1-63 | Hartford | 29 | 48 | 77 |
| Govedaris, Chris | 6:00 | 200 | Toronto, Ont. | 2- 2-70 | Toronto Jrs. | 41 | 38 | 79 |
| Hoover, Ron | 6:01 | 185 | North Bay, Ont. | 1- 9-65 | Western Mich. U.-Indianapolis | 32 | 27 | 59 |
| Hull, Jody | 6:02 | 200 | Cambridge, Ont. | 2- 2-69 | Hartford | 16 | 18 | 34 |
| Kasowski, Peter | 5:11 | 180 | Edmonton, Alta. | 3-19-69 | Swift Current | 58 | 73 | 131 |
| Kastelic, Ed | 6:04 | 215 | Toronto, Ont. | 1-29-64 | Binghamton-Hartford | 9 | 8 | 17 |
| Krygier, Todd | 5:11 | 180 | Northville, Mich. | 10-12-65 | Binghamton | 26 | 42 | 68 |
| Lawton, Brian | 6:00 | 190 | New Brunswick, N.J. | 6-29-65 | N.Y. Rangers-Hartford | 17 | 26 | 43 |
| Lindberg, Chris | 6:01 | 190 | Fort Francis, Ont. | 4-16-67 | Univ. of Minnesota-Duluth | 15 | 18 | 33 |
| MacDermid, Paul | 6:01 | 205 | Chesley, Ont. | 4-14-63 | Hartford | 17 | 27 | 44 |
| Martin, Tom | 6:02 | 200 | Kelowna, B.C. | 5-11-64 | Minnesota-Hartford | 11 | 17 | 28 |
| McKenzie, Jim | 6:03 | 205 | Gull Lake, Sask. | 11- 3-69 | Victoria | 15 | 27 | 42 |
| Moore, John | 6:03 | 205 | Montreal, Que. | 1- 9-67 | Yale Univ. | 3 | 3 | 6 |
| Picard, Michel | 5:11 | 190 | Beauport, Que. | 11- 7-69 | Trois-Rivieres | 59 | 81 | 140 |
| Quinn, Jim | 5:11 | 185 | Calgary, Alta. | 2-10-67 | Bowling Green State | 21 | 20 | 41 |
| Saumier, Raymond | 6:00 | 195 | Hull, Que. | 2-27-69 | Trois-Rivieres | 30 | 62 | 92 |
| Sceviour, Todd | 5:11 | 195 | Lacombe, Alta. | 2-18-67 | | | | |
| Thomson, Jim | 6:01 | 205 | Edmonton, Alta. | 12-30-65 | Washington-Hartford | 2 | 0 | 2 |
| Tippett, Dave | 5:10 | 180 | Moosomin, Sask. | 8-25-61 | Hartford | 17 | 24 | 41 |
| Tomlak, Mike | 6:03 | 205 | Thunder Bay, Ont. | 10-17-64 | Univ. of Western Ontario | 16 | 34 | 50 |
| Tory, Paul | 6:00 | 175 | Coquitlam, B.C. | 1-13-66 | Univ. of Illinois-Chicago | 5 | 8 | 13 |
| Verbeek, Pat | 5:09 | 190 | Sarnia, Ont. | 5-24-64 | New Jersey | 26 | 21 | 47 |
| Yake, Terry | 5:11 | 185 | New Westminster, B.C. | 10-22-68 | Binghamton-Hartford | 39 | 56 | 95 |
| Young, Scott | 6:00 | 190 | Clinton, Mass. | 10- 1-67 | Hartford | 19 | 40 | 59 |

## DEFENSEMEN

| Name | Hgt. | Wgt. | Place of Birth | Date | 1988-89 Club | G. | A. | Pts. |
|---|---|---|---|---|---|---|---|---|
| Babych, David | 6:02 | 215 | Edmonton, Alta. | 5-23-61 | Hartford | 6 | 41 | 47 |
| Battice, John | 6:01 | 182 | Brampton, Ont. | 2-25-69 | London | 5 | 19 | 24 |
| Beaulieu, Corey | 6:02 | 210 | Winnipeg, Man. | 9-10-69 | Moose Jaw | 3 | 20 | 23 |
| Burgers, Martin | 6:04 | 205 | Diepenveen, Holland | 4-21-60 | Fort Wayne | 4 | 7 | 11 |
| Burt, Adam | 6:00 | 190 | Detroit, Mich. | 1-15-69 | N. Bay-Binghamton-Hartford | 4 | 13 | 17 |
| Chapman, Brian | 6:00 | 195 | Brockville, Ont. | 2-10-68 | Binghamton | 5 | 25 | 30 |
| Cote, Sylvain | 5:11 | 185 | Durberger, Que. | 1-19-66 | Hartford | 8 | 9 | 17 |
| Culhane, Jim | 6:00 | 195 | Haileybury, Ont. | 3-13-65 | Binghamton | 6 | 11 | 17 |
| Herczeg, Don | 6:01 | 210 | Edmonton, Alta. | 6- 6-64 | Denver-Indianapolis | 0 | 3 | 3 |
| Jennings, Grant | 6:03 | 200 | Hudson Bay, Sask. | 5- 5-65 | Hartford-Binghamton | 3 | 10 | 13 |
| Ladouceur, Randy | 6:02 | 220 | Brockville, Ont. | 6-30-60 | Hartford | 2 | 5 | 7 |
| Laforge, Marc | 6:02 | 210 | Sudbury, Ont. | 1- 3-68 | Binghamton-Indianapolis | 4 | 6 | 10 |
| Lovsin, Ken | 5:11 | 190 | Peace River, Alta. | 12- 3-66 | Canadian Nat. Team | 0 | 10 | 10 |
| Maciver, Norm | 5:11 | 180 | Thunder Bay, Ont. | 9- 8-64 | N.Y. Rangers-Hartford | 1 | 32 | 33 |
| Quenneville, Joel | 6:01 | 200 | Windsor, Ont. | 9-15-58 | Hartford | 4 | 7 | 11 |
| Quinn, Doug | 6:02 | 205 | Red Deer, Alta. | 4- 2-65 | | | | |
| Samuelsson, Ulf | 6:01 | 195 | Fagersta, Sweden | 3-26-64 | Hartford | 9 | 26 | 35 |
| Shaw, Brad | 5:11 | 170 | Cambridge, Ont. | 4-28-64 | Hartford | 1 | 0 | 1 |
| Short, Mike | 6:06 | 210 | Scarborough, Ont. | | | | | |
| Trader, Larry | 6:02 | 185 | Barry's Bay, Ont. | 7- 7-63 | Binghamton | 11 | 40 | 51 |

## GOALTENDERS

| Name | Hgt. | Wgt. | Place of Birth | Date | 1988-89 Club | Mins. | GA. | SO. |
|---|---|---|---|---|---|---|---|---|
| Horn, Bill | 5:08 | 150 | Regina, Sask. | 4-16-67 | Western Michigan Univ. | 2181 | 153 | 0 |
| Liut, Mike | 6:02 | 195 | Weston, Ont. | 1- 7-56 | Hartford | 2006 | 142 | 1 |
| McKay, Ross | 5:11 | 175 | Edmonton, Alta | 3- 3-64 | Binghamton-Indianapolis | 1125 | 99 | 1 |
| Sidorkiewicz, Peter | 5:09 | 180 | Dabrown Bia., Poland | 6-29-63 | Hartford | 2635 | 133 | 4 |
| Whitmore, Kay | 5:11 | 175 | Sudbury, Ont. | 4-10-67 | Binghamton-Hartford | 3382 | 251 | 1 |

# Los Angeles Kings
**Smythe Division**

| | |
|---|---|
| Governor/President | Bruce McNall |
| Alternate Governors | Roy A. Mlakar, Rogatien Vachon |
| Executive Vice-President | Roy A. Mlakar |
| Vice-Presidents | Steven H. Nesenblatt, Nora J. Rothrock, Suzan A. Waks |
| Vice-President Administration/Finance | Robert Moor |
| General Manager | Rogatien Vachon |
| Coach | Tom Webster |
| Assistant Coaches | Cap Raeder, Rick Wilson |
| Administrative Assistant to General Manager | John Wolf |
| Special Assistant to General Manager | Ted O'Connor |
| Director of Player Personnel/Development | Nick Beverley |
| Director of Amateur Scouting | Bob Owen |
| Scouting Staff | Alex Smart, Kari Melanen, Jim Anderson, Serge Blanchard, Jan Lindgren, Joe Mahoney, Mark Miller, Al Murray, Don Perry |
| Executive Director, Communications and Public Relations | Scott J. Carmichael |
| Director of Media Relations | Nick Salata |
| Media Relations | Susan Carpenter |
| Trainers | Pete Demers, Mark O'Neill, Pete Millar |
| Home Ice | The Great Western Forum |
| Address | 3900 West Manchester Blvd., P. O. Box 17013, Inglewood, Calif. 90308 |
| Seating Capacity | 16,005 |
| Club Colors | Black, White and Silver |
| Phone | (213) 419-3160 |

Bruce McNall

Roy A. Mlakar

Rogatien Vachon

Tom Webster

# Los Angeles Kings 1989-90 Roster

## FORWARDS

| Name | Hgt. | Wgt. | Place of Birth | Date | 1988-89 Club | G. | A. | Pts. |
|---|---|---|---|---|---|---|---|---|
| Aivazoff, Micah | 6:01 | 192 | Powell River, B.C. | 5- 4-69 | Victoria | 35 | 65 | 100 |
| Allison, Mike | 6:00 | 200 | Fort Francis, Ont. | 3-28-61 | Los Angeles | 14 | 22 | 36 |
| Couturier, Sylvain | 6:02 | 205 | Greenfield Park, Que. | 4-23-68 | New Haven-Los Angeles | 19 | 23 | 42 |
| Crowder, Keith | 6:00 | 190 | Windsor, Ont. | 1- 6-59 | Boston | 15 | 18 | 33 |
| Duguay, Ron | 6:02 | 195 | Sudbury, Ont. | 7- 6-57 | Los Angeles | 7 | 17 | 24 |
| Duncanson, Craig | 6:00 | 190 | Naughton, Ont. | 3-17-67 | New Haven-Los Angeles | 25 | 39 | 64 |
| Elik, Todd | 6:02 | 190 | Brampton, Ont. | 4-15-66 | Colorado-New Haven | 31 | 40 | 71 |
| Fitzgerald, Sean | 6:01 | 208 | West Seneca, N.Y. | 1-12-67 | Oswego State | 51 | 26 | 77 |
| Fox, Jim | 5:08 | 175 | Coniston, Ont. | 5-18-60 | Los Angeles | (Did not play) | | |
| Gretzky, Wayne | 6:00 | 170 | Brantford, Ont. | 1-26-61 | Los Angeles | 54 | 114 | 168 |
| Horner, Steve | 6:01 | 195 | Cowansville, Que. | 6- 4-66 | Univ. of New Hampshire | 15 | 13 | 28 |
| Karialainen, Kyosti | 6:01 | 190 | Gavle, Sweden | 6-19-67 | Brynas, Sweden | 9 | 17 | 26 |
| Kasper, Steve | 5:08 | 175 | Montreal, Que. | 9-28-61 | Boston-Los Angeles | 19 | 31 | 50 |
| Kelly, Paul | 6:00 | 180 | Hamilton, Ont. | 4-17-67 | Utica-New Haven | 10 | 13 | 23 |
| Kontos, Chris | 6:01 | 195 | Toronto, Ont. | 12-10-63 | Los Angeles | 1 | 2 | 3 |
| Krushelnyski, Mike | 6:02 | 200 | Montreal, Que. | 4-27-60 | Los Angeles | 26 | 36 | 62 |
| Kudelski, Bob | 6:01 | 200 | Springfield, Mass. | 3- 3-64 | New Haven-Los Angeles | 33 | 22 | 55 |
| Lindholm, Mikael | 6:00 | 195 | Brynas, Sweden | 12-19-64 | Brynas, Sweden | 9 | 17 | 26 |
| Logan, Bob | 6:00 | 190 | Montreal, Que. | 2-22-64 | N. Haven-Rochester-Los Ang. | 23 | 34 | 57 |
| McDonough, Hubie | 5:09 | 180 | Manchester, N.H. | 7- 8-63 | New Haven-Los Angeles | 37 | 56 | 93 |
| McSorley, Marty | 6:01 | 225 | Hamilton, Ont. | 5-18-63 | Los Angeles | 10 | 17 | 27 |
| Miller, Jay | 6:02 | 210 | Wellesley, Mass. | 7-16-60 | Boston-Los Angeles | 7 | 7 | 14 |
| Nicholls, Bernie | 6:00 | 185 | Haliburton, Ont. | 6-24-61 | Los Angeles | 70 | 80 | 150 |
| Pasin, Dave | 6:01 | 205 | Edmonton, Alta. | 7- 8-66 | New Haven-Maine-Los Angeles | 27 | 28 | 55 |
| Robitaille, Luc | 6:01 | 190 | Montreal, Que. | 2-17-66 | Los Angeles | 46 | 52 | 98 |
| Sykes, Phil | 5:10 | 175 | Dawson Creek, B.C. | 3-18-59 | New Haven-Los Angeles | 9 | 18 | 27 |
| Taylor, Dave | 6:00 | 195 | Levack, Ont. | 12- 4-55 | Los Angeles | 26 | 37 | 63 |
| Tonelli, John | 6:01 | 200 | Milton, Ont. | 3-23-57 | Los Angeles | 31 | 33 | 64 |
| Van Kessel, John | 6:04 | 193 | Bridgewater, Ont. | 12-19-69 | North Bay | 7 | 13 | 20 |
| Walker, Gord | 6:00 | 175 | Castlegar, B.C. | 8-12-65 | New Haven-Los Angeles | 22 | 25 | 47 |
| Whyte, Sean | 6:00 | 198 | Sudbury, Ont. | 5- 4-70 | Guelph | 20 | 44 | 64 |
| Williams, Darryl | 5:11 | 185 | Mt. Pearl, Nfld. | 2- 9-68 | Belleville-New Haven | 29 | 26 | 55 |
| Wilson, Ross | 6:03 | 197 | The Pas, Man. | 6-26-69 | Peterborough | 28 | 11 | 39 |

## DEFENSEMEN

| Name | Hgt. | Wgt. | Place of Birth | Date | 1988-89 Club | G. | A. | Pts. |
|---|---|---|---|---|---|---|---|---|
| Baumgartner, Ken | 6:01 | 200 | Flin Flon, Man. | 3-11-66 | Los Angeles-New Haven | 2 | 6 | 8 |
| Chapdelaine, Rene | 6:01 | 195 | Weyburn, Sask. | 9-27-66 | Lake Superior State | 4 | 9 | 13 |
| DeGray, Dale | 6:00 | 200 | Ottawa, Ont. | 9- 1-63 | Los Angeles | 6 | 22 | 28 |
| Duchesne, Steve | 5:11 | 195 | Sept-Iles, Que. | 6-30-65 | Los Angeles | 25 | 50 | 75 |
| Germain, Eric | 6:01 | 195 | Quebec City, Que. | 6-26-66 | New Haven | 0 | 9 | 9 |
| Holden, Paul | 6:03 | 210 | Kitchener, Ont. | 3-15-70 | London | 11 | 21 | 32 |
| Jacques, Steve | 5:11 | 186 | Burnaby, B.C. | 2-21-69 | Tri-City | 18 | 34 | 52 |
| Kennedy, Dean | 6:02 | 200 | Redvers, Sask. | 1-18-63 | Los Angeles-N.Y. Rangers | 3 | 11 | 14 |
| Laidlaw, Tom | 6:02 | 205 | Brampton, Ont. | 4-15-58 | Los Angeles | 3 | 17 | 20 |
| Mann, Russ | 6:02 | 205 | Methuen, Mass. | 8-17-67 | St. Lawrence Univ. | 7 | 12 | 19 |
| Panek, Chris | 6:02 | 205 | Buffalo, N.Y. | 10-13-66 | New Haven-Flint | 5 | 20 | 25 |
| Prajsler, Petr | 6:02 | 200 | Hradec Kraloue, Cz. | 9-21-65 | New Haven-Los Angeles | 4 | 9 | 13 |
| Ricard, Eric | 6:04 | 220 | St. Cesaire, Que. | 2-16-69 | Granby | 5 | 31 | 36 |
| Robinson, Larry | 6:03 | 220 | Winchester, Ont. | 6- 2-51 | Montreal | 4 | 26 | 30 |
| Thompson, Brent | 6:02 | 175 | Calgary, Alta. | 1- 9-71 | Medicine Hat | 3 | 10 | 13 |
| Watters, Tim | 5:11 | 185 | Kamloops, B.C. | 7-25-59 | Los Angeles | 3 | 18 | 21 |
| Wiemer, Jim | 6:04 | 208 | Sudbury, Ont. | 1- 9-61 | Cape Breton-N.Haven-Los Ang. | 15 | 33 | 48 |
| Young, Scott | 6:01 | 195 | Burlington, Ont. | 5-26-65 | Colgate Univ.-New Haven | 16 | 23 | 39 |

## GOALTENDERS

| Name | Hgt. | Wgt. | Place of Birth | Date | 1988-89 Club | Mins. | GA. | SO. |
|---|---|---|---|---|---|---|---|---|
| Gosselin, Mario | 5:08 | 160 | Thetford Mines, Que. | 6-15-63 | Quebec-Halifax | 2247 | 155 | 0 |
| Healy, Glenn | 5:09 | 183 | Pickering, Ont. | 8-23-62 | Los Angeles | 2699 | 192 | 0 |
| Hrudey, Kelly | 5:10 | 180 | Edmonton, Alta. | 1-13-61 | N.Y. Islanders-Los Angeles | 3774 | 230 | 1 |
| Hyduke, John | 5:10 | 165 | Hibbing, Minn. | 6-23-67 | Univ. of Minnesota-Duluth | 1622 | 103 | 0 |
| Repp, Carl | 6:00 | 175 | Vancouver, B.C. | | Univ. of British Columbia | 1695 | 117 | 2 |
| Stauber, Robb | 6:00 | 170 | Duluth, Minn. | 11-25-67 | Univ. of Minnesota | 2024 | 82 | 0 |

# Minnesota North Stars
## Norris Division

| | |
|---|---|
| Co-Chairmen of the Board | George Gund III and Gordon Gund |
| President | Lou Nanne |
| Vice-President, General Manager | Jack Ferreira |
| Vice President, Communications/Sales | Dick Arneson |
| Vice-President, Corporate Relations | Paul Giel |
| Vice President, Met Center Operations | Jim Goddard |
| Vice President, Marketing | Frank Jirik |
| Vice President, Finance | George Wettstaedt |
| Assistant General Manager | Dean Lombardi |
| Coach | Pierre Page |
| Assistant Coaches | Dave Chambers, Craig Hartsburg, Doug Jarvis |
| Director of Professional Scouting | Chuck Grillo |
| Director of Amateur Scouting | Les Jackson |
| Scouts | Craig Button, Pat Funk, Herb Hammond, George Kingston, Mark Pezzin, Brad Robson, Larry Ross |
| Public Relations Director | Joe Janasz |
| Assistant Public Relations Director | Joan Preston |
| Community Relations Director | Patty Reid |
| Director of Administration | Peter Jocketty |
| Head Athletic Trainer | Dave Surprenant |
| Athletic Training Consultant | Doc Rose |
| Assistant Trainer | Dave Smith |
| Equipment Manager | Mark Baribeau |
| Home Ice | Metropolitan Sports Center |
| Address | 7901 Cedar Avenue S., Bloomington, Minn. 55420 |
| Seating Capacity | 15,093 |
| Club colors | Green, White, Gold and Black |
| Phone | (612) 853-9333 |

George Gund III

Gordon Gund

Jack Ferreira

Pierre Page

# Minnesota North Stars 1989-90 Roster

## FORWARDS

| Name | Hgt. | Wgt. | Place of Birth | Date | 1988-89 Club | G. | A. | Pts. |
|---|---|---|---|---|---|---|---|---|
| Archibald, Dave | 6:01 | 195 | Vancouver, B.C. | 4-14-69 | Minnesota | 14 | 19 | 33 |
| Babe, Warren | 6:03 | 200 | Medicine Hat, Alta. | 6- 7-68 | Kalamazoo-Minnesota | 20 | 27 | 47 |
| Barber, Don | 6:01 | 205 | Victoria, B.C. | 12- 2-64 | Kalamazoo-Minnesota | 22 | 22 | 44 |
| Bernard, Larry | 6:02 | 195 | Prince George, B.C. | 4-16-67 | Kalamazoo | 13 | 21 | 34 |
| Bellows, Brian | 5:11 | 195 | St. Catharines, Ont. | 9- 1-64 | Minnesota | 23 | 27 | 50 |
| Berezan, Perry | 6:02 | 190 | Edmonton, Alta. | 12- 5-64 | Calgary-Minnesota | 5 | 8 | 13 |
| Bischoff, Grant | 5:10 | 165 | Anoka, Minn. | 10-26-68 | Univ. of Minnesota | 21 | 16 | 37 |
| Blum, Ken | 6:01 | 175 | Hackensack, N.J. | 6- 8-71 | St. Joseph Prep. (N.J.) | 50 | 59 | 109 |
| Brooke, Bob | 6:01 | 200 | Acton, Mass. | 12-18-60 | Minnesota | 7 | 9 | 16 |
| Broten, Neal | 5:09 | 170 | Roseau, Minn. | 11-29-59 | Minnesota | 18 | 38 | 56 |
| Churla, Shane | 6:01 | 200 | Fernie, B.C. | 6-24-65 | Salt Lake-Calgary-Minnesota | 4 | 13 | 17 |
| Craig, Mike | 6:01 | 180 | London, Ont. | 6- 6-71 | Oshawa | 36 | 36 | 72 |
| DePalma, Larry | 6:00 | 190 | Trenton, Mich. | 10-27-65 | Minnesota | 5 | 7 | 12 |
| Duchesne, Gaetan | 5:11 | 200 | Quebec City, Que. | 7-11-62 | Quebec | 8 | 21 | 29 |
| Emmons, Gary | 5:09 | 180 | Winnipeg, Man. | 12-30-63 | Canadian Nat. Team | 16 | 26 | 42 |
| Evans, Kevin | 5:11 | 195 | Peterborough, Ont. | 7-10-65 | Kalamazoo | 22 | 32 | 54 |
| Fraser, Curt | 6:01 | 200 | Cincinnati, O. | 1-12-58 | Minnesota | 5 | 5 | 10 |
| Gagner, Dave | 5:10 | 185 | Chatham, Ont. | 12-11-64 | Minnesota | 35 | 43 | 78 |
| Gartner, Mike | 6:00 | 185 | Ottawa, Ont. | 10-29-59 | Washington-Minnesota | 33 | 36 | 69 |
| Gaudreau, Rob | 5:10 | 175 | Lincoln, R.I. | 1-20-70 | Providence College | 14 | 16 | 30 |
| Gavin, Stewart | 6:00 | 190 | Ottawa, Ont. | 3-15-60 | Minnesota | 8 | 18 | 26 |
| Gotaas, Steve | 5:09 | 170 | Camrose, Alta. | 5-10-67 | Kalamazoo-Minnesota | 34 | 41 | 75 |
| Hiltner, Mike | 6:01 | 190 | St. Cloud, Minn. | 3-22-66 | Minnesota | 15 | 17 | 32 |
| Hodge, Ken | 6:01 | 190 | St. Catharines, Ont. | 4-13-66 | Kalamazoo-Minnesota | 27 | 46 | 73 |
| Jerrard, Paul | 6:01 | 185 | Winnipeg, Man. | 4-30-65 | Kalamazoo-Minnesota | 16 | 26 | 42 |
| Kelfer, Mike | 5:10 | 185 | Peabody, Mass. | 1- 2-67 | Boston Univ. | 23 | 27 | 50 |
| McCrady, Scott | 6:01 | 195 | Calgary, Alta. | 10-30-68 | Kalamazoo | 8 | 29 | 37 |
| Modano, Mike | 6:03 | 190 | Livonia, Mich. | 6- 7-70 | Prince Albert | 39 | 66 | 105 |
| McRae, Basil | 6:02 | 205 | Orilla, Ont. | 1- 5-61 | Minnesota | 12 | 19 | 31 |
| Messier, Mitch | 6:02 | 185 | Regina, Sask. | 8-21-65 | Kalamazoo-Minnesota | 34 | 47 | 81 |
| McHugh, Mike | 5:10 | 190 | Bowdoin, Mass. | 8-16-65 | Kalamazoo | 17 | 29 | 46 |
| Norton, Darcy | 6:00 | 175 | Camrose, Alta. | 5- 2-67 | Kalamazoo | 39 | 38 | 77 |
| Pasek, Dusan | 6:01 | 200 | Bratislava, Czech. | 9- 7-60 | Minnesota | 4 | 10 | 14 |
| Quintin, J.F. | 6:01 | 190 | St. Jean, Que. | 5-28-69 | Shawinigan | 52 | 100 | 152 |
| Robinson, Scott | 6:02 | 200 | 100 Mile House, B.C. | 3-29-64 | Kalamazoo | 14 | 17 | 31 |
| Schreiber, Wally | 5:10 | 180 | Edmonton, Alta. | 4-15-62 | Minnesota | 2 | 5 | 7 |
| Smith, Randy | 6:04 | 200 | Saskatoon, Sask. | 7- 7-65 | Kalamazoo-Maine | 13 | 25 | 38 |
| Sullivan, Mike | 6:02 | 185 | Marshfield, Mass. | 2-27-68 | Boston Univ. | 19 | 17 | 36 |
| Tomlinson, Kirk | 5:11 | 190 | Toronto, Ont. | 5- 2-68 | Kitchener | 23 | 22 | 45 |
| Weisbrod, John | 6:01 | 185 | Syosset, N.Y. | 10- 8-68 | Harvard | 22 | 13 | 35 |

## DEFENSEMEN

| Name | Hgt. | Wgt. | Place of Birth | Date | 1988-89 Club | G. | A. | Pts. |
|---|---|---|---|---|---|---|---|---|
| Berger, Mike | 6:00 | 200 | Edmonton, Alta. | 6- 2-67 | Kalamazoo | 9 | 16 | 25 |
| Chambers, Shawn | 6:02 | 210 | Royal Oaks, Mich. | 10-11-66 | Minnesota | 5 | 19 | 24 |
| Gaetz, Link | 6:04 | 220 | Vancouver, B.C. | 10- 2-68 | Kalamazoo-Minnesota | 3 | 6 | 9 |
| Giles, Curt | 5:08 | 175 | The Pas, Man. | 11-30-58 | Minnesota | 5 | 10 | 15 |
| Hollyman, Rhys | 6:03 | 210 | Toronto, Ont. | 1-30-70 | Univ. of Miami-Ohio | 8 | 5 | 13 |
| Keczmer, Dan | 6:01 | 180 | Mt. Clemens, Mich. | 5-25-68 | Lake Superior State | 2 | 19 | 21 |
| Kolstad, Dean | 6:06 | 210 | Edmonton, Alta. | 6-16-68 | Kalamazoo-Minnesota | 11 | 28 | 39 |
| Larson, Reed | 6:00 | 195 | Minneapolis, Minn. | 7-30-56 | Edmonton-Islanders-Minnesota | 9 | 29 | 38 |
| MacLeod, Pat | 5:11 | 190 | Melford, Sask. | 6-15-69 | Kamloops | 11 | 34 | 45 |
| MacArthur, Ken | 6:02 | 185 | Rossland, B.C. | 3-15-68 | Univ. of Denver | 11 | 19 | 30 |
| Mullowney, Mike | 6:01 | 190 | Brighton, Mass. | 1-17-66 | Boston College | 2 | 7 | 9 |
| Murphy, Larry | 6:02 | 210 | Scarborough, Ont. | 3- 8-61 | Washington-Minnesota | 11 | 35 | 46 |
| Musil, Frantisek | 6:03 | 205 | Pardubice, Czech. | 12-17-64 | Minnesota | 1 | 19 | 20 |
| Olimb, Larry | 5:10 | 160 | Warroad, Minn. | 8-11-69 | Univ. of Minnesota | 10 | 29 | 39 |
| Pederson, Tom | 5:09 | 165 | Bloomington, Minn. | 1-14-70 | Univ. of Minnesota | 4 | 20 | 24 |
| Pitlick, Lance | 6:00 | 185 | Minneapolis, Minn. | 11- 5-67 | Univ. of Minnesota | 3 | 8 | 11 |
| Schmidt, Don | 5:10 | 185 | Calgary, Alta. | 7-13-68 | Kamloops | 5 | 9 | 14 |
| Schofield, David | 6:01 | 190 | Wayland, Mass. | 2-17-65 | Kalamazoo | 1 | 6 | 7 |
| Scremin, Claudio | 6:01 | 195 | Burnaby, B.C. | 5-28-68 | Univ. of Maine | 5 | 24 | 29 |
| Siren, Ville | 6:01 | 185 | Tempere, Finland | 2-10-64 | Pittsburgh-Minnesota | 3 | 10 | 13 |
| Tinordi, Mark | 6:04 | 205 | Red Deer, Alta. | 5- 9-66 | Minnesota | 2 | 3 | 5 |
| Viveiros, Emanuel | 6:00 | 175 | St. Albert, Alta. | 1- 8-66 | Kalamazoo | 11 | 28 | 39 |
| Wilkinson, Neil | 6:03 | 180 | Selkirk, Man. | 10-16-67 | Kalamazoo | 5 | 15 | 20 |
| Zettler, Rob | 6:03 | 190 | Sept. Iles, Que. | 3- 8-68 | Kalamazoo | 5 | 21 | 26 |
| Zmolek, Doug | 6:01 | 175 | Rochester, Minn. | 11- 3-70 | Rochester J.M.H.S. | 17 | 40 | 57 |

## GOALTENDERS

| Name | Hgt. | Wgt. | Place of Birth | Date | 1988-89 Club | Mins. | GA. | SO. |
|---|---|---|---|---|---|---|---|---|
| Blue, John | 5:09 | 170 | Huntington, Calif. | 2-19-66 | Kalamazoo-Virginia | 1540 | 107 | 0 |
| Casey, Jon | 5:10 | 155 | Grand Rapids, Minn. | 3-29-62 | Minnesota | 2961 | 151 | 1 |
| Dyck, Larry | 5:11 | 170 | Winkler, Man. | 12-15-65 | Kalamazoo | 2308 | 168 | 0 |
| Felicio, Mark | 5:07 | 170 | Smithfield, R.I. | 12- 1-68 | Ferris State | 1045 | 85 | 0 |
| Flaherty, Wade | 5:11 | 170 | Terrace, B.C. | 1-11-68 | Victoria | 2408 | 0 | 0 |
| Myllys, Jarmo | 5:08 | 150 | Savolinna, Finland | 5-29-65 | Kalamazoo-Minnesota | 1761 | 115 | 0 |
| Stolp, Jeff | 6:00 | 180 | Hibbing, Minn. | 6-20-70 | Univ. of Minnesota | 742 | 45 | 0 |
| Takko, Kari | 6:02 | 185 | Uusikaupunki, Finland | 6-23-62 | Minnesota | 1603 | 93 | 0 |

# Montreal Canadiens
## Adams Division

| | |
|---|---|
| President | Ronald Corey |
| Managing Director | Serge Savard |
| Senior Vice-President, Corporate Affairs | Jean Beliveau |
| Vice-President, Forum Operations | Aldo Giampaolo |
| Vice-President, Finance and Administration | Fred Steer |
| Assistant to Managing Director | Jacques Lemaire |
| Director of Recruitment and Assistant to Managing Director | Andre Boudrias |
| Coach | Pat Burns |
| Assistant Coach | Jacques Laperriere |
| Goaltending Instructor | Francois Allaire |
| Director of Player Development and Scout | Claude Ruel |
| Chief Scout | Doug Robinson |
| Director of Special Events | Camil Desroches |
| Director of Advertising Sales | Floyd Curry |
| Director of Public Relations | Claude Mouton |
| Director of Press Relations | Michele Lapointe |
| Club Physician | Dr. D.G. Kinnear |
| Head Sports Therapist | Gaetan Lefebvre |
| Head Trainer | Eddy Palchak |
| Assistant Trainers | Pierre Gervais, Sylvain Toupin |
| Home Ice | Montreal Forum |
| Address | 2313 St. Catherine Street West, Montreal, Que. H3H 1N2 |
| Seating Capacity | 16,197 |
| Club colors | Red, White and Blue |
| Phone | (514) 932-2582 |

**Ronald Corey**

**Serge Savard**

**Jean Beliveau**

**Pat Burns**

# Montreal Canadiens 1989-90 Roster

## FORWARDS

| Name | Hgt. | Wgt. | Place of Birth | Date | 1988-89 Club | G. | A. | Pts. |
|---|---|---|---|---|---|---|---|---|
| Brunet, Benoit | 5:11 | 184 | St. Anne-B'll'v'e, Que. | 8-24-68 | Sherbrooke-Montreal | 41 | 77 | 118 |
| Carbonneau, Guy | 5:11 | 180 | Sept.-Iles, Que. | 3-18-60 | Montreal | 26 | 30 | 56 |
| Cassels, Andrew | 6:00 | 167 | Bramalea, Ont. | 7-23-69 | Ottawa | 37 | 97 | 134 |
| Chorske, Tom | 6:01 | 185 | Minneapolis, Minn. | 9-18-66 | Univ. of Minnesota | 25 | 24 | 49 |
| Corson, Shayne | 6:00 | 175 | Barrie, Ont. | 8-13-66 | Montreal | 26 | 24 | 50 |
| Courtnall, Russ | 5:11 | 180 | Duncan, B.C. | 6-2-65 | Toronto-Montreal | 23 | 18 | 41 |
| Cristofoli, Ed | 6:02 | 205 | Trail, B.C. | 5-14-67 | Denver Univ. | 20 | 19 | 39 |
| Desjardins, Martin | 5:11 | 165 | St. Rose, Que. | 1-28-67 | Sherbrooke | 17 | 27 | 44 |
| Ferguson, John | 6:00 | 175 | Winnipeg, Man. | 7-7-67 | Providence College | 14 | 15 | 29 |
| Gilchrist, Brent | 5:11 | 175 | Moose Jaw, Sask. | 4-3-67 | Montreal-Sherbrooke | 14 | 21 | 35 |
| Keane, Mike | 5:10 | 175 | Winnipeg, Man. | 5-28-67 | Montreal | 16 | 19 | 35 |
| Lebeau, Stephan | 5:10 | 180 | Sherbrooke, Que. | 2-28-68 | Sherbrooke-Montreal | 70 | 65 | 135 |
| Lemieux, Claude | 6:01 | 206 | Buckingham, Que. | 7-16-65 | Montreal | 29 | 22 | 51 |
| Lemieux, Jocelyn | 5:10 | 200 | Mont Laurier, Que. | 11-18-67 | Sherbrooke-Montreal | 25 | 29 | 54 |
| Martinson, Steve | 6:01 | 205 | Minnetonka, Minn. | 6-21-59 | Montreal-Sherbrooke | 6 | 7 | 13 |
| McPhee, Mike | 6:01 | 200 | Riviere-Bourgeois, N.S. | 7-14-60 | Montreal | 19 | 22 | 41 |
| Naslund, Mats | 5:07 | 160 | Timra, Sweden | 10-31-59 | Montreal | 33 | 51 | 84 |
| Nesich, Jim | 5:11 | 170 | Dearborn, Mich. | 2-22-66 | Sherbrooke | 12 | 34 | 46 |
| Pederson, Mark | 6:02 | 190 | Prelate, Sask. | 1-14-68 | Sherbrooke | 43 | 38 | 81 |
| Richer, Stephane | 6:02 | 200 | Ripon, Que. | 6-7-66 | Montreal | 25 | 35 | 60 |
| Roberge, Mario | 5:11 | 185 | Quebec, Que. | 1-23-64 | Sherbrooke | 4 | 9 | 13 |
| Roberge, Serge | 6:01 | 195 | Quebec, Que. | 3-31-65 | Sherbrooke | 5 | 7 | 12 |
| Saumier, Marc | 5:08 | 185 | Hull, Que. | 4-18-67 | Peoria-Sherbrooke | 12 | 11 | 23 |
| Skrudland, Brian | 6:00 | 188 | Peace River, Alta. | 7-31-63 | Montreal | 12 | 29 | 41 |
| Smith, Bobby | 6:04 | 210 | North Sydney, N.S. | 2-12-58 | Montreal | 32 | 51 | 83 |
| Thibaudeau, Gilles | 5:10 | 180 | Montreal, Que. | 3-4-63 | Montreal | 6 | 6 | 12 |
| Walter, Ryan | 6:00 | 195 | New Westminster, B.C. | 4-23-58 | Montreal | 14 | 17 | 31 |
| Woodley, Dan | 5:11 | 185 | Oklahoma City, Okla. | 12-29-67 | Milwaukee-Sherbrooke | 18 | 28 | 46 |

## DEFENSEMEN

| Name | Hgt. | Wgt. | Place of Birth | Date | 1988-89 Club | G. | A. | Pts. |
|---|---|---|---|---|---|---|---|---|
| Bishop, Mike | 6:02 | 185 | Sarnia, Ont. | 6-15-66 | Colgate Univ. | 8 | 13 | 21 |
| Bisson, Steve | 6:01 | 193 | Ottawa, Ont. | 5-24-68 | North Bay-Sherbrooke | 8 | 19 | 27 |
| Charron, Eric | 6:03 | 192 | Verdun, Que. | 1-14-70 | Verdun | 4 | 31 | 35 |
| Chelios, Chris | 6:01 | 186 | Chicago, Ill. | 1-25-62 | Montreal | 15 | 58 | 73 |
| Daigneault, J.J. | 5:11 | 185 | Montreal, Que. | 10-12-65 | Hershey-Sherbrooke | 10 | 43 | 53 |
| Desjardins, Eric | 6:01 | 185 | Rouyn, Que. | 6-14-69 | Montreal | 2 | 12 | 14 |
| Dufresne, Donald | 6:01 | 190 | Quebec, Que. | 4-10-67 | Sherbrooke-Montreal | 0 | 13 | 13 |
| Gauthier, Luc | 5:09 | 195 | Longueuil, Que. | 4-19-64 | Sherbrooke | 8 | 20 | 28 |
| Green, Rick | 6:03 | 210 | Belleville, Ont. | 2-20-56 | Montreal | 1 | 14 | 15 |
| Lefebvre, Sylvain | 6:02 | 187 | Richmond, Que. | 10-14-67 | Sherbrooke | 15 | 32 | 47 |
| Ludwig, Craig | 6:03 | 217 | Rhinelander, Wis. | 3-15-61 | Montreal | 3 | 13 | 16 |
| Lumme, Jyrki | 6:01 | 190 | Tampere, Finland | 7-16-66 | Sherbrooke-Montreal | 5 | 14 | 19 |
| Odelein, Lyle | 5:10 | 185 | Quill Lake, Sask. | 7-21-68 | Sherbrooke-Flint | 17 | 16 | 33 |
| Richards, Todd | 6:00 | 180 | Robindale, Minn. | 10-20-66 | Univ. of Minnesota | 6 | 32 | 38 |
| Richer, Stephane | 5:11 | 200 | Hull, Que. | 4-23-66 | Sherbrooke | 7 | 26 | 33 |
| Schneider, Mathieu | 5:11 | 180 | Woonsocket, R.I. | 6-12-69 | Cornwall | 16 | 57 | 73 |
| Svoboda, Petr | 6:01 | 170 | Most, Czech. | 2-14-66 | Montreal | 8 | 37 | 45 |

## GOALTENDERS

| Name | Hgt. | Wgt. | Place of Birth | Date | 1988-89 Club | Mins. | GA. | SO. |
|---|---|---|---|---|---|---|---|---|
| Bergeron, Jean | 6:02 | 181 | Hauterive, Que. | 10-14-68 | Verdun-Sherbrooke | 2719 | 213 | 0 |
| Exelby, Randy | 5:09 | 170 | Toronto, Ont. | 8-13-65 | Sherbrooke-Montreal | 2938 | 146 | 6 |
| Gravel, Francois | 6:02 | 185 | St. Foy, Que. | 10-21-68 | Sherbrooke | 1625 | 95 | 2 |
| Hayward, Brian | 5:10 | 175 | Georgetown, Ont. | 6-25-60 | Montreal | 2091 | 101 | 1 |
| Roy, Patrick | 6:00 | 174 | Quebec, Que. | 10-5-65 | Montreal | 2744 | 113 | 4 |

# New Jersey Devils
## Patrick Division

| | |
|---|---|
| Chairman | John J. McMullen |
| President and General Manager | Lou Lamoriello |
| Executive Vice-President | Max McNab |
| Coach | Jim Schoenfeld |
| Assistant Coach | John Cunniff |
| Goaltending Coach | Bob Bellemore |
| Director of Player Personnel | Marshall Johnston |
| Assistant Director of Player Personnel | David Conte |
| Scouts | Tim Burke, Claude Carrier, Frank Jay, Russ LeClair, Ed Thomlinson, Milt Fisher, Glen Dirk, Dan Labraaten, Les Widdifield |
| Strength Coach | Dimitri Lopuchin |
| Director, Public and Media Relations | David Freed |
| Public Relations Assistants | Mike Levine, Tom Shine |
| Executive Offices | Byrne Meadowlands Arena |
| Home Ice | Byrne Meadowlands Arena |
| Address | Meadowlands Arena, P.O. Box 504, East Rutherford, N.J. 07073 |
| Seating Capacity | 19,040 |
| Club Colors | Red, Green and White |
| Phone | (201) 935-6050 |

John J. McMullen

Lou Lamoriello

Max McNab

Jim Schoenfeld

# New Jersey Devils 1989-90 Roster

| FORWARDS | Hgt. | Wgt. | Place of Birth | Date | 1988-89 Club | G. | A. | Pts. |
|---|---|---|---|---|---|---|---|---|
| Anderson, Perry | 6:01 | 225 | Barrie, Ont. | 10-14-61 | New Jersey | 3 | 6 | 9 |
| Brady, Neil | 6:03 | 190 | Montreal, Que. | 4-12-68 | Utica | 16 | 21 | 37 |
| Broten, Aaron | 5:10 | 180 | Roseau, Minn. | 11-14-60 | New Jersey | 16 | 43 | 59 |
| Brown, Doug | 5:11 | 180 | Southborough, Mass. | 6-12-64 | New Jersey-Utica | 16 | 14 | 30 |
| Budy, Tim | 6:00 | 190 | Selkirk, Man. | 2-14-67 | Colorado College-Utica | 23 | 23 | 46 |
| Cichocki, Chris | 5:11 | 185 | Detroit, Mich. | 9- 7-63 | Utica-New Jersey | 32 | 32 | 64 |
| Conacher, Pat | 5:08 | 190 | Edmonton, Alta. | 5- 1-59 | New Jersey | 7 | 5 | 12 |
| Crowder, Troy | 6:04 | 215 | Sudbury, Ont. | 5- 3-68 | Utica | 6 | 4 | 10 |
| Guerin, Bill | 6:02 | 190 | Wilbraham, Mass. | 11- 9-70 | Springfield Olympics | 32 | 37 | 69 |
| Johnson, Mark | 5:09 | 170 | Madison, Wis. | 9-22-57 | New Jersey | 13 | 25 | 38 |
| Korn, Jim | 6:04 | 220 | Hopkins, Minn. | 9-28-57 | New Jersey | 15 | 16 | 31 |
| Lanthier, Jean-Marc | 6:02 | 195 | Montreal, Que. | 3-27-63 | Utica-Maine | 30 | 42 | 72 |
| MacLean, John | 6:00 | 200 | Oshawa, Ont. | 11-20-64 | New Jersey | 42 | 45 | 87 |
| Madill, Jeff | 5:11 | 195 | Oshawa, Ont. | 6-21-67 | Utica | 23 | 25 | 48 |
| Maley, David | 6:02 | 205 | Beaver Dam, Wis. | 4-24-63 | New Jersey | 5 | 6 | 11 |
| Miller, Jason | 6:01 | 180 | Edmonton, Alta. | 3- 1-71 | Medicine Hat | 51 | 55 | 106 |
| Morris, Jon | 6:00 | 175 | Lowell, Mass. | 5- 6-66 | New Jersey | 0 | 2 | 2 |
| Muller, Kirk | 6:00 | 205 | Kingston, Ont. | 2- 8-66 | New Jersey | 31 | 43 | 74 |
| Ojanen, Janne | 6:02 | 190 | Tampere, Finland | 4- 9-68 | Utica-New Jersey | 23 | 38 | 61 |
| Poddubny, Walt | 6:01 | 205 | Thunder Bay, Ont. | 2-14-60 | Quebec | 38 | 37 | 75 |
| Rooney, Steve | 6:02 | 200 | Canton, Mass. | 6-28-62 | New Jersey | 3 | 1 | 4 |
| Shanahan, Brendan | 6:03 | 205 | Mimico, Ont. | 1-23-69 | New Jersey | 22 | 28 | 50 |
| Skalde, Jarrod | 6:00 | 180 | Niagara Falls, Ont. | 2-26-71 | Oshawa | 38 | 38 | 76 |
| Stewart, Al | 6:00 | 195 | Fort St. John, B.C. | 1-31-64 | Utica-New Jersey | 9 | 25 | 34 |
| Sundstrom, Patrik | 6:00 | 195 | Skelleftea, Sweden | 12-14-61 | New Jersey | 28 | 41 | 69 |
| Sundstrom, Peter | 6:00 | 180 | Skelleftea, Sweden | 12-14-61 | Washington | 4 | 2 | 6 |
| Todd, Kevin | 5:10 | 180 | Winnipeg, Man. | 5- 4-63 | Utica-New Jersey | 26 | 45 | 71 |
| Turgeon, Sylvain | 6:00 | 195 | Noranda, Que. | 1-17-65 | Hartford | 16 | 14 | 30 |
| Vilgrain, Claude | 6:01 | 195 | Port-au-Prince, Haiti | 3- 1-63 | Utica-Milwaukee | 32 | 43 | 75 |
| Ysebaert, Paul | 6:01 | 185 | Sarnia, Ont. | 5-15-66 | Utica-New Jersey | 36 | 48 | 84 |
| **DEFENSEMEN** | | | | | | | | |
| Albelin, Tommy | 6:01 | 200 | Stockholm, Sweden | 5-21-64 | Quebec-New Jersey | 9 | 28 | 37 |
| Blessman, John | 6:03 | 210 | Toronto, Ont. | 4-27-67 | Utica-Indianapolis | 4 | 8 | 12 |
| Daneyko, Ken | 6:00 | 210 | Windsor, Ont. | 4-16-64 | New Jersey | 5 | 5 | 10 |
| Driver, Bruce | 6:00 | 185 | Toronto, Ont. | 4-29-62 | New Jersey | 1 | 15 | 16 |
| Fetisov, Viacheslav | 6:01 | 200 | Moscow, USSR | 5-20-58 | Central Red Army | 9 | 8 | 17 |
| Huscroft, Jamie | 6:02 | 200 | Creston, B.C. | 1- 9-67 | Utica-New Jersey | 2 | 12 | 14 |
| Kurvers, Tom | 6:00 | 205 | Bloomington, Minn. | 9-14-62 | New Jersey | 16 | 50 | 66 |
| Laniel, Marc | 6:00 | 190 | Oshawa, Ont. | 1-16-68 | Utica | 6 | 28 | 34 |
| Marcinyshyn, Dave | 6:03 | 210 | Edmonton, Alta. | 2- 4-67 | Utica | 4 | 14 | 18 |
| O'Connor, Myles | 5:11 | 165 | Calgary, Alta. | 4- 2-67 | Univ. of Michigan-Utica | 3 | 31 | 34 |
| Ruotsalainen, Reijo | 5:08 | 170 | Oulu, Finland | 4- 1-60 | Bern | .. | .. | .. |
| Starikov, Sergei | 5:10 | 215 | Chelysbinsk, USSR | 12-4-58 | Central Red Army | 3 | 3 | 6 |
| Velischek, Randy | 6:01 | 200 | Montreal, Que. | 2-10-62 | New Jersey | 4 | 14 | 18 |
| Weinrich, Eric | 6:01 | 210 | Roanoke, Va. | 12-19-66 | Utica-New Jersey | 17 | 27 | 44 |
| Wolanin, Craig | 6:03 | 210 | Grosse Pointe, Mich. | 7-27-67 | New Jersey | 3 | 8 | 11 |
| Woods, Bob | 6:00 | 170 | Leroy, Sask. | 1-24-68 | Brandon-Utica | 26 | 51 | 77 |
| **GOALTENDERS** | | | | | | Mins. | GA. | SO. |
| Billington, Craig | 5:10 | 165 | London, Ont. | 9-11-66 | Utica-New Jersey | 2572 | 161 | 2 |
| Burke, Sean | 6:03 | 205 | Windsor, Ont. | 1-29-67 | New Jersey | 3590 | 230 | 3 |
| Delianedis, Dan | 5:09 | 185 | Worcester, Mass. | 7- 3-64 | Utica | 94 | 8 | 0 |
| Melanson, Roland | 5:10 | 180 | Moncton, N.B. | 6-28-60 | New Haven-Los Angeles | 1912 | 125 | 1 |
| Terreri, Chris | 5:09 | 160 | Providence, R.I. | 11-15-64 | Utica-New Jersey | 2716 | 150 | 0 |

# New York Islanders
## Patrick Division

| | |
|---|---|
| Owner | John O. Pickett, Jr. |
| Chairman of the Board and General Manager | William A. Torrey |
| President | John H. Krumpe |
| General Counsel | William M. Skehan |
| Vice-President/Administration | Joseph H. Dreyer |
| Vice-President/Finance | Arthur McCarthy |
| Vice-President/Media Sales | Arthur Adler |
| Coach | Al Arbour |
| Assistant Coach/Director of Hockey Administration | Darcy Regier |
| Assistant Coach | Lorne Henning |
| Assistant General Manager/Director of Scouting | Gerry Ehman |
| Scouting Staff | Harry Boyd, Richard Green, Hal Laycoe, Mario Saraceno, Jack Vivian, Earl Ingarfield, Bert Marshall |
| Publicity Director | Greg Bouris |
| Assistant Publicity Director | Catherine Schutte |
| Communications Consultant | Barney Kremenko |
| Controller | Ralph Sellitti |
| Trainer | Mark Aldridge |
| Assistant Trainers | Jim Pickard, Terry Murphy |
| Home Ice | Nassau Veterans Memorial Coliseum |
| Address | Uniondale, N. Y. 11553 |
| Seating Capacity | 16,297 |
| Club colors | Blue, White and Orange |
| Phone | (516) 794-4100 |

John O. Pickett, Jr.

Bill Torrey

Al Arbour

Gerry Ehman

# New York Islanders 1989-90 Roster

| FORWARDS | Hgt. | Wgt. | Place of Birth | Date | 1988-89 Club | G. | A. | Pts. |
|---|---|---|---|---|---|---|---|---|
| Byram, Shawn | 6:02 | 204 | Neepawa, Man. | 9-12-68 | Springfield | 5 | 11 | 16 |
| Chyzowski, Davis | 6:01 | 190 | Edmonton, Alta. | 7-11-71 | Kamloops | 56 | 48 | 104 |
| Clark, Kerry | 6:01 | 190 | Kelvington, Sask. | 8-21-68 | Springfield | 7 | 7 | 14 |
| Dalgarno, Brad | 6:03 | 215 | Vancouver, B.C. | 8-11-67 | N.Y. Islanders | 11 | 10 | 21 |
| Dallman, Rod | 5:11 | 185 | Quesnel, B.C. | 1-26-67 | Springfield | 12 | 12 | 24 |
| DiMaio, Rob | 5:08 | 175 | Calgary, Alta. | 2-19-68 | Springfield-N.Y. Islanders | 14 | 18 | 32 |
| Doucet, Wayne | 6:02 | 203 | Etibicoke, Ont. | 6-19-70 | Kingston-Springfield | 28 | 45 | 73 |
| Ens, Kelly | 6:02 | 194 | Saskatoon, Sask. | 6-15-69 | Lethbridge | 46 | 36 | 82 |
| Ewen, Dean | 6:01 | 185 | St. Albert, Alta. | 2-28-69 | Seattle-Springfield | 22 | 30 | 52 |
| Fitzgerald, Tom | 6:01 | 193 | Melrose, Mass. | 8-28-68 | Springfield-N.Y. Islanders | 27 | 23 | 50 |
| Flatley, Patrick | 6:02 | 197 | Toronto, Ont. | 10- 3-63 | N.Y. Islanders-Springfield | 11 | 16 | 27 |
| Fraser, Iain | 5:10 | 175 | Scarborough, Ont. | 8-10-69 | Oshawa | 33 | 57 | 90 |
| Gaucher, Yves | 5:11 | 189 | Valleyfield, Que. | 7-14-68 | Chicoutimi | 35 | 58 | 93 |
| Green, Travis | 6:00 | 196 | Creston, B.C. | 12-20-70 | Spokane | 51 | 51 | 102 |
| Grieve, Brent | 6:01 | 202 | Oshawa, Ont. | 5- 9-69 | Oshawa | 34 | 33 | 67 |
| Henry, Dale | 6:00 | 205 | Prince Albert, Sask. | 9-24-64 | Springfield-N.Y. Islanders | 15 | 23 | 38 |
| Huber, Phil | 5:10 | 194 | Calgary, Alta. | 1-10-69 | Kamloops | 54 | 68 | 122 |
| Kerr, Alan | 5:11 | 195 | Hazleton, B.C. | 3-28-64 | N.Y. Islanders | 20 | 18 | 38 |
| King, Derek | 6:01 | 210 | Hamilton, Ont. | 2-11-67 | N.Y. Islanders-Springfield | 18 | 29 | 47 |
| Kushner, Dale | 6:01 | 205 | Terrace, B.C. | 6-13-66 | Springfield | 5 | 8 | 13 |
| Lauer, Brad | 6:00 | 195 | Humboldt, Sask. | 10-27-66 | N.Y. Islanders-Springfield | 4 | 7 | 11 |
| LaFontaine, Pat | 5:10 | 177 | St. Louis, Mo. | 2-22-65 | N.Y. Islanders | 45 | 43 | 88 |
| LeBrun, Sean | 6:02 | 200 | Prince George, B.C. | 5- 2-69 | Tri-City | 52 | 73 | 125 |
| Makela, Mikko | 6:02 | 193 | Tampere, Finland | 2-28-65 | N.Y. Islanders | 17 | 28 | 45 |
| McLellan, Todd | 5:11 | 185 | Melville, Sask. | 10- 3-67 | Springfield | 7 | 19 | 26 |
| Stevens, Mike | 5:11 | 195 | Kitchener, Ont. | 12-30-65 | Springfield-N.Y. Islanders | 18 | 13 | 31 |
| Sutter, Brent | 5:11 | 180 | Viking, Alta. | 6-10-62 | N.Y. Islanders | 29 | 34 | 63 |
| Trottier, Bryan | 5:11 | 195 | Val Marie, Sask. | 7-17-56 | N.Y. Islanders | 17 | 28 | 45 |
| Volek, David | 6:00 | 185 | Czechoslovakia | 6-18-66 | N.Y. Islanders | 25 | 34 | 59 |
| Vukota, Mick | 6:02 | 195 | Saskatoon, Sask. | 9-14-66 | N.Y. Islanders-Springfield | 3 | 2 | 5 |
| Walsh, Mike | 6:02 | 195 | New York, N.Y. | 4- 3-62 | Springfield-N.Y. Islanders | 33 | 34 | 67 |
| Wood, Randy | 6:00 | 195 | Princeton, N.J. | 10-12-63 | N.Y. Islanders-Springfield | 16 | 14 | 30 |
| Young, Steve | 6:03 | 200 | Calgary, Alta. | 5-17-69 | Moose Jaw | 20 | 17 | 37 |
| DEFENSEMEN | | | | | | | | |
| Berg, Bill | 6:01 | 190 | St. Catharines, Ont. | 10-21-67 | Springfield-N.Y. Islanders | 18 | 34 | 52 |
| Bergevin, Marc | 6:00 | 185 | Montreal, Que. | 8-11-65 | Chicago-N.Y. Islanders | 2 | 13 | 15 |
| Brassard, Andre | 6:00 | 190 | Arvida, Que. | 4-18-68 | Trois-Rivieres | 10 | 40 | 50 |
| Cheveldayoff, Kevin | 6:00 | 202 | Saskatoon, Sask. | 2- 4-70 | Brandon | 4 | 12 | 16 |
| Chynoweth, Dean | 6:02 | 190 | Calgary, Alta. | 10-30-68 | N.Y. Islanders | 0 | 0 | 0 |
| Crossman, Doug | 6:02 | 190 | Peterborough, Ont. | 6-30-60 | Los Angeles | 10 | 15 | 25 |
| Diduck, Gerald | 6:02 | 207 | Edmonton, Alta. | 4- 6-65 | N.Y. Islanders | 11 | 21 | 32 |
| Evans, Shawn | 6:03 | 195 | Kingston, Ont. | 9- 7-65 | Springfield | 9 | 50 | 59 |
| Finley, Jeff | 6:02 | 185 | Edmonton, Alta. | 4-14-67 | Springfield-N.Y. Islanders | 3 | 16 | 19 |
| Lammens, Hank | 6:01 | 190 | Brockville, Ont. | 2-21-66 | Springfield | 1 | 13 | 14 |
| McBean, Wayne | 6:02 | 185 | Calgary, Alta. | 2-21-69 | Los Ang.-N. Haven-Islanders | 1 | 7 | 8 |
| Norton, Jeff | 6:02 | 190 | Cambridge, Mass. | 11-25-65 | N.Y. Islanders | 1 | 30 | 31 |
| Nylund, Gary | 6:04 | 210 | Surrey, B.C. | 10-28-63 | Chicago-N.Y. Islanders | 7 | 13 | 20 |
| Pilon, Richard | 6:00 | 202 | Saskatoon, Sask. | 4-30-68 | N.Y. Islanders | 0 | 14 | 14 |
| Pryor, Chris | 5:11 | 210 | St. Paul, Minn. | 1-31-61 | Springfield-N.Y. Islanders | 3 | 6 | 9 |
| Smith, Vern | 6:01 | 190 | Winnipeg, Man. | 5-30-64 | Springfield | 3 | 26 | 29 |
| GOALTENDERS | | | | | | Mins. | GA. | SO. |
| Fitzpatrick, Mark | 6:02 | 190 | Toronto, Ont. | 11-13-68 | N. Haven-Los Ang.-Islanders | 2563 | 159 | 1 |
| Hackett, Jeff | 6:01 | 175 | London, Ont. | 6- 1-68 | Springfield-N.Y. Islanders | 2338 | 155 | 0 |
| Lorenz, Danny | 5:10 | 167 | Murrayville, B.C. | 12-12-69 | Seattle-Springfield | 4213 | 252 | 3 |
| Maneluk, George | 5:11 | 185 | Winnipeg, Man. | 7-25-67 | Springfield | 1202 | 84 | 0 |

# New York Rangers
## Patrick Division

| | |
|---|---|
| President and Governor | Richard H. Evans |
| Executive Vice-President | John C. Diller |
| Vice-President and General Manager | Neil Smith |
| Vice-President and General Counsel | Kenneth W. Munoz |
| Senior Vice-President, Marketing and Communications | Michael D. Walker |
| Vice-President, Business Affairs and Administration | David Peterson |
| Vice-President, Communications | John Halligan |
| Assistant Vice-President, Legal Affairs | Kevin Billet |
| Director, Marketing | Kevin Kennedy |
| Assistant General Manager, Operations | Gord Stellick |
| Assistant General Manager, Player Development | Larry Pleau |
| Coach | Roger Neilson |
| Development Coach | Paul Theriault |
| Scouting Staff | Al Cerrone, John Chapman, Tony Feltrin, Lou Jankowski, George Kozak, Don Murdoch, Richard Rose, Dan Summers |
| Manager of Team Services | Matthew Loughran |
| Public Relations Manager | Barry Watkins |
| Public Relations Assistant | Ginger Killian |
| Statistician | Arthur Friedman |
| Team Physician and Orthopedic Surgeon | Barton Nisonson, M.D. |
| Medical Trainer | Dave Smith |
| Trainers | Jacques Cayer, Joe Murphy |
| Equipment Manager | Scott Luhrmann |
| Home Ice | Madison Square Garden |
| Address | 4 Pennsylvania Plaza, New York, N. Y. 10001 |
| Seating Capacity | 16,651 |
| Club colors | Blue, Red and White |
| Phone | (212) 563-8000 |

Richard H. Evans

John C. Diller

Neil Smith

Roger Neilson

# New York Rangers 1989-90 Roster

## FORWARDS

| | Hgt. | Wgt. | Place of Birth | Date | 1988-89 Club | G. | A. | Pts. |
|---|---|---|---|---|---|---|---|---|
| Bergeron, Martin | 6:00 | 180 | Verdun, Que. | 1-20-68 | Drummondville-Denver | 55 | 82 | 137 |
| Broten, Paul | 5:11 | 175 | Roseau, Minn. | 10-27-65 | Denver | 28 | 31 | 59 |
| Chyzowski, Barry | 6:00 | 170 | Edmonton, Alta. | 5-25-68 | Denver | 12 | 21 | 33 |
| Cyr, Paul | 5:11 | 205 | Port Alberni, B.C. | 10-31-63 | N.Y. Rangers | 0 | 0 | 0 |
| Dahlen, Ulf | 6:02 | 196 | Ostersund, Sweden | 2-12-67 | N.Y. Rangers | 24 | 19 | 43 |
| Dionne, Marcel | 5:08 | 190 | Drummondville, Que. | 8- 3-51 | N.Y. Rangers-Denver | 7 | 29 | 36 |
| Erixon, Jan | 6:00 | 196 | Skelleftea, Sweden | 7- 8-62 | N.Y. Rangers | 4 | 11 | 15 |
| Gagne, Simon | 6:04 | 202 | Montreal, Que. | 9-29-68 | Denver | 7 | 18 | 25 |
| Golden, Mike | 6:01 | 195 | Boston, Mass. | 6-14-65 | Denver | 12 | 10 | 22 |
| Graham, Robb | 6:04 | 205 | Bellevue, Wash. | 4- 7-68 | Denver | 14 | 22 | 36 |
| Granato, Tony | 5:10 | 175 | Downers Grove, Ill. | 7-25-64 | N.Y. Rangers | 36 | 27 | 63 |
| Janssens, Mark | 6:03 | 195 | Surrey, B.C. | 5-19-68 | Denver-N.Y. Rangers | 19 | 19 | 38 |
| Kisio, Kelly | 5:09 | 180 | Peace River, Alta. | 9-18-59 | N.Y. Rangers | 26 | 36 | 62 |
| Lacroix, Daniel | 6:02 | 185 | Montreal, Que. | 3-11-69 | Granby-Denver | 45 | 50 | 95 |
| Lafreniere, Jason | 5:11 | 185 | St. Catharines, Ont. | 12- 6-66 | Denver-N.Y. Rangers | 18 | 35 | 53 |
| Latos, James | 6:01 | 200 | Wakaw, Sask. | 1- 4-66 | Denver-N.Y. Rangers | 7 | 5 | 12 |
| McRae, Chris | 6:00 | 180 | Newmarket, Ont. | 8-26-65 | Toronto-Newmarket-Denver | 4 | 5 | 9 |
| Millen, Corey | 5:07 | 165 | Duluth, Minn. | 3-30-64 | Ambri Piotta, Switz. | 32 | 22 | 54 |
| Miller, Kevin | 5:10 | 180 | Lansing, Mich. | 9- 2-65 | Denver-N.Y. Rangers | 32 | 52 | 84 |
| Mullen, Brian | 5:10 | 180 | New York, N.Y. | 3-16-62 | N.Y. Rangers | 29 | 35 | 64 |
| Nilan, Chris | 6:00 | 205 | Boston, Mass. | 2- 9-58 | N.Y. Rangers | 7 | 7 | 14 |
| Ogrodnick, John | 6:00 | 206 | Ottawa, Ont. | 6-20-59 | N.Y. Rangers | 15 | 30 | 45 |
| Paterson, Joe | 6:02 | 207 | Toronto, Ont. | 6-25-60 | Den.-N. Haven-N.Y. Rangers | 5 | 5 | 10 |
| Poeschek, Rudy | 6:01 | 210 | Kamloops, B.C. | 9-29-66 | N.Y. Rangers-Denver | 0 | 2 | 2 |
| Ruff, Lindy | 6:02 | 200 | Warburg, Alta. | 2-17-60 | Buffalo-N.Y. Rangers | 6 | 16 | 22 |
| Sandstrom, Tomas | 6:02 | 204 | Jakobstad, Finland | 9- 4-64 | N.Y. Rangers | 32 | 56 | 88 |
| Turcotte, Darren | 6:00 | 185 | Boston, Mass. | 3- 2-68 | Denver-N.Y. Rangers | 28 | 31 | 59 |
| Walter, Bret | 6:01 | 195 | Calgary, Alta. | 4-28-68 | Denver | 12 | 10 | 22 |
| Wheeldon, Simon | 5:11 | 180 | Nelson, B.C. | 10- 2-68 | Denver-N.Y. Rangers | 50 | 57 | 107 |
| Wilson, Carey | 6:02 | 205 | Winnipeg, Man. | 5-19-62 | Hartford-N.Y. Rangers | 32 | 45 | 77 |

## DEFENSEMEN

| | Hgt. | Wgt. | Place of Birth | Date | 1988-89 Club | G. | A. | Pts. |
|---|---|---|---|---|---|---|---|---|
| Bloemberg, Jeff | 6:02 | 200 | Listowel, Ont. | 1-31-68 | Den.-N.Y. Rangers | 7 | 22 | 29 |
| Brochu, Stephane | 6:01 | 185 | Sherbrooke, Que. | 8-15-67 | Denver-N.Y. Rangers | 5 | 14 | 19 |
| Fiorentino, Peter | 6:01 | 200 | Niagara Falls, Ont. | 12-22-68 | Sault Ste. Marie-Denver | 5 | 24 | 29 |
| Greschner, Ron | 6:02 | 208 | Goodsoil, Sask. | 12-22-54 | N.Y. Rangers | 1 | 10 | 11 |
| Hardy, Mark | 5:11 | 195 | Senaden, Switzerland | 2- 1-59 | Minnesota-N.Y. Rangers | 4 | 16 | 20 |
| Horava, Miroslav | 6:00 | 190 | Kladno, Czech. | 8-18-61 | Kladno-N.Y. Rangers | 10 | 17 | 27 |
| Hurlbut, Mike | 6:02 | 195 | Kassens, N.Y. | 10- 7-66 | St. Lawrence-Denver | 8 | 27 | 35 |
| Larocque, Denis | 6:01 | 195 | Hawkesbury, Ont. | 10- 5-67 | New Haven-Denver | 4 | 10 | 14 |
| Laviolette, Peter | 6:02 | 200 | Norwood, Mass. | 12- 7-64 | Denver-N.Y. Rangers | 6 | 19 | 25 |
| Leetch, Brian | 5:11 | 185 | Corpus Christi, Tex. | 3- 3-68 | N.Y. Rangers | 23 | 48 | 71 |
| More, Jayson | 6:01 | 190 | Souris, Man. | 1-12-69 | Denver-N.Y. Rangers | 7 | 15 | 22 |
| Patrick, James | 6:02 | 192 | Winnipeg, Man. | 6-14-63 | N.Y. Rangers | 11 | 36 | 47 |
| Petit, Michel | 6:01 | 205 | St. Malo, Que. | 2-12-64 | N.Y. Rangers | 8 | 25 | 33 |
| Rochefort, Normand | 6:01 | 200 | Trois-Rivieres, Que. | 1-28-61 | N.Y. Rangers | 1 | 5 | 6 |
| Shaw, David | 6:02 | 204 | St. Thomas, Ont. | 5-25-64 | N.Y. Rangers | 6 | 11 | 17 |
| Shudra, Ron | 6:02 | 192 | Winnipeg, Man. | 11-28-67 | Cape Breton-Denver | 11 | 14 | 25 |

## GOALTENDERS

| | Hgt. | Wgt. | Place of Birth | Date | 1988-89 Club | Mins. | GA. | SO. |
|---|---|---|---|---|---|---|---|---|
| Brower, Scott | 6:00 | 185 | Viking, Alta. | 9-26-64 | Denver | 938 | 82 | 0 |
| Froese, Bob | 5:11 | 178 | St. Catharines, Ont. | 6-30-58 | N.Y. Rangers | 1621 | 102 | 1 |
| Richter, Mike | 5:10 | 185 | Abington, Pa. | 9-22-66 | Denver | 3031 | 217 | 1 |
| Rosati, Mike | 5:10 | 170 | Toronto, Ont. | 1- 7-68 | Niagara Falls | 2339 | 174 | 1 |
| Scott, Ron | 5:08 | 155 | Guelph, Ont. | 7-21-60 | Denver | 990 | 79 | 0 |
| Vanbiesbrouck, John | 5:08 | 179 | Detroit, Mich. | 9- 4-63 | N.Y. Rangers | 3207 | 197 | 0 |

# Philadelphia Flyers
### Patrick Division

| | |
|---|---|
| Chairman of the Executive Committee | Edward M. Snider |
| Chairman of the Board Emeritus | Joseph C. Scott |
| President | Jay T. Snider |
| Executive Vice-President | Keith Allen |
| Vice-President and General Manager | Bob Clarke |
| Coach | Paul Holmgren |
| Assistant General Manager | John Paddock |
| Assistant Coaches | Mike Eaves, Andy Murray |
| Goaltending Instructor | Bernie Parent |
| Physical Conditioning and Rehabilitation Coach | Pat Croce |
| Director of Pro Scouting | Bill Barber |
| Scouts | Inge Hammarstrom, Jerry Melnyk, Dennis Patterson, Glen Sonmor, Red Sullivan |
| Executive Vice-President, Administration | Ron Ryan |
| Vice-President, Communications | John Brogan |
| Director of Public Relations | Rodger Gottlieb |
| Director of Media Relations | Mark Piazza |
| Ticket Manager | Ceil Baker |
| Vice-President, Sales | Jack Betson |
| Director of Team Services | Joe Kadlec |
| Trainer | Dave Settlemyre |
| Assistant Trainer | Kurt Mundt |
| Controller | Bob Baer |
| Team Physician | Jeffrey Hartzell, M.D. |
| Home Ice | The Spectrum |
| Address | Pattison Place, Philadelphia, Pa. 19148 |
| Seating Capacity | 17,423 |
| Club colors | Orange, White and Black |
| Phone | (215) 465-4500 |

**Edward M. Snider**

**Bob Clarke**

**Paul Holmgren**

**Jay T. Snider**

# Philadelphia Flyers 1989-90 Roster

## FORWARDS

| Name | Hgt. | Wgt. | Place of Birth | Date | 1988-89 Club | G. | A. | Pts. |
|---|---|---|---|---|---|---|---|---|
| Acton, Keith | 5:08 | 170 | Stoufville, Ont. | 4-15-58 | Edmonton-Philadelphia | 14 | 25 | 39 |
| Armstrong, Bill | 6:02 | 195 | London, Ont. | 6-25-66 | W. Michigan Univ. | 23 | 19 | 42 |
| Berube, Craig | 6:01 | 205 | Calihoo, Alta. | 11-17-65 | Philadelphia-Hershey | 1 | 3 | 4 |
| Biggs, Don | 5:08 | 185 | Mississauga, Ont. | 4-7-65 | Hershey | 36 | 67 | 103 |
| Boivin, Claude | 6:02 | 200 | St. Foy, Que. | 3-1-70 | Drummondville | 20 | 37 | 57 |
| Bullard, Mike | 6:00 | 195 | Ottawa, Ont. | 3-10-61 | St. Louis-Philadelphia | 27 | 38 | 65 |
| Craven, Murray | 6:02 | 185 | Medicine Hat, Alta. | 7-20-64 | Philadelphia | 9 | 28 | 37 |
| Dobbin, Brian | 5:11 | 205 | Petrolia, Ont. | 8-18-66 | Philadelphia-Hershey | 43 | 49 | 92 |
| Eklund, Pelle | 5:10 | 175 | Stockholm, Sweden | 3-22-63 | Philadelphia | 18 | 51 | 69 |
| Fletcher, Steve | 6:03 | 205 | Montreal, Que. | 3-31-62 | Moncton-Hershey | 6 | 9 | 15 |
| Freer, Mark | 5:10 | 180 | Peterborough, Ont. | 7-14-68 | Hershey-Philadelphia | 30 | 50 | 80 |
| Harding, Jeff | 6:03 | 220 | Toronto, Ont. | 4-6-69 | Hershey-Philadelphia | 13 | 5 | 18 |
| Harper, Warren | 6:01 | 200 | Prince Albert, Sask. | 5-10-63 | Hershey | 20 | 20 | 40 |
| Hawley, Kent | 6:03 | 215 | Kingston, Ont. | 2-20-68 | Hershey | 9 | 17 | 26 |
| Horacek, Tony | 6:04 | 210 | Vancouver, B.C. | 2-3-67 | Indianapolis-Hershey | 11 | 13 | 24 |
| Jensen, Chris | 5:10 | 170 | Fort St. John, B.C. | 10-28-63 | Hershey | 27 | 31 | 58 |
| Kerr, Tim | 6:03 | 230 | Windsor, Ont. | 1-5-60 | Philadelphia | 48 | 40 | 88 |
| Kypreos, Nick | 6:00 | 195 | Toronto, Ont. | 6-4-66 | Hershey | 12 | 15 | 27 |
| Mellanby, Scott | 6:01 | 205 | Montreal, Que. | 6-11-66 | Philadelphia | 21 | 29 | 50 |
| Nachbaur, Don | 6:02 | 195 | Kitimat, B.C. | 1-30-59 | Hershey-Philadelphia | 25 | 31 | 56 |
| Poulin, Dave | 5:11 | 190 | Timmins, Ont. | 12-17-58 | Philadelphia | 18 | 17 | 35 |
| Propp, Brian | 5:11 | 190 | Lanigan, Sask. | 2-15-59 | Philadelphia | 32 | 46 | 78 |
| Rendall, Bruce | 6:01 | 190 | Thunder Bay, Ont. | 4-18-67 | Hershey-Indianapolis | 9 | 10 | 19 |
| Seabrooke, Glen | 6:00 | 190 | Peterborough, Ont. | 9-11-67 | Hershey-Philadelphia | 23 | 16 | 39 |
| Sinisalo, Ilkka | 6:00 | 200 | Valeakoski, Finland | 7-10-58 | Philadelphia | 1 | 6 | 7 |
| Smith, Derrick | 6:02 | 215 | Scarborough, Ont. | 1-22-65 | Philadelphia | 16 | 14 | 30 |
| Sulliman, Doug | 5:09 | 190 | Glace Bay, N.S. | 8-29-59 | Philadelphia | 6 | 6 | 12 |
| Sutter, Ron | 6:00 | 180 | Viking, Alta. | 12-2-63 | Philadelphia | 26 | 22 | 48 |
| Tocchet, Rick | 6:00 | 205 | Scarborough, Ont. | 4-9-64 | Philadelphia | 45 | 36 | 81 |
| Tookey, Tim | 5:11 | 190 | Edmonton, Alta. | 8-29-60 | Los Ang.-New Haven-Muskegon | 20 | 33 | 53 |

## DEFENSEMEN

| Name | Hgt. | Wgt. | Place of Birth | Date | 1988-89 Club | G. | A. | Pts. |
|---|---|---|---|---|---|---|---|---|
| Baron, Murray | 6:03 | 210 | Prince George, B.C. | 6-1-67 | U. of North Dakota-Hershey | 2 | 9 | 11 |
| Carkner, Terry | 6:03 | 212 | Smiths Falls, Ont. | 3-7-66 | Philadelphia | 11 | 32 | 43 |
| Chychrun, Jeff | 6:04 | 212 | LaSalle, Que. | 5-3-66 | Philadelphia | 1 | 4 | 5 |
| Fenyves, Dave | 5:11 | 192 | Dunnville, Ont. | 4-29-60 | Hershey-Philadelphia | 15 | 52 | 67 |
| Howe, Mark | 5:11 | 185 | Detroit, Mich. | 5-28-55 | Philadelphia | 9 | 29 | 38 |
| Huffman, Kerry | 6:02 | 200 | Peterborough, Ont. | 1-3-68 | Philadelphia-Hershey | 2 | 24 | 26 |
| Mantha, Moe | 6:02 | 210 | Lakewood, O. | 1-21-61 | Minnesota-Philadelphia | 4 | 14 | 18 |
| Murphy, Gord | 6:02 | 190 | Willowdale, Ont. | 3-23-67 | Philadelphia | 4 | 31 | 35 |
| Paddock, Gord | 6:00 | 187 | Hamiota, Man. | 2-15-64 | Hershey | 6 | 36 | 42 |
| Rumble, Darren | 6:01 | 200 | Barrie, Ont. | 1-23-69 | Kitchener | 11 | 28 | 39 |
| Sabol, Shawn | 6:02 | 215 | Fargo, N.D. | 7-13-66 | Hershey | 7 | 11 | 18 |
| Samuelsson, Kjell | 6:06 | 235 | Tingsryd, Sweden | 10-18-58 | Philadelphia | 3 | 14 | 17 |
| Sandelin, Scott | 6:00 | 180 | Hibbing, Minn. | 8-8-64 | Sherbrooke-Hershey | 6 | 18 | 24 |
| Stevens, John | 6:01 | 195 | Completon, N.B. | 5-4-66 | Hershey | 3 | 13 | 16 |
| Stothers, Mike | 6:04 | 212 | Toronto, Ont. | 2-22-62 | Hershey | 4 | 11 | 15 |
| Wells, Jay | 6:01 | 210 | Paris, Ont. | 5-18-59 | Philadelphia | 2 | 19 | 21 |

## GOALTENDERS

| Name | Hgt. | Wgt. | Place of Birth | Date | 1988-89 Club | Mins. | GA. | SO. |
|---|---|---|---|---|---|---|---|---|
| D'Amour, Marc | 5:09 | 190 | Sudbury, Ont. | 4-29-61 | Hershey-Philadelphia | 2193 | 127 | 0 |
| Gilmour, Darryl | 6:00 | 170 | Winnipeg, Man. | 2-13-67 | Hershey | 2093 | 144 | 0 |
| Hextall, Ron | 6:03 | 192 | Brandon, Man. | 5-3-64 | Philadelphia | 3756 | 202 | 0 |
| Hoffort, Bruce | 5:10 | 185 | N. Battleford, Sask. | 7-30-66 | Lake Superior State | 2595 | 117 | 0 |
| Laforest, Mark | 5:11 | 190 | Welland, Ont. | 7-10-62 | Philadelphia-Hershey | 1118 | 73 | 0 |
| Peeters, Pete | 6:01 | 195 | Edmonton, Alta. | 8-17-57 | Washington | 1854 | 88 | 4 |
| Perreault, Jocelyn | 6:03 | 196 | Montreal, Que. | 1-8-66 | Hershey | 394 | 22 | 0 |
| Roussel, Dominic | 6:01 | 185 | Hull, Que. | 2-22-70 | Shawinigan | 2555 | 171 | 0 |
| Wregget, Ken | 6:01 | 195 | Brandon, Man. | 3-25-64 | Toronto-Philadelphia | 2018 | 152 | 0 |

# Pittsburgh Penguins
### Patrick Division

| | |
|---|---|
| Chairman of the Board | Edward J. DeBartolo, Sr. |
| President | Marie Denise DeBartolo York |
| Vice-President and General Manager | Tony Esposito |
| General Counsel | Paul Martha |
| Secretary/Treasurer/Director | Anthony Liberati |
| Coach | Gene Ubriaco |
| Assistant Coaches | Rick Kehoe, Rick Paterson |
| Ontario/Central Collegiate Scout | Greg Malone |
| Ontario/Quebec Junior Leagues | Les Binkley |
| Minnesota Scout | John Gill |
| Director of Marketing | Tinsy Labrie |
| Director of Press Relations | Cindy Himes |
| Assistant Director of Press Relations | Harry Sanders |
| Trainer | Skip Thayer |
| Equipment Manager | Steve Latin |
| Home Ice | Civic Arena |
| Address | Civic Arena, Gate No. 9, Pittsburgh, Pa. 15219 |
| Seating Capacity | 16,025 |
| Club colors | Black, Gold and White |
| Phone | (412) 642-1800 |

Edward J. DeBartolo Sr.

Tony Esposito

Gene Ubriaco

# Pittsburgh Penguins 1989-90 Roster

## FORWARDS

| Name | Hgt. | Wgt. | Place of Birth | Date | 1988-89 Club | G. | A. | Pts. |
|---|---|---|---|---|---|---|---|---|
| Aitken, Brad | 6:02 | 200 | Scarborough, Ont. | 10-30-67 | Muskegon | 35 | 30 | 65 |
| Bourque, Phil | 6:01 | 203 | Chelmsford, Mass. | 6-8-62 | Pittsburgh | 17 | 26 | 43 |
| Brown, Rob | 5:11 | 185 | Kingston, Ont. | 4-10-68 | Pittsburgh | 49 | 66 | 115 |
| Callander, Jock | 6:01 | 188 | Regina, Sask. | 4-23-61 | Muskegon-Pittsburgh | 31 | 44 | 75 |
| Capuano, Dave | 6:02 | 190 | Cranston, R.I. | 7-27-68 | Univ. of Maine | 37 | 30 | 67 |
| Caufield, Jay | 6:04 | 230 | Philadelphia, Pa. | 7-17-60 | Pittsburgh | 1 | 4 | 5 |
| Cullen, John | 5:10 | 187 | Puslinch, Ont. | 8-2-64 | Pittsburgh | 12 | 37 | 49 |
| Daniels, Jeff | 6:01 | 197 | Oshawa, Ont. | 6-24-68 | Muskegon | 21 | 21 | 42 |
| Errey, Bob | 5:10 | 177 | Montreal, Que. | 9-21-64 | Pittsburgh | 26 | 32 | 58 |
| Frawley, Dan | 6:01 | 195 | Sturgeon Falls, Ont. | 6-2-62 | Pittsburgh-Muskegon | 15 | 20 | 35 |
| Gauthier, Daniel | 6:02 | 176 | Charlemagne, Que. | 5-17-70 | Victoriaville | 41 | 75 | 116 |
| Giffin, Lee | 6:00 | 181 | Chatham, Ont. | 4-1-67 | Muskegon | 30 | 44 | 74 |
| Gilhen, Randy | 5:10 | 180 | Zweibrucken, W. Ger. | 6-13-63 | Winnipeg | 5 | 3 | 8 |
| Hannan, Dave | 5:10 | 185 | Sudbury, Ont. | 11-26-61 | Pittsburgh | 10 | 20 | 30 |
| Heward, Jamie | 6:02 | 183 | Regina, Sask. | 3-30-71 | Regina | 31 | 28 | 59 |
| Kachowski, Mark | 5:10 | 196 | Edmonton, Alta. | 2-20-65 | Muskegon-Pittsburgh | 9 | 9 | 18 |
| Leach, Jamie | 6:01 | 198 | Winnipeg, Man. | 8-25-69 | Niagara Falls | 45 | 62 | 107 |
| Lemieux, Mario | 6:04 | 210 | Montreal, Que. | 10-5-65 | Pittsburgh | 85 | 114 | 199 |
| Loney, Troy | 6:03 | 205 | Bow Island, Alta. | 9-21-63 | Pittsburgh | 10 | 6 | 16 |
| Major, Mark | 6:03 | 227 | Toronto, Ont. | 3-20-70 | Kingston-North Bay | 25 | 31 | 56 |
| McBain, Andrew | 6:01 | 195 | Toronto, Ont. | 2-18-65 | Winnipeg | 37 | 40 | 77 |
| Michayluk, Dave | 5:10 | 180 | Wakaw, Sask. | 5-18-62 | Muskegon | 50 | 72 | 122 |
| Mick, Troy | 5:11 | 180 | Burnaby, B.C. | 3-30-69 | Portland | 49 | 87 | 136 |
| Mulvenna, Glenn | 5:11 | 182 | Calgary, Alta. | 2-18-67 | Muskegon-Flint | 12 | 16 | 28 |
| Needham, Mike | 5:10 | 198 | Calgary, Alta. | 4-4-70 | Kamloops | 24 | 27 | 51 |
| Quinn, Dan | 5:11 | 177 | Ottawa, Ont. | 6-1-65 | Pittsburgh | 34 | 60 | 94 |
| Recchi, Mark | 5:10 | 189 | Kamloops, Alta. | 2-1-68 | Muskegon-Pittsburgh | 51 | 50 | 101 |
| Smart, Jason | 6:04 | 212 | Prince George, B.C. | 1-23-70 | Saskatoon-Prince Albert | 7 | 20 | 27 |
| Stevens, Kevin | 6:03 | 210 | Brockton, Mass. | 4-15-65 | Muskegon-Pittsburgh | 36 | 44 | 80 |
| Wilson, Mitch | 5:08 | 189 | Kelowna, B.C. | 2-15-62 | Muskegon | 16 | 34 | 50 |

## DEFENSEMEN

| Name | Hgt. | Wgt. | Place of Birth | Date | 1988-89 Club | G. | A. | Pts. |
|---|---|---|---|---|---|---|---|---|
| Buskas, Rod | 6:01 | 207 | Wetaskiwin, Alta. | 1-7-61 | Pittsburgh | 1 | 5 | 6 |
| Coffey, Paul | 6:01 | 205 | Weston, Ont. | 6-1-61 | Pittsburgh | 30 | 83 | 113 |
| Dahlquist, Chris | 6:01 | 196 | Fridley, Minn. | 12-14-62 | Pittsburgh-Muskegon | 4 | 11 | 15 |
| Delorme, Gilbert | 6:01 | 205 | Boucherville, Que. | 11-25-62 | Detroit | 1 | 3 | 4 |
| Dineen, Gord | 6:00 | 195 | Toronto, Ont. | 9-21-62 | Minn.-Kalamazoo-Pittsburgh | 3 | 9 | 12 |
| Farrell, Scott | 5:11 | 190 | Richmond, B.C. | 4-15-70 | Spokane | 10 | 32 | 42 |
| Hillier, Randy | 6:01 | 186 | Toronto, Ont. | 3-30-60 | Pittsburgh | 1 | 23 | 24 |
| Hobson, Doug | 6:00 | 185 | Prince Albert, Sask. | 4-9-68 | Muskegon | 5 | 17 | 22 |
| Johnson, Jim | 6:01 | 190 | New Hope, Minn. | 8-9-62 | Pittsburgh | 2 | 14 | 16 |
| Kyte, Jim | 6:05 | 210 | Ottawa, Ont. | 3-21-64 | Winnipeg | 3 | 9 | 12 |
| Laus, Paul | 6:01 | 200 | Beamsville, Ont. | 9-26-70 | Niagara Falls | 1 | 10 | 11 |
| Mersh, Mike | 6:02 | 210 | Skokie, Ill. | 9-29-64 | Muskegon-Flint | 5 | 22 | 27 |
| Nelson, Todd | 6:00 | 201 | Prince Albert, Sask. | 5-11-69 | Prince Albert | 14 | 45 | 59 |
| Paek, Jim | 6:01 | 194 | Seoul, Korea | 4-7-67 | Muskegon | 3 | 54 | 57 |
| Pancoe, Don | 6:01 | 188 | St. George, Ont. | 2-23-69 | Niagara Falls | 1 | 17 | 18 |
| Stanton, Paul | 6:00 | 185 | Boston, Mass. | 6-22-67 | Univ. of Wisconsin | 7 | 29 | 36 |
| Stolk, Darren | 6:04 | 201 | Taber, Alta. | 7-22-68 | Medicine Hat | 8 | 43 | 51 |
| Taylor, Randy | 6:02 | 195 | Cornwall, Ont. | 7-30-65 | Flint-Indianapolis | 4 | 21 | 25 |
| Waver, Jeff | 5:10 | 189 | St. Boniface, Man. | 9-28-68 | Kingston-Muskegon | 30 | 43 | 73 |
| Wolf, Andrew | 5:11 | 196 | Richmond, B.C. | 5-29-69 | Victoria | 4 | 12 | 16 |
| Zalapski, Zarley | 6:01 | 204 | Edmonton, Alta. | 4-22-68 | Pittsburgh | 12 | 33 | 45 |

## GOALTENDERS

| Name | Hgt. | Wgt. | Place of Birth | Date | 1988-89 Club | Mins. | GA. | SO. |
|---|---|---|---|---|---|---|---|---|
| Barrasso, Tom | 6:03 | 207 | Boston, Mass. | 3-31-65 | Buffalo-Pittsburgh | 2951 | 187 | 0 |
| Pietrangelo, Frank | 5:10 | 182 | Niagara Falls, Ont. | 12-17-64 | Pittsburgh-Muskegon | 1429 | 83 | 1 |
| Racine, Bruce | 6:00 | 160 | Cornwall, Ont. | 8-9-66 | Muskegon | 3039 | 184 | 3 |
| Young, Wendell | 5:09 | 183 | Halifax, N.S. | 8-1-63 | Pittsburgh-Muskegon | 1315 | 99 | 0 |

# Quebec Nordiques
### Adams Division

| | |
|---|---|
| President and Governor | Marcel Aubut |
| Vice-President of Hockey Operations | Maurice Filion |
| General Manager | Martin Madden |
| Director of Personnel Development | Gilles Leger |
| Coach | Michel Bergeron |
| Associate Coaches | Guy Lapointe, Alain Chainey |
| Goaltending Coach | Serge Aubry |
| Scout-Professional Hockey and Special Assignments | Simon Nolet |
| Chief Scout | Pierre Gauthier |
| Assistant to the Chief Scout | Darwin Bennett |
| Scouts | P.A. Fontaine, Michel Georges, Guy Lafrance, Bob Manclni, Frank Moberg, Don Paarup, Andre Savard, Calle Tornquist |
| General Counsel | Jean Pelletier |
| Vice-President/Administration and Finance | Jean Laflamme |
| Vice-President/Marketing and Communications | Jean D. Legault |
| Supervisor of Press Relations | Jean Martineau |
| Coordinator of Information | Nicole Bouchard |
| Supervisor of Public Relations | Marius Fortier |
| Team Doctor | Dr. Pierre Beauchemin |
| Trainers | Rene Lacasse, Rene Lavigueur, Jacques Lavergne |
| Home Ice | Quebec Colisee |
| Address | 2205 Ave. du Colisee, Quebec, Que. G1L 4W7 |
| Seating Capacity | 15,399 |
| Club colors | Blue, White and Red |
| Phone | (418) 529-8441 |

**Marcel Aubut**

**Maurice Filion**

**Martin Madden**

**Michel Bergeron**

# Quebec Nordiques 1989-90 Roster

## FORWARDS

| Name | Hgt. | Wgt. | Place of Birth | Date | 1988-89 Club | G. | A. | Pts. |
|---|---|---|---|---|---|---|---|---|
| Baillargeon, Joel | 6:02 | 215 | Quebec, Que. | 10- 6-64 | Halifax-Quebec | 11 | 19 | 30 |
| Baker, Jamie | 5:11 | 180 | Nepean, Ont. | 8-31-66 | St. Lawrence University | 11 | 16 | 27 |
| DeBlois, Lucien | 5:11 | 200 | Joliette, Que. | 6-21-57 | N.Y. Rangers | 9 | 24 | 33 |
| Dore, Daniel | 6:03 | 202 | Ferme-Neuve, Que. | 4- 9-70 | Drummondville | 33 | 58 | 91 |
| Fortier, Marc | 6:00 | 192 | Windsor, Que. | 2-26-66 | Quebec-Halifax | 31 | 30 | 61 |
| Gillis, Paul | 5:11 | 198 | Toronto, Ont. | 12-31-63 | Quebec | 15 | 25 | 40 |
| Goulet, Michel | 6:01 | 195 | Peribonka, Que. | 4-21-60 | Quebec | 26 | 38 | 64 |
| Hopkins, Dean | 6:01 | 210 | Cobourg, Ont. | 6- 6-59 | Halifax-Quebec | 18 | 33 | 51 |
| Hough, Mike | 6:01 | 192 | Montreal, Que. | 2- 6-63 | Quebec-Halifax | 20 | 20 | 40 |
| Jackson, Jeff | 6:01 | 195 | Dresden, Ont. | 4-24-65 | Quebec | 4 | 6 | 10 |
| Jarvi, Iiro | 6:01 | 198 | Helsinki, Finland | 3-23-65 | Quebec | 11 | 30 | 41 |
| Kaminski, Kevin | 5:09 | 170 | Churchbridge, Sask. | 3-13-69 | Saskatoon | 25 | 43 | 68 |
| Kimble, Darin | 6:02 | 205 | Swift Current, Sask. | 11-22-68 | Halifax-Quebec | 11 | 7 | 18 |
| Lafleur, Guy | 6:00 | 185 | Thurso, Que. | 9-20-51 | N.Y. Rangers | 18 | 27 | 45 |
| Latta, David | 6:01 | 190 | Thunder Bay, Ont. | 1- 3-67 | Halifax-Quebec | 24 | 34 | 58 |
| Loiselle, Claude | 5:11 | 195 | Ottawa, Ont. | 5-29-63 | New Jersey | 7 | 14 | 21 |
| McRae, Ken | 6:01 | 195 | Winchester, Ont. | 4-23-68 | Halifax-Quebec | 26 | 32 | 58 |
| Mailhot, Jacques | 6:02 | 208 | Shawinigan, Que. | 12- 5-61 | Halifax-Quebec | 4 | 1 | 5 |
| Major, Bruce | 6:03 | 180 | Vernon, B.C. | 1- 3-67 | Univ. of Maine | 13 | 11 | 24 |
| Middendorf, Max | 6:04 | 210 | Syracuse, N.Y. | 12-18-67 | Halifax | 41 | 39 | 80 |
| Miller, Keith | 6:02 | 215 | Toronto, Ont. | 3-18-67 | Fort Wayne | 35 | 25 | 60 |
| Morin, Stephane | 6:00 | 174 | Montreal, Que. | 3-27-69 | Chicoutimi | 77 | 109 | 186 |
| Quinney, Ken | 5:10 | 186 | New Westminster, B.C. | 5-23-65 | Halifax | 41 | 49 | 90 |
| Routhier, Jean | 6:02 | 190 | Quebec, Que. | 2- 2-68 | Halifax | 13 | 13 | 26 |
| Sakic, Joe | 5:11 | 185 | Burnaby, B.C. | 7- 7-69 | Quebec | 23 | 39 | 62 |
| Severyn, Brent | 6:02 | 210 | Vegreville, Alta. | 2-22-66 | Halifax | 2 | 12 | 14 |
| Shaunessy, Scott | 6:04 | 220 | Newport, R.I. | 1-22-64 | Halifax-Quebec | 3 | 10 | 13 |
| Stastny, Peter | 6:01 | 199 | Bratislava, Czech. | 9-18-56 | Quebec | 35 | 50 | 85 |
| Stienburg, Trevor | 6:01 | 200 | Kingston, Ont. | 5-13-66 | Quebec | 6 | 3 | 9 |
| Vermette, Mark | 6:01 | 203 | Cochenour, Ont. | 10- 3-67 | Halifax-Quebec | 12 | 20 | 32 |

## DEFENSEMEN

| Name | Hgt. | Wgt. | Place of Birth | Date | 1988-89 Club | G. | A. | Pts. |
|---|---|---|---|---|---|---|---|---|
| Brown, Jeff | 6:01 | 202 | Ottawa, Ont. | 4-30-66 | Quebec | 21 | 47 | 68 |
| Bzdel, Gerald | 6:01 | 196 | Wynyard, Sask. | 3-13-68 | Halifax | 1 | 3 | 4 |
| Cirella, Joe | 6:03 | 210 | Hamilton, Ont. | 5- 9-63 | New Jersey | 3 | 19 | 22 |
| Dollas, Bobby | 6:02 | 212 | Montreal, Que. | 1-31-65 | Halifax-Quebec | 5 | 22 | 27 |
| Espe, David | 6:00 | 185 | St. Paul, Minn. | 11- 3-66 | Univ. of Minnesota | 0 | 11 | 11 |
| Finn, Steven | 6:00 | 198 | Laval, Que. | 8-20-66 | Quebec | 2 | 6 | 8 |
| Fogarty, Brian | 6:02 | 198 | Brantford, Ont. | 6-11-69 | Niagara Falls | 47 | 108 | 155 |
| Gronstrand, Jari | 6:03 | 197 | Tampere, Finland | 11-14-62 | Quebec-Halifax | 1 | 4 | 5 |
| Guerard, Stephane | 6:02 | 198 | St. Elizabeth, Que. | 4-12-68 | Halifax | 1 | 9 | 10 |
| Julien, Claude | 6:00 | 198 | Blind River, Ont. | 4-23-60 | Halifax | 8 | 52 | 60 |
| Leschyshyn, Curtis | 6:01 | 205 | Thompson, Man. | 9-21-69 | Quebec | 4 | 9 | 13 |
| Marois, Mario | 5:11 | 190 | Quebec, Que. | 12-15-57 | Winnipeg-Quebec | 3 | 12 | 15 |
| Moller, Randy | 6:02 | 207 | Red Deer, Alta. | 8-23-63 | Quebec | 7 | 22 | 29 |
| Picard, Robert | 6:02 | 212 | Montreal, Que. | 5-25-57 | Quebec | 7 | 14 | 21 |
| Richard, Jean | 5:11 | 178 | St. Raymond, Que. | 10- 8-66 | Halifax | 8 | 25 | 33 |
| Smyth, Greg | 6:03 | 212 | Oakville, Ont. | 4-23-66 | Halifax-Quebec | 3 | 10 | 13 |
| Sprott, Jim | 6:01 | 200 | Oakville, Ont. | 4-11-69 | London | 15 | 42 | 57 |

## GOALTENDERS

| Name | Hgt. | Wgt. | Place of Birth | Date | 1988-89 Club | Mins. | GA. | SO. |
|---|---|---|---|---|---|---|---|---|
| Brunetta, Mario | 6:03 | 180 | Quebec, Que. | 1-25-67 | Halifax-Quebec | 2124 | 143 | 0 |
| Fiset, Stephane | 6:00 | 175 | Montreal, Que. | 6-17-70 | Victoriaville | 2401 | 138 | 1 |
| Gordon, Scott | 5:09 | 175 | Brockton, Mass. | 2- 6-63 | Johnstown-Halifax | 1955 | 127 | 2 |
| Tugnutt, Ron | 5:11 | 155 | Scarborough, Ont. | 10-22-67 | Quebec-Halifax | 2735 | 161 | 1 |

# St. Louis Blues
### Norris Division

| | |
|---|---|
| Board of Directors | Michael F. Shanahan, Jerome V. LaBarbera, Jerry Clinton, James Kerley, Lewis N. Wolff |
| Chairman of the Board | Michael F. Shanahan |
| Vice-Chairman | Jerome V. LaBarbera |
| President | Jack Quinn |
| Vice-President/General Manager | Ronald Caron |
| Vice-President/Director of Public Relations and Marketing | Susie Mathieu |
| Director of Player Development | Bob Plager |
| Director of Scouting | Ted Hampson |
| Assistant Director of Scouting/Eastern Canada and U.S. | Jack Evans |
| Western Canada and U.S. Scout | Pat Ginnell |
| Head Coach | Brian Sutter |
| Assistant Coaches | Bob Berry, Joe Micheletti |
| Assistant Director of Public Relations/Media Relations | Mark Niebling |
| Assistant Director of Public Relations/Publications | Jeff Trammel |
| Trainer | Norm Mackie |
| Home Ice | The Arena |
| Address | 5700 Oakland Avenue, St. Louis, Missouri 63110 |
| Seating Capacity | 17,188 |
| Club colors | Blue, Gold, Red and White |
| Phone | (314) 781-5300 |

**Michael F. Shanahan**

**Ronald Caron**

**Jack Quinn**

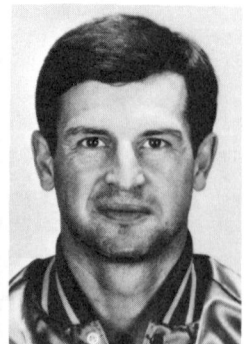
**Brian Sutter**

# St. Louis Blues 1989-90 Roster

| FORWARDS | Hgt. | Wgt. | Place of Birth | Date | 1988-89 Club | G. | A. | Pts. |
|---|---|---|---|---|---|---|---|---|
| Brind'Amour, Rod | 6:01 | 200 | Ottawa, Ont. | 8- 9-70 | Michigan State | 26 | 30 | 56 |
| Cavallini, Gino | 6:01 | 215 | Toronto, Ont. | 11-24-62 | St. Louis | 20 | 23 | 43 |
| Chase, Kelly | 5:11 | 200 | Porcupine, Sask. | 10-25-67 | Peoria | 14 | 7 | 21 |
| Coxe, Craig | 6:05 | 220 | Chula Vista, Calif. | 1-21-64 | St. Louis-Peoria | 2 | 14 | 16 |
| Ducolon, Toby | 6:00 | 195 | St. Albans, Vt. | 6-18-66 | Peoria | 17 | 33 | 50 |
| Emerson, Nelson | 5:11 | 165 | Hamilton, Ont. | 8-12-67 | Bowling Green State | 22 | 46 | 68 |
| Evans, Doug | 5:09 | 170 | Peterborough, Ont. | 6- 2-63 | St. Louis | 7 | 12 | 19 |
| Ewen, Todd | 6:02 | 220 | Saskatoon, Sask. | 3-22-66 | St. Louis | 4 | 5 | 9 |
| Felsner, Denny | 6:00 | 180 | Mt. Clemens, Mich. | 4-29-70 | Univ. of Michigan | 28 | 18 | 46 |
| Hrkac, Tony | 5:11 | 170 | Thunder Bay, Ont. | 7- 7-66 | St. Louis | 17 | 28 | 45 |
| Hull, Brett | 5:10 | 195 | Belleville, Ont. | 9- 9-64 | St. Louis | 41 | 43 | 84 |
| Lowry, Dave | 6:01 | 195 | Sudbury, Ont. | 2-14-65 | Peoria-St. Louis | 34 | 38 | 72 |
| MacLean, Paul | 6:02 | 205 | Grostenquin, France | 3- 9-58 | Detroit | 36 | 35 | 71 |
| MacLean, Terry | 6:01 | 178 | Montreal, Que. | 1-14-68 | Peoria | 18 | 30 | 48 |
| Meagher, Rick | 5:08 | 175 | Belleville, Ont. | 11- 2-53 | St. Louis | 15 | 14 | 29 |
| Miehm, Kevin | 6:02 | 190 | Kitchener, Ont. | 9-10-69 | Oshawa-Peoria | 44 | 79 | 123 |
| Momesso. Sergio | 6:03 | 215 | Montreal, Que. | 9- 4-65 | St. Louis | 9 | 17 | 26 |
| Oates, Adam | 5:11 | 185 | Weston, Ont. | 8-27-62 | Detroit | 16 | 62 | 78 |
| O'Brien, David | 6:01 | 180 | Brighton, Mass. | 9-13-66 | Binghamton | 3 | 12 | 15 |
| Osborne, Keith | 6:01 | 180 | Toronto, Ont. | 4- 2-69 | Niagara Falls | 45 | 64 | 109 |
| Raglan, Herb | 6:00 | 200 | Peterborough, Ont. | 9- 5-67 | St. Louis | 7 | 10 | 17 |
| Ronning, Cliff | 5:08 | 165 | Vancouver, B.C. | 10- 1-65 | St. Louis-Peoria | 35 | 51 | 86 |
| Smith, Darin | 6:02 | 204 | Vineland Sta., Ont. | 2-20-67 | Peoria | 13 | 17 | 30 |
| Thomlinson, Dave | 6:01 | 185 | Edmonton, Alta. | 10-22-66 | Peoria | 27 | 29 | 56 |
| Tuttle, Steve | 6:01 | 180 | Vancouver, B.C. | 1- 5-66 | St. Louis | 13 | 12 | 25 |
| Vesey, Jim | 6:01 | 200 | Columbus, Mass. | 10-29-65 | Peoria-St. Louis | 48 | 47 | 95 |
| Wolak, Mike | 5:10 | 155 | Utica, Mich. | 4-29-68 | Windsor-Peoria | 21 | 38 | 59 |
| Zezel, Peter | 5:11 | 200 | Toronto, Ont. | 4-22-65 | Philadelphia-St. Louis | 21 | 49 | 70 |
| **DEFENSEMEN** | | | | | | | | |
| Benning. Brian | 6:01 | 195 | Edmonton, Alta. | 6-10-66 | St. Louis | 8 | 26 | 34 |
| Cavallini, Paul | 6:01 | 210 | Toronto, Ont. | 10-13-65 | St. Louis | 4 | 20 | 24 |
| Corriveau, Rick | 5:11 | 206 | Welland, Ont. | 1- 6-71 | London | 4 | 10 | 14 |
| DeGaetano, Phil | 6:01 | 203 | Flushing, N.Y. | 8- 9-63 | Maine-Peoria | 7 | 21 | 28 |
| Dirk, Robert | 6:04 | 210 | Regina, Sask. | 8-20-66 | Peoria-St. Louis | 0 | 3 | 3 |
| Featherstone, Glen | 6:04 | 210 | Toronto, Ont. | 7- 8-68 | Peoria-St. Louis | 5 | 21 | 26 |
| Lalor, Mike | 6:03 | 200 | Buffalo, N.Y. | 3- 8-63 | Montreal-St. Louis | 2 | 18 | 20 |
| Laperriere, Daniel | 6:01 | 180 | Laval, Que. | 3-28-69 | St. Lawrence Univ. | 0 | 7 | 7 |
| Lavoie, Dominic | 6:02 | 195 | Montreal, Que. | 11-21-67 | Peoria-St. Louis | 11 | 31 | 42 |
| Marshall, Jason | 6:02 | 185 | Cranbrook, B.C. | 2-22-71 | Vernon | 10 | 30 | 40 |
| McPherson, Darwin | 6:01 | 195 | Flin Flon, Man. | 5-16-68 | Saskatoon | 4 | 13 | 17 |
| Paluch, Scott | 6:03 | 185 | Chicago, Ill. | 3- 9-66 | Peoria | 10 | 39 | 49 |
| Plavsic, Adrien | 6:01 | 190 | Monteal Que. | 1-13-70 | Canadian Nat. Team | 5 | 10 | 15 |
| Posma, Mike | 6:01 | 195 | Utica, N.Y. | 12-16-67 | Univ. of Western Michigan | 7 | 34 | 41 |
| Richter, Dave | 6:05 | 225 | St. Boniface, Man. | 4- 8-60 | St. Louis | 1 | 5 | 6 |
| Roberts, Gordie | 6:00 | 190 | Detroit, Mich. | 10- 2-57 | St. Louis | 2 | 24 | 26 |
| Robinson, Rob | 6:01 | 210 | St. Catharines, Ont. | 4-19-67 | Miami of Ohio-Peoria | 5 | 4 | 9 |
| Rolfe, Dan | 6:04 | 198 | Inglewood, Calif. | 12-25-67 | Ferris State | 0 | 2 | 2 |
| Skarda, Randy | 6:01 | 195 | St. Paul, Minn. | 5- 5-68 | Univ. of Minnesota | 6 | 24 | 30 |
| Tilley, Tom | 6:00 | 180 | Trenton, Ont. | 3-28-65 | St. Louis | 1 | 22 | 23 |
| Twist, Tony | 6:00 | 212 | Sherwood Pk., Alta. | 5- 9-68 | Peoria | 3 | 8 | 11 |
| Wilson, Rik | 6:00 | 210 | Long Beach, Calif. | 6-19-63 | West Germany | .. | .. | .. |

| GOALTENDERS | Hgt. | Wgt. | Place of Birth | Date | 1988-89 Club | Mins. | GA. | SO. |
|---|---|---|---|---|---|---|---|---|
| Jablonski, Pat | 6:00 | 175 | Toledo, O. | 6-20-67 | Peoria | 2051 | 163 | 1 |
| Joseph, Curtis | 5:10 | 170 | Keswick, Ont. | 4-29-67 | Univ. of Wisconsin | 2267 | 94 | 1 |
| Millen, Greg | 5:09 | 175 | Toronto, Ont. | 6-25-57 | St. Louis | 3019 | 170 | 6 |
| Riendeau, Vincent | 5:10 | 190 | St. Hyacinthe, Que. | 4-20-66 | St. Louis | 1842 | 108 | 0 |

# Toronto Maple Leafs
### Norris Division

| | |
|---|---|
| President, Governor and Managing Director | Harold E. Ballard |
| Chairman of the Board | Paul McNamara |
| Acting General Manager | Floyd Smith |
| Coach | Doug Carpenter |
| Assistant Coaches | Garry Lariviere, Mike Kitchen |
| Scouts | Johnny Bower, Frank Currie, Dick Duff, Floyd Smith, Jack Gardiner, Jim Bzdel, Bob Johnson, Doug Woods |
| Director of Public Relations | Bob Stellick |
| Treasurer | Donald Crump |
| Box Office Manager | I.M. 'Patty' Patoff |
| Trainers | Guy Kinnear, Dan Lemelin, Brian Papineau |
| Home Ice | Maple Leaf Gardens |
| Address | 60 Carlton Street, Toronto, Ont. M5B 1L1 |
| Seating Capacity | 16,382 (including standees) |
| Club Colors | Blue and White |
| Phone | (416) 977-1641 |

**Harold E. Ballard**

**Floyd Smith**

**Doug Carpenter**

# Toronto Maple Leafs 1989-90 Roster

## FORWARDS

| Name | Hgt. | Wgt. | Place of Birth | Date | 1988-89 Club | G. | A. | Pts. |
|---|---|---|---|---|---|---|---|---|
| Armstrong, Tim | 5:11 | 170 | Toronto, Ont. | 5-12-67 | Newmarket-Toronto | 17 | 24 | 41 |
| Bean, Tim | 6:01 | 200 | Sault Ste. Marie, Ont. | 3- 9-67 | Newmarket | 4 | 12 | 16 |
| Bellefeuille, Brian | 6:02 | 185 | Natick, Mass. | 3-21-67 | Univ. of Maine | 5 | 10 | 15 |
| Blaisdell, Mike | 6:01 | 200 | Moose Jaw, Sask. | 1-18-60 | Newmarket-Toronto | 17 | 7 | 24 |
| Brennan, Stephen | 6:01 | 190 | Winchester, Mass. | 3-22-67 | Clarkson Univ. | 3 | 4 | 7 |
| Chartrand, Steve | 5:09 | 158 | Verdun, Que. | 1- 8-69 | Drummondville | 74 | 83 | 157 |
| Clark, Wendel | 5:11 | 194 | Kelvington, Sask. | 10-25-66 | Toronto | 7 | 4 | 11 |
| Damphousse, Vincent | 6:01 | 190 | Montreal, Que. | 12-17-67 | Toronto | 26 | 42 | 68 |
| Daoust, Dan | 5:11 | 170 | Montreal, Que. | 2-29-60 | Toronto | 7 | 5 | 12 |
| Domi, Tie | 5:10 | 200 | Windsor, Ont. | 11- 1-69 | Peterborough | 14 | 16 | 30 |
| Eastwood, Michael | 6:02 | 190 | Ottawa, Ont. | 7- 1-67 | Univ. of Western Michigan | 10 | 13 | 23 |
| Elvenas, Roger | 6:01 | 183 | Lund, Sweden | 5-29-68 | Rogle | .. | .. | .. |
| Fergus, Tom | 6:03 | 210 | Chicago, Ill. | 6-16-62 | Toronto | 22 | 45 | 67 |
| Franceschetti, Lou | 6:00 | 190 | Toronto, Ont. | 3-28-58 | Washington-Baltimore | 15 | 17 | 32 |
| Gagne, Paul | 5:10 | 180 | Iroquois Falls, Ont. | 2- 6-62 | Newmarket-Toronto | 36 | 43 | 79 |
| Giguere, Stephane | 6:00 | 180 | Montreal, Que. | 2-21-68 | Flint | 4 | 10 | 14 |
| Hulst, Kent | 6:00 | 180 | St. Thomas, Ont. | 4- 8-68 | Belleville | 21 | 41 | 62 |
| Ihnacak, Peter | 6:01 | 200 | Poprad, Czech. | 5- 3-57 | Newmarket-Toronto | 16 | 32 | 48 |
| Jackson, Mike | 6:01 | 192 | Mississauga, Ont. | 2- 4-69 | Toronto Jrs. | 16 | 51 | 67 |
| Jarvis, Wes | 5:11 | 185 | Toronto, Ont. | 5-30-58 | Newmarket | 22 | 31 | 53 |
| Jobe, Trevor | 6:01 | 200 | Lethbridge, Alta. | 5-14-67 | Mewmarket | 23 | 24 | 47 |
| Kordic, John | 6:01 | 190 | Edmonton, Alta. | 3-22-65 | Montreal-Toronto | 1 | 2 | 3 |
| Lawless, Paul | 5:11 | 180 | Scarborough, Ont. | 9- 2-64 | Milwaukee-Toronto | 30 | 35 | 65 |
| Laxdal, Derek | 6:01 | 198 | St. Boniface, Man. | 2-21-66 | Newmarket-Toronto | 31 | 28 | 59 |
| Leeman, Gary | 5:11 | 180 | Toronto, Ont. | 2-19-64 | Toronto | 32 | 43 | 75 |
| Mallgrave, Matt | 6:00 | 180 | Washington, D.C. | 5- 3-70 | Harvard | 24 | 14 | 38 |
| Marois, Daniel | 6:01 | 190 | Montreal, Que. | 10- 3-68 | Toronto | 31 | 23 | 54 |
| McIntyre, John | 6:01 | 175 | Ravenswood, Ont. | 4-29-69 | Guelph-Newmarket | 30 | 28 | 58 |
| McKenna, Sean | 6:00 | 185 | Asbestos, Que. | 3- 7-62 | Newmarket-Toronto | 14 | 28 | 42 |
| Moes, Mike | 5:11 | 185 | Burlington, Ont. | 3-30-67 | Univ. of Michigan | 14 | 24 | 38 |
| Olczyk, Ed | 6:01 | 200 | Chicago, Ill. | 8-16-66 | Toronto | 38 | 52 | 90 |
| Osborne, Mark | 6:02 | 205 | Toronto, Ont. | 8-13-61 | Toronto | 16 | 30 | 46 |
| Pearson, Rob | 6:01 | 173 | Oshawa, Ont. | 8- 3-71 | Belleville | 8 | 12 | 20 |
| Pearson, Scott | 6:01 | 203 | Cornwall, Ont. | 12-19-69 | Kingston-Niag. Falls-Toronto | 35 | 43 | 78 |
| Reid, Dave | 6:00 | 205 | Toronto, Ont. | 5-15-64 | Toronto | 9 | 21 | 30 |
| Reynolds, Bobby | 5:11 | 175 | Flint, Mich. | 7-14-67 | Michigan State | 36 | 41 | 77 |
| Sacco, Joe | 6:01 | 180 | Medford, Mass. | 2- 4-69 | Boston Univ. | 21 | 19 | 40 |
| Shedden, Doug | 6:00 | 185 | Wallaceburg, Ont. | 4-29-61 | Newmarket-Toronto | 14 | 26 | 40 |
| Terrion, Greg | 5:11 | 175 | Marmora, Ont. | 5- 2-60 | Newmarket | 15 | 34 | 49 |
| Thornton, Scott | 6:02 | 200 | London, Ont. | 1- 9-71 | Belleville | 28 | 34 | 62 |
| Tomlinson, David | 5:11 | 177 | N. Vancouver, B.C. | 5- 8-68 | Boston Univ. | 16 | 30 | 46 |
| Whittemore, Todd | 6:01 | 175 | Taunton, Mass. | 6-20-67 | Providence College | 7 | 1 | 8 |

## DEFENSEMEN

| Name | Hgt. | Wgt. | Place of Birth | Date | 1988-89 Club | G. | A. | Pts. |
|---|---|---|---|---|---|---|---|---|
| Bancroft, Steve | 6:01 | 214 | Toronto, Ont. | 10- 6-70 | Belleville | 7 | 30 | 37 |
| Blad, Brian | 6:02 | 202 | Brockville, Ont. | 7-22-67 | Newmarket | 2 | 4 | 6 |
| Buckley, David | 6:04 | 195 | Newton, Mass. | 1-27-66 | Boston College | 3 | 7 | 10 |
| Burke, David | 6:01 | 182 | Detroit, Mich. | 10-15-70 | Cornell Univ. | 0 | 3 | 3 |
| Capuano, Jack | 6:02 | 210 | Cranston, R.I. | 7- 7-66 | Newmarket | 5 | 16 | 21 |
| Carney, Keith | 6:01 | 175 | Cumberland, R.I. | 2- 7-71 | Mt. St. Charles H.S. | 12 | 25 | 37 |
| Crowley, Ted | 6:02 | 188 | Concord, Mass. | 5- 3-70 | Lawrence Academy | 12 | 24 | 36 |
| Curran, Brian | 6:05 | 215 | Toronto, Ont. | 11- 5-63 | Toronto | 1 | 4 | 5 |
| Delay, Mike | 6:00 | 190 | Boston, Mass. | 8-31-69 | Boston College | 6 | 13 | 19 |
| Gill, Todd | 6:01 | 185 | Brockville, Ont. | 11- 9-65 | Toronto | 11 | 14 | 25 |
| Hammond, Ken | 6:01 | 190 | Port Credit, Ont. | 8-22-63 | Edmonton-N.Y. Rangers-Toronto | 0 | 3 | 3 |
| Hepple, Alan | 5:09 | 200 | Blaydon on Tyne, Eng. | 8-16-63 | Newmarket | 5 | 29 | 34 |
| Hoard, Brian | 6:04 | 218 | Oshawa, Ont. | 3-10-68 | Newmarket | 2 | 5 | 7 |
| Hotham, Greg | 5:11 | 185 | London, Ont. | 3- 7-56 | Newmarket | 9 | 42 | 51 |
| Iafrate, Al | 6:03 | 215 | Dearborn, Mich. | 3-21-66 | Toronto | 13 | 20 | 33 |
| Jensen, Chris | 5:10 | 160 | Ft. St. John, B.C. | 10-28-63 | Univ. of Wisconsin | 1 | 0 | 1 |
| Langille, Derek | 6:00 | 184 | Toronto, Ont. | 6-25-69 | North Bay | 20 | 38 | 58 |
| Marsh, Brad | 6:03 | 220 | London, Ont. | 3-31-58 | Toronto | 1 | 15 | 16 |
| Martin, Matt | 6:03 | 190 | Hamden, Ct. | 4-30-71 | Avon Old Farms H.S. | 9 | 23 | 32 |
| Ramage, Rob | 6:02 | 195 | Byron, Ont. | 1-11-59 | Calgary | 3 | 13 | 16 |
| Richardson, Luke | 6:04 | 210 | Ottawa, Ont. | 3-26-69 | Toronto | 2 | 7 | 9 |
| Root, Bill | 6:00 | 210 | Toronto, Ont. | 9- 6-59 | Newmarket | 10 | 22 | 32 |
| Sacco, David | 5:09 | 162 | Malden, Mass. | 7-31-70 | Boston Univ. | 14 | 29 | 43 |
| Serowick, Jeff | 6:00 | 190 | Manchester, N.H. | 10- 1-67 | Providence College | 3 | 14 | 17 |
| Shannon, Darryl | 6:02 | 190 | Barrie, Ont. | 6-21-68 | Newmarket-Toronto | 6 | 27 | 33 |
| Spangler, Ken | 5:11 | 190 | Edmonton, Alta. | 5- 2-67 | Flint-Baltimore | 4 | 18 | 22 |
| Taylor, Scott | 6:00 | 180 | Toronto, Ont. | 3-23-68 | Oshawa | 2 | 5 | 7 |
| Veitch, Darren | 6:00 | 190 | Saskatoon, Sask. | 4-24-60 | Toronto-Newmarket | 8 | 26 | 34 |

## GOALTENDERS

| Name | Hgt. | Wgt. | Place of Birth | Date | 1988-89 Club | Mins. | GA. | SO. |
|---|---|---|---|---|---|---|---|---|
| Anderson, Dean | 5:10 | 175 | Oshawa, Ont. | 7-14-66 | Flint-Newmarket | 806 | 86 | 1 |
| Bernhardt, Tim | 5:09 | 160 | Sarnia, Ont. | 1-17-58 | Newmarket | 2004 | 145 | 1 |
| Bester, Allan | 5:07 | 150 | Hamilton, Ont. | 3-26-64 | Toronto | 2460 | 156 | 2 |
| Ing, Peter | 6:00 | 165 | Toronto, Ont. | 4-28-69 | London-Windsor | 2891 | 180 | 3 |
| Reese, Jeff | 5:09 | 170 | Brantford, Ont. | 3-24-66 | Newmarket-Toronto | 2558 | 172 | 0 |
| Rhodes, Damian | 6:00 | 165 | St. Paul, Minn. | 5-28-69 | Michigan Tech | 2216 | 163 | 0 |

# Vancouver Canucks
### Smythe Division

| | |
|---|---|
| Chairman of the Board | Frank A. Griffiths |
| Vice-Chairman | Arthur R. Griffiths |
| President and General Manager | Pat Quinn |
| Vice President and Director of Hockey Operations | Brian Burke |
| Vice-President and Director of Marketing and Communications | Glen Ringdal |
| Senior Advisor | Jack Gordon |
| Director, Public and Media Relations | Darcy Rota |
| Coach | Bob McCammon |
| Assistant Coaches | Jack McIlhargey, Mike Murphy |
| Goaltending Consultant | Cesare Maniago |
| Director of Scouting | Mike Penny |
| Director of Pro Scouting | Murray Oliver |
| Scouts | Jack McCartan, Ken Slater, Ron Delorme, Ed McColgan, Paul McIntosh, Scott Carter, Jim Paulenko |
| Director of Community Relations and Ticket Sales | Lynn Harrison |
| Director of Hockey Information | Frank Bohmer |
| Trainers | Larry Ashley, Pat O'Neil, Ed Georgica |
| Home Ice | Pacific Coliseum |
| Address | 100 North Renfrew St., Vancouver, B.C. V5K 3N7 |
| Seating Capacity | 16,160 |
| Club Colors | White, Black, Red and Gold |
| Phone | (604) 254-5141 |

Frank A. Griffiths

Pat Quinn

Brian Burke

Bob McCammon

# Vancouver Canucks 1989-90 Roster

## FORWARDS

| Name | Hgt. | Wgt. | Place of Birth | Date | 1988-89 Club | G. | A. | Pts. |
|---|---|---|---|---|---|---|---|---|
| Adams, Greg | 6:03 | 190 | Nelson, B.C. | 8- 1-63 | Vancouver | 19 | 14 | 33 |
| Adams, Greg C. | 6:02 | 200 | Duncan, B.C. | 5-31-60 | Edmonton-Vancouver | 8 | 7 | 15 |
| Bakovic, Peter | 6:02 | 200 | Thunder Bay, Ont. | 1-31-65 | Milwaukee | 16 | 14 | 30 |
| Bozek, Steve | 5:11 | 180 | Kelowna, B.C. | 11-26-60 | Vancouver | 17 | 18 | 35 |
| Bradley, Brian | 5:10 | 180 | Kitchener, Ont. | 1-21-65 | Vancouver | 18 | 27 | 45 |
| Bruce, David | 5:11 | 185 | Thunder Bay, Ont. | 10- 7-64 | Vancouver | 7 | 7 | 14 |
| Charbonneau, Jose | 6:00 | 195 | Ferme-Nueve, Que. | 11-21-66 | Mont.-Sher.-Van.-Milwaukee | 24 | 22 | 46 |
| Crawford, Marc | 5:11 | 185 | Belleville, Ont. | 2-13-61 | Milwaukee | 23 | 30 | 53 |
| DeBoer, Peter | 6:00 | 195 | Windsor, Ont. | 6-13-68 | Windsor-Milwaukee | 45 | 47 | 92 |
| Hawkins, Todd | 6:01 | 195 | Kingston, Ont. | 8- 2-66 | Milwaukee-Vancouver | 12 | 14 | 26 |
| Johnson, Steve | 6:01 | 190 | Grand Forks, N.D. | 3- 3-66 | Milwaukee | 18 | 34 | 52 |
| Larionov, Igor | 5:09 | 165 | Voskresonk, U.S.S.R. | 12- 3-60 | Central Red Army | 15 | 12 | 27 |
| Lenardon, Tim | 6:02 | 185 | Trail, B.C. | 5-11-62 | Utica-Milwaukee | 34 | 32 | 66 |
| Linden, Trevor | 6:04 | 200 | Medicine Hat, Alta. | 4-11-70 | Vancouver | 30 | 29 | 59 |
| Mazur, Jay | 6:02 | 205 | Hamilton, Ont. | 1-22-65 | Milwaukee-Vancouver | 33 | 31 | 64 |
| Murphy, Rob | 6:03 | 205 | Hull, Que. | 4- 7-69 | Drummondville-Van.-Milwaukee | 19 | 28 | 47 |
| Pederson, Barry | 5:11 | 185 | Big River, Sask. | 3-13-61 | Vancouver | 15 | 26 | 41 |
| Rohlicek, Jeff | 6:00 | 180 | Park Ridge, Ill. | 1-27-66 | Milwaukee-Vancouver | 47 | 63 | 110 |
| Sandlak, Jim | 6:03 | 219 | Kitchener, Ont. | 12-12-66 | Vancouver | 20 | 20 | 40 |
| Skriko, Petri | 5:10 | 180 | Lapeenranta, Finland | 3-12-62 | Vancouver | 30 | 36 | 66 |
| Smith, Doug | 5:11 | 186 | Ottawa, Ont. | 5-17-63 | Edm.-Cape Breton-Vancouver | 15 | 16 | 31 |
| Smyl, Stan | 5:08 | 195 | Glendon, Alta. | 1-28-58 | Vancouver | 7 | 18 | 25 |
| Stanley, Darryl | 6:02 | 200 | Winnipeg, Man. | 12- 2-62 | Vancouver | 3 | 1 | 4 |
| Stern, Ronnie | 6:00 | 195 | Ste. Agathe, Que. | 1-11-67 | Milwaukee-Vancouver | 20 | 23 | 43 |
| Street, Keith | 6:00 | 170 | Moose Jaw, Sask. | 3-18-65 | Milwaukee | 10 | 11 | 21 |
| Sutter, Rich | 5:11 | 190 | Viking, Alta. | 12- 2-63 | Vancouver | 17 | 15 | 32 |
| Tanti, Tony | 5:09 | 185 | Toronto, Ont. | 9- 7-63 | Vancouver | 24 | 25 | 49 |
| Vargas, Ernie | 6:01 | 180 | St. Paul, Minn. | 3- 1-64 | Milwaukee | 16 | 35 | 51 |

## DEFENSEMEN

| Name | Hgt. | Wgt. | Place of Birth | Date | 1988-89 Club | G. | A. | Pts. |
|---|---|---|---|---|---|---|---|---|
| Agnew, Jim | 6:01 | 190 | Hartney, Man. | 3-21-66 | Milwaukee | 2 | 10 | 12 |
| Benning, Jim | 6:00 | 185 | Edmonton, Alta. | 4-29-63 | Vancouver | 3 | 9 | 12 |
| Butcher, Garth | 6:00 | 200 | Regina, Sask. | 1- 8-63 | Vancouver | 0 | 20 | 20 |
| Guy, Kevan | 6:03 | 200 | Edmonton, Alta. | 7-16-65 | Kitchener | 2 | 2 | 4 |
| Herniman, Steve | 6:04 | 210 | Windsor, Ont. | 6- 9-68 | Kitchener | 3 | 16 | 19 |
| Hunt, Chris | 6:00 | 195 | N. Battleford, Sask. | 1-28-67 | Milwaukee | 3 | 17 | 20 |
| Kidd, Ian | 5:11 | 195 | Gresham, Ore. | 5-11-64 | Milwaukee-Vancouver | 13 | 40 | 53 |
| Lidster, Doug | 6:01 | 200 | Kamloops, B.C. | 10-18-60 | Vancouver | 5 | 17 | 22 |
| Melnyk, Larry | 6:00 | 195 | Saskatoon, Sask. | 2-21-60 | Vancouver | 3 | 11 | 14 |
| Nordmark, Robert | 6:01 | 200 | Lulea, Sweden | 8-20-62 | Vancouver | 6 | 35 | 41 |
| Reinhart, Paul | 5:11 | 200 | Kitchener, Ont. | 1- 8-60 | Vancouver | 7 | 50 | 57 |
| Snepsts, Harold | 6:03 | 210 | Edmonton, Alta. | 10-24-54 | Vancouver | 0 | 8 | 8 |
| Valimont, Carl | 6:01 | 200 | Southington, Ct. | 3- 1-66 | Milwaukee | 4 | 33 | 37 |
| Veilleux, Steve | 6:00 | 198 | Lachenaie, Que. | 3- 9-69 | Trois-Rivieres-Milwaukee | 5 | 28 | 33 |

## GOALTENDERS

| Name | Hgt. | Wgt. | Place of Birth | Date | 1988-89 Club | Mins. | GA. | SO. |
|---|---|---|---|---|---|---|---|---|
| Gamble, Troy | 5:11 | 195 | New Glasgow, N.S. | 4- 7-67 | Milwaukee-Vancouver | 2500 | 150 | 0 |
| McLean, Kirk | 6:00 | 185 | Willowdale, Ont. | 6-26-66 | Vancouver | 2477 | 127 | 4 |
| Weeks, Steve | 5:11 | 170 | Scarborough, Ont. | 6-30-58 | Vancouver | 2056 | 102 | 0 |

# Washington Capitals
### Patrick Division

| | |
|---|---|
| Chairman and Governor | Abe Pollin |
| President and Alternate Governor | Richard M. Patrick |
| Vice-President and General Manager | David Poile |
| Legal Counselors and Alternate Governors | David M. Osnos, Peter F. O'Malley |
| Vice-President and Comptroller | Edmund Stelzer |
| Coach | Bryan Murray |
| Assistant Coaches | Doug MacLean, Rob Laird |
| Strength and Conditioning Coach | Frank Costello |
| Director of Player Personnel and Recruitment | Jack Button |
| Coordinator of Scouting | Hugh Rogers |
| Chief U.S. Scout | Jack Barzee |
| Chief Eastern Scout | Jack Ferguson |
| Chief Western Scout | Barry Trotz |
| Scouts | Gilles Cote, Fred Devereaux, Bruce Hamilton, Eje Johansson, Richard Rothermel, Bob Schmidt, Dan Sylvester, John Stanton, Darrell Young |
| Vice-President/Marketing | Lew Strudler |
| Director of Public Relations | Lou Corletto |
| Assistant Director of Marketing | Debi Angus |
| Director of Community Relations | Yvon Labre |
| Director of Promotions | Charles Copeland |
| Director of Season Subscriptions | Joanne Kowalski |
| Public Relations Assistant | David Ferry |
| Administrative Assistant to the General Manager | Pat Young |
| Trainer | Stan Wong |
| Assistant Trainer/Head Equipment Manager | Doug Shearer |
| Home Ice | Capital Centre |
| Address | Landover, Md. 20785 |
| Seating Capacity | 18,130 |
| Club Colors | Red, White and Blue |
| Phone | (301) 386-7000 |

**Abe Pollin**

**David Poile**

**Jack Button**

**Bryan Murray**

# Washington Capitals 1989-90 Roster

## FORWARDS

| Name | Hgt. | Wgt. | Place of Birth | Date | 1988-89 Club | G. | A. | Pts. |
|---|---|---|---|---|---|---|---|---|
| Bawa, Robin | 6:02 | 214 | Chemainos, B.C. | 3-26-66 | Baltimore | 23 | 24 | 47 |
| Bergland, Tim | 6:02 | 194 | Crookston, Minn. | 1-11-65 | Baltimore | 24 | 29 | 53 |
| Christian, Dave | 5:11 | 195 | Warroad, Minn. | 3-12-59 | Washington | 34 | 31 | 65 |
| Ciccarelli, Dino | 5:10 | 175 | Sarnia, Ont. | 2-8-60 | Minnesota-Washington | 44 | 30 | 74 |
| Corriveau, Yvon | 6:01 | 215 | Welland, Ont. | 2-8-67 | Baltimore-Washington | 19 | 25 | 44 |
| Courtnall, Geoff | 6:01 | 190 | Victoria, B.C. | 8-18-62 | Washington | 42 | 38 | 80 |
| Dickie, Gary | 5:11 | 187 | Regina, Sask. | 11-19-68 | Regina | 48 | 60 | 108 |
| Druce, John | 6:01 | 200 | Peterborough, Ont. | 2-23-66 | Washington-Baltimore | 10 | 18 | 28 |
| Gervais, Victor | 5:09 | 172 | Prince George, B.C. | 3-13-69 | Seattle | 54 | 65 | 119 |
| Gould, Bobby | 5:10 | 185 | Petrolia, Ont. | 9-2-57 | Washington | 5 | 13 | 18 |
| Greenlaw, Jeff | 6:01 | 230 | Toronto, Ont. | 2-28-68 | Baltimore | 12 | 15 | 27 |
| Hollett, Steve | 6:00 | 200 | St. John's, Nfld. | 6-12-67 | Fort Wayne | 27 | 21 | 48 |
| Holoien, Dean | 6:00 | 197 | Melford, Sask. | 4-18-69 | Saskatoon | 22 | 30 | 52 |
| Hunter, Dale | 5:10 | 198 | Petrolia, Ont. | 7-31-60 | Washington | 20 | 37 | 57 |
| Larter, Tyler | 5:10 | 190 | Charlottetown, P.E.I. | 3-12-68 | Baltimore | 9 | 19 | 28 |
| Leach, Steve | 5:11 | 198 | Cambridge, Mass. | 1-16-66 | Washington | 11 | 19 | 30 |
| Lindal, Kirby | 5:10 | 180 | Humboldt, Sask. | 1-12-68 | Medicine Hat | 67 | 55 | 122 |
| Lorentz, Dave | 5:09 | 182 | Kitchener, Ont. | 3-16-69 | Peterborough | 18 | 38 | 56 |
| Maltais, Steve | 6:02 | 204 | Arvida, Que. | 1-25-69 | Cornwall | 53 | 70 | 123 |
| May, Alan | 6:01 | 200 | Barrhead, Man. | 1-14-65 | Cape Breton-New Haven | 14 | 21 | 35 |
| McEwen, Dennis | 5:11 | 191 | Elliot Lake, Ont. | 1-30-68 | London | 50 | 42 | 92 |
| Millar, Mike | 5:11 | 175 | St. Catharines, Ont. | 4-28-65 | Baltimore-Washington | 53 | 38 | 91 |
| Miller, Kelly | 5:11 | 196 | Detroit, Mich. | 3-3-63 | Washington | 19 | 21 | 40 |
| Murray, Rob | 6:00 | 185 | Toronto, Ont. | 4-4-67 | Baltimore | 11 | 23 | 34 |
| Pivonka, Michal | 6:02 | 198 | Kladno, Czech. | 1-28-66 | Washington-Baltimore | 20 | 43 | 63 |
| Purves, John | 6:00 | 201 | Toronto, Ont. | 2-12-68 | North Bay | 39 | 63 | 102 |
| Richard, Mike | 5:10 | 194 | Scarborough, Ont. | 7-9-66 | Baltimore | 44 | 63 | 107 |
| Ridley, Mike | 6:01 | 200 | Winnipeg, Man. | 7-8-63 | Washington | 41 | 48 | 89 |
| Savage, Reggie | 5:10 | 179 | Montreal, Que. | 5-1-70 | Victoriaville | 58 | 55 | 113 |
| Seftel, Steve | 6:02 | 196 | Kitchener, Ont. | 5-14-68 | Baltimore | 12 | 15 | 27 |
| Taylor, Tim | 5:11 | 178 | Stratford, Ont. | 2-6-69 | London | 34 | 80 | 114 |
| Wickenheiser, Doug | 6:01 | 200 | Regina, Sask. | 3-30-61 | NYR-Team Canada-Balt.-Wash. | 10 | 25 | 35 |

## DEFENSEMEN

| Name | Hgt. | Wgt. | Place of Birth | Date | 1988-89 Club | G. | A. | Pts. |
|---|---|---|---|---|---|---|---|---|
| Babcock, Bob | 6:01 | 222 | Toronto, Ont. | 8-3-68 | Cornwall | 0 | 9 | 9 |
| Ballantyne, Jeff | 6:01 | 203 | Elmira, Ont. | 1-7-69 | Ottawa | 8 | 21 | 29 |
| Bartley, Wade | 6:01 | 190 | Kilarney, Man. | 5-16-71 | Univ. of North Dakota | 1 | 1 | 2 |
| Felix, Chris | 5:10 | 191 | Bramalea, Ont. | 5-27-64 | Baltimore-Washington | 8 | 37 | 45 |
| Ferner, Mark | 6:00 | 193 | Regina, Sask. | 9-5-65 | Rochester-Buffalo | 0 | 18 | 18 |
| Hatcher, Kevin | 6:04 | 225 | Detroit, Mich. | 9-9-66 | Washington | 13 | 27 | 40 |
| Houlder, Bill | 6:03 | 212 | Thunder Bay, Ont. | 5-11-67 | Baltimore-Washington | 10 | 39 | 49 |
| Johansson, Calle | 5:11 | 205 | Goteborg, Sweden | 2-14-67 | Buffalo-Washington | 3 | 18 | 21 |
| Kleinendorst, Scott | 6:03 | 215 | Grand Rapids, Minn. | 1-16-60 | Hartford-Washington | 0 | 1 | 1 |
| Kummu, Ryan | 6:03 | 205 | Kitchener, Ont. | 6-5-67 | RPI | 2 | 5 | 7 |
| Langway, Rod | 6:03 | 224 | Taiwan, Formosa | 5-3-57 | Washington | 2 | 19 | 21 |
| Mathieson, Jim | 6:01 | 209 | Kindersley, Sask. | 1-24-71 | Regina | 5 | 22 | 27 |
| Rouse, Bob | 6:01 | 210 | Surrey, B.C. | 6-18-64 | Minnesota-Washington | 4 | 15 | 19 |
| Sheehy, Neil | 6:02 | 214 | Int'l. Falls, Minn. | 2-9-60 | Washington | 3 | 4 | 7 |
| Smith, Dennis | 5:11 | 192 | Detroit, Mich. | 7-27-64 | Adirondack | 5 | 35 | 40 |
| Stevens, Scott | 6:01 | 209 | Kitchener, Ont. | 4-1-64 | Washington | 12 | 60 | 72 |
| Tutt, Brian | 6:01 | 195 | Small Well, Alta. | 6-9-62 | Team Canada-Baltimore | 1 | 23 | 24 |

## GOALTENDERS

| Name | Hgt. | Wgt. | Place of Birth | Date | 1988-89 Club | Mins. | GA. | SO. |
|---|---|---|---|---|---|---|---|---|
| Beaupre, Don | 5:09 | 165 | Waterloo, Ont. | 9-19-61 | Kalamazoo-Minn.-Balt.-Wash. | 2531 | 143 | 2 |
| Dafoe, Byron | 5:11 | 175 | Duncan, B.C. | 2-25-71 | Portland | 3279 | 291 | 1 |
| Hrivnak, Jim | 6:02 | 185 | Montreal, Que. | 5-28-68 | Merrimack College-Baltimore | 1797 | 104 | 2 |
| Kolzig, Olaf | 6:03 | 207 | Joh'sburg, S.Africa | 4-9-70 | Tri-City | 1671 | 97 | 1 |
| Mason, Bob | 6:01 | 180 | Int'l. Falls, Minn. | 4-22-61 | Quebec-Halifax | 2446 | 165 | 1 |
| Raymond, Alain | 5:10 | 180 | Rimouski, Que. | 6-24-65 | Baltimore | 2300 | 162 | 0 |
| Simpson, Shawn | 5:11 | 183 | Gloucester, Ont. | 8-10-63 | Oshawa-Baltimore | 1878 | 138 | 0 |

# Winnipeg Jets
### Smythe Division

| | |
|---|---|
| President and Governor | Barry L. Shenkarow |
| Alternate Governors | Michael A. Smith, Bill Davis |
| Vice-President and General Manager | Michael A. Smith |
| Assistant General Manager—Director of Hockey Operations | Dennis McDonald |
| Director of Finance and Administration | Don Binda |
| Coach | Bob Murdoch |
| Assistant Coaches | Alpo Suhonen, Clare Drake |
| Scouts | Joe Yannetti, Bill Lesuk, Tom Savage, Connie Broden |
| Executive Assistant to Vice-President and General Manager | Pat MacDonald |
| Vice-President of Marketing and Public Relations | Madeline Hanson |
| Director of Public Relations | Murray Harding |
| Director of Media Relations | Mike O'Hearn |
| Director of Community Relations | Lori Summers |
| Athletic Therapists | Chuck Badcock, Jim Ramsay |
| Equipment Manager | Craig Heisinger |
| Home Ice | Winnipeg Arena |
| Address | 15-1430 Maroons Road, Winnipeg, Man. R3G 0L5 |
| Seating Capacity | 15,405 |
| Club Colors | Blue, Red and White |
| Phone | (204) 783-5387 |

Barry L. Shenkarow

Michael A. Smith

Dennis McDonald

Bob Murdoch

# Winnipeg Jets 1989-90 Roster

| FORWARDS | Hgt. | Wgt. | Place of Birth | Date | 1988-89 Club | G. | A. | Pts. |
|---|---|---|---|---|---|---|---|---|
| Ashton, Brent | 6:01 | 210 | Saskatoon, Sask. | 5-18-60 | Winnipeg | 31 | 37 | 68 |
| Barnes, Stu | 5:10 | 175 | Edmonton, Alta. | 12-25-70 | Tri-City | 59 | 82 | 141 |
| Borrel, John | 6:02 | 190 | Shakopee, Minn. | 3-23-67 | Lowell University | 8 | 8 | 16 |
| Borsato, Luciano | 5:10 | 165 | Richmond Hill, Ont. | 1- 7-66 | Tappara, Finland | 31 | 36 | 67 |
| Boschman, Laurie | 6:00 | 185 | Major, Sask. | 6- 4-60 | Winnipeg | 10 | 26 | 36 |
| Cirone, Jason | 5:09 | 184 | Toronto, Ont. | 2-21-71 | Cornwall | 39 | 44 | 83 |
| Cole, Danton | 5:11 | 189 | Lansing, Mich. | 1-10-67 | Michigan State | 29 | 33 | 62 |
| Cunneyworth, Randy | 6:00 | 180 | Etobicoke, Ont. | 5-10-61 | Pittsburgh | 25 | 19 | 44 |
| DiPietro, Paul | 5:09 | 190 | Sault Ste. Marie, Ont. | 9- 8-70 | Sudbury | 29 | 48 | 77 |
| Donnelly, Gord | 6:01 | 202 | Montreal, Que. | 4- 5-62 | Quebec-Winnipeg | 10 | 10 | 20 |
| Draper, Kris | 5:11 | 188 | Toronto, Ont. | 5-24-71 | Canadian Nat. Team | 11 | 15 | 26 |
| Duncan, Iain | 6:01 | 200 | Toronto, Ont. | 8- 4-63 | Winnipeg | 14 | 30 | 44 |
| Elynuik, Pat | 6:00 | 185 | Foam Lake, Sask. | 10-30-67 | Winnipeg | 26 | 25 | 51 |
| Endean, Craig | 5:11 | 175 | Kamloops, B.C. | 4-13-68 | Fort Wayne-Moncton | 13 | 27 | 40 |
| Fenton, Paul | 5:11 | 180 | Springfield, Mass. | 12-22-64 | Los Angeles-Winnipeg | 16 | 12 | 28 |
| Hannigan, Jason | 6:00 | 188 | Stoney Creek, Ont. | 1-13-69 | Cornwall | 32 | 23 | 55 |
| Hawerchuk, Dale | 5:11 | 185 | Toronto, Ont. | 4- 4-63 | Winnipeg | 41 | 55 | 96 |
| Heise, Kevin | 6:01 | 169 | Regina, Sask. | 9- 0-68 | | .. | .. | .. |
| Hughes, Brent | 5:11 | 190 | New Westminster, B.C. | 4- 5-66 | Moncton-Winnipeg | 37 | 36 | 73 |
| Hunt, Brian | 6:00 | 185 | Toronto, Ont. | 2-12-69 | Oshawa | 30 | 56 | 86 |
| Jones, Brad | 6:00 | 180 | Sterling Hts., Mich. | 6-26-65 | Moncton-Winnipeg | 26 | 24 | 50 |
| Jones, Ron | 6:03 | 197 | Detroit, Mich. | 2- 7-69 | London | 27 | 36 | 63 |
| Joseph, Tony | 6:04 | 203 | Cornwall, Ont. | 3- 1-69 | Oshawa, Winnipeg | 21 | 16 | 37 |
| Kulak, Stu | 5:10 | 180 | Edmonton, Alta. | 3-10-63 | Moncton, Winnipeg | 32 | 29 | 61 |
| Kumpel, Mark | 6:00 | 190 | Wakefield, Mass. | 3- 7-61 | Moncton | 22 | 23 | 45 |
| Larose, Guy | 5:10 | 175 | Hull, Que. | 7-31-67 | Moncton-Winnipeg | 32 | 28 | 60 |
| Meadmore, Neil | 6:04 | 190 | Winnipeg, Man. | 10-23-59 | Moncton | 9 | 14 | 23 |
| McLlwain, Dave | 6:00 | 190 | Seaforth, Ont. | 1- 9-67 | Muskegon-Pittsburgh | 38 | 37 | 75 |
| McReynolds, Brian | 6:01 | 180 | Pentanguishene, Ont. | 1- 5-65 | Canadian Nat. Team | 9 | 25 | 34 |
| Paslawski, Greg | 5:11 | 190 | Kindersley, Sask. | 8-25-61 | St. Louis | 26 | 26 | 52 |
| Peltola, Pekka | 6:02 | 196 | Helsinki, Finland | 6-24-65 | HPK Finland | 28 | 30 | 58 |
| Schneider, Scott | 6:01 | 180 | Rochester, Minn. | 5-18-65 | Moncton | 29 | 36 | 65 |
| Selanne, Teemu | 6:00 | 176 | Helsinki, Finland | 7- 3-70 | Jokerit | 35 | 33 | 68 |
| Smail, Doug | 5:09 | 175 | Moose Jaw, Sask. | 9- 2-57 | Winnipeg | 14 | 15 | 29 |
| Steen, Thomas | 5:10 | 195 | Tocksmark, Sweden | 6- 8-60 | Winnipeg | 27 | 61 | 88 |
| Warus, Mike | 6:01 | 190 | Sudbury, Ont. | 1-16-64 | Moncton | 6 | 8 | 14 |
| Wilson, Ron | 5:09 | 175 | Toronto, Ont. | 5-13-66 | Moncton | 31 | 61 | 92 |
| DEFENSEMEN | | | | | | | | |
| Berry, Brad | 6:02 | 190 | Bashaw, Alta. | 4- 1-65 | Moncton-Winnipeg | 3 | 25 | 28 |
| Carlyle, Randy | 5:10 | 200 | Sudbury, Ont. | 4-19-56 | Winnipeg | 6 | 38 | 44 |
| Ellett, Dave | 6:01 | 200 | Cleveland, O. | 3-30-64 | Winnipeg | 22 | 34 | 56 |
| Flichel, Todd | 6:03 | 195 | Osgoode, Ont. | 9-14-64 | Moncton | 2 | 29 | 31 |
| Galloway, Kyle | 5:11 | 175 | Winnipeg, Man. | 11-10-69 | Univ. of Manitoba | 6 | 18 | 24 |
| Gosselin, Guy | 5:10 | 190 | Rochester, Minn. | 1- 6-64 | Moncton | 2 | 8 | 10 |
| Hervey, Matt | 5:11 | 205 | Whittier, Calif. | 5-16-66 | Moncton | 8 | 28 | 36 |
| Marchment, Bryan | 6:01 | 198 | Scarborough, Ont. | 5- 1-69 | Belleville | 14 | 36 | 50 |
| Norton, Chris | 6:02 | 200 | Oakville, Ont. | 3-11-65 | Moncton | 1 | 21 | 22 |
| Numminen, Teppo | 6:01 | 190 | Tampere, Finland | 7- 3-68 | Winnipeg | 1 | 14 | 15 |
| Olausson, Fredrik | 6:02 | 200 | Vaxsjo, Sweden | 10- 5-66 | Winnipeg | 15 | 47 | 62 |
| Taglianetti, Peter | 6:02 | 200 | Framingham, Mass. | 8-15-63 | Winnipeg | 1 | 14 | 15 |
| | | | | | | Mins. | GA. | SO. |
| GOALTENDERS | | | | | | | | |
| Beauregard, Stephane | 5:11 | 182 | Cowanville, Que. | 1-10-68 | Fort Wayne-Moncton | 1653 | 105 | 0 |
| Berthiaume, Daniel | 5:09 | 150 | Longueuil, Que. | 1-26-66 | Moncton-Winnipeg | 1525 | 120 | 0 |
| Draper, Tom | 5:11 | 180 | Outrement, Que. | 11-20-66 | Moncton | 2963 | 171 | 2 |
| Essensa, Bob | 6:00 | 160 | Toronto, Ont. | 1-14-65 | Fort Wayne-Winnipeg | 2389 | 138 | 1 |
| Furlan, Frank | 5:09 | 160 | Sherwood Park, Alta. | 3- 8-68 | Tri-City | 2662 | 191 | 0 |
| O'Neill, Mike | 5:07 | 160 | Montreal, Que. | 11- 3-67 | Yale University | 1490 | 93 | 0 |
| Reddick, Pokey | 5:08 | 170 | Halifax, N.S. | 10- 6-64 | Winnipeg | 2109 | 144 | 0 |
| Tabaracci, Richard | 5:10 | 183 | Toronto, Ont. | 1- 2-69 | Cornwall-Pittsburgh | 2482 | 167 | 1 |

Mario Lemieux

Joe Mullen

Luc Robitaille

# The Sporting News
## 1988-89 NHL All-Star Team

| First Team | Position | Second Team |
|---|---|---|
| Mario Lemieux, Pittsburgh | Center | Wayne Gretzky, Los Angeles |
| Joe Mullen, Calgary | Right Wing | Jari Kurri, Edmonton |
| Luc Robitaille, Los Angeles | Left Wing | Mats Naslund, Montreal |
| Paul Coffey, Pittsburgh | Defense | Ray Bourque, Boston |
| Chris Chelios, Montreal | Defense | Gary Suter, Calgary |
| Patrick Roy, Montreal | Goalie | Mike Vernon, Calgary |

THE SPORTING NEWS Player of the Year: Mario Lemieux, Pittsburgh
THE SPORTING NEWS Rookie of the Year: Brian Leetch, N.Y. Rangers
THE SPORTING NEWS Coach of the Year: Pat Burns, Montreal
THE SPORTING NEWS Executive of the Year: Bruce McNall, Los Angeles
Note: THE SPORTING NEWS All-Star Team is selected by the NHL Players.

Paul Coffey

Chris Chelios

Patrick Roy

**Montreal defenseman Chris Chelios is a first-time selection to The Sporting News' All-Star Team.**

**Calgary Flames right wing Joe Mullen.**

# 1988-89 FINAL NHL STANDINGS

## Prince of Wales Conference

### Charles F. Adams Division

|  | G. | W. | L. | T. | Pts. | G.F. | G.A. | Home | Away | Div. Rec. |
|---|---|---|---|---|---|---|---|---|---|---|
| Montreal Canadiens | 80 | 53 | 18 | 9 | 115 | 315 | 218 | 30-6-4 | 23-12-5 | 23-8-1 |
| Boston Bruins | 80 | 37 | 29 | 14 | 88 | 289 | 256 | 17-15-8 | 20-14-6 | 9-16-7 |
| Buffalo Sabres | 80 | 38 | 35 | 7 | 83 | 291 | 299 | 25-12-3 | 13-23-4 | 14-14-4 |
| Hartford Whalers | 80 | 37 | 38 | 5 | 79 | 299 | 290 | 21-17-2 | 16-21-3 | 13-18-1 |
| Quebec Nordiques | 80 | 27 | 46 | 7 | 61 | 269 | 342 | 16-20-4 | 11-26-3 | 12-15-5 |

### Lester Patrick Division

|  | G. | W. | L. | T. | Pts. | G.F. | G.A. | Home | Away | Div. Rec. |
|---|---|---|---|---|---|---|---|---|---|---|
| Washington Capitals | 80 | 41 | 29 | 10 | 92 | 305 | 259 | 25-12-3 | 16-17-7 | 16-17-2 |
| Pittsburgh Penguins | 80 | 40 | 33 | 7 | 87 | 347 | 349 | 24-13-3 | 16-20-4 | 19-12-4 |
| New York Rangers | 80 | 37 | 35 | 8 | 82 | 310 | 307 | 21-17-2 | 16-18-6 | 17-14-4 |
| Philadelphia Flyers | 80 | 36 | 36 | 8 | 80 | 307 | 285 | 22-15-3 | 14-21-5 | 19-14-2 |
| New Jersey Devils | 80 | 27 | 41 | 12 | 66 | 281 | 325 | 17-18-5 | 10-23-7 | 12-19-4 |
| New York Islanders | 80 | 28 | 47 | 5 | 61 | 265 | 325 | 19-18-3 | 9-29-2 | 12-19-4 |

## Clarence Campbell Conference

### James Norris Division

|  | G. | W. | L. | T. | Pts. | G.F. | G.A. | Home | Away | Div. Rec. |
|---|---|---|---|---|---|---|---|---|---|---|
| Detroit Red Wings | 80 | 34 | 34 | 12 | 80 | 313 | 316 | 20-14-6 | 14-20-6 | 15-13-4 |
| St. Louis Blues | 80 | 33 | 35 | 12 | 78 | 275 | 285 | 22-11-7 | 11-24-5 | 18-8-6 |
| Minnesota North Stars | 80 | 27 | 37 | 16 | 70 | 258 | 278 | 17-15-8 | 10-22-8 | 10-16-6 |
| Chicago Black Hawks | 80 | 27 | 41 | 12 | 66 | 297 | 335 | 16-14-10 | 11-27-2 | 12-13-7 |
| Toronto Maple Leafs | 80 | 28 | 46 | 6 | 62 | 259 | 342 | 15-20-5 | 13-26-1 | 12-17-3 |

### Conn Smythe Division

|  | G. | W. | L. | T. | Pts. | G.F. | G.A. | Home | Away | Div. Rec. |
|---|---|---|---|---|---|---|---|---|---|---|
| Calgary Flames | 80 | 54 | 17 | 9 | 117 | 354 | 226 | 32-4-4 | 22-13-5 | 21-7-4 |
| Los Angeles Kings | 80 | 42 | 31 | 7 | 91 | 376 | 335 | 25-12-3 | 17-19-4 | 12-16-4 |
| Edmonton Oilers | 80 | 38 | 34 | 8 | 84 | 325 | 306 | 21-16-3 | 17-18-5 | 13-17-2 |
| Vancouver Canucks | 80 | 33 | 39 | 8 | 74 | 251 | 253 | 19-15-6 | 14-24-2 | 13-16-3 |
| Winnipeg Jets | 80 | 26 | 42 | 12 | 64 | 300 | 355 | 17-18-5 | 9-24-7 | 11-14-7 |

# Top 20 Scorers for the Art Ross Memorial Trophy

*Indicates league-leading figure.

|  | Games | G. | A. | Pts. | Pen. |
|---|---|---|---|---|---|
| 1. Mario Lemieux, Pittsburgh | 76 | *85 | *114 | *199 | 100 |
| 2. Wayne Gretzky, Los Angeles | 78 | 54 | *114 | 168 | 26 |
| 3. Steve Yzerman, Detroit | 80 | 65 | 90 | 155 | 61 |
| 4. Bernie Nicholls, Los Angeles | 79 | 70 | 80 | 150 | 96 |
| 5. Rob Brown, Pittsburgh | 68 | 49 | 66 | 115 | 118 |
| 6. Paul Coffey, Pittsburgh | 75 | 30 | 83 | 113 | 195 |
| 7. Joe Mullen, Calgary | 79 | 51 | 59 | 110 | 16 |
| 8. Jari Kurri, Edmonton | 76 | 44 | 58 | 102 | 69 |
| 9. Jimmy Carson, Edmonton | 80 | 49 | 51 | 100 | 36 |
| 10. Luc Robitaille, Los Angeles | 78 | 46 | 52 | 98 | 65 |
| 11. Dale Hawerchuk, Winnipeg | 75 | 41 | 55 | 96 | 28 |
| 12. Dan Quinn, Pittsburgh | 79 | 34 | 60 | 94 | 102 |
| Mark Messier, Edmonton | 72 | 33 | 61 | 94 | 130 |
| 14. Gerard Gallant, Detroit | 76 | 39 | 54 | 93 | 230 |
| 15. Ed Olczyk, Toronto | 80 | 38 | 52 | 90 | 75 |
| 16. Kevin Dineen, Hartford | 79 | 45 | 44 | 89 | 167 |
| Mike Ridley, Washington | 80 | 41 | 48 | 89 | 49 |
| 18. Tim Kerr, Philadelphia | 69 | 48 | 40 | 88 | 73 |
| Pat LaFontaine, N.Y. Islanders | 79 | 45 | 43 | 88 | 26 |
| Pierre Turgeon, Buffalo | 80 | 34 | 54 | 88 | 26 |
| Tomas Sandstrom, N.Y. Rangers | 79 | 32 | 56 | 88 | 148 |
| Thomas Steen, Winnipeg | 80 | 27 | 61 | 88 | 80 |

# National Hockey League Team-by-Team Individual Scoring

*Indicates league-leading figure.

## Boston Bruins

| | Games | G. | A. | Pts. | Pen. |
|---|---|---|---|---|---|
| Cam Neely | 74 | 37 | 38 | 75 | 190 |
| Ken Linseman | 78 | 27 | 45 | 72 | 164 |
| Craig Janney | 62 | 16 | 46 | 62 | 12 |
| Randy Burridge | 80 | 31 | 30 | 61 | 39 |
| Ray Bourque | 60 | 18 | 43 | 61 | 52 |
| Glen Wesley | 77 | 19 | 35 | 54 | 61 |
| Bob Joyce | 77 | 18 | 31 | 49 | 46 |
| Greg Hawgood | 56 | 16 | 24 | 40 | 84 |
| Bobby Carpenter, Los Angeles | 39 | 11 | 15 | 26 | 16 |
| Boston | 18 | 5 | 9 | 14 | 10 |
| Totals | 57 | 16 | 24 | 40 | 26 |
| Andy Brickley | 71 | 13 | 22 | 35 | 20 |
| Keith Crowder | 69 | 15 | 18 | 33 | 147 |
| Garry Galley | 78 | 8 | 22 | 30 | 80 |
| Bob Sweeney | 75 | 14 | 14 | 28 | 104 |
| John Carter | 44 | 12 | 10 | 22 | 24 |
| Michael Thelven | 40 | 3 | 18 | 21 | 71 |
| Greg Johnston | 57 | 11 | 9 | 20 | 32 |
| Ray Neufeld, Winnipeg | 31 | 5 | 2 | 7 | 52 |
| Boston | 14 | 1 | 3 | 4 | 28 |
| Totals | 45 | 6 | 5 | 11 | 80 |
| Don Sweeney | 36 | 3 | 5 | 8 | 20 |
| Tom Lehmann | 26 | 4 | 2 | 6 | 10 |
| Allen Pedersen | 51 | 0 | 6 | 6 | 69 |
| Alain Cote | 31 | 2 | 3 | 5 | 51 |
| Bruce Shoebottom | 29 | 1 | 3 | 4 | 44 |
| Lyndon Byers | 49 | 0 | 4 | 4 | 218 |
| Bill O'Dwyer | 19 | 1 | 2 | 3 | 8 |
| Robert Cimetta | 7 | 2 | 0 | 2 | 0 |
| Paul Guay, Los Angeles | 2 | 0 | 0 | 0 | 2 |
| Boston | 5 | 0 | 2 | 2 | 0 |
| Totals | 7 | 0 | 2 | 2 | 2 |
| Gord Kluzak | 3 | 0 | 1 | 1 | 2 |
| Ray Podloski | 8 | 0 | 1 | 1 | 17 |
| Stephane Quintal | 26 | 0 | 1 | 1 | 29 |
| Rejean Lemelin (Goalie) | 40 | 0 | 1 | 1 | 6 |
| Andy Moog (Goalie) | 41 | 0 | 1 | 1 | 6 |
| Dale Dunbar | 1 | 0 | 0 | 0 | 0 |
| Ron Flockhart | 4 | 0 | 0 | 0 | 0 |
| Paul Beraldo | 7 | 0 | 0 | 0 | 4 |
| Carl Mokosak | 7 | 0 | 0 | 0 | 31 |

## Buffalo Sabres

| | Games | G. | A. | Pts. | Pen. |
|---|---|---|---|---|---|
| Pierre Turgeon | 80 | 34 | 54 | 88 | 26 |
| Phil Housley | 72 | 26 | 44 | 70 | 47 |
| Christian Ruuttu | 67 | 14 | 46 | 60 | 98 |
| Rick Vaive, Chicago | 30 | 12 | 13 | 25 | 60 |
| Buffalo | 28 | 19 | 13 | 32 | 64 |
| Totals | 58 | 31 | 26 | 57 | 124 |
| Dave Andreychuk | 56 | 28 | 24 | 52 | 40 |
| Doug Bodger, Pittsburgh | 10 | 1 | 4 | 5 | 7 |
| Buffalo | 61 | 7 | 40 | 47 | 52 |
| Totals | 71 | 8 | 44 | 52 | 59 |
| Mike Foligno | 75 | 27 | 22 | 49 | 156 |
| Benoit Hogue | 69 | 14 | 30 | 44 | 120 |
| John Tucker | 60 | 13 | 31 | 44 | 31 |
| Ray Sheppard | 67 | 22 | 21 | 43 | 15 |
| Scott Arniel | 80 | 18 | 23 | 41 | 46 |

**Boston Bruins defenseman Glen Wesley.**

|  | Games | G. | A. | Pts. | Pen. |
|---|---|---|---|---|---|
| Mark Napier | 66 | 11 | 17 | 28 | 33 |
| Grant Ledyard, Washington | 61 | 3 | 11 | 14 | 41 |
|     Buffalo | 13 | 1 | 5 | 6 | 8 |
|     Totals | 74 | 4 | 16 | 20 | 49 |
| Jeff Parker | 57 | 9 | 9 | 18 | 82 |
| Kevin Maguire | 60 | 8 | 10 | 18 | 241 |
| Uwe Krupp | 70 | 5 | 13 | 18 | 55 |
| Mike Hartman | 70 | 8 | 9 | 17 | 316 |
| Mike Ramsey | 56 | 2 | 14 | 16 | 84 |
| Shawn Anderson | 33 | 2 | 10 | 12 | 18 |
| Mike Donnelly | 22 | 4 | 6 | 10 | 10 |
| Larry Playfair, Los Angeles | 6 | 0 | 3 | 3 | 16 |
|     Buffalo | 42 | 0 | 3 | 3 | 110 |
|     Totals | 48 | 0 | 6 | 6 | 126 |
| Joe Reekie | 15 | 1 | 3 | 4 | 26 |
| Daren Puppa (Goalie) | 37 | 0 | 4 | 4 | 12 |
| Ken Priestlay | 15 | 2 | 0 | 2 | 2 |
| Scott Metcalfe | 9 | 1 | 1 | 2 | 13 |
| Jan Ludvig | 13 | 0 | 2 | 2 | 39 |
| Jacques Cloutier (Goalie) | 36 | 0 | 2 | 2 | 6 |
| Richie Dunn | 4 | 0 | 1 | 1 | 2 |
| Mikael Andersson | 14 | 0 | 1 | 1 | 4 |
| Bob Halkidis | 16 | 0 | 1 | 1 | 66 |
| Clint Malarchuk, Washington (Goalie) | 42 | 0 | 1 | 1 | 16 |
|     Buffalo (Goalie) | 7 | 0 | 0 | 0 | 2 |
|     Totals | 49 | 0 | 1 | 1 | 18 |
| Trent Kaese | 1 | 0 | 0 | 0 | 0 |
| Darren Eliot (Goalie) | 2 | 0 | 0 | 0 | 0 |
| Mark Ferner | 2 | 0 | 0 | 0 | 2 |
| Darrin Shannon | 3 | 0 | 0 | 0 | 0 |
| Steve Smith | 3 | 0 | 0 | 0 | 0 |
| Darcy Wakaluk (Goalie) | 6 | 0 | 0 | 0 | 0 |
| Brad Miller | 7 | 0 | 0 | 0 | 6 |

## Calgary Flames

|  | Games | G. | A. | Pts. | Pen. |
|---|---|---|---|---|---|
| Joe Mullen | 79 | 51 | 59 | 110 | 16 |
| Hakan Loob | 79 | 27 | 58 | 85 | 44 |
| Doug Gilmour | 72 | 26 | 59 | 85 | 44 |
| Joe Nieuwendyk | 77 | 51 | 31 | 82 | 40 |
| Al MacInnis | 79 | 16 | 58 | 74 | 136 |
| Gary Suter | 63 | 13 | 49 | 62 | 78 |
| Jiri Hrdina | 70 | 22 | 32 | 54 | 26 |
| Joel Otto | 72 | 23 | 30 | 53 | 213 |
| Brian MacLellan, Minnesota | 60 | 16 | 23 | 39 | 104 |
|     Calgary | 12 | 2 | 3 | 5 | 14 |
|     Totals | 72 | 18 | 26 | 44 | 118 |
| Gary Roberts | 71 | 22 | 16 | 38 | 250 |
| Colin Patterson | 74 | 14 | 24 | 38 | 56 |
| Jim Peplinski | 79 | 13 | 25 | 38 | 241 |
| Theo Fleury | 36 | 14 | 20 | 34 | 46 |
| Mark Hunter | 66 | 22 | 8 | 30 | 194 |
| Jamie Macoun | 72 | 8 | 19 | 27 | 78 |
| Brad McCrimmon | 72 | 5 | 17 | 22 | 96 |
| Dana Murzyn | 63 | 3 | 19 | 22 | 142 |
| Lanny McDonald | 51 | 11 | 7 | 18 | 26 |
| Rob Ramage | 68 | 3 | 13 | 16 | 156 |
| Tim Hunter | 75 | 3 | 9 | 12 | *375 |
| Ric Nattress | 38 | 1 | 8 | 9 | 47 |
| Mike Vernon (Goalie) | 52 | 0 | 4 | 4 | 18 |
| Rick Lessard | 6 | 0 | 1 | 1 | 2 |
| Ken Sabourin | 6 | 0 | 1 | 1 | 26 |
| Brian Glynn | 9 | 0 | 1 | 1 | 19 |
| Rick Wamsley (Goalie) | 35 | 0 | 1 | 1 | 8 |
| Rich Chernomaz | 1 | 0 | 0 | 0 | 0 |
| Stu Grimson | 1 | 0 | 0 | 0 | 5 |

**Buffalo Sabres center Pierre Turgeon.**

|  | Games | G. | A. | Pts. | Pen. |
|---|---|---|---|---|---|
| Sergei Priakin | 2 | 0 | 0 | 0 | 2 |
| Dave Reierson | 2 | 0 | 0 | 0 | 2 |
| Paul Ranheim | 5 | 0 | 0 | 0 | 0 |

## Chicago Black Hawks

|  | Games | G. | A. | Pts. | Pen. |
|---|---|---|---|---|---|
| Steve Larmer | 80 | 43 | 44 | 87 | 54 |
| Denis Savard | 58 | 23 | 59 | 82 | 110 |
| Dirk Graham | 80 | 33 | 45 | 78 | 91 |
| Doug Wilson | 66 | 15 | 47 | 62 | 69 |
| Dave Manson | 79 | 18 | 36 | 54 | 352 |
| Troy Murray | 79 | 21 | 30 | 51 | 113 |
| Adam Creighton, Buffalo | 24 | 7 | 10 | 17 | 44 |
|    Chicago | 43 | 15 | 14 | 29 | 92 |
|    Totals | 67 | 22 | 24 | 46 | 136 |
| Steve Thomas | 45 | 21 | 19 | 40 | 69 |
| Wayne Presley | 72 | 21 | 19 | 40 | 100 |
| Trent Yawney | 69 | 5 | 19 | 24 | 116 |
| Mike Hudson | 41 | 7 | 16 | 23 | 20 |
| Greg Gilbert, N.Y. Islanders | 55 | 8 | 13 | 21 | 45 |
|    Chicago | 4 | 0 | 0 | 0 | 0 |
|    Totals | 59 | 8 | 13 | 21 | 45 |
| Bob Bassen, N.Y. Islanders | 19 | 1 | 4 | 5 | 21 |
|    Chicago | 49 | 4 | 12 | 16 | 62 |
|    Totals | 68 | 5 | 16 | 21 | 83 |
| Jeremy Roenick | 20 | 9 | 9 | 18 | 4 |
| Steve Konroyd, N.Y. Islanders | 21 | 1 | 5 | 6 | 2 |
|    Chicago | 57 | 5 | 7 | 12 | 40 |
|    Totals | 78 | 6 | 12 | 18 | 42 |
| Keith Brown | 74 | 2 | 16 | 18 | 84 |
| Duane Sutter | 75 | 7 | 9 | 16 | 214 |
| Mike Eagles | 47 | 5 | 11 | 16 | 44 |
| Brian Noonan | 45 | 4 | 12 | 16 | 28 |
| Dan Vincelette | 66 | 11 | 4 | 15 | 119 |
| Everett Sanipass | 50 | 6 | 9 | 15 | 164 |
| Bob Murray | 15 | 2 | 4 | 6 | 27 |
| Alain Chevrier, Winnipeg (Goalie) | 22 | 0 | 4 | 4 | 2 |
|    Chicago (Goalie) | 27 | 0 | 0 | 0 | 0 |
|    Totals | 49 | 0 | 4 | 4 | 2 |
| Bob McGill | 68 | 0 | 4 | 4 | 155 |
| Dave Mackey | 23 | 1 | 2 | 3 | 78 |
| Darren Pang (Goalie) | 35 | 0 | 3 | 3 | 4 |
| Bill Gardner | 6 | 1 | 1 | 2 | 0 |
| Mario Doyon | 7 | 1 | 1 | 2 | 6 |
| Bruce Cassidy | 9 | 0 | 2 | 2 | 4 |
| Jari Torkki | 4 | 1 | 0 | 1 | 0 |
| Steve Ludzik | 6 | 1 | 0 | 1 | 8 |
| Bill Watson | 3 | 0 | 1 | 1 | 4 |
| Mike Stapleton | 7 | 0 | 1 | 1 | 7 |
| Ed Belfour (Goalie) | 23 | 0 | 1 | 1 | 6 |
| Chris Clifford (Goalie) | 1 | 0 | 0 | 0 | 0 |
| Kevin Paynter | 1 | 0 | 0 | 0 | 2 |
| Mike Rucinski | 1 | 0 | 0 | 0 | 0 |
| Warren Rychel | 2 | 0 | 0 | 0 | 17 |
| Jim Playfair | 7 | 0 | 0 | 0 | 28 |
| Wayne Van Dorp | 8 | 0 | 0 | 0 | 28 |
| Jimmy Waite (Goalie) | 11 | 0 | 0 | 0 | 0 |

## Detroit Red Wings

|  | Games | G. | A. | Pts. | Pen. |
|---|---|---|---|---|---|
| Steve Yzerman | 80 | 65 | 90 | 155 | 61 |
| Gerard Gallant | 76 | 39 | 54 | 93 | 230 |
| Adam Oates | 69 | 16 | 62 | 78 | 14 |
| Paul MacLean | 76 | 36 | 35 | 71 | 118 |
| Dave Barr | 73 | 27 | 32 | 59 | 69 |
| Steve Chiasson | 65 | 12 | 35 | 47 | 149 |

Detroit Red Wings left wing Gerard Gallant.

|  | Games | G. | A. | Pts. | Pen. |
|---|---|---|---|---|---|
| Shawn Burr | 79 | 19 | 27 | 46 | 78 |
| Lee Norwood | 66 | 10 | 32 | 42 | 100 |
| Petr Klima | 51 | 25 | 16 | 41 | 44 |
| Rick Zombo | 75 | 1 | 20 | 21 | 106 |
| Joey Kocur | 60 | 9 | 9 | 18 | 213 |
| Mike O'Connell | 66 | 1 | 15 | 16 | 41 |
| Jim Nill | 71 | 8 | 7 | 15 | 83 |
| Tim Higgins | 42 | 5 | 9 | 14 | 62 |
| Jeff Sharples | 46 | 4 | 9 | 13 | 26 |
| Doug Houda | 57 | 2 | 11 | 13 | 67 |
| Adam Graves | 56 | 7 | 5 | 12 | 60 |
| John Chabot | 52 | 2 | 10 | 12 | 6 |
| Torrie Robertson, Hartford | 27 | 2 | 4 | 6 | 84 |
|     Detroit | 12 | 2 | 2 | 4 | 63 |
|     Totals | 39 | 4 | 6 | 10 | 147 |
| Joe Murphy | 26 | 1 | 7 | 8 | 28 |
| Bob Probert | 25 | 4 | 2 | 6 | 106 |
| Dale Krentz | 16 | 3 | 3 | 6 | 4 |
| Kris King | 55 | 2 | 3 | 5 | 168 |
| Gilbert Delorme | 42 | 1 | 3 | 4 | 51 |
| Brent Fedyk | 5 | 2 | 0 | 2 | 0 |
| Greg Stefan (Goalie) | 46 | 0 | 2 | 2 | 41 |
| John Mokosak | 8 | 0 | 1 | 1 | 14 |
| Glen Hanlon (Goalie) | 39 | 0 | 1 | 1 | 12 |
| Jeff Brubaker | 1 | 0 | 0 | 0 | 0 |
| Miroslav Ihnacak | 1 | 0 | 0 | 0 | 0 |
| Tim Cheveldae (Goalie) | 2 | 0 | 0 | 0 | 0 |
| Randy McKay | 3 | 0 | 0 | 0 | 0 |
| Sam St. Laurent (Goalie) | 4 | 0 | 0 | 0 | 0 |
| John Blum | 6 | 0 | 0 | 0 | 8 |

## Edmonton Oilers

|  | Games | G. | A. | Pts. | Pen. |
|---|---|---|---|---|---|
| Jari Kurri | 76 | 44 | 58 | 102 | 69 |
| Jimmy Carson | 80 | 49 | 51 | 100 | 36 |
| Mark Messier | 72 | 33 | 61 | 94 | 130 |
| Esa Tikkanen | 67 | 31 | 47 | 78 | 92 |
| Craig Simpson | 66 | 35 | 41 | 76 | 80 |
| Glenn Anderson | 79 | 16 | 48 | 64 | 93 |
| Craig MacTavish | 80 | 21 | 31 | 52 | 55 |
| Charlie Huddy | 76 | 11 | 33 | 44 | 52 |
| Tomas Jonsson, N.Y. Islanders | 53 | 9 | 23 | 32 | 34 |
|     Edmonton | 20 | 1 | 10 | 11 | 22 |
|     Totals | 73 | 10 | 33 | 43 | 56 |
| Normand Lacombe | 64 | 17 | 11 | 28 | 57 |
| Miroslav Frycer, Detroit | 23 | 7 | 8 | 15 | 47 |
|     Edmonton | 14 | 5 | 5 | 10 | 18 |
|     Totals | 37 | 12 | 13 | 25 | 65 |
| Kevin Lowe | 76 | 7 | 18 | 25 | 98 |
| Steve Smith | 35 | 3 | 19 | 22 | 97 |
| Kevin McClelland | 79 | 6 | 14 | 20 | 161 |
| Craig Muni | 69 | 5 | 13 | 18 | 71 |
| Randy Gregg | 57 | 3 | 15 | 18 | 28 |
| Kelly Buchberger | 66 | 5 | 9 | 14 | 234 |
| Craig Redmond | 21 | 3 | 10 | 13 | 12 |
| Dave Hunter, Winnipeg | 34 | 3 | 1 | 4 | 61 |
|     Edmonton | 32 | 3 | 5 | 8 | 22 |
|     Totals | 66 | 6 | 6 | 12 | 83 |
| Mark Lamb | 20 | 2 | 8 | 10 | 14 |
| Chris Joseph | 44 | 4 | 5 | 9 | 54 |
| Doug Halward, Detroit | 18 | 0 | 1 | 1 | 36 |
|     Edmonton | 24 | 0 | 7 | 7 | 25 |
|     Totals | 42 | 0 | 8 | 8 | 61 |
| Jeff Beukeboom | 36 | 0 | 5 | 5 | 94 |
| Dave Brown, Philadelphia | 50 | 0 | 3 | 3 | 100 |
|     Edmonton | 22 | 0 | 2 | 2 | 56 |
|     Totals | 72 | 0 | 5 | 5 | 156 |

**Hartford Whalers right wing Kevin Dineen.**

|  | Games | G. | A. | Pts. | Pen. |
|---|---|---|---|---|---|
| Martin Gelinas | 6 | 1 | 2 | 3 | 0 |
| John LeBlanc | 2 | 1 | 0 | 1 | 0 |
| Alan May | 3 | 1 | 0 | 1 | 7 |
| Mike Ware | 2 | 0 | 1 | 1 | 11 |
| Grant Fuhr (Goalie) | 59 | 0 | 1 | 1 | 6 |
| Nick Fotiu | 1 | 0 | 0 | 0 | 0 |
| Francois Leroux | 2 | 0 | 0 | 0 | 0 |
| Selmar Odelein | 2 | 0 | 0 | 0 | 2 |
| Kim Issel | 4 | 0 | 0 | 0 | 0 |
| Glen Cochrane, Chicago | 6 | 0 | 0 | 0 | 13 |
| Edmonton | 12 | 0 | 0 | 0 | 52 |
| Totals | 18 | 0 | 0 | 0 | 65 |
| Bill Ranford (Goalie) | 29 | 0 | 0 | 0 | 2 |

## Hartford Whalers

|  | Games | G. | A. | Pts. | Pen. |
|---|---|---|---|---|---|
| Kevin Dineen | 79 | 45 | 44 | 89 | 167 |
| Ron Francis | 69 | 29 | 48 | 77 | 36 |
| Ray Ferraro | 80 | 41 | 35 | 76 | 86 |
| Scott Young | 76 | 19 | 40 | 59 | 27 |
| Dave Babych | 70 | 6 | 41 | 47 | 54 |
| Paul MacDermid | 74 | 17 | 27 | 44 | 141 |
| Brian Lawton, N.Y. Rangers | 30 | 7 | 10 | 17 | 39 |
| Hartford | 35 | 10 | 16 | 26 | 28 |
| Totals | 65 | 17 | 26 | 43 | 67 |
| Dave Tippett | 80 | 17 | 24 | 41 | 45 |
| John Anderson | 62 | 16 | 24 | 40 | 28 |
| Ulf Samuelsson | 71 | 9 | 26 | 35 | 181 |
| Jody Hull | 60 | 16 | 18 | 34 | 10 |
| Norm Maciver, N.Y. Rangers | 26 | 0 | 10 | 10 | 14 |
| Hartford | 37 | 1 | 22 | 23 | 24 |
| Totals | 63 | 1 | 32 | 33 | 38 |
| Sylvain Turgeon | 42 | 16 | 14 | 30 | 40 |
| Dean Evason | 67 | 11 | 17 | 28 | 60 |
| Don Maloney, N.Y. Rangers | 31 | 4 | 9 | 13 | 16 |
| Hartford | 21 | 3 | 11 | 14 | 23 |
| Totals | 52 | 7 | 20 | 27 | 39 |
| Sylvain Cote | 78 | 8 | 9 | 17 | 49 |
| Brent Peterson | 66 | 4 | 13 | 17 | 61 |
| Tom Martin, Minnesota | 4 | 1 | 1 | 2 | 4 |
| Hartford | 38 | 7 | 6 | 13 | 113 |
| Totals | 42 | 8 | 7 | 15 | 117 |
| Grant Jennings | 55 | 3 | 10 | 13 | 159 |
| Joel Quenneville | 69 | 4 | 7 | 11 | 32 |
| Jim Pavese, Detroit | 39 | 3 | 6 | 9 | 130 |
| Hartford | 5 | 0 | 0 | 0 | 5 |
| Totals | 44 | 3 | 6 | 9 | 135 |
| Randy Ladouceur | 75 | 2 | 5 | 7 | 95 |
| Peter Sidorkiewicz (Goalie) | 44 | 0 | 3 | 3 | 0 |
| Jim Thomson, Washington | 14 | 2 | 0 | 2 | 53 |
| Hartford | 5 | 0 | 0 | 0 | 14 |
| Totals | 19 | 2 | 0 | 2 | 67 |
| Dallas Gaume | 4 | 1 | 1 | 2 | 0 |
| Kay Whitmore (Goalie) | 3 | 0 | 2 | 2 | 0 |
| Mark Reeds | 7 | 0 | 2 | 2 | 6 |
| Ed Kastelic | 10 | 0 | 2 | 2 | 15 |
| Brad Shaw | 3 | 1 | 0 | 1 | 0 |
| Terry Yake | 2 | 0 | 0 | 0 | 0 |
| Allan Tuer | 4 | 0 | 0 | 0 | 23 |
| Adam Burt | 5 | 0 | 0 | 0 | 6 |
| Mike Liut (Goalie) | 35 | 0 | 0 | 0 | 0 |

## Los Angeles Kings

|  | Games | G. | A. | Pts. | Pen. |
|---|---|---|---|---|---|
| Wayne Gretzky | 78 | 54 | *114 | 168 | 26 |
| Bernie Nicholls | 79 | 70 | 80 | 150 | 96 |

**Los Angeles Kings center Bernie Nicholls.**

|  | Games | G. | A. | Pts. | Pen. |
|---|---|---|---|---|---|
| Luc Robitaille | 78 | 46 | 52 | 98 | 65 |
| Steve Duchesne | 79 | 25 | 50 | 75 | 92 |
| John Tonelli | 77 | 31 | 33 | 64 | 110 |
| Dave Taylor | 70 | 26 | 37 | 63 | 80 |
| Mike Krushelnyski | 78 | 26 | 36 | 62 | 110 |
| Steve Kasper, Boston | 49 | 10 | 16 | 26 | 49 |
| Los Angeles | 29 | 9 | 15 | 24 | 14 |
| Totals | 78 | 19 | 31 | 50 | 63 |
| Mike Allison | 55 | 14 | 22 | 36 | 122 |
| Dale DeGray | 63 | 6 | 22 | 28 | 97 |
| Marty McSorley | 66 | 10 | 17 | 27 | 350 |
| Doug Crossman | 74 | 10 | 15 | 25 | 53 |
| Igor Liba, N.Y. Rangers | 10 | 2 | 5 | 7 | 15 |
| Los Angeles | 27 | 5 | 13 | 18 | 21 |
| Totals | 37 | 7 | 18 | 25 | 36 |
| Ron Duguay | 70 | 7 | 17 | 24 | 48 |
| Tim Watters | 76 | 3 | 18 | 21 | 168 |
| Tom Laidlaw | 70 | 3 | 17 | 20 | 63 |
| Jay Miller, Boston | 37 | 2 | 4 | 6 | 168 |
| Los Angeles | 29 | 5 | 3 | 8 | 133 |
| Totals | 66 | 7 | 7 | 14 | 301 |
| Dean Kennedy, N.Y. Rangers | 16 | 0 | 1 | 1 | 40 |
| Los Angeles | 51 | 3 | 10 | 13 | 63 |
| Totals | 67 | 3 | 11 | 14 | 103 |
| Jim Wiemer | 9 | 2 | 3 | 5 | 20 |
| Robert Kudelski | 14 | 1 | 3 | 4 | 17 |
| Sylvain Couturier | 16 | 1 | 3 | 4 | 2 |
| Ken Baumgartner | 49 | 1 | 3 | 4 | 286 |
| Chris Kontos | 7 | 2 | 1 | 3 | 2 |
| Tim Tookey | 7 | 2 | 1 | 3 | 4 |
| Petr Prajsler | 2 | 0 | 3 | 3 | 0 |
| Kelly Hrudey, N.Y. Islanders (Goalie) | 50 | 0 | 1 | 1 | 17 |
| Los Angeles (Goalie) | 16 | 0 | 2 | 2 | 2 |
| Totals | 66 | 0 | 3 | 3 | 19 |
| Steve Richmond | 9 | 0 | 2 | 2 | 26 |
| Gord Walker | 11 | 1 | 0 | 1 | 2 |
| Hubie McDonough | 4 | 0 | 1 | 1 | 0 |
| Gilles Hamel, Winnipeg | 1 | 0 | 0 | 0 | 0 |
| Los Angeles | 11 | 0 | 1 | 1 | 2 |
| Totals | 12 | 0 | 1 | 1 | 2 |
| Phil Sykes | 23 | 0 | 1 | 1 | 8 |
| Glenn Healy (Goalie) | 48 | 0 | 1 | 1 | 28 |
| Jim Hofford | 1 | 0 | 0 | 0 | 2 |
| Bob Janecyk (Goalie) | 1 | 0 | 0 | 0 | 0 |
| Brian Wilks | 2 | 0 | 0 | 0 | 2 |
| Bob Logan | 4 | 0 | 0 | 0 | 0 |
| Roland Melanson (Goalie) | 4 | 0 | 0 | 0 | 4 |
| Craig Duncanson | 5 | 0 | 0 | 0 | 0 |
| Dave Pasin | 5 | 0 | 0 | 0 | 0 |

## Minnesota North Stars

|  | Games | G. | A. | Pts. | Pen. |
|---|---|---|---|---|---|
| Dave Gagner | 75 | 35 | 43 | 78 | 104 |
| Mike Gartner, Washington | 56 | 26 | 29 | 55 | 71 |
| Minnesota | 13 | 7 | 7 | 14 | 2 |
| Totals | 69 | 33 | 36 | 69 | 73 |
| Neal Broten | 68 | 18 | 38 | 56 | 57 |
| Marc Habscheid | 76 | 23 | 31 | 54 | 40 |
| Brian Bellows | 60 | 23 | 27 | 50 | 55 |
| Larry Murphy, Washington | 65 | 7 | 29 | 36 | 70 |
| Minnesota | 13 | 4 | 6 | 10 | 12 |
| Totals | 78 | 11 | 35 | 46 | 82 |
| Reed Larson, Edmonton | 10 | 2 | 7 | 9 | 15 |
| N.Y. Islanders | 33 | 7 | 13 | 20 | 35 |
| Minnesota | 11 | 0 | 9 | 9 | 18 |
| Totals | 54 | 9 | 29 | 38 | 68 |

**Minnesota North Stars center Dave Gagner.**

| | Games | G. | A. | Pts. | Pen. |
|---|---|---|---|---|---|
| David Archibald | 72 | 14 | 19 | 33 | 14 |
| Basil McRae | 78 | 12 | 19 | 31 | 365 |
| Stewart Gavin | 73 | 8 | 18 | 26 | 34 |
| Shawn Chambers | 72 | 5 | 19 | 24 | 80 |
| Frantisek Musil | 55 | 1 | 19 | 20 | 54 |
| Craig Hartsburg | 30 | 4 | 14 | 18 | 47 |
| Bob Brooke | 57 | 7 | 9 | 16 | 57 |
| Curt Giles | 76 | 5 | 10 | 15 | 77 |
| Dusan Pasek | 48 | 4 | 10 | 14 | 30 |
| Don Barber | 23 | 8 | 5 | 13 | 8 |
| Perry Berezan, Calgary | 35 | 4 | 4 | 8 | 21 |
| Minnesota | 16 | 1 | 4 | 5 | 4 |
| Totals | 51 | 5 | 8 | 13 | 25 |
| Ville Siren, Pittsburgh | 12 | 1 | 0 | 1 | 14 |
| Minnesota | 38 | 2 | 10 | 12 | 58 |
| Totals | 50 | 3 | 10 | 13 | 72 |
| Larry DePalma | 43 | 5 | 7 | 12 | 102 |
| Curt Fraser | 35 | 5 | 5 | 10 | 76 |
| Wally Schreiber | 25 | 2 | 5 | 7 | 10 |
| Dean Kolstad | 25 | 1 | 5 | 6 | 42 |
| Warren Babe | 14 | 2 | 3 | 5 | 19 |
| Mark Tinordi | 47 | 2 | 3 | 5 | 107 |
| Steve Gotaas | 12 | 1 | 3 | 4 | 6 |
| Terry Ruskowski | 3 | 1 | 1 | 2 | 2 |
| Ken Hodge | 5 | 1 | 1 | 2 | 0 |
| Link Gaetz | 12 | 0 | 2 | 2 | 53 |
| Shane Churla, Calgary | 5 | 0 | 0 | 0 | 25 |
| Minnesota | 13 | 1 | 0 | 1 | 54 |
| Totals | 18 | 1 | 0 | 1 | 79 |
| Mitch Messier | 3 | 0 | 1 | 1 | 0 |
| Dennis Maruk | 6 | 0 | 1 | 1 | 2 |
| Jon Casey (Goalie) | 55 | 0 | 1 | 1 | 10 |
| Mike Berger | 1 | 0 | 0 | 0 | 2 |
| Kevin Kaminski | 1 | 0 | 0 | 0 | 0 |
| Rob Zettler | 2 | 0 | 0 | 0 | 0 |
| Mike McHugh | 3 | 0 | 0 | 0 | 2 |
| Paul Jerrard | 5 | 0 | 0 | 0 | 4 |
| Jarmo Myllys (Goalie) | 6 | 0 | 0 | 0 | 0 |
| Kari Takko (Goalie) | 32 | 0 | 0 | 0 | 6 |

## Montreal Canadiens

| | Games | G. | A. | Pts. | Pen. |
|---|---|---|---|---|---|
| Mats Naslund | 77 | 33 | 51 | 84 | 14 |
| Bobby Smith | 80 | 32 | 51 | 83 | 69 |
| Chris Chelios | 80 | 15 | 58 | 73 | 185 |
| Stephane Richer | 68 | 25 | 35 | 60 | 61 |
| Guy Carbonneau | 79 | 26 | 30 | 56 | 44 |
| Claude Lemieux | 69 | 29 | 22 | 51 | 136 |
| Shayne Corson | 80 | 26 | 24 | 50 | 193 |
| Petr Svoboda | 71 | 8 | 37 | 45 | 147 |
| Russ Courtnall, Toronto | 9 | 1 | 1 | 2 | 4 |
| Montreal | 64 | 22 | 17 | 39 | 15 |
| Totals | 73 | 23 | 18 | 41 | 19 |
| Mike McPhee | 73 | 19 | 22 | 41 | 74 |
| Brian Skrudland | 71 | 12 | 29 | 41 | 84 |
| Mike Keane | 69 | 16 | 19 | 35 | 69 |
| Ryan Walter | 78 | 14 | 17 | 31 | 48 |
| Larry Robinson | 74 | 4 | 26 | 30 | 22 |
| Brent Gilchrist | 49 | 8 | 16 | 24 | 16 |
| Bob Gainey | 49 | 10 | 7 | 17 | 34 |
| Craig Ludwig | 74 | 3 | 13 | 16 | 73 |
| Rick Green | 72 | 1 | 14 | 15 | 25 |
| Eric Desjardins | 36 | 2 | 12 | 14 | 26 |
| Gilles Thibaudeau | 32 | 6 | 6 | 12 | 6 |
| Patrick Roy (Goalie) | 48 | 0 | 6 | 6 | 2 |
| Jyrki Lumme | 21 | 1 | 3 | 4 | 10 |

**New Jersey Devils center Kirk Muller.**

|  | Games | G. | A. | Pts. | Pen. |
|---|---|---|---|---|---|
| Steve Martinson | 25 | 1 | 0 | 1 | 87 |
| Stephan Lebeau | 1 | 0 | 1 | 1 | 2 |
| Jocelyn Lemieux | 1 | 0 | 1 | 1 | 0 |
| Benoit Brunet | 2 | 0 | 1 | 1 | 0 |
| Donald Dufresne | 13 | 0 | 1 | 1 | 43 |
| Randy Exelby (Goalie) | 1 | 0 | 0 | 0 | 0 |
| Brian Hayward (Goalie) | 36 | 0 | 0 | 0 | 10 |

## New Jersey Devils

|  | Games | G. | A. | Pts. | Pen. |
|---|---|---|---|---|---|
| John MacLean | 74 | 42 | 45 | 87 | 122 |
| Kirk Muller | 80 | 31 | 43 | 74 | 119 |
| Patrik Sundstrom | 65 | 28 | 41 | 69 | 36 |
| Tom Kurvers | 74 | 16 | 50 | 66 | 38 |
| Aaron Broten | 80 | 16 | 43 | 59 | 81 |
| Brendan Shanahan | 68 | 22 | 28 | 50 | 115 |
| Pat Verbeek | 77 | 26 | 21 | 47 | 189 |
| Mark Johnson | 40 | 13 | 25 | 38 | 24 |
| Tommy Albelin, Quebec | 14 | 2 | 4 | 6 | 27 |
|    New Jersey | 46 | 7 | 24 | 31 | 40 |
|    Totals | 60 | 9 | 28 | 37 | 67 |
| Jim Korn | 65 | 15 | 16 | 31 | 212 |
| Jack O'Callahan | 36 | 5 | 21 | 26 | 51 |
| Doug Brown | 63 | 15 | 10 | 25 | 15 |
| Joe Cirella | 80 | 3 | 19 | 22 | 155 |
| Claude Loiselle | 74 | 7 | 14 | 21 | 209 |
| Randy Velischek | 80 | 4 | 14 | 18 | 70 |
| Bruce Driver | 27 | 1 | 15 | 16 | 24 |
| Pat Conacher | 55 | 7 | 5 | 12 | 14 |
| Anders Carlsson | 47 | 4 | 8 | 12 | 20 |
| David Maley | 68 | 5 | 6 | 11 | 249 |
| Craig Wolanin | 56 | 3 | 8 | 11 | 69 |
| Ken Daneyko | 80 | 5 | 5 | 10 | 283 |
| Perry Anderson | 39 | 3 | 6 | 9 | 128 |
| Steve Rooney | 25 | 3 | 1 | 4 | 79 |
| Paul Ysebaert | 5 | 0 | 4 | 4 | 0 |
| Sean Burke (Goalie) | 62 | 0 | 3 | 3 | 54 |
| Jon Morris | 4 | 0 | 2 | 2 | 0 |
| Allan Stewart | 6 | 0 | 2 | 2 | 15 |
| Jamie Huscroft | 15 | 0 | 2 | 2 | 51 |
| George McPhee | 1 | 0 | 1 | 1 | 2 |
| Chris Cichocki | 2 | 0 | 1 | 1 | 2 |
| Janne Ojanen | 3 | 0 | 1 | 1 | 2 |
| Kevin Todd | 1 | 0 | 0 | 0 | 0 |
| Corey Foster | 2 | 0 | 0 | 0 | 0 |
| Eric Weinrich | 2 | 0 | 0 | 0 | 0 |
| Craig Billington (Goalie) | 3 | 0 | 0 | 0 | 0 |
| Chris Terreri (Goalie) | 8 | 0 | 0 | 0 | 2 |
| Bob Sauve (Goalie) | 15 | 0 | 0 | 0 | 0 |

## New York Islanders

|  | Games | G. | A. | Pts. | Pen. |
|---|---|---|---|---|---|
| Pat LaFontaine | 79 | 45 | 43 | 88 | 26 |
| Brent Sutter | 77 | 29 | 34 | 63 | 77 |
| Dave Volek | 77 | 25 | 34 | 59 | 24 |
| Bryan Trottier | 73 | 17 | 28 | 45 | 44 |
| Mikko Makela | 76 | 17 | 28 | 45 | 22 |
| Derek King | 60 | 14 | 29 | 43 | 14 |
| Alan Kerr | 71 | 20 | 18 | 38 | 144 |
| Gerald Diduck | 65 | 11 | 21 | 32 | 155 |
| Jeff Norton | 69 | 1 | 30 | 31 | 74 |
| Randy Wood | 77 | 15 | 13 | 28 | 44 |
| Patrick Flatley | 41 | 10 | 15 | 25 | 31 |
| Brad Dalgarno | 55 | 11 | 10 | 21 | 86 |
| Gary Nylund, Chicago | 23 | 3 | 2 | 5 | 63 |
|    N.Y. Islanders | 46 | 4 | 8 | 12 | 74 |
|    Totals | 69 | 7 | 10 | 17 | 137 |

**New York Rangers defenseman Brian Leetch.**

|  | Games | G. | A. | Pts. | Pen. |
|---|---|---|---|---|---|
| Marc Bergevin, Chicago | 11 | 0 | 0 | 0 | 18 |
| N.Y. Islanders | 58 | 2 | 13 | 15 | 62 |
| Totals | 69 | 2 | 13 | 15 | 80 |
| Richard Pilon | 62 | 0 | 14 | 14 | 242 |
| Raimo Helminen | 24 | 1 | 11 | 12 | 4 |
| Tom Fitzgerald | 23 | 3 | 5 | 8 | 10 |
| Rich Kromm | 20 | 1 | 6 | 7 | 4 |
| Wayne McBean, Los Angeles | 33 | 0 | 5 | 5 | 23 |
| N.Y. Islanders | 19 | 0 | 1 | 1 | 12 |
| Totals | 52 | 0 | 6 | 6 | 35 |
| Brad Lauer | 14 | 3 | 2 | 5 | 2 |
| Dale Henry | 22 | 2 | 2 | 4 | 66 |
| Mick Vukota | 48 | 2 | 2 | 4 | 237 |
| Ken Morrow | 34 | 1 | 3 | 4 | 32 |
| Bill Berg | 7 | 1 | 2 | 3 | 10 |
| Mike Walsh | 13 | 2 | 0 | 2 | 4 |
| Mark Fitzpatrick, Los Angeles (Goalie) | 17 | 0 | 1 | 1 | 2 |
| N.Y. Islanders (Goalie) | 11 | 0 | 1 | 1 | 2 |
| Totals | 28 | 0 | 2 | 2 | 4 |
| Mike Stevens | 9 | 1 | 0 | 1 | 14 |
| Rob DiMaio | 16 | 1 | 0 | 1 | 30 |
| Jeff Hackett (Goalie) | 13 | 0 | 1 | 1 | 2 |
| Rod Dallman | 1 | 0 | 0 | 0 | 15 |
| Jeff Finley | 4 | 0 | 0 | 0 | 6 |
| Dean Chynoweth | 6 | 0 | 0 | 0 | 48 |
| Chris Pryor | 7 | 0 | 0 | 0 | 25 |
| Billy Smith (Goalie) | 17 | 0 | 0 | 0 | 8 |

## New York Rangers

|  | Games | G. | A. | Pts. | Pen. |
|---|---|---|---|---|---|
| Tomas Sandstrom | 79 | 32 | 56 | 88 | 148 |
| Carey Wilson, Hartford | 34 | 11 | 11 | 22 | 14 |
| N.Y. Rangers | 41 | 21 | 34 | 55 | 45 |
| Totals | 75 | 32 | 45 | 77 | 59 |
| Brian Leetch | 68 | 23 | 48 | 71 | 50 |
| Brian Mullen | 78 | 29 | 35 | 64 | 60 |
| Tony Granato | 78 | 36 | 27 | 63 | 140 |
| Kelly Kisio | 70 | 26 | 36 | 62 | 91 |
| James Patrick | 68 | 11 | 36 | 47 | 41 |
| Guy Lafleur | 67 | 18 | 27 | 45 | 12 |
| Ulf Dahlen | 56 | 24 | 19 | 43 | 50 |
| John Ogrodnick | 60 | 13 | 29 | 42 | 14 |
| Lucien DeBlois | 73 | 9 | 24 | 33 | 107 |
| Michel Petit | 69 | 8 | 25 | 33 | 154 |
| Jason Lafreniere | 38 | 8 | 16 | 24 | 6 |
| Marcel Dionne | 37 | 7 | 16 | 23 | 20 |
| Lindy Ruff, Buffalo | 63 | 6 | 11 | 17 | 86 |
| N.Y. Rangers | 13 | 0 | 5 | 5 | 31 |
| Totals | 76 | 6 | 16 | 22 | 117 |
| Mark Hardy, Minnesota | 15 | 2 | 4 | 6 | 26 |
| N.Y. Rangers | 45 | 2 | 12 | 14 | 45 |
| Totals | 60 | 4 | 16 | 20 | 71 |
| David Shaw | 63 | 6 | 11 | 17 | 88 |
| Jan Erixon | 44 | 4 | 11 | 15 | 27 |
| Chris Nilan | 38 | 7 | 7 | 14 | 177 |
| Ron Greschner | 58 | 1 | 10 | 11 | 94 |
| Darren Turcotte | 20 | 7 | 3 | 10 | 4 |
| Kevin Miller | 24 | 3 | 5 | 8 | 2 |
| Normand Rochefort | 11 | 1 | 5 | 6 | 18 |
| Rudy Poeschek | 52 | 0 | 2 | 2 | 199 |
| John Vanbiesbrouck (Goalie) | 56 | 0 | 2 | 2 | 30 |
| Miroslav Horava | 6 | 0 | 1 | 1 | 0 |
| Simon Wheeldon | 6 | 0 | 1 | 1 | 2 |
| Joe Paterson | 20 | 0 | 1 | 1 | 84 |
| Bob Froese (Goalie) | 30 | 0 | 1 | 1 | 6 |
| Stephane Brochu | 1 | 0 | 0 | 0 | 0 |

**Philadelphia Flyers right wing Tim Kerr.**

|  | Games | G. | A. | Pts. | Pen. |
|---|---|---|---|---|---|
| Paul Cyr | 1 | 0 | 0 | 0 | 2 |
| Jim Latos | 1 | 0 | 0 | 0 | 0 |
| Jayson More | 1 | 0 | 0 | 0 | 0 |
| Mark Janssens | 5 | 0 | 0 | 0 | 0 |
| Jeff Bloemberg | 9 | 0 | 0 | 0 | 0 |
| Peter Laviolette | 12 | 0 | 0 | 0 | 6 |

## Philadelphia Flyers

|  | Games | G. | A. | Pts. | Pen. |
|---|---|---|---|---|---|
| Tim Kerr | 69 | 48 | 40 | 88 | 73 |
| Rick Tocchet | 66 | 45 | 36 | 81 | 183 |
| Brian Propp | 77 | 32 | 46 | 78 | 37 |
| Pelle Eklund | 79 | 18 | 51 | 69 | 23 |
| Mike Bullard, St. Louis | 20 | 4 | 12 | 16 | 46 |
| Philadelphia | 54 | 23 | 26 | 49 | 60 |
| Totals | 74 | 27 | 38 | 65 | 106 |
| Scott Mellanby | 76 | 21 | 29 | 50 | 183 |
| Ron Sutter | 55 | 26 | 22 | 48 | 80 |
| Terry Carkner | 78 | 11 | 32 | 43 | 149 |
| Keith Acton, Edmonton | 46 | 11 | 15 | 26 | 47 |
| Philadelphia | 25 | 3 | 10 | 13 | 64 |
| Totals | 71 | 14 | 25 | 39 | 111 |
| Mark Howe | 52 | 9 | 29 | 38 | 45 |
| Murray Craven | 51 | 9 | 28 | 37 | 52 |
| Dave Poulin | 69 | 18 | 17 | 35 | 49 |
| Gordon Murphy | 75 | 4 | 31 | 35 | 68 |
| Derrick Smith | 74 | 16 | 14 | 30 | 43 |
| Jay Wells | 67 | 2 | 19 | 21 | 184 |
| Moe Mantha, Minnesota | 16 | 1 | 6 | 7 | 10 |
| Philadelphia | 30 | 3 | 8 | 11 | 33 |
| Totals | 46 | 4 | 14 | 18 | 43 |
| Kjell Samuelsson | 69 | 3 | 14 | 17 | 140 |
| Al Secord, Toronto | 40 | 5 | 10 | 15 | 71 |
| Philadelphia | 20 | 1 | 0 | 1 | 40 |
| Totals | 60 | 6 | 10 | 16 | 111 |
| Doug Sulliman | 52 | 6 | 6 | 12 | 8 |
| Kerry Huffman | 29 | 0 | 11 | 11 | 31 |
| Ron Hextall (Goalie) | 64 | 0 | 8 | 8 | 113 |
| Ilkka Sinisalo | 13 | 1 | 6 | 7 | 2 |
| Jeff Chychrun | 80 | 1 | 4 | 5 | 245 |
| Mark Laforest (Goalie) | 17 | 0 | 4 | 4 | 4 |
| Ken Wregget, Toronto (Goalie) | 32 | 0 | 3 | 3 | 20 |
| Philadelphia (Goalie) | 3 | 0 | 0 | 0 | 0 |
| Totals | 35 | 0 | 3 | 3 | 20 |
| Magnus Roupe | 7 | 1 | 1 | 2 | 10 |
| Craig Berube | 53 | 1 | 1 | 2 | 199 |
| Don Nachbaur | 15 | 1 | 0 | 1 | 37 |
| Dave Fenyves | 1 | 0 | 1 | 1 | 0 |
| Glen Seabrooke | 3 | 0 | 1 | 1 | 0 |
| Mark Freer | 5 | 0 | 1 | 1 | 0 |
| Brian Dobbin | 14 | 0 | 1 | 1 | 8 |
| Marc D'Amour (Goalie) | 1 | 0 | 0 | 0 | 0 |
| Jeff Harding | 6 | 0 | 0 | 0 | 29 |

## Pittsburgh Penguins

|  | Games | G. | A. | Pts. | Pen. |
|---|---|---|---|---|---|
| Mario Lemieux | 76 | *85 | *114 | *199 | 100 |
| Rob Brown | 68 | 49 | 66 | 115 | 118 |
| Paul Coffey | 75 | 30 | 83 | 113 | 195 |
| Dan Quinn | 79 | 34 | 60 | 94 | 102 |
| Bob Errey | 76 | 26 | 32 | 58 | 124 |
| John Cullen | 79 | 12 | 37 | 49 | 112 |
| Zarley Zalapski | 58 | 12 | 33 | 45 | 57 |
| Randy Cunneyworth | 70 | 25 | 19 | 44 | 156 |
| Phil Bourque | 80 | 17 | 26 | 43 | 97 |
| Dave Hannan | 72 | 10 | 20 | 30 | 157 |
| Randy Hillier | 68 | 1 | 23 | 24 | 141 |

**Pittsburgh Penguins defenseman Paul Coffey.**

|  | Games | G. | A. | Pts. | Pen. |
|---|---|---|---|---|---|
| Troy Loney | 69 | 10 | 6 | 16 | 165 |
| Jim Johnson | 76 | 2 | 14 | 16 | 163 |
| Kevin Stevens | 24 | 12 | 3 | 15 | 19 |
| Jock Callander | 30 | 6 | 5 | 11 | 20 |
| Tom Barrasso, Buffalo (Goalie) | 10 | 0 | 3 | 3 | 21 |
|    Pittsburgh (Goalie) | 44 | 0 | 5 | 5 | 49 |
|    Totals | 54 | 0 | 8 | 8 | 70 |
| Dan Frawley | 46 | 3 | 4 | 7 | 66 |
| Steve Dykstra | 65 | 1 | 6 | 7 | 126 |
| Chris Dahlquist | 43 | 1 | 5 | 6 | 42 |
| Rod Buskas | 52 | 1 | 5 | 6 | 105 |
| Jay Caufield | 58 | 1 | 4 | 5 | 285 |
| Gord Dineen, Minnesota | 2 | 0 | 1 | 1 | 2 |
|    Pittsburgh | 38 | 1 | 2 | 3 | 44 |
|    Totals | 40 | 1 | 3 | 4 | 46 |
| Scott Bjugstad | 24 | 3 | 0 | 3 | 4 |
| Dave McLlwain | 24 | 1 | 2 | 3 | 4 |
| Mark Kachowski | 12 | 1 | 1 | 2 | 43 |
| Mark Recchi | 15 | 1 | 1 | 2 | 0 |
| Wendell Young (Goalie) | 22 | 0 | 2 | 2 | 4 |
| Steve Guenette (Goalie) | 11 | 0 | 1 | 1 | 0 |
| Rich Tabaracci (Goalie) | 1 | 0 | 0 | 0 | 2 |
| Perry Ganchar | 3 | 0 | 0 | 0 | 0 |
| Frank Pietrangelo (Goalie) | 15 | 0 | 0 | 0 | 2 |
| Richard Zemlak, Minnesota | 3 | 0 | 0 | 0 | 13 |
|    Pittsburgh | 31 | 0 | 0 | 0 | 135 |
|    Totals | 34 | 0 | 0 | 0 | 148 |

## Quebec Nordiques

|  | Games | G. | A. | Pts. | Pen. |
|---|---|---|---|---|---|
| Peter Stastny | 72 | 35 | 50 | 85 | 117 |
| Walt Poddubny | 72 | 38 | 37 | 75 | 107 |
| Jeff Brown | 78 | 21 | 47 | 68 | 62 |
| Michel Goulet | 69 | 26 | 38 | 64 | 67 |
| Joe Sakic | 70 | 23 | 39 | 62 | 24 |
| Iiro Jarvi | 75 | 11 | 30 | 41 | 40 |
| Paul Gillis | 79 | 15 | 25 | 40 | 163 |
| Marc Fortier | 57 | 20 | 19 | 39 | 45 |
| Anton Stastny | 55 | 7 | 30 | 37 | 12 |
| Gaetan Duchesne | 70 | 8 | 21 | 29 | 56 |
| Randy Moller | 74 | 7 | 22 | 29 | 136 |
| Robert Picard | 74 | 7 | 14 | 21 | 61 |
| Mike Hough | 46 | 9 | 10 | 19 | 39 |
| Ken McRae | 37 | 6 | 11 | 17 | 68 |
| Mario Marois, Winnipeg | 7 | 1 | 1 | 2 | 17 |
|    Quebec | 42 | 2 | 11 | 13 | 101 |
|    Totals | 49 | 3 | 12 | 15 | 118 |
| Curtis Leschyshyn | 71 | 4 | 9 | 13 | 71 |
| Dave Latta | 24 | 4 | 8 | 12 | 4 |
| Jeff Jackson | 33 | 4 | 6 | 10 | 28 |
| Alain Cote | 55 | 2 | 8 | 10 | 14 |
| Trevor Stienberg | 55 | 6 | 3 | 9 | 130 |
| Steven Finn | 77 | 2 | 6 | 8 | 235 |
| Darin Kimble | 26 | 3 | 1 | 4 | 149 |
| Lane Lambert | 13 | 2 | 2 | 4 | 23 |
| Jari Gronstrand | 25 | 1 | 3 | 4 | 14 |
| Mark Vermette | 12 | 0 | 4 | 4 | 7 |
| Bobby Dollas | 16 | 0 | 3 | 3 | 16 |
| Ron Tugnutt (Goalie) | 26 | 0 | 3 | 3 | 2 |
| Dean Hopkins | 5 | 0 | 2 | 2 | 4 |
| Mario Gosselin (Goalie) | 39 | 0 | 2 | 2 | 6 |
| Greg Smyth | 10 | 0 | 1 | 1 | 70 |
| Bob Mason (Goalie) | 22 | 0 | 1 | 1 | 2 |
| Scott Shaunessy | 4 | 0 | 0 | 0 | 16 |
| Joel Baillargeon | 5 | 0 | 0 | 0 | 4 |
| Mario Brunetta (Goalie) | 5 | 0 | 0 | 0 | 0 |
| Jacques Mailhot | 5 | 0 | 0 | 0 | 33 |

**St. Louis Blues right wing Brett Hull.**

## St. Louis Blues

| | Games | G. | A. | Pts. | Pen. |
|---|---|---|---|---|---|
| Brett Hull | 78 | 41 | 43 | 84 | 33 |
| Peter Zezel, Philadelphia | 26 | 4 | 13 | 17 | 15 |
|     St. Louis | 52 | 17 | 36 | 53 | 27 |
|     Totals | 78 | 21 | 49 | 70 | 42 |
| Bernie Federko | 66 | 22 | 45 | 67 | 54 |
| Cliff Ronning | 64 | 24 | 31 | 55 | 18 |
| Greg Paslawski | 75 | 26 | 26 | 52 | 18 |
| Tony Hrkac | 70 | 17 | 28 | 45 | 8 |
| Gino Cavallini | 74 | 20 | 23 | 43 | 79 |
| Tony McKegney | 71 | 25 | 17 | 42 | 58 |
| Brian Benning | 66 | 8 | 26 | 34 | 102 |
| Rick Meagher | 78 | 15 | 14 | 29 | 53 |
| Sergio Momesso | 53 | 9 | 17 | 26 | 139 |
| Gordie Roberts | 77 | 2 | 24 | 26 | 90 |
| Steve Tuttle | 53 | 13 | 12 | 25 | 6 |
| Paul Cavallini | 65 | 4 | 20 | 24 | 128 |
| Tom Tilley | 70 | 1 | 22 | 23 | 47 |
| Mike Lalor, Montreal | 12 | 1 | 4 | 5 | 15 |
|     St. Louis | 36 | 1 | 14 | 15 | 54 |
|     Totals | 48 | 2 | 18 | 20 | 69 |
| Doug Evans | 53 | 7 | 12 | 19 | 81 |
| Herb Raglan | 50 | 7 | 10 | 17 | 144 |
| Gaston Gingras | 52 | 3 | 10 | 13 | 6 |
| Todd Ewen | 34 | 4 | 5 | 9 | 171 |
| Craig Coxe | 41 | 0 | 7 | 7 | 127 |
| Dave Lowry | 21 | 3 | 3 | 6 | 11 |
| Dave Richter | 66 | 1 | 5 | 6 | 99 |
| Jim Vesey | 5 | 1 | 1 | 2 | 7 |
| Glen Featherstone | 18 | 0 | 2 | 2 | 22 |
| Robert Dirk | 9 | 0 | 1 | 1 | 11 |
| Vincent Riendeau (Goalie) | 32 | 0 | 1 | 1 | 4 |
| Dominic Lavoie | 1 | 0 | 0 | 0 | 0 |
| Tim Bothwell | 22 | 0 | 0 | 0 | 14 |
| Greg Millen (Goalie) | 52 | 0 | 0 | 0 | 4 |

## Toronto Maple Leafs

| | Games | G. | A. | Pts. | Pen. |
|---|---|---|---|---|---|
| Ed Olczyk | 80 | 38 | 52 | 90 | 75 |
| Gary Leeman | 61 | 32 | 43 | 75 | 66 |
| Vincent Damphousse | 80 | 26 | 42 | 68 | 75 |
| Tom Fergus | 80 | 22 | 45 | 67 | 48 |
| Dan Marois | 76 | 31 | 23 | 54 | 76 |
| Mark Osborne | 75 | 16 | 30 | 46 | 112 |
| Al Iafrate | 65 | 13 | 20 | 33 | 72 |
| Dave Reid | 77 | 9 | 21 | 30 | 22 |
| Todd Gill | 59 | 11 | 14 | 25 | 72 |
| Craig Laughlin | 66 | 10 | 13 | 23 | 41 |
| Borje Salming | 63 | 3 | 17 | 20 | 86 |
| Peter Ihnacak | 26 | 2 | 16 | 18 | 10 |
| Brad Marsh | 80 | 1 | 15 | 16 | 79 |
| Derek Laxdal | 41 | 9 | 6 | 15 | 65 |
| Chris Kotsopoulos | 57 | 1 | 14 | 15 | 44 |
| Dan Daoust | 68 | 7 | 5 | 12 | 54 |
| Wendel Clark | 15 | 7 | 4 | 11 | 66 |
| Darren Veitch | 37 | 3 | 7 | 10 | 16 |
| Rick Lanz | 32 | 1 | 9 | 10 | 18 |
| Luke Richardson | 55 | 2 | 7 | 9 | 106 |
| Paul Gagne | 16 | 3 | 2 | 5 | 6 |
| Brian Curran | 47 | 1 | 4 | 5 | 185 |
| Darryl Shannon | 14 | 1 | 3 | 4 | 6 |
| John Kordic, Montreal | 6 | 0 | 0 | 0 | 13 |
|     Toronto | 46 | 1 | 2 | 3 | 185 |
|     Totals | 52 | 1 | 2 | 3 | 198 |
| Ken Hammond, Edmonton | 5 | 0 | 1 | 1 | 8 |
|     N.Y. Rangers | 3 | 0 | 0 | 0 | 0 |

|  | Games | G. | A. | Pts. | Pen. |
|---|---|---|---|---|---|
| Toronto | 14 | 0 | 2 | 2 | 12 |
| Totals | 22 | 0 | 3 | 3 | 20 |
| Allan Bester (Goalie) | 43 | 0 | 2 | 2 | 2 |
| Mike Blaisdell | 9 | 1 | 0 | 1 | 4 |
| Tim Armstrong | 11 | 1 | 0 | 1 | 6 |
| Ken Yaremchuk | 11 | 1 | 0 | 1 | 2 |
| Sean McKenna | 3 | 0 | 1 | 1 | 0 |
| Scott Pearson | 9 | 0 | 1 | 1 | 2 |
| Doug Shedden | 1 | 0 | 0 | 0 | 2 |
| Chris McRae | 3 | 0 | 0 | 0 | 12 |
| Marty Dallman | 4 | 0 | 0 | 0 | 0 |
| Paul Lawless | 7 | 0 | 0 | 0 | 0 |
| Jeff Reese (Goalie) | 10 | 0 | 0 | 0 | 4 |

## Vancouver Canucks

|  | Games | G. | A. | Pts. | Pen. |
|---|---|---|---|---|---|
| Petri Skriko | 74 | 30 | 36 | 66 | 57 |
| Trevor Linden | 80 | 30 | 29 | 59 | 41 |
| Paul Reinhart | 64 | 7 | 50 | 57 | 44 |
| Tony Tanti | 77 | 24 | 25 | 49 | 69 |
| Brian Bradley | 71 | 18 | 27 | 45 | 42 |
| Barry Pederson | 62 | 15 | 26 | 41 | 22 |
| Robert Nordmark | 80 | 6 | 35 | 41 | 97 |
| Jim Sandlak | 72 | 20 | 20 | 40 | 99 |
| Steve Bozek | 71 | 17 | 18 | 35 | 64 |
| Greg Adams | 61 | 19 | 14 | 33 | 24 |
| Rich Sutter | 75 | 17 | 15 | 32 | 122 |
| Stan Smyl | 75 | 7 | 18 | 25 | 102 |
| Doug Lidster | 63 | 5 | 17 | 22 | 78 |
| Garth Butcher | 78 | 0 | 20 | 20 | 227 |
| Dan Hodgson | 23 | 4 | 13 | 17 | 25 |
| Greg C. Adams, Edmonton | 49 | 4 | 5 | 9 | 82 |
| Vancouver | 12 | 4 | 2 | 6 | 35 |
| Totals | 61 | 8 | 7 | 15 | 117 |
| David Bruce | 53 | 7 | 7 | 14 | 65 |
| Larry Melnyk | 74 | 3 | 11 | 14 | 82 |
| Jim Benning | 65 | 3 | 9 | 12 | 48 |
| Doug Smith, Edmonton | 19 | 1 | 1 | 2 | 9 |
| Vancouver | 10 | 3 | 4 | 7 | 4 |
| Totals | 29 | 4 | 5 | 9 | 13 |
| Harold Snepsts | 59 | 0 | 8 | 8 | 69 |
| Mel Bridgman | 15 | 4 | 3 | 7 | 10 |
| Jose Charbonneau, Montreal | 9 | 1 | 3 | 4 | 6 |
| Vancouver | 13 | 0 | 1 | 1 | 6 |
| Totals | 22 | 1 | 4 | 5 | 12 |
| Daryl Stanley | 20 | 3 | 1 | 4 | 14 |
| Kevan Guy | 45 | 2 | 2 | 4 | 34 |
| Ken Berry | 13 | 2 | 1 | 3 | 5 |
| Ronnie Stern | 17 | 1 | 0 | 1 | 49 |
| Randy Boyd | 2 | 0 | 1 | 1 | 0 |
| Rob Murphy | 8 | 0 | 1 | 1 | 2 |
| Kirk McLean (Goalie) | 42 | 0 | 1 | 1 | 6 |
| Ian Kidd | 1 | 0 | 0 | 0 | 0 |
| Jay Mazur | 1 | 0 | 0 | 0 | 0 |
| Jeff Rohlicek | 2 | 0 | 0 | 0 | 4 |
| Todd Hawkins | 4 | 0 | 0 | 0 | 9 |
| Troy Gamble (Goalie) | 5 | 0 | 0 | 0 | 0 |
| Steve Weeks (Goalie) | 35 | 0 | 0 | 0 | 4 |

## Washington Capitals

|  | Games | G. | A. | Pts. | Pen. |
|---|---|---|---|---|---|
| Mike Ridley | 80 | 41 | 48 | 89 | 49 |
| Geoff Courtnall | 79 | 42 | 38 | 80 | 110 |
| Dino Ciccarelli, Minnesota | 65 | 32 | 27 | 59 | 64 |
| Washington | 11 | 12 | 3 | 15 | 12 |
| Totals | 76 | 44 | 30 | 74 | 76 |

|  | Games | G. | A. | Pts. | Pen. |
|---|---|---|---|---|---|
| Bengt Gustafsson | 72 | 18 | 51 | 69 | 18 |
| Scott Stevens | 80 | 7 | 61 | 68 | 225 |
| Dave Christian | 80 | 34 | 31 | 65 | 12 |
| Dale Hunter | 80 | 20 | 37 | 57 | 219 |
| Kelly Miller | 78 | 19 | 21 | 40 | 45 |
| Kevin Hatcher | 62 | 13 | 27 | 40 | 101 |
| Stephen Leach | 74 | 11 | 19 | 30 | 92 |
| Michal Pivonka | 52 | 8 | 19 | 27 | 30 |
| Calle Johansson, Buffalo | 47 | 2 | 11 | 13 | 33 |
|     Washington | 12 | 1 | 7 | 8 | 4 |
|     Totals | 59 | 3 | 18 | 21 | 37 |
| Rod Langway | 76 | 2 | 19 | 21 | 67 |
| Bob Rouse, Minnesota | 66 | 4 | 13 | 17 | 124 |
|     Washington | 13 | 0 | 2 | 2 | 38 |
|     Totals | 79 | 4 | 15 | 19 | 162 |
| Bob Gould | 75 | 5 | 13 | 18 | 65 |
| Lou Franceschetti | 63 | 7 | 10 | 17 | 123 |
| John Druce | 48 | 8 | 7 | 15 | 62 |
| Mike Millar | 18 | 6 | 3 | 9 | 4 |
| Doug Wickenheiser, N.Y. Rangers | 1 | 1 | 0 | 1 | 0 |
|     Washington | 16 | 2 | 5 | 7 | 4 |
|     Totals | 17 | 3 | 5 | 8 | 4 |
| Chris Felix | 21 | 0 | 8 | 8 | 8 |
| Neil Sheehy | 72 | 3 | 4 | 7 | 184 |
| Peter Sundstrom | 35 | 4 | 2 | 6 | 14 |
| Yvon Corriveau | 33 | 3 | 2 | 5 | 62 |
| Bill Houlder | 8 | 0 | 3 | 3 | 4 |
| Scot Kleinendorst, Hartford | 24 | 0 | 1 | 1 | 36 |
|     Washington | 3 | 0 | 1 | 1 | 10 |
|     Totals | 27 | 0 | 2 | 2 | 46 |
| Kent Carlson | 2 | 1 | 0 | 1 | 0 |
| Pete Peeters (Goalie) | 33 | 0 | 1 | 1 | 8 |
| Shawn Cronin | 1 | 0 | 0 | 0 | 0 |
| Don Beaupre, Minnesota (Goalie) | 1 | 0 | 0 | 0 | 0 |
|     Washington (Goalie) | 11 | 0 | 0 | 0 | 6 |
|     Totals | 12 | 0 | 0 | 0 | 6 |

## Winnipeg Jets

|  | Games | G. | A. | Pts. | Pen. |
|---|---|---|---|---|---|
| Dale Hawerchuk | 75 | 41 | 55 | 96 | 28 |
| Thomas Steen | 80 | 27 | 61 | 88 | 80 |
| Andrew McBain | 80 | 37 | 40 | 77 | 71 |
| Brent Ashton | 75 | 31 | 37 | 68 | 36 |
| Fredrik Olausson | 75 | 15 | 47 | 62 | 32 |
| Dave Ellett | 75 | 22 | 34 | 56 | 62 |
| Pat Elynuik | 56 | 26 | 25 | 51 | 29 |
| Iain Duncan | 57 | 14 | 30 | 44 | 74 |
| Randy Carlyle | 78 | 6 | 38 | 44 | 78 |
| Laurie Boschman | 70 | 10 | 26 | 36 | 163 |
| Doug Smail | 47 | 14 | 15 | 29 | 52 |
| Paul Fenton, Los Angeles | 21 | 2 | 3 | 5 | 6 |
|     Winnipeg | 59 | 14 | 9 | 23 | 33 |
|     Totals | 80 | 16 | 12 | 28 | 39 |
| Gord Donnelly, Quebec | 16 | 4 | 0 | 4 | 46 |
|     Winnipeg | 57 | 6 | 10 | 16 | 228 |
|     Totals | 73 | 10 | 10 | 20 | 274 |
| Peter Taglianetti | 66 | 1 | 14 | 15 | 226 |
| Teppo Numminen | 69 | 1 | 14 | 15 | 36 |
| Jim Kyte | 74 | 3 | 9 | 12 | 190 |
| Brad Jones | 22 | 6 | 5 | 11 | 6 |
| Hannu Jarvenpaa | 53 | 4 | 7 | 11 | 41 |
| Brad Berry | 38 | 0 | 9 | 9 | 45 |
| Randy Gilhen | 64 | 5 | 3 | 8 | 38 |
| Brent Hughes | 28 | 3 | 2 | 5 | 82 |
| Alfie Turcotte | 14 | 1 | 3 | 4 | 2 |
| Stu Kulak | 18 | 2 | 0 | 2 | 24 |
| Markku Kyllonen | 9 | 0 | 2 | 2 | 2 |

**Washington Capitals right wing Dino Ciccarelli.**

| | Games | G. | A. | Pts. | Pen. |
|---|---|---|---|---|---|
| Anthony Joseph | 2 | 1 | 0 | 1 | 0 |
| Moe Lemay, Boston | 12 | 0 | 0 | 0 | 23 |
| Winnipeg | 10 | 1 | 0 | 1 | 14 |
| Totals | 22 | 1 | 0 | 1 | 37 |
| Guy Larose | 3 | 0 | 1 | 1 | 6 |
| Eldon Reddick (Goalie) | 41 | 0 | 1 | 1 | 6 |
| Darren Boyko | 1 | 0 | 0 | 0 | 0 |
| Todd Flichel | 1 | 0 | 0 | 0 | 0 |
| Tom Draper (Goalie) | 2 | 0 | 0 | 0 | 0 |
| Matt Hervey | 2 | 0 | 0 | 0 | 4 |
| Bryan Marchment | 2 | 0 | 0 | 0 | 2 |
| Paul Boutilier | 3 | 0 | 0 | 0 | 4 |
| Steve Fletcher | 3 | 0 | 0 | 0 | 5 |
| Daniel Berthiaume (Goalie) | 9 | 0 | 0 | 0 | 0 |
| Bob Essensa (Goalie) | 20 | 0 | 0 | 0 | 2 |

## Complete Goaltending Records

| | Games | Mins. | Goals | SO. | Avg. |
|---|---|---|---|---|---|
| Randy Exelby | 1 | 3 | 0 | 0 | 0.00 |
| Patrick Roy | 48 | 2744 | 113(2) | 4 | *2.47 |
| Brian Hayward | 36 | 2091 | 101(2) | 1 | 2.90 |
| MONTREAL TOTALS | 80 | 4849 | 218 | 5 | 2.70 |
| Mike Vernon | 52 | 2938 | 130 | 0 | 2.65 |
| Rick Wamsley | 35 | 1927 | 95(1) | 2 | 2.96 |
| CALGARY TOTALS | 80 | 4872 | 226 | 2 | 2.78 |
| Troy Gamble | 5 | 302 | 12(2) | 0 | 2.38 |
| Steve Weeks | 35 | 2056 | 102(7) | 0 | 2.98 |
| Kirk McLean | 42 | 2477 | 127(3) | 4 | 3.08 |
| VANCOUVER TOTALS | 80 | 4855 | 253 | 4 | 3.13 |
| Rejean Lemelin | 40 | 2392 | 120(3) | 0 | 3.01 |
| Andy Moog | 41 | 2482 | 133 | 1 | 3.22 |
| BOSTON TOTALS | 80 | 4882 | 256 | 1 | 3.15 |
| Pete Peeters | 33 | 1854 | 88 | 4 | 2.85 |
| Don Beaupre (a) | 11 | 578 | 28(1) | 1 | 2.91 |
| Clint Malarchuk (b) | 42 | 2428 | 141(1) | 1 | 3.48 |
| WASHINGTON TOTALS | 80 | 4865 | 259 | 6 | 3.19 |
| Don Beaupre (a) | 1 | 59 | 3(1) | 0 | 3.05 |
| Jon Casey | 55 | 2961 | 151(3) | 1 | 3.06 |
| Kari Takko | 32 | 1603 | 93(5) | 0 | 3.48 |
| Jarmo Myllys | 6 | 238 | 22 | 0 | 5.55 |
| MINNESOTA TOTALS | 80 | 4882 | 278 | 1 | 3.42 |
| Greg Millen | 52 | 3019 | 170(3) | *6 | 3.38 |
| Vincent Riendeau | 32 | 1842 | 108(4) | 0 | 3.52 |
| ST. LOUIS TOTALS | 80 | 4871 | 285 | 6 | 3.51 |
| Marc D'Amour | 1 | 19 | 0(1) | 0 | 0.00 |
| Ron Hextall | 64 | 3756 | 202(5) | 0 | 3.23 |
| Mark Laforest | 17 | 933 | 64 | 0 | 4.12 |
| Ken Wregget (c) | 3 | 130 | 13 | 0 | 6.00 |
| PHILADELPHIA TOTALS | 80 | 4854 | 285 | 0 | 3.52 |
| Peter Sidorkiewicz | 44 | 2635 | 133(1) | 4 | 3.03 |
| Kay Whitmore | 3 | 180 | 10 | 0 | 3.33 |
| Mike Liut | 35 | 2006 | 142(4) | 1 | 4.25 |
| HARTFORD TOTALS | 80 | 4834 | 290 | 5 | 3.60 |
| Clint Malarchuk (b) | 7 | 326 | 13 | 1 | 2.39 |
| Daren Puppa | 37 | 1908 | 107(1) | 1 | 3.36 |
| Jacques Cloutier | 36 | 1786 | 108(1) | 0 | 3.63 |
| Darcy Wakaluk | 6 | 214 | 15(1) | 0 | 4.21 |
| Tom Barrasso (d) | 10 | 545 | 45(1) | 0 | 4.95 |
| Darren Eliot | 2 | 67 | 7 | 0 | 6.27 |
| BUFFALO TOTALS | 80 | 4856 | 299 | 2 | 3.69 |
| Bill Ranford | 29 | 1509 | 88(1) | 1 | 3.50 |
| Grant Fuhr | 59 | 3341 | 213(4) | 1 | 3.83 |
| EDMONTON TOTALS | 80 | 4860 | 306 | 2 | 3.78 |

| | Games | Mins. | Goals | SO. | Avg. |
|---|---|---|---|---|---|
| John Vanbiesbrouck | 56 | 3207 | 197(4) | 0 | 3.69 |
| Bob Froese | 30 | 1621 | 102(4) | 1 | 3.78 |
| NEW YORK RANGERS TOTALS | 80 | 4844 | 307 | 1 | 3.80 |
| Glen Hanlon | 39 | 2092 | 124(3) | 1 | 3.56 |
| Sam St. Laurent | 4 | 141 | 9 | 0 | 3.83 |
| Greg Stefan | 46 | 2499 | 167(4) | 0 | 4.01 |
| Tim Cheveldae | 2 | 122 | 9 | 0 | 4.43 |
| DETROIT TOTALS | 80 | 4874 | 316 | 1 | 3.89 |
| Chris Terreri | 8 | 402 | 18(1) | 0 | 2.69 |
| Sean Burke | 62 | 3590 | *230(7) | 3 | 3.84 |
| Bob Sauve | 15 | 721 | 56(2) | 0 | 4.66 |
| Craig Billington | 3 | 140 | 11 | 0 | 4.71 |
| NEW JERSEY TOTALS | 80 | 4873 | 325 | 3 | 4.00 |
| Jeff Hackett | 13 | 662 | 39 | 0 | 3.53 |
| Mark Fitzpatrick (e) | 11 | 627 | 41 | 0 | 3.92 |
| Kelly Hrudey (f) | 50 | 2800 | 183(6) | 0 | 3.92 |
| Billy Smith | 17 | 730 | 54(2) | 0 | 4.44 |
| NEW YORK ISLANDERS TOTALS | 80 | 4832 | 325 | 0 | 4.04 |
| Chris Clifford | 1 | 4 | 0 | 0 | 0.00 |
| Alain Chevrier (g) | 27 | 1573 | 92(2) | 0 | 3.51 |
| Ed Belfour | 23 | 1148 | 74(1) | 0 | 3.87 |
| Darren Pang | 35 | 1644 | 120(1) | 0 | 4.38 |
| Jim Waite | 11 | 494 | 43(2) | 0 | 5.22 |
| CHICAGO TOTALS | 80 | 4874 | 335 | 0 | 4.12 |
| Kelly Hrudey (f) | 16 | 974 | 47(1) | 1 | 2.90 |
| Bob Janecyk | 1 | 30 | 2 | 0 | 4.00 |
| Mark Fitzpatrick (e) | 17 | 957 | 64(3) | 0 | 4.01 |
| Glenn Healy | 48 | 2699 | 192(7) | 0 | 4.27 |
| Roland Melanson | 4 | 178 | 19 | 0 | 6.40 |
| LOS ANGELES TOTALS | 80 | 4853 | 335 | 1 | 4.14 |
| Ron Tugnutt | 26 | 1367 | 82(1) | 0 | 3.60 |
| Mario Gosselin | 39 | 2064 | 146 | 0 | 4.24 |
| Bob Mason | 22 | 1168 | 92(1) | 0 | 4.73 |
| Mario Brunetta | 5 | 226 | 19(1) | 0 | 5.04 |
| QUEBEC TOTALS | 80 | 4840 | 342 | 0 | 4.24 |
| Allan Bester | 43 | 2460 | 156(5) | 2 | 3.80 |
| Ken Wregget (c) | 32 | 1888 | 139(1) | 0 | 4.42 |
| Jeff Reese | 10 | 486 | 40(1) | 0 | 4.94 |
| TORONTO TOTALS | 80 | 4845 | 342 | 2 | 4.24 |
| Frank Pietrangelo | 15 | 669 | 45(1) | 0 | 4.04 |
| Tom Barrasso (d) | 44 | 2406 | 162(4) | 0 | 4.04 |
| Steve Guenette | 11 | 574 | 41 | 0 | 4.29 |
| Wendell Young | 22 | 1150 | 92 | 0 | 4.80 |
| Rich Tabaracci | 1 | 33 | 4 | 0 | 7.27 |
| PITTSBURGH TOTALS | 80 | 4843 | 349 | 0 | 4.32 |
| Bob Essensa | 20 | 1102 | 68(2) | 1 | 3.70 |
| Eldon Reddick | 41 | 2109 | 144(3) | 0 | 4.10 |
| Alain Chevrier (g) | 22 | 1092 | 78(2) | 1 | 4.29 |
| Daniel Berthiaume | 9 | 443 | 44(2) | 0 | 5.96 |
| Tom Draper | 2 | 120 | 12 | 0 | 6.00 |
| WINNIPEG TOTALS | 80 | 4879 | 355 | 2 | 4.37 |

( )—Empty Net Goals. Do not count against an individual average.
(a)—Beaupre played for Washington and Minnesota.
(b)—Malarchuk played for Washington and Buffalo.
(c)—Wregget played for Philadelphia and Toronto.
(d)—Barrasso played for Buffalo and Pittsburgh.
(e)—Fitzpatrick played for New York Islanders and Los Angeles.
(f)—Hrudey played for New York Islanders and Los Angeles.
(g)—Chevrier played for Chicago and Winnipeg.
NOTE: Hrudey led all goaltenders in games played with 66 (50 with New York Islanders and 16 with Los Angeles), minutes played with 3,774 (2,800 with New York Islanders and 974 with Los Angeles) and tied for goals allowed with 230 (183 with New York Islanders and 47 with Los Angeles).

# NHL Miscellaneous Statistics

(Players are listed alphabetically)

| Player — Team | Games | Shots | Goals | Shooting Pct. | PPG | SHG | +/− |
|---|---|---|---|---|---|---|---|
| Keith Acton, Edmonton | 46 | 74 | 11 | 14.9 | 0 | 1 | + 9 |
| Philadelphia | 25 | 38 | 3 | 7.9 | 0 | 1 | + 1 |
| Totals | 71 | 112 | 14 | 12.5 | 0 | 2 | + 10 |
| Greg Adams, Vancouver | 61 | 144 | 19 | 13.2 | 9 | 0 | − 21 |
| Greg C. Adams, Edmonton | 49 | 49 | 4 | 8.2 | 0 | 0 | + 1 |
| Vancouver | 12 | 22 | 4 | 18.2 | 2 | 0 | + 2 |
| Totals | 61 | 71 | 8 | 11.3 | 2 | 0 | + 3 |
| Tommy Albelin, Quebec | 14 | 16 | 2 | 12.5 | 1 | 0 | − 6 |
| New Jersey | 46 | 82 | 7 | 8.5 | 1 | 1 | + 18 |
| Totals | 60 | 98 | 9 | 9.2 | 2 | 1 | + 12 |
| Mike Allison, Los Angeles | 55 | 71 | 14 | 19.7 | 6 | 0 | + 7 |
| Glenn Anderson, Edmonton | 79 | 212 | 16 | 7.5 | 7 | 0 | − 16 |
| John Anderson, Hartford | 62 | 132 | 16 | 12.1 | 1 | 0 | + 15 |
| Perry Anderson, New Jersey | 39 | 36 | 3 | 8.3 | 0 | 0 | + 5 |
| Shawn Anderson, Buffalo | 33 | 26 | 2 | 7.7 | 2 | 0 | + 3 |
| Mikael Andersson, Buffalo | 14 | 12 | 0 | 0.0 | 0 | 0 | − 1 |
| Dave Andreychuk, Buffalo | 56 | 145 | 28 | 19.3 | 7 | 0 | Even |
| David Archibald, Minnesota | 72 | 105 | 14 | 13.3 | 7 | 0 | − 11 |
| Tim Armstrong, Toronto | 11 | 5 | 1 | 20.0 | 0 | 0 | − 2 |
| Scott Arniel, Buffalo | 80 | 122 | 18 | 14.8 | 0 | 2 | + 10 |
| Brent Ashton, Winnipeg | 75 | 180 | 31 | 17.2 | 7 | 1 | − 5 |
| Warren Babe, Minnesota | 14 | 15 | 2 | 13.3 | 0 | 0 | + 3 |
| Dave Babych, Hartford | 70 | 172 | 6 | 3.5 | 4 | 0 | − 5 |
| Joel Baillergeon, Quebec | 5 | 2 | 0 | 0.0 | 0 | 0 | − 3 |
| Don Barber, Minnesota | 23 | 42 | 8 | 19.0 | 3 | 0 | + 2 |
| Dave Barr, Detroit | 73 | 140 | 27 | 19.3 | 5 | 2 | + 12 |
| Bob Bassen, N.Y. Islanders | 19 | 14 | 1 | 7.1 | 0 | 0 | Even |
| Chicago | 49 | 37 | 4 | 10.8 | 0 | 0 | + 5 |
| Totals | 68 | 51 | 5 | 9.8 | 0 | 0 | + 5 |
| Ken Baumgartner, Los Angeles | 49 | 15 | 1 | 6.7 | 0 | 0 | − 9 |
| Brian Bellows, Minnesota | 60 | 196 | 23 | 11.7 | 7 | 0 | − 14 |
| Brian Benning, St. Louis | 66 | 91 | 8 | 8.8 | 3 | 0 | − 23 |
| Jim Benning, Vancouver | 65 | 55 | 3 | 5.5 | 1 | 0 | − 4 |
| Paul Beraldo, Boston | 7 | 1 | 0 | 0.0 | 0 | 0 | − 2 |
| Perry Berezan, Calgary | 35 | 49 | 4 | 8.2 | 0 | 1 | + 5 |
| Minnesota | 16 | 16 | 1 | 6.3 | 0 | 0 | + 1 |
| Totals | 51 | 65 | 5 | 7.7 | 0 | 1 | + 6 |
| Bill Berg, N.Y. Islanders | 7 | 10 | 1 | 10.0 | 1 | 0 | − 2 |
| Mike Berger, Minnesota | 1 | 0 | 0 | 0.0 | 0 | 0 | − 1 |
| Marc Bergevin, Chicago | 11 | 9 | 0 | 0.0 | 0 | 0 | − 3 |
| N.Y. Islanders | 58 | 56 | 2 | 3.6 | 1 | 0 | + 2 |
| Totals | 69 | 65 | 2 | 3.1 | 1 | 0 | − 1 |
| Brad Berry, Winnipeg | 38 | 21 | 0 | 0.0 | 0 | 0 | − 8 |
| Ken Berry, Vancouver | 13 | 10 | 2 | 20.0 | 0 | 0 | + 2 |
| Craig Berube, Philadelphia | 53 | 31 | 1 | 3.2 | 0 | 0 | − 15 |
| Jeff Beukeboom, Edmonton | 36 | 26 | 0 | 0.0 | 0 | 0 | + 2 |
| Scott Bjugstad, Pittsburgh | 24 | 21 | 3 | 14.3 | 0 | 0 | − 12 |
| Mike Blaisdell, Toronto | 9 | 8 | 1 | 12.5 | 0 | 0 | − 5 |
| Jeff Bloemberg, N.Y. Rangers | 9 | 9 | 0 | 0.0 | 0 | 0 | + 2 |
| John Blum, Detroit | 6 | 3 | 0 | 0.0 | 0 | 0 | − 2 |
| Doug Bodger, Pittsburgh | 10 | 22 | 1 | 4.5 | 0 | 0 | + 6 |
| Buffalo | 61 | 134 | 7 | 5.2 | 6 | 0 | + 9 |
| Totals | 71 | 156 | 8 | 5.1 | 6 | 0 | + 15 |
| Laurie Boschman, Winnipeg | 70 | 113 | 10 | 8.8 | 3 | 0 | − 17 |
| Tim Bothwell, St. Louis | 22 | 10 | 0 | 0.0 | 0 | 0 | + 4 |
| Phil Bourque, Pittsburgh | 80 | 153 | 17 | 11.1 | 5 | 2 | − 22 |
| Ray Bourque, Boston | 60 | 243 | 18 | 7.4 | 6 | 0 | + 20 |
| Paul Boutilier, Winnipeg | 3 | 4 | 0 | 0.0 | 0 | 0 | + 2 |
| Randy Boyd, Vancouver | 2 | 6 | 0 | 0.0 | 0 | 0 | − 1 |
| Darren Boyko, Winnipeg | 1 | 0 | 0 | 0.0 | 0 | 0 | − 1 |
| Steve Bozek, Vancouver | 71 | 138 | 17 | 12.3 | 0 | 2 | + 1 |
| Brian Bradley, Vancouver | 71 | 151 | 18 | 11.9 | 6 | 0 | − 5 |
| Andy Brickley, Boston | 71 | 98 | 13 | 13.3 | 2 | 0 | + 4 |
| Mel Bridgman, Vancouver | 15 | 17 | 4 | 23.5 | 2 | 0 | − 4 |
| Stephane Brochu, N.Y. Rangers | 1 | 1 | 0 | 0.0 | 0 | 0 | + 1 |
| Bob Brooke, Minnesota | 57 | 77 | 7 | 9.1 | 0 | 1 | − 12 |
| Aaron Broten, New Jersey | 80 | 178 | 16 | 9.0 | 4 | 0 | − 7 |

| Player — Team | Games | Shots | Goals | Shooting Pct. | PPG | SHG | +/− |
|---|---|---|---|---|---|---|---|
| Neal Broten, Minnesota | 68 | 160 | 18 | 11.3 | 4 | 5 | + 1 |
| Dave Brown, Philadelphia | 50 | 28 | 0 | 0.0 | 0 | 0 | − 8 |
| Edmonton | 22 | 14 | 0 | 0.0 | 0 | 0 | − 4 |
| Totals | 72 | 42 | 0 | 0.0 | 0 | 0 | − 12 |
| Doug Brown, New Jersey | 63 | 110 | 15 | 13.6 | 4 | 0 | − 7 |
| Jeff Brown, Quebec | 78 | 276 | 21 | 7.6 | 13 | 1 | − 22 |
| Keith Brown, Chicago | 74 | 105 | 2 | 1.9 | 1 | 0 | − 5 |
| Rob Brown, Pittsburgh | 68 | 169 | 49 | 29.0 | 24 | 0 | + 27 |
| Jeff Brubaker, Detroit | 1 | 0 | 0 | 0.0 | 0 | 0 | Even |
| David Bruce, Vancouver | 53 | 86 | 7 | 8.1 | 1 | 0 | − 16 |
| Benoit Brunet, Montreal | 2 | 1 | 0 | 0.0 | 0 | 0 | Even |
| Kelly Buchberger, Edmonton | 66 | 57 | 5 | 8.8 | 1 | 0 | − 14 |
| Mike Bullard, St. Louis | 20 | 52 | 4 | 7.7 | 2 | 0 | + 1 |
| Philadelphia | 54 | 137 | 23 | 16.8 | 8 | 0 | + 1 |
| Totals | 74 | 189 | 27 | 14.3 | 10 | 0 | + 2 |
| Shawn Burr, Detroit | 79 | 149 | 19 | 12.8 | 1 | 4 | + 5 |
| Randy Burridge, Boston | 80 | 189 | 31 | 16.4 | 6 | 2 | + 19 |
| Adam Burt, Hartford | 5 | 1 | 0 | 0.0 | 0 | 0 | − 1 |
| Rod Buskas, Pittsburgh | 52 | 15 | 1 | 6.7 | 0 | 0 | − 2 |
| Garth Butcher, Vancouver | 78 | 101 | 0 | 0.0 | 0 | 0 | + 4 |
| Lyndon Byers, Boston | 49 | 25 | 0 | 0.0 | 0 | 0 | − 8 |
| Jock Callander, Pittsburgh | 30 | 35 | 6 | 17.1 | 2 | 0 | − 3 |
| Guy Carbonneau, Montreal | 79 | 142 | 26 | 18.3 | 1 | 2 | + 37 |
| Terry Carkner, Philadelphia | 78 | 84 | 11 | 13.1 | 2 | 1 | − 6 |
| Kent Carlson, Washington | 2 | 1 | 1 | 100.0 | 0 | 0 | + 2 |
| Anders Carlsson, New Jersey | 47 | 42 | 4 | 9.5 | 0 | 0 | + 3 |
| Randy Carlyle, Winnipeg | 78 | 124 | 6 | 4.8 | 2 | 0 | − 19 |
| Bobby Carpenter, Los Angeles | 39 | 91 | 11 | 12.1 | 3 | 0 | + 3 |
| Boston | 18 | 46 | 5 | 10.9 | 1 | 0 | + 4 |
| Totals | 57 | 137 | 16 | 11.7 | 4 | 0 | + 7 |
| Jimmy Carson, Edmonton | 80 | 240 | 49 | 20.4 | 19 | 0 | + 3 |
| John Carter, Boston | 44 | 96 | 12 | 12.5 | 4 | 1 | − 1 |
| Bruce Cassidy, Chicago | 9 | 12 | 0 | 0.0 | 0 | 0 | − 5 |
| Jay Caufield, Pittsburgh | 58 | 10 | 1 | 10.0 | 0 | 0 | − 4 |
| Gino Cavallini, St. Louis | 74 | 153 | 20 | 13.1 | 1 | 0 | + 2 |
| Paul Cavallini, St. Louis | 65 | 93 | 4 | 4.3 | 0 | 0 | + 25 |
| John Chabot, Detroit | 52 | 49 | 2 | 4.1 | 0 | 2 | − 18 |
| Shawn Chambers, Minnesota | 72 | 131 | 5 | 3.8 | 1 | 2 | − 4 |
| Jose Charbonneau, Montreal | 9 | 15 | 1 | 6.7 | 0 | 0 | − 1 |
| Vancouver | 13 | 16 | 0 | 0.0 | 0 | 0 | − 3 |
| Totals | 22 | 31 | 1 | 3.2 | 0 | 0 | − 4 |
| Chris Chelios, Montreal | 80 | 206 | 15 | 7.3 | 8 | 0 | + 35 |
| Rich Chernomaz, Calgary | 1 | 2 | 0 | 0.0 | 0 | 0 | − 1 |
| Steve Chiasson, Detroit | 65 | 187 | 12 | 6.4 | 5 | 2 | − 6 |
| Dave Christian, Washington | 80 | 177 | 34 | 19.2 | 16 | 1 | + 2 |
| Shane Churla, Calgary | 5 | 2 | 0 | 0.0 | 0 | 0 | − 3 |
| Minnesota | 13 | 6 | 1 | 16.7 | 0 | 0 | Even |
| Totals | 18 | 8 | 1 | 12.5 | 0 | 0 | − 3 |
| Jeff Chychrun, Philadelphia | 80 | 53 | 1 | 1.9 | 0 | 0 | + 11 |
| Dean Chynoweth, N.Y. Islanders | 6 | 0 | 0 | 0.0 | 0 | 0 | − 4 |
| Dino Ciccarelli, Minnesota | 65 | 208 | 32 | 15.4 | 13 | 0 | − 16 |
| Washington | 11 | 39 | 12 | 30.8 | 3 | 0 | + 10 |
| Totals | 76 | 247 | 44 | 17.8 | 16 | 0 | − 6 |
| Chris Cichocki, New Jersey | 2 | 2 | 0 | 0.0 | 0 | 0 | Even |
| Robert Cimetta, Boston | 7 | 4 | 2 | 50.0 | 0 | 0 | − 4 |
| Joe Cirella, New Jersey | 80 | 84 | 3 | 3.6 | 0 | 1 | − 14 |
| Wendel Clark, Toronto | 15 | 30 | 7 | 23.3 | 3 | 0 | − 3 |
| Jacques Cloutier, Buffalo | 36 | 0 | 0 | 0.0 | 0 | 0 | Even |
| Glen Cochrane, Chicago | 6 | 1 | 0 | 0.0 | 0 | 0 | − 1 |
| Edmonton | 12 | 3 | 0 | 0.0 | 0 | 0 | − 2 |
| Totals | 18 | 4 | 0 | 0.0 | 0 | 0 | − 3 |
| Paul Coffey, Pittsburgh | 75 | 342 | 30 | 8.8 | 11 | 0 | − 10 |
| Pat Conacher, New Jersey | 55 | 59 | 7 | 11.9 | 0 | 1 | − 7 |
| Yvon Corriveau, Washington | 33 | 39 | 3 | 7.7 | 0 | 0 | Even |
| Shayne Corson, Montreal | 80 | 133 | 26 | 19.5 | 10 | 0 | − 1 |
| Alain Cote, Quebec | 55 | 31 | 2 | 6.5 | 0 | 1 | − 1 |
| Alain G. Cote, Boston | 31 | 45 | 2 | 4.4 | 0 | 0 | − 9 |
| Sylvain Cote, Hartford | 78 | 130 | 8 | 6.2 | 1 | 0 | − 7 |
| Geoff Courtnall, Washington | 79 | 239 | 42 | 17.6 | 16 | 0 | + 11 |
| Russ Courtnall, Toronto | 9 | 11 | 1 | 9.1 | 0 | 1 | − 2 |

| Player — Team | Games | Shots | Goals | Shooting Pct. | PPG | SHG | +/− |
|---|---|---|---|---|---|---|---|
| Montreal | 64 | 136 | 22 | 16.2 | 7 | 0 | + 11 |
| Totals | 73 | 147 | 23 | 15.6 | 7 | 1 | + 9 |
| Sylvain Couturier, Los Angeles | 16 | 15 | 1 | 6.7 | 1 | 0 | − 3 |
| Craig Coxe, St. Louis | 41 | 15 | 0 | 0.0 | 0 | 0 | + 3 |
| Murray Craven, Philadelphia | 51 | 89 | 9 | 10.1 | 0 | 0 | + 4 |
| Adam Creighton, Buffalo | 24 | 42 | 7 | 16.7 | 3 | 0 | − 5 |
| Chicago | 43 | 113 | 15 | 13.3 | 8 | 0 | − 4 |
| Totals | 67 | 155 | 22 | 14.2 | 11 | 0 | − 9 |
| Shawn Cronin, Washington | 1 | 0 | 0 | 0.0 | 0 | 0 | Even |
| Doug Crossman, Los Angeles | 74 | 137 | 10 | 7.3 | 2 | 0 | − 11 |
| Keith Crowder, Boston | 69 | 121 | 15 | 12.4 | 5 | 0 | + 6 |
| John Cullen, Pittsburgh | 79 | 121 | 12 | 9.9 | 8 | 0 | − 25 |
| Randy Cunneyworth, Pittsburgh | 70 | 163 | 25 | 15.3 | 10 | 0 | − 22 |
| Brian Curran, Toronto | 47 | 18 | 1 | 5.6 | 0 | 0 | Even |
| Paul Cyr, N.Y. Rangers | 1 | 0 | 0 | 0.0 | 0 | 0 | Even |
| Ulf Dahlen, N.Y. Rangers | 56 | 147 | 24 | 16.3 | 8 | 0 | − 6 |
| Chris Dahlquist, Pittsburgh | 43 | 27 | 1 | 3.7 | 0 | 0 | − 8 |
| Brad Dalgarno, N.Y. Islanders | 55 | 83 | 11 | 13.3 | 2 | 0 | − 8 |
| Marty Dallman, Toronto | 4 | 2 | 0 | 0.0 | 0 | 0 | Even |
| Rod Dallman, N.Y. Islanders | 1 | 1 | 0 | 0.0 | 0 | 0 | − 1 |
| Vincent Damphousse, Toronto | 80 | 190 | 26 | 13.7 | 6 | 0 | − 8 |
| Ken Daneyko, New Jersey | 80 | 108 | 5 | 4.6 | 1 | 0 | − 22 |
| Dan Daoust, Toronto | 68 | 66 | 7 | 10.6 | 0 | 2 | − 20 |
| Lucien DeBlois, N.Y. Rangers | 73 | 117 | 9 | 7.7 | 0 | 0 | − 6 |
| Dale DeGray, Los Angeles | 63 | 87 | 6 | 6.9 | 0 | 0 | + 3 |
| Gilbert Delorme, Detroit | 42 | 23 | 1 | 4.3 | 0 | 0 | − 11 |
| Larry DePalma, Minnesota | 43 | 42 | 5 | 11.9 | 1 | 0 | − 14 |
| Eric Desjardins, Montreal | 36 | 39 | 2 | 5.1 | 1 | 0 | + 9 |
| Gerald Diduck, N.Y. Islanders | 65 | 132 | 11 | 8.3 | 6 | 0 | + 9 |
| Rob DiMaio, N.Y. Islanders | 16 | 16 | 1 | 6.3 | 0 | 0 | − 6 |
| Gord Dineen, Minnesota | 2 | 7 | 0 | 0.0 | 0 | 0 | − 4 |
| Pittsburgh | 38 | 25 | 1 | 4.0 | 0 | 0 | − 5 |
| Totals | 40 | 32 | 1 | 3.1 | 0 | 0 | − 9 |
| Kevin Dineen, Hartford | 79 | 294 | 45 | 15.3 | 20 | 1 | − 6 |
| Marcel Dionne, N.Y. Rangers | 37 | 74 | 7 | 9.5 | 4 | 0 | − 6 |
| Robert Dirk, St. Louis | 9 | 7 | 0 | 0.0 | 0 | 0 | − 3 |
| Brian Dobbin, Philadelphia | 14 | 13 | 0 | 0.0 | 0 | 0 | − 6 |
| Bobby Dollas, Quebec | 16 | 11 | 0 | 0.0 | 0 | 0 | − 11 |
| Gord Donnelly, Quebec | 16 | 14 | 4 | 28.6 | 1 | 0 | − 8 |
| Winnipeg | 57 | 53 | 6 | 11.3 | 0 | 0 | − 12 |
| Totals | 73 | 67 | 10 | 14.9 | 1 | 0 | − 20 |
| Mike Donnelly, Buffalo | 22 | 25 | 4 | 16.0 | 0 | 0 | − 1 |
| Mario Doyon, Chicago | 7 | 7 | 1 | 14.3 | 1 | 0 | + 2 |
| Bruce Driver, New Jersey | 27 | 69 | 1 | 1.4 | 1 | 0 | Even |
| John Druce, Washington | 48 | 59 | 8 | 13.6 | 0 | 0 | + 7 |
| Gaetan Duchesne, Quebec | 70 | 110 | 8 | 7.3 | 2 | 1 | Even |
| Steve Duchesne, Los Angeles | 79 | 215 | 25 | 11.6 | 8 | 5 | + 31 |
| Donald Dufresne, Montreal | 13 | 5 | 0 | 0.0 | 0 | 0 | + 3 |
| Ron Duguay, Los Angeles | 70 | 80 | 7 | 8.8 | 0 | 0 | + 23 |
| Dale Dunbar, Boston | 1 | 2 | 0 | 0.0 | 0 | 0 | Even |
| Iain Duncan, Winnipeg | 57 | 91 | 14 | 15.4 | 1 | 0 | − 17 |
| Craig Duncanson, Los Angeles | 5 | 1 | 0 | 0.0 | 0 | 0 | − 1 |
| Richie Dunn, Buffalo | 4 | 2 | 0 | 0.0 | 0 | 0 | − 1 |
| Steve Dykstra, Pittsburgh | 65 | 38 | 1 | 2.6 | 0 | 0 | − 12 |
| Mike Eagles, Chicago | 47 | 39 | 5 | 12.8 | 0 | 0 | − 8 |
| Pelle Eklund, Philadelphia | 79 | 121 | 18 | 14.9 | 8 | 1 | + 5 |
| Darren Eliot, Buffalo | 2 | 0 | 0 | 0.0 | 0 | 0 | Even |
| Dave Ellett, Winnipeg | 75 | 209 | 22 | 10.5 | 9 | 2 | − 18 |
| Pat Elynuik, Winnipeg | 56 | 100 | 26 | 26.0 | 5 | 0 | + 5 |
| Jan Erixon, N.Y. Rangers | 44 | 41 | 4 | 9.8 | 0 | 0 | − 3 |
| Bob Errey, Pittsburgh | 76 | 130 | 26 | 20.0 | 0 | 3 | + 40 |
| Doug Evans, St. Louis | 53 | 48 | 7 | 14.6 | 0 | 1 | + 3 |
| Dean Evason, Hartford | 67 | 95 | 11 | 11.6 | 0 | 0 | − 9 |
| Todd Ewen, St. Louis | 34 | 22 | 4 | 18.2 | 0 | 0 | + 4 |
| Glen Featherstone, St. Louis | 18 | 9 | 0 | 0.0 | 0 | 0 | − 3 |
| Bernie Federko, St. Louis | 66 | 115 | 22 | 19.1 | 9 | 0 | − 20 |
| Brent Fedyk, Detroit | 5 | 6 | 2 | 33.3 | 1 | 0 | − 1 |
| Chris Felix, Washington | 21 | 18 | 0 | 0.0 | 0 | 0 | + 7 |
| Paul Fenton, Los Angeles | 21 | 26 | 2 | 7.7 | 0 | 0 | − 1 |
| Winnipeg | 59 | 109 | 14 | 12.8 | 1 | 0 | − 15 |
| Totals | 80 | 135 | 16 | 11.9 | 1 | 0 | − 16 |

| Player — Team | Games | Shots | Goals | Shooting Pct. | PPG | SHG | +/− |
|---|---|---|---|---|---|---|---|
| Dave Fenyves, Philadelphia | 1 | 0 | 0 | 0.0 | 0 | 0 | Even |
| Tom Fergus, Toronto | 80 | 151 | 22 | 14.6 | 10 | 1 | − 38 |
| Mark Ferner, Buffalo | 2 | 0 | 0 | 0.0 | 0 | 0 | − 2 |
| Ray Ferraro, Hartford | 80 | 169 | 41 | 24.3 | 11 | 0 | + 1 |
| Jeff Finley, N.Y. Islanders | 4 | 1 | 0 | 0.0 | 0 | 0 | + 1 |
| Steven Finn, Quebec | 77 | 86 | 2 | 2.3 | 0 | 1 | − 21 |
| Tom Fitzgerald, N.Y. Islanders | 23 | 24 | 3 | 12.5 | 0 | 0 | + 1 |
| Patrick Flatley, N.Y. Islanders | 41 | 72 | 10 | 13.9 | 2 | 1 | − 5 |
| Steve Fletcher, Winnipeg | 3 | 1 | 0 | 0.0 | 0 | 0 | − 1 |
| Theoren Fleury, Calgary | 36 | 89 | 14 | 15.7 | 5 | 0 | + 5 |
| Todd Flichel, Winnipeg | 1 | 1 | 0 | 0.0 | 0 | 0 | − 1 |
| Ron Flockhart, Boston | 4 | 3 | 0 | 0.0 | 0 | 0 | − 3 |
| Mike Foligno, Buffalo | 75 | 144 | 27 | 18.8 | 11 | 0 | − 7 |
| Marc Fortier, Quebec | 57 | 90 | 20 | 22.2 | 2 | 2 | − 18 |
| Corey Foster, New Jersey | 2 | 2 | 0 | 0.0 | 0 | 0 | − 2 |
| Nick Fotiu, Edmonton | 1 | 0 | 0 | 0.0 | 0 | 0 | + 1 |
| Lou Franceschetti, Washington | 63 | 55 | 7 | 12.7 | 0 | 0 | − 4 |
| Ron Francis, Hartford | 69 | 156 | 29 | 18.6 | 8 | 0 | + 4 |
| Curt Fraser, Minnesota | 35 | 58 | 5 | 8.6 | 1 | 0 | − 15 |
| Dan Frawley, Pittsburgh | 46 | 37 | 3 | 8.1 | 0 | 0 | − 1 |
| Mark Freer, Philadelphia | 5 | 1 | 0 | 0.0 | 0 | 0 | Even |
| Miroslav Frycer, Detroit | 23 | 40 | 7 | 17.5 | 2 | 0 | − 4 |
| Edmonton | 14 | 33 | 5 | 15.2 | 2 | 0 | + 2 |
| Totals | 37 | 73 | 12 | 16.4 | 4 | 0 | − 2 |
| Link Gaetz, Minnesota | 12 | 8 | 0 | 0.0 | 0 | 0 | − 3 |
| Paul Gagne, Toronto | 16 | 14 | 3 | 21.4 | 1 | 0 | − 8 |
| Dave Gagner, Minnesota | 75 | 183 | 35 | 19.1 | 11 | 3 | + 13 |
| Bob Gainey, Montreal | 49 | 65 | 10 | 15.4 | 1 | 0 | + 13 |
| Gerard Gallant, Detroit | 76 | 221 | 39 | 17.6 | 13 | 0 | + 7 |
| Garry Galley, Boston | 78 | 145 | 8 | 5.5 | 2 | 1 | − 7 |
| Perry Ganchar, Pittsburgh | 3 | 3 | 0 | 0.0 | 0 | 0 | − 3 |
| Bill Gardner, Chicago | 6 | 4 | 1 | 25.0 | 1 | 0 | + 2 |
| Mike Gartner, Washington | 56 | 190 | 26 | 13.7 | 6 | 0 | + 8 |
| Minnesota | 13 | 33 | 7 | 21.2 | 3 | 0 | + 3 |
| Totals | 69 | 223 | 33 | 14.8 | 9 | 0 | + 11 |
| Dallas Gaume, Hartford | 4 | 5 | 1 | 20.0 | 0 | 0 | + 1 |
| Stewart Gavin, Minnesota | 73 | 129 | 8 | 6.2 | 0 | 1 | + 3 |
| Martin Gelinas, Edmonton | 6 | 14 | 1 | 7.1 | 0 | 0 | − 1 |
| Greg Gilbert, N.Y. Islanders | 55 | 73 | 8 | 11.0 | 0 | 0 | + 1 |
| Chicago | 4 | 2 | 0 | 0.0 | 0 | 0 | + 1 |
| Totals | 59 | 75 | 8 | 10.7 | 0 | 0 | + 2 |
| Brent Gilchrist, Montreal | 49 | 68 | 8 | 11.8 | 0 | 0 | + 9 |
| Curt Giles, Minnesota | 76 | 64 | 5 | 7.8 | 0 | 1 | + 2 |
| Randy Gilhen, Winnipeg | 64 | 76 | 5 | 6.6 | 0 | 1 | − 24 |
| Todd Gill, Toronto | 59 | 92 | 11 | 12.0 | 0 | 0 | − 3 |
| Paul Gillis, Quebec | 79 | 97 | 15 | 15.5 | 5 | 0 | − 14 |
| Doug Gilmour, Calgary | 72 | 161 | 26 | 16.1 | 11 | 0 | + 45 |
| Gaston Gingras, St. Louis | 52 | 98 | 3 | 3.1 | 2 | 0 | + 1 |
| Brian Glynn, Calgary | 9 | 4 | 0 | 0.0 | 0 | 0 | + 1 |
| Steve Gotaas, Minnesota | 12 | 18 | 1 | 5.6 | 1 | 0 | − 1 |
| Bob Gould, Washington | 75 | 91 | 5 | 5.5 | 0 | 1 | − 2 |
| Michel Goulet, Quebec | 69 | 162 | 26 | 16.0 | 11 | 0 | − 20 |
| Dirk Graham, Chicago | 80 | 217 | 33 | 15.2 | 5 | 10 | + 8 |
| Tony Granato, N.Y. Rangers | 78 | 234 | 36 | 15.4 | 4 | 4 | + 17 |
| Adam Graves, Detroit | 56 | 60 | 7 | 11.7 | 0 | 0 | − 5 |
| Rick Green, Montreal | 72 | 42 | 1 | 2.4 | 0 | 0 | + 19 |
| Randy Gregg, Edmonton | 57 | 42 | 3 | 7.1 | 1 | 0 | − 9 |
| Ron Greschner, N.Y. Rangers | 58 | 49 | 1 | 2.0 | 0 | 0 | + 9 |
| Wayne Gretzky, Los Angeles | 78 | 303 | 54 | 17.8 | 11 | 5 | + 15 |
| Stu Grimson, Calgary | 1 | 0 | 0 | 0.0 | 0 | 0 | Even |
| Jari Gronstrand, Quebec | 25 | 18 | 1 | 5.6 | 0 | 0 | − 9 |
| Paul Guay, Los Angeles | 2 | 2 | 0 | 0.0 | 0 | 0 | − 2 |
| Boston | 5 | 1 | 0 | 0.0 | 0 | 0 | Even |
| Totals | 7 | 3 | 0 | 0.0 | 0 | 0 | − 2 |
| Bengt Gustafsson, Washington | 72 | 107 | 18 | 16.8 | 5 | 4 | + 13 |
| Kevan Guy, Vancouver | 45 | 40 | 2 | 5.0 | 0 | 0 | − 14 |
| Marc Habscheid, Minnesota | 76 | 182 | 23 | 12.6 | 7 | 3 | + 2 |
| Bob Halkidis, Buffalo | 16 | 9 | 0 | 0.0 | 0 | 0 | − 1 |
| Doug Halward, Detroit | 18 | 5 | 0 | 0.0 | 0 | 0 | − 11 |
| Edmonton | 24 | 8 | 0 | 0.0 | 0 | 0 | − 3 |
| Totals | 42 | 13 | 0 | 0.0 | 0 | 0 | − 14 |

| Player — Team | Games | Shots | Goals | Shooting Pct. | PPG | SHG | +/− |
|---|---|---|---|---|---|---|---|
| Gilles Hamel, Winnipeg | 1 | 0 | 0 | 0.0 | 0 | 0 | Even |
| Los Angeles | 11 | 11 | 0 | 0.0 | 0 | 0 | − 3 |
| Totals | 12 | 11 | 0 | 0.0 | 0 | 0 | − 3 |
| Ken Hammond, Edmonton | 5 | 1 | 0 | 0.0 | 0 | 0 | − 2 |
| N.Y. Rangers | 3 | 2 | 0 | 0.0 | 0 | 0 | − 3 |
| Toronto | 14 | 9 | 0 | 0.0 | 0 | 0 | − 13 |
| Totals | 22 | 12 | 0 | 0.0 | 0 | 0 | − 18 |
| Dave Hannan, Pittsburgh | 72 | 72 | 10 | 13.9 | 2 | 1 | − 12 |
| Jeff Harding, Philadelphia | 6 | 11 | 0 | 0.0 | 0 | 0 | + 1 |
| Mark Hardy, Minnesota | 15 | 19 | 2 | 10.5 | 0 | 0 | − 1 |
| N.Y. Rangers | 45 | 51 | 2 | 3.9 | 0 | 0 | − 8 |
| Totals | 60 | 70 | 4 | 5.7 | 0 | 0 | − 9 |
| Mike Hartman, Buffalo | 70 | 91 | 8 | 8.8 | 1 | 0 | + 9 |
| Craig Hartsburg, Minnesota | 30 | 75 | 4 | 5.3 | 1 | 0 | − 8 |
| Kevin Hatcher, Washington | 62 | 148 | 13 | 8.8 | 3 | 0 | + 19 |
| Dale Hawerchuk, Winnipeg | 75 | 239 | 41 | 17.2 | 14 | 3 | − 30 |
| Greg Hawgood, Boston | 56 | 132 | 16 | 12.1 | 5 | 0 | + 4 |
| Todd Hawkins, Vancouver | 4 | 2 | 0 | 0.0 | 0 | 0 | − 1 |
| Glenn Healy, Los Angeles | 48 | 0 | 0 | 0.0 | 0 | 0 | Even |
| Raimo Helminen, N.Y. Islanders | 24 | 22 | 1 | 4.5 | 1 | 0 | − 15 |
| Dale Henry, N.Y. Islanders | 22 | 20 | 2 | 10.0 | 0 | 0 | − 4 |
| Matt Hervey, Winnipeg | 2 | 1 | 0 | 0.0 | 0 | 0 | + 2 |
| Tim Higgins, Detroit | 42 | 45 | 5 | 11.1 | 0 | 0 | Even |
| Randy Hillier, Pittsburgh | 68 | 37 | 1 | 2.7 | 0 | 1 | − 4 |
| Ken Hodge, Minnesota | 5 | 6 | 1 | 16.7 | 0 | 0 | + 1 |
| Dan Hodgson, Vancouver | 23 | 38 | 4 | 10.5 | 0 | 0 | + 3 |
| Jim Hofford, Los Angeles | 1 | 0 | 0 | 0.0 | 0 | 0 | + 2 |
| Benoit Hogue, Buffalo | 69 | 114 | 14 | 12.3 | 1 | 2 | − 5 |
| Dean Hopkins, Quebec | 5 | 6 | 0 | 0.0 | 0 | 0 | + 1 |
| Miroslav Horava, N.Y. Rangers | 6 | 7 | 0 | 0.0 | 0 | 0 | − 2 |
| Doug Houda, Detroit | 57 | 38 | 2 | 5.3 | 0 | 0 | + 17 |
| Mike Hough, Quebec | 46 | 51 | 9 | 17.6 | 1 | 3 | − 7 |
| Bill Houlder, Washington | 8 | 5 | 0 | 0.0 | 0 | 0 | + 7 |
| Phil Housley, Buffalo | 72 | 178 | 26 | 14.6 | 5 | 0 | + 6 |
| Mark Howe, Philadelphia | 52 | 95 | 9 | 9.5 | 5 | 1 | + 7 |
| Jiri Hrdina, Calgary | 70 | 147 | 22 | 15.0 | 6 | 0 | + 19 |
| Tony Hrkac, St. Louis | 70 | 133 | 17 | 12.8 | 5 | 0 | − 10 |
| Charlie Huddy, Edmonton | 76 | 178 | 11 | 6.2 | 5 | 2 | Even |
| Mike Hudson, Chicago | 41 | 45 | 7 | 15.6 | 0 | 1 | − 12 |
| Kerry Huffman, Philadelphia | 29 | 23 | 0 | 0.0 | 0 | 0 | Even |
| Brent Hughes, Winnipeg | 28 | 37 | 3 | 8.1 | 0 | 1 | − 7 |
| Brett Hull, St. Louis | 78 | 305 | 41 | 13.4 | 16 | 0 | − 17 |
| Jody Hull, Hartford | 60 | 82 | 16 | 19.5 | 6 | 0 | + 6 |
| Dale Hunter, Washington | 80 | 138 | 20 | 14.5 | 9 | 0 | − 3 |
| Dave Hunter, Winnipeg | 34 | 43 | 3 | 7.0 | 0 | 1 | − 3 |
| Edmonton | 32 | 44 | 3 | 6.8 | 0 | 0 | − 5 |
| Totals | 66 | 87 | 6 | 6.9 | 0 | 1 | − 8 |
| Mark Hunter, Calgary | 66 | 116 | 22 | 19.0 | 12 | 0 | + 4 |
| Tim Hunter, Calgary | 75 | 67 | 3 | 4.5 | 0 | 0 | + 22 |
| Jamie Huscroft, New Jersey | 15 | 9 | 0 | 0.0 | 0 | 0 | − 3 |
| Al Iafrate, Toronto | 65 | 105 | 13 | 12.4 | 1 | 2 | + 3 |
| Miroslav Ihnacak, Detroit | 1 | 1 | 0 | 0.0 | 0 | 0 | Even |
| Peter Ihnacak, Toronto | 26 | 30 | 2 | 6.7 | 0 | 0 | + 3 |
| Kim Issel, Edmonton | 4 | 1 | 0 | 0.0 | 0 | 0 | − 1 |
| Jeff Jackson, Quebec | 33 | 40 | 4 | 10.0 | 0 | 1 | − 15 |
| Craig Janney, Boston | 62 | 95 | 16 | 16.8 | 2 | 0 | + 20 |
| Mark Janssens, N.Y. Rangers | 5 | 4 | 0 | 0.0 | 0 | 0 | − 4 |
| Hannu Jarvenpaa, Winnipeg | 53 | 27 | 4 | 14.8 | 1 | 0 | − 14 |
| Iiro Jarvi, Quebec | 75 | 109 | 11 | 10.1 | 1 | 0 | − 13 |
| Grant Jennings, Hartford | 55 | 39 | 3 | 7.7 | 0 | 0 | + 17 |
| Paul Jerrard, Minnesota | 5 | 8 | 0 | 0.0 | 0 | 0 | + 1 |
| Calle Johansson, Buffalo | 47 | 53 | 2 | 3.8 | 0 | 0 | − 7 |
| Washington | 12 | 22 | 1 | 4.5 | 1 | 0 | + 1 |
| Totals | 59 | 75 | 3 | 4.0 | 1 | 0 | − 6 |
| Jim Johnson, Pittsburgh | 76 | 70 | 2 | 2.9 | 1 | 0 | + 7 |
| Mark Johnson, New Jersey | 40 | 95 | 13 | 13.7 | 4 | 0 | − 1 |
| Greg Johnston, Boston | 57 | 89 | 11 | 12.4 | 0 | 1 | + 7 |
| Brad Jones, Winnipeg | 22 | 25 | 6 | 24.0 | 0 | 1 | Even |
| Tomas Jonsson, N.Y. Islanders | 53 | 103 | 9 | 8.7 | 4 | 1 | − 13 |
| Edmonton | 20 | 46 | 1 | 2.2 | 1 | 0 | − 12 |
| Totals | 73 | 149 | 10 | 6.7 | 5 | 1 | − 25 |

| Player — Team | Games | Shots | Goals | Shooting Pct. | PPG | SHG | +/− |
|---|---|---|---|---|---|---|---|
| Anthony Joseph, Winnipeg | 2 | 4 | 1 | 25.0 | 0 | 0 | + 1 |
| Chris Joseph, Edmonton | 44 | 36 | 4 | 11.1 | 0 | 0 | − 9 |
| Bob Joyce, Boston | 77 | 142 | 18 | 12.7 | 7 | 0 | + 8 |
| Mark Kachowski, Pittsburgh | 12 | 3 | 1 | 33.3 | 0 | 0 | + 1 |
| Trent Kaese, Buffalo | 1 | 5 | 0 | 0.0 | 0 | 0 | Even |
| Kevin Kaminski, Minnesota | 1 | 0 | 0 | 0.0 | 0 | 0 | Even |
| Steve Kasper, Boston | 49 | 82 | 10 | 12.2 | 2 | 0 | − 2 |
| Los Angeles | 29 | 48 | 9 | 18.8 | 3 | 2 | Even |
| Totals | 78 | 130 | 19 | 14.6 | 5 | 2 | − 2 |
| Ed Kastelic, Hartford | 10 | 6 | 0 | 0.0 | 0 | 0 | Even |
| Mike Keane, Montreal | 69 | 90 | 16 | 17.8 | 5 | 0 | + 9 |
| Dean Kennedy, N.Y. Rangers | 16 | 7 | 0 | 0.0 | 0 | 0 | − 1 |
| Los Angeles | 51 | 38 | 3 | 7.9 | 0 | 0 | + 18 |
| Totals | 67 | 45 | 3 | 6.7 | 0 | 0 | + 17 |
| Alan Kerr, N.Y. Islanders | 71 | 147 | 20 | 13.6 | 6 | 0 | − 5 |
| Tim Kerr, Philadelphia | 69 | 236 | 48 | 20.3 | 25 | 0 | − 4 |
| Ian Kidd, Vancouver | 1 | 0 | 0 | 0.0 | 0 | 0 | − 1 |
| Darin Kimble, Quebec | 26 | 21 | 3 | 14.3 | 0 | 0 | − 5 |
| Chris King, Detroit | 55 | 34 | 2 | 5.9 | 0 | 0 | − 7 |
| Derek King, N.Y. Islanders | 60 | 103 | 14 | 13.6 | 4 | 0 | + 10 |
| Kelly Kisio, N.Y. Rangers | 70 | 128 | 26 | 20.3 | 2 | 0 | + 14 |
| Scot Kleinendorst, Hartford | 24 | 7 | 0 | 0.0 | 0 | 0 | − 11 |
| Washington | 3 | 0 | 0 | 0.0 | 0 | 0 | Even |
| Totals | 27 | 7 | 0 | 0.0 | 0 | 0 | − 11 |
| Petr Klima, Detroit | 51 | 145 | 25 | 17.2 | 1 | 0 | + 5 |
| Gord Kluzak, Boston | 3 | 4 | 0 | 0.0 | 0 | 0 | − 2 |
| Joey Kocur, Detroit | 60 | 76 | 9 | 11.8 | 1 | 0 | − 4 |
| Dean Kolstad, Minnesota | 25 | 41 | 1 | 2.4 | 1 | 0 | − 5 |
| Steve Konroyd, N.Y. Islanders | 21 | 30 | 1 | 3.3 | 0 | 0 | − 5 |
| Chicago | 57 | 102 | 5 | 4.9 | 0 | 0 | − 11 |
| Totals | 78 | 132 | 6 | 4.5 | 0 | 0 | − 16 |
| Chris Kontos, Los Angeles | 7 | 9 | 2 | 22.2 | 1 | 0 | + 2 |
| John Kordic, Montreal | 6 | 2 | 0 | 0.0 | 0 | 0 | − 1 |
| Toronto | 46 | 33 | 1 | 3.0 | 0 | 0 | − 13 |
| Totals | 52 | 35 | 1 | 2.9 | 0 | 0 | − 14 |
| Jim Korn, New Jersey | 65 | 65 | 15 | 23.1 | 4 | 0 | − 3 |
| Chris Kotsopoulos, Toronto | 57 | 66 | 1 | 1.5 | 0 | 0 | − 4 |
| Dale Krentz, Detroit | 16 | 27 | 3 | 11.1 | 0 | 0 | − 3 |
| Rich Kromm, N.Y. Islanders | 20 | 12 | 1 | 8.3 | 0 | 0 | − 3 |
| Uwe Krupp, Buffalo | 70 | 51 | 5 | 9.8 | 0 | 1 | Even |
| Mike Krushelnyski, Los Angeles | 78 | 143 | 26 | 18.2 | 5 | 0 | + 9 |
| Robert Kudelski, Los Angeles | 14 | 15 | 1 | 6.7 | 0 | 0 | − 5 |
| Stu Kulak, Winnipeg | 18 | 18 | 2 | 11.1 | 1 | 0 | − 6 |
| Jari Kurri, Edmonton | 76 | 214 | 44 | 20.6 | 10 | 5 | + 19 |
| Tom Kurvers, New Jersey | 74 | 190 | 16 | 8.4 | 5 | 0 | + 11 |
| Markku Kyllonen, Winnipeg | 9 | 7 | 0 | 0.0 | 0 | 0 | − 3 |
| Jim Kyte, Winnipeg | 74 | 56 | 3 | 5.4 | 0 | 0 | − 25 |
| Normand Lacombe, Edmonton | 64 | 71 | 17 | 23.9 | 2 | 0 | + 2 |
| Randy Ladouceur, Hartford | 75 | 56 | 2 | 3.6 | 0 | 0 | − 23 |
| Guy Lafleur, N.Y. Rangers | 67 | 122 | 18 | 14.8 | 6 | 0 | + 1 |
| Pat LaFontaine, N.Y. Islanders | 79 | 288 | 45 | 15.6 | 16 | 0 | − 8 |
| Jason Lafreniere, N.Y. Rangers | 38 | 42 | 8 | 19.0 | 3 | 0 | − 3 |
| Tom Laidlaw, Los Angeles | 70 | 31 | 3 | 9.7 | 0 | 0 | + 30 |
| Mike Lalor, Montreal | 12 | 12 | 1 | 8.3 | 0 | 0 | − 1 |
| St. Louis | 36 | 40 | 1 | 2.5 | 0 | 0 | + 15 |
| Totals | 48 | 52 | 2 | 3.8 | 0 | 0 | + 14 |
| Mark Lamb, Edmonton | 20 | 20 | 2 | 10.0 | 1 | 0 | + 4 |
| Lane Lambert, Quebec | 13 | 19 | 2 | 10.5 | 0 | 0 | − 2 |
| Rod Langway, Washington | 76 | 80 | 2 | 2.5 | 0 | 0 | + 12 |
| Rick Lanz, Toronto | 32 | 56 | 1 | 1.8 | 0 | 0 | − 17 |
| Steve Larmer, Chicago | 80 | 269 | 43 | 16.0 | 19 | 1 | + 2 |
| Guy Larose, Winnipeg | 3 | 2 | 0 | 0.0 | 0 | 0 | − 1 |
| Reed Larson, Edmonton | 10 | 19 | 2 | 10.5 | 0 | 1 | + 1 |
| N.Y. Islanders | 33 | 77 | 7 | 9.1 | 6 | 0 | − 8 |
| Minnesota | 11 | 19 | 0 | 0.0 | 0 | 0 | − 3 |
| Totals | 54 | 115 | 9 | 7.8 | 6 | 1 | − 10 |
| Jim Latos, N.Y. Rangers | 1 | 0 | 0 | 0.0 | 0 | 0 | − 1 |
| Dave Latta, Quebec | 24 | 30 | 4 | 13.3 | 1 | 0 | − 8 |
| Brad Lauer, N.Y. Islanders | 14 | 21 | 3 | 14.3 | 0 | 0 | − 2 |
| Craig Laughlin, Toronto | 66 | 87 | 10 | 11.5 | 0 | 0 | − 22 |
| Peter Laviolette, N.Y. Rangers | 12 | 2 | 0 | 0.0 | 0 | 0 | + 2 |

| Player — Team | Games | Shots | Goals | Shooting Pct. | PPG | SHG | +/− |
|---|---|---|---|---|---|---|---|
| Dominic Lavoie, St. Louis | 1 | 1 | 0 | 0.0 | 0 | 0 | + 2 |
| Paul Lawless, Toronto | 7 | 11 | 0 | 0.0 | 0 | 0 | − 2 |
| Brian Lawton, N.Y. Rangers | 30 | 58 | 7 | 12.1 | 3 | 0 | − 2 |
| Hartford | 35 | 70 | 10 | 14.3 | 7 | 0 | − 9 |
| Totals | 65 | 128 | 17 | 13.3 | 10 | 0 | − 11 |
| Derek Laxdal, Toronto | 41 | 41 | 9 | 22.0 | 1 | 0 | − 11 |
| Stephen Leach, Washington | 74 | 145 | 11 | 7.6 | 4 | 0 | − 4 |
| Stephane Lebeau, Montreal | 1 | 1 | 0 | 0.0 | 0 | 0 | + 1 |
| John LeBlanc, Edmonton | 2 | 5 | 1 | 20.0 | 0 | 0 | Even |
| Grant Ledyard, Washington | 61 | 81 | 3 | 3.7 | 1 | 0 | + 1 |
| Buffalo | 13 | 25 | 1 | 4.0 | 0 | 0 | + 1 |
| Totals | 74 | 106 | 4 | 3.8 | 1 | 0 | + 2 |
| Gary Leeman, Toronto | 61 | 195 | 32 | 16.4 | 7 | 1 | + 5 |
| Brian Leetch, N.Y. Rangers | 68 | 268 | 23 | 8.6 | 8 | 3 | + 8 |
| Tom Lehmann, Boston | 26 | 26 | 4 | 15.4 | 1 | 1 | − 7 |
| Moe Lemay, Boston | 12 | 6 | 0 | 0.0 | 0 | 0 | − 5 |
| Winnipeg | 10 | 15 | 1 | 6.7 | 0 | 0 | − 3 |
| Totals | 22 | 21 | 1 | 4.8 | 0 | 0 | − 8 |
| Claude Lemieux, Montreal | 69 | 220 | 29 | 13.2 | 7 | 0 | + 14 |
| Jocelyn Lemieux, Montreal | 1 | 0 | 0 | 0.0 | 0 | 0 | − 1 |
| Mario Lemieux, Pittsburgh | 76 | 313 | 85 | 27.2 | 31 | 13 | + 41 |
| Francois Leroux, Edmonton | 2 | 0 | 0 | 0.0 | 0 | 0 | + 1 |
| Curtis Leschyshyn, Quebec | 71 | 58 | 4 | 6.9 | 1 | 1 | − 32 |
| Rick Lessard, Calgary | 6 | 0 | 0 | 0.0 | 0 | 0 | − 2 |
| Igor Liba, N.Y. Rangers | 10 | 14 | 2 | 14.3 | 1 | 0 | + 1 |
| Los Angeles | 27 | 28 | 5 | 17.9 | 1 | 0 | − 4 |
| Totals | 37 | 42 | 7 | 16.7 | 2 | 0 | − 3 |
| Doug Lidster, Vancouver | 63 | 116 | 5 | 4.3 | 3 | 0 | − 4 |
| Trevor Linden, Vancouver | 80 | 186 | 30 | 16.1 | 10 | 1 | − 10 |
| Ken Linseman, Boston | 78 | 159 | 27 | 17.0 | 13 | 1 | + 15 |
| Bob Logan, Los Angeles | 4 | 0 | 0 | 0.0 | 0 | 0 | Even |
| Claude Loiselle, New Jersey | 74 | 92 | 7 | 7.6 | 0 | 1 | − 10 |
| Troy Loney, Pittsburgh | 69 | 90 | 10 | 11.1 | 0 | 0 | − 5 |
| Hakan Loob, Calgary | 79 | 223 | 27 | 12.1 | 5 | 0 | + 28 |
| Kevin Lowe, Edmonton | 76 | 85 | 7 | 8.2 | 0 | 0 | + 26 |
| Dave Lowry, St. Louis | 21 | 22 | 3 | 13.6 | 0 | 1 | + 1 |
| Jan Ludvig, Buffalo | 13 | 11 | 0 | 0.0 | 0 | 0 | − 1 |
| Craig Ludwig, Montreal | 74 | 83 | 3 | 3.6 | 0 | 1 | + 33 |
| Steve Ludzik, Chicago | 6 | 7 | 1 | 14.3 | 0 | 0 | Even |
| Jyrki Lumme, Montreal | 21 | 18 | 1 | 5.6 | 1 | 0 | + 3 |
| Paul MacDermid, Hartford | 74 | 113 | 17 | 15.0 | 5 | 0 | + 1 |
| Al MacInnis, Calgary | 79 | 277 | 16 | 5.8 | 8 | 0 | + 38 |
| Norm Maciver, N.Y. Rangers | 26 | 36 | 0 | 0.0 | 0 | 0 | − 3 |
| Hartford | 37 | 51 | 1 | 2.0 | 1 | 0 | Even |
| Totals | 63 | 87 | 1 | 1.1 | 1 | 0 | − 3 |
| Dave Mackey, Chicago | 23 | 15 | 1 | 6.7 | 0 | 0 | − 1 |
| John MacLean, New Jersey | 74 | 266 | 42 | 15.8 | 14 | 0 | + 26 |
| Paul MacLean, Detroit | 76 | 148 | 36 | 24.3 | 16 | 0 | + 7 |
| Brian MacLellan, Minnesota | 60 | 114 | 16 | 14.0 | 7 | 0 | Even |
| Calgary | 12 | 23 | 2 | 8.7 | 0 | 0 | + 3 |
| Totals | 72 | 137 | 18 | 13.1 | 7 | 0 | + 3 |
| Jamie Macoun, Calgary | 72 | 89 | 8 | 9.0 | 0 | 0 | + 40 |
| Craig MacTavish, Edmonton | 80 | 120 | 21 | 17.5 | 2 | 4 | + 10 |
| Kevin Maguire, Buffalo | 60 | 35 | 8 | 22.9 | 0 | 0 | + 9 |
| Jacques Mailhot, Quebec | 5 | 0 | 0 | 0.0 | 0 | 0 | Even |
| Mikko Makela, N.Y. Islanders | 76 | 123 | 17 | 13.8 | 4 | 0 | − 16 |
| David Maley, New Jersey | 68 | 63 | 5 | 7.9 | 0 | 0 | − 27 |
| Don Maloney, N.Y. Rangers | 31 | 38 | 4 | 10.5 | 0 | 0 | + 2 |
| Hartford | 21 | 34 | 3 | 8.8 | 1 | 0 | + 1 |
| Totals | 52 | 72 | 7 | 9.7 | 1 | 0 | + 3 |
| Dave Manson, Chicago | 79 | 224 | 18 | 8.0 | 8 | 1 | + 5 |
| Moe Mantha, Minnesota | 16 | 32 | 1 | 3.1 | 1 | 0 | + 1 |
| Philadelphia | 30 | 71 | 3 | 4.2 | 2 | 0 | − 5 |
| Totals | 46 | 103 | 4 | 3.9 | 3 | 0 | − 4 |
| Bryan Marchment, Winnipeg | 2 | 1 | 0 | 0.0 | 0 | 0 | Even |
| Dan Marois, Toronto | 76 | 146 | 31 | 21.2 | 7 | 0 | − 4 |
| Mario Marois, Winnipeg | 7 | 10 | 1 | 10.0 | 1 | 0 | − 6 |
| Quebec | 42 | 61 | 2 | 3.3 | 0 | 0 | − 15 |
| Totals | 49 | 71 | 3 | 4.2 | 1 | 0 | − 21 |
| Brad Marsh, Toronto | 80 | 69 | 1 | 1.4 | 0 | 0 | − 16 |
| Tom Martin, Minnesota | 4 | 6 | 1 | 16.7 | 0 | 0 | + 1 |

| Player — Team | Games | Shots | Goals | Shooting Pct. | PPG | SHG | +/− |
|---|---|---|---|---|---|---|---|
| Hartford | 38 | 40 | 7 | 17.5 | 0 | 0 | + 8 |
| Totals | 42 | 46 | 8 | 17.4 | 0 | 0 | + 9 |
| Steve Martinson, Montreal | 25 | 8 | 1 | 12.5 | 0 | 0 | − 1 |
| Dennis Maruk, Minnesota | 6 | 6 | 0 | 0.0 | 0 | 0 | Even |
| Alan May, Edmonton | 3 | 3 | 1 | 33.3 | 0 | 0 | Even |
| Jay Mazur, Vancouver | 1 | 0 | 0 | 0.0 | 0 | 0 | Even |
| Andrew McBain, Winnipeg | 80 | 180 | 37 | 20.6 | 20 | 1 | − 35 |
| Wayne McBean, Los Angeles | 33 | 19 | 0 | 0.0 | 0 | 0 | − 9 |
| N. Y. Islanders | 19 | 17 | 0 | 0.0 | 0 | 0 | − 4 |
| Totals | 52 | 36 | 0 | 0.0 | 0 | 0 | − 13 |
| Kevin McClelland, Edmonton | 79 | 43 | 6 | 14.0 | 0 | 0 | − 10 |
| Brad McCrimmon, Calgary | 72 | 78 | 5 | 6.4 | 2 | 1 | + 43 |
| Lanny McDonald, Calgary | 51 | 72 | 11 | 15.3 | 0 | 0 | − 1 |
| Hubie McDonough, Los Angeles | 4 | 3 | 0 | 0.0 | 0 | 0 | + 2 |
| Bob McGill, Chicago | 68 | 38 | 0 | 0.0 | 0 | 0 | + 9 |
| Mike McHugh, Minnesota | 3 | 1 | 0 | 0.0 | 0 | 0 | − 1 |
| Randy McKay, Detroit | 3 | 2 | 0 | 0.0 | 0 | 0 | − 1 |
| Tony McKegney, St. Louis | 71 | 154 | 25 | 16.2 | 7 | 0 | − 1 |
| Sean McKenna, Toronto | 3 | 1 | 0 | 0.0 | 0 | 0 | − 1 |
| Dave McLlwain, Pittsburgh | 24 | 14 | 1 | 7.1 | 0 | 0 | − 11 |
| George McPhee, New Jersey | 1 | 0 | 0 | 0.0 | 0 | 0 | + 1 |
| Mike McPhee, Montreal | 73 | 154 | 19 | 12.3 | 1 | 1 | + 14 |
| Basil McRae, Minnesota | 78 | 122 | 12 | 9.8 | 4 | 0 | − 8 |
| Chris McRae, Toronto | 3 | 0 | 0 | 0.0 | 0 | 0 | Even |
| Ken McRae, Quebec | 37 | 47 | 6 | 12.8 | 1 | 0 | − 9 |
| Marty McSorley, Los Angeles | 66 | 87 | 10 | 11.5 | 2 | 0 | + 3 |
| Rick Meagher, St. Louis | 78 | 109 | 15 | 13.8 | 0 | 1 | + 9 |
| Scott Mellanby, Philadelphia | 76 | 202 | 21 | 10.4 | 11 | 0 | − 13 |
| Larry Melnyk, Vancouver | 74 | 59 | 3 | 5.1 | 0 | 1 | + 3 |
| Mark Messier, Edmonton | 72 | 164 | 33 | 20.1 | 6 | 6 | − 5 |
| Mitch Messier, Minnesota | 3 | 3 | 0 | 0.0 | 0 | 0 | − 1 |
| Scott Metcalf, Buffalo | 9 | 11 | 1 | 9.1 | 0 | 0 | − 1 |
| Mike Millar, Washington | 18 | 37 | 6 | 16.2 | 3 | 0 | − 4 |
| Brad Miller, Buffalo | 7 | 0 | 0 | 0.0 | 0 | 0 | − 1 |
| Kelly Miller, Washington | 78 | 121 | 19 | 15.7 | 2 | 1 | + 13 |
| Kevin Miller, N. Y. Rangers | 24 | 40 | 3 | 7.5 | 0 | 0 | − 1 |
| Jay Miller, Boston | 37 | 14 | 2 | 14.3 | 0 | 0 | − 6 |
| Los Angeles | 29 | 16 | 5 | 31.3 | 0 | 0 | − 3 |
| Totals | 66 | 30 | 7 | 23.3 | 0 | 0 | − 9 |
| Carl Mokosak, Boston | 7 | 3 | 0 | 0.0 | 0 | 0 | − 2 |
| John Mokosak, Detroit | 8 | 0 | 0 | 0.0 | 0 | 0 | Even |
| Randy Moller, Quebec | 74 | 117 | 7 | 6.0 | 2 | 0 | + 2 |
| Sergio Momesso, St. Louis | 53 | 81 | 9 | 11.1 | 0 | 0 | − 1 |
| Jayson More, N. Y. Rangers | 1 | 0 | 0 | 0.0 | 0 | 0 | − 1 |
| Jon Morris, New Jersey | 4 | 1 | 0 | 0.0 | 0 | 0 | Even |
| Ken Morrow, N. Y. Islanders | 34 | 27 | 1 | 3.7 | 0 | 0 | − 7 |
| Brian Mullen, N. Y. Rangers | 78 | 217 | 29 | 13.4 | 8 | 3 | + 7 |
| Joe Mullen, Calgary | 79 | 270 | 51 | 18.9 | 13 | 1 | + 51 |
| Kirk Muller, New Jersey | 80 | 182 | 31 | 17.0 | 12 | 1 | − 23 |
| Craig Muni, Edmonton | 69 | 40 | 5 | 12.5 | 0 | 0 | + 43 |
| Gordon Murphy, Philadelphia | 75 | 116 | 4 | 3.4 | 3 | 0 | − 3 |
| Joe Murphy, Detroit | 26 | 29 | 1 | 3.4 | 0 | 0 | − 7 |
| Larry Murphy, Washington | 65 | 129 | 7 | 5.4 | 3 | 0 | − 5 |
| Minnesota | 13 | 31 | 4 | 12.9 | 3 | 0 | + 5 |
| Totals | 78 | 160 | 11 | 6.9 | 6 | 0 | Even |
| Rob Murphy, Vancouver | 8 | 10 | 0 | 0.0 | 0 | 0 | − 1 |
| Bob Murray, Chicago | 15 | 19 | 2 | 10.5 | 2 | 0 | − 4 |
| Troy Murray, Chicago | 79 | 156 | 21 | 13.5 | 5 | 2 | Even |
| Dana Murzyn, Calgary | 63 | 91 | 3 | 3.3 | 0 | 1 | + 26 |
| Frantisek Musil, Minnesota | 55 | 78 | 1 | 1.3 | 0 | 0 | + 4 |
| Don Nachbaur, Philadelphia | 15 | 10 | 1 | 10.0 | 0 | 0 | − 1 |
| Mark Napier, Buffalo | 66 | 92 | 11 | 12.0 | 0 | 2 | − 3 |
| Mats Naslund, Montreal | 77 | 165 | 33 | 20.0 | 14 | 0 | + 34 |
| Ric Nattress, Calgary | 38 | 28 | 1 | 3.6 | 0 | 0 | + 12 |
| Cam Neely, Boston | 74 | 235 | 37 | 15.7 | 18 | 0 | + 14 |
| Ray Neufeld, Winnipeg | 31 | 47 | 5 | 10.6 | 0 | 0 | − 9 |
| Boston | 14 | 16 | 1 | 6.3 | 0 | 0 | − 2 |
| Totals | 45 | 63 | 6 | 9.5 | 0 | 0 | − 11 |
| Bernie Nicholls, Los Angeles | 79 | 385 | 70 | 18.2 | 21 | 8 | + 30 |
| Joe Nieuwendyk, Calgary | 77 | 215 | 21 | 23.7 | 19 | 3 | + 26 |
| Chris Nilan, N. Y. Rangers | 38 | 39 | 7 | 17.9 | 0 | 0 | − 8 |

| Player — Team | Games | Shots | Goals | Shooting Pct. | PPG | SHG | +/− |
|---|---|---|---|---|---|---|---|
| Jim Nill, Detroit | 71 | 39 | 8 | 20.5 | 0 | 1 | − 1 |
| Brian Noonan, Chicago | 45 | 84 | 4 | 4.8 | 2 | 0 | − 2 |
| Robert Nordmark, Vancouver | 80 | 156 | 6 | 3.8 | 5 | 0 | − 4 |
| Jeff Norton, N. Y. Islanders | 69 | 126 | 1 | 0.8 | 1 | 0 | − 24 |
| Lee Norwood, Detroit | 66 | 97 | 10 | 10.3 | 4 | 1 | + 6 |
| Teppo Numminen, Winnipeg | 69 | 85 | 1 | 1.2 | 0 | 1 | − 11 |
| Gary Nyland, Chicago | 23 | 26 | 3 | 11.5 | 0 | 0 | − 4 |
| N. Y. Islanders | 46 | 48 | 4 | 8.3 | 0 | 0 | − 15 |
| Totals | 69 | 74 | 7 | 9.5 | 0 | 0 | − 19 |
| Adam Oates, Detroit | 69 | 127 | 16 | 12.6 | 2 | 0 | − 1 |
| Selmar Odelein, Edmonton | 2 | 0 | 0 | 0.0 | 0 | 0 | − 1 |
| John Ogrodnick, N. Y. Rangers | 60 | 149 | 13 | 8.7 | 1 | 0 | Even |
| Janne Ojanen, New Jersey | 3 | 1 | 0 | 0.0 | 0 | 0 | − 1 |
| Fredrik Olausson, Winnipeg | 75 | 178 | 15 | 8.4 | 4 | 0 | + 6 |
| Ed Olczyk, Toronto | 80 | 249 | 38 | 15.3 | 11 | 2 | Even |
| Mark Osborne, Toronto | 75 | 118 | 16 | 13.6 | 5 | 0 | − 5 |
| Joel Otto, Calgary | 72 | 123 | 23 | 18.7 | 10 | 2 | + 12 |
| Jack O'Callahan, New Jersey | 36 | 96 | 5 | 5.2 | 5 | 0 | Even |
| Mike O'Connell, Detroit | 66 | 49 | 1 | 2.0 | 0 | 0 | − 8 |
| Bill O'Dwyer, Boston | 19 | 18 | 1 | 5.6 | 0 | 0 | − 4 |
| Jeff Parker, Buffalo | 57 | 78 | 9 | 11.5 | 0 | 0 | + 3 |
| Dusan Pasek, Minnesota | 48 | 86 | 4 | 4.7 | 1 | 0 | − 8 |
| Dave Pasin, Los Angeles | 5 | 2 | 0 | 0.0 | 0 | 0 | − 1 |
| Greg Paslawski, St. Louis | 75 | 179 | 26 | 14.5 | 8 | 0 | + 8 |
| Joe Paterson, N.Y. Rangers | 20 | 8 | 0 | 0.0 | 0 | 0 | − 3 |
| James Patrick, N.Y. Rangers | 68 | 147 | 11 | 7.5 | 6 | 0 | + 3 |
| Colin Patterson, Calgary | 74 | 103 | 14 | 13.6 | 0 | 0 | + 44 |
| Jim Pavese, Detroit | 39 | 27 | 3 | 11.1 | 0 | 0 | − 1 |
| Hartford | 5 | 6 | 0 | 0.0 | 0 | 0 | − 1 |
| Totals | 44 | 33 | 3 | 9.1 | 0 | 0 | − 2 |
| Kevin Paynter, Chicago | 1 | 0 | 0 | 0.0 | 0 | 0 | − 1 |
| Scott Pearson, Toronto | 9 | 6 | 0 | 0.0 | 0 | 0 | Even |
| Allen Pedersen, Boston | 51 | 24 | 0 | 0.0 | 0 | 0 | − 3 |
| Barry Pederson, Vancouver | 62 | 98 | 15 | 15.3 | 7 | 1 | + 5 |
| Jim Peplinski, Calgary | 79 | 103 | 13 | 12.6 | 0 | 0 | + 6 |
| Brent Peterson, Hartford | 66 | 56 | 4 | 7.1 | 0 | 0 | + 2 |
| Michel Petit, N.Y. Rangers | 69 | 132 | 8 | 6.1 | 5 | 0 | − 15 |
| Robert Picard, Quebec | 74 | 102 | 7 | 6.9 | 2 | 1 | − 28 |
| Richard Pilon, N.Y. Islanders | 62 | 47 | 0 | 0.0 | 0 | 0 | − 9 |
| Michal Pivonka, Washington | 52 | 73 | 8 | 11.0 | 1 | 0 | + 9 |
| Jim Playfair, Chicago | 7 | 1 | 0 | 0.0 | 0 | 0 | + 1 |
| Larry Playfair, Los Angeles | 6 | 4 | 0 | 0.0 | 0 | 0 | + 3 |
| Buffalo | 42 | 6 | 0 | 0.0 | 0 | 0 | − 10 |
| Totals | 48 | 10 | 0 | 0.0 | 0 | 0 | − 7 |
| Walt Poddubny, Quebec | 72 | 197 | 38 | 19.3 | 14 | 0 | − 18 |
| Ray Podloski, Boston | 8 | 3 | 0 | 0.0 | 0 | 0 | − 1 |
| Rudy Poeschek, N.Y. Rangers | 52 | 17 | 0 | 0.0 | 0 | 0 | − 8 |
| Dave Poulin, Philadelphia | 69 | 81 | 18 | 22.2 | 1 | 5 | + 4 |
| Petr Prajsler, Los Angeles | 2 | 1 | 0 | 0.0 | 0 | 0 | + 4 |
| Wayne Presley, Chicago | 72 | 132 | 21 | 15.9 | 4 | 3 | − 3 |
| Sergei Priakin, Calgary | 2 | 2 | 0 | 0.0 | 0 | 0 | + 1 |
| Ken Priestlay, Buffalo | 15 | 20 | 2 | 10.0 | 0 | 0 | − 8 |
| Bob Probert, Detroit | 25 | 23 | 4 | 17.4 | 1 | 0 | − 11 |
| Brian Propp, Philadelphia | 77 | 245 | 32 | 13.1 | 13 | 2 | + 16 |
| Chris Pryor, N.Y. Islanders | 7 | 2 | 0 | 0.0 | 0 | 0 | − 6 |
| Mike Pucinski, Chicago | 1 | 0 | 0 | 0.0 | 0 | 0 | Even |
| Joel Quenneville, Hartford | 69 | 45 | 4 | 8.9 | 0 | 0 | + 3 |
| Dan Quinn, Pittsburgh | 79 | 200 | 34 | 17.0 | 16 | 0 | − 37 |
| Stephane Quintal, Boston | 26 | 23 | 0 | 0.0 | 0 | 0 | − 5 |
| Herb Raglan, St. Louis | 50 | 86 | 7 | 8.1 | 0 | 0 | − 8 |
| Rob Ramage, Calgary | 68 | 91 | 3 | 3.3 | 2 | 0 | + 26 |
| Mike Ramsey, Buffalo | 56 | 63 | 2 | 3.2 | 0 | 0 | + 5 |
| Paul Ranheim, Calgary | 5 | 4 | 0 | 0.0 | 0 | 0 | − 3 |
| Mark Recchi, Pittsburgh | 15 | 11 | 1 | 9.1 | 0 | 0 | − 2 |
| Craig Redmond, Edmonton | 21 | 29 | 3 | 10.3 | 3 | 0 | − 10 |
| Mark Reeds, Hartford | 7 | 6 | 0 | 0.0 | 0 | 0 | − 1 |
| Joe Reekie, Buffalo | 15 | 14 | 1 | 7.1 | 1 | 0 | + 6 |
| Dave Reid, Toronto | 77 | 87 | 9 | 10.3 | 1 | 1 | + 12 |
| Dave Reierson, Calgary | 2 | 1 | 0 | 0.0 | 0 | 0 | + 1 |
| Paul Reinhart, Vancouver | 64 | 133 | 7 | 5.3 | 3 | 0 | − 4 |
| Luke Richardson, Toronto | 55 | 59 | 2 | 3.4 | 0 | 0 | − 15 |

| Player — Team | Games | Shots | Goals | Shooting Pct. | PPG | SHG | +/− |
|---|---|---|---|---|---|---|---|
| Stephane Richer, Montreal | 68 | 214 | 25 | 11.7 | 11 | 0 | + 4 |
| Steve Richmond, Los Angeles | 9 | 1 | 0 | 0.0 | 0 | 0 | + 2 |
| Dave Richter, St. Louis | 66 | 23 | 1 | 4.3 | 0 | 0 | − 21 |
| Mike Ridley, Washington | 80 | 187 | 41 | 21.9 | 16 | 0 | + 17 |
| Gary Roberts, Calgary | 71 | 123 | 22 | 17.9 | 0 | 1 | + 32 |
| Gordie Roberts, St. Louis | 77 | 52 | 2 | 3.8 | 0 | 0 | + 7 |
| Torrie Robertson, Hartford | 27 | 21 | 2 | 9.5 | 0 | 0 | − 3 |
| Detroit | 12 | 5 | 2 | 40.0 | 0 | 0 | Even |
| Totals | 39 | 26 | 4 | 15.4 | 0 | 0 | − 3 |
| Larry Robinson, Montreal | 74 | 79 | 4 | 5.1 | 0 | 0 | + 23 |
| Luc Robitaille, Los Angeles | 78 | 237 | 46 | 19.4 | 10 | 0 | + 5 |
| Normand Rochefort, N.Y. Rangers | 11 | 14 | 1 | 7.1 | 0 | 0 | Even |
| Jeremy Roenick, Chicago | 20 | 52 | 9 | 17.3 | 2 | 0 | + 4 |
| Jeff Rohlicek, Vancouver | 2 | 2 | 0 | 0.0 | 0 | 0 | Even |
| Cliff Ronning, St. Louis | 64 | 150 | 24 | 16.0 | 16 | 0 | + 3 |
| Steve Rooney, New Jersey | 25 | 23 | 3 | 13.0 | 0 | 0 | − 9 |
| Magnus Roupe, Philadelphia | 7 | 15 | 1 | 6.7 | 0 | 0 | + 1 |
| Bob Rouse, Minnesota | 66 | 66 | 4 | 6.1 | 0 | 1 | − 5 |
| Washington | 13 | 19 | 0 | 0.0 | 0 | 0 | + 2 |
| Totals | 79 | 85 | 4 | 4.7 | 0 | 1 | − 3 |
| Lindy Ruff, Buffalo | 63 | 69 | 6 | 8.7 | 0 | 0 | − 17 |
| N.Y. Rangers | 13 | 19 | 0 | 0.0 | 0 | 0 | − 6 |
| Totals | 76 | 88 | 6 | 6.8 | 0 | 0 | − 23 |
| Terry Ruskowski, Minnesota | 3 | 2 | 1 | 50.0 | 0 | 0 | + 1 |
| Christian Ruuttu, Buffalo | 67 | 149 | 14 | 9.4 | 5 | 0 | + 13 |
| Warren Rychel, Chicago | 2 | 3 | 0 | 0.0 | 0 | 0 | − 1 |
| Ken Sabourin, Calgary | 6 | 2 | 0 | 0.0 | 0 | 0 | + 3 |
| Joe Sakic, Quebec | 70 | 148 | 23 | 15.5 | 10 | 0 | − 36 |
| Borje Salming, Toronto | 63 | 58 | 3 | 5.2 | 1 | 0 | + 7 |
| Kjell Samuelsson, Philadelphia | 69 | 60 | 3 | 5.0 | 0 | 1 | + 13 |
| Ulf Samuelsson, Hartford | 71 | 122 | 9 | 7.4 | 3 | 0 | + 23 |
| Jim Sandlak, Vancouver | 72 | 164 | 20 | 12.2 | 9 | 0 | + 8 |
| Tomas Sandstrom, N.Y. Rangers | 79 | 240 | 32 | 13.3 | 11 | 2 | + 5 |
| Everett Sanipass, Chicago | 50 | 51 | 6 | 11.8 | 0 | 0 | − 7 |
| Denis Savard, Chicago | 58 | 182 | 23 | 12.6 | 7 | 5 | − 5 |
| Wally Schreiber, Minnesota | 25 | 41 | 2 | 4.9 | 1 | 0 | − 5 |
| Glen Seabrooke, Philadelphia | 3 | 0 | 0 | 0.0 | 0 | 0 | − 1 |
| Al Secord, Toronto | 40 | 52 | 5 | 9.6 | 1 | 0 | − 13 |
| Philadelphia | 20 | 15 | 1 | 6.7 | 0 | 0 | − 7 |
| Totals | 60 | 67 | 6 | 9.0 | 1 | 0 | − 20 |
| Brendan Shanahan, New Jersey | 68 | 152 | 22 | 14.5 | 9 | 0 | + 2 |
| Darrin Shannon, Buffalo | 3 | 0 | 0 | 0.0 | 0 | 0 | − 2 |
| Darryl Shannon, Toronto | 14 | 16 | 1 | 6.3 | 0 | 0 | + 5 |
| Jeff Sharples, Detroit | 46 | 48 | 4 | 8.3 | 3 | 0 | + 5 |
| Scott Shaunessy, Quebec | 4 | 0 | 0 | 0.0 | 0 | 0 | Even |
| Brad Shaw, Hartford | 3 | 2 | 1 | 50.0 | 1 | 0 | 1 |
| David Shaw, N.Y. Rangers | 63 | 85 | 6 | 7.1 | 3 | 1 | + 14 |
| Doug Shedden, Toronto | 1 | 2 | 0 | 0.0 | 0 | 0 | − 1 |
| Neil Sheehy, Washington | 72 | 22 | 3 | 13.6 | 0 | 0 | − 1 |
| Ray Sheppard, Buffalo | 67 | 147 | 22 | 15.0 | 7 | 0 | − 7 |
| Bruce Shoebottom, Boston | 29 | 19 | 1 | 5.3 | 0 | 0 | + 5 |
| Craig Simpson, Edmonton | 66 | 121 | 35 | 28.9 | 17 | 0 | − 3 |
| Ilkka Sinisalo, Philadelphia | 13 | 15 | 1 | 6.7 | 0 | 0 | + 6 |
| Ville Siren, Pittsburgh | 12 | 11 | 1 | 9.1 | 0 | 0 | Even |
| Minnesota | 38 | 39 | 2 | 5.1 | 0 | 0 | Even |
| Totals | 50 | 50 | 3 | 6.0 | 0 | 0 | Even |
| Petri Skriko, Vancouver | 74 | 204 | 30 | 14.7 | 9 | 0 | − 3 |
| Brian Skrudland, Montreal | 71 | 98 | 12 | 12.2 | 1 | 1 | + 22 |
| Doug Smail, Winnipeg | 47 | 68 | 14 | 20.6 | 0 | 2 | + 12 |
| Bobby Smith, Montreal | 80 | 195 | 32 | 16.4 | 6 | 0 | + 25 |
| Derrick Smith, Philadelphia | 74 | 115 | 16 | 13.9 | 0 | 1 | − 4 |
| Doug Smith, Edmonton | 19 | 15 | 1 | 6.7 | 0 | 0 | − 1 |
| Vancouver | 10 | 12 | 3 | 25.0 | 1 | 0 | + 3 |
| Totals | 29 | 27 | 4 | 14.8 | 1 | 0 | + 2 |
| Steve Smith, Buffalo | 3 | 2 | 0 | 0.0 | 0 | 0 | Even |
| J. Steve Smith, Edmonton | 35 | 47 | 3 | 6.4 | 0 | 0 | + 5 |
| Stan Smyl, Vancouver | 75 | 89 | 7 | 7.9 | 1 | 0 | Even |
| Greg Smyth, Quebec | 10 | 3 | 0 | 0.0 | 0 | 0 | − 9 |
| Harold Snepsts, Vancouver | 59 | 27 | 0 | 0.0 | 0 | 0 | − 3 |
| Daryl Stanley, Vancouver | 20 | 12 | 3 | 25.0 | 0 | 0 | + 3 |
| Mike Stapleton, Chicago | 7 | 6 | 0 | 0.0 | 0 | 0 | − 1 |

| Player — Team | Games | Shots | Goals | Shooting Pct. | PPG | SHG | +/- |
|---|---|---|---|---|---|---|---|
| Anton Stastny, Quebec | 55 | 84 | 7 | 8.3 | 3 | 0 | −19 |
| Peter Stastny, Quebec | 72 | 195 | 35 | 17.9 | 13 | 0 | −23 |
| Thomas Steen, Winnipeg | 80 | 173 | 27 | 15.6 | 9 | 1 | +14 |
| Ronnie Stern, Vancouver | 17 | 13 | 1 | 7.7 | 0 | 0 | −6 |
| Kevin Stevens, Pittsburgh | 24 | 52 | 12 | 23.1 | 4 | 0 | −8 |
| Mike Stevens, N.Y. Islanders | 9 | 9 | 1 | 11.1 | 0 | 0 | −1 |
| Scott Stevens, Washington | 80 | 195 | 7 | 3.6 | 6 | 0 | +1 |
| Allan Stewart, New Jersey | 6 | 4 | 0 | 0.0 | 0 | 0 | −2 |
| Trevor Stienberg, Quebec | 55 | 65 | 6 | 9.2 | 1 | 0 | −17 |
| Doug Sulliman, Philadelphia | 52 | 52 | 6 | 11.5 | 0 | 1 | −8 |
| Patrik Sundstrom, New Jersey | 65 | 156 | 28 | 17.9 | 12 | 1 | +22 |
| Peter Sundstrom, Washington | 35 | 39 | 4 | 10.3 | 0 | 0 | −5 |
| Gary Suter, Calgary | 63 | 216 | 13 | 6.0 | 8 | 0 | +26 |
| Brent Sutter, N.Y. Islanders | 77 | 187 | 29 | 15.5 | 17 | 2 | −12 |
| Duane Sutter, Chicago | 75 | 83 | 7 | 8.4 | 0 | 0 | −11 |
| Rich Sutter, Vancouver | 75 | 125 | 17 | 13.6 | 1 | 3 | +3 |
| Ron Sutter, Philadelphia | 55 | 106 | 26 | 24.5 | 4 | 1 | +25 |
| Petr Svoboda, Montreal | 71 | 131 | 8 | 6.1 | 4 | 0 | +28 |
| Bob Sweeney, Boston | 75 | 117 | 14 | 12.0 | 2 | 1 | −19 |
| Don Sweeney, Boston | 36 | 35 | 3 | 8.6 | 0 | 0 | −6 |
| Phil Sykes, Los Angeles | 23 | 5 | 0 | 0.0 | 0 | 0 | −3 |
| Peter Taglianetti, Winnipeg | 66 | 72 | 1 | 1.4 | 1 | 0 | −23 |
| Tony Tanti, Vancouver | 77 | 211 | 24 | 11.4 | 8 | 0 | −10 |
| Dave Taylor, Los Angeles | 70 | 141 | 26 | 18.4 | 7 | 0 | +10 |
| Michael Thelven, Boston | 40 | 68 | 3 | 4.4 | 1 | 1 | +10 |
| Gilles Thibaudeau, Montreal | 32 | 42 | 6 | 14.3 | 1 | 0 | +5 |
| Steve Thomas, Chicago | 45 | 124 | 21 | 16.9 | 8 | 0 | −2 |
| Jim Thomson, Washington | 14 | 9 | 2 | 22.2 | 0 | 0 | −3 |
| Hartford | 5 | 3 | 0 | 0.0 | 0 | 0 | −3 |
| Totals | 19 | 12 | 2 | 16.7 | 0 | 0 | −6 |
| Esa Tikkanen, Edmonton | 67 | 151 | 31 | 20.5 | 6 | 8 | +10 |
| Tom Tilley, St. Louis | 70 | 77 | 1 | 1.3 | 0 | 0 | +1 |
| Mark Tinordi, Minnesota | 47 | 39 | 2 | 5.1 | 0 | 0 | −9 |
| Dave Tippett, Hartford | 80 | 165 | 17 | 10.3 | 1 | 2 | −6 |
| Rick Tocchet, Philadelphia | 66 | 220 | 45 | 20.5 | 16 | 1 | −1 |
| Kevin Todd, New Jersey | 1 | 0 | 0 | 0.0 | 0 | 0 | −1 |
| John Tonelli, Los Angeles | 77 | 156 | 31 | 19.9 | 1 | 1 | +9 |
| Tim Tookey, Los Angeles | 7 | 8 | 2 | 25.0 | 0 | 0 | −3 |
| Jari Torkki, Chicago | 4 | 2 | 1 | 50.0 | 1 | 0 | −2 |
| Bryan Trottier, N.Y. Islanders | 73 | 163 | 17 | 10.4 | 5 | 0 | −7 |
| John Tucker, Buffalo | 60 | 94 | 13 | 13.8 | 3 | 0 | −5 |
| Allan Tuer, Hartford | 4 | 0 | 0 | 0.0 | 0 | 0 | −2 |
| Alfie Turcotte, Winnipeg | 14 | 10 | 1 | 10.0 | 0 | 0 | −6 |
| Darren Turcotte, N.Y. Rangers | 20 | 49 | 7 | 14.3 | 2 | 0 | Even |
| Pierre Turgeon, Buffalo | 80 | 182 | 34 | 18.7 | 19 | 0 | −2 |
| Sylvain Turgeon, Hartford | 42 | 122 | 16 | 13.1 | 7 | 0 | −11 |
| Steve Tuttle, St. Louis | 53 | 82 | 13 | 15.9 | 0 | 1 | +3 |
| Rick Vaive, Chicago | 30 | 57 | 12 | 21.1 | 9 | 0 | −5 |
| Buffalo | 28 | 81 | 19 | 23.5 | 7 | 0 | +7 |
| Totals | 58 | 138 | 31 | 22.5 | 16 | 0 | +2 |
| Wayne Van Dorp, Chicago | 8 | 4 | 0 | 0.0 | 0 | 0 | +1 |
| Darren Veitch, Toronto | 37 | 69 | 3 | 4.3 | 1 | 0 | −17 |
| Randy Velischek, New Jersey | 80 | 77 | 4 | 5.2 | 0 | 1 | −2 |
| Pat Verbeek, New Jersey | 77 | 175 | 26 | 14.9 | 9 | 0 | −18 |
| Mark Vermette, Quebec | 12 | 10 | 0 | 0.0 | 0 | 0 | −7 |
| Jim Vesey, St. Louis | 5 | 5 | 1 | 20.0 | 0 | 0 | −1 |
| Dan Vincelette, Chicago | 66 | 76 | 11 | 14.5 | 1 | 0 | −9 |
| Dave Volek, N.Y. Islanders | 77 | 229 | 25 | 10.9 | 9 | 0 | −11 |
| Mick Vukota, N.Y. Islanders | 48 | 19 | 2 | 10.5 | 0 | 0 | −17 |
| Gord Walker, Los Angeles | 11 | 13 | 1 | 7.7 | 0 | 0 | −2 |
| Mike Walsh, N.Y. Islanders | 13 | 11 | 2 | 18.2 | 0 | 0 | −7 |
| Ryan Walter, Montreal | 78 | 104 | 14 | 13.5 | 1 | 1 | +23 |
| Mike Ware, Edmonton | 2 | 0 | 0 | 0.0 | 0 | 0 | +1 |
| Bill Watson, Chicago | 3 | 2 | 0 | 0.0 | 0 | 0 | Even |
| Tim Watters, Los Angeles | 76 | 62 | 3 | 4.8 | 0 | 0 | +17 |
| Eric Weinrich, New Jersey | 2 | 3 | 0 | 0.0 | 0 | 0 | −1 |
| Jay Wells, Philadelphia | 67 | 67 | 2 | 3.0 | 0 | 0 | −3 |
| Glen Wesley, Boston | 77 | 181 | 19 | 10.5 | 8 | 1 | +23 |
| Simon Wheeldon, N.Y. Rangers | 6 | 2 | 0 | 0.0 | 0 | 0 | −1 |
| Doug Wickenheiser, N.Y. Rangers | 1 | 4 | 1 | 25.0 | 0 | 0 | +1 |
| Washington | 16 | 29 | 2 | 6.9 | 1 | 0 | Even |

| Player — Team | Games | Shots | Goals | Shooting Pct. | PPG | SHG | +/− |
|---|---|---|---|---|---|---|---|
| Totals | 17 | 33 | 3 | 9.1 | 1 | 0 | + 1 |
| Jim Wiemer, Los Angeles | 9 | 17 | 2 | 11.8 | 0 | 1 | + 2 |
| Brian Wilks, Los Angeles | 2 | 2 | 0 | 0.0 | 0 | 0 | Even |
| Carey Wilson, Hartford | 34 | 56 | 11 | 19.6 | 4 | 0 | − 12 |
| N. Y. Rangers | 41 | 108 | 21 | 19.4 | 10 | 0 | + 1 |
| Totals | 75 | 164 | 32 | 19.5 | 14 | 0 | − 11 |
| Doug Wilson, Chicago | 66 | 248 | 15 | 6.0 | 4 | 1 | + 8 |
| Craig Wolanin, New Jersey | 56 | 70 | 3 | 4.3 | 0 | 0 | − 9 |
| Randy Wood, N.Y. Islanders | 77 | 115 | 15 | 13.0 | 0 | 0 | − 18 |
| Terry Yake, Hartford | 2 | 0 | 0 | 0.0 | 0 | 0 | + 1 |
| Ken Yaremchuk, Toronto | 11 | 13 | 1 | 7.7 | 0 | 0 | − 5 |
| Trent Yawney, Chicago | 69 | 75 | 5 | 6.7 | 3 | 1 | − 5 |
| Scott Young, Hartford | 76 | 203 | 19 | 9.4 | 6 | 0 | − 21 |
| Paul Ysebaert, New Jersey | 5 | 4 | 0 | 0.0 | 0 | 0 | + 2 |
| Steve Yzerman, Detroit | 80 | 388 | 65 | 16.8 | 17 | 3 | + 17 |
| Zarley Zalapski, Pittsburgh | 58 | 95 | 12 | 12.6 | 5 | 1 | + 9 |
| Richard Zemlak, Minnesota | 3 | 1 | 0 | 0.0 | 0 | 0 | + 1 |
| Pittsburgh | 31 | 2 | 0 | 0.0 | 0 | 0 | − 4 |
| Totals | 34 | 3 | 0 | 0.0 | 0 | 0 | − 3 |
| Rob Zettler, Minnesota | 2 | 0 | 0 | 0.0 | 0 | 0 | + 1 |
| Peter Zezel, Philadelphia | 26 | 34 | 4 | 11.8 | 0 | 0 | − 13 |
| St. Louis | 52 | 115 | 17 | 14.8 | 5 | 1 | − 1 |
| Totals | 78 | 149 | 21 | 14.1 | 5 | 1 | − 14 |
| Rick Zombo, Detroit | 75 | 64 | 1 | 1.6 | 1 | 0 | + 22 |

## NHL Departmental Leaders

### Goals
1. Mario Lemieux, Pittsburgh ............ 85
2. Bernie Nicholls, Los Angeles ........ 70
3. Steve Yzerman, Detroit ................ 65
4. Wayne Gretzky, Los Angeles ........ 54
5. Joe Nieuwendyk, Calgary ............ 51
   Joe Mullen, Calgary .................... 51

### Assists
1. Mario Lemieux, Pittsburgh ............ 114
   Wayne Gretzky, Los Angeles ........ 114
3. Steve Yzerman, Detroit ................ 90
4. Paul Coffey, Pittsburgh ................ 83
5. Bernie Nicholls, Los Angeles ........ 80

### Power-Play Goals
1. Mario Lemieux, Pittsburgh ............ 31
2. Tim Kerr, Philadelphia .................. 25
3. Rob Brown, Pittsburgh .................. 24
4. Bernie Nicholls, Los Angeles ........ 21
5. Kevin Dineen, Hartford ................ 20
   Andrew McBain, Winnipeg ............ 20

### Shorthanded Goals
1. Mario Lemieux, Pittsburgh ............ 13
2. Dirk Graham, Chicago .................. 10
3. Esa Tikkanen, Edmonton .............. 8
   Bernie Nicholls, Los Angeles ........ 8
5. Mark Messier, Edmonton .............. 6

### Game-Winning Goals
1. Joe Nieuwendyk, Calgary ............ 11
2. Guy Carbonneau, Montreal .......... 10
3. Mike Ridley, Washington .............. 9
4. Dino Ciccarelli, Minnesota-Washington ... 8
   Jari Kurri, Edmonton .................... 8
   Mario Lemieux, Pittsburgh ............ 8
   Mike Krushelnyski, Los Angeles .... 8

### Shooting Percentage (150 Shots)
1. Rob Brown, Pittsburgh .................. 29.0
2. Mario Lemieux, Pittsburgh ............ 27.2
3. Ray Ferraro, Hartford .................. 24.3
4. Joe Nieuwendyk, Calgary ............ 23.7
5. Mike Ridley, Washington .............. 21.9

### Shots on Goal
1. Steve Yzerman, Detroit ................ 388
2. Bernie Nicholls, Los Angeles ........ 385
3. Paul Coffey, Pittsburgh ................ 342
4. Mario Lemieux, Pittsburgh ............ 313
5. Brett Hull, St. Louis ...................... 305

### Plus/Minus Leaders
1. Joe Mullen, Calgary .................... +51
2. Doug Gilmour, Calgary ................ +45
3. Colin Patterson, Calgary .............. +44
4. Brad McCrimmon, Calgary .......... +43
   Craig Muni, Edmonton ................ +43

### Worst Plus/Minus Players
1. Tom Fergus, Toronto .................... −38
2. Dan Quinn, Pittsburgh .................. −37
3. Joe Sakic, Quebec ...................... −36
4. Andrew McBain, Winnipeg .......... −35
5. Curtis Leschyshyn, Quebec .......... −32

### Penalty Minutes
1. Tim Hunter, Calgary .................... 375
2. Basil McRae, Minnesota .............. 365
3. Dave Manson, Chicago ................ 352
4. Marty McSorley, Los Angeles ...... 350
5. Mike Hartman, Buffalo ................ 316

# Miscellaneous Goaltending Statistics

(Players are listed alphabetically)

| | Games | W. | L. | T. | Goals | Saves | Sv. Pct. | Goal Interval |
|---|---|---|---|---|---|---|---|---|
| Tom Barrasso, Buffalo | 10 | 2 | 7 | 0 | 45 | 240 | 84.2 | 12:07 |
| Pittsburgh | 44 | 18 | 15 | 7 | 162 | 1283 | 88.8 | 14:51 |
| Totals | 54 | 20 | 22 | 7 | 207 | 1523 | 88.0 | 14:16 |
| Don Beaupre, Minnesota | 1 | 0 | 1 | 0 | 3 | 23 | 88.5 | 19:40 |
| Washington | 11 | 5 | 4 | 0 | 28 | 241 | 89.6 | 20:38 |
| Totals | 12 | 5 | 5 | 0 | 31 | 264 | 89.5 | 20:33 |
| Ed Belfour, Chicago | 23 | 4 | 12 | 3 | 74 | 531 | 87.8 | 15:31 |
| Daniel Berthiaume, Winnipeg | 9 | 0 | 8 | 0 | 44 | 211 | 82.7 | 10:04 |
| Allan Bester, Toronto | 43 | 17 | 20 | 3 | 156 | 1264 | 89.0 | 15:46 |
| Craig Billington, New Jersey | 3 | 1 | 1 | 0 | 11 | 54 | 83.1 | 12:44 |
| Mario Brunetta, Quebec | 5 | 1 | 3 | 0 | 19 | 98 | 83.8 | 11:53 |
| Sean Burke, New Jersey | 62 | 22 | 31 | 9 | 230 | 1593 | 87.4 | 15:37 |
| Jon Casey, Minnesota | 55 | 18 | 17 | 12 | 151 | 1358 | 90.0 | 19:37 |
| Tim Cheveldae, Detroit | 2 | 0 | 2 | 0 | 9 | 65 | 87.8 | 13:34 |
| Alain Chevrier, Winnipeg | 22 | 8 | 8 | 2 | 78 | 476 | 85.9 | 14:00 |
| Chicago | 27 | 13 | 11 | 2 | 92 | 648 | 87.6 | 17:06 |
| Totals | 49 | 21 | 19 | 4 | 170 | 1124 | 86.9 | 15:41 |
| Chris Clifford, Chicago | 1 | 0 | 0 | 0 | 0 | 0 | 0.0 | 0:00 |
| Jacques Cloutier, Buffalo | 36 | 15 | 14 | 0 | 108 | 749 | 87.4 | 16:32 |
| Marc D'Amour, Philadelphia | 1 | 0 | 0 | 0 | 0 | 14 | 100.0 | 0:00 |
| Tom Draper, Winnipeg | 2 | 1 | 1 | 0 | 12 | 54 | 81.8 | 10:00 |
| Darren Eliot, Buffalo | 2 | 0 | 0 | 0 | 7 | 36 | 83.7 | 9:34 |
| Bob Essensa, Winnipeg | 20 | 6 | 8 | 3 | 68 | 506 | 88.2 | 16:13 |
| Randy Exelby, Montreal | 1 | 0 | 0 | 0 | 0 | 1 | 100.0 | 0:00 |
| Mark Fitzpatrick, Los Angeles | 17 | 6 | 7 | 3 | 64 | 502 | 88.7 | 14:57 |
| N.Y. Islanders | 11 | 3 | 5 | 2 | 41 | 272 | 86.9 | 15:17 |
| Totals | 28 | 9 | 12 | 5 | 105 | 774 | 88.1 | 15:05 |
| Bob Froese, N.Y. Rangers | 30 | 9 | 14 | 4 | 102 | 689 | 87.1 | 15:53 |
| Grant Fuhr, Edmonton | 59 | 23 | 26 | 6 | 213 | 1501 | 87.6 | 15:41 |
| Troy Gamble, Vancouver | 5 | 2 | 3 | 0 | 12 | 128 | 91.4 | 25:10 |
| Mario Gosselin, Quebec | 39 | 11 | 19 | 3 | 146 | 959 | 86.8 | 14:08 |
| Steve Guenette, Pittsburgh | 11 | 5 | 6 | 0 | 41 | 267 | 86.7 | 14:00 |
| Jeff Hackett, N.Y. Islanders | 13 | 4 | 7 | 0 | 39 | 290 | 88.1 | 16:58 |
| Glen Hanlon, Detroit | 39 | 13 | 14 | 8 | 124 | 931 | 88.2 | 16:52 |
| Brian Hayward, Montreal | 36 | 20 | 13 | 3 | 101 | 793 | 88.7 | 20:42 |
| Glenn Healy, Los Angeles | 48 | 25 | 19 | 2 | 192 | 1317 | 87.3 | 14:04 |
| Ron Hextall, Philadelphia | 64 | 30 | 28 | 6 | 202 | 1658 | 89.1 | 18:35 |
| Kelly Hrudey, N.Y. Islanders | 50 | 18 | 24 | 3 | 183 | 1274 | 87.4 | 15:18 |
| Los Angeles | 16 | 10 | 4 | 2 | 47 | 444 | 90.4 | 20:43 |
| Totals | 66 | 28 | 28 | 5 | 230 | 1718 | 88.2 | 16:25 |
| Bob Janecyk, Los Angeles | 1 | 0 | 0 | 0 | 2 | 20 | 90.9 | 15:00 |
| Mark Laforest, Philadelphia | 17 | 5 | 7 | 2 | 64 | 433 | 87.1 | 14:35 |
| Rejean Lemelin, Boston | 40 | 19 | 15 | 6 | 120 | 941 | 88.7 | 19:56 |
| Mike Liut, Hartford | 35 | 13 | 19 | 1 | 142 | 885 | 86.2 | 14:08 |
| Clint Malarchuk, Washington | 42 | 16 | 18 | 7 | 141 | 1004 | 87.7 | 17:13 |
| Buffalo | 7 | 3 | 1 | 1 | 13 | 129 | 90.8 | 25:05 |
| Totals | 49 | 19 | 19 | 8 | 154 | 1133 | 88.0 | 17:53 |
| Bob Mason, Quebec | 22 | 5 | 14 | 1 | 92 | 535 | 85.3 | 12:42 |
| Kirk McLean, Vancouver | 42 | 20 | 17 | 3 | 127 | 1042 | 89.1 | 19:30 |
| Roland Melanson, Los Angeles | 4 | 1 | 1 | 0 | 19 | 90 | 82.6 | 9:22 |
| Greg Millen, St. Louis | 52 | 22 | 20 | 7 | 170 | 1241 | 88.0 | 17:46 |
| Andy Moog, Boston | 41 | 18 | 14 | 8 | 133 | 946 | 87.7 | 18:40 |
| Jarmo Myllys, Minnesota | 6 | 1 | 4 | 0 | 22 | 116 | 84.1 | 10:49 |
| Darren Pang, Chicago | 35 | 10 | 11 | 6 | 120 | 795 | 86.9 | 13:42 |
| Pete Peeters, Washington | 33 | 20 | 7 | 3 | 88 | 702 | 88.9 | 21:04 |
| Frank Pietrangelo, Pittsburgh | 15 | 5 | 3 | 0 | 45 | 364 | 89.0 | 14:52 |
| Daren Puppa, Buffalo | 37 | 17 | 10 | 6 | 107 | 854 | 88.9 | 17:50 |
| Bill Ranford, Edmonton | 29 | 15 | 8 | 2 | 88 | 630 | 87.7 | 17:09 |
| Eldon Reddick, Winnipeg | 41 | 11 | 17 | 7 | 144 | 988 | 87.3 | 14:39 |
| Jeff Reese, Toronto | 10 | 2 | 6 | 1 | 40 | 246 | 86.0 | 12:09 |
| Vincent Riendeau, St. Louis | 32 | 11 | 15 | 5 | 108 | 728 | 87.1 | 17:04 |
| Patrick Roy, Montreal | 48 | 33 | 5 | 6 | 113 | 1115 | 90.8 | 24:17 |
| Bob Sauve, New Jersey | 15 | 4 | 5 | 1 | 56 | 277 | 83.2 | 12:53 |
| Peter Sidorkiewicz, Hartford | 44 | 22 | 18 | 4 | 133 | 1074 | 89.0 | 19:49 |
| Billy Smith, N.Y. Islanders | 17 | 3 | 11 | 0 | 54 | 310 | 85.2 | 13:31 |
| Greg Stefan, Detroit | 46 | 21 | 17 | 3 | 167 | 1123 | 87.1 | 14:58 |

| | Games | W. | L. | T. | Goals | Saves | Sv. Pct. | Goal Interval |
|---|---|---|---|---|---|---|---|---|
| Sam St. Laurent, Detroit | 4 | 0 | 1 | 1 | 9 | 82 | 90.1 | 15:40 |
| Rich Tabaracci, Pittsburgh | 1 | 0 | 0 | 0 | 4 | 17 | 81.0 | 8:15 |
| Kari Takko, Minnesota | 32 | 8 | 15 | 4 | 93 | 829 | 89.9 | 17:14 |
| Chris Terreri, New Jersey | 8 | 0 | 4 | 2 | 18 | 152 | 89.4 | 22:20 |
| Ron Tugnutt, Quebec | 26 | 10 | 10 | 3 | 82 | 674 | 89.2 | 16:40 |
| John Vanbiesbrouck, N.Y. Rangers | 56 | 28 | 21 | 4 | 197 | 1469 | 88.2 | 16:17 |
| Mike Vernon, Calgary | 52 | 37 | 6 | 5 | 130 | 1133 | 89.7 | 22:36 |
| Jimmy Waite, Chicago | 11 | 0 | 7 | 1 | 43 | 210 | 83.0 | 11:29 |
| Darcy Wakaluk, Buffalo | 6 | 1 | 3 | 0 | 15 | 75 | 83.3 | 14:16 |
| Rick Wamsley, Calgary | 35 | 17 | 11 | 4 | 95 | 701 | 88.1 | 20:17 |
| Steve Weeks, Vancouver | 35 | 11 | 19 | 5 | 102 | 851 | 89.3 | 20:10 |
| Kay Whitmore, Hartford | 3 | 2 | 1 | 0 | 10 | 86 | 89.6 | 18:00 |
| Ken Wregget, Toronto | 32 | 9 | 20 | 2 | 139 | 898 | 86.6 | 13:35 |
| Philadelphia | 3 | 1 | 1 | 0 | 13 | 60 | 82.2 | 10:00 |
| Totals | 35 | 10 | 21 | 2 | 152 | 958 | 86.3 | 13:17 |
| Wendell Young, Pittsburgh | 22 | 12 | 9 | 0 | 92 | 581 | 86.3 | 12:30 |

## Goaltending Departmental Leaders

### Games Played
1. Kelly Hrudey, N.Y. Islanders-Los Angeles ......... 66
2. Ron Hextall, Philadelphia ............................... 64
3. Sean Burke, New Jersey ................................. 62
4. Grant Fuhr, Edmonton .................................... 59
5. John Vanbiesbrouck, N.Y. Rangers ................. 56

### Games Won Leaders
1. Mike Vernon, Calgary ..................................... 37
2. Patrick Roy, Montreal .................................... 33
3. Ron Hextall, Philadelphia ............................... 30
4. John Vanbiesbrouck, N.Y. Rangers ................. 28
   Kelly Hrudey, N.Y. Islanders-Los Angeles ......... 28

### Games Lost Leaders
1. Sean Burke, New Jersey ................................. 31
2. Ron Hextall, Philadelphia ............................... 28
   Kelly Hrudey, N.Y. Isl.-Los Angeles ................. 28
4. Grant Fuhr, Edmonton .................................... 26
5. Tom Barrasso, Buffalo-Pittsburgh .................... 22

### Goals Allowed Leaders
1. Sean Burke, New Jersey ................................. 230
   Kelly Hrudey, N.Y. Islanders-Los Angeles ......... 230
3. Grant Fuhr, Edmonton .................................... 213
4. Tom Barrasso, Buffalo-Pittsburgh .................... 207
5. Ron Hextall, Philadelphia ............................... 202

### Save Leaders
1. Kelly Hrudey, N.Y. Islanders-Los Angeles ......... 1718
2. Ron Hextall, Philadelphia ............................... 1658
3. Sean Burke, New Jersey ................................. 1593
4. Tom Barrasso, Buffalo-Pittsburgh .................... 1523
5. Grant Fuhr, Edmonton .................................... 1501

### Save Percentage Leaders
1. Patrick Roy, Montreal .................................... 90.8
2. Jon Casey, Minnesota .................................... 90.0
3. Kari Takko, Minnesota .................................... 89.9
4. Mike Vernon, Calgary ..................................... 89.7
5. Steve Weeks, Vancouver ................................. 89.3

### Goal Interval Leaders
1. Patrick Roy, Montreal .................................... 24:28
2. Mike Vernon, Calgary ..................................... 22:60
3. Pete Peeters, Washington ............................... 21:07
4. Brian Hayward, Montreal ................................ 20:70
5. Rick Wamsley, Calgary ................................... 20:28

### Minutes Played
1. Kelly Hrudey, N.Y. Islanders-Los Angeles ......... 3774
2. Ron Hextall, Philadelphia ............................... 3756
3. Sean Burke, New Jersey ................................. 3590
4. Grant Fuhr, Edmonton .................................... 3341
5. John Vanbiesbrouck, N.Y. Rangers ................. 3207

### Goals Against Average
1. Patrick Roy, Montreal .................................... 2.47
2. Mike Vernon, Calgary ..................................... 2.65
3. Pete Peeters, Washington ............................... 2.85
4. Brian Hayward, Montreal ................................ 2.90
5. Rick Wamsley, Calgary ................................... 2.96

### Shutouts
1. Greg Millen, St. Louis .................................... 6
2. Pete Peeters, Washington ............................... 4
   Kirk McLean, Vancouver ................................. 4
   Peter Sidorkiewicz, Hartford ........................... 4
   Patrick Roy, Montreal .................................... 4

# 1989 Stanley Cup Playoffs

## Top 10 Playoff Scoring Leaders

| | Games | G. | A. | Pts. | Pen. |
|---|---|---|---|---|---|
| 1. Al MacInnis, Calgary | 22 | 7 | *24 | *31 | 46 |
| 2. Tim Kerr, Philadelphia | 19 | 14 | 11 | 25 | 27 |
| 3. Joe Mullen, Calgary | 21 | *16 | 8 | 24 | 4 |
| 4. Brian Propp, Philadelphia | 18 | 14 | 9 | 23 | 14 |
| 5. Doug Gilmour, Calgary | 22 | 11 | 11 | 22 | 20 |
| Wayne Gretzky, Los Angeles | 11 | 5 | 17 | 22 | 0 |
| 7. Mario Lemieux, Pittsburgh | 11 | 12 | 7 | 19 | 16 |
| Bobby Smith, Montreal | 21 | 11 | 8 | 19 | 46 |
| Denis Savard, Chicago | 16 | 8 | 11 | 19 | 10 |
| Joel Otto, Calgary | 22 | 6 | 13 | 19 | 46 |
| Chris Chelios, Montreal | 21 | 4 | 15 | 19 | 28 |

*Indicates a league-leading figure.

## Preliminary Rounds
### (Division Semifinals)
(Best-of-seven Series)

#### ADAMS DIVISION

| | W. | L. | Pts. | GF. | GA. |
|---|---|---|---|---|---|
| Montreal Canadiens | 4 | 0 | 8 | 18 | 11 |
| Hartford Whalers | 0 | 4 | 0 | 11 | 18 |
| Boston Bruins | 4 | 1 | 8 | 16 | 14 |
| Buffalo Sabres | 1 | 4 | 2 | 14 | 16 |

(Montreal won Adams Division semifinal, 4-0)
Wed. April 5—Hartford 2, at Montreal 6
Thur. April 6—Hartford 2, at Montreal 3
Sat. April 8—Montreal 5, at Hartford 4 (a)
Sun. April 9—Montreal 4, at Hartford 3 (b)
 (a)—Stephane Richer scored at 5:01 of overtime for Montreal.
 (b)—Russ Courtnall scored at 15:12 of overtime for Montreal.

(Boston won Adams Division semifinal, 4-1)
Wed. April 5—Buffalo 6, at Boston 0
Thur. April 6—Buffalo 3, at Boston 5
Sat. April 8—Boston 4, at Buffalo 2
Sun. April 9—Boston 3, at Buffalo 2
Tues. April 11—Buffalo 1, at Boston 4

#### PATRICK DIVISION

| | W. | L. | Pts. | GF. | GA. |
|---|---|---|---|---|---|
| Philadelphia Flyers | 4 | 2 | 8 | 25 | 19 |
| Washington Capitals | 2 | 4 | 4 | 19 | 25 |
| Pittsburgh Penguins | 4 | 0 | 8 | 19 | 11 |
| New York Rangers | 0 | 4 | 0 | 11 | 19 |

(Philadelphia won Patrick Division semifinal, 4-2)
Wed. April 5—Philadelphia 2, at Washington 3
Thur. April 6—Philadelphia 3, at Washington 2
Sat. April 8—Washington 4, at Philadelphia 3 (c)
Sun. April 9—Washington 2, at Philadelphia 5
Tues. April 11—Philadelphia 8, at Washington 5
Thur. April 13—Washington 3, at Philadelphia 4
 (c)—Kelly Miller scored at 0:51 of overtime for Washington.

(Pittsburgh won Patrick Division semifinal, 4-0)
Wed. April 5—N.Y. Rangers 1, at Pittsburgh 3
Thur. April 6—N.Y. Rangers 4, at Pittsburgh 7
Sat. April 8—Pittsburgh 5, at N.Y. Rangers 3
Sun. April 9—Pittsburgh 4, at N.Y. Rangers 3

#### NORRIS DIVISION

| | W. | L. | Pts. | GF. | GA. |
|---|---|---|---|---|---|
| Chicago Black Hawks | 4 | 2 | 8 | 25 | 18 |
| Detroit Red Wings | 2 | 4 | 4 | 18 | 25 |
| St. Louis Blues | 4 | 1 | 8 | 23 | 15 |
| Minnesota North Stars | 1 | 4 | 2 | 15 | 23 |

(Chicago won Norris Division semifinal, 4-2)
Wed. April 5—Chicago 2, at Detroit 3
Thur. April 6—Chicago 5, at Detroit 4 (d)
Sat. April 8—Detroit 2, at Chicago 4
Sun. April 9—Detroit 2, at Chicago 3
Tues. April 11—Chicago 4, at Detroit 6
Thur. April 13—Detroit 1, at Chicago 7
 (d)—Duane Sutter scored at 14:36 of overtime for Chicago.

(St. Louis won Norris Division semifinal, 4-1)
Wed. April 5—Minnesota 3, at St. Louis 4 (e)
Thur. April 6—Minnesota 3, at St. Louis 4 (f)
Sat. April 8—St. Louis 5, at Minnesota 3
Sun. April 9—St. Louis 4, at Minnesota 5
Tues. April 11—Minnesota 1, at St. Louis 6
 (e)—Brett Hull scored at 11:55 of overtime for St. Louis.
 (f)—Rick Meagher scored at 5:30 of overtime for St. Louis.

## SMYTHE DIVISION

|  | W. | L. | Pts. | GF. | GA. |
|---|---|---|---|---|---|
| Calgary Flames | 4 | 3 | 8 | 26 | 20 |
| Vancouver Canucks | 3 | 4 | 6 | 20 | 26 |

(Calgary won Smythe Division semifinal, 4-3)
Wed. April 5—Vancouver 4, at Calgary 3 (g)
Thur. April 6—Vancouver 2, at Calgary 5
Sat. April 8—Calgary 4, at Vancouver 0
Sun. April 9—Calgary 3, at Vancouver 5
Tues. April 11—Vancouver 0, at Calgary 4
Thur. April 13—Calgary 3, at Vancouver 6
Sat. April 15—Vancouver 3, at Calgary 4 (h)

(g)—Paul Reinhart scored at 2:47 of overtime for Vancouver.
(h)—Joel Otto scored at 19:21 of overtime for Calgary.

|  | W. | L. | Pts. | GF. | GA. |
|---|---|---|---|---|---|
| Los Angeles Kings | 4 | 3 | 8 | 25 | 20 |
| Edmonton Oilers | 3 | 4 | 6 | 20 | 25 |

(Los Angeles won Smythe Division semifinal, 4-3)
Wed. April 5—Edmonton 4, at Los Angeles 3
Thur. April 6—Edmonton 2, at Los Angeles 5
Sat. April 8—Los Angeles 0, at Edmonton 4
Sun. April 9—Los Angeles 3, at Edmonton 4
Tues. April 11—Edmonton 2, at Los Angeles 4
Thur. April 13—Los Angeles 4, at Edmonton 1
Sat. April 15—Edmonton 3, at Los Angeles 6

# Quarterfinal Rounds
## (Division Finals)
(Best-of-seven Series)

### ADAMS DIVISION

|  | W. | L. | Pts. | GF. | GA. |
|---|---|---|---|---|---|
| Montreal Canadiens | 4 | 1 | 8 | 16 | 13 |
| Boston Bruins | 1 | 4 | 2 | 13 | 16 |

(Montreal won Division final, 4-1)
Mon. April 17—Boston 2, at Montreal 3
Wed. April 19—Boston 2, at Montreal 3 (i)
Fri. April 21—Montreal 5, at Boston 4
Sun. April 23—Montreal 2, at Boston 3
Tues. April 25—Boston 2, at Montreal 3

(i)—Bobby Smith scored at 12:24 of overtime for Montreal.

### NORRIS DIVISION

|  | W. | L. | Pts. | GF. | GA. |
|---|---|---|---|---|---|
| Chicago Black Hawks | 4 | 1 | 8 | 19 | 12 |
| St. Louis Blues | 1 | 4 | 2 | 12 | 19 |

(Chicago won Division final, 4-1)
Tues. April 18—Chicago 3, at St. Louis 1
Thur. April 20—Chicago 4, at St. Louis 5 (k)
Sat. April 22—St. Louis 2, at Chicago 5
Mon. April 24—St. Louis 2, at Chicago 3
Wed. April 26—Chicago 4, at St. Louis 2

(k)—Tony Hrkac scored at 33:49 of overtime for St. Louis.

### PATRICK DIVISION

|  | W. | L. | Pts. | GF. | GA. |
|---|---|---|---|---|---|
| Philadelphia Flyers | 4 | 3 | 8 | 31 | 24 |
| Pittsburgh Penguins | 3 | 4 | 6 | 24 | 31 |

(Philadelphia won Division final, 4-3)
Mon. April 17—Philadelphia 3, at Pittsburgh 4
Wed. April 19—Philadelphia 4, at Pittsburgh 2
Fri. April 21—Pittsburgh 4, at Philadelphia 3 (j)
Sun. April 23—Pittsburgh 1, at Philadelphia 4
Tues. April 25—Philadelphia 7, at Pittsburgh 10
Thur. April 27—Pittsburgh 2, at Philadelphia 6
Sat. April 29—Philadelphia 4, at Pittsburgh 1

(j)—Phil Bourque scored at 12:08 of overtime for Pittsburgh.

### SMYTHE DIVISION

|  | W. | L. | Pts. | GF. | GA. |
|---|---|---|---|---|---|
| Calgary Flames | 4 | 0 | 8 | 22 | 11 |
| Los Angeles Kings | 0 | 4 | 0 | 11 | 22 |

(Calgary won Division final, 4-0)
Tues. April 18—Los Angeles 3, at Calgary 4 (l)
Thur. April 20—Los Angeles 3, at Calgary 8
Sat. April 22—Calgary 5, at Los Angeles 2
Mon. April 24—Calgary 5, at Los Angeles 3

(l)—Doug Gilmour scored at 7:47 of overtime for Calgary.

# Semifinal Rounds
## (Conference Championships)
(Best-of-seven Series)

### PRINCE OF WALES CONFERENCE

|  | W. | L. | Pts. | GF. | GA. |
|---|---|---|---|---|---|
| Montreal Canadiens | 4 | 2 | 8 | 17 | 8 |
| Philadelphia Flyers | 2 | 4 | 4 | 8 | 17 |

(Montreal won Conference title, 4-2)
Mon. May 1—Philadelphia 3, at Montreal 1
Wed. May 3—Philadelphia 0, at Montreal 3
Fri. May 5—Montreal 5, at Philadelphia 1
Sun. May 7—Montreal 3, at Philadelphia 0
Tues. May 9—Philadelphia 2, at Montreal 1 (m)
Thur. May 11—Montreal 4, at Philadelphia 2

(m)—Dave Poulin scored at 5:02 of overtime for Philadelphia.

### CLARENCE CAMPBELL CONFERENCE

|  | W. | L. | Pts. | GF. | GA. |
|---|---|---|---|---|---|
| Calgary Flames | 4 | 1 | 8 | 15 | 8 |
| Chicago Black Hawks | 1 | 4 | 2 | 8 | 15 |

(Calgary won Conference title, 4-1)
Tues. May 2—Chicago 0, at Calgary 3
Thur. May 4—Chicago 4, at Calgary 2
Sat. May 6—Calgary 5, at Chicago 2
Mon. May 8—Calgary 2, at Chicago 1 (n)
Wed. May 10—Chicago 1, at Calgary 3

(n)—Al MacInnis scored at 15:05 of overtime for Calgary.

# Finals for the Stanley Cup
(Best-of-seven Series)

|  | W. | L. | Pts. | GF. | GA. |
|---|---|---|---|---|---|
| Calgary Flames | 4 | 2 | 8 | 19 | 16 |
| Montreal Canadiens | 2 | 4 | 4 | 16 | 19 |

(Calgary Flames won Stanley Cup Championship Series, 4-2)

Sun. May 14—Montreal 2, at Calgary 3
Wed. May 17—Montreal 4, at Calgary 2
Fri. May 19—Calgary 3, at Montreal 4 (2 OT)
Sun. May 21—Calgary 4, at Montreal 2
Tues. May 23—Montreal 2, at Calgary 3
Thur. May 25—Calgary 4, at Montreal 2

### Game 1—Sunday, May 14 at Calgary (Calgary won, 3-2)

Montreal ...................... 2  0  0—2
Calgary ........................ 2  1  0—3

FIRST PERIOD: 1. Montreal, Richer (Corson, Chelios) PPG 2:43; 2. Calgary, MacInnis (Otto, Mullen) PPG 6:51; 3. Calgary, MacInnis (Otto, Peplinski) 8:33; 4. Montreal, Robinson (Smith, Keane) 10:02. Penalties: Peplinski, Calgary 0:49; Robinson, Montreal 6:33; Roy, Montreal (served by Courtnall) 10:29; Carbonneau, Montreal 18:51; Gilmour, Calgary 18:51; Skrudland, Montreal 19:22.

SECOND PERIOD: 5. Calgary, Fleury (Macoun, T. Hunter) 11:45. Penalties: Peplinski, Calgary 6:07; Smith, Montreal 6:15; Macoun, Calgary 7:42; McCrimmon, Calgary 14:20.

THIRD PERIOD: No scoring. Penalties: Ludwig, Montreal 1:36; Smith, Montreal, misconduct 19:39.

Shots Against:
  Roy (Montreal) .................................... 13   12   10 — 35
  Vernon (Calgary) ..................................  6   16    9 — 31
Attendance: 20,062.

### Game 2—Wednesday, May 17 at Calgary (Montreal won, 4-2)

Montreal ...................... 1  1  2—4
Calgary ........................ 0  2  0—2

FIRST PERIOD: 1. Montreal, Robinson (McPhee, Skrudland) 4:18. Penalties: McCrimmon, Calgary 2:14; Gilchrist, Montreal 5:31; Chelios, Montreal 7:15; Corson, Montreal 10:48; Peplinski, Calgary 10:48; McPhee, Montreal 16:35; T. Hunter, Calgary 16:35; Corson, Montreal 20:00; Roberts, Calgary 20:00.

SECOND PERIOD: 2. Montreal, Smith (Keane, Chelios) PPG 1:55; 3. Calgary, Nieuwendyk (MacLellan) 5:14; 4. Calgary, Otto (Mullen, MacInnis) PPG 13:49. Penalties: Murzyn, Calgary 1:23; Gilchrist, Montreal 2:58; Svoboda, Montreal 7:56; Skrudland, Montreal 13:32; Murzyn, Calgary 16:07; Chelios, Montreal 18:18; McPhee, Montreal 19:48; MacLellan, Calgary 19:48.

THIRD PERIOD: 5. Montreal, Chelios (Skrudland, Svoboda) 8:01; 6. Montreal, Courtnall (Chelios, Svoboda) PPG 9:35. Penalties: T. Hunter, Calgary 2:31; Keane, Montreal 3:11; Roberts, Calgary 8:13; Naslund, Montreal 11:21; Nieuwendyk, Calgary 13:19; Chelios, Montreal 13:19.

Shots Against:
  Roy (Montreal) ....................................  8   16    8 — 32
  Vernon (Calgary) .................................. 11    4    8 — 23
Attendance: 20,062.

### Game 3—Friday, May 19 at Montreal (Montreal won, 4-3)

Calgary ........................ 1  1  1  0  0—3
Montreal ...................... 1  0  2  0  1—4

FIRST PERIOD: 1. Montreal, McPhee (unassisted) 1:32; 2. Calgary, Mullen (McCrimmon, Gilmour) 17:15. Penalties: Gilmour, Calgary 0:34; Chelios, Montreal 0:34; Ramage, Calgary 2:57; M. Hunter, Calgary 6:42; Ludwig, Montreal 6:42; Fleury, Calgary 7:10; Svoboda, Montreal 11:06; MacInnis, Calgary 11:39; Ludwig, Montreal 12:07; Smith, Montreal 14:25; Patterson, Calgary 17:15; Desjardins, Montreal 17:15; MacInnis, Calgary 20:00; Skrudland, Montreal 20:00.

SECOND PERIOD: 3. Calgary, Mullen (MacInnis, Fleury) PPG 15:35. Penalties: Carbonneau, Montreal 0:49; Macoun, Calgary 4:04; McCrimmon, Calgary 6:15; Macoun, Calgary 6:58; Skrudland, Montreal 6:58; Skrudland, Montreal 14:25; Ramage, Calgary 16:08; Murzyn, Calgary 19:00; Skrudland, Montreal 19:00.

THIRD PERIOD: 4. Montreal, Smith (Naslund, Svoboda) 1:36; 5. Calgary, Gilmour (T. Hunter) 13:02; 6. Montreal, Naslund (unassisted) 19:19. Penalties: MacInnis, Calgary 10:11; Corson, Montreal 10:11.

FIRST OVERTIME: No scoring. Penalties: T. Hunter, Calgary 11:38; Corson, Montreal 11:38; MacInnis, Calgary 16:09; Smith, Montreal 16:09; M. Hunter, Calgary 17:34; Skrudland, Montreal 17:34; Ramage, Calgary 17:59; Corson, Montreal 17:59.

SECOND OVERTIME: 7. Montreal, Walter (Richer) 18:08. Penalties: MacInnis, Calgary 9:25; Gainey, Montreal 9:25; M. Hunter, Calgary 16:08.

Shots Against:
  Vernon (Calgary) ..................................  4   7   6   12   6 — 35
  Roy (Montreal) .................................... 13   7   8    5   4 — 37
Attendance: 17,899.

### Game 4—Sunday, May 21 at Montreal (Calgary won, 4-2)

| | | | |
|---|---|---|---|
| Calgary | 0 | 2 | 2—4 |
| Montreal | 0 | 0 | 2—2 |

FIRST PERIOD: No scoring. Penalties: Svoboda, Montreal 5:44; MacInnis, Calgary 9:46; Keane, Montreal 11:07; Ramage, Calgary 15:19; Carbonneau, Montreal 18:03; Gainey, Montreal 18:19.

SECOND PERIOD: 1. Calgary, Gilmour (unassisted) 11:56; 2. Calgary, Mullen (MacInnis, Otto) PPG 18:43. Penalties: MacInnis, Calgary 7:03; Gilmour, Calgary 9:47; Svoboda, Montreal 13:22; Patterson, Calgary 15:38; Robinson, Montreal 18:18; Otto, Calgary 19:56.

THIRD PERIOD: 3. Montreal, Courtnall (McPhee, Chelios) 10:59; 4. Calgary, MacInnis (Otto) 18:22; 5. Montreal, Lemieux (Robinson) 19:33; 6. Calgary, Mullen (Gilmour, Patterson) PPG—ENG 19:49. Penalties: Montreal bench (served by Lemieux) 5:57; Macoun, Calgary 12:47; Nattress, Calgary, misconduct 12:47; Lemieux, Montreal 19:33; Patterson, Calgary, minor-misconduct 19:49; Richer, Montreal, misconduct 19:49; Courtnall, Montreal, misconduct 19:49.

Shots Against:
| | | | |
|---|---|---|---|
| Vernon (Calgary) | 3 | 10 | 6 — 19 |
| Roy (Montreal) | 13 | 9 | 13 — 35 |

Attendance: 17,907.

### Game 5—Tuesday, May 23 at Calgary (Calgary won, 3-2)

| | | | |
|---|---|---|---|
| Montreal | 1 | 1 | 0—2 |
| Calgary | 3 | 0 | 0—3 |

FIRST PERIOD: 1. Calgary, Otto (Peplinski, M. Hunter) 0:28; 2. Calgary, Mullen (Gilmour, Ramage) 8:15; 3. Montreal, Smith (Chelios, Naslund) PPG 13:24; 4. Calgary, MacInnis (Ramage, Otto) PPG 19:31. Penalties: Corson, Montreal 2:31; Walter, Montreal 6:10; Mullen, Calgary 9:14; Peplinski, Calgary 11:57; Peplinski, Calgary 13:50; Green, Montreal 19:18.

SECOND PERIOD: 5. Montreal, Keane (Smith, Gainey) 14:17. Penalties: Lemieux, Montreal 18:20.

THIRD PERIOD: No scoring. Penalties: MacInnis, Calgary 8:40; Smith, Montreal 9:32; Lemieux, Montreal 10:06; Vernon, Calgary (served by Roberts) 10:06; Corson, Montreal 16:28; MacLellan, Calgary 16:28.

Shots Against:
| | | | |
|---|---|---|---|
| Roy (Montreal) | 10 | 13 | 5 — 28 |
| Vernon (Calgary) | 10 | 7 | 11 — 28 |

Attendance: 20,062.

### Game 6—Thursday, May 25 at Montreal (Calgary won, 4-2)

| | | | |
|---|---|---|---|
| Calgary | 1 | 1 | 2—4 |
| Montreal | 0 | 1 | 1—2 |

FIRST PERIOD: 1. Calgary, Patterson (Murzyn, MacInnis) 18:51. Penalties: Mullen, Calgary 0:54; Chelios, Montreal 5:09; Naslund, Montreal 8:20; M. Hunter, Calgary 9:53; Skrudland, Montreal 9:53; Murzyn, Calgary 10:26; Roberts, Calgary 18:30; Ramage, Calgary 18:30; Corson, Montreal 18:30; Smith, Montreal 18:30.

SECOND PERIOD: 2. Montreal, Lemieux (Skrudland, Chelios) 1:23; 3. Calgary, McDonald (Nieuwendyk, Loob) 4:24. Penalties: McDonald, Calgary 2:13; M. Hunter, Calgary 4:53; Walter, Montreal 4:53; Vernon, Calgary (served by Roberts) 6:37; Loob, Calgary 6:37; Corson, Montreal 6:37; Ludwig, Montreal 11:08; Nattress, Calgary 16:36.

THIRD PERIOD: 4. Calgary, Gilmour (Otto, MacInnis) PPG 11:02; 5. Montreal, Green (McPhee, Lemieux) 11:53; 6. Calgary, Gilmour (Mullen, Macoun) ENG 18:57. Penalties: M. Hunter, Calgary 2:17; Skrudland, Montreal 2:17; Courtnall, Montreal 10:46; MacInnis, Calgary 18:34; Lemieux, Montreal, minor-misconduct 18:34.

Shots Against:
| | | | |
|---|---|---|---|
| Vernon (Calgary) | 9 | 7 | 6 — 22 |
| Roy (Montreal) | 4 | 8 | 7 — 19 |

Attendance: 17,909.

# Team-by-Team Playoff Scoring

## Boston Bruins
(Lost Adams Division finals to Montreal, 4-1)

| | Games | G. | A. | Pts. | Pen. |
|---|---|---|---|---|---|
| Craig Janney | 10 | 4 | 9 | 13 | 21 |
| Cam Neely | 10 | 7 | 2 | 9 | 8 |
| Michael Thelven | 10 | 1 | 7 | 8 | 8 |
| Bob Joyce | 9 | 5 | 2 | 7 | 2 |
| Randy Burridge | 10 | 5 | 2 | 7 | 8 |
| Bob Sweeney | 10 | 2 | 4 | 6 | 19 |
| Ray Neufeld | 10 | 2 | 3 | 5 | 9 |
| Ray Bourque | 10 | 0 | 4 | 4 | 6 |
| John Carter | 10 | 1 | 2 | 3 | 6 |
| Bobby Carpenter | 8 | 1 | 1 | 2 | 4 |
| Andy Brickley | 10 | 0 | 2 | 2 | 0 |
| Keith Crowder | 10 | 0 | 2 | 2 | 37 |
| Greg Hawgood | 10 | 0 | 2 | 2 | 2 |
| Bruce Shoebottom | 10 | 0 | 2 | 2 | 35 |
| Glen Wesley | 10 | 0 | 2 | 2 | 4 |
| Greg Johnston | 10 | 1 | 0 | 1 | 6 |
| Andy Moog (Goalie) | 6 | 0 | 1 | 1 | 0 |
| Garry Galley | 9 | 0 | 1 | 1 | 33 |
| Robert Cimetta | 1 | 0 | 0 | 0 | 15 |
| Carl Mokosak | 1 | 0 | 0 | 0 | 0 |
| Lyndon Byers | 2 | 0 | 0 | 0 | 0 |
| Rejean Lemelin (Goalie) | 4 | 0 | 0 | 0 | 2 |
| Allen Pedersen | 10 | 0 | 0 | 0 | 2 |

## Buffalo Sabres
(Lost Adams Division semifinals to Boston, 4-1)

| | Games | G. | A. | Pts. | Pen. |
|---|---|---|---|---|---|
| Pierre Turgeon | 5 | 3 | 5 | 8 | 2 |
| Mike Foligno | 5 | 3 | 1 | 4 | 21 |
| Phil Housley | 5 | 1 | 3 | 4 | 2 |
| Rick Vaive | 5 | 2 | 1 | 3 | 8 |
| Grant Ledyard | 5 | 1 | 2 | 3 | 2 |
| John Tucker | 3 | 0 | 3 | 3 | 0 |
| Dave Andreychuk | 5 | 0 | 3 | 3 | 0 |
| Doug Bodger | 5 | 1 | 1 | 2 | 11 |
| Mark Napier | 3 | 1 | 0 | 1 | 0 |
| Scott Arniel | 5 | 1 | 0 | 1 | 4 |
| Mike Ramsey | 5 | 1 | 0 | 1 | 11 |
| Ray Sheppard | 1 | 0 | 1 | 1 | 0 |
| Shawn Anderson | 5 | 0 | 1 | 1 | 4 |
| Uwe Krupp | 5 | 0 | 1 | 1 | 4 |
| Clint Malarchuk (Goalie) | 1 | 0 | 0 | 0 | 2 |
| Larry Playfair | 1 | 0 | 0 | 0 | 0 |
| Christian Ruuttu | 2 | 0 | 0 | 0 | 2 |
| Darrin Shannon | 2 | 0 | 0 | 0 | 0 |
| Ken Priestlay | 3 | 0 | 0 | 0 | 2 |
| Jacques Cloutier (G.) | 4 | 0 | 0 | 0 | 0 |
| Mike Hartman | 5 | 0 | 0 | 0 | 34 |
| Benoit Hogue | 5 | 0 | 0 | 0 | 17 |
| Kevin Maguire | 5 | 0 | 0 | 0 | 36 |
| Jeff Parker | 5 | 0 | 0 | 0 | 26 |

## Calgary Flames
(Winners of 1989 Stanley Cup Playoffs)

| | Games | G. | A. | Pts. | Pen. |
|---|---|---|---|---|---|
| Al MacInnis | 22 | 7 | *24 | *31 | 46 |
| Joe Mullen | 21 | *16 | 8 | 24 | 4 |
| Doug Gilmour | 22 | 11 | 11 | 22 | 20 |
| Joel Otto | 22 | 6 | 13 | 19 | 46 |
| Hakan Loob | 22 | 8 | 9 | 17 | 4 |
| Joe Nieuwendyk | 22 | 10 | 4 | 14 | 10 |
| Colin Patterson | 22 | 3 | 10 | 13 | 24 |
| Gary Roberts | 22 | 5 | 7 | 12 | 57 |
| Rob Ramage | 20 | 1 | 11 | 12 | 26 |
| Theo Fleury | 22 | 5 | 6 | 11 | 24 |
| Jamie Macoun | 22 | 3 | 6 | 9 | 30 |
| Jim Peplinski | 20 | 1 | 6 | 7 | 75 |
| Brian MacLellan | 21 | 3 | 2 | 5 | 19 |
| Mark Hunter | 10 | 2 | 2 | 4 | 23 |
| Lanny McDonald | 14 | 1 | 3 | 4 | 29 |
| Tim Hunter | 19 | 0 | 4 | 4 | 32 |
| Gary Suter | 5 | 0 | 3 | 3 | 10 |
| Ric Nattress | 19 | 0 | 3 | 3 | 20 |
| Dana Murzyn | 21 | 0 | 3 | 3 | 20 |
| Brad McCrimmon | 22 | 0 | 3 | 3 | 30 |
| Sergei Priakin | 1 | 0 | 0 | 0 | 0 |
| Ken Sabourin | 1 | 0 | 0 | 0 | 0 |
| Rick Wamsley (Goalie) | 1 | 0 | 0 | 0 | 0 |
| Jiri Hrdina | 4 | 0 | 0 | 0 | 0 |
| Mike Vernon (Goalie) | 22 | 0 | 0 | 0 | 14 |

## Chicago Black Hawks
(Lost Campbell Conference finals to Calgary, 4-1)

| | Games | G. | A. | Pts. | Pen. |
|---|---|---|---|---|---|
| Denis Savard | 16 | 8 | 11 | 19 | 10 |
| Steve Larmer | 16 | 8 | 9 | 17 | 22 |
| Wayne Presley | 14 | 7 | 5 | 12 | 18 |
| Adam Creighton | 15 | 5 | 6 | 11 | 44 |
| Trent Yawney | 15 | 3 | 6 | 9 | 20 |
| Troy Murray | 16 | 3 | 6 | 9 | 25 |
| Steve Thomas | 12 | 3 | 5 | 8 | 10 |
| Dave Manson | 16 | 0 | 8 | 8 | *84 |
| Dirk Graham | 16 | 2 | 4 | 6 | 38 |
| Greg Gilbert | 15 | 1 | 5 | 6 | 20 |
| Bob Murray | 16 | 2 | 3 | 5 | 22 |
| Duane Sutter | 16 | 3 | 1 | 4 | 15 |
| Jeremy Roenick | 10 | 1 | 3 | 4 | 7 |
| Keith Brown | 13 | 1 | 3 | 4 | 25 |
| Doug Wilson | 4 | 1 | 2 | 3 | 0 |
| Mike Hudson | 10 | 1 | 2 | 3 | 18 |
| Steve Konroyd | 16 | 2 | 0 | 2 | 10 |
| Bob Bassen | 10 | 1 | 1 | 2 | 34 |
| Alain Chevrier (Goalie) | 16 | 0 | 1 | 1 | 0 |
| Wayne Van Dorp | 16 | 0 | 1 | 1 | 17 |
| Bruce Cassidy | 1 | 0 | 0 | 0 | 0 |
| Brian Noonan | 1 | 0 | 0 | 0 | 0 |
| Darren Pang (Goalie) | 2 | 0 | 0 | 0 | 0 |
| Everett Sanipass | 3 | 0 | 0 | 0 | 2 |
| Dan Vincelette | 5 | 0 | 0 | 0 | 4 |
| Bob McGill | 16 | 0 | 0 | 0 | 33 |

## Detroit Red Wings
(Lost Norris Division semifinals to Chicago 4-2)

| | Games | G. | A. | Pts. | Pen. |
|---|---|---|---|---|---|
| Steve Yzerman | 6 | 5 | 5 | 10 | 2 |
| Adam Oates | 6 | 0 | 8 | 8 | 2 |
| Petr Klima | 6 | 2 | 4 | 6 | 19 |
| Dave Barr | 6 | 3 | 1 | 4 | 6 |
| Steve Chiasson | 5 | 2 | 1 | 3 | 6 |
| Shawn Burr | 6 | 1 | 2 | 3 | 6 |
| Gerard Gallant | 6 | 1 | 2 | 3 | 40 |
| Lee Norwood | 6 | 1 | 2 | 3 | 16 |
| Paul MacLean | 5 | 1 | 1 | 2 | 8 |

|  | Games | G. | A. | Pts. | Pen. |
|---|---|---|---|---|---|
| John Chabot | 6 | 1 | 1 | 2 | 0 |
| Torrie Robertson | 6 | 1 | 0 | 1 | 17 |
| Joey Kocur | 3 | 0 | 1 | 1 | 6 |
| Gilbert Delorme | 6 | 0 | 1 | 1 | 2 |
| Doug Houda | 6 | 0 | 1 | 1 | 0 |
| Rick Zombo | 6 | 0 | 1 | 1 | 16 |
| Tim Higgins | 1 | 0 | 0 | 0 | 0 |
| Jeff Sharples | 1 | 0 | 0 | 0 | 0 |
| Glen Hanlon (Goalie) | 2 | 0 | 0 | 0 | 0 |
| Kris King | 2 | 0 | 0 | 0 | 2 |
| Randy McKay | 2 | 0 | 0 | 0 | 2 |
| Adam Graves | 5 | 0 | 0 | 0 | 4 |
| Greg Stefan (Goalie) | 5 | 0 | 0 | 0 | 4 |
| Jim Nill | 6 | 0 | 0 | 0 | 25 |
| Mike O'Connell | 6 | 0 | 0 | 0 | 4 |

## Edmonton Oilers
(Lost Smythe Division semifinals to Los Angeles, 4-3)

|  | Games | G. | A. | Pts. | Pen. |
|---|---|---|---|---|---|
| Mark Messier | 7 | 1 | 11 | 12 | 8 |
| Jari Kurri | 7 | 3 | 5 | 8 | 6 |
| Steve Smith | 7 | 2 | 2 | 4 | 20 |
| Esa Tikkanen | 7 | 1 | 3 | 4 | 12 |
| Jimmy Carson | 7 | 2 | 1 | 3 | 6 |
| Normand Lacombe | 7 | 2 | 1 | 3 | 21 |
| Glenn Anderson | 7 | 1 | 2 | 3 | 8 |
| Kevin Lowe | 7 | 1 | 2 | 3 | 4 |
| Craig Muni | 7 | 0 | 3 | 3 | 8 |
| Tomas Jonsson | 4 | 2 | 0 | 2 | 6 |
| Charlie Huddy | 7 | 2 | 0 | 2 | 4 |
| Craig Simpson | 7 | 2 | 0 | 2 | 10 |
| Mark Lamb | 6 | 0 | 2 | 2 | 8 |
| Kevin McClelland | 7 | 0 | 2 | 2 | 16 |
| Randy Gregg | 7 | 1 | 0 | 1 | 6 |
| Craig MacTavish | 7 | 0 | 1 | 1 | 8 |
| Jeff Beukeboom | 1 | 0 | 0 | 0 | 2 |
| John LeBlanc | 1 | 0 | 0 | 0 | 0 |
| Doug Halward | 2 | 0 | 0 | 0 | 0 |
| Dave Hunter | 6 | 0 | 0 | 0 | 0 |
| Dave Brown | 7 | 0 | 0 | 0 | 6 |
| Grant Fuhr (Goalie) | 7 | 0 | 0 | 0 | 0 |

## Hartford Whalers
(Lost Adams Division semifinals to Montreal, 4-0)

|  | Games | G. | A. | Pts. | Pen. |
|---|---|---|---|---|---|
| Dave Babych | 4 | 1 | 5 | 6 | 2 |
| Dean Evason | 4 | 1 | 2 | 3 | 10 |
| Joel Quenneville | 4 | 0 | 3 | 3 | 4 |
| Ray Ferraro | 4 | 2 | 0 | 2 | 4 |
| Scott Young | 4 | 2 | 0 | 2 | 4 |
| Paul MacDermid | 4 | 1 | 1 | 2 | 16 |
| Ron Francis | 4 | 0 | 2 | 2 | 0 |
| Ulf Samuelsson | 4 | 0 | 2 | 2 | 2 |
| Sylvain Turgeon | 4 | 0 | 2 | 2 | 4 |
| Brian Lawton | 3 | 1 | 0 | 1 | 0 |
| Brad Shaw | 3 | 1 | 0 | 1 | 0 |
| Kevin Dineen | 4 | 1 | 0 | 1 | 10 |
| Grant Jennings | 4 | 1 | 0 | 1 | 17 |
| Brent Peterson | 2 | 0 | 1 | 1 | 4 |
| Sylvain Cote | 3 | 0 | 1 | 1 | 4 |
| John Anderson | 4 | 0 | 1 | 1 | 2 |
| Dave Tippett | 4 | 0 | 1 | 1 | 0 |
| Jody Hull | 1 | 0 | 0 | 0 | 2 |
| Randy Ladouceur | 1 | 0 | 0 | 0 | 10 |
| Norm Maciver | 1 | 0 | 0 | 0 | 2 |
| Tom Martin | 1 | 0 | 0 | 0 | 4 |

|  | Games | G. | A. | Pts. | Pen. |
|---|---|---|---|---|---|
| Jim Pavese | 1 | 0 | 0 | 0 | 0 |
| Peter Sidorkiewicz (G.) | 2 | 0 | 0 | 0 | 0 |
| Kay Whitmore (Goalie) | 2 | 0 | 0 | 0 | 0 |
| Don Maloney | 4 | 0 | 0 | 0 | 8 |

## Los Angeles Kings
(Lost Smythe Division finals to Calgary, 4-0)

|  | Games | G. | A. | Pts. | Pen. |
|---|---|---|---|---|---|
| Wayne Gretzky | 11 | 5 | 17 | 22 | 0 |
| Bernie Nicholls | 11 | 7 | 9 | 16 | 12 |
| Chris Kontos | 11 | 9 | 0 | 9 | 8 |
| Steve Duchesne | 11 | 4 | 4 | 8 | 12 |
| Luc Robitaille | 11 | 2 | 6 | 8 | 10 |
| Steve Kasper | 11 | 1 | 5 | 6 | 10 |
| Dave Taylor | 11 | 1 | 5 | 6 | 19 |
| Tom Laidlaw | 11 | 2 | 3 | 5 | 6 |
| Mike Krushelnyski | 11 | 1 | 4 | 5 | 4 |
| Jim Wiemer | 10 | 2 | 1 | 3 | 19 |
| Dale DeGray | 8 | 1 | 2 | 3 | 12 |
| Dean Kennedy | 11 | 0 | 2 | 2 | 8 |
| Marty McSorley | 11 | 0 | 2 | 2 | 33 |
| Mike Allison | 7 | 1 | 0 | 1 | 10 |
| Doug Crossman | 2 | 0 | 1 | 1 | 2 |
| Jay Miller | 11 | 0 | 1 | 1 | 63 |
| Tim Watters | 11 | 0 | 1 | 1 | 6 |
| Petr Prajsler | 1 | 0 | 0 | 0 | 0 |
| Igor Liba | 2 | 0 | 0 | 0 | 2 |
| Glenn Healy (Goalie) | 3 | 0 | 0 | 0 | 0 |
| Phil Sykes | 3 | 0 | 0 | 0 | 8 |
| Ken Baumgartner | 5 | 0 | 0 | 0 | 8 |
| John Tonelli | 6 | 0 | 0 | 0 | 8 |
| Kelly Hrudey (Goalie) | 10 | 0 | 0 | 0 | 0 |
| Ron Duguay | 11 | 0 | 0 | 0 | 6 |

## Minnesota North Stars
(Lost Norris Division semifinals to St. Louis, 4-1)

|  | Games | G. | A. | Pts. | Pen. |
|---|---|---|---|---|---|
| Brian Bellows | 5 | 2 | 3 | 5 | 8 |
| Stewart Gavin | 5 | 3 | 1 | 4 | 10 |
| Neal Broten | 5 | 2 | 2 | 4 | 4 |
| Marc Habscheid | 5 | 1 | 3 | 4 | 13 |
| Bob Brooke | 5 | 3 | 0 | 3 | 2 |
| Perry Berezan | 5 | 1 | 2 | 3 | 4 |
| Don Barber | 4 | 1 | 1 | 2 | 2 |
| Frantisek Musil | 5 | 1 | 1 | 2 | 4 |
| Shawn Chambers | 3 | 0 | 2 | 2 | 0 |
| Larry Murphy | 5 | 0 | 2 | 2 | 8 |
| Dusan Pasek | 2 | 1 | 0 | 1 | 0 |
| Steve Gotaas | 3 | 0 | 1 | 1 | 5 |
| David Archibald | 5 | 0 | 1 | 1 | 0 |
| Warren Babe | 2 | 0 | 0 | 0 | 0 |
| Larry DePalma | 2 | 0 | 0 | 0 | 6 |
| Mike Modano | 2 | 0 | 0 | 0 | 0 |
| Reed Larson | 3 | 0 | 0 | 0 | 4 |
| Kari Takko (Goalie) | 3 | 0 | 0 | 0 | 0 |
| Jon Casey (Goalie) | 4 | 0 | 0 | 0 | 2 |
| Ville Siren | 4 | 0 | 0 | 0 | 4 |
| Mike Gartner | 5 | 0 | 0 | 0 | 6 |
| Curt Giles | 5 | 0 | 0 | 0 | 4 |
| Basil McRae | 5 | 0 | 0 | 0 | 58 |
| Mark Tinordi | 5 | 0 | 0 | 0 | 0 |

## Montreal Canadiens
(Lost Stanley Cup finals to Calgary, 4-2)

|  | Games | G. | A. | Pts. | Pen. |
|---|---|---|---|---|---|
| Bobby Smith | 21 | 11 | 8 | 19 | 46 |

|  | Games | G. | A. | Pts | Pen. |
|---|---|---|---|---|---|
| Chris Chelios | 21 | 4 | 15 | 19 | 28 |
| Mats Naslund | 21 | 4 | 11 | 15 | 6 |
| Russ Courtnall | 21 | 8 | 5 | 13 | 18 |
| Petr Svoboda | 21 | 1 | 11 | 12 | 16 |
| Stephane Richer | 21 | 6 | 5 | 11 | 14 |
| Mike McPhee | 20 | 4 | 7 | 11 | 30 |
| Brian Skrudland | 21 | 3 | 7 | 10 | 40 |
| Larry Robinson | 21 | 2 | 8 | 10 | 12 |
| Guy Carbonneau | 21 | 4 | 5 | 9 | 10 |
| Shayne Corson | 21 | 4 | 5 | 9 | 65 |
| Ryan Walter | 21 | 3 | 5 | 8 | 6 |
| Claude Lemieux | 18 | 4 | 3 | 7 | 58 |
| Mike Keane | 21 | 4 | 3 | 7 | 17 |
| Bob Gainey | 16 | 1 | 4 | 5 | 8 |
| Donald Dufresne | 6 | 1 | 1 | 2 | 4 |
| Brent Gilchrist | 9 | 1 | 1 | 2 | 10 |
| Eric Desjardins | 14 | 1 | 1 | 2 | 6 |
| Rick Green | 21 | 1 | 1 | 2 | 6 |
| Patrick Roy (Goalie) | 19 | 0 | 2 | 2 | 16 |
| Craig Ludwig | 21 | 0 | 2 | 2 | 24 |
| Steve Martinson | 1 | 0 | 0 | 0 | 10 |
| Brian Hayward (Goalie) | 2 | 0 | 0 | 0 | 0 |

## New York Rangers
(Lost Patrick Division semifinals to Pittsburgh, 4-0)

|  | Games | G. | A. | Pts | Pen. |
|---|---|---|---|---|---|
| Brian Leetch | 4 | 3 | 2 | 5 | 2 |
| Tomas Sandstrom | 4 | 3 | 2 | 5 | 12 |
| Carey Wilson | 4 | 1 | 2 | 3 | 2 |
| John Ogrodnick | 3 | 2 | 0 | 2 | 0 |
| Tony Granato | 4 | 1 | 1 | 2 | 21 |
| Michel Petit | 4 | 0 | 2 | 2 | 27 |
| David Shaw | 4 | 0 | 2 | 2 | 30 |
| Guy Lafleur | 4 | 1 | 0 | 1 | 0 |
| Bob Froese (Goalie) | 2 | 0 | 1 | 1 | 0 |
| Brian Mullen | 3 | 0 | 1 | 1 | 4 |
| Jan Erixon | 4 | 0 | 1 | 1 | 2 |
| Ron Greschner | 4 | 0 | 1 | 1 | 6 |
| Mark Hardy | 4 | 0 | 1 | 1 | 31 |
| Chris Nilan | 4 | 0 | 1 | 1 | 28 |
| James Patrick | 4 | 0 | 1 | 1 | 2 |
| Mike Richter (Goalie) | 1 | 0 | 0 | 0 | 0 |
| Darren Turcotte | 1 | 0 | 0 | 0 | 0 |
| Lindy Ruff | 2 | 0 | 0 | 0 | 17 |
| John Vanbiesbrouck (G.) | 2 | 0 | 0 | 0 | 0 |
| Jason Lafreniere | 3 | 0 | 0 | 0 | 17 |
| Ulf Dahlen | 4 | 0 | 0 | 0 | 0 |
| Lucien DeBlois | 4 | 0 | 0 | 0 | 4 |
| Kelly Kisio | 4 | 0 | 0 | 0 | 9 |

## Philadelphia Flyers
(Lost Prince of Wales Conference finals to Montreal, 4-2)

|  | Games | G. | A. | Pts | Pen. |
|---|---|---|---|---|---|
| Tim Kerr | 19 | 14 | 11 | 25 | 27 |
| Brian Propp | 18 | 14 | 9 | 23 | 14 |
| Mark Howe | 19 | 0 | 15 | 15 | 10 |
| Rick Tocchet | 16 | 6 | 6 | 12 | 69 |
| Mike Bullard | 19 | 3 | 9 | 12 | 32 |
| Dave Poulin | 19 | 6 | 5 | 11 | 16 |
| Pelle Eklund | 19 | 3 | 8 | 11 | 2 |
| Ron Sutter | 19 | 1 | 9 | 10 | 51 |
| Scott Mellanby | 19 | 4 | 5 | 9 | 28 |
| Gordon Murphy | 19 | 2 | 7 | 9 | 13 |
| Derrick Smith | 19 | 5 | 2 | 7 | 12 |
| Terry Carkner | 19 | 1 | 5 | 6 | 28 |
| Keith Acton | 16 | 2 | 3 | 5 | 18 |

|  | Games | G. | A. | Pts | Pen. |
|---|---|---|---|---|---|
| Kjell Samuelsson | 19 | 1 | 3 | 4 | 24 |
| Al Secord | 14 | 0 | 4 | 4 | 31 |
| Ilkka Sinisalo | 8 | 1 | 1 | 2 | 0 |
| Jay Wells | 18 | 0 | 2 | 2 | 51 |
| Jeff Chychrun | 19 | 0 | 2 | 2 | 65 |
| Ron Hextall (Goalie) | 15 | 1 | 0 | 1 | 28 |
| Murray Craven | 1 | 0 | 0 | 0 | 2 |
| Moe Mantha | 1 | 0 | 0 | 0 | 0 |
| Brian Dobbin | 2 | 0 | 0 | 0 | 17 |
| Doug Sulliman | 4 | 0 | 0 | 0 | 0 |
| Ken Wregget (Goalie) | 5 | 0 | 0 | 0 | 16 |
| Craig Berube | 16 | 0 | 0 | 0 | 56 |

## Pittsburgh Penguins
(Lost Patrick Division finals to Philadelphia, 4-3)

|  | Games | G. | A. | Pts | Pen. |
|---|---|---|---|---|---|
| Mario Lemieux | 11 | 12 | 7 | 19 | 16 |
| Paul Coffey | 11 | 2 | 13 | 15 | 31 |
| Kevin Stevens | 11 | 3 | 7 | 10 | 16 |
| Dan Quinn | 11 | 6 | 3 | 9 | 10 |
| John Cullen | 11 | 3 | 6 | 9 | 28 |
| Zarley Zalapski | 11 | 1 | 8 | 9 | 13 |
| Rob Brown | 11 | 5 | 3 | 8 | 22 |
| Randy Cunneyworth | 11 | 3 | 5 | 8 | 26 |
| Jock Callander | 10 | 2 | 5 | 7 | 10 |
| Phil Bourque | 11 | 4 | 1 | 5 | 66 |
| Jim Johnson | 11 | 0 | 5 | 5 | 44 |
| Troy Loney | 11 | 1 | 3 | 4 | 24 |
| Bob Errey | 11 | 1 | 2 | 3 | 12 |
| Gord Dineen | 11 | 0 | 2 | 2 | 8 |
| Dave McLlwain | 3 | 0 | 1 | 1 | 0 |
| Dave Hannan | 8 | 0 | 1 | 1 | 4 |
| Randy Hillier | 9 | 0 | 1 | 1 | 49 |
| Tom Barrasso (Goalie) | 11 | 0 | 1 | 1 | 8 |
| Steve Dykstra | 1 | 0 | 0 | 0 | 2 |
| Wendell Young (Goalie) | 1 | 0 | 0 | 0 | 0 |
| Richard Zemlak | 1 | 0 | 0 | 0 | 10 |
| Chris Dahlquist | 2 | 0 | 0 | 0 | 0 |
| Jay Caufield | 9 | 0 | 0 | 0 | 28 |
| Rod Buskas | 10 | 0 | 0 | 0 | 23 |

## St. Louis Blues
(Lost Norris Division finals to Chicago, 4-1)

|  | Games | G. | A. | Pts | Pen. |
|---|---|---|---|---|---|
| Peter Zezel | 10 | 6 | 6 | 12 | 4 |
| Bernie Federko | 10 | 4 | 8 | 12 | 0 |
| Brett Hull | 10 | 5 | 5 | 10 | 6 |
| Gordie Roberts | 10 | 1 | 7 | 8 | 8 |
| Sergio Momesso | 10 | 2 | 5 | 7 | 24 |
| Rick Meagher | 10 | 3 | 2 | 5 | 6 |
| Dave Lowry | 10 | 0 | 5 | 5 | 4 |
| Paul Cavallini | 10 | 2 | 2 | 4 | 14 |
| Cliff Ronning | 7 | 1 | 3 | 4 | 0 |
| Greg Paslawski | 9 | 2 | 1 | 3 | 2 |
| Steve Tuttle | 6 | 1 | 2 | 3 | 0 |
| Doug Evans | 7 | 1 | 2 | 3 | 16 |
| Herb Raglan | 8 | 1 | 2 | 3 | 13 |
| Tom Tilley | 10 | 1 | 2 | 3 | 17 |
| Rod Brind'Amour | 5 | 2 | 0 | 2 | 4 |
| Tony Hrkac | 4 | 1 | 1 | 2 | 0 |
| Brian Benning | 7 | 1 | 1 | 2 | 11 |
| Mike Lalor | 10 | 1 | 1 | 2 | 14 |
| Gino Cavallini | 9 | 0 | 2 | 2 | 17 |
| Tony McKegney | 3 | 0 | 1 | 1 | 0 |
| Gaston Gingras | 7 | 0 | 1 | 1 | 2 |
| Todd Ewen | 2 | 0 | 0 | 0 | 21 |

|  | Games | G. | A. | Pts. | Pen. |
|---|---|---|---|---|---|
| Glen Featherstone | 6 | 0 | 0 | 0 | 25 |
| Greg Millen (Goalie) | 10 | 0 | 0 | 0 | 2 |

|  | Games | G. | A. | Pts. | Pen. |
|---|---|---|---|---|---|
| Greg C. Adams | 7 | 0 | 0 | 0 | 21 |
| Stan Smyl | 7 | 0 | 0 | 0 | 9 |

## Vancouver Canucks
(Lost Smythe Division semifinals to Calgary, 4-3)

|  | Games | G. | A. | Pts. | Pen. |
|---|---|---|---|---|---|
| Brian Bradley | 7 | 3 | 4 | 7 | 10 |
| Trevor Linden | 7 | 3 | 4 | 7 | 8 |
| Petri Skriko | 7 | 1 | 5 | 6 | 0 |
| Robert Nordmark | 7 | 3 | 2 | 5 | 8 |
| Greg Adams | 7 | 2 | 3 | 5 | 2 |
| Paul Reinhart | 7 | 2 | 3 | 5 | 4 |
| Tony Tanti | 7 | 0 | 5 | 5 | 4 |
| Rich Sutter | 7 | 2 | 1 | 3 | 12 |
| Mel Bridgman | 7 | 1 | 2 | 3 | 10 |
| Jim Sandlak | 6 | 1 | 1 | 2 | 2 |
| Garth Butcher | 7 | 1 | 1 | 2 | 22 |
| Doug Lidster | 7 | 1 | 1 | 2 | 9 |
| Steve Bozek | 7 | 0 | 2 | 2 | 4 |
| Ronnie Stern | 3 | 0 | 1 | 1 | 17 |
| Harold Snepsts | 7 | 0 | 1 | 1 | 6 |
| Kevan Guy | 1 | 0 | 0 | 0 | 0 |
| Jim Benning | 3 | 0 | 0 | 0 | 0 |
| Steve Weeks (Goalie) | 3 | 0 | 0 | 0 | 2 |
| Larry Melnyk | 4 | 0 | 0 | 0 | 2 |
| Doug Smith | 4 | 0 | 0 | 0 | 6 |
| Kirk McLean (Goalie) | 5 | 0 | 0 | 0 | 0 |

## Washington Capitals
(Lost Patrick Division semifinals to Philadelphia, 4-2)

|  | Games | G. | A. | Pts. | Pen. |
|---|---|---|---|---|---|
| Geoff Courtnall | 6 | 2 | 5 | 7 | 12 |
| Dino Ciccarelli | 6 | 3 | 3 | 6 | 12 |
| Bengt Gustafsson | 4 | 2 | 3 | 5 | 6 |
| Kevin Hatcher | 6 | 1 | 4 | 5 | 20 |
| Scott Stevens | 6 | 1 | 4 | 5 | 11 |
| Mike Ridley | 6 | 0 | 5 | 5 | 2 |
| Michal Pivonka | 6 | 3 | 1 | 4 | 10 |
| Dale Hunter | 6 | 0 | 4 | 4 | 27 |
| Calle Johansson | 6 | 1 | 2 | 3 | 0 |
| Bob Rouse | 6 | 2 | 0 | 2 | 4 |
| Dave Christian | 6 | 1 | 1 | 2 | 0 |
| Bob Gould | 6 | 0 | 2 | 2 | 0 |
| Lou Franceschetti | 6 | 1 | 0 | 1 | 8 |
| Stephen Leach | 6 | 1 | 0 | 1 | 12 |
| Kelly Miller | 6 | 1 | 0 | 1 | 2 |
| Chris Felix | 1 | 0 | 1 | 1 | 0 |
| Yvon Corriveau | 1 | 0 | 0 | 0 | 0 |
| John Druce | 1 | 0 | 0 | 0 | 0 |
| Doug Wickenheiser | 5 | 0 | 0 | 0 | 2 |
| Rod Langway | 6 | 0 | 0 | 0 | 6 |
| Pete Peeters (Goalie) | 6 | 0 | 0 | 0 | 2 |
| Neil Sheehy | 6 | 0 | 0 | 0 | 19 |

# Complete Stanley Cup Goaltending

|  | Games | Mins. | Goals | SO. | Avg. |
|---|---|---|---|---|---|
| Patrick Roy | 19 | 1206 | 42(2) | 2 | *2.09 |
| Brian Hayward | 2 | 124 | 7 | 0 | 3.39 |
| Montreal Totals | 21 | 1336 | 51 | 2 | 2.29 |
| Mike Vernon | *22 | *1381 | *52(1) | *3 | 2.26 |
| Rick Wamsley | 1 | 20 | 2 | 0 | 6.00 |
| Calgary Totals | 22 | 1403 | 55 | 3 | 2.35 |
| Darren Pang | 2 | 10 | 0 | 0 | 0.00 |
| Alain Chevrier | 16 | 1013 | 44(1) | 0 | 2.61 |
| Chicago Totals | 16 | 1024 | 45 | 0 | 2.64 |
| Andy Moog | 6 | 359 | 14 | 0 | 2.34 |
| Rejean Lemelin | 4 | 252 | 16 | 0 | 3.81 |
| Boston Totals | 10 | 612 | 30 | 0 | 2.94 |
| Ken Wregget | 5 | 268 | 10(1) | 0 | 2.24 |
| Ron Hextall | 15 | 886 | 49 | 0 | 3.32 |
| Philadelphia Totals | 19 | 1158 | 60 | 0 | 3.11 |
| Greg Millen | 10 | 649 | 34 | 0 | 3.14 |
| St. Louis Totals | 10 | 651 | 34 | 0 | 3.13 |
| Jacques Cloutier | 4 | 238 | 10(1) | 1 | 2.52 |
| Clint Malarchuk | 1 | 59 | 5 | 0 | 5.08 |
| Buffalo Totals | 5 | 300 | 16 | 1 | 3.20 |
| Steve Weeks | 3 | 140 | 8 | 0 | 3.43 |
| Kirk McLean | 5 | 302 | 18 | 0 | 3.58 |
| Vancouver Totals | 7 | 442 | 26 | 0 | 3.53 |
| Grant Fuhr | 7 | 417 | 24(1) | 1 | 3.45 |
| Edmonton Totals | 7 | 420 | 25 | 1 | 3.57 |
| Wendell Young | 1 | 39 | 1 | 0 | 1.54 |
| Tom Barrasso | 11 | 631 | 40(1) | 0 | 3.80 |
| Pittsburgh Totals | 11 | 672 | 42 | 0 | 3.75 |
| Glenn Healy | 3 | 97 | 6 | 0 | 3.71 |
| Kelly Hrudey | 10 | 566 | 35(1) | 0 | 3.71 |
| Los Angeles Totals | 11 | 668 | 42 | 0 | 3.77 |

|  | Games | Mins. | Goals | SO. | Avg. |
|---|---|---|---|---|---|
| Greg Stefan | 5 | 294 | 18 | 0 | 3.67 |
| Glen Hanlon | 2 | 78 | 7 | 0 | 5.38 |
| Detroit Totals | 6 | 375 | 25 | 0 | 4.00 |
| Peter Sidorkiewicz | 2 | 124 | 8 | 0 | 3.87 |
| Kay Whitmore | 2 | 135 | 10 | 0 | 4.44 |
| Hartford Totals | 4 | 260 | 18 | 0 | 4.15 |
| Pete Peeters | 6 | 359 | 24(1) | 0 | 4.01 |
| Washington Totals | 6 | 361 | 25 | 0 | 4.16 |
| Kari Takko | 3 | 105 | 7 | 0 | 4.00 |
| Jon Casey | 4 | 211 | 16 | 0 | 4.55 |
| Minnesota Totals | 5 | 317 | 23 | 0 | 4.35 |
| John Vanbiesbrouck | 2 | 107 | 6(1) | 0 | 3.36 |
| Mike Richter | 1 | 58 | 4 | 0 | 4.14 |
| Bob Froese | 2 | 72 | 8 | 0 | 6.67 |
| New York Rangers Totals | 4 | 240 | 19 | 0 | 4.75 |

( )—Empty Net Goals. Not counted against an individual goalie's average.

## Individual Stanley Cup Leaders

| | | |
|---|---|---|
| Goals | Joe Mullen, Calgary— | 16 |
| Assists | Al MacInnis, Calgary— | 24 |
| Points | Al MacInnis, Calgary— | 31 |
| Penalty Minutes | Dave Manson, Chicago— | 84 |
| Goaltender's average (360 minutes) | Patrick Roy, Montreal— | 2.09 |
| Shutouts | Mike Vernon, Calgary— | 3 |

## Individual 1988-89 NHL Trophy Winners

ART ROSS TROPHY (Scoring leader) ................................................. Mario Lemieux, Pittsburgh
HART MEMORIAL TROPHY (Most Valuable) .................................... Wayne Gretzky, Los Angeles
JAMES NORRIS MEMORIAL TROPHY (Top Defenseman) ................ Chris Chelios, Montreal
VEZINA TROPHY (Top Goaltender) .................................................. Patrick Roy, Montreal
BILL JENNINGS TROPHY (Goaltending Trophy) ................................ Patrick Roy, Montreal
 Brian Hayward, Montreal
CALDER MEMORIAL TROPHY (Top Rookie) ..................................... Brian Leetch, N.Y. Rangers
LADY BYNG TROPHY (Most Gentlemanly) ....................................... Joe Mullen, Calgary
CONN SMYTHE TROPHY (Playoff MVP) ............................................ Al MacInnis, Calgary
BILL MASTERTON MEMORIAL TROPHY
 (Perseverance, Sportsmanship and Dedication) .......................... Tim Kerr, Philadelphia
FRANK J. SELKE TROPHY (Best Defensive Forward) ......................... Guy Carbonneau, Montreal
JACK ADAMS AWARD (Coach of the Year) ..................................... Pat Burns, Montreal
KING CLANCY TROPHY (Humanitarian Contributions) ..................... Bryan Trottier, N.Y. Islanders

# Year-By-Year NHL Standings

From 1917-18 through the 1925-26 season, National Hockey League champions played against the Pacific Coast Hockey League for the Stanley Cup. So, only Stanley Cup championships are designated in the following club records for that period.

Key to standings: *—Missed playoffs. †—Eliminated in first round of new playoff format (1974-75). a—Eliminated in quarterfinal round. b—Eliminated in semifinal round. c—Eliminated in final round. xx—Stanley Cup champion.

NOTE: Records for Edmonton Oilers, Hartford Whalers, Quebec Nordiques and Winnipeg Jets include World Hockey Association results prior to their entrance into NHL in 1979-80. Key to WHA standings: *—Missed playoffs. †—Preliminary round (established for 1975-76 season). a—Eliminated in quarterfinal round. b—Eliminated in semifinal round. c—Eliminated in final round. xx—Avco World Cup champion.

## Boston Bruins

| Season | W. | L. | T. | Pts. | GF. | GA. | Position |
|---|---|---|---|---|---|---|---|
| 1924-25 | 6 | 24 | 0 | 12 | 49 | 119 | Sixth |
| 1925-26 | 17 | 15 | 4 | 38 | 92 | 85 | Fourth |
| 1926-27 | 21 | 20 | 3 | 45 | 97 | 89 | Second—c |
| 1927-28 | 20 | 13 | 11 | 51 | 77 | 70 | First—b |
| 1928-29 | 26 | 13 | 5 | 57 | 89 | 52 | First—xx |
| 1929-30 | 38 | 5 | 1 | 77 | 179 | 98 | First—c |
| 1930-31 | 28 | 10 | 6 | 62 | 143 | 90 | First—b |
| 1931-32 | 15 | 21 | 12 | 42 | 122 | 117 | Fourth—* |
| 1932-33 | 25 | 15 | 8 | 58 | 124 | 88 | First—b |
| 1933-34 | 18 | 25 | 5 | 41 | 111 | 130 | Fourth—* |
| 1934-35 | 26 | 16 | 6 | 58 | 129 | 112 | First—b |
| 1935-36 | 22 | 20 | 6 | 50 | 92 | 83 | Second—a |
| 1936-37 | 23 | 18 | 7 | 53 | 120 | 110 | Second—a |
| 1937-38 | 30 | 11 | 7 | 67 | 142 | 89 | First—b |
| 1938-39 | 36 | 10 | 2 | 74 | 156 | 76 | First—xx |
| 1939-40 | 31 | 12 | 5 | 67 | 170 | 98 | First—b |
| 1940-41 | 27 | 8 | 13 | 67 | 168 | 102 | First—xx |
| 1941-42 | 25 | 17 | 6 | 56 | 160 | 118 | Third—b |
| 1942-43 | 24 | 17 | 9 | 57 | 195 | 176 | Second—c |
| 1943-44 | 19 | 26 | 5 | 43 | 223 | 268 | Fifth—* |
| 1944-45 | 16 | 30 | 4 | 36 | 179 | 219 | Fourth—b |
| 1945-46 | 24 | 18 | 8 | 56 | 167 | 156 | Second—c |
| 1946-47 | 26 | 23 | 11 | 63 | 190 | 175 | Third—b |
| 1947-48 | 23 | 24 | 13 | 59 | 167 | 168 | Third—b |
| 1948-49 | 29 | 23 | 8 | 66 | 178 | 163 | Second—b |
| 1949-50 | 22 | 32 | 16 | 60 | 198 | 228 | Fifth—* |
| 1950-51 | 22 | 30 | 18 | 62 | 178 | 197 | Fourth—b |
| 1951-52 | 25 | 29 | 16 | 66 | 162 | 176 | Fourth—b |
| 1952-53 | 28 | 29 | 13 | 69 | 152 | 172 | Third—c |
| 1953-54 | 32 | 28 | 10 | 74 | 177 | 181 | Fourth—b |
| 1954-55 | 23 | 26 | 21 | 67 | 169 | 188 | Fourth—b |
| 1955-56 | 23 | 34 | 13 | 59 | 147 | 185 | Fifth—* |
| 1956-57 | 34 | 24 | 12 | 80 | 195 | 174 | Third—c |
| 1957-58 | 27 | 28 | 15 | 69 | 199 | 194 | Fourth—c |
| 1958-59 | 32 | 29 | 9 | 73 | 205 | 215 | Second—b |
| 1959-60 | 28 | 34 | 8 | 64 | 220 | 241 | Fifth—* |
| 1960-61 | 15 | 42 | 13 | 43 | 176 | 254 | Sixth—* |
| 1961-62 | 15 | 47 | 8 | 38 | 177 | 306 | Sixth—* |
| 1962-63 | 14 | 39 | 17 | 45 | 198 | 281 | Sixth—* |
| 1963-64 | 18 | 40 | 12 | 48 | 170 | 212 | Sixth—* |
| 1964-65 | 21 | 43 | 6 | 48 | 166 | 253 | Sixth—* |
| 1965-66 | 21 | 43 | 6 | 48 | 174 | 275 | Fifth—* |
| 1966-67 | 17 | 43 | 10 | 44 | 182 | 253 | Sixth—* |
| 1967-68 | 37 | 27 | 10 | 84 | 259 | 216 | Third—a |
| 1968-69 | 42 | 18 | 16 | 100 | 303 | 221 | Second—b |
| 1969-70 | 40 | 17 | 19 | 99 | 277 | 216 | Second—xx |
| 1970-71 | 57 | 14 | 7 | 121 | 399 | 207 | First—a |
| 1971-72 | 54 | 13 | 11 | 119 | 330 | 204 | First—xx |
| 1972-73 | 51 | 22 | 5 | 107 | 330 | 235 | Second—a |
| 1973-74 | 52 | 17 | 9 | 113 | 349 | 221 | First—c |
| 1974-75 | 40 | 26 | 14 | 94 | 345 | 245 | Second—† |
| 1975-76 | 48 | 15 | 17 | 113 | 313 | 237 | First—b |
| 1976-77 | 49 | 23 | 8 | 106 | 312 | 240 | First—c |
| 1977-78 | 51 | 18 | 11 | 113 | 333 | 218 | First—c |
| 1978-79 | 43 | 23 | 14 | 100 | 316 | 270 | First—b |
| 1979-80 | 46 | 21 | 13 | 105 | 310 | 234 | Second—a |
| 1980-81 | 37 | 30 | 13 | 87 | 316 | 272 | Second—† |

| Season | W. | L. | T. | Pts. | GF. | GA. | Position |
|---|---|---|---|---|---|---|---|
| 1981-82 | 43 | 27 | 10 | 96 | 323 | 285 | Second—a |
| 1982-83 | 50 | 20 | 10 | 110 | 327 | 228 | First—b |
| 1983-84 | 49 | 25 | 6 | 104 | 336 | 261 | First—† |
| 1984-85 | 36 | 34 | 10 | 82 | 303 | 287 | Fourth—† |
| 1985-86 | 37 | 31 | 12 | 86 | 311 | 288 | Third—† |
| 1986-87 | 39 | 34 | 7 | 85 | 301 | 276 | Third—† |
| 1987-88 | 44 | 30 | 6 | 94 | 300 | 251 | Second—c |
| 1988-89 | 37 | 29 | 14 | 88 | 289 | 256 | Second—a |
|  | 1994 | 1568 | 630 | 4618 | 13476 | 12404 |  |

## Buffalo Sabres

| Season | W. | L. | T. | Pts. | GF. | GA. | Position |
|---|---|---|---|---|---|---|---|
| 1970-71 | 24 | 39 | 15 | 63 | 217 | 291 | Fifth—* |
| 1971-72 | 16 | 43 | 19 | 51 | 203 | 289 | Sixth—* |
| 1972-73 | 37 | 27 | 14 | 88 | 257 | 219 | Fourth—a |
| 1973-74 | 32 | 34 | 12 | 76 | 242 | 250 | Fifth—* |
| 1974-75 | 49 | 16 | 15 | 113 | 354 | 240 | First—c |
| 1975-76 | 46 | 21 | 13 | 105 | 339 | 240 | Second—a |
| 1976-77 | 48 | 24 | 8 | 104 | 301 | 220 | Second—a |
| 1977-78 | 44 | 19 | 17 | 105 | 288 | 215 | Second—a |
| 1978-79 | 36 | 28 | 16 | 88 | 280 | 263 | Second—† |
| 1979-80 | 47 | 17 | 16 | 110 | 318 | 201 | First—b |
| 1980-81 | 39 | 20 | 21 | 99 | 327 | 250 | First—a |
| 1981-82 | 39 | 26 | 15 | 93 | 307 | 273 | Third—† |
| 1982-83 | 38 | 29 | 13 | 89 | 318 | 285 | Third—a |
| 1983-84 | 48 | 25 | 7 | 103 | 315 | 257 | Second—† |
| 1984-85 | 38 | 28 | 14 | 90 | 290 | 237 | Third—† |
| 1985-86 | 37 | 37 | 6 | 80 | 296 | 291 | Fifth—* |
| 1986-87 | 28 | 44 | 8 | 64 | 280 | 308 | Fifth—* |
| 1987-88 | 37 | 32 | 11 | 85 | 283 | 305 | Third—† |
| 1988-89 | 38 | 35 | 7 | 83 | 291 | 299 | Third—† |
|  | 721 | 544 | 247 | 1689 | 5506 | 4933 |  |

## Calgary Flames

| Season | W. | L. | T. | Pts. | GF. | GA. | Position |
|---|---|---|---|---|---|---|---|
| 1972-73 | 25 | 38 | 15 | 65 | 191 | 239 | Seventh—* |
| 1973-74 | 30 | 34 | 14 | 74 | 214 | 238 | Fourth—a |
| 1974-75 | 34 | 31 | 15 | 83 | 243 | 233 | Fourth—* |
| 1975-76 | 35 | 33 | 12 | 82 | 262 | 237 | Third—† |
| 1976-77 | 34 | 34 | 12 | 80 | 264 | 265 | Third—† |
| 1977-78 | 34 | 27 | 19 | 87 | 274 | 252 | Third—† |
| 1978-79 | 41 | 31 | 8 | 90 | 327 | 280 | Fourth—† |
| 1979-80 | 35 | 32 | 13 | 83 | 282 | 269 | Fourth—† |
| 1980-81 | 39 | 27 | 14 | 92 | 329 | 298 | Third—b |
| 1981-82 | 29 | 34 | 17 | 75 | 334 | 345 | Third—† |
| 1982-83 | 32 | 34 | 14 | 78 | 321 | 317 | Second—a |
| 1983-84 | 34 | 32 | 14 | 82 | 311 | 314 | Second—a |
| 1984-85 | 41 | 27 | 12 | 94 | 363 | 302 | Third—† |
| 1985-86 | 40 | 31 | 9 | 89 | 354 | 315 | Second—c |
| 1986-87 | 46 | 31 | 3 | 95 | 318 | 289 | Second—† |
| 1987-88 | 48 | 23 | 9 | 105 | 397 | 305 | First—a |
| 1988-89 | 54 | 17 | 9 | 117 | 354 | 226 | First—xx |
|  | 631 | 516 | 209 | 1471 | 5138 | 4729 |  |

## Chicago Black Hawks

| Season | W. | L. | T. | Pts. | GF. | GA. | Position |
|---|---|---|---|---|---|---|---|
| 1926-27 | 19 | 22 | 3 | 41 | 115 | 116 | Third—a |
| 1927-28 | 7 | 34 | 3 | 17 | 68 | 134 | Fifth—* |
| 1928-29 | 7 | 29 | 8 | 22 | 33 | 85 | Fifth—* |
| 1929-30 | 21 | 18 | 5 | 47 | 117 | 111 | Second—a |
| 1930-31 | 24 | 17 | 3 | 51 | 108 | 78 | Second—c |
| 1931-32 | 18 | 19 | 11 | 47 | 86 | 101 | Second—a |
| 1932-33 | 16 | 20 | 12 | 44 | 88 | 101 | Fourth—* |
| 1933-34 | 20 | 17 | 11 | 51 | 88 | 83 | Second—xx |
| 1934-35 | 26 | 17 | 5 | 57 | 118 | 88 | Second—a |
| 1935-36 | 21 | 19 | 8 | 50 | 93 | 92 | Third—a |
| 1936-37 | 14 | 27 | 7 | 35 | 99 | 131 | Fourth—* |
| 1937-38 | 14 | 25 | 9 | 37 | 97 | 139 | Third—xx |
| 1938-39 | 12 | 28 | 8 | 32 | 91 | 132 | Seventh—* |

| Season | W. | L. | T. | Pts. | GF. | GA. | Position |
|---|---|---|---|---|---|---|---|
| 1939-40 | 23 | 19 | 6 | 52 | 112 | 120 | Fourth—a |
| 1940-41 | 16 | 25 | 7 | 39 | 112 | 139 | Fifth—b |
| 1941-42 | 22 | 23 | 3 | 47 | 145 | 155 | Fourth—a |
| 1942-43 | 17 | 18 | 15 | 49 | 179 | 180 | Fifth—* |
| 1943-44 | 22 | 23 | 5 | 49 | 178 | 187 | Fourth—c |
| 1944-45 | 13 | 30 | 7 | 33 | 141 | 194 | Fifth—* |
| 1945-46 | 23 | 20 | 7 | 53 | 200 | 178 | Third—b |
| 1946-47 | 19 | 37 | 4 | 42 | 193 | 274 | Sixth—* |
| 1947-48 | 20 | 34 | 6 | 46 | 195 | 225 | Sixth—* |
| 1948-49 | 21 | 31 | 8 | 50 | 173 | 211 | Fifth—* |
| 1949-50 | 22 | 38 | 10 | 54 | 203 | 244 | Sixth—* |
| 1950-51 | 13 | 47 | 10 | 36 | 171 | 280 | Sixth—* |
| 1951-52 | 17 | 44 | 9 | 43 | 158 | 241 | Sixth—* |
| 1952-53 | 27 | 28 | 15 | 69 | 169 | 175 | Fourth—b |
| 1953-54 | 12 | 51 | 7 | 31 | 133 | 242 | Sixth—* |
| 1954-55 | 13 | 40 | 17 | 43 | 161 | 235 | Sixth—* |
| 1955-56 | 19 | 39 | 12 | 50 | 155 | 216 | Sixth—* |
| 1956-57 | 16 | 39 | 15 | 47 | 169 | 225 | Sixth—* |
| 1957-58 | 24 | 39 | 7 | 55 | 163 | 202 | Fifth—* |
| 1958-59 | 28 | 29 | 13 | 69 | 197 | 208 | Third—b |
| 1959-60 | 28 | 29 | 13 | 69 | 191 | 180 | Third—b |
| 1960-61 | 29 | 24 | 17 | 75 | 198 | 180 | Third—xx |
| 1961-62 | 31 | 26 | 13 | 75 | 217 | 186 | Third—c |
| 1962-63 | 32 | 21 | 17 | 81 | 194 | 178 | Second—b |
| 1963-64 | 36 | 22 | 12 | 84 | 218 | 169 | Second—b |
| 1964-65 | 34 | 28 | 8 | 76 | 224 | 176 | Third—c |
| 1965-66 | 37 | 25 | 8 | 82 | 240 | 187 | Second—b |
| 1966-67 | 41 | 17 | 12 | 94 | 264 | 170 | First—b |
| 1967-68 | 32 | 26 | 16 | 80 | 212 | 222 | Fourth—b |
| 1968-69 | 34 | 33 | 9 | 77 | 280 | 246 | Sixth—* |
| 1969-70 | 45 | 22 | 9 | 99 | 250 | 170 | First—b |
| 1970-71 | 49 | 20 | 9 | 107 | 277 | 184 | First—c |
| 1971-72 | 46 | 17 | 15 | 107 | 256 | 166 | First—b |
| 1972-73 | 42 | 27 | 9 | 93 | 284 | 225 | First—c |
| 1973-74 | 41 | 14 | 23 | 105 | 272 | 164 | Second—b |
| 1974-75 | 37 | 35 | 8 | 82 | 268 | 241 | Third—a |
| 1975-76 | 32 | 30 | 18 | 82 | 254 | 261 | First—a |
| 1976-77 | 26 | 43 | 11 | 63 | 240 | 298 | Third—† |
| 1977-78 | 32 | 29 | 19 | 83 | 230 | 220 | First—a |
| 1978-79 | 29 | 36 | 15 | 73 | 244 | 277 | First—a |
| 1979-80 | 34 | 27 | 19 | 87 | 241 | 250 | First—a |
| 1980-81 | 31 | 33 | 16 | 78 | 304 | 315 | Second—† |
| 1981-82 | 30 | 38 | 12 | 72 | 332 | 363 | Fourth—b |
| 1982-83 | 47 | 23 | 10 | 104 | 338 | 268 | First—b |
| 1983-84 | 30 | 42 | 8 | 68 | 277 | 311 | Fourth—† |
| 1984-85 | 38 | 35 | 7 | 83 | 309 | 299 | Second—b |
| 1985-86 | 39 | 33 | 8 | 86 | 351 | 349 | First—† |
| 1986-87 | 29 | 37 | 14 | 72 | 290 | 310 | Third—† |
| 1987-88 | 30 | 41 | 9 | 69 | 284 | 328 | Third—† |
| 1988-89 | 27 | 41 | 12 | 66 | 297 | 335 | Fourth—b |
| | 1654 | 1820 | 652 | 3960 | 12344 | 12750 | |

## Detroit Red Wings

| Season | W. | L. | T. | Pts. | GF. | GA. | Position |
|---|---|---|---|---|---|---|---|
| 1926-27 | 12 | 28 | 4 | 28 | 76 | 105 | Fifth—* |
| 1927-28 | 19 | 19 | 6 | 44 | 88 | 79 | Fourth—* |
| 1928-29 | 19 | 16 | 9 | 47 | 72 | 63 | Third—a |
| 1929-30 | 14 | 24 | 6 | 34 | 117 | 133 | Fourth—* |
| 1930-31 | 16 | 21 | 7 | 39 | 102 | 105 | Fourth—* |
| 1931-32 | 18 | 20 | 10 | 46 | 95 | 108 | Third—a |
| 1932-33 | 25 | 15 | 8 | 58 | 111 | 93 | Second—b |
| 1933-34 | 24 | 14 | 10 | 58 | 113 | 98 | First—c |
| 1934-35 | 19 | 22 | 7 | 45 | 127 | 114 | Fourth—* |
| 1935-36 | 24 | 16 | 8 | 56 | 124 | 103 | First—xx |
| 1936-37 | 25 | 14 | 9 | 59 | 128 | 102 | First—xx |
| 1937-38 | 12 | 25 | 11 | 35 | 99 | 133 | Fourth—* |
| 1938-39 | 18 | 24 | 6 | 42 | 107 | 128 | Fifth—b |
| 1939-40 | 16 | 26 | 6 | 38 | 90 | 126 | Fifth—b |
| 1940-41 | 21 | 16 | 11 | 53 | 112 | 102 | Third—c |
| 1941-42 | 19 | 25 | 4 | 42 | 140 | 147 | Fifth—c |

| Season | W. | L. | T. | Pts. | GF. | GA. | Position |
|---|---|---|---|---|---|---|---|
| 1942-43 | 25 | 14 | 11 | 61 | 169 | 124 | First—xx |
| 1943-44 | 26 | 18 | 6 | 58 | 214 | 177 | Second—b |
| 1944-45 | 31 | 14 | 5 | 67 | 218 | 161 | Second—c |
| 1945-46 | 20 | 20 | 10 | 50 | 146 | 159 | Fourth—b |
| 1946-47 | 22 | 27 | 11 | 55 | 190 | 193 | Fourth—b |
| 1947-48 | 30 | 18 | 12 | 72 | 187 | 148 | Second—c |
| 1948-49 | 34 | 19 | 7 | 75 | 195 | 145 | First—c |
| 1949-50 | 37 | 19 | 14 | 88 | 229 | 164 | First—xx |
| 1950-51 | 44 | 13 | 13 | 101 | 236 | 139 | First—b |
| 1951-52 | 44 | 14 | 12 | 100 | 215 | 133 | First—xx |
| 1952-53 | 36 | 16 | 18 | 90 | 222 | 133 | First—b |
| 1953-54 | 37 | 19 | 14 | 88 | 191 | 132 | First—xx |
| 1954-55 | 42 | 17 | 11 | 95 | 204 | 134 | First—xx |
| 1955-56 | 30 | 24 | 16 | 76 | 183 | 148 | Second—c |
| 1956-57 | 38 | 20 | 12 | 88 | 198 | 157 | First—b |
| 1957-58 | 29 | 29 | 12 | 70 | 176 | 207 | Third—b |
| 1958-59 | 25 | 37 | 8 | 58 | 167 | 218 | Sixth—* |
| 1959-60 | 26 | 29 | 15 | 67 | 186 | 197 | Fourth—b |
| 1960-61 | 25 | 29 | 16 | 66 | 195 | 215 | Fourth—c |
| 1961-62 | 23 | 33 | 14 | 60 | 184 | 219 | Fifth—* |
| 1962-63 | 32 | 25 | 13 | 77 | 200 | 194 | Fourth—c |
| 1963-64 | 30 | 29 | 11 | 71 | 191 | 204 | Fourth—c |
| 1964-65 | 40 | 23 | 7 | 87 | 224 | 175 | First—b |
| 1965-66 | 31 | 27 | 12 | 74 | 221 | 194 | Fourth—c |
| 1966-67 | 27 | 39 | 4 | 58 | 212 | 241 | Fifth—* |
| 1967-68 | 27 | 35 | 12 | 66 | 245 | 257 | Sixth—* |
| 1968-69 | 33 | 31 | 12 | 78 | 239 | 221 | Fifth—* |
| 1969-70 | 40 | 21 | 15 | 95 | 246 | 199 | Third—a |
| 1970-71 | 22 | 45 | 11 | 55 | 209 | 308 | Seventh—* |
| 1971-72 | 33 | 35 | 10 | 76 | 261 | 262 | Fifth—* |
| 1972-73 | 37 | 29 | 12 | 86 | 265 | 243 | Fifth—* |
| 1973-74 | 29 | 39 | 10 | 68 | 255 | 319 | Sixth—* |
| 1974-75 | 23 | 45 | 12 | 58 | 259 | 335 | Fourth—* |
| 1975-76 | 26 | 44 | 10 | 62 | 226 | 300 | Fourth—* |
| 1976-77 | 16 | 55 | 9 | 41 | 183 | 309 | Fifth—* |
| 1977-78 | 32 | 34 | 14 | 78 | 252 | 266 | Second—a |
| 1978-79 | 23 | 41 | 16 | 62 | 252 | 295 | Fifth—* |
| 1979-80 | 26 | 43 | 11 | 63 | 268 | 306 | Fifth—* |
| 1980-81 | 19 | 43 | 18 | 56 | 252 | 339 | Fifth—* |
| 1981-82 | 21 | 47 | 12 | 54 | 270 | 351 | Sixth—* |
| 1982-83 | 21 | 44 | 15 | 57 | 263 | 344 | Fifth—* |
| 1983-84 | 31 | 42 | 7 | 69 | 298 | 323 | Third—† |
| 1984-85 | 27 | 41 | 12 | 66 | 313 | 357 | Third—† |
| 1985-86 | 17 | 57 | 6 | 40 | 266 | 415 | Fifth—* |
| 1986-87 | 34 | 36 | 10 | 78 | 260 | 274 | Second—b |
| 1987-88 | 41 | 28 | 11 | 93 | 322 | 269 | First—b |
| 1988-89 | 34 | 34 | 12 | 80 | 313 | 316 | First—† |
|  | 1697 | 1766 | 663 | 4057 | 12371 | 12658 |  |

## Edmonton Oilers

| Season | W. | L. | T. | Pts. | GF. | GA. | Position |
|---|---|---|---|---|---|---|---|
| 1972-73 | 38 | 37 | 3 | 79 | 269 | 256 | Fifth—* |
| 1973-74 | 38 | 37 | 3 | 79 | 268 | 269 | Third—a |
| 1974-75 | 36 | 38 | 4 | 76 | 279 | 279 | Fifth—* |
| 1975-76 | 27 | 49 | 5 | 59 | 268 | 345 | Fourth—a |
| 1976-77 | 34 | 43 | 4 | 72 | 243 | 304 | Fourth—a |
| 1977-78 | 38 | 39 | 3 | 79 | 309 | 307 | Fifth—a |
| 1978-79 | 48 | 30 | 2 | 98 | 340 | 266 | First—c |
| 1979-80 | 28 | 39 | 13 | 69 | 301 | 322 | Fourth—† |
| 1980-81 | 29 | 35 | 16 | 74 | 328 | 327 | Fourth—a |
| 1981-82 | 48 | 17 | 15 | 111 | 417 | 295 | First—† |
| 1982-83 | 47 | 21 | 12 | 106 | 424 | 315 | First—c |
| 1983-84 | 57 | 18 | 5 | 119 | 446 | 314 | First—xx |
| 1984-85 | 49 | 20 | 11 | 109 | 401 | 298 | First—xx |
| 1985-86 | 56 | 17 | 7 | 119 | 426 | 310 | First—a |
| 1986-87 | 50 | 24 | 6 | 106 | 372 | 284 | First—xx |
| 1987-88 | 44 | 25 | 11 | 99 | 363 | 288 | Second—xx |
| 1988-89 | 38 | 34 | 8 | 84 | 325 | 306 | Third—† |
|  | 705 | 523 | 128 | 1538 | 5779 | 5085 |  |

## Hartford Whalers

| Season | W. | L. | T. | Pts. | GF. | GA. | Position |
|---|---|---|---|---|---|---|---|
| 1972-73 | 46 | 30 | 2 | 94 | 318 | 263 | First—xx |
| 1973-74 | 43 | 31 | 4 | 90 | 291 | 260 | First—a |
| 1974-75 | 43 | 30 | 5 | 91 | 274 | 279 | First—a |
| 1975-76 | 33 | 40 | 7 | 73 | 255 | 290 | Third—b |
| 1976-77 | 35 | 40 | 6 | 76 | 275 | 290 | Fourth—a |
| 1977-78 | 44 | 31 | 5 | 93 | 335 | 269 | Second—c |
| 1978-79 | 37 | 34 | 9 | 83 | 298 | 287 | Fourth—b |
| 1979-80 | 27 | 34 | 19 | 73 | 303 | 312 | Fourth—† |
| 1980-81 | 21 | 41 | 18 | 60 | 292 | 372 | Fourth—* |
| 1981-82 | 21 | 41 | 18 | 60 | 264 | 351 | Fifth—* |
| 1982-83 | 19 | 54 | 7 | 45 | 261 | 403 | Fifth—* |
| 1983-84 | 28 | 42 | 10 | 66 | 288 | 320 | Fifth—* |
| 1984-85 | 30 | 41 | 9 | 69 | 268 | 318 | Fifth—* |
| 1985-86 | 40 | 36 | 4 | 84 | 332 | 302 | Fourth—a |
| 1986-87 | 43 | 30 | 7 | 93 | 287 | 270 | First—† |
| 1987-88 | 35 | 38 | 7 | 77 | 249 | 267 | Fourth—† |
| 1988-89 | 37 | 38 | 5 | 79 | 299 | 290 | Fourth—† |
|  | 582 | 631 | 142 | 1306 | 4894 | 5143 |  |

## Los Angeles Kings

| Season | W. | L. | T. | Pts. | GF. | GA. | Position |
|---|---|---|---|---|---|---|---|
| 1967-68 | 31 | 33 | 10 | 72 | 200 | 224 | Second—a |
| 1968-69 | 24 | 42 | 10 | 58 | 185 | 260 | Fourth—b |
| 1969-70 | 14 | 52 | 10 | 38 | 168 | 290 | Sixth—* |
| 1970-71 | 25 | 40 | 13 | 63 | 239 | 303 | Fifth—* |
| 1971-72 | 20 | 49 | 9 | 49 | 206 | 305 | Seventh—* |
| 1972-73 | 31 | 36 | 11 | 73 | 232 | 245 | Sixth—* |
| 1973-74 | 33 | 33 | 12 | 78 | 233 | 231 | Third—a |
| 1974-75 | 42 | 17 | 21 | 105 | 269 | 185 | Second-† |
| 1975-76 | 38 | 33 | 9 | 85 | 263 | 265 | Second—a |
| 1976-77 | 34 | 31 | 15 | 83 | 271 | 241 | Second—a |
| 1977-78 | 31 | 34 | 15 | 77 | 243 | 245 | Third—† |
| 1978-79 | 34 | 34 | 12 | 80 | 292 | 286 | Third—† |
| 1979-80 | 30 | 36 | 14 | 74 | 290 | 313 | Second—† |
| 1980-81 | 43 | 24 | 13 | 99 | 337 | 290 | Second—† |
| 1981-82 | 24 | 41 | 15 | 63 | 314 | 369 | Fourth—a |
| 1982-83 | 27 | 41 | 12 | 66 | 308 | 365 | Fifth—* |
| 1983-84 | 23 | 44 | 13 | 59 | 309 | 376 | Fifth—* |
| 1984-85 | 34 | 32 | 14 | 82 | 339 | 326 | Fourth—† |
| 1985-86 | 23 | 49 | 8 | 54 | 284 | 389 | Fifth—† |
| 1986-87 | 31 | 41 | 8 | 70 | 318 | 341 | Fourth—† |
| 1987-88 | 30 | 42 | 8 | 68 | 318 | 359 | Fourth—† |
| 1988-89 | 42 | 31 | 7 | 91 | 376 | 335 | Second—a |
|  | 664 | 715 | 259 | 1587 | 5994 | 6543 |  |

## Minnesota North Stars

| Season | W. | L. | T. | Pts. | GF. | GA. | Position |
|---|---|---|---|---|---|---|---|
| 1967-68 | 27 | 32 | 15 | 69 | 191 | 226 | Fourth—b |
| 1968-69 | 18 | 43 | 15 | 51 | 189 | 270 | Sixth—* |
| 1969-70 | 19 | 35 | 22 | 60 | 224 | 257 | Third—a |
| 1970-71 | 28 | 34 | 16 | 72 | 191 | 223 | Fourth—b |
| 1971-72 | 37 | 29 | 12 | 86 | 212 | 191 | Second—a |
| 1972-73 | 37 | 30 | 11 | 85 | 254 | 230 | Third—a |
| 1973-74 | 23 | 38 | 17 | 63 | 235 | 275 | Seventh—* |
| 1974-75 | 23 | 50 | 7 | 53 | 221 | 341 | Fourth—* |
| 1975-76 | 20 | 53 | 7 | 47 | 195 | 303 | Fourth—* |
| 1976-77 | 23 | 39 | 18 | 64 | 240 | 310 | Second—† |
| 1977-78 | 18 | 53 | 9 | 45 | 218 | 325 | Fifth—* |
| 1978-79 | 28 | 40 | 12 | 68 | 257 | 289 | Fourth—* |
| 1979-80 | 36 | 28 | 16 | 88 | 311 | 253 | Third—b |
| 1980-81 | 35 | 28 | 17 | 87 | 291 | 263 | Third—c |
| 1981-82 | 37 | 23 | 20 | 94 | 346 | 288 | First—† |
| 1982-83 | 40 | 24 | 16 | 96 | 321 | 290 | Second—a |
| 1983-84 | 39 | 31 | 10 | 88 | 345 | 344 | First—b |
| 1984-85 | 25 | 43 | 12 | 62 | 268 | 321 | Fourth—a |
| 1985-86 | 38 | 33 | 9 | 85 | 327 | 305 | Second—† |
| 1986-87 | 30 | 40 | 10 | 70 | 296 | 314 | Fifth—* |
| 1987-88 | 19 | 48 | 13 | 51 | 242 | 349 | Fifth—* |
| 1988-89 | 27 | 37 | 16 | 70 | 258 | 278 | Third—† |
|  | 627 | 811 | 300 | 1554 | 5632 | 6245 |  |

## Montreal Canadiens

| Season | W. | L. | T. | Pts. | GF. | GA. | Position |
|---|---|---|---|---|---|---|---|
| 1917-18 | 13 | 9 | 0 | 26 | 115 | 84 | First and Third |
| 1918-19 | 10 | 8 | 0 | 20 | 88 | 78 | Second |
| 1919-20 | 13 | 11 | 0 | 26 | 129 | 113 | Second |
| 1920-21 | 13 | 11 | 0 | 26 | 112 | 99 | Third |
| 1921-22 | 12 | 11 | 1 | 25 | 88 | 94 | Third |
| 1922-23 | 13 | 9 | 2 | 28 | 73 | 61 | Second |
| 1923-24 | 13 | 11 | 0 | 26 | 59 | 48 | Second—xx |
| 1924-25 | 17 | 11 | 2 | 36 | 93 | 56 | Third |
| 1925-26 | 11 | 24 | 1 | 23 | 79 | 108 | Seventh |
| 1926-27 | 28 | 14 | 2 | 58 | 99 | 67 | Second—c |
| 1927-28 | 26 | 11 | 7 | 59 | 116 | 48 | First—b |
| 1928-29 | 22 | 7 | 15 | 59 | 71 | 43 | First—b |
| 1929-30 | 21 | 14 | 9 | 51 | 142 | 114 | Second—xx |
| 1930-31 | 26 | 10 | 8 | 60 | 129 | 89 | First—xx |
| 1931-32 | 25 | 16 | 7 | 57 | 128 | 111 | First—b |
| 1932-33 | 18 | 25 | 5 | 41 | 92 | 115 | Third—a |
| 1933-34 | 22 | 20 | 6 | 50 | 99 | 101 | Second—a |
| 1934-35 | 19 | 23 | 6 | 44 | 110 | 145 | Third—a |
| 1935-36 | 11 | 26 | 11 | 33 | 82 | 123 | Fourth—* |
| 1936-37 | 24 | 18 | 6 | 54 | 115 | 111 | First—b |
| 1937-38 | 18 | 17 | 13 | 49 | 123 | 128 | Third—a |
| 1938-39 | 15 | 24 | 9 | 39 | 115 | 146 | Sixth—a |
| 1939-40 | 10 | 33 | 5 | 25 | 90 | 167 | Seventh—* |
| 1940-41 | 16 | 26 | 6 | 38 | 121 | 147 | Sixth—a |
| 1941-42 | 18 | 27 | 3 | 39 | 134 | 173 | Sixth—a |
| 1942-43 | 19 | 19 | 12 | 50 | 181 | 191 | Fourth—b |
| 1943-44 | 38 | 5 | 7 | 83 | 234 | 109 | First—xx |
| 1944-45 | 38 | 8 | 4 | 80 | 228 | 121 | First—b |
| 1945-46 | 28 | 17 | 5 | 61 | 172 | 134 | First—xx |
| 1946-47 | 34 | 16 | 10 | 78 | 189 | 138 | First—c |
| 1947-48 | 20 | 29 | 11 | 51 | 147 | 169 | Fifth—* |
| 1948-49 | 28 | 23 | 9 | 65 | 152 | 126 | Third—b |
| 1949-50 | 29 | 22 | 19 | 77 | 172 | 150 | Second—b |
| 1950-51 | 25 | 30 | 15 | 65 | 173 | 184 | Third—c |
| 1951-52 | 34 | 26 | 10 | 78 | 195 | 164 | Second—c |
| 1952-53 | 28 | 23 | 19 | 75 | 155 | 148 | Second—xx |
| 1953-54 | 35 | 24 | 11 | 81 | 195 | 141 | Second—c |
| 1954-55 | 41 | 18 | 11 | 93 | 228 | 157 | Second—c |
| 1955-56 | 45 | 15 | 10 | 100 | 222 | 131 | First—xx |
| 1956-57 | 35 | 23 | 12 | 82 | 210 | 155 | Second—xx |
| 1957-58 | 43 | 17 | 10 | 96 | 250 | 158 | First—xx |
| 1958-59 | 39 | 18 | 13 | 91 | 258 | 158 | First—xx |
| 1959-60 | 40 | 18 | 12 | 92 | 255 | 178 | First—xx |
| 1960-61 | 41 | 19 | 10 | 92 | 254 | 188 | First—b |
| 1961-62 | 42 | 14 | 14 | 98 | 259 | 166 | First—b |
| 1962-63 | 28 | 19 | 23 | 79 | 225 | 183 | Third—b |
| 1963-64 | 36 | 21 | 13 | 85 | 209 | 167 | First—b |
| 1964-65 | 36 | 23 | 11 | 83 | 211 | 185 | Second—xx |
| 1965-66 | 41 | 21 | 8 | 90 | 239 | 173 | First—xx |
| 1966-67 | 32 | 25 | 13 | 77 | 202 | 188 | Second—c |
| 1967-68 | 42 | 22 | 10 | 94 | 236 | 167 | First—xx |
| 1968-69 | 46 | 19 | 11 | 103 | 271 | 202 | First—xx |
| 1969-70 | 38 | 22 | 16 | 92 | 244 | 201 | Fifth—* |
| 1970-71 | 42 | 23 | 13 | 97 | 291 | 216 | Third—xx |
| 1971-72 | 46 | 16 | 16 | 108 | 307 | 205 | Third—a |
| 1972-73 | 52 | 10 | 16 | 120 | 329 | 184 | First—xx |
| 1973-74 | 45 | 24 | 9 | 99 | 293 | 240 | Second—a |
| 1974-75 | 47 | 14 | 19 | 113 | 374 | 225 | First—b |
| 1975-76 | 58 | 11 | 11 | 127 | 337 | 174 | First—xx |
| 1976-77 | 60 | 8 | 12 | 132 | 387 | 171 | First—xx |
| 1977-78 | 59 | 10 | 11 | 129 | 359 | 183 | First—xx |
| 1978-79 | 52 | 17 | 11 | 115 | 337 | 204 | First—xx |
| 1979-80 | 47 | 20 | 13 | 107 | 328 | 240 | First—a |
| 1980-81 | 45 | 22 | 13 | 103 | 332 | 232 | First—† |
| 1981-82 | 46 | 17 | 17 | 109 | 360 | 223 | First—† |
| 1982-83 | 42 | 24 | 14 | 98 | 350 | 286 | Second—† |
| 1983-84 | 35 | 40 | 5 | 75 | 286 | 295 | Fourth—b |
| 1984-85 | 41 | 27 | 12 | 94 | 309 | 262 | First—a |
| 1985-86 | 40 | 33 | 7 | 87 | 330 | 280 | Second—xx |
| 1986-87 | 41 | 29 | 10 | 92 | 277 | 241 | Second—b |

| Season | W. | L. | T. | Pts. | GF. | GA. | Position |
|---|---|---|---|---|---|---|---|
| 1987-88 | 45 | 22 | 13 | 103 | 298 | 238 | First—a |
| 1988-89 | 53 | 18 | 9 | 115 | 315 | 218 | First—c |
| | 2311 | 1357 | 684 | 5306 | 14767 | 11418 | |

## New Jersey Devils

| Season | W. | L. | T. | Pts. | GF. | GA. | Position |
|---|---|---|---|---|---|---|---|
| 1974-75 | 15 | 54 | 11 | 41 | 184 | 328 | Fifth—* |
| 1975-76 | 12 | 56 | 12 | 36 | 190 | 351 | Fifth—* |
| 1976-77 | 20 | 46 | 14 | 54 | 226 | 307 | Fifth—* |
| 1977-78 | 19 | 40 | 21 | 59 | 257 | 305 | Second—† |
| 1978-79 | 15 | 53 | 12 | 42 | 210 | 331 | Fourth—* |
| 1979-80 | 19 | 48 | 13 | 51 | 234 | 308 | Sixth—* |
| 1980-81 | 22 | 45 | 13 | 57 | 258 | 344 | Fifth—* |
| 1981-82 | 18 | 49 | 13 | 49 | 241 | 362 | Fifth—* |
| 1982-83 | 17 | 49 | 14 | 48 | 230 | 338 | Fifth—* |
| 1983-84 | 17 | 56 | 7 | 41 | 231 | 350 | Fifth—* |
| 1984-85 | 22 | 48 | 10 | 54 | 263 | 346 | Fifth—* |
| 1985-86 | 28 | 49 | 3 | 59 | 300 | 374 | Fifth—* |
| 1986-87 | 29 | 45 | 6 | 64 | 293 | 368 | Sixth—* |
| 1987-88 | 38 | 36 | 6 | 82 | 295 | 296 | Fourth—b |
| 1988-89 | 27 | 41 | 12 | 66 | 281 | 325 | Fifth—* |
| | 318 | 715 | 167 | 803 | 3693 | 5036 | |

## New York Islanders

| Season | W. | L. | T. | Pts. | GF. | GA. | Position |
|---|---|---|---|---|---|---|---|
| 1972-73 | 12 | 60 | 6 | 30 | 170 | 347 | Eighth—* |
| 1973-74 | 19 | 41 | 18 | 56 | 182 | 247 | Eighth—* |
| 1974-75 | 33 | 25 | 22 | 88 | 264 | 221 | Third—b |
| 1975-76 | 42 | 21 | 17 | 101 | 297 | 190 | Second—b |
| 1976-77 | 47 | 21 | 12 | 106 | 288 | 193 | Second—b |
| 1977-78 | 48 | 17 | 15 | 111 | 334 | 210 | First—a |
| 1978-79 | 51 | 15 | 14 | 116 | 358 | 214 | First—b |
| 1979-80 | 39 | 28 | 13 | 91 | 281 | 247 | Second—xx |
| 1980-81 | 48 | 18 | 14 | 110 | 355 | 260 | First—xx |
| 1981-82 | 54 | 16 | 10 | 118 | 385 | 250 | First—xx |
| 1982-83 | 42 | 26 | 12 | 96 | 302 | 226 | Second—xx |
| 1983-84 | 50 | 26 | 4 | 104 | 357 | 269 | First—c |
| 1984-85 | 40 | 34 | 6 | 86 | 345 | 312 | Third—a |
| 1985-86 | 39 | 29 | 12 | 90 | 327 | 284 | Third—† |
| 1986-87 | 35 | 33 | 12 | 82 | 279 | 281 | Third—a |
| 1987-88 | 39 | 31 | 10 | 88 | 308 | 267 | First—† |
| 1988-89 | 28 | 47 | 5 | 61 | 265 | 325 | Sixth—* |
| | 666 | 488 | 202 | 1534 | 5097 | 4343 | |

## New York Rangers

| Season | W. | L. | T. | Pts. | GF. | GA. | Position |
|---|---|---|---|---|---|---|---|
| 1926-27 | 25 | 13 | 6 | 56 | 95 | 72 | First—a |
| 1927-28 | 19 | 16 | 9 | 47 | 94 | 79 | Second—xx |
| 1928-29 | 21 | 13 | 10 | 52 | 72 | 65 | Second—c |
| 1929-30 | 17 | 17 | 10 | 44 | 136 | 143 | Third—b |
| 1930-31 | 19 | 16 | 9 | 47 | 106 | 87 | Third—b |
| 1931-32 | 23 | 17 | 8 | 54 | 134 | 112 | First—c |
| 1932-33 | 23 | 17 | 8 | 54 | 135 | 107 | Third—xx |
| 1933-34 | 21 | 19 | 8 | 50 | 120 | 113 | Third—a |
| 1934-35 | 22 | 20 | 6 | 50 | 137 | 139 | Third—b |
| 1935-36 | 19 | 17 | 12 | 50 | 91 | 96 | Fourth—* |
| 1936-37 | 19 | 20 | 9 | 47 | 117 | 106 | Third—c |
| 1937-38 | 27 | 15 | 6 | 60 | 149 | 96 | Second—a |
| 1938-39 | 26 | 16 | 6 | 58 | 149 | 105 | Second—b |
| 1939-40 | 27 | 11 | 10 | 64 | 136 | 77 | Second—xx |
| 1940-41 | 21 | 19 | 8 | 50 | 143 | 125 | Fourth—a |
| 1941-42 | 29 | 17 | 2 | 60 | 177 | 143 | First—b |
| 1942-43 | 11 | 31 | 8 | 30 | 161 | 253 | Sixth—* |
| 1943-44 | 6 | 39 | 5 | 17 | 162 | 310 | Sixth—* |
| 1944-45 | 11 | 29 | 10 | 32 | 154 | 247 | Sixth—* |
| 1945-46 | 13 | 28 | 9 | 35 | 144 | 191 | Sixth—* |
| 1946-47 | 22 | 32 | 6 | 50 | 167 | 186 | Fifth—* |
| 1947-48 | 21 | 26 | 13 | 55 | 176 | 201 | Fourth—b |
| 1948-49 | 18 | 31 | 11 | 47 | 133 | 172 | Sixth—* |
| 1949-50 | 28 | 31 | 11 | 67 | 170 | 189 | Fourth—c |
| 1950-51 | 20 | 29 | 21 | 61 | 169 | 201 | Fifth—* |

| Season | W. | L. | T. | Pts. | GF. | GA. | Position |
|---|---|---|---|---|---|---|---|
| 1951-52 | 23 | 34 | 13 | 59 | 192 | 219 | Fifth—* |
| 1952-53 | 17 | 37 | 16 | 50 | 152 | 211 | Sixth—* |
| 1953-54 | 29 | 31 | 10 | 68 | 161 | 182 | Fifth—* |
| 1954-55 | 17 | 35 | 18 | 52 | 150 | 210 | Fifth—* |
| 1955-56 | 32 | 28 | 10 | 74 | 204 | 203 | Third—b |
| 1956-57 | 26 | 30 | 14 | 66 | 184 | 227 | Fourth—b |
| 1957-58 | 32 | 25 | 13 | 77 | 195 | 188 | Second—b |
| 1958-59 | 26 | 32 | 12 | 64 | 201 | 217 | Fifth—* |
| 1959-60 | 17 | 38 | 15 | 49 | 187 | 247 | Sixth—* |
| 1960-61 | 22 | 38 | 10 | 54 | 204 | 248 | Fifth—* |
| 1961-62 | 26 | 32 | 12 | 64 | 195 | 207 | Fourth—b |
| 1962-63 | 22 | 36 | 12 | 56 | 211 | 233 | Fifth—* |
| 1963-64 | 22 | 38 | 10 | 54 | 186 | 242 | Fifth—* |
| 1964-65 | 20 | 38 | 12 | 52 | 179 | 246 | Fifth—* |
| 1965-66 | 18 | 41 | 11 | 47 | 195 | 261 | Sixth—* |
| 1966-67 | 30 | 28 | 12 | 72 | 188 | 189 | Fourth—b |
| 1967-68 | 39 | 23 | 12 | 90 | 226 | 183 | Second—a |
| 1968-69 | 41 | 26 | 9 | 91 | 231 | 196 | Third—a |
| 1969-70 | 38 | 22 | 16 | 92 | 246 | 189 | Fourth—a |
| 1970-71 | 49 | 18 | 11 | 109 | 259 | 177 | Second—b |
| 1971-72 | 48 | 17 | 13 | 109 | 317 | 192 | Second—c |
| 1972-73 | 47 | 23 | 8 | 102 | 297 | 208 | Third—b |
| 1973-74 | 40 | 24 | 14 | 94 | 300 | 251 | Third—b |
| 1974-75 | 37 | 29 | 14 | 88 | 319 | 276 | Second—† |
| 1975-76 | 29 | 42 | 9 | 67 | 262 | 333 | Fourth—* |
| 1976-77 | 29 | 37 | 14 | 72 | 272 | 310 | Fourth—* |
| 1977-78 | 30 | 37 | 13 | 73 | 279 | 280 | Fourth—† |
| 1978-79 | 40 | 29 | 11 | 91 | 316 | 292 | Third—c |
| 1979-80 | 38 | 32 | 10 | 86 | 308 | 284 | Third—a |
| 1980-81 | 30 | 36 | 14 | 74 | 312 | 317 | Fourth—b |
| 1981-82 | 39 | 27 | 14 | 92 | 316 | 306 | Second—a |
| 1982-83 | 35 | 35 | 10 | 80 | 306 | 287 | Fourth—a |
| 1983-84 | 42 | 29 | 9 | 93 | 314 | 304 | Fourth—† |
| 1984-85 | 26 | 44 | 10 | 62 | 295 | 345 | Fourth—† |
| 1985-86 | 36 | 38 | 6 | 78 | 280 | 276 | Fourth—b |
| 1986-87 | 34 | 38 | 8 | 76 | 307 | 323 | Fourth—† |
| 1987-88 | 36 | 34 | 10 | 82 | 300 | 283 | Fourth—* |
| 1988-89 | 37 | 35 | 8 | 82 | 310 | 307 | Third—† |
|  | 1707 | 1755 | 664 | 4078 | 12783 | 13064 |  |

## Philadelphia Flyers

| Season | W. | L. | T. | Pts. | GF. | GA. | Position |
|---|---|---|---|---|---|---|---|
| 1967-68 | 31 | 32 | 11 | 73 | 173 | 179 | First—a |
| 1968-69 | 20 | 35 | 21 | 61 | 174 | 225 | Third—a |
| 1969-70 | 17 | 35 | 24 | 58 | 197 | 225 | Fifth—* |
| 1970-71 | 28 | 33 | 17 | 73 | 207 | 225 | Third—a |
| 1971-72 | 26 | 38 | 14 | 66 | 200 | 236 | Fifth—* |
| 1972-73 | 37 | 30 | 11 | 85 | 296 | 256 | Second—b |
| 1973-74 | 50 | 16 | 12 | 112 | 273 | 164 | First—xx |
| 1974-75 | 51 | 18 | 11 | 113 | 293 | 181 | First—xx |
| 1975-76 | 51 | 13 | 16 | 118 | 348 | 209 | First—c |
| 1976-77 | 48 | 16 | 16 | 112 | 323 | 213 | First—b |
| 1977-78 | 45 | 20 | 15 | 105 | 296 | 200 | Second—b |
| 1978-79 | 40 | 25 | 15 | 95 | 281 | 248 | Second—a |
| 1979-80 | 48 | 12 | 20 | 116 | 327 | 254 | First—c |
| 1980-81 | 41 | 24 | 15 | 97 | 313 | 249 | Second—a |
| 1981-82 | 38 | 31 | 11 | 87 | 325 | 313 | Third—† |
| 1982-83 | 49 | 23 | 8 | 106 | 326 | 240 | First—† |
| 1983-84 | 44 | 26 | 10 | 98 | 350 | 290 | Third—† |
| 1984-85 | 53 | 20 | 7 | 113 | 348 | 240 | First—c |
| 1985-86 | 53 | 23 | 4 | 110 | 335 | 241 | First—† |
| 1986-87 | 46 | 26 | 8 | 100 | 310 | 245 | First—c |
| 1987-88 | 38 | 33 | 9 | 85 | 292 | 292 | Second—† |
| 1988-89 | 36 | 36 | 8 | 80 | 307 | 285 | Fourth—b |
|  | 890 | 565 | 283 | 2063 | 6294 | 5310 |  |

## Pittsburgh Penguins

| Season | W. | L. | T. | Pts. | GF. | GA. | Position |
|---|---|---|---|---|---|---|---|
| 1967-68 | 27 | 34 | 13 | 67 | 195 | 216 | Fifth—* |
| 1968-69 | 20 | 45 | 11 | 51 | 189 | 252 | Fifth—* |
| 1969-70 | 26 | 38 | 12 | 64 | 182 | 238 | Second—b |

| Season | W. | L. | T. | Pts. | GF. | GA. | Position |
|---|---|---|---|---|---|---|---|
| 1970-71 | 21 | 37 | 20 | 62 | 221 | 240 | Sixth—* |
| 1971-72 | 26 | 38 | 14 | 66 | 220 | 258 | Fourth—a |
| 1972-73 | 32 | 37 | 9 | 73 | 257 | 265 | Fifth—* |
| 1973-74 | 28 | 41 | 9 | 65 | 242 | 273 | Fifth—* |
| 1974-75 | 37 | 28 | 15 | 89 | 326 | 289 | Third—a |
| 1975-76 | 35 | 33 | 12 | 82 | 339 | 303 | Third—† |
| 1976-77 | 34 | 33 | 13 | 81 | 240 | 252 | Third—† |
| 1977-78 | 25 | 37 | 18 | 68 | 254 | 321 | Fourth—* |
| 1978-79 | 36 | 31 | 13 | 85 | 281 | 279 | Second—a |
| 1979-80 | 30 | 37 | 13 | 73 | 251 | 303 | Third—† |
| 1980-81 | 30 | 37 | 13 | 73 | 302 | 345 | Third—† |
| 1981-82 | 31 | 36 | 13 | 75 | 310 | 337 | Fourth—† |
| 1982-83 | 18 | 53 | 9 | 45 | 257 | 394 | Sixth—* |
| 1983-84 | 16 | 58 | 6 | 38 | 254 | 390 | Sixth—* |
| 1984-85 | 24 | 51 | 5 | 53 | 276 | 385 | Fifth—* |
| 1985-86 | 34 | 38 | 8 | 76 | 313 | 305 | Fifth—* |
| 1986-87 | 30 | 38 | 12 | 72 | 297 | 290 | Fifth—* |
| 1987-88 | 36 | 35 | 9 | 81 | 319 | 316 | Sixth—* |
| 1988-89 | 40 | 33 | 7 | 87 | 347 | 349 | Second—a |
|  | 636 | 848 | 254 | 1526 | 5630 | 6600 |  |

## Quebec Nordiques

| Season | W. | L. | T. | Pts. | GF. | GA. | Position |
|---|---|---|---|---|---|---|---|
| 1972-73 | 33 | 40 | 5 | 71 | 276 | 313 | Fifth—* |
| 1973-74 | 38 | 36 | 4 | 80 | 306 | 280 | Fifth—* |
| 1974-75 | 46 | 32 | 0 | 92 | 331 | 299 | First—c |
| 1975-76 | 50 | 27 | 4 | 104 | 371 | 316 | Second—a |
| 1976-77 | 47 | 31 | 3 | 97 | 353 | 295 | First—xx |
| 1977-78 | 40 | 37 | 3 | 83 | 349 | 347 | Fourth—b |
| 1978-79 | 41 | 34 | 5 | 87 | 288 | 271 | Second—b |
| 1979-80 | 25 | 44 | 11 | 61 | 248 | 313 | Fifth—* |
| 1980-81 | 30 | 32 | 18 | 78 | 314 | 318 | Fourth—† |
| 1981-82 | 33 | 31 | 16 | 82 | 356 | 345 | Fourth—b |
| 1982-83 | 34 | 34 | 12 | 80 | 343 | 336 | Fourth—† |
| 1983-84 | 42 | 28 | 10 | 94 | 360 | 278 | Third—a |
| 1984-85 | 41 | 30 | 9 | 91 | 323 | 275 | Second—b |
| 1985-86 | 43 | 31 | 6 | 92 | 330 | 289 | First—† |
| 1986-87 | 31 | 39 | 10 | 72 | 267 | 276 | Fourth—a |
| 1987-88 | 32 | 43 | 5 | 69 | 271 | 306 | Fifth—* |
| 1988-89 | 27 | 46 | 7 | 61 | 269 | 342 | Fifth—* |
|  | 633 | 592 | 128 | 1394 | 5355 | 5199 |  |

## St. Louis Blues

| Season | W. | L. | T. | Pts. | GF. | GA. | Position |
|---|---|---|---|---|---|---|---|
| 1967-68 | 27 | 31 | 16 | 70 | 177 | 191 | Third—c |
| 1968-69 | 37 | 25 | 14 | 88 | 204 | 157 | First—c |
| 1969-70 | 37 | 27 | 12 | 86 | 224 | 179 | First—c |
| 1970-71 | 34 | 25 | 19 | 87 | 223 | 208 | Second—a |
| 1971-72 | 28 | 39 | 11 | 67 | 208 | 247 | Third—b |
| 1972-73 | 32 | 34 | 12 | 76 | 233 | 251 | Fourth—a |
| 1973-74 | 26 | 40 | 12 | 64 | 206 | 248 | Sixth—* |
| 1974-75 | 35 | 31 | 14 | 84 | 269 | 267 | Second—† |
| 1975-76 | 29 | 37 | 14 | 72 | 249 | 290 | Third—† |
| 1976-77 | 32 | 39 | 9 | 73 | 239 | 276 | First—a |
| 1977-78 | 20 | 47 | 13 | 53 | 195 | 304 | Fourth—* |
| 1978-79 | 18 | 50 | 12 | 48 | 249 | 348 | Third—* |
| 1979-80 | 34 | 34 | 12 | 80 | 266 | 278 | Second—† |
| 1980-81 | 45 | 18 | 17 | 107 | 352 | 281 | First—a |
| 1981-82 | 32 | 40 | 8 | 72 | 315 | 349 | Third—a |
| 1982-83 | 25 | 40 | 15 | 65 | 285 | 316 | Fourth—† |
| 1983-84 | 32 | 41 | 7 | 71 | 293 | 316 | Second—a |
| 1984-85 | 37 | 31 | 12 | 86 | 299 | 288 | First—† |
| 1985-86 | 37 | 34 | 9 | 83 | 302 | 291 | Third—b |
| 1986-87 | 32 | 33 | 15 | 79 | 281 | 293 | First—† |
| 1987-88 | 34 | 38 | 8 | 76 | 278 | 294 | Second—a |
| 1988-89 | 33 | 35 | 12 | 78 | 275 | 285 | Second—a |
|  | 696 | 769 | 273 | 1665 | 5622 | 5957 |  |

## Toronto Maple Leafs

| Season | W. | L. | T. | Pts. | GF. | GA. | Position |
|---|---|---|---|---|---|---|---|
| 1917-18 | 13 | 9 | 0 | 26 | 108 | 109 | Second, First |
| 1918-19 | 5 | 13 | 0 | 10 | 64 | 92 | Third |
| 1919-20 | 12 | 12 | 0 | 24 | 119 | 106 | Third |
| 1920-21 | 15 | 9 | 0 | 30 | 105 | 100 | First |
| 1921-22 | 13 | 10 | 1 | 27 | 98 | 97 | Second—xx |
| 1922-23 | 13 | 10 | 1 | 27 | 82 | 88 | Third |
| 1923-24 | 10 | 14 | 0 | 20 | 59 | 85 | Third |
| 1924-25 | 19 | 11 | 0 | 38 | 90 | 84 | Second |
| 1925-26 | 12 | 21 | 3 | 27 | 92 | 114 | Sixth |
| 1926-27 | 15 | 24 | 5 | 35 | 79 | 94 | Fifth—* |
| 1927-28 | 18 | 18 | 8 | 44 | 89 | 88 | Fourth—* |
| 1928-29 | 21 | 18 | 5 | 47 | 85 | 69 | Third—b |
| 1929-30 | 17 | 21 | 6 | 40 | 116 | 124 | Fourth—* |
| 1930-31 | 22 | 13 | 9 | 53 | 118 | 99 | Second—a |
| 1931-32 | 23 | 18 | 7 | 53 | 155 | 127 | Second—xx |
| 1932-33 | 24 | 18 | 6 | 54 | 119 | 111 | First—c |
| 1933-34 | 26 | 13 | 9 | 61 | 174 | 119 | First—b |
| 1934-35 | 30 | 14 | 4 | 64 | 157 | 111 | First—c |
| 1935-36 | 23 | 19 | 6 | 52 | 126 | 106 | Second—c |
| 1936-37 | 22 | 21 | 5 | 49 | 119 | 115 | Third—a |
| 1937-38 | 24 | 15 | 9 | 57 | 151 | 127 | First—c |
| 1938-39 | 19 | 20 | 9 | 47 | 114 | 107 | Third—c |
| 1939-40 | 25 | 17 | 6 | 56 | 134 | 110 | Third—c |
| 1940-41 | 28 | 14 | 6 | 62 | 145 | 99 | Second—b |
| 1941-42 | 27 | 18 | 3 | 57 | 158 | 136 | Second—xx |
| 1942-43 | 22 | 19 | 9 | 53 | 198 | 159 | Third—b |
| 1943-44 | 23 | 23 | 4 | 50 | 214 | 174 | Third—b |
| 1944-45 | 24 | 22 | 4 | 52 | 183 | 161 | Third—xx |
| 1945-46 | 19 | 24 | 7 | 45 | 174 | 185 | Fifth—* |
| 1946-47 | 31 | 19 | 10 | 72 | 209 | 172 | Second—xx |
| 1947-48 | 32 | 15 | 13 | 77 | 182 | 143 | First—xx |
| 1948-49 | 22 | 25 | 13 | 57 | 147 | 161 | Fourth—xx |
| 1949-50 | 31 | 27 | 12 | 74 | 176 | 173 | Third—b |
| 1950-51 | 41 | 16 | 13 | 95 | 212 | 138 | Second—xx |
| 1951-52 | 29 | 25 | 16 | 74 | 168 | 157 | Third—b |
| 1952-53 | 27 | 30 | 13 | 67 | 156 | 167 | Fifth—* |
| 1953-54 | 32 | 24 | 14 | 78 | 152 | 131 | Third—b |
| 1954-55 | 24 | 24 | 22 | 70 | 147 | 135 | Third—b |
| 1955-56 | 24 | 33 | 13 | 61 | 153 | 181 | Fourth—b |
| 1956-57 | 21 | 34 | 15 | 57 | 174 | 192 | Fifth—* |
| 1957-58 | 21 | 38 | 11 | 53 | 192 | 226 | Sixth—* |
| 1958-59 | 27 | 32 | 11 | 65 | 189 | 201 | Fourth—c |
| 1959-60 | 35 | 26 | 9 | 79 | 199 | 195 | Second—c |
| 1960-61 | 39 | 19 | 12 | 90 | 234 | 176 | Second—b |
| 1961-62 | 37 | 22 | 11 | 85 | 232 | 180 | Second—xx |
| 1962-63 | 35 | 23 | 12 | 82 | 221 | 180 | First—xx |
| 1963-64 | 33 | 25 | 12 | 78 | 192 | 172 | Third—xx |
| 1964-65 | 30 | 26 | 14 | 74 | 204 | 173 | Fourth—b |
| 1965-66 | 34 | 25 | 11 | 79 | 208 | 187 | Third—b |
| 1966-67 | 32 | 27 | 11 | 75 | 204 | 211 | Third—xx |
| 1967-68 | 33 | 31 | 10 | 76 | 209 | 176 | Fifth—* |
| 1968-69 | 35 | 26 | 15 | 85 | 234 | 217 | Fourth—a |
| 1969-70 | 29 | 34 | 13 | 71 | 222 | 242 | Sixth—* |
| 1970-71 | 37 | 33 | 8 | 82 | 248 | 211 | Fourth—a |
| 1971-72 | 33 | 31 | 14 | 80 | 209 | 208 | Fourth—a |
| 1972-73 | 27 | 41 | 10 | 64 | 247 | 279 | Sixth—* |
| 1973-74 | 35 | 27 | 16 | 86 | 274 | 230 | Fourth—a |
| 1974-75 | 31 | 33 | 16 | 78 | 280 | 309 | Third—a |
| 1975-76 | 34 | 31 | 15 | 83 | 294 | 276 | Third—b |
| 1976-77 | 33 | 32 | 15 | 81 | 301 | 285 | Third—a |
| 1977-78 | 41 | 29 | 10 | 92 | 271 | 237 | Third—b |
| 1978-79 | 34 | 33 | 13 | 81 | 267 | 252 | Third—a |
| 1979-80 | 35 | 40 | 5 | 75 | 304 | 327 | Fourth—† |
| 1980-81 | 28 | 37 | 15 | 71 | 322 | 367 | Fifth—† |
| 1981-82 | 20 | 44 | 16 | 56 | 298 | 380 | Fifth—* |
| 1982-83 | 28 | 40 | 12 | 68 | 293 | 330 | Third—† |
| 1983-84 | 26 | 45 | 9 | 61 | 303 | 387 | Fifth—* |
| 1984-85 | 20 | 52 | 8 | 48 | 253 | 358 | Fifth—* |
| 1985-86 | 25 | 48 | 7 | 57 | 311 | 386 | Fourth—a |
| 1986-87 | 32 | 42 | 6 | 70 | 286 | 319 | Fourth—a |

| Season | W. | L. | T. | Pts. | GF. | GA. | Position |
|---|---|---|---|---|---|---|---|
| 1987-88 | 21 | 49 | 10 | 52 | 273 | 345 | Fourth—† |
| 1988-89 | 28 | 46 | 6 | 62 | 259 | 342 | Fifth—* |
| | 1866 | 1837 | 649 | 4381 | 13534 | 13410 | |

## Vancouver Canucks

| Season | W. | L. | T. | Pts. | GF. | GA. | Position |
|---|---|---|---|---|---|---|---|
| 1970-71 | 24 | 46 | 8 | 56 | 229 | 296 | Sixth—* |
| 1971-72 | 20 | 50 | 8 | 48 | 203 | 297 | Seventh—* |
| 1972-73 | 22 | 47 | 9 | 53 | 233 | 339 | Seventh—* |
| 1973-74 | 24 | 43 | 11 | 59 | 224 | 296 | Seventh—* |
| 1974-75 | 38 | 32 | 10 | 86 | 271 | 254 | First—a |
| 1975-76 | 33 | 32 | 15 | 81 | 271 | 272 | Second—† |
| 1976-77 | 25 | 42 | 13 | 63 | 235 | 294 | Fourth—* |
| 1977-78 | 20 | 43 | 17 | 57 | 239 | 320 | Third—* |
| 1978-79 | 25 | 42 | 13 | 63 | 217 | 291 | Second—† |
| 1979-80 | 27 | 37 | 16 | 70 | 256 | 281 | Third—† |
| 1980-81 | 28 | 32 | 20 | 76 | 289 | 301 | Third—† |
| 1981-82 | 30 | 33 | 17 | 77 | 290 | 286 | Second—c |
| 1982-83 | 30 | 35 | 15 | 75 | 303 | 309 | Third—† |
| 1983-84 | 32 | 39 | 9 | 73 | 306 | 328 | Third—† |
| 1984-85 | 25 | 46 | 9 | 59 | 284 | 401 | Fifth—* |
| 1985-86 | 23 | 44 | 13 | 59 | 282 | 333 | Fourth—† |
| 1986-87 | 29 | 43 | 8 | 66 | 302 | 314 | Fifth—* |
| 1987-88 | 25 | 46 | 9 | 59 | 273 | 320 | Fifth—* |
| 1988-89 | 33 | 39 | 8 | 74 | 251 | 253 | Fourth—† |
| | 513 | 771 | 228 | 1254 | 4958 | 5785 | |

## Washington Capitals

| Season | W. | L. | T. | Pts. | GF. | GA. | Position |
|---|---|---|---|---|---|---|---|
| 1974-75 | 8 | 67 | 5 | 21 | 181 | 446 | Fifth—* |
| 1975-76 | 11 | 59 | 10 | 32 | 224 | 394 | Fifth—* |
| 1976-77 | 24 | 42 | 14 | 62 | 221 | 307 | Fourth—* |
| 1977-78 | 17 | 49 | 14 | 48 | 195 | 321 | Fifth—* |
| 1978-79 | 24 | 41 | 15 | 63 | 273 | 338 | Fourth—* |
| 1979-80 | 27 | 40 | 13 | 67 | 261 | 293 | Fifth—* |
| 1980-81 | 26 | 36 | 18 | 70 | 286 | 317 | Fifth—* |
| 1981-82 | 26 | 41 | 13 | 65 | 319 | 338 | Fifth—* |
| 1982-83 | 39 | 25 | 16 | 94 | 306 | 283 | Third—† |
| 1983-84 | 48 | 27 | 5 | 101 | 308 | 226 | Second—a |
| 1984-85 | 46 | 25 | 9 | 101 | 322 | 240 | Second—† |
| 1985-86 | 50 | 23 | 7 | 107 | 315 | 272 | Second—a |
| 1986-87 | 38 | 32 | 10 | 86 | 285 | 278 | Second—† |
| 1987-88 | 38 | 33 | 9 | 85 | 281 | 249 | Second—a |
| 1988-89 | 41 | 29 | 10 | 92 | 305 | 259 | First—† |
| | 463 | 569 | 168 | 1094 | 4082 | 4561 | |

## Winnipeg Jets

| Season | W. | L. | T. | Pts. | GF. | GA. | Position |
|---|---|---|---|---|---|---|---|
| 1972-73 | 43 | 31 | 4 | 90 | 285 | 249 | First—c |
| 1973-74 | 34 | 39 | 5 | 73 | 264 | 296 | Fourth—a |
| 1974-75 | 38 | 35 | 5 | 81 | 322 | 293 | Third—* |
| 1975-76 | 52 | 27 | 2 | 106 | 345 | 254 | First—xx |
| 1976-77 | 46 | 32 | 2 | 94 | 366 | 291 | Second—c |
| 1977-78 | 50 | 28 | 2 | 102 | 381 | 270 | First—xx |
| 1978-79 | 39 | 35 | 6 | 84 | 307 | 306 | Third—xx |
| 1979-80 | 20 | 49 | 11 | 51 | 214 | 314 | Fifth—* |
| 1980-81 | 9 | 57 | 14 | 32 | 246 | 400 | Sixth—* |
| 1981-82 | 33 | 33 | 14 | 80 | 319 | 332 | Second—† |
| 1982-83 | 33 | 39 | 8 | 74 | 311 | 333 | Fourth—† |
| 1983-84 | 31 | 38 | 11 | 73 | 340 | 374 | Third—† |
| 1984-85 | 43 | 27 | 10 | 96 | 358 | 332 | Second—a |
| 1985-86 | 26 | 47 | 7 | 59 | 295 | 372 | Third—† |
| 1986-87 | 40 | 32 | 8 | 88 | 279 | 271 | Third—a |
| 1987-88 | 33 | 36 | 11 | 77 | 292 | 310 | Third—† |
| 1988-89 | 26 | 42 | 12 | 64 | 300 | 355 | Fifth—* |
| | 596 | 627 | 132 | 1324 | 5224 | 5352 | |

# NHL Stanley Cup Winners

| SEASON | TEAM | COACH |
|---|---|---|
| 1917-18 | Toronto Arenas | Dick Carroll |
| 1919-20 | Ottawa Senators | Pete Green |
| 1920-21 | Ottawa Senators | Pete Green |
| 1921-22 | Toronto St. Pats | Eddie Powers |
| 1922-23 | Ottawa Senators | Pete Green |
| 1923-24 | Montreal Canadiens | Leo Dandurand |
| 1924-25 | Victoria Cougars | Lester Patrick |
| 1925-26 | Montreal Maroons | Eddie Gerard |
| 1926-27 | Ottawa Senators | Dave Gill |
| 1927-28 | New York Rangers | Lester Patrick |
| 1928-29 | Boston Bruins | Cy Denneny |
| 1929-30 | Montreal Canadiens | Cecil Hart |
| 1930-31 | Montreal Canadiens | Cecil Hart |
| 1931-32 | Toronto Maple Leafs | Dick Irvin |
| 1932-33 | New York Rangers | Lester Patrick |
| 1933-34 | Chicago Black Hawks | Tommy Gorman |
| 1934-35 | Montreal Maroons | Tommy Gorman |
| 1935-36 | Detroit Red Wings | Jack Adams |
| 1936-37 | Detroit Red Wings | Jack Adams |
| 1937-38 | Chicago Black Hawks | Bill Stewart |
| 1938-39 | Boston Bruins | Art Ross |
| 1939-40 | New York Rangers | Frank Boucher |
| 1940-41 | Boston Bruins | Cooney Weiland |
| 1941-42 | Toronto Maple Leafs | Hap Day |
| 1942-43 | Detroit Red Wings | Jack Adams |
| 1943-44 | Montreal Canadiens | Dick Irvin |
| 1944-45 | Toronto Maple Leafs | Hap Day |
| 1945-46 | Montreal Canadiens | Dick Irvin |
| 1946-47 | Toronto Maple Leafs | Hap Day |
| 1947-48 | Toronto Maple Leafs | Hap Day |
| 1948-49 | Toronto Maple Leafs | Hap Day |
| 1949-50 | Detroit Red Wings | Tommy Ivan |
| 1950-51 | Toronto Maple Leafs | Joe Primeau |
| 1951-52 | Detroit Red Wings | Tommy Ivan |
| 1952-53 | Montreal Canadiens | Dick Irvin |
| 1953-54 | Detroit Red Wings | Tommy Ivan |
| 1954-55 | Detroit Red Wings | Jimmy Skinner |
| 1955-56 | Montreal Canadiens | Toe Blake |
| 1956-57 | Montreal Canadiens | Toe Blake |
| 1957-58 | Montreal Canadiens | Toe Blake |
| 1958-59 | Montreal Canadiens | Toe Blake |
| 1959-60 | Montreal Canadiens | Toe Blake |
| 1960-61 | Chicago Black Hawks | Rudy Pilous |
| 1961-62 | Toronto Maple Leafs | Punch Imlach |
| 1962-63 | Toronto Maple Leafs | Punch Imlach |
| 1963-64 | Toronto Maple Leafs | Punch Imlach |
| 1964-65 | Montreal Canadiens | Toe Blake |
| 1965-66 | Montreal Canadiens | Toe Blake |
| 1966-67 | Toronto Maple Leafs | Punch Imlach |
| 1967-68 | Montreal Canadiens | Toe Blake |
| 1968-69 | Montreal Canadiens | Claude Ruel |
| 1969-70 | Boston Bruins | Harry Sinden |
| 1970-71 | Montreal Canadiens | Al MacNeil |
| 1971-72 | Boston Bruins | Tom Johnson |
| 1972-73 | Montreal Canadiens | Scotty Bowman |
| 1973-74 | Philadelphia Flyers | Fred Shero |
| 1974-75 | Philadelphia Flyers | Fred Shero |
| 1975-76 | Montreal Canadiens | Scotty Bowman |
| 1976-77 | Montreal Canadiens | Scotty Bowman |
| 1977-78 | Montreal Canadiens | Scotty Bowman |
| 1978-79 | Montreal Canadiens | Scotty Bowman |
| 1979-80 | New York Islanders | Al Arbour |
| 1980-81 | New York Islanders | Al Arbour |
| 1981-82 | New York Islanders | Al Arbour |
| 1982-83 | New York Islanders | Al Arbour |
| 1983-84 | Edmonton Oilers | Glen Sather |
| 1984-85 | Edmonton Oilers | Glen Sather |
| 1985-86 | Montreal Canadiens | Jean Perron |
| 1986-87 | Edmonton Oilers | Glen Sather |
| 1987-88 | Edmonton Oilers | Glen Sather |
| 1988-89 | Calgary Flames | Terry Crisp |

NOTE: 1918-19 series between Montreal and Seattle cancelled after five games because of influenza epidemic.

# Stanley Cup Playoff Records

## Team
1—Most Stanley Cup Championships: Montreal Canadiens (23).
2—Most Final Series Appearances: Montreal Canadiens (31).
3—Most Years in Playoffs: Montreal Canadiens (64).
4—Most Consecutive Stanley Cup Championships: Montreal Canadiens (5).
5—Most Consecutive Playoff Appearances: Boston Bruins (22).
6—Most Goals, One Team, One Game: Edmonton (13) vs. Los Angeles, April 9, 1987.
7—Most Goals, One Team, One Period: Montreal Canadiens (7) vs. Toronto, March 30, 1944—3rd period.
8—Most Consecutive Playoff Game Victories: Edmonton Oilers (12).

## Individual
1—Most Years in Playoffs: Gordie Howe (Detroit 19, Hartford 1)—20.
2—Most Consecutive Years in Playoffs: Brad Park (N.Y. Rangers, Boston, Detroit)—17.
3—Most Playoff Games: Larry Robinson (Montreal)—203.
4—Most Points in Playoffs: Wayne Gretzky (Edmonton, Los Angeles)—274.
5—Most Goals in Playoffs: Wayne Gretzky (Edmonton, Los Angeles)—86.
6—Most Assists in Playoffs: Wayne Gretzky (Edmonton, Los Angeles)—188.
7—Most Shutouts in Playoffs: Jacques Plante (Montreal, St. Louis)—14.
8—Most Games Played by Goaltender: Billy Smith (N.Y. Islanders)—131.
9—Most Points One Year: Wayne Gretzky (Edmonton)—47 in 1984-85.
10—Most Goals One Year:
    Reggie Leach (Philadelphia)—19 in 1975-76.
    Jari Kurri (Edmonton)—19 in 1984-85.
11—Most Assists One Year: Wayne Gretzky (Edmonton)—31 in 1987-88.
12—Most Points By Defenseman One Year: Paul Coffey (Edmonton)—37 in 1984-85.
13—Most Goals By Defenseman One Year: Paul Coffey (Edmonton)—12 in 1984-85.
14—Most Assists By Defenseman One Year: Paul Coffey (Edmonton)—25 in 1984-85.
15—Most Penalty Minutes One Year: Chris Nilan (Montreal)—141 in 1985-86.
16—Most Shutouts One Year:
    Clint Benedict (Montreal Maroons)—4 in 1927-28.
    Dave Kerr (N.Y. Rangers)—4 in 1936-37.
    Frank McCool (Toronto)—4 in 1944-45.
    Terry Sawchuk (Detroit)—4 in 1951-52.
    Bernie Parent (Philadelphia)—4 in 1974-75.
    Ken Dryden (Montreal)—4 in 1976-77.
17—Most Consecutive Shutouts: Frank McCool (Toronto)—3 in 1944-45.
18—Most Points One Game:
    Patrik Sundstrom (New Jersey)—8 vs. Washington, April 22, 1988.
    Mario Lemieux (Pittsburgh)—8 vs. Philadelphia, April 25, 1989.
19—Most Goals One Game:
    Maurice Richard (Montreal)—5 vs. Toronto, March 23, 1944.
    Darryl Sittler (Toronto)—5 vs. Philadelphia, April 22, 1976.
    Reggie Leach (Philadelphia)—5 vs. Boston, May 6, 1976.
    Mario Lemieux (Pittsburgh)—5 vs. Philadelphia, April 25, 1989.
20—Most Assists One Game:
    Mikko Leinonen (N.Y. Rangers)—6 vs. Philadelphia, April 8, 1982.
    Wayne Gretzky (Edmonton)—6 vs. Los Angeles, April 9, 1987.
21—Most Penalty Minutes in Playoffs: Dave (Tiger) Williams (Toronto, Vancouver, Los Angeles)—455.

# Individual Awards

## Art Ross Trophy
### (Leading Scorer—Regular Season)

(Originally Leading Scorer Trophy. Present trophy presented to NHL by Art Ross, former manager-coach of Boston Bruins, in 1947. In event of tie, player with most goals receives the award.)

| | Games | G. | A. | Pts. |
|---|---|---|---|---|
| 1917-18—Joe Malone, Montreal | 20 | 44 | ** | 44 |
| 1918-19—Newsy Lalonde, Montreal | 17 | 23 | 9 | 32 |
| 1919-20—Joe Malone, Quebec Bulldogs | 24 | 39 | 6 | 45 |
| 1920-21—Newsy Lalonde, Montreal | 24 | 33 | 8 | 41 |
| 1921-22—Punch Broadbelt, Ottawa | 24 | 32 | 14 | 46 |
| 1922-23—Babe Dye, Toronto | 22 | 26 | 11 | 37 |
| 1923-24—Cy Denneny, Ottawa | 21 | 22 | 1 | 23 |
| 1924-25—Babe Dye, Toronto | 29 | 38 | 6 | 44 |
| 1925-26—Nels Stewart, Montreal Maroons | 36 | 34 | 8 | 42 |
| 1926-27—Bill Cook, New York Rangers | 44 | 33 | 4 | 37 |
| 1927-28—Howie Morenz, Montreal | 43 | 33 | 18 | 51 |
| 1928-29—Ace Bailey, Toronto | 44 | 22 | 10 | 32 |
| 1929-30—Cooney Weiland, Boston | 44 | 43 | 30 | 73 |
| 1930-31—Howie Morenz, Montreal | 39 | 28 | 23 | 51 |
| 1931-32—Harvey Jackson, Toronto | 48 | 28 | 25 | 53 |
| 1932-33—Bill Cook, New York Rangers | 48 | 28 | 22 | 50 |
| 1933-34—Charlie Conacher, Toronto | 42 | 32 | 20 | 52 |
| 1934-35—Charlie Conacher, Toronto | 48 | 36 | 21 | 57 |
| 1935-36—Dave Schriner, New York Americans | 48 | 19 | 26 | 45 |
| 1936-37—Dave Schriner, New York Americans | 48 | 21 | 25 | 46 |
| 1937-38—Gordie Drillon, Toronto | 48 | 26 | 26 | 52 |
| 1938-39—Toe Blake, Montreal | 48 | 24 | 23 | 47 |
| 1939-40—Milt Schmidt, Boston | 48 | 22 | 30 | 52 |
| 1940-41—Bill Cowley, Boston | 46 | 17 | 45 | 62 |
| 1941-42—Bryan Hextall, New York Rangers | 48 | 24 | 32 | 56 |
| 1942-43—Doug Bentley, Chicago | 50 | 33 | 40 | 73 |
| 1943-44—Herbie Cain, Boston | 48 | 36 | 46 | 82 |
| 1944-45—Elmer Lach, Montreal | 50 | 26 | 54 | 80 |
| 1945-46—Max Bentley, Chicago | 47 | 31 | 30 | 61 |
| 1946-47—Max Bentley, Chicago | 60 | 29 | 43 | 72 |
| 1947-48—Elmer Lach, Montreal | 60 | 30 | 31 | 61 |
| 1948-49—Roy Conacher, Chicago | 60 | 26 | 42 | 68 |
| 1949-50—Ted Lindsay, Detroit | 69 | 23 | 55 | 78 |
| 1950-51—Gordie Howe, Detroit | 70 | 43 | 43 | 86 |
| 1951-52—Gordie Howe, Detroit | 70 | 47 | 39 | 86 |
| 1952-53—Gordie Howe, Detroit | 70 | 49 | 46 | 95 |
| 1953-54—Gordie Howe, Detroit | 70 | 33 | 48 | 81 |
| 1954-55—Bernie Geoffrion, Montreal | 70 | 38 | 37 | 75 |
| 1955-56—Jean Beliveau, Montreal | 70 | 47 | 41 | 88 |
| 1956-57—Gordie Howe, Detroit | 70 | 44 | 45 | 89 |
| 1957-58—Dickie Moore, Montreal | 70 | 36 | 48 | 84 |
| 1958-59—Dickie Moore, Montreal | 70 | 41 | 55 | 96 |
| 1959-60—Bobby Hull, Chicago | 70 | 39 | 42 | 81 |
| 1960-61—Bernie Geoffrion, Montreal | 64 | 50 | 45 | 95 |
| 1961-62—Bobby Hull, Chicago | 70 | 50 | 34 | 84 |
| 1962-63—Gordie Howe, Detroit | 70 | 38 | 48 | 86 |
| 1963-64—Stan Mikita, Chicago | 70 | 39 | 50 | 89 |
| 1964-65—Stan Mikita, Chicago | 70 | 28 | 59 | 87 |
| 1965-66—Bobby Hull, Chicago | 65 | 54 | 43 | 97 |
| 1966-67—Stan Mikita, Chicago | 70 | 35 | 62 | 97 |
| 1967-68—Stan Mikita, Chicago | 72 | 40 | 47 | 87 |
| 1968-69—Phil Esposito, Boston | 74 | 49 | 77 | 126 |
| 1969-70—Bobby Orr, Boston | 76 | 33 | 87 | 120 |
| 1970-71—Phil Esposito, Boston | 78 | 76 | 76 | 152 |
| 1971-72—Phil Esposito, Boston | 76 | 66 | 67 | 133 |
| 1972-73—Phil Esposito, Boston | 78 | 55 | 75 | 130 |
| 1973-74—Phil Esposito, Boston | 78 | 68 | 77 | 145 |
| 1974-75—Bobby Orr, Boston | 80 | 46 | 89 | 135 |
| 1975-76—Guy Lafleur, Montreal | 80 | 56 | 69 | 125 |
| 1976-77—Guy Lafleur, Montreal | 80 | 56 | 80 | 136 |
| 1977-78—Guy Lafleur, Montreal | 78 | 60 | 72 | 132 |
| 1978-79—Bryan Trottier, New York Islanders | 76 | 47 | 87 | 134 |
| 1979-80—Marcel Dionne, Los Angeles | 80 | 53 | 84 | 137 |

|  | Games | G. | A. | Pts. |
|---|---|---|---|---|
| 1980-81—Wayne Gretzky, Edmonton | 80 | 55 | 109 | 164 |
| 1981-82—Wayne Gretzky, Edmonton | 80 | 92 | 120 | 212 |
| 1982-83—Wayne Gretzky, Edmonton | 80 | 71 | 125 | 196 |
| 1983-84—Wayne Gretzky, Edmonton | 74 | 87 | 118 | 205 |
| 1984-85—Wayne Gretzky, Edmonton | 80 | 73 | 135 | 208 |
| 1985-86—Wayne Gretzky, Edmonton | 80 | 52 | 163 | 215 |
| 1986-87—Wayne Gretzky, Edmonton | 79 | 62 | 121 | 183 |
| 1987-88—Mario Lemieux, Pittsburgh | 77 | 70 | 98 | 168 |
| 1988-89—Mario Lemieux, Pittsburgh | 76 | 85 | 114 | 199 |

**—Number of assists not recorded.

## Hart Memorial Trophy
### (Most Valuable Player)

1923-24—Frank Nighbor, Ottawa
1924-25—Billy Burch, Hamilton
1925-26—Nels Stewart, Montreal Maroons
1926-27—Herb Gardiner, Montreal
1927-28—Howie Morenz, Montreal
1928-29—Roy Worters, N.Y. Americans
1929-30—Nels Stewart, Montreal Maroons
1930-31—Howie Morenz, Montreal
1931-32—Howie Morenz, Montreal
1932-33—Eddie Shore, Boston
1933-34—Aurel Joliat, Montreal
1934-35—Eddie Shore, Boston
1935-36—Eddie Shore, Boston
1936-37—Babe Siebert, Montreal
1937-38—Eddie Shore, Boston
1938-39—Toe Blake, Montreal
1939-40—Ebbie Goodfellow, Detroit
1940-41—Bill Cowley, Boston
1941-42—Tom Anderson, N.Y. Americans
1942-43—Bill Cowley, Boston
1943-44—Babe Pratt, Toronto
1944-45—Elmer Lach, Montreal
1945-46—Max Bentley, Chicago
1946-47—Maurice Richard, Montreal
1947-48—Buddy O'Connor, N.Y. Rangers
1948-49—Sid Abel, Detroit
1949-50—Chuck Rayner, N.Y. Rangers
1950-51—Milt Schmidt, Boston
1951-52—Gordie Howe, Detroit
1952-53—Gordie Howe, Detroit
1953-54—Al Rollins, Chicago
1954-55—Ted Kennedy, Toronto
1955-56—Jean Beliveau, Montreal
1956-57—Gordie Howe, Detroit
1957-58—Gordie Howe, Detroit
1958-59—Andy Bathgate, N.Y. Rangers
1959-60—Gordie Howe, Detroit
1960-61—Bernie Geoffrion, Montreal
1961-62—Jacques Plante, Montreal
1962-63—Gordie Howe, Detroit
1963-64—Jean Beliveau, Montreal
1964-65—Bobby Hull, Chicago
1965-66—Bobby Hull, Chicago
1966-67—Stan Mikita, Chicago
1967-68—Stan Mikita, Chicago
1968-69—Phil Esposito, Boston
1969-70—Bobby Orr, Boston
1970-71—Bobby Orr, Boston
1971-72—Bobby Orr, Boston
1972-73—Bobby Clarke, Philadelphia
1973-74—Phil Esposito, Boston
1974-75—Bobby Clarke, Philadelphia
1975-76—Bobby Clarke, Philadelphia
1976-77—Guy Lafleur, Montreal
1977-78—Guy Lafleur, Montreal
1978-79—Bryan Trottier, N.Y. Islanders
1979-80—Wayne Gretzky, Edmonton
1980-81—Wayne Gretzky, Edmonton
1981-82—Wayne Gretzky, Edmonton
1982-83—Wayne Gretzky, Edmonton
1983-84—Wayne Gretzky, Edmonton
1984-85—Wayne Gretzky, Edmonton
1985-86—Wayne Gretzky, Edmonton
1986-87—Wayne Gretzky, Edmonton
1987-88—Mario Lemieux, Pittsburgh
1988-89—Wayne Gretzky, Los Angeles

## Penalty Leaders

|  | Games | Penalty Minutes |
|---|---|---|
| 1926-27—Nels Stewart, Montreal Maroons | 44 | 133 |
| 1927-28—Eddie Shore, Boston | 44 | 165 |
| 1928-29—Merv "Red" Dutton, Montreal Maroons | 44 | 139 |
| 1929-30—Joe Lamb, Ottawa Senators | 44 | 119 |
| 1930-31—Harvey Rockburn, Detroit | 42 | 118 |
| 1931-32—Merv "Red" Dutton, N.Y. Americans | 47 | 107 |
| 1932-33—Red Horner, Toronto | 47 | 144 |
| 1933-34—Red Horner, Toronto | 42 | 126* |
| 1934-35—Red Horner, Toronto | 46 | 125 |
| 1935-36—Red Horner, Toronto | 43 | 167 |
| 1936-37—Red Horner, Toronto | 48 | 124 |
| 1937-38—Red Horner, Toronto | 47 | 82* |
| 1938-39—Red Horner, Toronto | 48 | 85 |
| 1939-40—Red Horner, Toronto | 30 | 87 |
| 1940-41—Jimmy Orlando, Detroit | 48 | 99 |
| 1941-42—Jimmy Orlando, Detroit | 48 | 81** |
| 1942-43—Jimmy Orlando, Detroit | 40 | 89* |
| 1943-44—Mike McMahon, Montreal Canadiens | 42 | 98 |
| 1944-45—Pat Egan, Boston | 48 | 86 |
| 1945-46—Jack Stewart, Detroit | 47 | 73 |

|  | Games | Penalty Minutes |
|---|---|---|
| 1946-47—Gus Mortson, Toronto | 60 | 133 |
| 1947-48—Bill Barilko, Toronto | 57 | 147 |
| 1948-49—Bill Ezinicki, Toronto | 52 | 145 |
| 1949-50—Bill Ezinicki, Toronto | 67 | 144 |
| 1950-51—Gus Mortson, Toronto | 60 | 142 |
| 1951-52—Walter "Gus" Kyle, Boston | 69 | 127 |
| 1952-53—Maurice Richard, Montreal Canadiens | 70 | 112 |
| 1953-54—Gus Mortson, Chicago | 68 | 132 |
| 1954-55—Fernie Flaman, Boston | 70 | 150 |
| 1955-56—Lou Fontinato, N.Y. Rangers | 70 | 202 |
| 1956-57—Gus Mortson, Chicago | 70 | 147 |
| 1957-58—Lou Fontinato, N.Y. Rangers | 70 | 152 |
| 1958-59—Ted Lindsay, Chicago | 70 | 184 |
| 1959-60—Carl Brewer, Toronto | 67 | 150 |
| 1960-61—Pierre Pilote, Chicago | 70 | 165 |
| 1961-62—Lou Fontinato, Montreal | 54 | 167 |
| 1962-63—Howie Young, Detroit | 64 | 273 |
| 1963-64—Vic Hadfield, N.Y. Rangers | 69 | 151 |
| 1964-65—Carl Brewer, Toronto | 70 | 177 |
| 1965-66—Reg Fleming, N.Y. Rangers | 69 | 166 |
| 1966-67—John Ferguson, Montreal | 67 | 177 |
| 1967-68—Barclay Plager, St. Louis | 49 | 153 |
| 1968-69—Forbes Kennedy, Philadelphia-Toronto | 77 | 219 |
| 1969-70—Keith Magnuson, Chicago | 76 | 213 |
| 1970-71—Keith Magnuson, Chicago | 76 | 291 |
| 1971-72—Bryan Watson, Pittsburgh | 75 | 212 |
| 1972-73—Dave Schultz, Philadelphia | 76 | 259 |
| 1973-74—Dave Schultz, Philadelphia | 73 | 348 |
| 1974-75—Dave Schultz, Philadelphia | 76 | 472 |
| 1975-76—Steve Durbano, Pittsburgh-Kansas City | 69 | 370 |
| 1976-77—Dave Williams, Toronto | 77 | 338 |
| 1977-78—Dave Schultz, Los Angeles-Pittsburgh | 74 | 405 |
| 1978-79—Dave Williams, Toronto | 77 | 298 |
| 1979-80—Jimmy Mann, Winnipeg | 72 | 287 |
| 1980-81—Dave Williams, Vancouver | 77 | 333 |
| 1981-82—Paul Baxter, Pittsburgh | 76 | 407 |
| 1982-83—Randy Holt, Washington | 70 | 275 |
| 1983-84—Chris Nilan, Montreal | 76 | 338 |
| 1984-85—Chris Nilan, Montreal | 77 | 358 |
| 1985-86—Joey Kocur, Detroit | 59 | 377 |
| 1986-87—Dave Williams, Los Angeles | 76 | 358 |
| 1987-88—Bob Probert, Detroit | 74 | 398 |
| 1988-89—Tim Hunter, Calgary | 75 | 375 |

\*—Match Misconduct penalty not included in total minutes.
\*\*—Three Match misconduct penalties not included in total minutes. 1946-47 was first season that Match penalties were automatically included in penalty totals.

## James Norris Memorial Trophy
### (Outstanding Defenseman)

1953-54—Red Kelly, Detroit
1954-55—Doug Harvey, Montreal
1955-56—Doug Harvey, Montreal
1956-57—Doug Harvey, Montreal
1957-58—Doug Harvey, Montreal
1958-59—Tom Johnson, Montreal
1959-60—Doug Harvey, Montreal
1960-61—Doug Harvey, Montreal
1961-62—Doug Harvey, N.Y. Rangers
1962-63—Pierre Pilote, Chicago
1963-64—Pierre Pilote, Chicago
1964-65—Pierre Pilote, Chicago
1965-66—Jacques Laperriere, Montreal
1966-67—Harry Howell, N.Y. Rangers
1967-68—Bobby Orr, Boston
1968-69—Bobby Orr, Boston
1969-70—Bobby Orr, Boston
1970-71—Bobby Orr, Boston
1971-72—Bobby Orr, Boston
1972-73—Bobby Orr, Boston
1973-74—Bobby Orr, Boston
1974-75—Bobby Orr, Boston
1975-76—Denis Potvin, N.Y. Islanders
1976-77—Larry Robinson, Montreal
1977-78—Denis Potvin, N.Y. Islanders
1978-79—Denis Potvin, N.Y. Islanders
1979-80—Larry Robinson, Montreal
1980-81—Randy Carlyle, Pittsburgh
1981-82—Doug Wilson, Chicago
1982-83—Rod Langway, Washington
1983-84—Rod Langway, Washington
1984-85—Paul Coffey, Edmonton
1985-86—Paul Coffey, Edmonton
1986-87—Ray Bourque, Boston
1987-88—Ray Bourque, Boston
1988-89—Chris Chelios, Montreal

## Vezina Trophy

(Awarded to goalkeeper(s) having played a minimum 25 games for the team with fewest goals scored against. Beginning with 1981-82 season, awarded to outstanding goaltender.)

| Season | Goaltender | Games | Goals | SO. | Avg. |
|---|---|---|---|---|---|
| 1926-27 | George Hainsworth, Montreal | 44 | 67 | 14 | 1.52 |
| 1927-28 | George Hainsworth, Montreal | 44 | 48 | 13 | 1.09 |
| 1928-29 | George Hainsworth, Montreal | 44 | 43 | 22 | 0.98 |
| 1929-30 | Tiny Thompson, Boston | 44 | 98 | 3 | 2.23 |
| 1930-31 | Roy Worters, N.Y. Americans | 44 | 74 | 8 | 1.68 |
| 1931-32 | Charlie Gardiner, Chicago | 48 | 101 | 4 | 2.10 |
| 1932-33 | Tiny Thompson, Boston | 48 | 88 | 11 | 1.83 |
| 1933-34 | Charlie Gardiner, Chicago | 48 | 83 | 10 | 1.73 |
| 1934-35 | Lorne Chabot, Chicago | 48 | 88 | 8 | 1.83 |
| 1935-36 | Tiny Thompson, Boston | 48 | 82 | 10 | 1.71 |
| 1936-37 | Normie Smith, Detroit | 48 | 102 | 6 | 2.13 |
| 1937-38 | Tiny Thompson, Boston | 48 | 89 | 7 | 1.85 |
| 1938-39 | Frank Brimsek, Boston | 43 | 69 | 10 | 1.60 |
| 1939-40 | Dave Kerr, N.Y. Rangers | 48 | 77 | 8 | 1.60 |
| 1940-41 | Turk Broda, Toronto | 48 | 99 | 4 | 2.06 |
| 1941-42 | Frank Brimsek, Boston | 47 | 112 | 3 | 2.38 |
| 1942-43 | Johnny Mowers, Detroit | 50 | 124 | 6 | 2.48 |
| 1943-44 | Bill Durnan, Montreal | 50 | 109 | 2 | 2.18 |
| 1944-45 | Bill Durnan, Montreal | 50 | 121 | 1 | 2.42 |
| 1945-46 | Bill Durnan, Montreal | 40 | 104 | 4 | 2.60 |
| 1946-47 | Bill Durnan, Montreal | 60 | 138 | 4 | 2.30 |
| 1947-48 | Turk Broda, Toronto | 60 | 143 | 5 | 2.38 |
| 1948-49 | Bill Durnan, Montreal | 60 | 126 | 10 | 2.10 |
| 1949-50 | Bill Durnan, Montreal | 64 | 141 | 8 | 2.20 |
| 1950-51 | Al Rollins, Toronto | 40 | 70 | 5 | 1.75 |
| 1951-52 | Terry Sawchuk, Detroit | 70 | 139 | 11 | 1.98 |
| 1952-53 | Terry Sawchuk, Detroit | 70 | 133 | 12 | 1.94 |
| 1953-54 | Harry Lumley, Toronto | 69 | 128 | 13 | 1.85 |
| 1954-55 | Terry Sawchuk, Detroit | 68 | 132 | 12 | 1.94 |
| 1955-56 | Jacques Plante, Montreal | 64 | 119 | 7 | 1.86 |
| 1956-57 | Jacques Plante, Montreal | 61 | 123 | 9 | 2.02 |
| 1957-58 | Jacques Plante, Montreal | 57 | 119 | 9 | 2.09 |
| 1958-59 | Jacques Plante, Montreal | 67 | 144 | 9 | 2.15 |
| 1959-60 | Jacques Plante, Montreal | 69 | 175 | 3 | 2.54 |
| 1960-61 | Johnny Bower, Toronto | 58 | 145 | 2 | 2.50 |
| 1961-62 | Jacques Plante, Montreal | 70 | 166 | 4 | 2.37 |
| 1962-63 | Glenn Hall, Chicago | 66 | 166 | 5 | 2.51 |
| 1963-64 | Charlie Hodge, Montreal | 62 | 140 | 8 | 2.26 |
| 1964-65 | Terry Sawchuk, Toronto | 36 | 92 | 1 | 2.56 |
|  | Johnny Bower, Toronto | 34 | 81 | 3 | 2.38 |
| 1965-66 | Lorne Worsley, Montreal | 48 | 114 | 2 | 2.36 |
|  | Charlie Hodge, Montreal | 21 | 56 | 1 | 2.58 |
| 1966-67 | Glenn Hall, Chicago | 32 | 66 | 2 | 2.38 |
|  | Denis DeJordy, Chicago | 44 | 104 | 4 | 2.46 |
| 1967-68 | Lorne Worsley, Montreal | 40 | 73 | 6 | 1.98 |
|  | Rogatien Vachon, Montreal | 39 | 92 | 4 | 2.48 |
| 1968-69 | Glenn Hall, St. Louis | 41 | 85 | 8 | 2.17 |
|  | Jacques Plante, St. Louis | 37 | 70 | 5 | 1.96 |
| 1969-70 | Tony Esposito, Chicago | 63 | 136 | 15 | 2.17 |
| 1970-71 | Ed Giacomin, N.Y. Rangers | 45 | 95 | 8 | 2.15 |
|  | Gilles Villemure, N.Y. Rangers | 34 | 78 | 4 | 2.29 |
| 1971-72 | Tony Esposito, Chicago | 48 | 82 | 9 | 1.76 |
|  | Gary Smith, Chicago | 28 | 62 | 5 | 2.41 |
| 1972-73 | Ken Dryden, Montreal | 54 | 119 | 6 | 2.26 |
| 1973-74 | Bernie Parent, Philadelphia | 73 | 136 | 12 | 1.89 |
|  | Tony Esposito, Chicago | 70 | 141 | 10 | 2.04 |
| 1974-75 | Bernie Parent, Philadelphia | 68 | 137 | 12 | 2.03 |
| 1975-76 | Ken Dryden, Montreal | 62 | 121 | 8 | 2.03 |
| 1976-77 | Ken Dryden, Montreal | 56 | 117 | 10 | 2.14 |
|  | Michel Larocque, Montreal | 26 | 53 | 4 | 2.09 |
| 1977-78 | Ken Dryden, Montreal | 52 | 105 | 5 | 2.05 |
|  | Michel Larocque, Montreal | 30 | 77 | 1 | 2.67 |
| 1978-79 | Ken Dryden, Montreal | 47 | 108 | 5 | 2.30 |
|  | Michel Larocque, Montreal | 34 | 94 | 3 | 2.84 |
| 1979-80 | Bob Sauve, Buffalo | 32 | 74 | 4 | 2.36 |
|  | Don Edwards, Buffalo | 49 | 125 | 4 | 2.57 |
| 1980-81 | Richard Sevigny, Montreal | 33 | 71 | 2 | 2.40 |
|  | Michel Larocque, Montreal | 28 | 82 | 1 | 3.03 |
|  | Denis Herron, Montreal | 25 | 67 | 1 | 3.50 |

|  | Games | Goals | SO. | Avg. |
|---|---|---|---|---|
| 1981-82—Billy Smith, N.Y. Islanders | 46 | 133 | 0 | 2.97 |
| 1982-83—Pete Peeters, Boston | 62 | 142 | 8 | 2.36 |
| 1983-84—Tom Barrasso, Buffalo | 42 | 117 | 2 | 2.84 |
| 1984-85—Pelle Lindbergh, Philadelphia | 65 | 194 | 2 | 3.02 |
| 1985-86—John Vanbiesbrouck, N.Y. Rangers | 61 | 184 | 3 | 3.32 |
| 1986-87—Ron Hextall, Philadelphia | 66 | 190 | 1 | 3.00 |
| 1987-88—Grant Fuhr, Edmonton | 75 | 246 | 4 | 3.43 |
| 1988-89—Patrick Roy, Montreal | 48 | 113 | 4 | 2.47 |

## Bill Jennings Trophy

(Awarded to goalkeeper(s) having played a minimum of 25 games for the team with fewest goals scored against, beginning with 1981-82 season.)

|  | Games | Goals | SO. | Avg. |
|---|---|---|---|---|
| 1981-82—Denis Herron, Montreal | 27 | 68 | 3 | 2.64 |
| Rick Wamsley, Montreal | 38 | 101 | 2 | 2.75 |
| 1982-83—Roland Melanson, N.Y. Islanders | 44 | 109 | 1 | 2.66 |
| Billy Smith, N.Y. Islanders | 41 | 112 | 1 | 2.87 |
| 1983-84—Pat Riggin, Washington | 41 | 102 | 4 | 2.66 |
| Al Jensen, Washington | 43 | 117 | 4 | 2.91 |
| 1984-85—Tom Barrasso, Buffalo | 54 | 144 | 5 | 2.66 |
| Bob Sauve, Buffalo | 27 | 84 | 0 | 3.22 |
| 1985-86—Bob Froese, Philadelphia | 51 | 116 | 5 | 2.55 |
| Darren Jensen, Philadelphia | 29 | 88 | 2 | 3.68 |
| 1986-87—Brian Hayward, Montreal | 37 | 102 | 1 | 2.81 |
| Patrick Roy, Montreal | 46 | 131 | 1 | 2.93 |
| 1987-88—Brian Hayward, Montreal | 39 | 107 | 2 | 2.86 |
| Patrick Roy, Montreal | 45 | 125 | 3 | 2.90 |
| 1988-89—Patrick Roy, Montreal | 48 | 113 | 4 | 2.47 |
| Brian Hayward, Montreal | 36 | 101 | 1 | 2.90 |

## Calder Memorial Trophy
### (Rookie of the Year)

(Award was originally Leading Rookie Award. Named Calder Trophy in 1936-37 and became Calder Memorial Trophy when NHL President Frank Calder passed away—1942-43 season.)

1932-33—Carl Voss, Detroit
1933-34—Russ Blinco, Montreal Maroons
1934-35—Dave Schriner, N.Y. Americans
1935-36—Mike Karakas, Chicago
1936-37—Syl Apps, Toronto
1937-38—Cully Dahlstrom, Chicago
1938-39—Frank Brimsek, Boston
1939-40—Kilby Macdonald, N.Y. Rangers
1940-41—John Quilty, Montreal
1941-42—Grant Warwick, N.Y. Rangers
1942-43—Gaye Stewart, Toronto
1943-44—Gus Bodnar, Toronto
1944-45—Frank McCool, Toronto
1945-46—Edgar Laprade, N.Y. Rangers
1946-47—Howie Meeker, Toronto
1947-48—Jim McFadden, Detroit
1948-49—Pentti Lund, N.Y. Rangers
1949-50—Jack Gelineau, Boston
1950-51—Terry Sawchuk, Detroit
1951-52—Bernie Geoffrion, Montreal
1952-53—Lorne Worsley, N.Y. Rangers
1953-54—Camille Henry, N.Y. Rangers
1954-55—Ed Litzenberger, Chicago
1955-56—Glenn Hall, Detroit
1956-57—Larry Regan, Boston
1957-58—Frank Mahovlich, Toronto
1958-59—Ralph Backstrom, Montreal
1951-60—Bill Hay, Chicago
1960-61—Dave Keon, Toronto
1961-62—Bobby Rousseau, Montreal
1962-63—Kent Douglas, Toronto
1963-64—Jacques Laperriere, Montreal
1964-65—Roger Crozier, Detroit
1965-66—Brit Selby, Toronto
1966-67—Bobby Orr, Boston
1967-68—Derek Sanderson, Boston
1968-69—Danny Grant, Minnesota
1969-70—Tony Esposito, Chicago
1970-71—Gilbert Perreault, Buffalo
1971-72—Ken Dryden, Montreal
1972-73—Steve Vickers, N.Y. Rangers
1973-74—Denis Potvin, N.Y. Islanders
1974-75—Eric Vail, Atlanta
1975-76—Bryan Trottier, N.Y. Islanders
1976-77—Willi Plett, Atlanta
1977-78—Mike Bossy, N.Y. Islanders
1978-79—Bobby Smith, Minnesota
1979-80—Ray Bourque, Boston
1980-81—Peter Stastny, Quebec
1981-82—Dale Hawerchuk, Winnipeg
1982-83—Steve Larmer, Chicago
1983-84—Tom Barrasso, Buffalo
1984-85—Mario Lemieux, Pittsburgh
1985-86—Gary Suter, Calgary
1986-87—Luc Robitaille, Los Angeles
1987-88—Joe Nieuwendyk, Calgary
1988-89—Brian Leetch, N.Y. Rangers

## Lady Byng Memorial Trophy
### (Most Gentlemanly Player)

(Originally Lady Byng Trophy. After winning award seven times, Frank Boucher received permanent possession and a new trophy was donated to NHL in 1936. After Lady Byng's death in 1949, NHL changed name to Lady Byng Memorial Trophy.)

1924-25—Frank Nighbor, Ottawa
1925-26—Frank Nighbor, Ottawa

1926-27—Billy Burch, N.Y. Americans
1927-28—Frank Boucher, N.Y. Rangers
1928-29—Frank Boucher, N.Y. Rangers
1929-30—Frank Boucher, N.Y. Rangers
1930-31—Frank Boucher, N.Y. Rangers
1931-32—Joe Primeau, Toronto
1932-33—Frank Boucher, N.Y. Rangers
1933-34—Frank Boucher, N.Y. Rangers
1934-35—Frank Boucher, N.Y. Rangers
1935-36—Doc Romnes, Chicago
1936-37—Marty Barry, Detroit
1937-38—Gordie Drillon, Toronto
1938-39—Clint Smith, N.Y. Rangers
1939-40—Bobby Bauer, Boston
1940-41—Bobby Bauer, Boston
1941-42—Syl Apps, Toronto
1942-43—Max Bentley, Chicago
1943-44—Clint Smith, Chicago
1944-45—Bill Mosienko, Chicago
1945-46—Toe Blake, Montreal
1946-47—Bobby Bauer, Boston
1947-48—Buddy O'Connor, N.Y. Rangers
1948-49—Bill Quackenbush, Detroit
1949-50—Edgar Laprade, N.Y. Rangers
1950-51—Red Kelly, Detroit
1951-52—Sid Smith, Toronto
1952-53—Red Kelly, Detroit
1953-54—Red Kelly, Detroit
1954-55—Sid Smith, Toronto
1955-56—Earl Reibel, Detroit
1956-57—Andy Hebenton, N.Y. Rangers
1957-58—Camille Henry, N.Y. Rangers
1958-59—Alex Delvecchio, Detroit
1959-60—Don McKenney, Boston
1960-61—Red Kelly, Toronto
1961-62—Dave Keon, Toronto
1962-63—Dave Keon, Toronto
1963-64—Ken Wharram, Chicago
1964-65—Bobby Hull, Chicago
1965-66—Alex Delvecchio, Detroit
1966-67—Stan Mikita, Chicago
1967-68—Stan Mikita, Chicago
1968-69—Alex Delvecchio, Detroit
1969-70—Phil Goyette, St. Louis
1970-71—John Bucyk, Boston
1971-72—Jean Ratelle, N.Y. Rangers
1972-73—Gilbert Perreault, Buffalo
1973-74—John Bucyk, Boston
1974-75—Marcel Dionne, Detroit
1975-76—Jean Ratelle, N.Y. R.-Boston
1976-77—Marcel Dionne, Los Angeles
1977-78—Butch Goring, Los Angeles
1978-79—Bob MacMillan, Atlanta
1979-80—Wayne Gretzky, Edmonton
1980-81—Butch Goring, N.Y. Islanders
1981-82—Rick Middleton, Boston
1982-83—Mike Bossy, N.Y. Islanders
1983-84—Mike Bossy, N.Y. Islanders
1984-85—Jari Kurri, Edmonton
1985-86—Mike Bossy, N.Y. Islanders
1986-87—Joe Mullen, Calgary
1987-88—Mats Naslund, Montreal
1988-89—Joe Mullen, Calgary

## Conn Smythe Trophy
### (Most Valuable Player in Playoffs)

1964-65—Jean Beliveau, Montreal
1965-66—Roger Crozier, Detroit
1966-67—Dave Keon, Toronto
1967-68—Glenn Hall, St. Louis
1968-69—Serge Savard, Montreal
1969-70—Bobby Orr, Boston
1970-71—Ken Dryden, Montreal
1971-72—Bobby Orr, Boston
1972-73—Yvan Cournoyer, Montreal
1973-74—Bernie Parent, Philadelphia
1974-75—Bernie Parent, Philadelphia
1975-76—Reggie Leach, Philadelphia
1976-77—Guy Lafleur, Montreal
1977-78—Larry Robinson, Montreal
1978-79—Bob Gainey, Montreal
1979-80—Bryan Trottier, N.Y. Islanders
1980-81—Butch Goring, N.Y. Islanders
1981-82—Mike Bossy, N. Y. Islanders
1982-83—Billy Smith, N.Y. Islanders
1983-84—Mark Messier, Edmonton
1984-85—Wayne Gretzky, Edmonton
1985-86—Patrick Roy, Montreal
1986-87—Ron Hextall, Philadelphia
1987-88—Wayne Gretzky, Edmonton
1988-89—Al MacInnis, Calgary

## Bill Masterton Memorial Trophy
(Presented by Professional Hockey Writers' Association to player who best exemplifies the qualities of perseverance, sportsmanship and dedication to hockey.)

1967-68—Claude Provost, Montreal
1968-69—Ted Hampson, Oakland
1969-70—Pit Martin, Chicago
1970-71—Jean Ratelle, N.Y. Rangers
1971-72—Bobby Clarke, Philadelphia
1972-73—Lowell MacDonald, Pittsburgh
1973-74—Henri Richard, Montreal
1974-75—Don Luce, Buffalo
1975-76—Rod Gilbert, N.Y. Rangers
1976-77—Ed Westfall, N.Y. Islanders
1977-78—Butch Goring, Los Angeles
1978-79—Serge Savard, Montreal
1979-80—Al MacAdam, Minnesota
1980-81—Blake Dunlop, St. Louis
1981-82—Glenn Resch, Colorado
1982-83—Lanny McDonald, Calgary
1983-84—Brad Park, Detroit
1984-85—Anders Hedberg, N.Y. Rangers
1985-86—Charlie Simmer, Boston
1986-87—Doug Jarvis, Hartford
1987-88—Bob Bourne, Los Angeles
1988-89—Tim Kerr, Philadelphia

## Frank J. Selke Trophy
### (Best Defensive Forward)

1977-78—Bob Gainey, Montreal
1978-79—Bob Gainey, Montreal
1979-80—Bob Gainey, Montreal
1980-81—Bob Gainey, Montreal
1981-82—Steve Kasper, Boston
1982-83—Bobby Clarke, Philadelphia
1983-84—Doug Jarvis, Washington
1984-85—Craig Ramsay, Buffalo
1985-86—Troy Murray, Chicago
1986-87—Dave Poulin, Philadelphia
1987-88—Guy Carbonneau, Montreal
1988-89—Guy Carbonneau, Montreal

## Jack Adams Award
### (Coach of the Year)

1973-74—Fred Shero, Philadelphia
1974-75—Bob Pulford, Los Angeles
1975-76—Don Cherry, Boston
1976-77—Scotty Bowman, Montreal
1977-78—Bobby Kromm, Detroit
1978-79—Al Arbour, N.Y. Islanders
1979-80—Pat Quinn, Philadelphia
1980-81—Red Berenson, St. Louis
1981-82—Tom Watt, Winnipeg
1982-83—Orval Tessier, Chicago
1983-84—Bryan Murray, Washington
1984-85—Mike Keenan, Philadelphia
1985-86—Glen Sather, Edmonton
1986-87—Jacques Demers, Detroit
1987-88—Jacques Demers, Detroit
1988-89—Pat Burns, Montreal

## King Clancy Trophy
### (Humanitarian Contributions)

1987-88—Lanny McDonald, Calgary
1988-89—Bryan Trottier, N.Y. Islanders

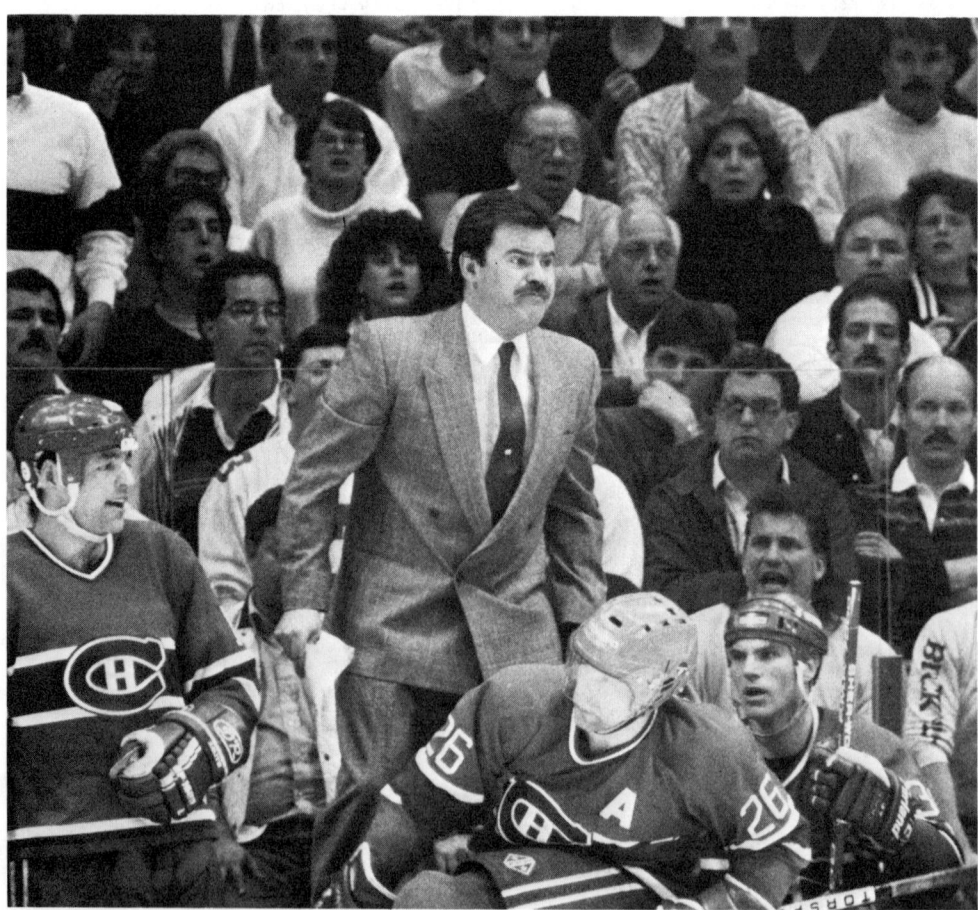

**Montreal's Pat Burns won the Jack Adams Award as NHL Coach of the Year in his rookie campaign.**

# NHL Entry Draft—June 17, 1989

## FIRST ROUND

| NHL Club | PLAYER | (Pos) | 1988-89 CLUB (League) |
|---|---|---|---|
| 1—Quebec | Mats Sundin | (RW) | Nacka, Sweden |
| 2—New York Islanders | Dave Chyzowski | (LW) | Kamloops (WHL) |
| 3—Toronto | Scott Thornton | (C) | Belleville (OHL) |
| 4—Winnipeg | Stu Barnes | (C) | Tri-City (WHL) |
| 5—New Jersey | Bill Guerin | (RW) | Springfield (Mass.) Jr. |
| 6—Chicago | Adam Bennett | (D) | Sudbury (OHL) |
| 7—Minnesota | Doug Zmolek | (D) | John Marshall H.S. (Minn.) |
| 8—Vancouver | Jason Herter | (D) | University of North Dakota |
| 9—St. Louis | Jason Marshall | (D) | Vernon (B.C.) Tier II |
| 10—Hartford | Robert Holik | (C) | Jihlava, Czech. |
| 11—Detroit | Mike Sillinger | (C) | Regina (WHL) |
| 12—Toronto (from Philadelphia) | Rob Pearson | (RW) | Belleville (OHL) |
| 13—Montreal (from N.Y. Rangers) | Lindsay Vallis | (RW) | Seattle (WHL) |
| 14—Buffalo | Kevin Haller | (D) | Regina (WHL) |
| 15—Edmonton | Jason Soules | (D) | Niagara Falls (OHL) |
| 16—Pittsburgh | Jamie Heward | (RW) | Regina (WHL) |
| 17—Boston | Shayne Stevenson | (RW) | Kitchener (OHL) |
| 18—N.J. (from L.A. & Edm.) | Jason Miller | (C) | Medicine Hat (WHL) |
| 19—Washington | Olaf Kolzig | (G) | Tri-City (WHL) |
| 20—N.Y. Rangers (from Mont.) | Steven Rice | (RW) | Kitchener (OHL) |
| 21—Toronto (from Calgary) | Steve Bancroft | (D) | Belleville (OHL) |

## SECOND ROUND

| NHL Club | PLAYER | (Pos) | 1988-89 CLUB (League) |
|---|---|---|---|
| 22—Quebec | Adam Foote | (D) | Sault Ste. Marie (OHL) |
| 23—New York Islanders | Travis Green | (C) | Spokane (WHL) |
| 24—Calgary (from Toronto) | Kent Manderville | (LW) | Notre Dame (Sask.) Tier II |
| 25—Winnipeg | Dan Ratushny | (D) | Cornell University |
| 26—New Jersey | Jarrod Skalde | (C) | Oshawa (OHL) |
| 27—Chicago | Michael Speer | (D) | Guelph (OHL) |
| 28—Minnesota | Mike Craig | (RW) | Oshawa (OHL) |
| 29—Vancouver | Robert Woodward | (LW) | Deerfield H.S. (Ill.) |
| 30—Montreal (from St. Louis) | Patrice Brisebois | (D) | Laval (QMJL) |
| 31—St. Louis (from Hartford) | Rick Corriveau | (D) | London (OHL) |
| 32—Detroit | Bob Boughner | (D) | Sault Ste. Marie (OHL) |
| 33—Philadelphia | Greg Johnson | (C) | Thunder Bay (Ont.) Jr. A. |
| 34—Philadelphia (from NY Rang.) | Patrik Juhlin | (LW) | Vasteras, Sweden |
| 35—Washington (from Buffalo) | Byron Dafoe | (G) | Portland (WHL) |
| 36—Edmonton | Richard Borgo | (RW) | Kitchener (OHL) |
| 37—Pittsburgh | Paul Laus | (D) | Niagara Falls (OHL) |
| 38—Boston | Mike Parson | (G) | Guelph (OHL) |
| 39—Los Angeles | Brent Thompson | (D) | Medicine Hat (WHL) |
| 40—N.Y. Rangers (from Wash.) | Jason Prosofsky | (RW) | Medicine Hat (WHL) |
| 41—Montreal | Steve Larouche | (C) | Trois-Rivieres (QMJL) |
| 42—Calgary | Ted Drury | (C) | Fairfield Prep. (Ct.) |

## THIRD ROUND

| NHL Club | PLAYER | (Pos) | 1988-89 CLUB (League) |
|---|---|---|---|
| 43—Quebec | Stephane Morin | (C) | Chicoutimi (QMJL) |
| 44—New York Islanders | Jason Zent | (LW) | Nichols H.S. (N.Y.) |
| 45—N.Y. Rangers (from Toronto) | Rob Zamuner | (C) | Guelph (OHL) |
| 46—Winnipeg (from New Jersey) | Jason Cirone | (C) | Cornwall (OHL) |
| 47—New Jersey | Scott Pellerin | (LW) | University of Maine |
| 48—Chicago | Bob Kellogg | (D) | Springfield (Mass.) Jr. B |
| 49—N.Y. Rangers (from Minn.) | Louie Debrusk | (LW) | London (OHL) |
| 50—Calgary (from Vancouver) | Veli-Pekka Kautonen | (D) | IFK Helsinki, Finland |
| 51—Montreal (from St. Louis) | Pierre Sevigny | (LW) | Verdun (QMJL) |
| 52—Hartford | Blair Atcheynum | (RW) | Moose Jaw (WHL) |
| 53—Detroit | Niklas Lidstrom | (D) | Vasteras, Sweden |
| 54—Quebec (from Philadelphia) | John Tanner | (G) | Peterborough (OHL) |
| 55—St. Louis (from NYR & Wpg.) | Denny Felsner | (LW) | Univerity of Michigan |
| 56—Buffalo | Scott Thomas | (RW) | Nichols H.S. (N.Y.) |
| 57—Boston (from Edmonton) | Wes Walz | (C) | Lethbridge (WHL) |
| 58—Pittsburgh | John Brill | (RW) | Grand Rapids H.S. (Minn.) |
| 59—Washington (from Boston) | Jim Mathieson | (D) | Regina (WHL) |
| 60—Minnesota (from Los Angeles) | Murray Garbutt | (C) | Medicine Hat (WHL) |
| 61—Washington | Jason Woolley | (D) | Michigan State University |
| 62—Winnipeg (from Mtl. & St.L.) | Kris Draper | (C) | Canadian Nationals |
| 63—Calgary | Corey Lyons | (RW) | Lethbridge (WHL) |

## FOURTH ROUND

| NHL Club | PLAYER | (Pos) | 1988-89 CLUB (League) |
|---|---|---|---|
| 64—Winnipeg (from Quebec) | Mark Brownschidle | (D) | Boston University |
| 65—New York Islanders | Brent Grieve | (LW) | Oshawa (OHL) |
| 66—Toronto | Matt Martin | (D) | Avon Old Farms H.S. (Ct.) |
| 67—N.Y. Rangers (from Winnipeg) | Jim Cummins | (RW) | Michigan State University |
| 68—Quebec (from New Jersey) | Niclas Andersson | (RW) | Frolunda, Sweden |
| 69—Winnipeg (from Chicago) | Allain Roy | (G) | Harvard University |
| 70—Calgary (from Minnesota) | Robert Reichel | (C) | Litvinov, Czech. |
| 71—Vancouver | Brett Hauer | (D) | Richfield H.S. (Minn.) |
| 72—Philadelphia (from St. Louis) | Reid Simpson | (LW) | Prince Albert (WHL) |
| 73—Hartford | Jim McKenzie | (LW) | Victoria (WHL) |
| 74—Detroit | Sergei Fedorov | (C) | CSKA, Russia |
| 75—Minnesota (from Philadelphia) | Jean Francois Quintin | (C) | Shawinigan (QMJL) |
| 76—Quebec (from N.Y. Rangers) | Eric Dubois | (D) | Laval (QMJL) |
| 77—Buffalo | Doug MacDonald | (C) | University of Wisconsin |
| 78—Edmonton | Josef Beranek | (C) | Litvinov, Czech. |
| 79—Pittsburgh | Todd Nelson | (D) | Prince Albert (WHL) |
| 80—Boston | Jackson Penney | (C) | Victoria (WHL) |
| 81—Los Angeles | Jim Maher | (D) | Univ. of Illinois-Chicago |
| 82—Washington | Trent Klatt | (C) | Osseo H.S. (Minn.) |
| 83—Montreal | Andre Racicot | (G) | Granby (QMJL) |
| 84—Calgary | Ryan O'Leary | (C) | Hermantown H.S. (Minn.) |

## FIFTH ROUND

| NHL Club | PLAYER | (Pos) | 1988-89 CLUB (League) |
|---|---|---|---|
| 85—Quebec | Kevin Kaiser | (LW) | Univ. of Minnesota-Duluth |
| 86—New York Islanders | Jace Reed | (D) | Grand Rapids H.S. (Minn.) |
| 87—Minnesota (from Toronto) | Pat MacLeod | (D) | Kamloops (WHL) |
| 88—N.Y. Rangers (from Winnipeg) | Aaron Miller | (D) | Niagara (N.Y.) Jr. A. |
| 89—New Jersey | Mike Heinke | (G) | Avon Old Farms H.S. (Ct.) |
| 90—N.Y. Islanders (from Chicago) | Steve Young | (RW) | Moose Jaw (WHL) |
| 91—Minnesota | Bryan Schoen | (G) | Minnetonka H.S. (Minn.) |
| 92—Edmonton (from Vancouver) | Peter White | (LW) | Michigan State University |
| 93—St. Louis | Daniel Laperriere | (D) | St. Lawrence University |
| 94—Hartford | James Black | (C) | Portland (WHL) |
| 95—Detroit | Shawn McCosh | (C) | Niagara Falls (OHL) |
| 96—Toronto (from Philadelphia) | Keith Carney | (D) | Mount St. Charles H.S. (R.I.) |
| 97—Minnesota (from N.Y. Rangers) | Rhys Hollyman | (D) | Miami University (O.) |
| 98—Buffalo | Ken Sutton | (D) | Saskatoon (WHL) |
| 99—N.Y. Islanders (from Edm.) | Kevin O'Sullivan | (D) | Catholic Memorial H.S. (Mass.) |
| 100—Pittsburgh | Tom Nevers | (C) | Edina H.S. (Minn.) |
| 101—Boston | Mark Montanari | (C) | Kitchener (OHL) |
| 102—Los Angeles | Eric Ricard | (D) | Granby (QMJL) |
| 103—Los Angeles (from Wash.) | Thomas Newman | (G) | Blaine H.S. (Minn.) |
| 104—Montreal | Marc Deschamps | (D) | Cornell University |
| 105—Calgary | Toby Kearney | (LW) | Belmont Hill H.S. (Mass.) |

## SIXTH ROUND

| NHL Club | PLAYER | (Pos) | 1988-89 CLUB (League) |
|---|---|---|---|
| 106—Quebec | Dan Lambert | (D) | Swift Current (WHL) |
| 107—Buffalo (from N.Y. Islanders) | Bill Pye | (G) | Northern Michigan University |
| 108—Toronto | David Burke | (D) | Cornell University |
| 109—Winnipeg | Dan Bylsma | (LW) | Bowling Green State Univ. |
| 110—New Jersey | David Emma | (C) | Boston College |
| 111—Chicago | Tommi Pullola | (C) | Sport Fin Div. I |
| 112—Minnesota | Scott Cashman | (G) | Kanata (Ont.) Tier II |
| 113—Vancouver | Pavel Bure | (RW) | USSR |
| 114—St. Louis | David Roberts | (LW) | Avon Old Farms H.S. (Ct.) |
| 115—Hartford | Jerome Bechard | (LW) | Moose Jaw (WHL) |
| 116—Detroit | Dallas Drake | (C) | Northern Michigan University |
| 117—Philadelphia | Niklas Eriksson | (C) | Sweden |
| 118—New York Rangers | Joby Messier | (D) | Michigan State University |
| 119—Buffalo | Mike Barkley | (RW) | University of Maine |
| 120—Edmonton | Anatoli Semenov | (C) | Moscow Dynamo |
| 121—Pittsburgh | Mike Markovich | (D) | University of Denver |
| 122—Boston | Stephen Foster | (D) | Catholic Memorial H.S. (Mass.) |
| 123—Los Angeles | Daniel Rydmark | (C) | Farjestad, Sweden |
| 124—St. Louis (from Washington) | Derek Frenette | (LW) | Ferris State University |
| 125—Toronto (from Montreal) | Michael Doers | (RW) | Northwood Prep (N.Y.) |
| 126—Pittsburgh (from Calgary) | Mike Needham | (RW) | Kamloops (WHL) |

## SEVENTH ROUND

| NHL Club | PLAYER | (Pos) | 1988-89 CLUB (League) |
|---|---|---|---|
| 127—Quebec | Sergei Mylnikov | (G) | Tractor Tjelsabinski, USSR |
| 128—New York Islanders | Jon Larson | (D) | Roseau H.S. (Minn.) |
| 129—Toronto | Keith Merkler | (LW) | Portledge H.S. (N.Y.) |
| 130—Winnipeg | Pekka Peltola | (RW) | HPK Finland |
| 131—Winnipeg (from New Jersey) | Doug Evans | (D) | University of Michigan |
| 132—Chicago | Tracy Egeland | (LW) | Prince Albert (WHL) |
| 133—N.Y. Islanders (from Minn.) | Brett Harkins | (LW) | Detroit Compuware |
| 134—Vancouver | James Revenberg | (RW) | Windsor (OHL) |
| 135—St. Louis | Jeff Batters | (D) | University of Alaska-Anchorage |
| 136—Hartford | Scott Daniels | (LW) | Regina (WHL) |
| 137—Detroit | Scott Zygulski | (D) | Culver Mil. Academy (Ind.) |
| 138—Philadelphia | John Callahan Jr. | (C) | Belmont Hill H.S. (Mass.) |
| 139—New York Rangers | Greg Leahy | (C) | Portland (WHL) |
| 140—Edmonton (from Buffalo) | Davis Payne | (LW) | Michigan Tech University |
| 141—Edmonton | Sergei Yashin | (LW) | Moscow Dynamo |
| 142—Pittsburgh | Patrick Schafhauser | (D) | Hill Murray H.S. (Minn.) |
| 143—Boston | Otto Hascak | (RW) | Dukla Trencin, Czech. |
| 144—Los Angeles | Ted Kramer | (RW) | University of Michigan |
| 145—Washington | Dave Lorentz | (LW) | Peterborough (OHL) |
| 146—Montreal | Craig Ferguson | (C) | Yale University |
| 147—Calgary | Alex Nikolic | (LW) | Cornell University |

## EIGHTH ROUND

| NHL Club | PLAYER | (Pos) | 1988-89 CLUB (League) |
|---|---|---|---|
| 148—Quebec | Paul Krake | (G) | University of Alaska-Anchorage |
| 149—New York Islanders | Phil Huber | (LW) | Kamloops (WHL) |
| 150—Toronto | Derek Langille | (D) | North Bay (OHL) |
| 151—Winnipeg | Jim Solly | (C) | Bowling Green State Univ. |
| 152—New Jersey | Sergei Starikow | (D) | ZSKA Moscow |
| 153—Chicago | Milan Tichy | (D) | Skoda Plzen, Czech. |
| 154—Minnesota | Jonathan Pratt | (C) | Pingree H.S. (Mass.) |
| 155—Vancouver | Rob Sangster | (LW) | Kitchener (OHL) |
| 156—St. Louis | Kevin Plager | (RW) | Parkway North H.S. (Mo.) |
| 157—Hartford | Raymond Saumier | (RW) | Trois-Rivieres (QMJL) |
| 158—Detroit | Andy Suhy | (D) | Western Michigan University |
| 159—Philadelphia | Sverre Sears | (D) | Belmont Hill H.S. (Mass.) |
| 160—New York Rangers | Greg Spenrath | (LW) | Tri-City (WHL) |
| 161—Buffalo | Derek Plante | (C) | Cloquet H.S. (Minn.) |
| 162—Edmonton | Darcy Martini | (D) | Michigan Tech University |
| 163—Pittsburgh | Dave Shute | (C) | Victoria (WHL) |
| 164—Boston | Rick Allain | (D) | Kitchener (OHL) |
| 165—Los Angeles | Sean Whyte | (C) | Guelph (OHL) |
| 166—Washington | Dean Holoien | (D) | Saskatoon (WHL) |
| 167—Montreal | Patrick Lebeau | (LW) | St. Jean (QMJL) |
| 168—Calgary | Kevin Wortman | (D) | American International Col. |

## NINTH ROUND

| NHL Club | PLAYER | (Pos) | 1988-89 CLUB (League) |
|---|---|---|---|
| 169—Quebec | Viacheslav Bykov | (C) | ZSKA Moscow |
| 170—New York Islanders | Matthew Robbins | (C) | New Hampton (N.H.) |
| 171—Toronto | Jeffrey St. Laurent | (RW) | Berwick (Me.) |
| 172—Winnipeg | Stephane Gauvin | (LW) | Cornell University |
| 173—New Jersey | Andre Faust | (C) | Princeton University |
| 174—Chicago | Jason Greyerbiehl | (LW) | Colgate University |
| 175—Minnesota | Kenneth Blum | (C) | St. Joseph Prep. (N.J.) |
| 176—Vancouver | Sandy Moger | (RW) | Lake Superior State |
| 177—St. Louis | John Roderick | (D) | Rindge & Latin H.S. (Mass.) |
| 178—Hartford | Michel Picard | (LW) | Trois-Rivieres (QMJL) |
| 179—Detroit | Bob Jones | (D) | Sault Ste. Marie (OHL) |
| 180—Philadelphia | Glen Wisser | (RW) | Philadelphia Jr. B |
| 181—New York Rangers | Mark Bavis | (C) | Cushing Academy (Ct.) |
| 182—Los Angeles (from Buffalo) | Jim Giacin | (LW) | Culver Mil. Academy (Ind.) |
| 183—Buffalo (from Edmonton) | Donald Audette | (RW) | Laval (QMJL) |
| 184—Pittsburgh | Andrew Wolf | (D) | Victoria (WHL) |
| 185—Boston | James Lavish | (RW) | Deerfield Academy (Mass.) |
| 186—Los Angeles | Martin Maskarinec | (D) | Sparta Praha, Czech. |
| 187—Washington | Victor Gervais | (C) | Seattle (WHL) |
| 188—Montreal | Roy Mitchell | (D) | Portland (WHL) |
| 189—Calgary | Sergei Gomolyakov | (C) | Tractor Tselsabinsk, USSR |

## TENTH ROUND

| NHL Club | PLAYER | (Pos) | 1988-89 CLUB (League) |
|---|---|---|---|
| 190—Quebec | Andrei Khumutov | (RW) | ZSKA Moscow |
| 191—New York Islanders | Vladimir Malakhov | (D) | ZSKA Moscow |
| 192—Toronto | Justin Tomberlin | (C) | Greenway H.S. (Minn.) |
| 193—Winnipeg | Joe Larson | (C) | Minnetonka H.S. (Minn.) |
| 194—Buffalo (from New Jersey) | Mark Astley | (D) | Lake Superior State |
| 195—Chicago | Matt Saunders | (LW) | Northeastern University |
| 196—Minnesota | Artur Irbe | (G) | Dynamo Riga, USSR |
| 197—Vancouver | Gus Morschauser | (G) | Kitchener (OHL) |
| 198—St. Louis | John Valo | (D) | Detroit Compuware |
| 199—Hartford | Trevor Buchanan | (LW) | Kamloops (WHL) |
| 200—Detroit | Greg Bignell | (D) | Belleville (OHL) |
| 201—Philadelphia | Al Kummu | (D) | Humbolt (Sask.) Tier II |
| 202—New York Rangers | Roman Oksyuta | (RW) | Himik, USSR |
| 203—Buffalo | John Nelson | (C) | Toronto (OHL) |
| 204—Detroit (from Edmonton) | Rick Judson | (LW) | University of Illinois-Chicago |
| 205—Pittsburgh | Greg Hagen | (RW) | Hill Murray H.S. (Minn.) |
| 206—Boston | Geoff Simpson | (D) | Estevan (B.C.) Tier II |
| 207—Los Angeles | Jim Hiller | (RW) | Melville (B.C.) Tier II |
| 208—Washington | Jiri Vykoukal | (D) | Olomouc, Czech. |
| 209—Montreal | Ed Henrich | (D) | Nichols H.S. (N.Y.) |
| 210—Calgary | Dan Sawyer | (D) | Ramapo Rangers Jr. B (N.J.) |

## ELEVENTH ROUND

| NHL Club | PLAYER | (Pos) | 1988-89 CLUB (League) |
|---|---|---|---|
| 211—Quebec | Byron Witkowski | (LW) | Nipiwan (Sask.) Tier II |
| 212—New York Islanders | Kelly Ens | (C) | Lethbridge (WHL) |
| 213—Toronto | Mike Jackson | (RW) | Toronto (OHL) |
| 214—Winnipeg | Bradley Podiak | (LW) | Wayzata H.S. (Minn.) |
| 215—New Jersey | Jason Simon | (LW) | Windsor (OHL) |
| 216—Chicago | Mike Kozak | (RW) | Clarkson University |
| 217—Minnesota | Tom Pederson | (D) | University of Minnesota |
| 218—Vancouver | Hayden O'Rear | (D) | Lathrop H.S. (Ala.) |
| 219—St. Louis | Brian Lukowski | (G) | Niagara (N.Y.) Jr. A |
| 220—Hartford | John Battice | (D) | London (OHL) |
| 221—Detroit | Vladimir Konstantivov | (D) | ZSKA Moscow |
| 222—Philadelphia | Matt Brait | (D) | St. Michael's (Ont.) Jr. B |
| 223—New York Rangers | Steve Locke | (LW) | Niagara Falls (OHL) |
| 224—Buffalo | Todd Henderson | (G) | Thunder Bay (Ont.) Jr. A |
| 225—Edmonton | Roman Bozek | (RW) | Budejovice, Czech. |
| 226—Pittsburgh | Scott Farrell | (D) | Spokane (WHL) |
| 227—Boston | David Franzosa | (LW) | Boston College |
| 228—Los Angeles | Steve Jaques | (D) | Tri-City (WHL) |
| 229—Washington | Andri Sidorov | (W) | Sokol Kiev (USSR) |
| 230—Montreal | Justin Duberman | (RW) | University of North Dakota |
| 231—Calgary | Alexander Yudin | (D) | Dynamo Moscow |

## TWELFTH ROUND

| NHL Club | PLAYER | (Pos) | 1988-89 CLUB (League) |
|---|---|---|---|
| 232—Quebec | Noel Rahn | (C) | Edina H.S. (Minn.) |
| 233—New York Islanders | Iain Fraser | (C) | Oshawa (OHL) |
| 234—Toronto | Steve Chartrand | (LW) | Drummondville (QMJL) |
| 235—Winnipeg | Genneyna Davydov | (RW) | ZSKA Moscow |
| 236—New Jersey | Peter Larsson | (C) | Sodertalje, Sweden |
| 237—Chicago | Michael Doneghey | (G) | Catholic Memorial H.S. (Mass.) |
| 238—Minnesota | Helmut Balderis | (RW) | Dynamo Riga, USSR |
| 239—Vancouver | Darcy Cahill | (C) | Cornwall (OHA) |
| 240—Winnipeg (from St. Louis) | Sergei Kharin | (RW) | Krylja Moscow |
| 241—Hartford | Peter Kasowski | (C) | Swift Current (WHL) |
| 242—Detroit | Joseph Frederick | (RW) | Madison (Wis.) Jr. A |
| 243—Philadelphia | James Pollio | (LW) | Vermont Academy |
| 244—New York Rangers | Ken MacDermid | (RW) | Hull (QMJL) |
| 245—Buffalo | Michael Bavis | (RW) | Cushing Academy (Ct.) |
| 246—Detroit (from Edmonton) | Jason Glickman | (G) | Hull (QMJL) |
| 247—Pittsburgh | Jason Smart | (C) | Saskatoon (WHL) |
| 248—Vancouver (from Boston) | Jan Bergman | (D) | Sodertalje, Sweden |
| 249—Los Angeles | Kevin Sneddon | (D) | Harvard University |
| 250—Washington | Ken House | (C) | Miami University (O.) |
| 251—Montreal | Steve Cadieux | (C) | Shawinigan (QMJL) |
| 252—Calgary | Kenneth Kennholt | (D) | Djurgarden, Sweden |

# INDIVIDUAL RECORDS

## SINGLE SEASON RECORDS

**1—GOALS**
  NHL—Wayne Gretzky, Edmonton Oilers—92 (1981-82 season).
  WHA—Bobby Hull, Winnipeg Jets—77 (1974-75 season).
  CHL—Alain Caron, St. Louis Braves—77 (1963-64 season).
  AHL—Stephan Lebeau, Sherbrooke Canadiens—70 (1988-89 season).
  IHL—Dan Lecours, Milwaukee Admirals—75 (1982-83 season).

**2—ASSISTS**
  NHL—Wayne Gretzky, Edmonton Oilers—163 (1985-86 season).
  WHA—Andre Lacroix, San Diego Mariners—106 (1974-75 season).
  CHL—Richie Hansen, Salt Lake Golden Eagles—81 (1981-82 season).
  AHL—George "Red" Sullivan, Hershey Bears—89 (1953-54 season).
  IHL—John Cullen, Flint Spirits—109 (1987-88 season).

**3—POINTS**
  NHL—Wayne Gretzky, Edmonton Oilers—215 (1985-86 season).
  WHA—Marc Tardif, Quebec Nordiques—154 (1977-78 season).
  CHL—Alain Caron, St. Louis Braves—125 (1963-64 season).
  AHL—Stephan Lebeau, Sherbrooke Canadiens—134 (1988-89 season).
  IHL—John Cullen, Flint Spirits—157 (1987-88 season).

**4—PENALTY MINUTES**
  NHL—Dave Schultz, Philadelphia Flyers—472 (1974-75 season).
  WHA—Curt Brackenbury, Minnesota Fighting Saints and Quebec Nordiques—365 (1975-76 season).
  CHL—Randy Holt, Dallas Black Hawks—411 (1974-75 season).
  AHL—Robert Ray, Rochester Americans—446 (1988-89 season).
  IHL—Kevin Evans, Kalamazoo—648 (1986-87 season).

**5—SHUTOUTS**
  NHL—George Hainsworth, Montreal Canadiens—22 (1928-29 season).

### Modern Era
  NHL—Tony Esposito, Chicago Black Hawks—15 (1969-70 season).
  WHA—Gerry Cheevers, Cleveland Crusaders—5 (1972-73 season).
      Joe Daley, Winnipeg Jets—5 (1975-76 season).
  CHL—Marcel Pelletier, St. Paul Rangers—9 (1963-64 season).
  AHL—Gordie Bell, Buffalo Bisons—9 (1942-43 season).
  IHL—Charlie Hodge, Cincinnati Mohawks—10 (1953-54 season).

**6—GOALS AGAINST AVERAGE**
  NHL—George Hainsworth, Montreal Canadiens—0.98 (1928-29 season).
  WHA—Don McLeod, Houston Aeros—2.57 (1973-74 season).
  CHL—Russ Gillow, Oklahoma City Blazers—2.16 (1967-68 season).
  AHL—Frank Brimsek, Providence Reds—1.79 (1937-38 season).
  IHL—Glenn Ramsay, Cincinnati Mohawks—1.88 (1956-57 season).

## CAREER (Regular Season Only)
(No WHA Records Listed for Most Seasons Played.)

**1—MOST SEASONS**
  NHL—Gordie Howe, Detroit Red Wings and Hartford Whalers—26 (1946-47 through 1970-71 and 1979-80).
  CHL—Richie Hansen, Fort Worth Texans, Salt Lake Golden Eagles, Wichita Wind—9 (1975-76 through 1983-84 seasons).
  AHL—Fred Glover, Indianapolis Caps, St. Louis Flyers, Cleveland Barons—20.
      Willie Marshall, Pittsburgh Hornets, Rochester Americans, Hershey Bears, Providence Reds, Baltimore Clippers—20.
  IHL—Glenn Ramsay, Cincinnati Mohawks, Fort Wayne Komets, Troy Bruins, Toledo Blades, St. Paul Saints, Omaha Knights, Des Moines Oak Leafs, Toledo Hornets, Port Huron Flags—18 (1956-57 through 1973-74).

**2—GAMES PLAYED**
  NHL—Gordie Howe, Detroit Red Wings and Hartford Whalers—1,767 (26 seasons).
  WHA—Andre Lacroix, Philadelphia Blazers, New York Golden Blades, Jersey Knights, San Diego Mariners, Houston Aeros and New England Whalers—551 (7 seasons).
  CHL—Richie Hansen, Fort Worth Texans, Salt Lake Golden Eagles, Wichita Wind—575 (9 seasons).
  AHL—Willie Marshall, Pittsburgh Hornets, Rochester Americans, Hershey Bears, Providence Reds, Baltimore Clippers—1,205 (20 seasons).
  IHL—Glenn Ramsay, Cincinnati Mohawks, Fort Wayne Komets, Troy Bruins, Toledo Blades, St. Paul Saints, Omaha Knights, Des Moines Oak Leafs, Toledo Hornets, Port Huron Flags—1,053 (18 seasons).

### 3—GOALS SCORED
**NHL**—Gordie Howe, Detroit Red Wings, Hartford Whalers—801 (26 seasons).
**WHA**—Marc Tardif, Quebec Nordiques—316 (6 seasons).
**CHL**—Richie Hansen, Fort Worth Texans, Salt Lake Golden Eagles, Wichita Wind—204 (9 seasons).
**AHL**—Willie Marshall, Pittsburgh Hornets, Rochester Americans, Hershey Bears, Providence Reds, Baltimore Clippers—523 (20 seasons).
**IHL**—Joe Kastelic, Fort Wayne Komets, Troy Bruins, Louisville Rebels, Muskegon Zephyrs, Muskegon Mohawks—526 (15 seasons).

### 4—ASSISTS
**NHL**—Wayne Gretzky, Edmonton Oilers, Los Angeles Kings—1,200.
**WHA**—Andre Lacroix, Philadelphia Blazers, Jersey Knights, San Diego Mariners, Houston Aeros, New England Whalers—547 (7 seasons).
**CHL**—Richie Hansen, Fort Worth Texans, Salt Lake Golden Eagles, Wichita Wind—374 (9 seasons).
**AHL**—Willie Marshall, Pittsburgh Hornets, Hershey Bears, Rochester Americans, Providence Reds, Baltimore Clippers—852 (20 seasons).
**IHL**—Len Thornson, Huntington Hornets, Indianapolis Chiefs, Fort Wayne Komets—826 (13 seasons).

### 5—TOTAL POINTS
**NHL**—Gordie Howe, Detroit Red Wings, Hartford Whalers—1,850 (26 seasons).
**WHA**—Andre Lacroix, Philadelphia Blazers, Jersey Knights, San Diego Mariners, Houston Aeros, New England Whalers—798 (7 seasons).
**CHL**—Richie Hansen, Fort Worth Texans, Salt Lake Golden Eagles, Wichita Wind—578 (9 seasons).
**AHL**—Willie Marshall, Pittsburgh Hornets, Hershey Bears, Rochester Americans, Providence Reds, Baltimore Clippers—1,375 (20 seasons).
**IHL**—Len Thornson, Huntington Hornets, Indianapolis Chiefs, Fort Wayne Komets—1,252 (13 seasons).

### 6—PENALTY MINUTES
**NHL**—Dave (Tiger) Williams, Toronto Maple Leafs, Vancouver Canucks, Detroit Red Wings, Los Angeles Kings, Hartford Whalers—3,966 (13 seasons).
**WHA**—Paul Baxter, Cleveland Crusaders, Quebec Nordiques—962 (5 seasons).
**CHL**—Brad Gassoff, Tulsa Oilers, Dallas Black Hawks—899 (5 seasons).
**AHL**—Fred Glover, Indianapolis Caps, St. Louis Flyers, Cleveland Barons— 2,402 (20 seasons).
**IHL**—Gord Malinoski, Dayton Gems, Saginaw Gears—2,175 (9 seasons).

### 7—SHUTOUTS
**NHL**—Terry Sawchuk, Detroit Red Wings, Boston Bruins, Los Angeles Kings, New York Rangers, Toronto Maple Leafs—103 (20 seasons).
**WHA**—Ernie Wakely, Winnipeg Jets, San Diego Mariners, Houston Aeros—16 (6 seasons).
**CHL**—Michel Dumas, Dallas Black Hawks—12 (4 seasons).
  Mike Veisor, Dallas Black Hawks—12 (5 seasons).
**AHL**—Johnny Bower, Cleveland Barons, Providence Reds—45 (11 seasons).
**IHL**—Glenn Ramsay, Cincinnati Mohawks, Fort Wayne Komets, Troy Bruins, Toledo Blades, St. Paul Saints, Omaha Knights, Des Moines Oak Leafs, Toledo Hornets, Port Huron Flags—45 (18 seasons).

## SINGLE GAME RECORDS
### 1—GOALS
**NHL**—Joe Malone, Quebec Bulldogs (January 31, 1920 vs. Toronto St. Pats)—7.

#### Modern Era
**NHL**—Syd Howe, Detroit Red Wings (Feb. 3, 1944 vs. N.Y. Rangers)—6.
  Gordon Berenson, St. Louis Blues (Nov. 7, 1968 vs. Philadelphia)—6.
  Darryl Sittler, Toronto Maple Leafs (Feb. 7, 1976 vs. Boston Bruins)—6.
**WHA**—Ron Ward, New York Raiders (January 4, 1973 vs. Ottawa)—5.
  Ron Climie, Edmonton Oilers (vs. N.Y. Golden Blades, November 6, 1973)—5.
  Andre Hinse, Houston Aeros (Jan. 16, 1975 vs. Edmonton)—5.
  Vaclav Nedomansky, Toronto Toros (Nov. 13, 1975 vs. Denver Spurs)—5.
  Wayne Connelly, Minnesota Fighting Saints (Nov. 27, 1975 vs. Cincinnati Stingers)—5.
  Ron Ward, Cleveland Crusaders (Nov. 30, 1975 vs. Toronto Toros)—5.
  Real Cloutier, Quebec Nordiques (Oct. 26, 1976 vs. Phoenix Roadrunners)—5.
**CHL**—Jim Mayer, Dallas Black Hawks (February 23, 1979)—6.
**AHL**—Bob Heron, Pittsburgh Hornets (1941-42)—6.
  Harry Pidhirny, Springfield Indians (1953-54)—6.
  Camille Henry, Providence Reds (1955-56)—6.
**IHL**—Pierre Brillant, Indianapolis Chiefs (Feb. 18, 1959)—6.
  Bryan McLay, Muskegon Zephyrs (Mar. 8, 1961)—6.
  Elliott Chorley, St. Paul Saints (Jan. 17, 1962)—6.
  Joe Kastelic, Muskegon Zephyrs (Mar. 1, 1962)—6.
  Tom St. James, Flint Generals (Mar. 15, 1985)—6.

**2—ASSISTS**
  **NHL**—Billy Taylor, Detroit Red Wings (Mar. 16, 1947 vs. Chicago)—7.
       Wayne Gretzky, Edmonton Oilers (Feb. 15, 1980 vs. Washington)—7.
  **WHA**—Jim Harrison, Alberta Oilers (January 30, 1973 vs. New York)—7.
       Jim Harrison, Cleveland Crusaders (Nov. 30, 1975 vs. Toronto Toros)—7.
  **CHL**—Art Stratton, St. Louis Braves (1966-67)—6.
       Ron Ward, Tulsa Oilers (1967-68)—6.
       Bill Hogaboam, Omaha Knights, January 15, 1972—6.
       Jim Wiley, Tulsa Oilers (1974-75)—6.
  **AHL**—Art Stratton, Buffalo Bisons (Mar. 17, 1963 vs. Pittsburgh)—9.
  **IHL**—Jean-Paul Denis, St. Paul Saints (Jan. 17, 1962)—9.

**3—POINTS**
  **NHL**—Darryl Sittler, Toronto Maple Leafs (Feb. 7, 1976 vs. Boston Bruins)—10.
  **WHA**—Jim Harrison, Alberta Oilers (January 30, 1973 vs. New York)—10.
  **CHL**—Steve Vickers, Omaha Knights (Jan. 15, 1972 vs. Kansas City)—8.
  **AHL**—Art Stratton, Buffalo Bisons (Mar. 17, 1963 vs. Pittsburgh)—9.
  **IHL**—Elliott Chorley, St. Paul Saints (Jan. 17, 1962)—11.
       Jean-Paul Denis, St. Paul Saints (Jan. 17, 1962)—11.

**4—PENALTY MINUTES**
  **NHL**—Randy Holt, Los Angeles Kings (March 11, 1979 vs. Philadelphia)—67.
  **WHA**—Dave Hanson, Birmingham Bulls (Feb. 5, 1978 vs. Indianapolis)—46.
  **CHL**—Gary Rissling, Birmingham Bulls (Dec. 5, 1980 vs. Salt Lake)—49.
  **AHL**—Wally Weir, Rochester Americans (Jan. 16, 1981 vs. New Brunswick)—54.
  **IHL**—Willie Prognitz, Dayton Gems (Oct. 29, 1977)—63.

## DEFENSEMEN'S RECORDS
### SINGLE SEASON

**1—GOALS**
  **NHL**—Paul Coffey, Edmonton Oilers (1985-86 season)—48.
  **WHA**—Kevin Morrison, Jersey Knights (1973-74 season)—24.
  **CHL**—Dan Poulin, Nashville South Stars (1981-82 season)—29.
  **AHL**—Greg Tebbutt, Baltimore Skipjacks (1982-83 season)—28.
  **IHL**—Roly McLenahan, Cincinnati Mohawks (1955-56 season)—34.

**2—ASSISTS**
  **NHL**—Bobby Orr, Boston Bruins (1970-71 season)—102.
  **WHA**—J. C. Tremblay, Quebec Nordiques (1975-76 season)—77.
  **CHL**—Barclay Plager, Omaha Knights (1963-64 season)—61.
  **AHL**—Craig Levie, Nova Scotia Voyageurs (1980-81 season)—62.
       Shawn Evans, Nova Scotia Oilers (1987-88 season)—62.
  **IHL**—Gerry Glaude, Muskegon Zephyrs (1962-63 season)—86.

**3—POINTS**
  **NHL**—Bobby Orr, Boston Bruins (1970-71 season)—139.
  **WHA**—J. C. Tremblay, Quebec Nordiques (1972-73 and 1975-76 seasons)—89.
  **CHL**—Dan Poulin, Nashville South Stars (1981-82 season)—85.
  **AHL**—Greg Tebbutt, Baltimore Skipjacks (1982-83 season)—84.
  **IHL**—Gerry Glaude, Muskegon Zephyrs (1962-63 season)—101.

# American Hockey League

425 Union Street, West Springfield, Mass. 01089
Phone— (413) 781-2030
FAX (413) 733-4767

Chairman of the Board—Robert W. Clarke
President and Treasurer—Jack A. Butterfield
Vice-President and General Counsel—Richard F. Canning
Vice-President, Secretary—Gordon C. Anziano

## Board Of Governors
Adirondack—Bill Dineen
Baltimore—Tom Ebright
Binghamton—James R. McCoy
Cape Breton—Bruce MacGregor
Halifax—Gilles Leger
Hershey—Frank Mathers
Maine—Ed Anderson
Moncton—Gary O'Neill
New Haven—Macgregor Kilpatrick
Newmarket—To be announced
Rochester—George Bergantz
Sherbrooke—Andre Boudrias
Springfield—James J. Coogan
Utica—Lou Lamoriello
Honorary Governor—George Sage

## Adirondack Red Wings
President—Michael Ilitch
Governor/Gen. Mang.—Bill Dineen
Executive Vice President—Jim Lites
Vice-President—Jim Devellano
Director of Operations—Jack Kelley
Coach—Barry Melrose
Dir. of Marketing and Promotions—Don Ostrom
Director of Media Relations—Bill Miller
Dir. of P.R./Broadcaster—Bob Crawford
Trainer—David Casey
Home Ice—Glens Falls Civic Center
Address—1 Civic Center Plaza,
Glens Falls, N.Y. 12801
Seating Capacity—4,804
NHL Affiliation—Detroit Red Wings
Phone— (518) 798-0366

## Baltimore Skipjacks
President and Governor—Tom Ebright
Alt. Gov./Gen. Mgr./Coach—Terry Murray
Asst. G.M./Marketing—Ketch Secor
Director of Operations—Stacey M. Riggs
Vice-President/Communications—Jim Riggs
P.R./Admin. Asst.—Scott Smith
Head Trainer—J.P. Mattingly
Home Ice—Baltimore Arena
Address—Suite 412,
201 W. Baltimore Street
Baltimore, Md. 21201
Seating Capacity—11,025
NHL Affiliation—Washington Capitals
Phone— (301) 727-0703

## Binghamton Whalers
President and Governor—James R. McCoy
Vice President—Robert W. Carr, Jr.
Secretary/Treasurer—Tom Mitchell
General Manager/Alt. Governor—Tom Mitchell
Coach—Doug McKay
Trainer—Jon Smith
Equipment Manager—Mark Dumas
Director of Mark./Comm.—Bob Ohrablo
Administrative Assistant—Mary Kelly
Home Ice—Broome County
Veterans Memorial Arena
Address—One Stuart Street
Binghamton, N.Y. 13901
Seating Capacity—4,849
NHL Affiliation—Hartford Whalers
Phone— (607) 723-8937

## Cape Breton Oilers
President—Glen Sather
Governor/Vice President—Bruce MacGregor
General Manager—Dave Andrews
Coach—Don McAdam
Office Manager—Patricia Bates
Director of Player Personnel—Barry Fraser
Home Ice—Centre 200
Address—481 George Street
Sydney, Nova Scotia B1P 6R7
Seating Capacity—4,500
NHL Affiliation—Edmonton Oilers
Phone— (902) 562-0780

## Halifax Citadels
Governor—Gilles Leger
V.P./Mark., Media, Comm.—Michael E. Doyle
Coach/General Manager—To be announced
Director of Sales—Michael E. Doyle
Home Ice—Halifax Metro-Centre
Address—5284 Duke Street
Halifax, N.S. B3J 3L2
Seating Capacity—9,952
NHL Affiliation—Quebec Nordiques
Phone— (902) 421-1600

## Hershey Bears
President/Chief Exec. Officer—J. Bruce McKinney
Gov., Pres. & Gen. Mgr.—Frank Mathers
Assistant General Manager—Doug Yingst
Coach—Kevin McCarthy
Assistant Coach—Al Hill
Trainer—Dan Stuck
Home Ice—Hersheypark Arena
Address—P.O. Box 866
Hershey, Pa. 17033
Seating Capacity—7,256
NHL Affiliation—Philadelphia Flyers
Phone— (717) 534-3380

## Maine Mariners
Governor and President—Ed Anderson
Alternate Governor—Harry Sinden
Coach—Rick Bowness
Broadcaster/Public Relations—Scott Wykoff
Administrative Assistant—Susan Small
Head Trainer—Jerry Foster
Home Ice—Cumberland County
Civic Center
Address—P.O. Box 1219
Portland, Me. 04104
Seating Capacity—6,734
NHL Affiliation—Boston Bruins
Phone— (207) 775-3411

## Moncton Hawks
Governor—Gary O'Neill
Coach/General Manager—Dave Farrish
Manager—Don Canning
Pub. Rel./Marketing—Scott Mathews
Home Ice—Moncton Coliseum
Address—P.O. Box 2940, Station A
　　Moncton, N.B. E1C 8T8
Seating Capacity—6,802
NHL Affiliation—Winnipeg Jets
Phone—(506) 857-4000

## New Haven Nighthawks
Governor—Macgregor Kilpatrick
President—Roy Mlakar
Director of Operations—Pat Hickey
Dir. Hockey Oper./Coach—Marcel Comeau
Director of Press Relations—Jan MacDonald
Trainers—Sal Lombardi & Scott Green
Home Ice—Veterans Memorial Coliseum
Address—P.O. Box 1444
　　New Haven, Conn. 06506
Seating Capacity—5,933
NHL Affiliation—Los Angeles Kings
Phone—(203) 787-0101

## Newmarket Saints
President—Harold Ballard
Governor/General Manager—To be announced
Coach—Paul Gardner
Assistant Coach—Mike Kitch
Marketing Assistant—Chris Reed
Trainer—Ken Garrett
Home Ice—Newmarket Recreation Complex
Address—100 Eagle Street, West
　　P.O. Box 116
　　Newmarket, Ont., L3Y 4W3
Seating Capacity—2,556
NHL Affiliation—Toronto Maple Leafs
Phone—(416) 895-7078

## Rochester Americans
Chairman of the Board—Lawrence Lovejoy
Governor—George Bergantz
General Manager—Randy Scott
Coach—John Van Boxmeer
P.R. Dir./Broadcast—Don Stevens
Director of Media Relations—Steve Rossi
Executive Assistant—Michele Butz
Athletic Trainer—Kent Weisbeck
Equipment Manager—J.C. Ihrig
Home Ice—Rochester War Memorial
Address—100 Exchange Street
　　Rochester, N.Y. 14614
Seating Capacity—6,973
NHL Affiliation—Buffalo Sabres
Phone—(716) 454-5335

## Sherbrooke Canadiens
President—George Guilbault
Governor/Gen. Mgr.—Andre Boudrias
Coach—Jean Hamel
Director of Operations—Claude Larose
Asst. Dir. of Operations—Francois St. Cyr
Trainer—Bob Boulanger
Home Ice—Sherbrooke Sports Palace
Address—360 Parc Street
　　Sherbrooke, Que. J1E 2J9
Seating Capacity—4,328
NHL Affiliation—Montreal Canadiens
Phone—(819) 566-2114

## Springfield Indians
President—Peter R. Cooney
Governor—James J. Coogan
Alternate Governor—William A. Torrey
General Manager—Bruce Landon
Coach—Jim Roberts
Business Manager—Martha Dalley
Broadcaster/Publicity Dir.—John H. Forslund
Trainer—Ed Tyburski
Equipment Manager—Ralph Calvanese
Home Ice—Springfield Civic Center
Address—P.O. Box 4896
　　Springfield, Mass. 01101
Seating Capacity—7,602
NHL Affiliation—New York Islanders
Phone—(413) 736-4546

## Utica Devils
President and Governor—Lou Lamoriello
Exec. Dir./Alt. Gov.—Brian Petrovek
General Manager/Coach—Tom McVie
Associate Coach—Bob Hoffmeyer
Director of Marketing—Paul D'Aiuto
Asst. Dir. Mark.—Virginia Roher
Dir. Public/Media Rel.—Bill Dowsland
Marketing/Administrative Asst.—Donna Dewar
Home Ice—Utica Memorial Auditorium
Address—400 Oriskany St., West
　　Utica, N.Y. 13502
Seating Capacity—3,971
NHL Affiliation—New Jersey Devils
Phone—(315) 724-2126

# 1988-89 Final AHL Standings

## North Division

| | G. | W. | L. | T. | Pts. | GF. | GA. |
|---|---|---|---|---|---|---|---|
| Sherbrooke Canadiens | 80 | 47 | 24 | 9 | 103 | 348 | 261 |
| Halifax Citadels | 80 | 42 | 30 | 8 | 92 | 345 | 300 |
| Moncton Hawks | 80 | 37 | 34 | 9 | 83 | 320 | 313 |
| New Haven Nighthawks | 80 | 35 | 35 | 10 | 80 | 325 | 309 |
| Maine Mariners | 80 | 32 | 40 | 8 | 72 | 262 | 317 |
| Springfield Indians | 80 | 32 | 44 | 4 | 68 | 287 | 341 |
| Cape Breton Oilers | 80 | 27 | 47 | 6 | 60 | 308 | 388 |

## South Division

| | G. | W. | L. | T. | Pts. | GF. | GA. |
|---|---|---|---|---|---|---|---|
| Adirondack Red Wings | 80 | 47 | 27 | 6 | 100 | 369 | 294 |
| Hershey Bears | 80 | 40 | 30 | 10 | 90 | 361 | 309 |
| Utica Devils | 80 | 37 | 34 | 9 | 83 | 309 | 295 |
| Newmarket Saints | 80 | 38 | 36 | 6 | 82 | 339 | 334 |
| Rochester Americans | 80 | 38 | 37 | 5 | 81 | 305 | 302 |
| Baltimore Skipjacks | 80 | 30 | 46 | 4 | 64 | 317 | 347 |
| Binghamton Whalers | 80 | 28 | 46 | 6 | 62 | 307 | 392 |

## Top 20 Scorers for the John B. Sollenberger Trophy

| | Games | G. | A. | Pts. | Pen. |
|---|---|---|---|---|---|
| 1. Stephan Lebeau, Sherbrooke | 78 | **70 | 64 | ***134 | 47 |
| 2. Murray Eaves, Adirondack | 80 | 46 | 72 | 118 | 84 |
| 3. Benoit Brunet, Sherbrooke | 73 | 41 | *76 | 117 | 95 |
| 4. Mike Richard, Baltimore | 80 | 44 | 63 | 107 | 51 |
| 5. Don Biggs, Hershey | 76 | 36 | 67 | 103 | 158 |
| 6. Terry Yake, Binghamton | 75 | 39 | 56 | 95 | 57 |
| 7. Ken Priestlay, Rochester | 64 | 56 | 37 | 93 | 60 |
| 8. Hubie McDonough, New Haven | 74 | 37 | 55 | 92 | 41 |
| Ron Wilson, Moncton | 80 | 31 | 61 | 92 | 110 |
| 10. Brian Dobbin, Hershey | 59 | 43 | 48 | 91 | 61 |
| 11. Ken Quinney, Halifax | 72 | 41 | 49 | 90 | 65 |
| 12. Scott McCrory, Baltimore | 80 | 38 | 51 | 89 | 25 |
| 13. Bruce Boudreau, Springfield | 50 | 28 | 36 | 64 | 42 |
| Newmarket | 20 | 7 | 16 | 23 | 12 |
| Totals | 70 | 35 | 52 | 87 | 54 |
| 14. Mike Millar, Baltimore | 53 | 47 | 35 | 82 | 58 |
| Mark Lamb, Cape Breton | 54 | 33 | 49 | 82 | 29 |
| 16. Mark Pederson, Sherbrooke | 75 | 43 | 38 | 81 | 53 |
| 17. Max Middendorf, Halifax | 72 | 41 | 39 | 80 | 85 |
| Paul Ysebaert, Utica | 56 | 36 | 44 | 80 | 22 |
| 19. Mark Lofthouse, Hershey | 74 | 32 | 47 | 79 | 71 |
| Mark Freer, Hershey | 75 | 30 | 49 | 79 | 77 |

**Established new record, breaking old record of 61 set in 1985-86 by Paul Gardner of Rochester.
***Established new record, breaking old record of 130 set in 1984-85 by Paul Gardner of Binghamton.

## Adirondack Red Wings

| | Games | G. | A. | Pts. | Pen. |
|---|---|---|---|---|---|
| Murray Eaves | 80 | 46 | 72 | 118 | 84 |
| Glenn Merkosky | 76 | 31 | 46 | 77 | 13 |
| Rob Doyle | 70 | 24 | 52 | 76 | 44 |
| Miroslav Ihnacak | 62 | 34 | 37 | 71 | 32 |
| Brent Fedyk | 66 | 40 | 28 | 68 | 33 |
| Joe Murphy | 47 | 31 | 35 | 66 | 66 |
| Randy McKay | 58 | 29 | 34 | 63 | 170 |
| Lou Crawford | 74 | 23 | 23 | 46 | 179 |
| Dale Krentz | 36 | 21 | 20 | 41 | 30 |
| Dennis Smith | 75 | 5 | 35 | 40 | 176 |
| John Mokosak | 65 | 4 | 31 | 35 | 195 |
| David Korol | 73 | 3 | 24 | 27 | 57 |
| J. F. Sauve | 16 | 7 | 19 | 26 | 18 |
| Daniel Shank | 43 | 5 | 20 | 25 | 113 |
| Mike Gober | 41 | 15 | 7 | 22 | 55 |
| Adam Graves | 14 | 10 | 11 | 21 | 28 |
| John Blum | 56 | 1 | 19 | 20 | 168 |
| Dean Morton | 66 | 2 | 15 | 17 | 186 |
| Rob Nichols | 56 | 8 | 7 | 15 | 154 |
| Joe Ferras | 35 | 7 | 8 | 15 | 8 |
| John Chabot | 8 | 3 | 12 | 15 | 0 |
| Peter Dineen | 32 | 2 | 12 | 14 | 61 |
| Jeff Brubaker | 63 | 3 | 10 | 13 | 137 |
| Tim Higgins | 14 | 7 | 4 | 11 | 24 |
| Bruce Bell, Halifax | 12 | 0 | 6 | 6 | 6 |
| Adirondack | 9 | 1 | 4 | 5 | 4 |
| Totals | 21 | 1 | 10 | 11 | 10 |
| Petr Klima | 5 | 5 | 1 | 6 | 4 |
| Jeff Sharples | 10 | 0 | 4 | 4 | 8 |
| Doug Houda | 7 | 0 | 3 | 3 | 8 |
| Rob Schena | 9 | 1 | 1 | 2 | 2 |
| Sam St. Laurent (Goalie) | 34 | 0 | 2 | 2 | 10 |
| Doug Halward | 4 | 1 | 0 | 1 | 0 |

|  | Games | G. | A. | Pts. | Pen. |
|---|---|---|---|---|---|
| Tom Bissett | 5 | 0 | 1 | 1 | 0 |
| Pete Richards, N.H. (G.) | 1 | 0 | 0 | 0 | 0 |
| Adirondack (G.) | 4 | 0 | 1 | 1 | 0 |
| Totals | 5 | 0 | 1 | 1 | 0 |
| Mark Reimer (Goalie) | 18 | 0 | 0 | 0 | 2 |
| Tim Cheveldae (Goalie) | 30 | 0 | 0 | 0 | 4 |

## Baltimore Skipjacks

|  | Games | G. | A. | Pts. | Pen. |
|---|---|---|---|---|---|
| Mike Richard | 80 | 44 | 63 | 107 | 51 |
| Scott McCrory | 80 | 38 | 51 | 89 | 25 |
| Mike Millar | 53 | 47 | 35 | 82 | 58 |
| Tim Bergland | 78 | 24 | 29 | 53 | 39 |
| Robin Bawa | 75 | 23 | 24 | 47 | 205 |
| Bill Houlder | 65 | 10 | 36 | 46 | 50 |
| Jim Thomson | 41 | 25 | 16 | 41 | 129 |
| Yvon Corriveau | 33 | 16 | 23 | 39 | 65 |
| Chris Felix | 50 | 8 | 29 | 37 | 44 |
| Michal Pivonka | 31 | 12 | 24 | 36 | 19 |
| Rob Murray | 80 | 11 | 23 | 34 | 235 |
| Tyler Larter | 71 | 9 | 19 | 28 | 189 |
| Jeff Greenlaw | 55 | 12 | 15 | 27 | 115 |
| Steve Seftel | 58 | 12 | 15 | 27 | 70 |
| Rob Whistle | 61 | 2 | 24 | 26 | 30 |
| Lou Franceschetti | 10 | 8 | 7 | 15 | 30 |
| Dave Farrish | 60 | 2 | 13 | 15 | 62 |
| John Druce | 16 | 2 | 11 | 13 | 10 |
| Shawn Cronin | 75 | 3 | 9 | 12 | 267 |
| Kent Carlson | 28 | 2 | 8 | 10 | 69 |
| Dallas Eakins | 62 | 0 | 10 | 10 | 139 |
| Frank DiMuzio | 33 | 5 | 3 | 8 | 30 |
| Brian Tutt | 6 | 1 | 5 | 6 | 6 |
| Doug Wickenheiser | 2 | 0 | 5 | 5 | 0 |
| Ken Spangler | 12 | 0 | 3 | 3 | 33 |
| Claude Dumas | 1 | 1 | 0 | 1 | 0 |
| David Wensley | 2 | 0 | 1 | 1 | 0 |
| Alain Raymond (Goalie) | 41 | 0 | 1 | 1 | 2 |
| Shawn Simpson (Goalie) | 1 | 0 | 0 | 0 | 0 |
| Pat Beauchesne | 2 | 0 | 0 | 0 | 4 |
| Alain Guay | 3 | 0 | 0 | 0 | 9 |
| Jim Hrivnak (Goalie) | 10 | 0 | 0 | 0 | 0 |
| Don Beaupre (Goalie) | 30 | 0 | 0 | 0 | 9 |
| Mark Hatcher | 50 | 0 | 0 | 0 | 156 |

## Binghamton Whalers

|  | Games | G. | A. | Pts. | Pen. |
|---|---|---|---|---|---|
| Terry Yake | 75 | 39 | 56 | 95 | 57 |
| Todd Krygier | 76 | 26 | 42 | 68 | 77 |
| Dallas Gaume | 57 | 23 | 43 | 66 | 16 |
| Mark Reeds | 69 | 26 | 34 | 60 | 18 |
| Roger Kortko | 79 | 22 | 36 | 58 | 28 |
| Chris Brant | 65 | 28 | 28 | 56 | 138 |
| Larry Trader | 65 | 11 | 40 | 51 | 72 |
| Charles Bourgeois | 76 | 9 | 35 | 44 | 239 |
| Mark LaVarre | 37 | 20 | 21 | 41 | 70 |
| Gary Callaghan | 72 | 23 | 17 | 40 | 33 |
| Bob Bodak | 44 | 15 | 25 | 40 | 135 |
| Brian Chapman | 71 | 5 | 25 | 30 | 216 |
| Dave Rowbotham | 63 | 10 | 12 | 22 | 0 |
| Mike Vellucci | 37 | 9 | 9 | 18 | 59 |
| Jim Culhane | 72 | 6 | 11 | 17 | 200 |
| Ed Kastelic | 35 | 9 | 6 | 15 | 124 |
| Ted Fauss | 53 | 4 | 11 | 15 | 66 |
| David O'Brien | 53 | 3 | 12 | 15 | 11 |
| Lindsay Carson | 24 | 4 | 10 | 14 | 35 |
| Brian Verbeek | 27 | 9 | 3 | 12 | 50 |

|  | Games | G. | A. | Pts. | Pen. |
|---|---|---|---|---|---|
| Al Tuer | 43 | 1 | 7 | 8 | 234 |
| Kay Whitmore (Goalie) | 56 | 0 | 6 | 6 | 50 |
| John Torchetti | 10 | 3 | 2 | 5 | 0 |
| Mark LaForge | 38 | 2 | 2 | 4 | 179 |
| Adam Burt | 5 | 0 | 2 | 2 | 13 |
| Scot Kleinendorst | 4 | 0 | 1 | 1 | 19 |
| Ross McKay (Goalie) | 19 | 0 | 1 | 1 | 2 |
| Grant Jennings | 2 | 0 | 0 | 0 | 2 |
| Richard Brodeur (G.) | 6 | 0 | 0 | 0 | 2 |
| Sean Evoy (Goalie) | 9 | 0 | 0 | 0 | 0 |
| Brent Regan | 9 | 0 | 0 | 0 | 2 |

## Cape Breton Oilers

|  | Games | G. | A. | Pts. | Pen. |
|---|---|---|---|---|---|
| Mark Lamb | 54 | 33 | 49 | 82 | 29 |
| Shaun VanAllen | 76 | 32 | 42 | 74 | 81 |
| Fabian Joseph | 70 | 32 | 34 | 66 | 30 |
| Dan Currie | 77 | 29 | 36 | 65 | 29 |
| Kim Issel | 65 | 34 | 28 | 62 | 62 |
| Brian Wilks, New Haven | 44 | 15 | 19 | 34 | 48 |
| Cape Breton | 12 | 4 | 11 | 15 | 27 |
| Totals | 56 | 19 | 30 | 49 | 75 |
| Larry Floyd | 70 | 16 | 33 | 49 | 40 |
| Craig Redmond | 44 | 13 | 22 | 35 | 28 |
| Selmar Odelein | 63 | 8 | 21 | 29 | 150 |
| John English, N. H. | 49 | 5 | 19 | 24 | 197 |
| Cape Breton | 13 | 0 | 3 | 3 | 80 |
| Totals | 62 | 5 | 22 | 27 | 277 |
| Robert MacInnis | 62 | 8 | 18 | 26 | 170 |
| Dave Pichette | 39 | 5 | 21 | 26 | 20 |
| Nicolas Beaulieu | 60 | 10 | 13 | 23 | 85 |
| Doug Smith | 24 | 11 | 11 | 22 | 69 |
| Mike Glover | 61 | 9 | 11 | 20 | 156 |
| David Haas | 61 | 9 | 9 | 18 | 325 |
| Jim Ennis | 67 | 3 | 15 | 18 | 94 |
| Brad MacGregor | 31 | 8 | 8 | 16 | 8 |
| John Hanna | 20 | 7 | 9 | 16 | 12 |
| Mike Ware | 48 | 1 | 11 | 12 | 317 |
| Mario Barbe | 70 | 1 | 11 | 12 | 137 |
| Jamie Nicolls | 23 | 3 | 4 | 7 | 18 |
| John Leblanc | 3 | 4 | 0 | 4 | 0 |
| Jack MacKeigan | 11 | 2 | 2 | 4 | 16 |
| Jeff Beukeboom | 8 | 0 | 4 | 4 | 36 |
| Darren Welsh | 8 | 0 | 4 | 4 | 0 |
| Jeff Leverman | 5 | 0 | 3 | 3 | 4 |
| Duane Saulnier | 3 | 1 | 1 | 2 | 0 |
| Chris Joseph | 5 | 1 | 1 | 2 | 18 |
| Darren Beals (Goalie) | 14 | 0 | 1 | 1 | 4 |
| W. Skorodenski (G.) | 25 | 0 | 1 | 1 | 15 |
| David Roach (Goalie) | 33 | 0 | 1 | 1 | 4 |
| Ivan Matulik | 1 | 0 | 0 | 0 | 0 |
| Jeff Crossman | 2 | 0 | 0 | 0 | 4 |
| Don Martin | 3 | 0 | 0 | 0 | 2 |
| Greg Ware | 3 | 0 | 0 | 0 | 15 |
| Ron Shudra | 5 | 0 | 0 | 0 | 0 |
| Daryl Reaugh (Goalie) | 13 | 0 | 0 | 0 | 4 |

## Halifax Citadels

|  | Games | G. | A. | Pts. | Pen. |
|---|---|---|---|---|---|
| Ken Quinney | 72 | 41 | 49 | 90 | 65 |
| Max Middendorf | 72 | 41 | 39 | 80 | 85 |
| Lane Lambert | 59 | 25 | 35 | 60 | 162 |
| Claude Julien | 79 | 8 | 52 | 60 | 72 |
| Ladislav Tresl | 67 | 24 | 35 | 59 | 28 |
| Jaroslav Sevcik | 78 | 17 | 41 | 58 | 17 |
| Dean Hopkins | 53 | 18 | 31 | 49 | 116 |

|  | Games | G. | A. | Pts. | Pen. |
|---|---|---|---|---|---|
| Dave Latta | 42 | 20 | 26 | 46 | 36 |
| Ken McRae | 41 | 20 | 21 | 41 | 87 |
| Jean Richard | 57 | 8 | 25 | 33 | 38 |
| Joel Baillargeon | 53 | 11 | 19 | 30 | 122 |
| Mark Vermette | 52 | 12 | 16 | 28 | 30 |
| Jean Routhier | 52 | 13 | 13 | 26 | 189 |
| Stephan Roy | 42 | 8 | 16 | 24 | 28 |
| Bobby Dollas | 57 | 5 | 19 | 24 | 65 |
| Marc Fortier | 16 | 11 | 11 | 22 | 14 |
| Mike Hough | 22 | 11 | 10 | 21 | 87 |
| Anton Stastny | 16 | 9 | 5 | 14 | 4 |
| Darin Kimble | 39 | 8 | 6 | 14 | 188 |
| Brent Severyn | 47 | 2 | 12 | 14 | 141 |
| Tom McMurchy | 11 | 10 | 3 | 13 | 18 |
| Scott Shaunessy | 41 | 3 | 10 | 13 | 106 |
| Greg Smyth | 43 | 3 | 9 | 12 | 310 |
| Stephan Guerard | 37 | 1 | 9 | 10 | 140 |
| Keith Miller | 12 | 6 | 3 | 9 | 6 |
| Tommy Albelin | 8 | 2 | 5 | 7 | 4 |
| Daniel Poudrier | 7 | 2 | 4 | 6 | 2 |
| Jacques Mailhot | 35 | 4 | 1 | 5 | 259 |
| Gerald Bzdel | 36 | 1 | 3 | 4 | 46 |
| Dave Allison | 12 | 1 | 2 | 3 | 29 |
| Craig Jenkins | 2 | 0 | 2 | 2 | 0 |
| Mario Gosselin (Goalie) | 3 | 0 | 1 | 1 | 0 |
| Jari Gronstrand | 8 | 0 | 1 | 1 | 6 |
| Bob Mason (Goalie) | 23 | 0 | 1 | 1 | 0 |
| Scott Gordon (Goalie) | 2 | 0 | 0 | 0 | 0 |
| Ron Tugnutt (Goalie) | 24 | 0 | 0 | 0 | 4 |
| Mario Brunetta (Goalie) | 36 | 0 | 0 | 0 | 14 |

## Hershey Bears

|  | Games | G. | A. | Pts. | Pen. |
|---|---|---|---|---|---|
| Don Biggs | 76 | 36 | 67 | 103 | 158 |
| Brian Dobbin | 59 | 43 | 48 | 91 | 61 |
| Mark Lofthouse | 74 | 32 | 47 | 79 | 71 |
| Mark Freer | 75 | 30 | 49 | 79 | 77 |
| Dave Fenyves | 79 | 15 | 51 | 66 | 41 |
| Chris Jensen | 45 | 27 | 31 | 58 | 66 |
| Don Nachbaur | 49 | 24 | 31 | 55 | 172 |
| Gord Paddock | 75 | 6 | 36 | 42 | 105 |
| Warren Harper | 66 | 20 | 20 | 40 | 72 |
| Glen Seabrooke | 51 | 23 | 15 | 38 | 19 |
| Al Hill | 62 | 13 | 20 | 33 | 63 |
| Nick Kypreos | 28 | 12 | 15 | 27 | 19 |
| Kent Hawley | 54 | 9 | 17 | 26 | 47 |
| Scott Sandelin, Sher. | 12 | 0 | 9 | 9 | 8 |
|    Hershey | 39 | 6 | 9 | 15 | 38 |
|    Totals | 51 | 6 | 18 | 24 | 46 |
| Jeff Harding | 34 | 13 | 5 | 18 | 64 |
| Shawn Sabol | 58 | 7 | 11 | 18 | 134 |
| Ray Allison | 15 | 6 | 11 | 17 | 18 |
| Mitch Lamoureux | 9 | 9 | 7 | 16 | 14 |
| John Stevens | 78 | 3 | 13 | 16 | 129 |
| Bruce Rendall | 37 | 7 | 8 | 15 | 12 |
| Ross Fitzpatrick | 11 | 6 | 9 | 15 | 4 |
| Steve Fletcher, Moncton | 23 | 1 | 1 | 2 | 89 |
|    Hershey | 29 | 5 | 8 | 13 | 91 |
|    Totals | 52 | 6 | 9 | 15 | 180 |
| Mike Stothers | 76 | 4 | 11 | 15 | 262 |
| Kerry Huffman | 29 | 2 | 13 | 15 | 16 |
| Magnus Roupe | 12 | 2 | 6 | 8 | 17 |
| Mike Murray | 19 | 1 | 2 | 3 | 8 |
| Murray Baron | 9 | 0 | 3 | 3 | 8 |
| Craig Berube | 7 | 0 | 2 | 2 | 19 |
| Craig Kitteringham | 2 | 0 | 0 | 0 | 4 |
| Mark Laforest (Goalie) | 3 | 0 | 0 | 0 | 0 |

|  | Games | G. | A. | Pts. | Pen. |
|---|---|---|---|---|---|
| Jocelyn Perreault (G.) | 8 | 0 | 0 | 0 | 4 |
| Tony Horacek | 10 | 0 | 0 | 0 | 38 |
| Darryl Gilmour (Goalie) | 38 | 0 | 0 | 0 | 8 |
| Marc D'Amour (Goalie) | 39 | 0 | 0 | 0 | 14 |

## Maine Mariners

|  | Games | G. | A. | Pts. | Pen. |
|---|---|---|---|---|---|
| Steve Tsujiura | 79 | 15 | 41 | 56 | 67 |
| Ray Podloski | 71 | 20 | 34 | 54 | 70 |
| Paul Guay, New Haven | 4 | 4 | 6 | 10 | 20 |
|    Maine | 61 | 15 | 29 | 44 | 77 |
|    Totals | 65 | 19 | 35 | 54 | 97 |
| Darren Lowe | 78 | 29 | 24 | 53 | 36 |
| Paul Beraldo | 73 | 25 | 28 | 53 | 134 |
| Carl Mokosak | 53 | 20 | 18 | 38 | 337 |
| Scott Harlow | 30 | 16 | 17 | 33 | 8 |
| Scott Drevitch | 75 | 10 | 21 | 31 | 51 |
| Jeff Lamb | 58 | 11 | 15 | 26 | 64 |
| Randy Smith | 33 | 9 | 16 | 25 | 34 |
| Don Sweeney | 42 | 8 | 17 | 25 | 24 |
| Alain Cote | 37 | 5 | 16 | 21 | 111 |
| David Jensen | 18 | 12 | 8 | 20 | 2 |
| John Carter | 24 | 13 | 6 | 19 | 12 |
| Dan Dorian, Utica | 15 | 7 | 4 | 11 | 19 |
|    Maine | 16 | 2 | 3 | 5 | 13 |
|    Totals | 31 | 9 | 7 | 16 | 32 |
| Stephan Quintal | 16 | 4 | 10 | 14 | 28 |
| Tommy Lehmann | 26 | 1 | 13 | 14 | 12 |
| Greg Johnston | 15 | 5 | 7 | 12 | 31 |
| Phil DeGaetano | 42 | 3 | 9 | 12 | 156 |
| Ron Flockhart | 9 | 5 | 6 | 11 | 0 |
| Greg Hawgood | 21 | 2 | 9 | 11 | 41 |
| Dale Dunbar | 65 | 1 | 9 | 10 | 49 |
| Mike Neill | 64 | 0 | 10 | 10 | 200 |
| Mitch Molloy | 47 | 1 | 8 | 9 | 177 |
| Bruce Shoebottom | 44 | 0 | 8 | 8 | 265 |
| Bernie Johnston | 11 | 2 | 3 | 5 | 0 |
| David Buda | 5 | 3 | 1 | 4 | 2 |
| Jay Fraser | 11 | 2 | 2 | 4 | 14 |
| Lyndon Byers | 4 | 1 | 3 | 4 | 2 |
| Graeme Townshend | 5 | 2 | 1 | 3 | 11 |
| Peter Buckridge | 12 | 2 | 1 | 3 | 0 |
| Stan Drulia | 3 | 1 | 1 | 2 | 0 |
| Maurice Mansi | 5 | 1 | 1 | 2 | 4 |
| Nevin Markwart | 1 | 0 | 1 | 1 | 0 |
| Ryan Stewart, Moncton | 1 | 0 | 0 | 0 | 0 |
|    Maine | 7 | 1 | 0 | 1 | 7 |
|    Totals | 8 | 1 | 0 | 1 | 7 |
| Tom McComb | 10 | 0 | 1 | 1 | 2 |
| Joe Flaherty | 16 | 0 | 1 | 1 | 21 |
| Norm Foster (Goalie) | 47 | 0 | 1 | 1 | 4 |
| Sylvain Mayer | 1 | 0 | 0 | 0 | 0 |
| Jay Rose | 1 | 0 | 0 | 0 | 7 |
| Larry Rusconi | 1 | 0 | 0 | 0 | 0 |
| Greg Drechsel | 2 | 0 | 0 | 0 | 0 |
| Joe Gurney | 2 | 0 | 0 | 0 | 0 |
| Dave Mellen | 2 | 0 | 0 | 0 | 7 |
| Terry Taillefer (Goalie) | 3 | 0 | 0 | 0 | 0 |
| Bill Whitfield | 3 | 0 | 0 | 0 | 7 |
| Alan Tigert | 5 | 0 | 0 | 0 | 2 |
| John McLean | 6 | 0 | 0 | 0 | 0 |
| Daniel Mecrones | 6 | 0 | 0 | 0 | 0 |
| Mike Jeffrey (Goalie) | 44 | 0 | 0 | 0 | 19 |

## Moncton Hawks

|  | Games | G. | A. | Pts. | Pen. |
|---|---|---|---|---|---|
| Ron Wilson | 80 | 31 | 61 | 92 | 110 |

|  | Games | G. | A. | Pts. | Pen. |
|---|---|---|---|---|---|
| Brent Hughes | 54 | 34 | 34 | 68 | 286 |
| Alfie Turcotte | 54 | 27 | 39 | 66 | 74 |
| Scott Schneider | 64 | 29 | 36 | 65 | 51 |
| Paul Boutilier | 77 | 6 | 54 | 60 | 101 |
| Guy Larose | 72 | 32 | 27 | 59 | 176 |
| Stu Kulak | 51 | 30 | 29 | 59 | 98 |
| Mark Kumpel | 53 | 22 | 23 | 45 | 25 |
| Brad Jones | 44 | 20 | 19 | 39 | 62 |
| Matt Hervey | 73 | 8 | 28 | 36 | 295 |
| Markku Kyllonen | 60 | 14 | 20 | 34 | 16 |
| Todd Flichel | 74 | 2 | 29 | 31 | 81 |
| Moe Lemay, Maine | 13 | 6 | 2 | 8 | 32 |
|    Moncton | 16 | 9 | 11 | 20 | 21 |
|    Totals | 29 | 15 | 13 | 28 | 53 |
| Neil Meadmore | 53 | 9 | 14 | 23 | 257 |
| Chris Norton | 60 | 1 | 21 | 22 | 49 |
| Brad Berry | 38 | 3 | 16 | 19 | 39 |
| Mike Warus | 35 | 6 | 8 | 14 | 127 |
| Craig Endean | 18 | 3 | 9 | 12 | 16 |
| Pat Elynuik | 7 | 8 | 2 | 10 | 2 |
| Darren Boyko | 18 | 3 | 7 | 10 | 2 |
| Jamie Husgen | 35 | 3 | 7 | 10 | 58 |
| Guy Gosselin | 58 | 2 | 8 | 10 | 56 |
| Sean Clement | 65 | 2 | 8 | 10 | 64 |
| Luciano Borsato | 6 | 2 | 5 | 7 | 4 |
| Len Nielsen | 14 | 4 | 1 | 5 | 4 |
| Robin Bartel | 23 | 0 | 4 | 4 | 19 |
| Martin Lacroix | 13 | 1 | 2 | 3 | 0 |
| Hannu Jarvenpaa | 4 | 1 | 0 | 1 | 0 |
| Tom Draper (Goalie) | 54 | 0 | 1 | 1 | 23 |
| Serge Amyor | 1 | 0 | 0 | 0 | 0 |
| Stephan Dugal | 1 | 0 | 0 | 0 | 2 |
| Mike McNeil | 1 | 0 | 0 | 0 | 0 |
| Alain Tousegnant | 1 | 0 | 0 | 0 | 2 |
| Mike Bycina | 2 | 0 | 0 | 0 | 0 |
| Stephan Beauregard (G) | 15 | 0 | 0 | 0 | 2 |
| Daniel Berthiaume (G.) | 21 | 0 | 0 | 0 | 27 |

## New Haven Nighthawks

|  | Games | G. | A. | Pts. | Pen. |
|---|---|---|---|---|---|
| Hubie McDonough | 74 | 37 | 55 | 92 | 41 |
| Craig Duncanson | 69 | 25 | 39 | 64 | 200 |
| Bob Logan, Rochester | 5 | 2 | 2 | 4 | 2 |
|    New Haven | 66 | 21 | 32 | 53 | 27 |
|    Totals | 71 | 23 | 34 | 57 | 29 |
| Dave Pasin, Maine | 11 | 2 | 5 | 7 | 6 |
|    New Haven | 48 | 25 | 23 | 48 | 42 |
|    Totals | 59 | 27 | 28 | 55 | 48 |
| Bob Kudelski | 60 | 32 | 19 | 51 | 43 |
| Gordie Walker | 60 | 21 | 25 | 46 | 50 |
| Francois Breault | 68 | 21 | 24 | 45 | 51 |
| Jim Wiemer, Cape B't'n. | 51 | 12 | 29 | 41 | 80 |
|    New Haven | 3 | 1 | 1 | 2 | 2 |
|    Totals | 54 | 13 | 30 | 43 | 82 |
| Steve Richmond | 49 | 6 | 35 | 41 | 114 |
| Sylvain Couturier | 44 | 18 | 20 | 38 | 33 |
| Mario Chitaroni | 54 | 12 | 24 | 36 | 97 |
| Todd Elik | 43 | 11 | 25 | 36 | 31 |
| Alan May, Cape Breton | 50 | 12 | 13 | 25 | 214 |
|    New Haven | 12 | 2 | 8 | 10 | 99 |
|    Totals | 62 | 14 | 21 | 35 | 313 |
| Gilles Hamel, Moncton | 14 | 7 | 5 | 12 | 10 |
|    New Haven | 34 | 9 | 9 | 18 | 12 |
|    Totals | 48 | 16 | 14 | 30 | 22 |
| Tim Tookey | 33 | 11 | 18 | 29 | 30 |
| Phil Sykes | 34 | 9 | 17 | 26 | 23 |

|  | Games | G. | A. | Pts. | Pen. |
|---|---|---|---|---|---|
| Brad Hyatt | 61 | 3 | 21 | 24 | 46 |
| Chris Panek | 41 | 4 | 18 | 22 | 13 |
| Dan Gratton | 29 | 5 | 13 | 18 | 41 |
| Darryl Williams | 15 | 5 | 5 | 10 | 24 |
| Petr Prajsler | 43 | 4 | 6 | 10 | 96 |
| Eric Germain | 55 | 0 | 9 | 9 | 93 |
| Tom Pratt | 35 | 1 | 7 | 8 | 53 |
| Brett MacDonald | 15 | 2 | 4 | 6 | 6 |
| Mark Vichorek | 23 | 1 | 5 | 6 | 26 |
| John Miner | 7 | 2 | 3 | 5 | 4 |
| Tom Karalis | 11 | 2 | 3 | 5 | 8 |
| Denis Larocque | 15 | 2 | 2 | 4 | 51 |
| Ken Baumgartner | 10 | 1 | 3 | 4 | 26 |
| Michael Dark | 7 | 0 | 4 | 4 | 4 |
| Wayne McBean | 7 | 1 | 1 | 2 | 2 |
| Scott Young | 7 | 1 | 1 | 2 | 4 |
| Roland Melanson (G.) | 29 | 0 | 2 | 2 | 22 |
| Michael Boyce | 10 | 0 | 1 | 1 | 2 |
| Mark Fitzpatrick (G.) | 18 | 0 | 1 | 1 | 10 |
| Bob Janecyk (Goalie) | 34 | 0 | 1 | 1 | 4 |
| Ray LeBlanc (Goalie) | 1 | 0 | 0 | 0 | 0 |
| Mike Mersch | 1 | 0 | 0 | 0 | 4 |
| Al Loring (Goalie) | 2 | 0 | 0 | 0 | 0 |
| Doug Crossman | 3 | 0 | 0 | 0 | 0 |
| Pat Mayer | 6 | 0 | 0 | 0 | 35 |
| Joe Paterson | 7 | 0 | 0 | 0 | 24 |

## Newmarket Saints

|  | Games | G. | A. | Pts. | Pen. |
|---|---|---|---|---|---|
| Bruce Boudreau, Spring. | 50 | 28 | 36 | 64 | 42 |
|    Newmarket | 20 | 7 | 16 | 23 | 12 |
|    Totals | 70 | 35 | 52 | 87 | 54 |
| Paul Gagne | 56 | 33 | 41 | 74 | 29 |
| Daryl Evans | 64 | 29 | 30 | 59 | 16 |
| Ken Yaremchuk | 55 | 25 | 33 | 58 | 145 |
| Wes Jarvis | 52 | 22 | 31 | 53 | 38 |
| Greg Hotham | 73 | 9 | 42 | 51 | 62 |
| Greg Terrion | 60 | 15 | 34 | 49 | 64 |
| Trevor Jobe | 75 | 23 | 24 | 47 | 90 |
| Marty Dallman | 37 | 26 | 20 | 46 | 24 |
| Derek Laxdal | 34 | 22 | 22 | 44 | 53 |
| Sean McKenna | 61 | 14 | 27 | 41 | 35 |
| Tim Armstrong | 37 | 16 | 24 | 40 | 38 |
| Doug Shedden | 29 | 14 | 26 | 40 | 6 |
| Alan Hepple | 72 | 5 | 29 | 34 | 122 |
| Bill Root | 66 | 10 | 22 | 32 | 39 |
| Peter Ihnacak | 38 | 14 | 16 | 30 | 8 |
| Darryl Shannon | 61 | 5 | 24 | 29 | 37 |
| Darren Veitch | 33 | 5 | 19 | 24 | 29 |
| Mike Blaisdell | 40 | 16 | 7 | 23 | 48 |
| Jack Capuano | 74 | 5 | 16 | 21 | 52 |
| Tim Bean | 44 | 4 | 12 | 16 | 55 |
| Mark Kirton | 37 | 4 | 8 | 12 | 18 |
| Taylor Hall, Maine | 8 | 0 | 1 | 1 | 7 |
|    Newmarket | 9 | 5 | 5 | 10 | 14 |
|    Totals | 17 | 5 | 6 | 11 | 21 |
| Brian Hoard | 54 | 2 | 5 | 7 | 208 |
| Brian Blad | 59 | 2 | 4 | 6 | 149 |
| Gerard Waslen | 18 | 4 | 1 | 5 | 11 |
| Chris McRae | 18 | 3 | 1 | 4 | 85 |
| Jeff Reese (Goalie) | 37 | 0 | 3 | 3 | 16 |
| John McIntyre | 3 | 0 | 2 | 2 | 7 |
| Tim Bernhardt (Goalie) | 37 | 0 | 2 | 2 | 0 |
| Jim Ralph (Goalie) | 17 | 0 | 1 | 1 | 0 |
| Dean Anderson (Goalie) | 2 | 0 | 0 | 0 | 0 |

## Rochester Americans

| | Games | G. | A. | Pts. | Pen. |
|---|---|---|---|---|---|
| Ken Priestlay | 64 | 56 | 37 | 93 | 60 |
| Mike Donnelly | 53 | 32 | 37 | 69 | 53 |
| Jody Gage | 65 | 31 | 38 | 69 | 50 |
| Jim Jackson | 73 | 19 | 50 | 69 | 14 |
| Scott Metcalfe | 60 | 20 | 31 | 51 | 241 |
| Mikael Andersson | 56 | 18 | 33 | 51 | 12 |
| Richie Dunn | 69 | 9 | 35 | 44 | 81 |
| Kevin Kerr | 66 | 20 | 18 | 38 | 306 |
| Robert Ray | 74 | 11 | 18 | 29 | *446 |
| Don McSween | 66 | 7 | 22 | 29 | 45 |
| Francois Guay | 45 | 6 | 20 | 26 | 34 |
| Grant Tkachuk | 64 | 12 | 13 | 25 | 26 |
| Geordie Robertson | 32 | 11 | 12 | 23 | 12 |
| Trent Kaese | 45 | 9 | 11 | 20 | 68 |
| Shawn Anderson | 31 | 5 | 14 | 19 | 24 |
| Shawn Whitham | 46 | 4 | 15 | 19 | 75 |
| Mark Ferner | 55 | 0 | 18 | 18 | 97 |
| Keith Gretzky | 23 | 3 | 13 | 16 | 0 |
| Steve Smith | 48 | 2 | 12 | 14 | 79 |
| Jeff Capello | 39 | 6 | 7 | 13 | 22 |
| Grant Martin | 6 | 7 | 5 | 12 | 6 |
| Paul Brydges | 51 | 8 | 3 | 11 | 36 |
| Jim Hofford | 34 | 1 | 9 | 10 | 139 |
| Wayne Van Dorp | 28 | 3 | 6 | 9 | 202 |
| Jeff Parker | 6 | 2 | 4 | 6 | 9 |
| Bob Halkidis | 16 | 0 | 6 | 6 | 64 |
| Joe Reekie | 21 | 1 | 2 | 3 | 56 |
| Dave Moylan | 20 | 0 | 2 | 2 | 15 |
| Darcy Wakaluk (Goalie) | 33 | 0 | 2 | 2 | 10 |
| Jacques Cloutier (G.) | 11 | 0 | 1 | 1 | 2 |
| Kenton Rein (Goalie) | 15 | 0 | 1 | 1 | 34 |
| Brian Ford (Goalie) | 19 | 0 | 1 | 1 | 0 |
| Darren Eliot (Goalie) | 23 | 0 | 1 | 1 | 4 |
| Graeme Bonar | 1 | 0 | 0 | 0 | 2 |
| Brad Miller | 3 | 0 | 0 | 0 | 4 |
| Ed Hospodar | 5 | 0 | 0 | 0 | 10 |

## Sherbrooke Canadiens

| | Games | G. | A. | Pts. | Pen. |
|---|---|---|---|---|---|
| Stephan Lebeau | 78 | *70 | 64 | *134 | 47 |
| Benoit Brunet | 73 | 41 | *76 | 117 | 95 |
| Mark Pederson | 75 | 43 | 38 | 81 | 53 |
| Jocelyn Lemieux | 73 | 25 | 28 | 53 | 134 |
| J.J. Daigneault, Hershey | 12 | 0 | 10 | 10 | 13 |
| Sherbooke | 63 | 10 | 33 | 43 | 48 |
| Totals | 75 | 10 | 43 | 53 | 61 |
| Sylvain Lefebvre | 77 | 15 | 32 | 47 | 119 |
| Jim Nesich | 74 | 12 | 34 | 46 | 112 |
| Martin Desjardins | 70 | 17 | 27 | 44 | 104 |
| Rocky Dundas | 63 | 12 | 29 | 41 | 212 |
| Ron Chyzowski | 62 | 15 | 25 | 40 | 14 |
| Martin Nicoletti | 75 | 15 | 24 | 39 | 148 |
| Stephane Richer | 70 | 7 | 26 | 33 | 158 |
| Jose Charbonneau | 33 | 13 | 15 | 28 | 95 |
| Luc Gauthier | 77 | 8 | 20 | 28 | 178 |
| Dan Woodley | 30 | 9 | 16 | 25 | 69 |
| Jyrki Lumme | 26 | 4 | 11 | 15 | 10 |
| Mario Roberge | 58 | 4 | 9 | 13 | 249 |
| Steven Martinson | 10 | 5 | 7 | 12 | 61 |
| Serge Roberge | 65 | 5 | 7 | 12 | 352 |
| Donald Dufresne | 47 | 0 | 12 | 12 | 170 |
| Brent Gilchrist | 7 | 6 | 5 | 11 | 7 |
| Rob Bryden | 13 | 8 | 2 | 10 | 15 |
| Lyle Odelein | 33 | 3 | 4 | 7 | 120 |
| Steve Bisson | 4 | 0 | 3 | 3 | 4 |

## Springfield Indians

| | Games | G. | A. | Pts. | Pen. |
|---|---|---|---|---|---|
| Randy Exelby (Goalie) | 52 | 0 | 3 | 3 | 46 |
| Brad McCaughey | 1 | 1 | 0 | 1 | 0 |
| Francois Gravel (Goalie) | 33 | 0 | 1 | 1 | 12 |
| Eric Charron | 1 | 0 | 0 | 0 | 0 |
| Jean Bergeron (Goalie) | 5 | 0 | 0 | 0 | 2 |
| Marc Saumier | 5 | 0 | 0 | 0 | 7 |
| Mike Walsh | 68 | 31 | 34 | 65 | 73 |
| Stu Burnie | 74 | 28 | 36 | 64 | 49 |
| Shawn Evans | 68 | 9 | 50 | 59 | 125 |
| Bill Berg | 69 | 17 | 32 | 49 | 122 |
| Richard Kromm | 48 | 21 | 26 | 47 | 15 |
| Tom Fitzgerald | 61 | 24 | 18 | 42 | 43 |
| Dale Henry | 50 | 13 | 21 | 34 | 83 |
| Rob DiMaio | 40 | 13 | 18 | 31 | 67 |
| Mike Stevens | 42 | 17 | 13 | 30 | 120 |
| Vern Smith | 80 | 3 | 26 | 29 | 121 |
| Tim Hanley, New Haven | 1 | 0 | 0 | 0 | 5 |
| Maine | 4 | 0 | 0 | 0 | 0 |
| Springfield | 33 | 13 | 15 | 28 | 10 |
| Totals | 38 | 13 | 15 | 28 | 15 |
| Todd McLellan | 37 | 7 | 19 | 26 | 17 |
| Rod Dallman | 67 | 12 | 12 | 24 | 360 |
| Jeff Finley | 65 | 3 | 16 | 19 | 55 |
| Raimo Helminen | 16 | 6 | 11 | 17 | 0 |
| Shawn Byram | 45 | 5 | 11 | 16 | 195 |
| Kerry Clark | 63 | 7 | 7 | 14 | 264 |
| Doug Weiss | 32 | 3 | 11 | 14 | 42 |
| Hank Lammens | 69 | 1 | 13 | 14 | 55 |
| Chris McSorley | 26 | 5 | 8 | 13 | 119 |
| Dale Kushner | 45 | 5 | 8 | 13 | 132 |
| Chris Pryor | 54 | 3 | 6 | 9 | 205 |
| Brad Lauer | 8 | 1 | 5 | 6 | 0 |
| Duncan MacPherson | 24 | 1 | 5 | 6 | 69 |
| Derek King | 4 | 4 | 0 | 4 | 0 |
| Wayne Doucet | 6 | 2 | 2 | 4 | 4 |
| Doug Keans, Balt. (G.) | 4 | 0 | 0 | 0 | 2 |
| Springfield (G.) | 32 | 0 | 4 | 4 | 14 |
| Totals | 36 | 0 | 4 | 4 | 16 |
| Randy Wood | 1 | 1 | 1 | 2 | 0 |
| Patrick Flatley | 2 | 1 | 1 | 2 | 2 |
| Glenn Johannesen | 5 | 1 | 1 | 2 | 20 |
| Jeff Hackett (Goalie) | 29 | 0 | 2 | 2 | 6 |
| Paul Houck | 2 | 1 | 0 | 1 | 0 |
| Mick Vukota | 3 | 1 | 0 | 1 | 33 |
| Richard Durose (Goalie) | 1 | 0 | 0 | 0 | 0 |
| Peter McGeough | 2 | 0 | 0 | 0 | 0 |
| Duane Joyce | 3 | 0 | 0 | 0 | 0 |
| Danny Lorenz (Goalie) | 4 | 0 | 0 | 0 | 2 |
| Dean Ewen | 6 | 0 | 0 | 0 | 26 |
| George Maneluk (G.) | 24 | 0 | 0 | 0 | 6 |

## Utica Devils

| | Games | G. | A. | Pts. | Pen. |
|---|---|---|---|---|---|
| Paul Ysebaert | 56 | 36 | 44 | 80 | 22 |
| Jean Marc Lanthier, Me. | 24 | 7 | 16 | 23 | 16 |
| Utica | 55 | 23 | 26 | 49 | 22 |
| Totals | 79 | 30 | 42 | 72 | 38 |
| Kevin Todd | 78 | 26 | 45 | 71 | 62 |
| Chris Cichocki | 59 | 32 | 31 | 63 | 50 |
| Janne Ojanen | 72 | 23 | 37 | 60 | 10 |
| Tim Lenardon | 63 | 28 | 27 | 55 | 48 |
| Claude Vilgrain | 55 | 23 | 30 | 53 | 41 |
| Jeff Madill | 69 | 23 | 25 | 48 | 225 |

| | Games | G. | A. | Pts. | Pen. | | Games | G. | A. | Pts. | Pen. |
|---|---|---|---|---|---|---|---|---|---|---|---|
| Eric Weinrich | 80 | 17 | 27 | 44 | 70 | Troy Crowder | 62 | 6 | 4 | 10 | 152 |
| Neil Brady | 75 | 16 | 21 | 37 | 56 | John Walker | 14 | 2 | 5 | 7 | 11 |
| Marc Laniel | 80 | 6 | 28 | 34 | 43 | Anders Carlsson | 7 | 2 | 4 | 6 | 4 |
| Murray Brumwell | 73 | 5 | 29 | 34 | 29 | George McPhee | 8 | 3 | 2 | 5 | 31 |
| Alan Stewart | 72 | 9 | 23 | 32 | 110 | John Blessman | 26 | 2 | 3 | 5 | 46 |
| Lyle Phair, New Haven | 11 | 2 | 3 | 5 | 4 | Doug Brown | 4 | 1 | 4 | 5 | 0 |
| Utica | 58 | 5 | 19 | 24 | 24 | Chris Terreri (Goalie) | 39 | 0 | 4 | 4 | 6 |
| Totals | 69 | 7 | 22 | 29 | 28 | Terry McCutcheon | 6 | 2 | 0 | 2 | 2 |
| Paul Kelly, New Haven | 12 | 4 | 5 | 9 | 22 | Bob Woods | 11 | 0 | 1 | 1 | 2 |
| Utica | 34 | 6 | 8 | 14 | 25 | Myles O'Connor | 1 | 0 | 0 | 0 | 0 |
| Totals | 46 | 10 | 13 | 23 | 47 | Tim Budy | 3 | 0 | 0 | 0 | 2 |
| Dave Marcinyshyn | 74 | 4 | 14 | 18 | 101 | Dan Delianedis (Goalie) | 3 | 0 | 0 | 0 | 0 |
| Jamie Huscroft | 41 | 2 | 10 | 12 | 215 | Craig Billington (G.) | 41 | 0 | 0 | 0 | 10 |

## Complete AHL Goaltending

| | Games | Mins. | Goals | SO. | Avg. |
|---|---|---|---|---|---|
| Tim Cheveldae | 30 | 1694 | 98(3) | 1 | 3.47 |
| Mark Reimer | 18 | 900 | 64(3) | 0 | 4.27 |
| Sam St. Laurent | 34 | 2054 | 113(4) | 0 | 3.30 |
| Pete Richards (a) | 4 | 181 | 9 | 0 | 2.98 |
| Adirondack Totals | 80 | 4829 | 294 | 1 | 3.65 |
| Alain Raymond | 41 | 2301 | 162(3) | 0 | 4.22 |
| Shawn Simpson | 1 | 60 | 7 | 0 | 7.00 |
| Doug Keans (b) | 4 | 239 | 17(1) | 0 | 4.27 |
| Don Beaupre | 30 | 1715 | 102 | 0 | 3.57 |
| Jim Hrivnak | 10 | 502 | 55 | 0 | 6.57 |
| Baltimore Totals | 80 | 4817 | 347 | 0 | 4.32 |
| Sean Evoy | 9 | 472 | 45 | 0 | 5.72 |
| Ross McKay | 19 | 938 | 81 | 1 | 5.18 |
| Kay Whitmore | *56 | *3200 | *241(4) | 1 | 4.52 |
| Richard Brodeur | 6 | 222 | 21 | 0 | 5.68 |
| Binghamton Totals | 80 | 4832 | 392 | 2 | 4.87 |
| Darren Beals | 14 | 738 | 65(3) | 0 | 5.28 |
| David Roach | 33 | 1810 | 130(4) | 1 | 4.31 |
| Daryl Reaugh | 13 | 778 | 72(1) | 0 | 5.55 |
| Warren Skorodenski | 25 | 1497 | 111(2) | 0 | 4.45 |
| Cape Breton Totals | 80 | 4823 | 388 | 1 | 4.83 |
| Scott Gordon | 2 | 116 | 10 | 0 | 5.17 |
| Ron Tugnutt | 24 | 1368 | 79(1) | 1 | 3.46 |
| Mario Gosselin | 3 | 183 | 9 | 0 | 2.95 |
| Mario Brunetta | 36 | 1898 | 124(2) | 0 | 3.92 |
| Bob Mason | 23 | 1278 | 73(2) | 1 | 3.43 |
| Halifax Totals | 80 | 4843 | 300 | 2 | 3.72 |
| Marc D'Amour | 39 | 2174 | 127(3) | 0 | 3.51 |
| Darryl Gilmour | 38 | 2093 | 144(4) | 0 | 4.13 |
| Jocelyn Perreault | 8 | 394 | 22 | 0 | 3.35 |
| Mark Laforest | 3 | 185 | 9 | 0 | 2.92 |
| Hershey Totals | 80 | 4846 | 309 | 0 | 3.83 |
| Norm Foster | 47 | 2411 | 156(2) | 1 | 3.88 |
| Mike Jeffrey | 44 | 2368 | 148 | 1 | 3.75 |
| Terry Taillefer | 3 | 71 | 11 | 0 | 9.30 |
| Maine Totals | 80 | 4850 | 317 | 2 | 3.92 |
| Stephan Beauregard | 15 | 824 | 62 | 0 | 4.51 |
| Tom Draper | 54 | 2962 | 171(2) | 2 | 3.46 |
| Daniel Berthiaume | 21 | 1083 | 76(2) | 0 | 4.21 |
| Moncton Totals | 80 | 4869 | 313 | 2 | 3.86 |
| Mark Fitzpatrick | 18 | 980 | 54(1) | 1 | 3.31 |
| Bob Janecyk | 34 | 1992 | 131 | 1 | 3.95 |
| Al Loring | 2 | 104 | 10 | 0 | 5.77 |
| Ray LeBlanc | 1 | 20 | 3 | 0 | 9.00 |
| Roland Melanson | 29 | 1734 | 106(3) | 1 | 3.67 |
| Pete Richards (a) | 1 | 20 | 1 | 0 | 3.00 |
| New Haven Totals | 80 | 4850 | 309 | 3 | 3.82 |

|  | Games | Mins. | Goals | SO. | Avg. |
|---|---|---|---|---|---|
| Tim Bernhardt | 37 | 2004 | 145(1) | 1 | 4.34 |
| Jim Ralph | 17 | 721 | 48(2) | 0 | 3.99 |
| Jeff Reese | 37 | 2072 | 132(2) | 0 | 3.82 |
| Dean Anderson | 2 | 38 | 4 | 0 | 6.32 |
| Newmarket Totals | 80 | 4835 | 334 | 1 | 4.14 |
| Jacques Cloutier | 11 | 527 | 41 | 0 | 4.67 |
| Kenton Rein | 15 | 676 | 39 | 2 | 3.46 |
| Darcy Wakaluk | 33 | 1566 | 97(5) | 1 | 3.72 |
| Darren Eliot | 23 | 969 | 59 | 0 | 3.65 |
| Brian Ford | 19 | 1075 | 60(1) | 2 | 3.35 |
| Rochester Totals | 80 | 4813 | 302 | 5 | 3.76 |
| Randy Exelby | 52 | 2935 | 146 | *6 | *2.98 |
| Francois Gravel | 33 | 1625 | 95(2) | 2 | 3.51 |
| Jean Bergeron | 5 | 302 | 18 | 0 | 3.58 |
| Sherbrooke Totals | 80 | 4862 | 261 | 8 | 3.22 |
| Jeff Hackett | 29 | 1677 | 116(3) | 0 | 4.15 |
| George Maneluk | 24 | 1202 | 84 | 0 | 4.19 |
| Doug Keans (b) | 32 | 1737 | 124(2) | 0 | 4.28 |
| Richard Durose | 1 | 1 | 0 | 0 | 0.00 |
| Danny Lorenz | 4 | 210 | 12 | 0 | 3.43 |
| Springfield Totals | 80 | 4827 | 341 | 0 | 4.24 |
| Craig Billington | 41 | 2432 | 150(2) | 2 | 3.70 |
| Dan Delianedis | 3 | 94 | 8 | 0 | 5.11 |
| Chris Terreri | 39 | 2314 | 132(3) | 0 | 3.42 |
| Utica Totals | 80 | 4840 | 295 | 2 | 3.66 |

( )—Empty Net Goals. Do no count against a Goaltender's average.
(a)—Richards played for Adirondack and New Haven.
(b)—Keans played for Baltimore and Springfield.

## Individual 1988-89 Leaders

| | | |
|---|---|---|
| Goals | Stephan Lebeau, Sherbrooke— | 70 |
| Assists | Benoit Brunet, Sherbrooke— | 76 |
| Points | Stephan Lebeau, Sherbrooke— | 134 |
| Penalty Minutes | Robert Ray, Rochester— | 446 |
| Goaltending Average (25 Games) | Randy Exelby, Sherbrooke— | 2.98 |
| Shutouts | Randy Exelby, Sherbrooke— | 6 |

## 1989 Calder Cup Playoffs

(All series best of seven)

### Quarterfinals

Series "A"
|  | W. | L. | Pts. | GF. | GA. |
|---|---|---|---|---|---|
| New Haven | 4 | 2 | 8 | 28 | 26 |
| Sherbrooke | 2 | 4 | 4 | 26 | 28 |

(New Haven wins series, 4 games to 2)

Series "C"
|  | W. | L. | Pts. | GF. | GA. |
|---|---|---|---|---|---|
| Adirondack | 4 | 1 | 8 | 28 | 20 |
| Newmarket | 1 | 4 | 2 | 20 | 28 |

(Adirondack wins series, 4 games to 1)

Series "B"
|  | W. | L. | Pts. | GF. | GA. |
|---|---|---|---|---|---|
| Moncton | 4 | 0 | 8 | 21 | 9 |
| Halifax | 0 | 4 | 0 | 9 | 21 |

(Moncton wins series, 4 games to 0)

Series "D"
|  | W. | L. | Pts. | GF. | GA. |
|---|---|---|---|---|---|
| Hershey | 4 | 1 | 8 | 24 | 8 |
| Utica | 1 | 4 | 2 | 8 | 24 |

(Hershey wins series, 4 games to 1)

### Semifinals

Series "E"
|  | W. | L. | Pts. | GF. | GA. |
|---|---|---|---|---|---|
| New Haven | 4 | 2 | 8 | 27 | 19 |
| Moncton | 2 | 4 | 4 | 19 | 27 |

(New Haven wins series, 4 games to 2)

Series "F"
|  | W. | L. | Pts. | GF. | GA. |
|---|---|---|---|---|---|
| Adirondack | 4 | 3 | 8 | 21 | 18 |
| Hershey | 3 | 4 | 6 | 18 | 21 |

(Adirondack wins series, 4 games to 3)

### Finals—For the Calder Cup

Series "G"
|  | W. | L. | Pts. | GF. | GA. |
|---|---|---|---|---|---|
| Adirondack | 4 | 1 | 8 | 34 | 19 |
| New Haven | 1 | 4 | 2 | 19 | 34 |

(Adirondack wins series, and Calder Cup, 4 games to 1)

## Top 10 Playoff Scorers

| | Games | G. | A. | Pts. | Pen. |
|---|---|---|---|---|---|
| 1. Hubie McDonough, New Haven | 17 | 10 | **21 | ***31 | 6 |
| 2. Murray Eaves, Adirondack | 16 | *13 | 12 | 25 | 10 |
| 3. Todd Elik, New Haven | 17 | 10 | 12 | 22 | 44 |
| 4. Rob Doyle, Adirondack | 17 | 8 | 13 | 21 | 27 |
| 5. Daniel Shank, Adirondack | 17 | 11 | 8 | 19 | 102 |
| Glenn Merkosky, Adirondack | 17 | 8 | 11 | 19 | 10 |
| 7. Adam Graves, Adirondack | 14 | 11 | 7 | 18 | 17 |
| J. F. Sauve, Adirondack | 17 | 6 | 12 | 18 | 6 |
| 9. Joe Murphy, Adirondack | 16 | 6 | 11 | 17 | 17 |
| 10. Dave Pasin, New Haven | 17 | 8 | 8 | 16 | 47 |

**Tied playoff record of 21 now shared by Frank Mario (1946-47 with Hershey), Dough McMurdy (1948-49 with Springfield) and Jean-Francois Sauve (1982-83 with Rochester).

***Established new playoff record, breaking old record of 28 set in 1982-83 by Jean-Francois Sauve of Rochester.

## Team-by-Team Playoff Scoring

### Adirondack Red Wings
(Winners of 1989 Calder Cup Playoffs)

| | Games | G. | A. | Pts. | Pen. |
|---|---|---|---|---|---|
| Murray Eaves | 16 | *13 | 12 | 25 | 10 |
| Rob Doyle | 17 | 8 | 13 | 21 | 27 |
| Daniel Shank | 17 | 11 | 8 | 19 | 102 |
| Glenn Merkosky | 17 | 8 | 11 | 19 | 10 |
| Adam Graves | 14 | 11 | 7 | 18 | 17 |
| J.F. Sauve | 17 | 6 | 12 | 18 | 6 |
| Joe Murphy | 16 | 6 | 11 | 17 | 17 |
| Brent Fedyk | 15 | 7 | 8 | 15 | 23 |
| Randy McKay | 14 | 4 | 7 | 11 | 60 |
| Miroslav Ihnacak | 13 | 4 | 3 | 7 | 16 |
| Peter Dineen | 17 | 2 | 5 | 7 | 22 |
| Dennis Smith | 17 | 1 | 6 | 7 | 47 |
| Lou Crawford | 9 | 0 | 6 | 6 | 32 |
| John Mokosak | 17 | 0 | 5 | 5 | 49 |
| David Korol | 17 | 1 | 2 | 3 | 8 |
| Rob Nichols | 11 | 0 | 3 | 3 | 30 |
| Yves Racine | 2 | 1 | 1 | 2 | 0 |
| Bruce Bell | 2 | 0 | 1 | 1 | 2 |
| Sam St. Laurent (Goalie) | 16 | 0 | 1 | 1 | 0 |
| Dean Morton | 8 | 0 | 1 | 1 | 13 |
| John Blum | 12 | 0 | 1 | 1 | 18 |
| Pete Richards (Goalie) | 1 | 0 | 0 | 0 | 0 |
| Serge Anglehardt | 2 | 0 | 0 | 0 | 0 |
| Tim Cheveldae (Goalie) | 2 | 0 | 0 | 0 | 0 |
| Mike Gober | 2 | 0 | 0 | 0 | 4 |

### Halifax Citadels
(Lost quarterfinals to Moncton, 4-0)

| | Games | G. | A. | Pts. | Pen. |
|---|---|---|---|---|---|
| Ken Quinney | 4 | 3 | 0 | 3 | 0 |
| Max Middendorf | 4 | 1 | 2 | 3 | 6 |
| Jean Routhier | 4 | 1 | 1 | 2 | 16 |
| Jaroslav Sevcik | 4 | 1 | 1 | 2 | 2 |
| Claude Julien | 4 | 0 | 2 | 2 | 4 |
| Lane Lambert | 4 | 0 | 2 | 2 | 2 |
| Dave Latta | 4 | 0 | 2 | 2 | 0 |
| Tom McMurchy | 3 | 0 | 2 | 2 | 2 |
| Joel Baillargeon | 4 | 1 | 0 | 1 | 26 |
| Bobby Dollas | 4 | 1 | 0 | 1 | 14 |
| Jean Richard | 4 | 1 | 0 | 1 | 4 |
| Dean Hopkins | 3 | 0 | 1 | 1 | 6 |
| Greg Smyth | 4 | 0 | 1 | 1 | 35 |
| Ladislav Tresl | 4 | 0 | 1 | 1 | 4 |
| Jacques Mailhot | 1 | 0 | 0 | 0 | 5 |
| Stephan Roy | 1 | 0 | 0 | 0 | 0 |
| Mark Vermette | 1 | 0 | 0 | 0 | 0 |
| Bob Mason (Goalie) | 2 | 0 | 0 | 0 | 0 |
| Mario Brunetta (Goalie) | 3 | 0 | 0 | 0 | 0 |
| Daniel Poudrier | 3 | 0 | 0 | 0 | 2 |
| Stephan Guerard | 4 | 0 | 0 | 0 | 8 |

### Hershey Bears
(Lost semifinals to Adirondack, 4-3)

| | Games | G. | A. | Pts. | Pen. |
|---|---|---|---|---|---|
| Don Biggs | 11 | 5 | 9 | 14 | 30 |
| Brian Dobbin | 11 | 7 | 6 | 13 | 12 |
| Ray Allison | 12 | 4 | 7 | 11 | 6 |
| Mark Freer | 12 | 4 | 6 | 10 | 2 |
| Chris Jensen | 10 | 4 | 5 | 9 | 29 |
| Nick Kypreos | 12 | 4 | 5 | 9 | 11 |
| Dave Fenyves | 12 | 2 | 6 | 8 | 6 |
| Mark Lofthouse | 12 | 3 | 4 | 7 | 20 |
| Mitch Lamoureux | 9 | 1 | 4 | 5 | 14 |
| Don Nachbaur | 12 | 0 | 5 | 5 | 58 |
| Ross Fitzpatrick | 9 | 2 | 2 | 4 | 4 |
| Scott Sandelin | 8 | 2 | 1 | 3 | 4 |
| Jeff Harding | 8 | 1 | 2 | 3 | 33 |
| Al Hill | 8 | 2 | 0 | 2 | 10 |
| John Stevens | 12 | 1 | 1 | 2 | 29 |
| Mike Stothers | 9 | 0 | 2 | 2 | 29 |
| Mark Laforest (Goalie) | 12 | 0 | 2 | 2 | 8 |
| Shawn Sabol | 12 | 0 | 2 | 2 | 35 |
| Gord Paddock | 12 | 0 | 1 | 1 | 17 |
| Warren Harper | 1 | 0 | 0 | 0 | 0 |

### Moncton Hawks
(Lost semifinals to New Haven, 4-2)

| | Games | G. | A. | Pts. | Pen. |
|---|---|---|---|---|---|
| Brent Hughes | 10 | 9 | 4 | 13 | 40 |
| Alfie Turcotte | 10 | 3 | 9 | 12 | 17 |
| Stu Kulak | 10 | 5 | 6 | 11 | 16 |
| Moe Lemay | 10 | 3 | 6 | 9 | 25 |
| Paul Boutilier | 10 | 2 | 7 | 9 | 4 |
| Guy Larose | 10 | 4 | 4 | 8 | 37 |
| Scott Scheider | 6 | 2 | 6 | 8 | 4 |
| Mark Kumpel | 10 | 3 | 4 | 7 | 0 |
| Chris Norton | 10 | 3 | 2 | 5 | 15 |
| Ron Wilson | 8 | 1 | 4 | 5 | 20 |
| Todd Flichel | 10 | 1 | 4 | 5 | 25 |
| Matt Hervey | 10 | 1 | 2 | 3 | 42 |

|  | Games | G. | A. | Pts. | Pen. |
|---|---|---|---|---|---|
| Guy Gosselin | 10 | 1 | 1 | 2 | 2 |
| Markku Kyllonen | 5 | 1 | 0 | 1 | 0 |
| Brad Jones | 7 | 1 | 0 | 1 | 22 |
| Robin Bartel | 10 | 0 | 1 | 1 | 18 |
| Neil Meadmore | 10 | 0 | 1 | 1 | 80 |
| Daniel Berthiaume (G.) | 3 | 0 | 0 | 0 | 0 |
| Darren Boyko | 4 | 0 | 0 | 0 | 0 |
| Tom Draper (Goalie) | 7 | 0 | 0 | 0 | 2 |

## New Haven Nighthawks
(Lost finals to Adirondack, 4-1)

|  | Games | G. | A. | Pts. | Pen. |
|---|---|---|---|---|---|
| Hubie McDonough | 17 | 10 | *21 | *31 | 6 |
| Todd Elik | 17 | 10 | 12 | 22 | 44 |
| Dave Pasin | 17 | 8 | 8 | 16 | 47 |
| Gordie Walker | 17 | 7 | 8 | 15 | 23 |
| John Miner | 17 | 3 | 12 | 15 | 40 |
| Bob Kudelski | 17 | 8 | 5 | 13 | 12 |
| Steve Richmond | 17 | 3 | 10 | 13 | 84 |
| Craig Duncanson | 17 | 4 | 8 | 12 | 60 |
| Alan May | 16 | 6 | 3 | 9 | *105 |
| Mario Chitaroni | 16 | 2 | 7 | 9 | 57 |
| Jim Wiemer | 7 | 2 | 5 | 7 | 2 |
| Petr Prajsler | 16 | 3 | 3 | 6 | 34 |
| Mark Vichorek | 17 | 2 | 4 | 6 | 18 |
| Bob Logan | 13 | 2 | 3 | 5 | 9 |
| Francois Breault | 16 | 2 | 3 | 5 | 12 |
| Sylvain Couturier | 10 | 2 | 2 | 4 | 11 |
| Eric Germain | 17 | 0 | 3 | 3 | 23 |
| Roland Melanson (G.) | 17 | 0 | 1 | 1 | 8 |
| Gilles Hamel | 1 | 0 | 0 | 0 | 0 |
| Brad Hyatt | 1 | 0 | 0 | 0 | 10 |
| Al Loring (Goalie) | 1 | 0 | 0 | 0 | 0 |
| Scott Young | 6 | 0 | 0 | 0 | 2 |

## Newmarket Saints
(Lost quarterfinals to Adirondack, 4-1)

|  | Games | G. | A. | Pts. | Pen. |
|---|---|---|---|---|---|
| Ken Yaremchuk | 5 | 7 | 7 | 14 | 12 |
| Paul Gagne | 5 | 4 | 4 | 8 | 5 |
| Wes Jarvis | 5 | 2 | 4 | 6 | 4 |
| Greg Hotham | 5 | 1 | 4 | 5 | 0 |
| Darren Veitch | 5 | 0 | 4 | 4 | 4 |
| Darryl Shannon | 5 | 0 | 3 | 3 | 10 |
| Derek Laxdal | 2 | 2 | 0 | 2 | 5 |
| Kent Hulst | 2 | 1 | 1 | 2 | 2 |
| Daryl Evans | 5 | 1 | 1 | 2 | 0 |
| John McIntyre | 5 | 1 | 1 | 2 | 20 |
| Sean McKenna | 5 | 1 | 1 | 2 | 4 |
| Bruce Boudreau | 4 | 0 | 1 | 1 | 6 |
| Greg Terrion | 4 | 0 | 1 | 1 | 2 |
| Brian Blad | 5 | 0 | 1 | 1 | 5 |
| Alan Hepple | 5 | 0 | 1 | 1 | 23 |
| Trevor Jobe | 5 | 0 | 1 | 1 | 12 |

|  | Games | G. | A. | Pts. | Pen. |
|---|---|---|---|---|---|
| Dean Anderson (Goalie) | 1 | 0 | 0 | 0 | 0 |
| Jack Capuano | 1 | 0 | 0 | 0 | 0 |
| Brian Hoard | 2 | 0 | 0 | 0 | 12 |
| Jim Ralph (Goalie) | 5 | 0 | 0 | 0 | 2 |
| Bill Root | 5 | 0 | 0 | 0 | 18 |

## Sherbrooke Canadiens
(Lost quarterfinals to New Haven, 4-2)

|  | Games | G. | A. | Pts. | Pen. |
|---|---|---|---|---|---|
| Mark Pederson | 6 | 7 | 5 | 12 | 4 |
| Martin Desjardins | 6 | 2 | 7 | 9 | 21 |
| Dan Woodley | 4 | 1 | 6 | 7 | 5 |
| Stephan Lebeau | 6 | 1 | 4 | 5 | 8 |
| Jocelyn Lemieux | 4 | 3 | 1 | 4 | 6 |
| J.J. Daigneault | 6 | 1 | 3 | 4 | 2 |
| Sylvain Lefebvre | 6 | 1 | 3 | 4 | 4 |
| Jyrki Lumme | 6 | 1 | 3 | 4 | 4 |
| Rob Bryden | 6 | 3 | 0 | 3 | 6 |
| Jim Nesich | 6 | 1 | 2 | 3 | 10 |
| Stephane Richer | 6 | 1 | 2 | 3 | 18 |
| Rocky Dundas | 2 | 2 | 0 | 2 | 8 |
| Benoit Brunet | 6 | 2 | 0 | 2 | 4 |
| Lyle Odelein | 3 | 0 | 2 | 2 | 5 |
| Mario Roberge | 6 | 0 | 2 | 2 | 8 |
| Serge Roberge | 6 | 0 | 1 | 1 | 10 |
| Francois Gravel (Goalie) | 1 | 0 | 0 | 0 | 0 |
| Martin Nicoletti | 5 | 0 | 0 | 0 | 13 |
| Randy Exelby (Goalie) | 6 | 0 | 0 | 0 | 12 |
| Luc Gauthier | 6 | 0 | 0 | 0 | 10 |

## Utica Devils
(Lost quarterfinals to Hershey, 4-1)

|  | Games | G. | A. | Pts. | Pen. |
|---|---|---|---|---|---|
| Jean Lanthier | 3 | 3 | 0 | 3 | 2 |
| Neil Brady | 4 | 0 | 3 | 3 | 0 |
| Janne Ojanen | 5 | 0 | 3 | 3 | 0 |
| Kevin Todd | 4 | 2 | 0 | 2 | 6 |
| Claude Vilgrain | 5 | 0 | 2 | 2 | 2 |
| George McPhee | 3 | 1 | 0 | 1 | 26 |
| Jeff Madill | 4 | 1 | 0 | 1 | 35 |
| Alan Stewart | 5 | 1 | 0 | 1 | 4 |
| Chris Cichocki | 5 | 0 | 1 | 1 | 2 |
| Marc Laniel | 5 | 0 | 1 | 1 | 2 |
| Eric Weinrich | 5 | 0 | 1 | 1 | 8 |
| Paul Ysebaert | 5 | 0 | 1 | 1 | 4 |
| Troy Crowder | 2 | 0 | 0 | 0 | 25 |
| Chris Terreri (Goalie) | 2 | 0 | 0 | 0 | 0 |
| Paul Kelly | 3 | 0 | 0 | 0 | 6 |
| Lyle Phair | 3 | 0 | 0 | 0 | 2 |
| Craig Billington (G.) | 4 | 0 | 0 | 0 | 2 |
| Bob Woods | 4 | 0 | 0 | 0 | 2 |
| Murray Brumwell | 5 | 0 | 0 | 0 | 2 |
| Jamie Huscroft | 5 | 0 | 0 | 0 | 40 |
| Dave Marcinyshyn | 5 | 0 | 0 | 0 | 13 |

## Complete Calder Cup Goaltending

| | Games | Mins. | Goals | SO. | Avg. |
|---|---|---|---|---|---|
| Pete Richards, Adirondack | 1 | 10 | 0 | 0 | 0.00 |
| Dean Anderson, Newmarket | 1 | 30 | 1(1) | 0 | 2.00 |
| Mark Laforest, Hershey | 12 | 744 | 27(2) | 1 | *2.18 |
| Sam St. Laurent, Adirondack | 16 | 956 | 47(1) | *2 | 2.95 |
| Tom Draper, Moncton | 7 | 419 | 24(1) | 0 | 3.44 |
| Daniel Berthiaume, Moncton | 3 | 180 | 11 | 0 | 3.67 |
| Al Loring, New Haven | 1 | 30 | 2 | 0 | 4.00 |
| Roland Melanson, New Haven | *17 | *1019 | *74(3) | 1 | 4.36 |
| Randy Exelby, Sherbrooke | 6 | 329 | 24(1) | 0 | 4.38 |
| Chris Terreri, Utica | 2 | 80 | 6 | 0 | 4.50 |
| Francois Gravel, Sherbrooke | 1 | 40 | 3 | 0 | 4.50 |
| Craig Billington, Utica | 4 | 220 | 18 | 0 | 4.91 |
| Mario Brunetta, Halifax | 3 | 142 | 12 | 0 | 5.07 |
| Jim Ralph, Newmarket | 5 | 269 | 23(3) | 0 | 5.13 |
| Tim Cheveldae, Adirondack | 2 | 99 | 9 | 0 | 5.45 |
| Bob Mason, Halifax | 2 | 97 | 9 | 0 | 5.57 |

( )—Empty Net Goals. Do not count against a Goaltender's average.

## Individual AHL Playoff Leaders

| | | |
|---|---|---|
| Goals | Murray Eaves, Adirondack— | 13 |
| Assists | Hubie McDonough, New Haven— | 21 |
| Points | Hubie McDonough, New Haven— | 31 |
| Penalty Minutes | Alan May, New Haven— | 105 |
| Goaltender's Average | Mark Laforest, Hershey— | 2.18 |
| Shutouts | Sam St. Laurent, Adirondack— | 2 |

★★★★★★★★★★★★★★★★★★★★★★★★★★★★★★★★★★★★★★★★★★★★★★★★★

## AHL 1988-89 ALL-STARS

| First Team | Position | Second Team |
|---|---|---|
| Randy Exelby, Sherbrooke | Goalie | Tom Draper, Moncton |
| Dave Fenyves, Hershey | Defense | Sylvain Lefebvre, Sherbrooke |
| Paul Boutilier, Moncton | Defense | Claude Julien, Halifax |
| Stephan Lebeau, Sherbrooke | Center | Murray Eaves, Adirondack |
| Brian Dobbin, Hershey | Right Wing | Mike Millar, Baltimore |
| Benoit Brunet, Sherbrooke | Left Wing | Ron Wilson, Moncton |

★★★★★★★★★★★★★★★★★★★★★★★★★★★★★★★★★★★★★★★★★★★★★★★★★

## AHL 1988-89 TROPHY WINNERS

| | |
|---|---|
| John B. Sollenberger Trophy (Leading Scorer) | Stephan Lebeau, Sherbrooke |
| Les Cunningham Plaque (Most Valuable Player) | Stephan Lebeau, Sherbrooke |
| Harry (Hap) Holmes Memorial Trophy (Top Team Goaltending) | Randy Exelby, Sherbrooke |
| | Francois Gravel, Sherbrooke |
| Dudley (Red) Garrett Memorial Trophy (Top Rookie) | Stephan Lebeau, Sherbrooke |
| Eddie Shore Plaque (Outstanding Defenseman) | Dave Fenyves, Hershey |
| Fred Hunt Memorial Award (Sportsmanship, Determination, Dedication) | Murray Eaves, Adirondack |
| Louis A.R. Pieri Memorial Award (Top AHL Coach) | Tom McVie, Utica |
| Baz Bastien Trophy (Coaches pick as top AHL Goalie) | Randy Exelby, Sherbrooke |
| Jack Butterfield Trophy (Calder Cup Playoffs MVP) | Sam St. Laurent, Adirondack |

# AHL All-Time Trophy Winners

## John B. Sollenberger Trophy
### Leading Scorer

(Originally called Wally Kilrea Trophy, later changed to Carl Liscombe Trophy and during summer of 1955 given current name)

| Season | Player, Team | Games | G. | A. | Pts. | Pen. |
|---|---|---|---|---|---|---|
| 1936-37 | Jack Markle, Syracuse | 48 | 21 | 39 | 60 | 2 |
| 1937-38 | Jack Markle, Syracuse | 48 | 22 | 32 | 54 | 8 |
| 1938-39 | Don Deacon, Pittsburgh | 46 | 24 | 41 | 65 | 41 |
| 1939-40 | Norm Locking, Syracuse | 55 | 31 | 32 | 63 | 12 |
| 1940-41 | Les Cunningham, Cleveland | 56 | 22 | 42 | 64 | 10 |
| 1941-42 | Pete Kelly, Springfield | 46 | 34 | 44 | 78 | 11 |
| 1942-43 | Wally Kilrea, Hershey | 56 | 31 | 68 | 99 | 8 |
| 1943-44 | Tommy Burlington, Cleveland | 52 | 33 | 49 | 82 | 17 |
| 1944-45 | Bob Gracie, Pittsburgh | 58 | 40 | 55 | 95 | 4 |
|  | Bob Walton, Pittsburgh | 58 | 37 | 58 | 95 | 17 |
| 1945-46 | Les Douglas, Indianapolis | 62 | 44 | 46 | 90 | 35 |
| 1946-47 | Phil Hergesheimer, Philadelphia | 64 | 48 | 44 | 92 | 20 |
| 1947-48 | Carl Liscombe, Providence | 68 | 50 | 68 | 118 | 10 |
| 1948-49 | Sid Smith, Pittsburgh | 68 | 55 | 57 | 112 | 4 |
| 1949-50 | Les Douglas, Cleveland | 67 | 32 | 68 | 100 | 27 |
| 1950-51 | Ab DeMarco, Buffalo | 64 | 37 | 76 | 113 | 35 |
| 1951-52 | Ray Powell, Providence | 67 | 35 | 62 | 97 | 6 |
| 1952-53 | Eddie Olson, Cleveland | 61 | 32 | 54 | 86 | 33 |
| 1953-54 | George Sullivan, Hershey | 69 | 30 | 89 | 119 | 54 |
| 1954-55 | Eddie Olson, Cleveland | 60 | 41 | 47 | 88 | 48 |
| 1955-56 | Zellio Toppazzini, Providence | 64 | 42 | 71 | 113 | 44 |
| 1956-57 | Fred Glover, Cleveland | 64 | 42 | 57 | 99 | 111 |
| 1957-58 | Willie Marshall, Hershey | 68 | 40 | 64 | 104 | 56 |
| 1958-59 | Bill Hicke, Rochester | 69 | 41 | 56 | 97 | 41 |
| 1959-60 | Fred Glover, Cleveland | 72 | 38 | 69 | 107 | 143 |
| 1960-61 | Bill Sweeney, Springfield | 70 | 40 | 68 | 108 | 26 |
| 1961-62 | Bill Sweeney, Springfield | 70 | 40 | 61 | 101 | 14 |
| 1962-63 | Bill Sweeney, Springfield | 69 | 38 | 65 | 103 | 16 |
| 1963-64 | Gerry Ehman, Rochester | 66 | 36 | 49 | 85 | 26 |
| 1964-65 | Art Stratton, Buffalo | 71 | 25 | 84 | 109 | 32 |
| 1965-66 | Dick Gamble, Rochester | 71 | 47 | 51 | 98 | 22 |
| 1966-67 | Gordon Labossiere, Quebec | 72 | 40 | 55 | 95 | 71 |
| 1967-68 | Simon Nolet, Quebec | 70 | 44 | 52 | 96 | 45 |
| 1968-69 | Jeannot Gilbert, Hershey | 71 | 35 | 65 | 100 | 13 |
| 1969-70 | Jude Drouin, Montreal | 65 | 37 | 69 | 106 | 88 |
| 1970-71 | Fred Speck, Baltimore | 72 | 31 | 61 | 92 | 40 |
| 1971-72 | Don Blackburn, Providence | 76 | 34 | 65 | 99 | 12 |
| 1972-73 | Yvon Lambert, Nova Scotia | 76 | 52 | 52 | 104 | 84 |
| 1973-74 | Steve West, New Haven | 76 | 50 | 60 | 110 | 41 |
| 1974-75 | Doug Gibson, Rochester | 75 | 44 | 72 | 116 | 81 |
| 1975-76 | Jean-Guy Gratton, Hershey | 73 | 35 | 58 | 93 | 38 |
| 1976-77 | Andre Peloffy, Springfield | 79 | 42 | 57 | 99 | 106 |
| 1977-78 | Gord Brooks, Philadelphia | 81 | 42 | 56 | 98 | 40 |
|  | Rick Adduono, Rochester | 76 | 38 | 60 | 98 | 34 |
| 1978-79 | Bernie Johnston, Maine | 70 | 29 | 66 | 95 | 40 |
| 1979-80 | Norm Dube, Nova Scotia | 77 | 40 | 61 | 101 | 51 |
| 1980-81 | Mark Lofthouse, Hershey | 74 | 48 | 55 | 103 | 131 |
| 1981-82 | Mike Kasczyki, New Brunswick | 80 | 36 | 82 | 118 | 67 |
| 1982-83 | Ross Yates, Binghamton | 77 | 41 | 84 | 125 | 28 |
| 1983-84 | Claude Larose, Sherbrooke | 80 | 53 | 67 | 120 | 6 |
| 1984-85 | Paul Gardner, Binghamton | 64 | 51 | 79 | 130 | 10 |
| 1985-86 | Paul Gardner, Rochester | 71 | 61 | 51 | 112 | 16 |
| 1986-87 | Tim Tookey, Hershey | 80 | 51 | 73 | 124 | 45 |
| 1987-88 | Bruce Boudreau, Springfield | 80 | 42 | 74 | 116 | 84 |
| 1988-89 | Stephan Lebeau, Sherbrooke | 78 | 70 | 64 | 134 | 47 |

## Les Cunningham Plaque
### Most Valuable Player

1947-48—Carl Liscombe, Providence
1948-49—Carl Liscombe, Providence
1949-50—Les Douglas, Cleveland
1950-51—Ab DeMarco, Buffalo
1951-52—Ray Powell, Providence
1952-53—Eddie Olson, Cleveland
1953-54—George "Red" Sullivan, Hershey
1954-55—Ross Lowe, Springfield

1955-56—Johnny Bower, Providence
1956-57—Johnny Bower, Providence
1957-58—Johnny Bower, Cleveland
1958-59—Bill Hicke, Rochester
         Rudy Migay, Rochester (tie)
1959-60—Fred Glover, Cleveland
1960-61—Phil Maloney, Buffalo
1961-62—Fred Glover, Cleveland
1962-63—Denis DeJordy, Buffalo
1963-64—Fred Glover, Cleveland
1964-65—Art Stratton, Buffalo
1965-66—Dick Gamble, Rochester
1966-67—Mike Nykoluk, Hershey
1967-68—Dave Creighton, Providence
1968-69—Gilles Villemure, Buffalo
1969-70—Gilles Villemure, Buffalo
1970-71—Fred Speck, Baltimore
1971-72—Garry Peters, Boston

1972-73—Billy Inglis, Cincinnati
1973-74—Art Stratton, Rochester
1974-75—Doug Gibson, Rochester
1975-76—Ron Andruff, Nova Scotia
1976-77—Doug Gibson, Rochester
1977-78—Blake Dunlop, Maine
1978-79—Rocky Saganiuk, New Brunswick
1979-80—Norm Dube, Nova Scotia
1980-81—Pelle Lindbergh, Maine
1981-82—Mike Kasczyki, New Brunswick
1982-83—Ross Yates, Binghamton
1983-84—Mal Davis, Rochester
         Garry Lariviere, St. Catharines (tie)
1984-85—Paul Gardner, Binghamton
1985-86—Paul Gardner, Rochester
1986-87—Tim Tookey, Hershey
1987-88—Jody Gage, Rochester
1988-89—Stephan Lebeau, Sherbrooke

## Harry (Hap) Holmes Memorial Trophy

(Awarded to outstanding goaltender. Beginning with 1983-84, awarded to top team goaltending with each goaltender having played a minimum 25 games for the team with fewest goals scored against.)

| | Games | Goals | SO. | Avg. |
|---|---|---|---|---|
| 1936-37—Bert Gardiner, Philadelphia | 47 | 108 | 4 | 2.29 |
| 1937-38—Frank Brimsek, Providence | 48 | 86 | 5 | 1.79 |
| 1938-39—Alfie Moore, Hershey | 53 | 105 | 7 | 1.98 |
| 1939-40—Moe Roberts, Cleveland | 56 | 130 | 5 | 2.32 |
| 1940-41—Chuck Rayner, Springfield | 36 | 87 | 6 | 2.42 |
| 1941-42—Bill Beveridge, Cleveland | 31 | 73 | 8 | 2.35 |
| 1942-43—Gordie Bell, Buffalo | 52 | 125 | 9 | 2.40 |
| 1943-44—Nick Damore, Hershey | 54 | 133 | 4 | 2.46 |
| 1944-45—Yves Nadon, Buffalo | 30 | 87 | 3 | 2.90 |
| 1945-46—Connie Dion, St. Louis-Buffalo | 42 | 124 | 1 | 2.95 |
| 1946-47—Baz Bastien, Pittsburgh | 40 | 140 | 7 | 2.60 |
| 1947-48—Baz Bastien, Pittsburgh | 68 | 170 | 5 | 2.50 |
| 1948-49—Baz Bastien, Pittsburgh | 68 | 175 | 6 | 2.57 |
| 1949-50—Gil Mayer, Pittsburgh | 50 | 142 | 4 | 2.84 |
| 1950-51—Gil Mayer, Pittsburgh | 71 | 174 | 6 | 2.45 |
| 1951-52—Johnny Bower, Cleveland | 68 | 165 | 3 | 2.43 |
| 1952-53—Gil Mayer, Pittsburgh | 62 | 146 | 6 | 2.35 |
| 1953-54—Jacques Plante, Buffalo | 55 | 148 | 3 | 2.69 |
| 1954-55—Gil Mayer, Pittsburgh | 64 | 179 | 3 | 2.80 |
| 1955-56—Gil Mayer, Pittsburgh | 56 | 151 | 5 | 2.70 |
| 1956-57—Johnny Bower, Providence | 57 | 138 | 4 | 2.42 |
| 1957-58—Johnny Bower, Cleveland | 64 | 140 | 8 | 2.19 |
| 1958-59—Bob Perreault, Hershey | 50 | 134 | 6 | 2.68 |
| 1959-60—Ed Chadwick, Rochester | 67 | 184 | 4 | 2.75 |
| 1960-61—Marcel Paille, Springfield | 67 | 188 | 8 | 2.81 |
| 1961-62—Marcel Paille, Springfield | 45 | 115 | 2 | 2.56 |
| 1962-63—Denis DeJordy, Buffalo | 67 | 187 | 6 | 2.79 |
| 1963-64—Roger Crozier, Pittsburgh | 44 | 103 | 4 | 2.34 |
| 1964-65—Gerry Cheevers, Rochester | 72 | 195 | 5 | 2.68 |
| 1965-66—Les Binkley, Cleveland | 66 | 192 | 2 | 2.93 |
| 1966-67—Andre Gill, Hershey | 56 | 161 | 4 | 2.90 |
| 1967-68—Bob Perreault, Rochester | 57 | 149 | 6 | 2.88 |
| 1968-69—Gilles Villemure, Buffalo | 62 | 148 | 6 | 2.41 |
| 1969-70—Gilles Villemure, Buffalo | 65 | 156 | 8 | 2.52 |
| 1970-71—Gary Kurt, Cleveland | 42 | 101 | 3 | 2.67 |
| 1971-72—Dan Bouchard, Boston | 50 | 122 | 4 | 2.51 |
| Ross Brooks, Boston | 30 | 65 | 1 | 2.38 |
| 1972-73—Michel Larocque, Nova Scotia | 47 | 114 | 1 | 2.50 |
| 1973-74—Jim Shaw, Nova Scotia | 41 | 104 | 3 | 2.68 |
| Dave Elenbaas, Nova Scotia | 39 | 109 | 3 | 2.96 |
| 1974-75—Ed Walsh, Nova Scotia | 46 | 128 | 2 | 2.77 |
| Dave Elenbaas, Nova Scotia | 30 | 93 | 1 | 3.15 |
| 1975-76—Dave Elenbaas, Nova Scotia | 48 | 114 | 5 | 2.42 |
| Ed Walsh, Nova Scotia | 31 | 91 | 2 | 3.06 |
| 1976-77—Ed Walsh, Nova Scotia | 40 | 115 | 3 | 2.86 |
| Dave Elenbaas, Nova Scotia | 31 | 81 | 5 | 2.61 |
| 1977-78—Bob Holland, Nova Scotia | 38 | 120 | 1 | 3.17 |
| Maurice Barrette, Nova Scotia | 39 | 107 | 2 | 2.74 |

|  | Games | Goals | SO. | Avg. |
|---|---|---|---|---|
| 1978-79—Pete Peeters, Maine | 35 | 100 | 2 | 2.90 |
| Robbie Moore, Maine | 26 | 84 | 1 | 3.38 |
| 1979-80—Rick St. Croix, Maine | 46 | 132 | 1 | 2.90 |
| Robbie Moore, Maine | 32 | 106 | 1 | 3.48 |
| 1980-81—Pelle Lindbergh, Maine | 51 | 165 | 1 | 3.26 |
| Robbie Moore, Maine | 25 | 92 | 1 | 3.86 |
| 1981-82—Bob Janecyk, New Brunswick | 53 | 153 | 2 | 2.85 |
| Warren Skorodenski, New Brunswick | 28 | 70 | 3 | 2.55 |
| 1982-83—Brian Ford, Fredericton | 27 | 84 | 0 | 3.49 |
| Clint Malarchuk, Fredericton | 25 | 78 | 1 | 3.11 |
| 1983-84—Brian Ford, Fredericton | 36 | 105 | 2 | 2.94 |
| 1984-85—Jon Casey, Baltimore | 46 | 116 | 4 | 2.63 |
| 1985-86—Sam St. Laurent, Maine | 50 | 161 | 1 | 3.38 |
| Karl Friesen, Maine | 35 | 115 | 2 | 3.48 |
| 1986-87—Vincent Riendeau, Sherbrooke | 41 | 114 | 2 | 2.89 |
| 1987-88—Vincent Riendeau, Sherbrooke | 44 | 112 | 4 | 2.67 |
| Jocelyn Perreault, Sherbrooke | 25 | 77 | 0 | 3.71 |
| 1988-89—Randy Exelby, Sherbrooke | 52 | 146 | 6 | 2.98 |
| Francois Gravel, Sherbrooke | 33 | 95 | 2 | 3.51 |

## Dudley (Red) Garrett Memorial Trophy
### Top Rookie

1947-48—Bob Solinger, Cleveland
1948-49—Terry Sawchuk, Indianapolis
1949-50—Paul Meger, Buffalo
1950-51—Wally Hergesheimer, Cleveland
1951-52—Earl "Dutch" Reibel, Indianapolis
1952-53—Guyle Fielder, St. Louis
1953-54—Don Marshall, Buffalo
1954-55—Jimmy Anderson, Springfield
1955-56—Bruce Cline, Providence
1956-57—Boris "Bo" Elik, Cleveland
1957-58—Bill Sweeney, Providence
1958-59—Bill Hicke, Rochester
1959-60—Stan Baluik, Providence
1960-61—Ronald "Chico" Maki, Buffalo
1961-62—Les Binkley, Cleveland
1962-63—Doug Robinson, Buffalo
1963-64—Roger Crozier, Pittsburgh
1964-65—Ray Cullen, Buffalo
1965-66—Mike Walton, Rochester
1966-67—Bob Rivard, Quebec
1967-68—Gerry Desjardins, Cleveland
1968-69—Ron Ward, Rochester
1969-70—Jude Drouin, Montreal
1970-71—Fred Speck, Baltimore
1971-72—Terry Caffery, Cleveland
1972-73—Ron Anderson, Boston
1973-74—Rick Middleton, Providence
1974-75—Jerry Holland, Providence
1975-76—Greg Holst, Providence
Pierre Mondou, Nova Scotia (tie)
1976-77—Rod Schutt, Nova Scotia
1977-78—Norm Dupont, Nova Scotia
1978-79—Mike Meeker, Binghamton
1979-80—Daryl Sutter, New Brunswick
1980-81—Pelle Lindbergh, Maine
1981-82—Bob Sullivan, Binghamton
1982-83—Mitch Lamoureux, Baltimore
1983-84—Claude Verret, Rochester
1984-85—Steve Thomas, St. Catharines
1985-86—Ron Hextall, Hershey
1986-87—Brett Hull, Moncton
1987-88—Mike Richard, Binghamton
1988-89—Stephan Lebeau, Sherbrooke

## Eddie Shore Plaque
### Outstanding Defenseman

1958-59—Steve Kraftcheck, Rochester
1959-60—Larry Hillman, Providence
1960-61—Bob McCord, Springfield
1961-62—Kent Douglas, Springfield
1962-63—Marc Reaume, Hershey
1963-64—Ted Harris, Cleveland
1964-65—Al Arbour, Rochester
1965-66—Jim Morrison, Quebec
1966-67—Bob McCord, Pittsburgh
1967-68—Bill Needham, Cleveland
1968-69—Bob Blackburn, Buffalo
1969-70—Noel Price, Springfield
1970-71—Marshall Johnston, Cleveland
1971-72—Noel Price, Nova Scotia
1972-73—Ray McKay, Cincinnati
1973-74—Gordon Smith, Springfield
1974-75—Joe Zanussi, Providence
1975-76—Noel Price, Nova Scotia
1976-77—Brian Engblom, Nova Scotia
1977-78—Terry Murray, Maine
1978-79—Terry Murray, Maine
1979-80—Rick Vasko, Adirondack
1980-81—Craig Levie, Nova Scotia
1981-82—Dave Farrish, New Brunswick
1982-83—Greg Tebbutt, Baltimore
1983-84—Garry Lariviere, St. Catharines
1984-85—Richie Dunn, Binghamton
1985-86—Jim Wiemer, New Haven
1986-87—Brad Shaw, Binghamton
1987-88—Dave Fenyves, Hershey
1988-89—Dave Fenyves, Hershey

## Fred Hunt Memorial Award
### Sportsmanship, Determination and Dedication

1977-78—Blake Dunlop, Maine
1978-79—Bernie Johnston, Maine
1979-80—Norm Dube, Nova Scotia
1980-81—Tony Cassolato, Hershey
1981-82—Mike Kasczyki, New Brunswick
1982-83—Ross Yates, Binghamton
1983-84—Claude Larose, Sherbrooke
1984-85—Paul Gardner, Binghamton
1985-86—Steve Tsujiura, Maine
1986-87—Glenn Merkosky, Adirondack
1987-88—Bruce Boudreau, Springfield
1988-89—Murray Eaves, Adirondack

## Louis A. R. Pieri Memorial Award
### Top AHL Coach

| | |
|---|---|
| 1967-68—Vic Stasiuk, Quebec | 1979-80—Doug Gibson, Hershey |
| 1968-69—Frank Mathers, Hershey | 1980-81—Bob McCammon, Maine |
| 1969-70—Fred Shero, Buffalo | 1981-82—Orval Tessier, New Brunswick |
| 1970-71—Terry Reardon, Baltimore | 1982-83—Jacques Demers, Fredericton |
| 1971-72—Al MacNeil, Nova Scotia | 1983-84—Gene Ubriaco, Baltimore |
| 1972-73—Floyd Smith, Cincinnati | 1984-85—Bill Dineen, Adirondack |
| 1973-74—Don Cherry, Rochester | 1985-86—Bill Dineen, Adirondack |
| 1974-75—John Muckler, Providence | 1986-87—Larry Pleau, Binghamton |
| 1975-76—Chuck Hamilton, Hershey | 1987-88—John Paddock, Hershey |
| 1976-77—Al MacNeil, Nova Scotia | Mike Milbury, Maine (tie) |
| 1977-78—Bob McCammon, Maine | 1988-89—Tom McVie, Utica |
| 1978-79—Parker MacDonald, New Haven | |

### Baz Bastien Trophy
#### Coaches pick as top AHL Goalie

1983-84—Brian Ford, Fredericton
1984-85—Jon Casey, Baltimore
1985-86—Sam St. Laurent, Maine
1986-87—Mark Laforest, Adirondack
1987-88—Wendell Young, Hershey
1988-89—Randy Exelby, Sherbrooke

### Jack Butterfield Trophy
#### Calder Cup Playoffs MVP

1983-84—Bud Stefanski, Maine
1984-85—Brian Skrudland, Sherbrooke
1985-86—Tim Tookey, Hershey
1986-87—Dave Fenyves, Rochester
1987-88—Wendell Young, Hershey
1988-89—Sam St. Laurent, Adirondack

# AHL All-Time Championship Teams

| REGULAR SEASON | | | PLAYOFFS (Calder Cup) |
|---|---|---|---|
| Div. | Championship Team (Coach) | Year | Championship Team (Coach) |
| E | Philadelphia (Herb Gardiner) | 1936-37 | Syracuse Stars (E. Powers) |
| W | Syracuse (Eddie Powers) | | |
| E | Providence (Bun Cook) | 1937-38 | Providence Reds (Bun Cook) |
| W | Cleveland (Bill Cook) | | |
| E | Philadelphia (Herb Gardiner) | 1938-39 | Cleveland Barons (Bill Cook) |
| W | Hershey (Herb Mitchell) | | |
| E | Providence (Bun Cook) | 1939-40 | Providence Reds (Bun Cook) |
| W | Indianapolis (Herb Lewis) | | |
| E | Providence (Bun Cook) | 1940-41 | Cleveland Barons (Bill Cook) |
| W | Cleveland (Bill Cook) | | |
| E | Springfield (Johnny Mitchell) | 1941-42 | Indianapolis Caps (Herb Lewis) |
| W | Indianapolis (Herb Lewis) | | |
| | Hershey (Cooney Weiland) | 1942-43 | Buffalo Bisons (Art Chapman) |
| E | Hershey (Cooney Weiland) | 1943-44 | Buffalo Bisons (Art Chapman) |
| W | Cleveland (Bun Cook) | | |
| E | Buffalo (Art Chapman) | 1944-45 | Cleveland Barons (Bun Cook) |
| W | Cleveland (Bun Cook) | | |
| E | Buffalo (Frank Beisler) | 1945-46 | Buffalo Bisons (Frank Beisler) |
| W | Indianapolis (Earl Seibert) | | |
| E | Hershey (Don Penniston) | 1946-47 | Hershey Bears (Don Penniston) |
| W | Cleveland (Bun Cook) | | |
| E | Providence (Terry Reardon) | 1947-48 | Cleveland Barons (Bun Cook) |
| W | Cleveland (Bun Cook) | | |
| E | Providence (Terry Reardon) | 1948-49 | Providence Reds (Terry Reardon) |
| W | St. Louis (Ebbie Goodfellow) | | |
| E | Buffalo (Roy Goldsworthy) | 1949-50 | Indianapolis Caps (Ott Heller) |
| W | Cleveland (Bun Cook) | | |
| E | Buffalo (Roy Goldsworthy) | 1950-51 | Cleveland Barons (Bun Cook) |
| W | Cleveland (Bun Cook) | | |
| E | Hershey (John Crawford) | 1951-52 | Pittsburgh Hornets (King Clancy) |
| W | Pittsburgh (King Clancy) | | |
| | Cleveland (Bun Cook) | 1952-53 | Cleveland Barons (Bun Cook) |
| | Buffalo (Frank Eddolls) | 1953-54 | Cleveland Barons (Bun Cook) |
| | Pittsburgh (Howie Meeker) | 1954-55 | Pittsburgh Hornets (Howie Meeker) |

| REGULAR SEASON | | PLAYOFFS (Calder Cup) | |
|---|---|---|---|
| Div. | Championship Team (Coach) | Year | Championship Team (Coach) |
| | Providence (John Crawford) | 1955-56 | Providence Reds (John Crawford) |
| | Providence (John Crawford) | 1956-57 | Cleveland Barons (Jack Gordon) |
| | Hershey (Frank Mathers) | 1957-58 | Hershey Bears (Frank Mathers) |
| | Buffalo (Bobby Kirk) | 1958-59 | Hershey Bears (Frank Mathers) |
| | Springfield (Pat Egan) | 1959-60 | Springfield Indians (Pat Egan) |
| | Springfield (Pat Egan) | 1960-61 | Springfield Indians (Pat Egan) |
| E— | Springfield (Pat Egan) | 1961-62 | Springfield Indians (Pat Egan) |
| W— | Cleveland (Jack Gordon) | | |
| E— | Providence (Fern Flaman) | 1962-63 | Buffalo Bisons (Billy Reay) |
| W— | Buffalo (Billy Reay) | | |
| E— | Quebec (Floyd Curry) | 1963-64 | Cleveland Barons (Fred Glover) |
| W— | Pittsburgh (Vic Stasiuk) | | |
| E— | Quebec (Bernie Geoffrion) | 1964-65 | Rochester Americans (Joe Crozier) |
| W— | Rochester (Joe Crozier) | | |
| E— | Quebec (Bernie Geoffrion) | 1965-66 | Rochester Americans (Joe Crozier) |
| W— | Rochester (Joe Crozier) | | |
| E— | Hershey (Frank Mathers) | 1966-67 | Pittsburgh Hornets (Baz Bastien) |
| W— | Pittsburgh (Baz Bastien) | | |
| E— | Hershey (Frank Mathers) | 1967-68 | Rochester Americans (Joe Crozier) |
| W— | Rochester (Joe Crozier) | | |
| E— | Hershey (Frank Mathers) | 1968-69 | Hershey Bears (Frank Mathers) |
| W— | Buffalo (Fred Shero) | | |
| E— | Montreal (Al MacNeil) | 1969-70 | Buffalo Bisons (Fred Shero) |
| W— | Buffalo (Fred Shero) | | |
| E— | Providence (Larry Wilson) | 1970-71 | Springfield Kings (John Wilson) |
| W— | Baltimore (Terry Reardon) | | |
| E— | Boston (Armond Guidolin) | 1971-72 | Nova Scotia Voyageurs (Al MacNeil) |
| W— | Baltimore (Terry Reardon) | | |
| E— | Nova Scotia (Al MacNeil) | 1972-73 | Cincinnati Swords (Floyd Smith) |
| W— | Cincinnati (Floyd Smith) | | |
| N— | Rochester (Don Cherry) | 1973-74 | Hershey Bears (Chuck Hamilton) |
| S— | Baltimore (Terry Reardon) | | |
| N— | Providence (John Muckler) | 1974-75 | Springfield Indians (Ron Stewart) |
| S— | Virginia (Doug Barkley) | | |
| N— | Nova Scotia (Al MacNeil) | 1975-76 | Nova Scotia Voyageurs (Al MacNeil) |
| S— | Hershey (Chuck Hamilton) | | |
| | Nova Scotia (Al MacNeil) | 1976-77 | Nova Scotia Voyageurs (Al MacNeil) |
| N— | Maine (Bob McCammon) | 1977-78 | Maine Mariners (Bob McCammon) |
| S— | Rochester (Duane Rupp) | | |
| N— | Maine (Bob McCammon) | 1978-79 | Maine Mariners (Bob McCammon) |
| S— | New Haven (Parker MacDonald) | | |
| N— | New Brunswick (Crozier-Angotti) | 1979-80 | Hershey Bears (Doug Gibson) |
| S— | New Haven (Parker MacDonald) | | |
| N— | Maine (Bob McCammon) | 1980-81 | Adirondack Red Wings (Tom Webster, J. P. LeBlanc) |
| S— | Hershey (Bryan Murray) | | |
| N— | New Brunswick (Orval Tessier) | 1981-82 | New Brunswick (Orval Tessier) |
| S— | Binghamton (Larry Kish) | | |
| N— | Fredericton (Jacques Demers) | 1982-83 | Rochester (Mike Keenan) |
| S— | Rochester (Mike Keenan) | | |
| N— | Fredericton (Earl Jessiman) | 1983-84 | Maine (John Paddock) |
| S— | Baltimore (Gene Ubriaco) | | |
| N— | Maine (McVie-Paddock) | 1984-85 | Sherbrooke (Pierre Creamer) |
| S— | Binghamton (Larry Pleau) | | |
| N— | Adirondack (Bill Dineen) | 1985-86 | Adirondack (Bill Dineen) |
| S— | Hershey (John Paddock) | | |
| N— | Sherbrooke (Pierre Creamer) | 1986-87 | Rochester (John Van Boxmeer) |
| S— | Rochester (John Van Boxmeer)* | | |
| N— | Maine (Mike Milbury) | 1987-88 | Hershey (John Paddock) |
| S— | Hershey (John Paddock) | | |
| N— | Sherbrooke (Jean Hamel) | 1988-89 | Adirondack (Bill Dineen) |
| S— | Adirondack (Bill Dineen) | | |

*Rochester awarded division championship based on season series record.

# International Hockey League

(Organized, December 21, 1945)

Commissioner—N. Thomas Berry Jr.
3850 Priority Way
South Drive
Suite 104
Indianapolis, Ind. 46240
(317) 573-3888
FAX (317) 573-3880
Mike Meyers—Director of Information

## Flint Spirits
Governor—Don Chambers
General Manager—Don Waddell
Coach—Paul Theriault
Director of Public Relations—To be announced
Home Ice—I.M.A. Sports Arena (4,021)
Address—3501 Lapeer Road
Flint, Mich. 48503
Affiliation—New York Rangers
Phone— (313) 743-1780

## Fort Wayne Komets
Governor/General Manager—David Welker
Coach—Al Sims
P.R./Dir. of Marketing—Pete Mahlock
Home Ice—Allen County Memorial Coliseum (8,022)
Address—1010 Memorial Way, Suite 210
Fort Wayne, Ind. 46805
Affiliations—Quebec Nordiques, Washington Capitals
and Winnipeg Jets
Phone— (219) 484-7825

## Indianapolis Ice
Governor—Horn Chen
Director of Operations—Ray Compton
Coach—Darryl Sutter
Director of Marketing—Dave Paitson
Director of Public Relations—Brad Beery
Home Ice—Indiana State Fairgrounds Coliseum
Address—1202 East 38th Street
Indianapolis, Ind. 46205
Affiliation—Chicago Black Hawks
Phone— (317) 924-1234

## Kalamazoo Wings
Governor—Ted Parfet
Alt. Gov./Gen. Man.—Bill Inglis
Coach—John Marks
Director of Public Relations—Steve Doherty
Director of Broadcasting—Mike Miller
Home Ice—Wings Stadium (5,121)
Address—3620 Van Rick Dr.,
Kalamazoo, Mich. 49002
Affiliation—Minnesota North Stars
Phone— (616) 349-9772

## Milwaukee Admirals
Governor—Joseph E. Tierney Jr.
Alt. Gov./Gen. Man.—Phil Wittliff
Coach—Ron Lapointe
Dir. of Sales and Marketing—Mike Wojciechowski
Dir. of P.R./Communications—Doug Petitt
Home Ice—Bradley Center
Address—1001 North 4th Street
Milwaukee, Wis. 53203
Affiliation—Vancouver Canucks
Phone— (414) 225-2400

## Muskegon Lumberjacks
Governor and General Manager—Larry Gordon
Alternate Governor—John Snider
Coach—B.J. MacDonald
Director of Public Relations—Bob Heethuis
Director of Sales—Leo Hunstiger
Home Ice—L.C. Walker Sports Arena (5,061)
Address—470 W. Western Ave.
Muskegon, Mich. 49440
Affiliation—Pittsburgh Penguins
Phone— (616) 726-5058

## Peoria Rivermen
Governor—Bruce Saurs
General Manager—Denis Cyr
Coach—Wayne Thomas
Director of Public Relations—Brad Johnson
Home Ice—Peoria Civic Center (9,228)
Address—201 S.W. Jefferson
Peoria, Ill. 61602
Affiliation—St. Louis Blues
Phone— (309) 673-8900

## Phoenix Roadrunners
Governor—Lyle Abraham
General Manager—Adam Keller
Coach—Garry Unger
Director of Sales—Ian MacPhee
Director Public Relations—Chuck Badone
Home Ice—Veterans Memorial Coliseum (13,737)
Address—1826 West McDowell Road
Phoenix, Ariz. 85005
Affiliations—Buffalo Sabres, Edmonton Oilers and
Los Angeles Kings
Phone— (602) 340-0001

## Saginaw Hawks
Governor—Eugene Chardoul, M.D.
Gen. Man./Coach—Dennis Desrosiers
Dir. Mkt./P.R.—Jim Nightingale
Home Ice—Saginaw Civic Center (5,463)
Address—118 North Washington
Saginaw, Mich. 48607
Affiliation—To be announced
Phone— (517) 754-3940

## Salt Lake Golden Eagles
Governor—Art Teece
General Manager—Mike Runge
Coach—Bob Francis
Director of Marketing—Dale Borg
Director of Public Relations—Mark Kelly
Home Ice—Salt Palace (10,594)
Address—100 S.W. Temple
Salt Lake City, Utah 84101
Affiliation—Calgary Flames
Phone— (801) 521-6120

# 1988-89 Final IHL Standings

## East Division

|  | G. | W. | L. | T. | Pts. | GF. | GA. |
|---|---|---|---|---|---|---|---|
| Muskegon Lumberjacks | 82 | 57 | 18 | 7 | 121 | 433 | 308 |
| Saginaw Hawks | 82 | 46 | 26 | 10 | 102 | 378 | 294 |
| Fort Wayne Komets | 82 | 46 | 30 | 6 | 98 | 293 | 274 |
| Kalamazoo Wings | 82 | 39 | 36 | 7 | 85 | 345 | 350 |
| Flint Spirits | 82 | 22 | 54 | 6 | 50 | 287 | 428 |

## West Division

|  | G. | W. | L. | T. | Pts. | GF. | GA. |
|---|---|---|---|---|---|---|---|
| Salt Lake Golden Eagles | 82 | 56 | 22 | 4 | 116 | 369 | 294 |
| Milwaukee Admirals | 82 | 54 | 23 | 5 | 113 | 399 | 323 |
| Denver Rangers | 82 | 33 | 42 | 7 | 73 | 323 | 394 |
| Peoria Rivermen | 82 | 31 | 42 | 9 | 71 | 339 | 383 |
| Indianapolis Ice | 82 | 26 | 54 | 2 | 54 | 312 | 430 |

NOTE: O. (Overtime) column includes overtime losses and shootout losses (teams receive a point for either).

## Top 20 Scorers for the Leo P. Lamoureux Memorial Trophy

|  | Games | G. | A. | Pts. | Pen. |
|---|---|---|---|---|---|
| 1. Dave Michayluk, Muskegon | 80 | 50 | 72 | *122 | 84 |
| 2. Michel Mongeau, Flint | 82 | 41 | *76 | 117 | 57 |
| 3. Jeff Rohlicek, Milwaukee | 78 | 47 | 63 | 110 | 106 |
| 4. Mike Rucinski, Saginaw | 81 | 35 | 72 | 107 | 40 |
| 5. Simon Wheeldon, Denver | 74 | 50 | 56 | 106 | 77 |
| 6. Rich Chernomaz, Salt Lake | 81 | 33 | 68 | 101 | 122 |
| 7. Ron Handy, Indianapolis | 81 | 43 | 57 | 100 | 52 |
| 8. Mark Recchi, Muskegon | 63 | 50 | 49 | 99 | 86 |
| 9. Paul Ranheim, Salt Lake | 75 | *68 | 29 | 97 | 16 |
| 10. Jim Vesey, Peoria | 76 | 47 | 46 | 93 | 137 |
| 11. Scott Gruhl, Muskegon | 79 | 37 | 55 | 92 | 163 |
| 12. Peter Lappin, Salt Lake | 81 | 48 | 42 | 90 | 50 |
| 13. Randy Bucyk, Salt Lake | 79 | 28 | 59 | 87 | 24 |
| 14. Yves Heroux, Flint | 82 | 43 | 42 | 85 | 98 |
| 15. Dan Hodgson, Milwaukee | 47 | 27 | 55 | 82 | 47 |
| 16. Mitch Messier, Kalamazoo | 67 | 34 | 46 | 80 | 71 |
| Bruce Cassidy, Saginaw | 72 | 16 | 64 | 80 | 80 |
| 18. Randy Boyd, Milwaukee | 73 | 24 | 55 | 79 | 218 |
| 19. Steve Ludzik, Saginaw | 65 | 21 | 57 | 78 | 129 |
| 20. D'Arcy Norton, Kalamazoo | 75 | 39 | 38 | 77 | 79 |

## Denver Rangers

|  | Games | G. | A. | Pts. | Pen. |
|---|---|---|---|---|---|
| Simon Wheeldon | 74 | 50 | 56 | 106 | 77 |
| Kevin Miller | 55 | 29 | 47 | 76 | 19 |
| Paul Broten | 77 | 28 | 31 | 59 | 133 |
| Darren Turcotte | 40 | 21 | 28 | 49 | 32 |
| Mark Janssens | 38 | 19 | 19 | 38 | 104 |
| Rob Graham | 67 | 14 | 22 | 36 | 72 |
| Todd Elik | 28 | 20 | 15 | 35 | 22 |
| Barry Chyzowski | 69 | 12 | 21 | 33 | 48 |
| Jason Lafreniere | 24 | 10 | 19 | 29 | 17 |
| Jeff Bloemberg | 64 | 7 | 22 | 29 | 55 |
| Ron Shudra | 64 | 11 | 14 | 25 | 44 |
| Simon Gagne | 69 | 7 | 18 | 25 | 78 |
| Peter Laviolette | 57 | 6 | 19 | 25 | 120 |
| Brad Stepan | 55 | 13 | 11 | 24 | 112 |
| Ken Hammond | 38 | 5 | 18 | 23 | 24 |
| Michael Golden | 36 | 12 | 10 | 22 | 21 |
| Bret Walter | 47 | 12 | 10 | 22 | 41 |
| Jayson More | 62 | 7 | 15 | 22 | 138 |
| Stephane Brochu | 67 | 5 | 14 | 19 | 109 |
| Marcel Dionne | 9 | 0 | 13 | 13 | 6 |
| Craig Redmond | 10 | 0 | 13 | 13 | 6 |
| Jim Latos | 37 | 7 | 5 | 12 | 157 |
| Denis Larocque | 30 | 2 | 8 | 10 | 39 |
| Joe Paterson | 9 | 5 | 4 | 9 | 31 |
| Steve Nemeth | 11 | 5 | 2 | 7 | 8 |
| Chris McRae | 23 | 1 | 4 | 5 | 121 |
| Michael Boyce | 21 | 0 | 5 | 5 | 29 |
| Mike Richter (Goalie) | 57 | 0 | 5 | 5 | 8 |
| Jeff Crossman | 7 | 1 | 2 | 3 | 17 |
| John Ogrodnick | 3 | 2 | 0 | 2 | 0 |
| David Giacomin | 7 | 2 | 0 | 2 | 0 |
| Michael Hurlbut | 8 | 0 | 2 | 2 | 13 |
| Barry Nelson | 4 | 1 | 0 | 1 | 9 |
| Martin Bergeron | 1 | 0 | 1 | 1 | 0 |
| Daniel Lacroix | 2 | 0 | 1 | 1 | 0 |
| Don Mercier | 20 | 0 | 1 | 1 | 20 |
| Scott Brower, Flint (G.) | 5 | 0 | 0 | 0 | 0 |
| Denver (Goalie) | 19 | 0 | 1 | 1 | 0 |
| Totals | 24 | 0 | 1 | 1 | 0 |
| Rudy Poeschek | 2 | 0 | 0 | 0 | 6 |
| Daryl Seltenreich, Flint | 2 | 0 | 0 | 0 | 0 |
| Denver | 3 | 0 | 0 | 0 | 2 |
| Totals | 5 | 0 | 0 | 0 | 2 |
| Peter Fiorentino | 10 | 0 | 0 | 0 | 39 |
| Ron Scott (Goalie) | 18 | 0 | 0 | 0 | 0 |

## Flint Spirits

| | Games | G. | A. | Pts. | Pen. |
|---|---|---|---|---|---|
| Michel Mongeau | 82 | 41 | *76 | 117 | 57 |
| Yves Heroux | 82 | 43 | 42 | 85 | 98 |
| Mike Hoffman | 76 | 33 | 39 | 72 | 46 |
| Lonnie Loach, Saginaw | 32 | 7 | 6 | 13 | 27 |
| Flint | 41 | 22 | 26 | 48 | 30 |
| Totals | 73 | 29 | 32 | 61 | 57 |
| Peter Horachek | 63 | 10 | 22 | 32 | 37 |
| Troy Vollhoffer, Musk. | 2 | 0 | 0 | 0 | 9 |
| Flint | 63 | 6 | 23 | 29 | 186 |
| Totals | 65 | 6 | 23 | 29 | 195 |
| Glenn Mulvenna, Musk. | 11 | 3 | 2 | 5 | 0 |
| Flint | 32 | 9 | 14 | 23 | 12 |
| Totals | 43 | 12 | 16 | 28 | 12 |
| Brett MacDonald | 57 | 3 | 24 | 27 | 53 |
| Rob Bryden | 28 | 14 | 12 | 26 | 22 |
| Randy Taylor, Ind. | 44 | 2 | 15 | 17 | 31 |
| Flint | 31 | 2 | 6 | 8 | 11 |
| Totals | 75 | 4 | 21 | 25 | 42 |
| Mario Chitaroni | 21 | 10 | 11 | 21 | 59 |
| Graeme Bonar, Ind. | 38 | 11 | 8 | 19 | 19 |
| Flint | 3 | 1 | 0 | 1 | 0 |
| Totals | 41 | 12 | 8 | 20 | 19 |
| Ken Spangler | 37 | 4 | 15 | 19 | 97 |
| Doug Wickenheiser | 21 | 9 | 7 | 16 | 18 |
| Shawn Whitham | 17 | 3 | 13 | 16 | 18 |
| Dan Gratton | 20 | 5 | 9 | 14 | 8 |
| Stephane Giguere | 53 | 4 | 10 | 14 | 80 |
| Darwin McC'tch'n, Ind. | 34 | 2 | 6 | 8 | 99 |
| Flint | 37 | 2 | 4 | 6 | 89 |
| Totals | 71 | 4 | 10 | 14 | 188 |
| Mark Vichorek | 44 | 4 | 9 | 13 | 47 |
| Maurice Mansi | 16 | 2 | 11 | 13 | 2 |
| Gerrard Waslen | 13 | 4 | 7 | 11 | 7 |
| Glen Goodall | 9 | 5 | 4 | 9 | 4 |
| Jim Andonoff | 34 | 1 | 7 | 8 | 25 |
| Rick Boyd, Ind. | 27 | 2 | 1 | 3 | 113 |
| Flint | 27 | 4 | 0 | 4 | 73 |
| Totals | 54 | 6 | 1 | 7 | 186 |
| Trent Kaese | 9 | 2 | 3 | 5 | 61 |
| Bob Kennedy | 24 | 2 | 3 | 5 | 10 |
| Steve Shaunessy, Musk. | 11 | 0 | 2 | 2 | 40 |
| Flint | 21 | 1 | 2 | 3 | 81 |
| Totals | 32 | 1 | 4 | 5 | 121 |
| John Devereaux | 11 | 3 | 1 | 4 | 11 |
| Tim Bean | 3 | 1 | 3 | 4 | 4 |
| Chris Panek | 8 | 2 | 1 | 3 | 9 |
| Bill Whitfield | 12 | 1 | 2 | 3 | 2 |
| Mark Dumont | 4 | 1 | 1 | 2 | 0 |
| Mitch Malloy | 5 | 1 | 1 | 2 | 21 |
| Terry McCutcheon | 5 | 1 | 1 | 2 | 2 |
| Scott Taylor | 7 | 0 | 2 | 2 | 22 |
| Gary Kruzich (Goalie) | 30 | 0 | 2 | 2 | 8 |
| Keith Gretzky | 2 | 0 | 1 | 1 | 0 |
| Paul Kelly | 4 | 0 | 1 | 1 | 0 |
| Kent Hulst | 7 | 0 | 1 | 1 | 4 |
| Jay Starke | 12 | 0 | 1 | 1 | 14 |
| Garry Garland, Denver | 11 | 0 | 0 | 0 | 57 |
| Flint | 4 | 0 | 1 | 1 | 30 |
| Totals | 15 | 0 | 1 | 1 | 87 |
| Jack Bowkus | 1 | 0 | 0 | 0 | 0 |
| Peter Buckeridge | 1 | 0 | 0 | 0 | 0 |
| Bill Huard | 1 | 0 | 0 | 0 | 2 |
| Frank Lattuca | 1 | 0 | 0 | 0 | 2 |
| Chris Mills | 1 | 0 | 0 | 0 | 0 |
| Bob Wensley | 1 | 0 | 0 | 0 | 0 |
| Dwight Mullins | 2 | 0 | 0 | 0 | 15 |
| Doug Stromback | 2 | 0 | 0 | 0 | 0 |
| Victor Posa | 3 | 0 | 0 | 0 | 21 |
| Alex Daviault | 5 | 0 | 0 | 0 | 12 |
| Kenton Rein (Goalie) | 8 | 0 | 0 | 0 | 5 |
| Dean Anderson (Goalie) | 14 | 0 | 0 | 0 | 6 |
| Mark Reimer (Goalie) | 17 | 0 | 0 | 0 | 0 |

## Fort Wayne Komets

| | Games | G. | A. | Pts. | Pen. |
|---|---|---|---|---|---|
| Mike McNeill | 75 | 27 | 35 | 62 | 12 |
| Keith Miller | 54 | 35 | 25 | 60 | 13 |
| Byron Lomow | 81 | 22 | 35 | 57 | 207 |
| Colin Chin | 76 | 21 | 35 | 56 | 71 |
| Steve Hollett | 79 | 27 | 21 | 48 | 39 |
| Joe Stefan | 61 | 17 | 29 | 46 | 28 |
| Al Sims | 61 | 7 | 30 | 37 | 32 |
| Brian Dowd | 62 | 9 | 24 | 33 | 39 |
| Claude Dumas | 71 | 12 | 20 | 32 | 40 |
| Brian McKee | 47 | 8 | 22 | 30 | 42 |
| Craig Channell | 79 | 5 | 25 | 30 | 168 |
| Craig Endean | 34 | 10 | 18 | 28 | 0 |
| Brian Hannon | 27 | 12 | 11 | 23 | 6 |
| Bob Fowler | 67 | 9 | 12 | 21 | 62 |
| Derek Ray | 45 | 12 | 8 | 20 | 72 |
| Guy Jacob, Flint | 25 | 9 | 6 | 15 | 38 |
| Fort Wayne | 13 | 2 | 2 | 4 | 24 |
| Totals | 38 | 11 | 8 | 19 | 62 |
| Ron Pessetti | 57 | 3 | 14 | 17 | 29 |
| Don Martin | 40 | 11 | 5 | 16 | 123 |
| Jim Burton | 21 | 3 | 13 | 16 | 8 |
| Mike Natyshuk | 48 | 5 | 9 | 14 | 95 |
| Martin Burgers | 63 | 4 | 7 | 11 | 100 |
| Carey Lucyk | 76 | 1 | 10 | 11 | 94 |
| Tony Camazzola | 12 | 2 | 3 | 5 | 26 |
| David Wensley | 11 | 1 | 2 | 3 | 4 |
| Len Neilsen | 7 | 1 | 1 | 2 | 2 |
| Tim Hrynewich, Flint | 5 | 0 | 1 | 1 | 4 |
| Fort Wayne | 4 | 0 | 1 | 1 | 8 |
| Totals | 9 | 0 | 2 | 2 | 12 |
| Rick Knickle (Goalie) | 47 | 0 | 1 | 1 | 2 |
| Steve Averill (Goalie) | 1 | 0 | 0 | 0 | 0 |
| Mike Lekun | 1 | 0 | 0 | 0 | 2 |
| Len Soccio | 1 | 0 | 0 | 0 | 17 |
| Bob Curtis | 2 | 0 | 0 | 0 | 2 |
| Al Loring (Goalie) | 2 | 0 | 0 | 0 | 0 |
| S. Beauregard (G.) | 16 | 0 | 0 | 0 | 0 |
| Bob Essensa (Goalie) | 22 | 0 | 0 | 0 | 0 |

## Indianapolis Ice

| | Games | G. | A. | Pts. | Pen. |
|---|---|---|---|---|---|
| Ron Handy | 81 | 43 | 57 | 100 | 52 |
| Brent Sapergia | 52 | 43 | 33 | 76 | 246 |
| Bob Lakso | 82 | 38 | 34 | 72 | 10 |
| Rick Barkovich | 78 | 32 | 35 | 67 | 81 |
| Paul Houck | 81 | 22 | 37 | 59 | 51 |
| Mark Teevens | 78 | 30 | 22 | 52 | 51 |
| Alain Lemieux | 29 | 18 | 26 | 44 | 90 |
| Glenn Johannesen | 76 | 18 | 23 | 41 | 235 |
| Shane Doyle | 62 | 4 | 36 | 40 | 224 |
| Tony Horacek | 43 | 11 | 13 | 24 | 138 |
| Dwaine Hutton, Flint | 14 | 5 | 5 | 10 | 22 |
| Indianapolis | 31 | 8 | 5 | 13 | 85 |
| Totals | 45 | 13 | 10 | 23 | 107 |
| Brad Beck | 34 | 4 | 15 | 19 | 103 |
| Mike Murray | 17 | 5 | 11 | 16 | 2 |

|  | Games | G. | A. | Pts. | Pen. |
|---|---|---|---|---|---|
| Jimmy Mann | 38 | 5 | 10 | 15 | 275 |
| Gary Stewart, Milw. | 1 | 0 | 0 | 0 | 2 |
| Indianapolis | 48 | 1 | 14 | 15 | 103 |
| Totals | 49 | 1 | 14 | 15 | 105 |
| Tom Karalis, Flint | 38 | 1 | 6 | 7 | 170 |
| Indianapolis | 26 | 0 | 8 | 8 | 132 |
| Totals | 64 | 1 | 14 | 15 | 302 |
| Scott Clements | 23 | 2 | 6 | 8 | 35 |
| John Blessman | 31 | 2 | 5 | 7 | 60 |
| Dave Allison | 34 | 0 | 7 | 7 | 105 |
| Chris McSorley | 39 | 2 | 4 | 6 | 222 |
| Duncan MacPhearson | 33 | 1 | 4 | 5 | 23 |
| Todd Carlile | 4 | 0 | 5 | 5 | 8 |
| Bruce Rendall | 15 | 2 | 2 | 4 | 9 |
| Kurt Lackton | 9 | 1 | 2 | 3 | 11 |
| Mike Vellucci | 12 | 1 | 2 | 3 | 43 |
| Don Perkins | 15 | 0 | 3 | 3 | 8 |
| Don Herczeg, Denver | 8 | 0 | 0 | 0 | 53 |
| Indianapolis | 15 | 0 | 3 | 3 | 52 |
| Totals | 23 | 0 | 3 | 3 | 105 |
| Alan Perry (Goalie) | 47 | 0 | 3 | 3 | 29 |
| Doug Dadswell, S.L. (G.) | 32 | 0 | 2 | 2 | 10 |
| Indianapolis (G.) | 24 | 0 | 1 | 1 | 16 |
| Totals | 56 | 0 | 3 | 3 | 26 |
| Mark LaForge | 14 | 0 | 2 | 2 | 138 |
| Geoff Benic | 10 | 1 | 0 | 1 | 51 |
| Kerry Clarke | 3 | 0 | 1 | 1 | 12 |
| Dave Hanson | 3 | 0 | 1 | 1 | 9 |
| Shawn Byram | 1 | 0 | 0 | 0 | 2 |
| Doug Weiss | 1 | 0 | 0 | 0 | 0 |
| Bob Bilton | 2 | 0 | 0 | 0 | 0 |
| Scott Johnson | 2 | 0 | 0 | 0 | 2 |
| Tim Hoover | 3 | 0 | 0 | 0 | 2 |
| Jaime McKinley | 4 | 0 | 0 | 0 | 5 |
| Ross McKay (Goalie) | 5 | 0 | 0 | 0 | 0 |
| Jocelyn Perreault (G.) | 5 | 0 | 0 | 0 | 4 |
| Marc D'Amour (Goalie) | 6 | 0 | 0 | 0 | 0 |
| Kevin Herom | 7 | 0 | 0 | 0 | 21 |

## Kalamazoo Wings

|  | Games | G. | A. | Pts. | Pen. |
|---|---|---|---|---|---|
| Mitch Messier | 67 | 34 | 46 | 80 | 71 |
| D'Arcy Norton | 75 | 39 | 38 | 77 | 79 |
| Steve Gotaas, Musk. | 19 | 9 | 16 | 25 | 34 |
| Kalamazoo | 30 | 24 | 22 | 46 | 12 |
| Totals | 49 | 33 | 38 | 71 | 46 |
| Ken Hodge | 72 | 26 | 45 | 71 | 34 |
| Kevin Evans | 54 | 22 | 32 | 54 | 328 |
| Mike McHugh | 70 | 17 | 29 | 46 | 89 |
| Wally Schreiber, Ft.W. | 32 | 15 | 16 | 31 | 51 |
| Kalamazoo | 5 | 5 | 7 | 12 | 2 |
| Totals | 37 | 20 | 23 | 43 | 53 |
| Warren Babe | 62 | 18 | 24 | 42 | 102 |
| Paul Jerrard, Denver | 2 | 1 | 1 | 2 | 21 |
| Kalamazoo | 68 | 15 | 25 | 40 | 195 |
| Totals | 70 | 16 | 26 | 42 | 216 |
| Emanuel Viveiros | 54 | 11 | 29 | 40 | 37 |
| Scott McCrady | 73 | 8 | 29 | 37 | 169 |
| Larry Bernard, Denver | 21 | 4 | 5 | 9 | 44 |
| Kalamazoo | 45 | 9 | 16 | 25 | 47 |
| Totals | 66 | 13 | 21 | 34 | 91 |
| Dean Kolstad | 51 | 10 | 23 | 33 | 91 |
| Mike Hiltner, Ft. W. | 2 | 0 | 0 | 0 | 0 |
| Kalamazoo | 52 | 15 | 17 | 32 | 46 |
| Totals | 54 | 15 | 17 | 32 | 46 |
| Don Barber | 39 | 14 | 17 | 31 | 23 |

|  | Games | G. | A. | Pts. | Pen. |
|---|---|---|---|---|---|
| Steve Harrison, Flint | 31 | 4 | 16 | 20 | 30 |
| Kalamazoo | 16 | 4 | 7 | 11 | 8 |
| Totals | 47 | 8 | 23 | 31 | 38 |
| Scott Robinson | 49 | 14 | 16 | 30 | 127 |
| Rob Zettler | 80 | 5 | 21 | 26 | 79 |
| Mike Berger | 67 | 9 | 16 | 25 | 96 |
| Joe Lockwood | 49 | 14 | 10 | 24 | 27 |
| Neil Wilkinson | 39 | 5 | 15 | 20 | 96 |
| Randy Smith | 23 | 4 | 9 | 13 | 2 |
| Stephane Roy | 20 | 5 | 4 | 9 | 27 |
| Brent Jarrett | 12 | 1 | 8 | 9 | 8 |
| Gord Dineen | 25 | 2 | 6 | 8 | 49 |
| Link Gaetz | 37 | 3 | 4 | 7 | 192 |
| David Schofield | 24 | 1 | 6 | 7 | 30 |
| Dennis Maruk | 5 | 1 | 5 | 6 | 4 |
| Scott Bjugstad | 4 | 5 | 0 | 5 | 4 |
| Larry Dyck (Goalie) | 41 | 0 | 4 | 4 | 18 |
| Jordon Fois | 9 | 1 | 0 | 1 | 0 |
| Dave Gagner | 1 | 0 | 1 | 1 | 4 |
| John Blue (Goalie) | 17 | 0 | 1 | 1 | 4 |
| Jarmo Myllys (Goalie) | 30 | 0 | 1 | 1 | 4 |
| Eddie Courtenay | 2 | 0 | 0 | 0 | 0 |
| Don Beaupre (Goalie) | 3 | 0 | 0 | 0 | 0 |
| Kirk Tomlinson | 3 | 0 | 0 | 0 | 12 |
| Mark Tinordi | 10 | 0 | 0 | 0 | 35 |

## Milwaukee Admirals

|  | Games | G. | A. | Pts. | Pen. |
|---|---|---|---|---|---|
| Jeff Rohlicek | 78 | 47 | 63 | 110 | 106 |
| Dan Hodgson | 47 | 27 | 55 | 82 | 47 |
| Randy Boyd | 73 | 24 | 55 | 79 | 218 |
| John LeBlanc | 61 | 39 | 31 | 70 | 42 |
| Paul Lawless | 53 | 30 | 35 | 65 | 58 |
| Jay Mazur | 73 | 33 | 31 | 64 | 86 |
| Marc Crawford | 53 | 23 | 30 | 53 | 166 |
| Ian Kidd | 76 | 13 | 40 | 53 | 124 |
| Steve Johnson | 64 | 18 | 34 | 52 | 37 |
| Ernie Vargas | 61 | 16 | 35 | 51 | 89 |
| Ron Stern | 45 | 19 | 23 | 42 | 280 |
| Carl Valimont | 79 | 4 | 33 | 37 | 56 |
| Peter Bakovic | 40 | 16 | 14 | 30 | 211 |
| Todd Hawkins | 63 | 12 | 14 | 26 | 307 |
| Claude Vilgrain | 23 | 9 | 13 | 22 | 26 |
| Keith Street | 40 | 10 | 11 | 21 | 22 |
| Dan Woodley | 30 | 9 | 12 | 21 | 48 |
| Curtis Hunt | 65 | 3 | 17 | 20 | 226 |
| Tim Molle | 76 | 7 | 12 | 19 | 338 |
| Dave Saunders | 21 | 6 | 12 | 18 | 21 |
| Andy Gribble, Flint | 14 | 1 | 3 | 4 | 4 |
| Milwaukee | 27 | 2 | 8 | 10 | 2 |
| Totals | 41 | 3 | 11 | 14 | 6 |
| Jaime Husgen | 22 | 2 | 12 | 14 | 42 |
| Jose Charbonneau | 13 | 8 | 5 | 13 | 46 |
| Jim Agnew | 47 | 2 | 10 | 12 | 181 |
| Tim Lenardon | 15 | 6 | 5 | 11 | 27 |
| Ken Berry | 5 | 4 | 4 | 8 | 2 |
| Rob Murphy | 8 | 4 | 2 | 6 | 4 |
| Robin Bartel | 26 | 1 | 5 | 6 | 59 |
| Mike MacWilliam, Flint | 18 | 0 | 0 | 0 | 92 |
| Milwaukee | 6 | 1 | 1 | 2 | 28 |
| Totals | 24 | 1 | 1 | 2 | 120 |
| Troy Gamble (Goalie) | 42 | 0 | 2 | 2 | 27 |
| Peter DeBoer | 2 | 0 | 1 | 1 | 0 |
| Steve Veilleux | 1 | 0 | 0 | 0 | 0 |
| Darren Jensen (Goalie) | 11 | 0 | 0 | 0 | 4 |
| Frank Caprice (Goalie) | 39 | 0 | 0 | 0 | 2 |

## Muskegon Lumberjacks

|  | Games | G. | A. | Pts. | Pen. |
|---|---|---|---|---|---|
| Dave Michayluk | 80 | 50 | 72 | *122 | 84 |
| Mark Recchi | 63 | 50 | 49 | 99 | 86 |
| Scott Gruhl | 79 | 37 | 55 | 92 | 163 |
| Lee Giffin | 63 | 30 | 44 | 74 | 93 |
| Perry Ganchar | 70 | 39 | 34 | 73 | 114 |
| Dave McIlwain | 46 | 37 | 35 | 72 | 51 |
| Brad Aitken | 74 | 35 | 30 | 65 | 139 |
| Kevin Stevens | 45 | 24 | 41 | 65 | 113 |
| Jock Callander | 48 | 25 | 39 | 64 | 40 |
| Todd Charlesworth | 74 | 10 | 53 | 63 | 85 |
| Jim Paek | 80 | 3 | 54 | 57 | 96 |
| Mitch Wilson | 61 | 16 | 34 | 50 | 382 |
| Jeff Daniels | 58 | 21 | 21 | 42 | 58 |
| Dave Goertz | 74 | 1 | 32 | 33 | 102 |
| Dan Frawley | 24 | 12 | 16 | 28 | 35 |
| Mike Mersch, Flint | 55 | 5 | 20 | 25 | 101 |
| Muskegon | 16 | 0 | 2 | 2 | 26 |
| Totals | 71 | 5 | 22 | 27 | 127 |
| Doug Hobson | 62 | 5 | 17 | 22 | 82 |
| Tim Tookey | 18 | 7 | 14 | 21 | 7 |
| Mark Kachowski | 57 | 8 | 8 | 16 | 167 |
| Kevin MacDonald | 64 | 2 | 13 | 15 | 190 |
| Richard Zemlak, Kal. | 2 | 1 | 3 | 4 | 22 |
| Muskegon | 18 | 5 | 4 | 9 | 55 |
| Totals | 20 | 6 | 7 | 13 | 77 |
| Pat Mayer | 56 | 0 | 13 | 13 | 314 |
| Chris Dahlquist | 10 | 3 | 6 | 9 | 14 |
| Tom Pratt, Flint | 22 | 1 | 2 | 3 | 38 |
| Muskegon | 14 | 1 | 3 | 4 | 15 |
| Totals | 36 | 2 | 5 | 7 | 53 |
| Bruce Racine (Goalie) | 51 | 0 | 5 | 5 | 2 |
| Jeff Waver | 3 | 0 | 1 | 1 | 0 |
| Frank Pietrangelo (G.) | 13 | 0 | 1 | 1 | 2 |
| Jeff Cooper, Ind. (G.) | 9 | 0 | 1 | 1 | 2 |
| Saginaw (Goalie) | 4 | 0 | 0 | 0 | 0 |
| Muskegon (Goalie) | 7 | 0 | 0 | 0 | 0 |
| Totals | 20 | 0 | 1 | 1 | 2 |
| Wendell Young (Goalie) | 2 | 0 | 0 | 0 | 0 |

## Peoria Rivermen

|  | Games | G. | A. | Pts. | Pen. |
|---|---|---|---|---|---|
| Jim Vesey | 76 | 47 | 46 | 93 | 137 |
| Peter Douris | 81 | 28 | 41 | 69 | 32 |
| Brad McCaughey | 71 | 30 | 38 | 68 | 14 |
| Dave Lowry | 58 | 31 | 35 | 66 | 45 |
| David Thomlinson | 64 | 27 | 29 | 56 | 154 |
| Shane MacEachern | 73 | 17 | 37 | 54 | 83 |
| Toby Ducolon | 73 | 17 | 33 | 50 | 58 |
| Scott Paluch | 81 | 10 | 39 | 49 | 92 |
| Wayne Gagne | 64 | 8 | 41 | 49 | 58 |
| Terry MacLean | 73 | 18 | 30 | 48 | 46 |
| Scott Harlow | 45 | 16 | 26 | 42 | 22 |
| Dominic Lavoie | 69 | 11 | 31 | 42 | 98 |
| Marc Saumier, Flint | 17 | 2 | 5 | 7 | 62 |
| Peoria | 41 | 12 | 12 | 24 | 204 |
| Totals | 58 | 14 | 17 | 31 | 266 |
| Cliff Ronning | 12 | 11 | 20 | 31 | 8 |
| Darin Smith | 62 | 13 | 17 | 30 | 127 |
| Glen Featherstone | 37 | 5 | 19 | 24 | 97 |
| Kelly Chase | 38 | 14 | 7 | 21 | 278 |
| Phil DeGaetano | 31 | 4 | 12 | 16 | 55 |
| Darren Taylor | 40 | 6 | 6 | 12 | 149 |
| Tony Twist | 67 | 3 | 8 | 11 | 312 |
| Lyle Odelein | 36 | 2 | 8 | 10 | 116 |
| Craig Coxe | 8 | 2 | 7 | 9 | 38 |
| Mike Wolak, Flint | 2 | 0 | 1 | 1 | 4 |
| Peoria | 8 | 2 | 4 | 6 | 16 |
| Totals | 10 | 2 | 5 | 7 | 20 |
| Tim Bothwell | 14 | 0 | 7 | 7 | 14 |
| Rob Robinson | 11 | 2 | 0 | 2 | 6 |
| Kevin Miehm | 3 | 1 | 1 | 2 | 0 |
| Ron Flockhart | 2 | 0 | 2 | 2 | 0 |
| Robert Dirk | 22 | 0 | 2 | 2 | 54 |
| Darrell May (Goalie) | 52 | 0 | 2 | 2 | 24 |
| Rob Whistle | 4 | 0 | 1 | 1 | 4 |
| Marty Raus | 7 | 0 | 0 | 0 | 21 |
| Ned Desmond | 9 | 0 | 0 | 0 | 17 |
| Robert Dumas | 10 | 0 | 0 | 0 | 51 |
| Pat Jablonski (Goalie) | 35 | 0 | 0 | 0 | 10 |

## Saginaw Hawks

|  | Games | G. | A. | Pts. | Pen. |
|---|---|---|---|---|---|
| Mike Rucinski | 81 | 35 | 72 | 107 | 40 |
| Bruce Cassidy | 72 | 16 | 64 | 80 | 80 |
| Steve Ludzik | 65 | 21 | 57 | 78 | 129 |
| Jari Torkki | 72 | 30 | 42 | 72 | 22 |
| Bill Gardner | 74 | 27 | 45 | 72 | 10 |
| Mike Stapleton | 69 | 21 | 47 | 68 | 162 |
| Sean Williams | 77 | 32 | 27 | 59 | 75 |
| Bill Watson | 42 | 26 | 24 | 50 | 18 |
| Mario Doyon | 71 | 16 | 32 | 48 | 69 |
| Dave Mackey | 57 | 22 | 23 | 45 | 223 |
| Guy Phillips | 62 | 20 | 17 | 37 | 31 |
| Mike Hudson | 30 | 15 | 17 | 32 | 10 |
| Brian Noonan | 19 | 18 | 13 | 31 | 36 |
| Warren Rychel | 50 | 15 | 14 | 29 | 226 |
| Kent Paynter | 69 | 12 | 14 | 26 | 148 |
| Everett Sanipass | 23 | 9 | 12 | 21 | 76 |
| Dale Marquette | 46 | 11 | 8 | 19 | 35 |
| Marty Nanne | 36 | 4 | 10 | 14 | 47 |
| Mark Kurzawski | 75 | 2 | 11 | 13 | 71 |
| Gary Moscaluk | 68 | 0 | 12 | 12 | 108 |
| Bob Murray | 18 | 3 | 7 | 10 | 14 |
| Jim Playfair | 23 | 3 | 6 | 9 | 73 |
| Wayne Van Dorp | 11 | 4 | 3 | 7 | 60 |
| Mark Paterson | 17 | 1 | 3 | 4 | 42 |
| Ryan McGill | 8 | 2 | 0 | 2 | 12 |
| Ed Belfour (Goalie) | 29 | 0 | 1 | 1 | 47 |
| Ray LeBlanc, Flint (G.) | 15 | 0 | 0 | 0 | 8 |
| Saginaw (Goalie) | 29 | 0 | 1 | 1 | 6 |
| Totals | 44 | 0 | 1 | 1 | 14 |
| Darren Pang (Goalie) | 2 | 0 | 0 | 0 | 0 |
| Dan Vincelette | 2 | 0 | 0 | 0 | 14 |
| Jimmy Waite (Goalie) | 5 | 0 | 0 | 0 | 0 |
| Chris Clifford (Goalie) | 7 | 0 | 0 | 0 | 0 |
| John Reid, Ind. (Goalie) | 5 | 0 | 0 | 0 | 12 |
| Saginaw (Goalie) | 12 | 0 | 0 | 0 | 17 |
| Totals | 17 | 0 | 0 | 0 | 29 |

## Salt Lake Golden Eagles

|  | Games | G. | A. | Pts. | Pen. |
|---|---|---|---|---|---|
| Rich Chernomaz | 81 | 33 | 68 | 101 | 122 |
| Paul Ranheim | 75 | *68 | 29 | 97 | 16 |
| Peter Lappin | 81 | 48 | 42 | 90 | 50 |
| Randy Bucyk | 79 | 28 | 59 | 87 | 24 |
| Jim Johannson | 82 | 35 | 40 | 75 | 87 |
| Theoren Fleury | 40 | 37 | 37 | 74 | 81 |
| Marc Bureau | 76 | 28 | 36 | 64 | 119 |
| Dave Reierson | 76 | 7 | 46 | 53 | 70 |

|  | Games | G. | A. | Pts. | Pen. |  | Games | G. | A. | Pts. | Pen. |
|---|---|---|---|---|---|---|---|---|---|---|---|
| Rick Lessard | 76 | 10 | 42 | 52 | 239 | Brian Glynn | 31 | 3 | 10 | 13 | 105 |
| Martin Simard | 71 | 13 | 15 | 28 | 221 | Doug Clarke | 35 | 5 | 7 | 12 | 20 |
| Stu Grimson | 72 | 9 | 18 | 27 | *397 | Jeff Wenaas | 17 | 2 | 8 | 10 | 6 |
| Rick Hayward | 72 | 4 | 20 | 24 | 313 | Kevin Grant | 3 | 0 | 1 | 1 | 5 |
| Jim Leavins | 25 | 8 | 13 | 21 | 14 | Wayne Cowley (Goalie) | 29 | 0 | 1 | 1 | 12 |
| Chris Biotti | 57 | 6 | 14 | 20 | 44 | S. Guenette, Musk. (G.) | 10 | 0 | 0 | 0 | 2 |
| Ken Sabourin | 74 | 2 | 18 | 20 | 197 | Salt Lake (Goalie) | 30 | 0 | 1 | 1 | 26 |
| Mark Holmes | 52 | 6 | 12 | 18 | 46 | Totals | 40 | 0 | 1 | 1 | 28 |
| Shane Churla | 32 | 3 | 13 | 16 | 278 | Ron Petranella (Goalie) | 1 | 0 | 0 | 0 | 0 |
| Michael Dark | 36 | 3 | 12 | 15 | 57 | Bob Bodak | 4 | 0 | 0 | 0 | 2 |
| Doug Pickell | 47 | 7 | 6 | 13 | 79 |  |  |  |  |  |  |

## Complete IHL Goaltending

|  | Games | Mins. | Goals | SO. | Avg. |
|---|---|---|---|---|---|
| Mike Richter | *57 | 3031 | 217(7) | 1 | 4.30 |
| Ron Scott | 18 | 990 | 79(3) | 0 | 4.79 |
| Scott Brower (a) | 20 | 938 | 82(1) | 0 | 5.25 |
| Shootout losses |  |  | 5 |  |  |
| Denver Totals | 82 | 4959 | 394 | 1 | 4.77 |
| Kenton Rein | 8 | 439 | 29 | 0 | 3.96 |
| Ray LeBlanc (b) | 15 | 852 | 67(1) | 0 | 4.72 |
| Gary Kruzich | 30 | 1637 | 132(2) | 1 | 4.84 |
| Mark Reimer | 17 | 1022 | 83 | 0 | 4.87 |
| Scott Brower (a) | 5 | 235 | 22 | 0 | 5.62 |
| Dean Anderson | 16 | 770 | 82(4) | 1 | 6.39 |
| Shootout losses |  |  | 6 |  |  |
| Flint Totals | 82 | 4955 | 428 | 2 | 5.18 |
| Stephane Beauregard | 16 | 830 | 43(2) | 0 | 3.10 |
| Rick Knickle | 47 | 2719 | 141(2) | 1 | 3.11 |
| Bob Essensa | 22 | 1287 | 70(1) | 0 | 3.26 |
| Steve Averill | 1 | 65 | 5 | 0 | 4.61 |
| Al Loring | 2 | 83 | 8 | 0 | 5.78 |
| Shootout losses |  |  | 2 |  |  |
| Fort Wayne Totals | 82 | 4984 | 274 | 1 | 3.30 |
| Marc D'Amour | 6 | 324 | 20(1) | 0 | 3.70 |
| Jeff Cooper (c) | 9 | 491 | 32(1) | 0 | 3.91 |
| John Reid (d) | 5 | 244 | 16 | 0 | 3.93 |
| Alan Perry | 47 | 2266 | 195(1) | 0 | 5.16 |
| Ross McKay | 5 | 187 | 18(1) | 0 | 5.78 |
| Doug Dadswell (e) | 24 | 1207 | 122 | 0 | 6.06 |
| Jocelyn Perreault | 5 | 214 | 22 | 0 | 6.17 |
| Shootout losses |  |  | 1 |  |  |
| Indianapolis Totals | 82 | 4933 | 430 | 0 | 5.23 |
| Don Beaupre | 3 | 179 | 9 | 1 | 3.02 |
| Jarmo Myllys | 28 | 1523 | 93(2) | 0 | 3.66 |
| John Blue | 17 | 970 | 69(1) | 0 | 4.27 |
| Larry Dyck | 42 | 2308 | 168(4) | 0 | 4.37 |
| Shootout losses |  |  | 4 |  |  |
| Kalamazoo Totals | 82 | 4980 | 350 | 1 | 4.22 |
| Troy Gamble | 42 | 2198 | 138 | 0 | 3.77 |
| Darren Jensen | 11 | 555 | 36(1) | 0 | 3.89 |
| Frank Caprice | 39 | 2204 | 143(2) | 2 | 3.89 |
| Shootout losses |  |  | 3 |  |  |
| Milwaukee Totals | 82 | 4957 | 323 | 2 | 3.91 |
| Frank Pietrangelo | 13 | 760 | 38 | 1 | 3.00 |
| Wendell Young | 2 | 125 | 7 | 0 | 3.36 |
| Bruce Racine | 51 | *3039 | 184(2) | *3 | 3.63 |
| Steve Guenette (f) | 10 | 597 | 39(1) | 0 | 3.92 |
| Jeff Cooper (c) | 7 | 428 | 31 | 0 | 4.35 |
| Shootout losses |  |  | 6 |  |  |
| Muskegon Totals | 82 | 4949 | 308 | 4 | 3.73 |
| Darrell May | 52 | 2908 | 202(6) | 0 | 4.17 |
| Pat Jablonski | 35 | 2051 | 163(4) | 1 | 4.77 |
| Shootout losses |  |  | 8 |  |  |
| Peoria Totals | 82 | 4959 | 383 | 1 | 4.63 |

|  | Games | Mins. | Goals | SO. | Avg. |
|---|---|---|---|---|---|
| Jimmy Waite | 5 | 304 | 10 | 0 | 1.97 |
| Ed Belfour | 29 | 1760 | 92(2) | 0 | 3.10 |
| John Reid (d) | 12 | 633 | 37(1) | 0 | 3.51 |
| Ray LeBlanc (b) | 29 | 1655 | 99 | 0 | 3.59 |
| Darren Pang | 2 | 89 | 6 | 0 | 4.04 |
| Jeff Cooper (c) | 4 | 226 | 16 | 0 | 4.25 |
| Chris Clifford | 7 | 321 | 23(1) | 0 | 4.30 |
| Shootout losses | ... | .... | 7 | .... | .... |
| Saginaw Totals | 82 | 4988 | 294 | 0 | 3.54 |
| Steve Guenette (f) | 30 | 1810 | 82(1) | 2 | 2.72 |
| Doug Dadswell (e) | 32 | 1723 | 110(2) | 0 | 3.83 |
| Wayne Cowley | 29 | 1423 | 94(1) | 0 | 3.96 |
| Ron Petranella | 1 | 2 | 1 | 0 | 30.00 |
| Shootout losses | ... | .... | 3 | .... | .... |
| Salt Lake Totals | 82 | 4958 | 294 | 2 | 3.56 |

( )—Empty Net Goals. Do not count against a Goaltender's average.
(a)—Brower played for Denver and Flint.
(b)—LeBlanc played for Flint and Saginaw.
(c)—Cooper played for Indianapolis, Muskegon and Saginaw.
(d)—Reid played for Indianapolis and Saginaw.
(e)—Dadswell played for Indianapolis and Salt Lake.
(f)—Guenette played for Muskegon and Salt Lake.

NOTE: Doug Dadswell led in goals allowed with 232 (122 with Indianapolis and 110 with Salt Lake) and Steve Guenette led in goals-against average with 3.02 (3.92 with Muskegon and 2.72 with Salt Lake).

## Individual 1988-89 Leaders

| | | |
|---|---|---|
| Goals | Paul Ranheim, Salt Lake— | 68 |
| Assists | Michel Mongeau, Flint— | 76 |
| Points | Dave Michayluk, Muskegon— | 122 |
| Penalty Minutes | Stu Grimson, Salt Lake— | 397 |
| Goaltending Average (2,000 Minutes) | Steve Guenette, S.L.-Musk.— | 3.02 |
| Shutouts | Bruce Racine, Muskegon— | 3 |

# 1988-89 Turner Cup Playoffs
(All series best-of-seven)

## Quarterfinals

**Series "A"**

|  | W. | L. | Pts. | GF. | GA. |
|---|---|---|---|---|---|
| Muskegon | 4 | 0 | 8 | 26 | 10 |
| Peoria | 0 | 4 | 0 | 10 | 26 |

(Muskegon wins series, 4 games to 0)

**Series "B"**

|  | W. | L. | Pts. | GF. | GA. |
|---|---|---|---|---|---|
| Salt Lake | 4 | 0 | 8 | 22 | 11 |
| Denver | 0 | 4 | 0 | 11 | 22 |

(Salt Lake wins series, 4 games to 0)

**Series "C"**

|  | W. | L. | Pts. | GF. | GA. |
|---|---|---|---|---|---|
| Milwaukee | 4 | 2 | 8 | 22 | 20 |
| Kalamazoo | 2 | 4 | 4 | 20 | 22 |

(Milwaukee wins series, 4 games to 2)

**Series "D"**

|  | W. | L. | Pts. | GF. | GA. |
|---|---|---|---|---|---|
| Fort Wayne | 4 | 2 | 8 | 17 | 12 |
| Saginaw | 2 | 4 | 4 | 12 | 17 |

(Fort Wayne wins series, 4 games to 2)

## Semifinals

**Series "E"**

|  | W. | L. | Pts. | GF. | GA. |
|---|---|---|---|---|---|
| Muskegon | 4 | 1 | 8 | 25 | 18 |
| Fort Wayne | 1 | 4 | 2 | 18 | 25 |

(Muskegon wins series, 4 games to 1)

**Series "F"**

|  | W. | L. | Pts. | GF. | GA. |
|---|---|---|---|---|---|
| Salt Lake | 4 | 1 | 8 | 20 | 15 |
| Milwaukee | 1 | 4 | 2 | 15 | 20 |

(Salt Lake wins series, 4 games to 1)

## Finals for the Turner Cup

**Series "G"**

|  | W. | L. | Pts. | GF. | GA. |
|---|---|---|---|---|---|
| Muskegon | 4 | 1 | 8 | 22 | 16 |
| Salt Lake | 1 | 4 | 2 | 16 | 22 |

(Muskegon wins series, and Turner Cup, 4 games to 1)

## Top 10 Playoff Scorers

|  | Games | G. | A. | Pts. | Pen. |
|---|---|---|---|---|---|
| 1. Dave Michayluk, Muskegon | 13 | *9 | 12 | *21 | 24 |
| Mark Recchi, Muskegon | 14 | 7 | *14 | *21 | 28 |
| 3. Scott Gruhl, Muskegon | 14 | 8 | 11 | 19 | 37 |
| 4. Peter Lappin, Salt Lake | 14 | *9 | 9 | 18 | 4 |
| 5. Perry Ganchar, Muskegon | 14 | 7 | 8 | 15 | 6 |
| Todd Charlesworth, Muskegon | 14 | 2 | 13 | 15 | 8 |
| 7. Dan Hodgson, Milwaukee | 11 | 6 | 7 | 13 | 10 |
| Jim Leavins, Salt Lake | 14 | 2 | 11 | 13 | 6 |
| 9. Marc Bureau, Salt Lake | 14 | 7 | 5 | 12 | 31 |
| Rich Chernomaz, Salt Lake | 14 | 7 | 5 | 12 | 47 |
| Jeff Rohlicek, Milwaukee | 11 | 6 | 6 | 12 | 8 |
| Lee Giffin, Muskegon | 12 | 5 | 7 | 12 | 8 |

# Team-by-Team Playoff Scoring

## Denver Rangers
(Lost quarterfinals to Salt Lake, 4 games to 0)

|  | Games | G. | A. | Pts. | Pen. |
|---|---|---|---|---|---|
| Mike Golden | 3 | 3 | 1 | 4 | 0 |
| Mark Janssens | 4 | 3 | 0 | 3 | 18 |
| Kevin Miller | 4 | 2 | 1 | 3 | 0 |
| Rob Graham | 1 | 1 | 2 | 3 | 0 |
| Mike Hurlbut | 4 | 1 | 2 | 3 | 2 |
| Paul Broten | 4 | 0 | 2 | 2 | 6 |
| Denis Larocque | 4 | 0 | 2 | 2 | 10 |
| Simon Wheeldon | 4 | 0 | 2 | 2 | 6 |
| Simon Gagne | 4 | 1 | 0 | 1 | 7 |
| Daniel Lacroix | 2 | 0 | 1 | 1 | 0 |
| Jayson More | 3 | 0 | 1 | 1 | 26 |
| Jeff Bloemberg | 1 | 0 | 0 | 0 | 0 |
| Scott Brower (Goalie) | 1 | 0 | 0 | 0 | 0 |
| Chris McRae | 2 | 0 | 0 | 0 | 20 |
| Ron Shudra | 2 | 0 | 0 | 0 | 0 |
| Bret Walter | 2 | 0 | 0 | 0 | 0 |
| Stephane Brochu | 3 | 0 | 0 | 0 | 0 |
| Barry Chyzowski | 3 | 0 | 0 | 0 | 4 |
| Peter Laviolette | 3 | 0 | 0 | 0 | 4 |
| Brad Stepan | 3 | 0 | 0 | 0 | 6 |
| Peter Fiorentino | 4 | 0 | 0 | 0 | 24 |
| Jim Latos | 4 | 0 | 0 | 0 | 17 |
| Mike Richter (Goalie) | 4 | 0 | 0 | 0 | 0 |

## Fort Wayne Komets
(Lost semifinals to Muskegon, 4 games to 1)

|  | Games | G. | A. | Pts. | Pen. |
|---|---|---|---|---|---|
| Craig Endean | 10 | 4 | 7 | 11 | 6 |
| Colin Chin | 11 | 5 | 4 | 9 | 8 |
| Brian McKee | 11 | 3 | 5 | 8 | 17 |
| Brian Hannon | 9 | 2 | 6 | 8 | 9 |
| Keith Miller | 10 | 4 | 3 | 7 | 9 |
| Craig Channell | 11 | 0 | 7 | 7 | 32 |
| Byron Lomow | 11 | 3 | 3 | 6 | 68 |

|  | Games | G. | A. | Pts. | Pen. |
|---|---|---|---|---|---|
| Jim Burton | 11 | 2 | 4 | 6 | 8 |
| Mike McNeill | 11 | 1 | 5 | 6 | 2 |
| Joe Stefan | 11 | 3 | 1 | 4 | 4 |
| Al Sims | 6 | 2 | 2 | 4 | 2 |
| Steve Hollett | 10 | 2 | 2 | 4 | 4 |
| Steve Maltais | 4 | 2 | 1 | 3 | 0 |
| Brian Dowd | 6 | 0 | 3 | 3 | 8 |
| Guy Jacob | 8 | 1 | 1 | 2 | 39 |
| Bob Fowler | 9 | 1 | 0 | 1 | 8 |
| Carey Lucyk | 10 | 0 | 1 | 1 | 17 |
| Claude Dumas | 1 | 0 | 0 | 0 | 0 |
| Mike Natyshuk | 3 | 0 | 0 | 0 | 0 |
| Rick Knickle (Goalie) | 4 | 0 | 0 | 0 | 6 |
| Ron Pessetti | 5 | 0 | 0 | 0 | 0 |
| Martin Burgers | 8 | 0 | 0 | 0 | 14 |
| S. Beauregard (G.) | 9 | 0 | 1 | 1 | 0 |

## Kalamazoo Wings
(Lost quarterfinals to Milwaukee, 4 games to 2)

|  | Games | G. | A. | Pts. | Pen. |
|---|---|---|---|---|---|
| Mitch Messier | 6 | 4 | 3 | 7 | 0 |
| Ken Hodge | 6 | 1 | 5 | 6 | 16 |
| Steve Gotaas | 5 | 2 | 3 | 5 | 2 |
| D'Arcy Norton | 6 | 2 | 3 | 5 | 15 |
| Warren Babe | 6 | 1 | 4 | 5 | 24 |
| Steve Harrison | 6 | 1 | 4 | 5 | 8 |
| Mike McHugh | 6 | 3 | 1 | 4 | 17 |
| Scott McCrady | 6 | 0 | 4 | 4 | 24 |
| Paul Jerrard | 6 | 2 | 1 | 3 | 37 |
| Scott Robinson | 6 | 1 | 2 | 3 | 21 |
| Mike Berger | 6 | 0 | 2 | 2 | 8 |
| Mike Hiltner | 2 | 1 | 0 | 1 | 0 |
| Jordon Fois | 6 | 1 | 0 | 1 | 0 |
| Dean Kolstad | 6 | 1 | 0 | 1 | 23 |
| Rob Zettler | 6 | 0 | 1 | 1 | 26 |
| Larry Bernard | 1 | 0 | 0 | 0 | 5 |
| Eddie Courtenay | 1 | 0 | 0 | 0 | 0 |
| Brent Jarrett | 1 | 0 | 0 | 0 | 0 |
| Joe Lockwood | 3 | 0 | 0 | 0 | 0 |
| Link Gaetz | 5 | 0 | 0 | 0 | 56 |
| Jarmo Myllys (Goalie) | 6 | 0 | 0 | 0 | 0 |

## Milwaukee Admirals
(Lost semifinals to Salt Lake, 4 games to 1)

|  | Games | G. | A. | Pts. | Pen. |
|---|---|---|---|---|---|
| Dan Hodgson | 11 | 6 | 7 | 13 | 10 |
| Jeff Rohlicek | 11 | 6 | 6 | 12 | 8 |
| Jay Mazur | 11 | 6 | 5 | 11 | 2 |
| Carl Valimont | 11 | 2 | 8 | 10 | 12 |
| Peter Bakovic | 11 | 4 | 4 | 8 | 46 |
| Rob Murphy | 11 | 3 | 5 | 8 | 34 |
| Marc Crawford | 11 | 2 | 5 | 7 | 26 |
| Randy Boyd | 9 | 0 | 6 | 6 | 26 |
| Jose Charbonneau | 10 | 3 | 2 | 5 | 23 |
| Tim Lenardon | 10 | 2 | 3 | 5 | 25 |
| Curtis Hunt | 11 | 1 | 2 | 3 | 43 |
| Peter DeBoer | 1 | 0 | 2 | 2 | 2 |
| Ian Kidd | 4 | 0 | 2 | 2 | 7 |
| Jim Agnew | 11 | 0 | 2 | 2 | 34 |
| Ron Stern | 5 | 1 | 0 | 1 | 11 |
| Ernie Vargas | 8 | 1 | 0 | 1 | .6 |
| Jaime Husgen | 4 | 0 | 1 | 1 | 2 |
| Todd Hawkins | 9 | 0 | 1 | 1 | 33 |
| Mike MacWilliams | 1 | 0 | 0 | 0 | 0 |
| Frank Caprice (Goalie) | 2 | 0 | 0 | 0 | 0 |
| Steve Johnson | 2 | 0 | 0 | 0 | 0 |

|  | Games | G. | A. | Pts. | Pen. |
|---|---|---|---|---|---|
| Steve Veilleux | 4 | 0 | 0 | 0 | 13 |
| Tim Molle | 10 | 0 | 0 | 0 | 39 |
| Troy Gamble (Goalie) | 11 | 0 | 0 | 0 | 0 |

## Muskegon Lumberjacks
(Winners of 1989 Turner Cup Playoffs)

|  | Games | G. | A. | Pts. | Pen. |
|---|---|---|---|---|---|
| Dave Michayluk | 13 | *9 | 12 | *21 | 24 |
| Mark Recchi | 14 | 7 | *14 | *21 | 28 |
| Scott Gruhl | 14 | 8 | 11 | 19 | 37 |
| Perry Ganchar | 14 | 7 | 8 | 15 | 6 |
| Todd Charlesworth | 14 | 2 | 13 | 15 | 8 |
| Lee Giffin | 12 | 5 | 7 | 12 | 8 |
| Tim Tookey | 8 | 2 | 9 | 11 | 4 |
| Jim Paek | 14 | 1 | 10 | 11 | 24 |
| Dave McLlwain | 7 | 8 | 2 | 10 | 6 |
| Dan Frawley | 14 | 6 | 4 | 10 | 31 |
| Jock Callander | 7 | 5 | 5 | 10 | 30 |
| Brad Aitken | 13 | 5 | 5 | 10 | 75 |
| Mitch Wilson | 11 | 4 | 5 | 9 | 83 |
| Jeff Daniels | 11 | 3 | 5 | 8 | 11 |
| Mike Mersch | 13 | 0 | 6 | 6 | 38 |
| Kevin MacDonald | 11 | 2 | 3 | 5 | 22 |
| Dave Goertz | 14 | 0 | 4 | 4 | 10 |
| Mark Kachowski | 8 | 1 | 2 | 3 | 17 |
| Richard Zemlak | 8 | 1 | 1 | 2 | 35 |
| Doug Hobson | 1 | 0 | 1 | 1 | 11 |
| Jeff Waver | 1 | 0 | 0 | 0 | 0 |
| Tom Pratt | 2 | 0 | 0 | 0 | 2 |
| Bruce Racine (Goalie) | 5 | 0 | 0 | 0 | 0 |
| Frank Pietrangelo (G.) | 9 | 0 | 0 | 0 | 6 |

## Peoria Rivermen
(Lost quarterfinals to Muskegon, 4 games to 0)

|  | Games | G. | A. | Pts. | Pen. |
|---|---|---|---|---|---|
| Brad McCaughey | 4 | 2 | 2 | 4 | 0 |
| Marc Saumier | 4 | 2 | 1 | 3 | 22 |
| Terry MacLean | 3 | 1 | 2 | 3 | 2 |
| Peter Douris | 4 | 1 | 2 | 3 | 0 |
| Wayne Gagne | 4 | 1 | 2 | 3 | 6 |
| Jim Vesey | 4 | 1 | 2 | 3 | 6 |
| Scott Paluch | 4 | 1 | 1 | 2 | 31 |
| Kevin Miehm | 4 | 0 | 2 | 2 | 0 |
| Darin Smith | 4 | 1 | 0 | 1 | 7 |
| Dave Thomlinson | 3 | 0 | 1 | 1 | 8 |
| Phil DeGaetano | 4 | 0 | 1 | 1 | 8 |
| Shane MacEachern | 4 | 0 | 1 | 1 | 2 |
| Mike Wolak | 1 | 0 | 0 | 0 | 0 |
| Darrell May (Goalie) | 2 | 0 | 0 | 0 | 2 |
| Pat Jablonski (Goalie) | 3 | 0 | 0 | 0 | 0 |
| Toby Ducolon | 4 | 0 | 0 | 0 | 9 |
| Robert Dumas | 4 | 0 | 0 | 0 | 23 |
| Dominic Lavoie | 4 | 0 | 0 | 0 | 4 |
| Marty Raus | 4 | 0 | 0 | 0 | 2 |

## Saginaw Hawks
(Lost quarterfinals to Fort Wayne, 4 games to 2)

|  | Games | G. | A. | Pts. | Pen. |
|---|---|---|---|---|---|
| Mike Rucinski | 6 | 2 | 4 | 6 | 14 |
| Bill Gardner | 6 | 3 | 1 | 4 | 0 |
| Kent Paynter | 6 | 2 | 2 | 4 | 17 |
| Mike Stapleton | 6 | 1 | 3 | 4 | 4 |
| Jari Torkki | 6 | 2 | 1 | 3 | 4 |
| Sean Williams | 6 | 0 | 3 | 3 | 0 |
| Bill Watson | 3 | 1 | 1 | 2 | 0 |

|  | Games | G. | A. | Pts. | Pen. |  | Games | G. | A. | Pts. | Pen. |
|---|---|---|---|---|---|---|---|---|---|---|---|
| Dale Marquette | 6 | 1 | 1 | 2 | 2 | Marc Bureau | 14 | 7 | 5 | 12 | 31 |
| Bruce Cassidy | 6 | 0 | 2 | 2 | 6 | Rich Chernomaz | 14 | 7 | 5 | 12 | 47 |
| Jim Playfair | 6 | 0 | 2 | 2 | 20 | Randy Bucyk | 14 | 5 | 5 | 10 | 4 |
| Steve Ludzik | 6 | 0 | 1 | 1 | 16 | Paul Ranheim | 14 | 5 | 5 | 10 | 8 |
| Ray LeBlanc (Goalie) | 1 | 0 | 0 | 0 | 0 | Brian Glynn | 14 | 3 | 7 | 10 | 31 |
| Brian Noonan | 1 | 0 | 0 | 0 | 0 | Dave Reierson | 13 | 1 | 8 | 9 | 12 |
| Gary Moscaluk | 3 | 0 | 0 | 0 | 0 | Rick Hayward | 10 | 4 | 3 | 7 | 42 |
| Ed Belfour (Goalie) | 5 | 0 | 0 | 0 | 4 | Chris Biotti | 12 | 3 | 4 | 7 | 16 |
| Guy Phillips | 5 | 0 | 0 | 0 | 0 | Jim Johannson | 13 | 2 | 5 | 7 | 13 |
| Mario Doyon | 6 | 0 | 0 | 0 | 8 | Rick Lessard | 14 | 1 | 6 | 7 | 35 |
| Mark Kurzawski | 6 | 0 | 0 | 0 | 12 | Brian Deasley | 7 | 3 | 2 | 5 | 25 |
| Ryan McGill | 6 | 0 | 0 | 0 | 42 | Stu Grimson | 14 | 2 | 3 | 5 | *86 |
| Warren Rychel | 6 | 0 | 0 | 0 | 51 | Martin Simard | 14 | 4 | 0 | 4 | 45 |
|  |  |  |  |  |  | Stephane Matteau | 9 | 0 | 4 | 4 | 13 |
|  |  |  |  |  |  | Mark Holmes | 4 | 0 | 2 | 2 | 7 |

### Salt Lake Golden Eagles
(Lost finals to Muskegon, 4 games to 1)

|  | Games | G. | A. | Pts. | Pen. |  | Games | G. | A. | Pts. | Pen. |
|---|---|---|---|---|---|---|---|---|---|---|---|
| Peter Lappin | 14 | *9 | 9 | 18 | 4 | Ken Sabourin | 11 | 0 | 1 | 1 | 26 |
| Jim Leavins | 14 | 2 | 11 | 13 | 6 | Wayne Cowley (Goalie) | 2 | 0 | 1 | 1 | 0 |
|  |  |  |  |  |  | Doug Pickell | 2 | 0 | 0 | 0 | 0 |
|  |  |  |  |  |  | Kevin Grant | 3 | 0 | 0 | 0 | 12 |
|  |  |  |  |  |  | Steve Guenette (Goalie) | 13 | 0 | 0 | 0 | 4 |

## Complete Turner Cup Goaltending

|  | Games | Mins. | Goals | SO. | Avg. |
|---|---|---|---|---|---|
| Scott Brower, Denver | 1 | 31 | 1 | 0 | 1.94 |
| Stephane Beauregard, Fort Wayne | 9 | 484 | 21 | *1 | *2.60 |
| Ed Belfour, Saginaw | 5 | 298 | 14 | 0 | 2.82 |
| Bruce Racine, Muskegon | 5 | 300 | 15 | 0 | 3.00 |
| Ray LeBlanc, Saginaw | 1 | 59 | 3 | 0 | 3.05 |
| Frank Pietrangelo, Muskegon | 9 | 566 | 29 | 0 | 3.07 |
| Jarmo Myllys, Kalamazoo | 6 | 419 | 22 | 0 | 3.15 |
| Troy Gamble, Milwaukee | 11 | 640 | 35 | 0 | 3.28 |
| Frank Caprice, Milwaukee | 2 | 91 | 5 | 0 | 3.30 |
| Steve Guenette, Salt Lake | *13 | *782 | *44(1) | 0 | 3.38 |
| Rick Knickle, Fort Wayne | 4 | 173 | 15(1) | 0 | 5.20 |
| Wayne Cowley, Salt Lake | 2 | 69 | 6 | 0 | 5.22 |
| Darrell May, Peoria | 2 | 137 | 13 | 0 | 5.69 |
| Pat Jablonski, Peoria | 3 | 130 | 13 | 0 | 6.00 |
| Mike Richter, Denver | 4 | 210 | 21 | 0 | 6.00 |

( )—Empty Net Goals. Do not count against a Goaltender's average.

## Individual IHL Playoff Leaders

| | | |
|---|---|---|
| Goals | Peter Lappin, Salt Lake— | 9 |
| | Dave Michayluk, Muskegon— | 9 |
| Assists | Mark Recchi, Muskegon— | 14 |
| Points | Dave Michayluk, Muskegon— | 21 |
| | Mark Recchi, Muskegon— | 21 |
| Penalty Minutes | Stu Grimson, Salt Lake— | 86 |
| Goaltending Average | Stephane Beauregard, Fort Wayne— | 2.60 |
| Shutouts | Stephane Beauregard, Fort Wayne— | 1 |

★★★★★★★★★★★★★★★★★★★★★★★★★★★★★★★★★★★★★★★★★★

## IHL 1988-89 All-Stars

| First Team | Position | Second Team |
|---|---|---|
| Rick Knickle, Fort Wayne | Goal | Steve Guenette, Salt Lake |
| Randy Boyd, Milwaukee | Defense | Todd Charlesworth, Muskegon |
| Rick Lessard, Salt Lake | Defense | Craig Channell, Fort Wayne |
| Bruce Cassidy, Saginaw | | |
| Jeff Rohlicek, Milwaukee | Center | Simon Wheeldon, Denver |
| Jim Vesey, Peoria | Right Wing | Mark Recchi, Muskegon |
| Dave Michayluk, Muskegon | Left Wing | Paul Ranheim, Salt Lake |

★★★★★★★★★★★★★★★★★★★★★★★★★★★★★★★★★★★★★★★★★★

## IHL 1988-89 Trophy Winners

| | |
|---|---|
| James Gatschene Memorial Trophy (Most Valuable Player) | Dave Michayluk, Muskegon |
| Leo P. Lamoureux Memorial Trophy (Leading Scorer) | Dave Michayluk, Muskegon |
| James Norris Memorial Trophy (Outstanding Goaltender) | Rick Knickle, Fort Wayne |
| Governors Trophy (Outstanding Defenseman) | Randy Boyd, Milwaukee |
| Garry F. Longman Memorial Trophy (Outstanding Rookie) | Paul Ranheim, Salt Lake |
| Ken McKenzie Trophy (Outstanding American-Born Rookie) | Paul Ranheim, Salt Lake |
| Commissioner's Trophy (Coach of the Year) | B.J. MacDonald, Muskegon |
| | Phil Russell, Muskegon |
| Turner Cup Playoff MVP | Dave Michayluk, Muskegon |
| Fred A. Huber Trophy (Regular Season Champion) | Muskegon Lumberjacks |
| Joseph Turner Memorial Cup Winner (Playoff Champion) | Muskegon Lumberjacks |

## IHL All-Time Trophy Winners
## James Gatschene Memorial Trophy
### Most Valuable Player

1946-47—Herb Jones, Det. Auto Club
1947-48—Lyle Dowell, Det. Bright's Goodyears
1948-49—Bob McFadden, Det. Jerry Lynch
1949-50—Dick Kowcinak, Sarnia
1950-51—John McGrath, Toledo
1951-52—Ernie Dick, Chatham
1952-53—Donnie Marshall, Cincinnati
1953-54—No award given
1954-55—Phil Goyette, Cincinnati
1955-56—George Hayes, Grand Rapids
1956-57—Pierre Brillant, Indianapolis
1957-58—Pierre Brillant, Indianapolis
1958-59—Len Thornson, Fort Wayne
1959-60—Billy Reichart, Minneapolis
1960-61—Len Thornson, Fort Wayne
1961-62—Len Thornson, Fort Wayne
1962-63—Len Thornson, Fort Wayne
       Eddie Lang, Fort Wayne (tie)
1963-64—Len Thornson, Fort Wayne
1964-65—Chick Chalmers, Toledo
1965-66—Gary Schall, Muskegon
1966-67—Len Thornson, Fort Wayne
1967-68—Len Thornson, Fort Wayne
        Don Westbrooke, Dayton (tie)
1968-69—Don Westbrooke, Dayton
1969-70—Cliff Pennington, Des Moines
1970-71—Lyle Carter, Muskegon
1971-72—Len Fontaine, Port Huron
1972-73—Gary Ford, Muskegon
1973-74—Pete Mara, Des Moines
1974-75—Gary Ford, Muskegon
1975-76—Len Fontaine, Port Huron
1976-77—Tom Mellor, Toledo
1977-78—Dan Bonar, Fort Wayne
1978-79—Terry McDougall, Fort Wayne
1979-80—Al Dumba, Fort Wayne
1980-81—Marcel Comeau, Saginaw
1981-82—Brent Jarrett, Kalamazoo
1982-83—Claude Noel, Toledo
1983-84—Darren Jensen, Fort Wayne
1984-85—Scott Gruhl, Muskegon
1985-86—Darrell May, Peoria
1986-87—Jeff Pyle, Saginaw
        Jock Callander, Muskegon (tie)
1987-88—John Cullen, Flint
1988-89—Dave Michayluk, Muskegon

## Leo P. Lamoureux Memorial Trophy
### Leading Scorer
(Originally called George H. Wilkinson Trophy
from 1946-47 through 1959-60.)

1946-47—Harry Marchand, Windsor
1947-48—Dick Kowcinak, Det. Auto Club
1948-49—Leo Richard, Toledo
1949-50—Dick Kowcinak, Sarnia
1950-51—Herve Parent, Grand Rapids
1951-52—George Parker, Grand Rapids
1952-53—Alex Irving, Milwaukee
1953-54—Don Hall, Johnstown
1954-55—Phil Goyette, Cincinnati
1955-56—Max Mekilok, Cincinnati
1956-57—Pierre Brillant, Indianapolis
1957-58—Warren Hynes, Cincinnati
1958-59—George Ranieri, Louisville
1959-60—Chick Chalmers, Louisville
1960-61—Ken Yackel, Minneapolis
1961-62—Len Thornson, Fort Wayne
1962-63—Moe Bartoli, Minneapolis
1963-64—Len Thornson, Fort Wayne
1964-65—Lloyd Maxfield, Port Huron
1965-66—Bob Rivard, Fort Wayne
1966-67—Len Thornson, Fort Wayne
1967-68—Gary Ford, Muskegon
1968-69—Don Westbrooke, Dayton
1969-70—Don Westbrooke, Dayton
1970-71—Darrel Knibbs, Muskegon
1971-72—Gary Ford, Muskegon
1972-73—Gary Ford, Muskegon
1973-74—Pete Mara, Des Moines
1974-75—Rick Bragnalo, Dayton
1975-76—Len Fontaine, Port Huron
1976-77—Jim Koleff, Flint
1977-78—Jim Johnston, Flint
1978-79—Terry McDougall, Fort Wayne
1979-80—Al Dumba, Fort Wayne
1980-81—Marcel Comeau, Saginaw
1981-82—Brent Jarrett, Kalamazoo
1982-83—Dale Yakiwchuk, Milwaukee
1983-84—Wally Schreiber, Fort Wayne
1984-85—Scott MacLeod, Salt Lake
1985-86—Scott MacLeod, Salt Lake
1986-87—Jock Callander, Muskegon
        Jeff Pyle, Saginaw (tie)
1987-88—John Cullen, Flint
1988-89—Dave Michayluk, Muskegon

## James Norris Memorial Trophy
### Outstanding Goaltender

1955-56—Bill Tibbs, Troy
1956-57—Glenn Ramsey, Cincinnati
1957-58—Glenn Ramsey, Cincinnati
1958-59—Don Rigazio, Louisville
1959-60—Rene Zanier, Fort Wayne
1960-61—Ray Mikulan, Minneapolis
1961-62—Glenn Ramsey, Omaha
1962-63—Glenn Ramsey, Omaha
1963-64—Glenn Ramsey, Toledo
1964-65—Chuck Adamson, Fort Wayne
1965-66—Bob Sneddon, Port Huron
1966-67—Glenn Ramsey, Toledo
1967-68—Tim Tabor, Muskegon
          Bob Perani, Muskegon
1968-69—Pat Rupp, Dayton
          John Adams, Dayton
1969-70—Gaye Cooley, Des Moines
          Bob Perreault, Des Moines
1970-71—Lyle Carter, Muskegon
1971-72—Glenn Resch, Muskegon
1972-73—Robbie Irons, Fort Wayne
          Don Atchison, Fort Wayne
1973-74—Bill Hughes, Muskegon
1974-75—Bob Volpe, Flint
          Merlin Jenner, Flint
1975-76—Don Cutts, Muskegon
1976-77—Terry Richardson, Kalamazoo
1977-78—Lorne Molleken, Saginaw
          Pierre Chagnon, Saginaw
1978-79—Gord Laxton, Grand Rapids
1979-80—Larry Lozinski, Kalamazoo
1980-81—Claude Legris, Kalamazoo
          Georges Gagnon, Kalamazoo
1981-82—Lorne Molleken, Toledo
          Dave Tardich, Toledo
1982-83—Lorne Molleken, Toledo
1983-84—Darren Jensen, Fort Wayne
1984-85—Rick Heinz, Peoria
1985-86—Rick St. Croix, Fort Wayne
          Pokey Reddick, Fort Wayne
1986-87—Alain Raymond, Fort Wayne
          Michel Dufour, Fort Wayne
1987-88—Steve Guenette, Muskegon
1988-89—Rick Knickle, Fort Wayne

## Governors Trophy
### Outstanding Defenseman

1964-65—Lionel Repka, Fort Wayne
1965-66—Bob Lemieux, Muskegon
1966-67—Larry Mavety, Port Huron
1967-68—Carl Brewer, Muskegon
1968-69—Al Breaule, Dayton
          Moe Benoit, Dayton (tie)
1969-70—John Gravel, Toledo
1970-71—Bob LaPage, Des Moines
1971-72—Rick Pagnutti, Fort Wayne
1972-73—Bob McCammon, Port Huron
1973-74—Dave Simpson, Dayton
1974-75—Murry Flegel, Muskegon
1975-76—Murry Flegel, Muskegon
1976-77—Tom Mellor, Toledo
1977-78—Michel LaChance, Milwaukee
1978-79—Guido Tenesi, Grand Rapids
1979-80—John Gibson, Saginaw
1980-81—Larry Goodenough, Saginaw
1981-82—Don Waddell, Saginaw
1982-83—Jim Burton, Fort Wayne
          Kevin Willison, Milwaukee (tie)
1983-84—Kevin Willison, Milwaukee
1984-85—Lee Norwood, Peoria
1985-86—Jim Burton, Fort Wayne
1986-87—Jim Burton, Fort Wayne
1987-88—Phil Bourque, Muskegon
1988-89—Randy Boyd, Milwaukee

## Garry F. Longman Memorial Trophy
### Outstanding Rookie

1961-62—Dave Richardson, Fort Wayne
1962-63—John Gravel, Omaha
1963-64—Don Westbrooke, Toledo
1964-65—Bob Thomas, Toledo
1965-66—Frank Golembrowsky, Port Huron
1966-67—Kerry Bond, Columbus
1967-68—Gary Ford, Muskegon
1968-69—Doug Volmar, Columbus
1969-70—Wayne Zuk, Toledo
1970-71—Corky Agar, Flint
          Herb Howdle, Dayton (tie)
1971-72—Glenn Resch, Muskegon
1972-73—Danny Gloor, Des Moines
1973-74—Frank DeMarco, Des Moines
1974-75—Rick Bragnalo, Dayton
1975-76—Sid Veysey, Fort Wayne
1976-77—Ron Zanussi, Fort Wayne
          Garth MacGuigan, Muskegon (tie)
1977-78—Dan Bonar, Fort Wayne
1978-79—Wes Jarvis, Port Huron
1979-80—Doug Robb, Milwaukee
1980-81—Scott Vanderburgh, Kalamazoo
1981-82—Scott Howson, Toledo
1982-83—Tony Fiore, Flint
1983-84—Darren Jensen, Fort Wayne
1984-85—Gilles Thibaudeau, Flint
1985-86—Guy Benoit, Muskegon
1986-87—Michel Mongeau, Saginaw
1987-88—Ed Belfour, Saginaw
          John Cullen, Flint (tie)
1988-89—Paul Ranheim, Salt Lake

## Ken McKenzie Trophy
### Outstanding American-Born Rookie

1977-78—Mike Eruzione, Toledo
1978-79—Jon Fontas, Saginaw
1979-80—Bob Janecyk, Fort Wayne
1980-81—Mike Labianca, Toledo
          Steve Janaszak, Fort Wayne (tie)
1981-82—Steve Salvucci, Saginaw
1982-83—Paul Fenton, Peoria
1983-84—Mike Krensing, Muskegon
1984-85—Bill Schafhauser, Kalamazoo
1985-86—Brian Noonan, Saginaw
1986-87—Ray LeBlanc, Flint
1987-88—Dan Woodley, Flint
1988-89—Paul Ranheim, Salt Lake

## Commissioner's Trophy
### Coach of the Year

1984-85—Rick Ley, Muskegon
    Pat Kelly, Peoria (tie)
1985-86—Rob Laird, Fort Wayne
1986-87—Wayne Thomas, Salt Lake

1987-88—Rick Dudley, Flint
1988-89—B. J. MacDonald, Muskegon
    Phil Russell, Muskegon

## Turner Cup Playoff MVP

1984-85—Denis Cyr, Peoria
1985-86—Jock Callander, Muskegon
1986-87—Rick Heinz, Salt Lake

1987-88—Peter Lappin, Salt Lake
1988-89—Dave Michayluk, Muskegon

## IHL All-Time Championship Teams

(Regular season championship award originally called
J.P. McGuire Trophy from 1946-47 through 1953-54.)

| Fred A. Huber Trophy Regular Season Champion | | | Joseph Turner Memorial Cup Winners Playoff Champion | |
|---|---|---|---|---|
| Championship Team | (Coach) | Year | Championship Team | (Coach) |
| No Trophy Awarded | | 1945-46 | Detroit Auto Club | (Jack Ward) |
| Windsor Staffords | (Jack Ward) | 1946-47 | Windsor Spitfires | (Ebbie Goodfellow) |
| Windsor Spitfires | (Dent-Goodfellow) | 1947-48 | Toledo Mercurys | (Andy Mulligan) |
| Toledo Mercurys | (Andy Mulligan) | 1948-49 | Windsor Hettche Spitfires | (Jimmy Skinner) |
| Sarnia Sailors | (Dick Kowcinak) | 1949-50 | Chatham Maroons | (Bob Stoddart) |
| Grand Rapid Rockets | (Lou Trudell) | 1950-51 | Toledo Mercurys | (Alex Wood) |
| Grand Rapid Rockets | (Lou Trudell) | 1951-52 | Toledo Mercurys | (Alex Wood) |
| Cincinnati Mohawks | (Buddy O'Conner) | 1952-53 | Cincinnati Mohawks | (Buddy O'Conner) |
| Cincinnati Mohawks | (Roly McLenahan) | 1953-54 | Cincinnati Mohawks | (Roly McLenahan) |
| Cincinnati Mohawks | (Roly McLenahan) | 1954-55 | Cincinnati Mohawks | (Roly McLenahan) |
| Cincinnati Mohawks | (Roly McLenahan) | 1955-56 | Cincinnati Mohawks | (Roly McLenahan) |
| Cincinnati Mohawks | (Roly McLenahan) | 1956-57 | Cincinnati Mohawks | (Roly McLenahan) |
| Cincinnati Mohawks | (Bill Gould) | 1957-58 | Indianapolis Chiefs | (Leo Lamoureux) |
| Louisville Rebels | (Leo Gasparini) | 1958-59 | Louisville Rebels | (Leo Gasparini) |
| Fort Wayne Komets | (Ken Ullyot) | 1959-60 | St. Paul Saints | (Fred Shero) |
| Minneapolis Millers | (Ken Yackel) | 1960-61 | St. Paul Saints | (Fred Shero) |
| Muskegon Zephyrs | (Moose Lallo) | 1961-62 | Muskegon Zephyrs | (Moose Lallo) |
| Fort Wayne Komets | (Ken Ullyot) | 1962-63 | Fort Wayne Komets | (Ken Ullyot) |
| Toledo Blades | (Moe Benoit) | 1963-64 | Toledo Blades | (Moe Benoit) |
| Port Huron Flags | (Lloyd Maxfield) | 1964-65 | Fort Wayne Komets | (Eddie Long) |
| Muskegon Mohawks | (Moose Lallo) | 1965-66 | Port Huron Flags | (Lloyd Maxfield) |
| Dayton Gems | (Warren Back) | 1966-67 | Toledo Blades | (Terry Slater) |
| Muskegon Mohawks | (Moose Lallo) | 1967-68 | Muskegon Mohawks | (Moose Lallo) |
| Dayton Gems | (Larry Wilson) | 1968-69 | Dayton Gems | (Larry Wilson) |
| Muskegon Mohawks | (Moose Lallo) | 1969-70 | Dayton Gems | (Larry Wilson) |
| Muskegon Mohawks | (Moose Lallo) | 1970-71 | Port Huron Flags | (Ted Garvin) |
| Muskegon Mohawks | (Moose Lallo) | 1971-72 | Port Huron Flags | (Ted Garvin) |
| Fort Wayne Komets | (Marc Boileau) | 1972-73 | Fort Wayne Komets | (Marc Boileau) |
| Des Moines Capitals | (Dan Belisle) | 1973-74 | Des Moines Capitals | (Dan Belisle) |
| Muskegon Mohawks | (Moose Lallo) | 1974-75 | Toledo Goaldiggers | (Ted Garvin) |
| Dayton Gems | (Ivan Prediger) | 1975-76 | Dayton Gems | (Ivan Prediger) |
| Saginaw Gears | (Don Perry) | 1976-77 | Saginaw Gears | (Don Perry) |
| Fort Wayne Komets | (Gregg Pilling) | 1977-78 | Toledo Goaldiggers | (Ted Garvin) |
| Grand Rapids Owls | (Moe Bartoli) | 1978-79 | Kalamazoo Wings | (Bill Purcell) |
| Kalamazoo Wings | (Doug McKay) | 1979-80 | Kalamazoo Wings | (Doug McKay) |
| Kalamazoo Wings | (Doug McKay) | 1980-81 | Saginaw Gears | (Don Perry) |
| Toledo Goaldiggers | (Bill Inglis) | 1981-82 | Toledo Goaldiggers | (Bill Inglis) |
| Toledo Goaldiggers | (Bill Inglis) | 1982-83 | Toledo Goaldiggers | (Bill Inglis) |
| Fort Wayne Komets | (Ron Ullyot) | 1983-84 | Flint Generals | (Dennis Desrosiers) |
| Peoria Rivermen | (Pat Kelly) | 1984-85 | Peoria Rivermen | (Pat Kelly) |
| Fort Wayne Komets | (Rob Laird) | 1985-86 | Muskegon Lumberjacks | (Rick Ley) |
| Fort Wayne Komets | (Rob Laird) | 1986-87 | Salt Lake Golden Eagles | (Wayne Thomas) |
| Muskegon Lumberjacks | (Rick Ley) | 1987-88 | Salt Lake Golden Eagles | (Paul Baxter) |
| Muskegon Lumberjacks | (B. J. MacDonald) | 1988-89 | Muskegon Lumberjacks | (B. J. MacDonald) |

# East Coast Hockey League

(Known as Atlantic Coast Hockey League from 1981-82 through 1986-87,
and All American Hockey League during 1987-88.)

## 1988-89 Final ECHL Standings

|  | G. | W. | L. | Pts. | GF. | GA. |
|---|---|---|---|---|---|---|
| Erie Panthers | 60 | 37 | 20(3) | 77 | 327 | 256 |
| Johnstown Chiefs | 60 | 32 | 22(6) | 70 | 295 | 251 |
| Knoxville Cherokees | 60 | 32 | 27(1) | 65 | 266 | 286 |
| Carolina Thunderbirds | 60 | 27 | 32(1) | 55 | 266 | 329 |
| Virginia Lancers | 60 | 22 | 30(8) | 52 | 266 | 298 |

( )—Indicates number of games lost in overtime and are worth one point.

### Top 10 ECHL Scorers

|  | Games | G. | A. | Pts. | Pen. |
|---|---|---|---|---|---|
| 1. Daryl Harpe, Erie | 60 | 38 | *84 | *122 | 181 |
| 2. Tom Sasso, Johnstown | 60 | 36 | 65 | 101 | 4 |
| 3. Rob Hrytsak, Johnstown | 56 | 40 | 49 | 89 | 86 |
| 4. Doug Stromback, Erie | 53 | 40 | 45 | 85 | 77 |
| 5. Mike Chighisola, Virginia | 59 | *45 | 38 | 83 | 122 |
| Scott Johnson, Knoxville | 56 | 28 | 55 | 83 | 181 |
| 7. Joe Gurney, Johnstown | 57 | 38 | 43 | 81 | 149 |
| Rob Bennett, Erie | 49 | 13 | 47 | 60 | 144 |
| Knoxville | 11 | 3 | 18 | 21 | 10 |
| Totals | 60 | 16 | 65 | 81 | 154 |
| 9. J.F. Nault, Johnstown | 52 | 24 | 54 | 78 | 148 |
| 10. Patrick Noiseux, Knoxville | 58 | 38 | 35 | 73 | 95 |
| Steve Climo, Virginia | 59 | 33 | 40 | 73 | 14 |
| Mike Marcinkiewicz, Johnstown | 53 | 32 | 41 | 73 | 171 |

### Carolina Thunderbirds

|  | Games | G. | A. | Pts. | Pen. |
|---|---|---|---|---|---|
| Brian Hannon | 39 | 30 | 37 | 67 | 23 |
| Blair McReynolds | 48 | 18 | 39 | 57 | 31 |
| Bob Wensley | 60 | 21 | 32 | 53 | 92 |
| John Devereaux | 28 | 18 | 31 | 49 | 32 |
| Bill Huard | 40 | 27 | 21 | 48 | 177 |
| Frank Lattuca | 51 | 8 | 38 | 46 | 24 |
| Jay Fraser | 37 | 16 | 28 | 44 | 62 |
| John Torchetti | 30 | 16 | 26 | 42 | 46 |
| E.J. Sauer, Johnstown | 2 | 0 | 0 | 0 | 0 |
| Virginia | 4 | 0 | 2 | 2 | 2 |
| Carolina | 34 | 21 | 17 | 38 | 61 |
| Totals | 40 | 21 | 19 | 40 | 63 |
| Scott Allen | 40 | 16 | 21 | 37 | 43 |
| Steve Plaskon | 21 | 9 | 19 | 28 | 126 |
| John Dzikowski | 17 | 10 | 12 | 22 | 36 |
| Michel Lanouette | 28 | 5 | 17 | 22 | 192 |
| Mike Kuzmich | 18 | 6 | 15 | 21 | 11 |
| Dan Pineau, Johnstown | 15 | 8 | 7 | 15 | 16 |
| Carolina | 5 | 0 | 0 | 0 | 6 |
| Totals | 20 | 8 | 7 | 15 | 22 |
| Dan Gardiner | 18 | 4 | 10 | 14 | 6 |
| Garry Garland | 23 | 4 | 10 | 14 | 151 |
| Scott Rettew | 5 | 4 | 8 | 12 | 15 |
| Jeff Greene | 33 | 5 | 6 | 11 | 84 |
| Randy Irving | 25 | 1 | 9 | 10 | 64 |
| Rick McCarthy | 9 | 4 | 5 | 9 | 4 |
| Mike O'Shea, Virginia | 9 | 0 | 2 | 2 | 6 |
| Knoxville | 25 | 0 | 4 | 4 | 52 |
| Carolina | 11 | 0 | 3 | 3 | 11 |
| Totals | 45 | 0 | 9 | 9 | 69 |
| Chris Seychel | 10 | 6 | 2 | 8 | 50 |
| Victor Posa | 10 | 4 | 4 | 8 | 93 |
| Mark Johnson | 24 | 0 | 7 | 7 | 77 |
| Dan Burrows | 18 | 3 | 2 | 5 | 44 |
| Troy Nelson | 13 | 2 | 3 | 5 | 2 |
| Dean Dixon | 5 | 1 | 3 | 4 | 2 |
| Jack Carcia | 6 | 1 | 2 | 3 | 0 |
| David Chiappelli | 3 | 0 | 3 | 3 | 4 |
| Gary Willett, Knox. (G.) | 6 | 0 | 1 | 1 | 0 |
| Carolina (G.) | 17 | 0 | 2 | 2 | 2 |
| Totals | 23 | 0 | 3 | 3 | 2 |
| Marc Marchand | 2 | 1 | 1 | 2 | 0 |
| Dan Gatenby (Goalie) | 6 | 0 | 2 | 2 | 16 |
| Clancy Cosgrove | 2 | 1 | 0 | 1 | 0 |
| Matt Winnicki | 2 | 0 | 1 | 1 | 7 |
| Shaun O'Sullivan (G.) | 4 | 0 | 1 | 1 | 19 |
| Kenton Rein (Goalie) | 4 | 0 | 1 | 1 | 2 |
| Nick Vitucci (Goalie) | 22 | 0 | 1 | 1 | 2 |
| Doug Smith | 28 | 0 | 1 | 1 | 179 |
| Mike Torillo | 1 | 0 | 0 | 0 | 0 |
| Toby O'Brien (Goalie) | 3 | 0 | 0 | 0 | 14 |
| Darren Srochenski | 3 | 0 | 0 | 0 | 2 |
| Bob Dore | 4 | 0 | 0 | 0 | 6 |

### Erie Panthers

|  | Games | G. | A. | Pts. | Pen. |
|---|---|---|---|---|---|
| Daryl Harpe | 60 | 38 | *84 | *122 | 181 |
| Doug Stromback, Johns. | 3 | 0 | 2 | 2 | 0 |
| Erie | 50 | 40 | 43 | 83 | 77 |
| Totals | 53 | 40 | 45 | 85 | 77 |
| Hank Banas | 60 | 39 | 32 | 71 | 76 |
| Kelly Szautner | 49 | 22 | 42 | 64 | 42 |
| Darryl Moise | 52 | 10 | 51 | 61 | 136 |

|  | Games | G. | A. | Pts. | Pen. |
|---|---|---|---|---|---|
| Terry McCutcheon | 32 | 28 | 30 | 58 | 45 |
| Harry Geary, Knoxville | 37 | 15 | 34 | 49 | 167 |
| Erie | 8 | 6 | 3 | 9 | 32 |
| Totals | 45 | 21 | 37 | 58 | 199 |
| Grant Ottenbreit | 58 | 24 | 32 | 56 | 307 |
| Rick Lambert, Knoxville | 48 | 17 | 20 | 37 | 79 |
| Erie | 8 | 4 | 5 | 9 | 6 |
| Totals | 56 | 21 | 25 | 46 | 85 |
| Doug Marsden | 24 | 27 | 18 | 45 | 23 |
| Steve Wienke | 59 | 3 | 28 | 31 | 167 |
| George Swarbrick | 38 | 9 | 21 | 30 | 42 |
| Chris Walsh | 36 | 12 | 17 | 29 | 8 |
| Joe DeMitchell | 12 | 7 | 7 | 14 | 2 |
| Darren Miciak | 43 | 6 | 7 | 13 | 216 |
| Pat Carli | 26 | 2 | 9 | 11 | 23 |
| Antti Autere, Carolina | 9 | 0 | 1 | 1 | 13 |
| Erie | 31 | 1 | 9 | 10 | 37 |
| Totals | 40 | 1 | 10 | 11 | 50 |
| Brian Kunkle | 10 | 4 | 4 | 8 | 16 |
| Rob Gador | 5 | 0 | 7 | 7 | 0 |
| Boyd Lomow | 10 | 5 | 1 | 6 | 32 |
| Perry Faffard | 3 | 0 | 3 | 3 | 0 |
| Bob VanBiesbrouck | 3 | 0 | 3 | 3 | 2 |
| Terry Mattson | 5 | 1 | 1 | 2 | 2 |
| Tom Thornton | 5 | 0 | 1 | 1 | 0 |
| Ralph Russo, Carolina | 1 | 0 | 0 | 0 | 0 |
| Erie | 5 | 0 | 1 | 1 | 2 |
| Totals | 6 | 0 | 1 | 1 | 2 |
| Paul Kenny (Goalie) | 34 | 0 | 1 | 1 | 55 |
| Lubo Dzurilla | 4 | 0 | 0 | 0 | 0 |
| Tony Mongillo (Goalie) | 31 | 0 | 0 | 0 | 27 |

## Johnstown Chiefs

|  | Games | G. | A. | Pts. | Pen. |
|---|---|---|---|---|---|
| Tom Sasso | 60 | 36 | 65 | 101 | 4 |
| Rob Hrytsak | 56 | 40 | 49 | 89 | 86 |
| Joe Gurney | 57 | 38 | 43 | 81 | 149 |
| J.F. Nault | 52 | 24 | 54 | 78 | 148 |
| Mike Marcinkiewicz | 53 | 32 | 41 | 73 | 171 |
| Jeff Salzbrunn | 49 | 32 | 23 | 55 | 117 |
| Darren Servatius | 59 | 8 | 45 | 53 | 177 |
| Ed Harding | 58 | 14 | 25 | 39 | 151 |
| Brock Kelly | 54 | 5 | 26 | 31 | *365 |
| Jamie Evans | 32 | 10 | 20 | 30 | 33 |
| Ron Servatius | 59 | 5 | 25 | 30 | 199 |
| Scott Brown | 30 | 16 | 13 | 29 | 52 |
| Quintin Brickley | 21 | 5 | 19 | 24 | 6 |
| Bob Kennedy | 21 | 5 | 7 | 12 | 13 |
| Dan Mercrones | 7 | 3 | 5 | 8 | 2 |
| Mike Hiltner | 4 | 2 | 5 | 7 | 7 |
| Tony Lopilato | 5 | 2 | 4 | 6 | 0 |
| Mike Black | 15 | 2 | 1 | 3 | 6 |
| Lance Carlsen (Goalie) | 25 | 0 | 2 | 2 | 29 |
| Scott Gordon (Goalie) | 31 | 0 | 2 | 2 | 8 |
| Dana Heinze (Goalie) | 1 | 0 | 0 | 0 | 0 |
| Gary Brush | 2 | 0 | 0 | 0 | 0 |
| Sylvan LaJeanesse | 4 | 0 | 0 | 0 | 0 |

## Knoxville Cherokees

|  | Games | G. | A. | Pts. | Pen. |
|---|---|---|---|---|---|
| Scott Johnson | 56 | 28 | 55 | 83 | 181 |
| Bob Bennett, Erie | 49 | 13 | 47 | 60 | 144 |
| Knoxville | 11 | 3 | 18 | 21 | 10 |
| Totals | 60 | 16 | 65 | 81 | 154 |
| Patrick Noiseux | 58 | 38 | 35 | 73 | 95 |
| Peter Buckridge | 37 | 33 | 33 | 66 | 38 |

|  | Games | G. | A. | Pts. | Pen. |
|---|---|---|---|---|---|
| Rob McDougal, Erie | 41 | 23 | 28 | 51 | 62 |
| Knoxville | 9 | 4 | 2 | 6 | 0 |
| Totals | 50 | 27 | 30 | 57 | 62 |
| Sean Donohue | 55 | 28 | 25 | 53 | 114 |
| Greg Batters | 47 | 20 | 24 | 44 | 359 |
| Tim Hanley | 25 | 22 | 21 | 43 | 43 |
| Alex Daviault | 44 | 10 | 21 | 31 | 326 |
| Tim Brown | 55 | 18 | 12 | 30 | 37 |
| Sean Mangan | 59 | 3 | 19 | 22 | 100 |
| Greg Davies | 38 | 5 | 14 | 19 | 159 |
| Tom Benson | 26 | 0 | 18 | 18 | 56 |
| Dick Popiel | 23 | 4 | 12 | 16 | 30 |
| Tim Skaggs, Johnstown | 30 | 5 | 4 | 9 | 48 |
| Knoxville | 3 | 0 | 1 | 1 | 17 |
| Totals | 33 | 5 | 5 | 10 | 65 |
| Frank O'Brien, Virginia | 5 | 0 | 0 | 0 | 4 |
| Johnstown | 33 | 1 | 8 | 9 | 36 |
| Knoxville | 6 | 0 | 0 | 0 | 19 |
| Totals | 44 | 1 | 8 | 9 | 59 |
| Ron Aubrey, Erie | 28 | 3 | 4 | 7 | 182 |
| Knoxville | 6 | 1 | 0 | 1 | 48 |
| Totals | 34 | 4 | 4 | 8 | 230 |
| Bob Palinski | 16 | 2 | 5 | 7 | 14 |
| Peter Richards (Goalie) | 32 | 0 | 6 | 6 | 71 |
| Jack Bowkus | 5 | 2 | 3 | 5 | 23 |
| Rick Bazzola | 1 | 2 | 1 | 3 | 0 |
| Bill Gregorie | 11 | 0 | 2 | 2 | 40 |
| Al Loring (Goalie) | 32 | 0 | 2 | 2 | 35 |
| Scott Willman | 6 | 1 | 0 | 1 | 4 |
| Tom Craven | 1 | 0 | 0 | 0 | 0 |
| Rick Farmer | 1 | 0 | 0 | 0 | 0 |
| Steve Farmer | 1 | 0 | 0 | 0 | 0 |
| Bob Gingerich | 2 | 0 | 0 | 0 | 0 |
| Glenn Mulvenna | 2 | 0 | 0 | 0 | 5 |
| M. Schwalb, Carol. (G.) | 17 | 0 | 0 | 0 | 15 |
| Knoxville (G.) | 3 | 0 | 0 | 0 | 2 |
| Totals | 20 | 0 | 0 | 0 | 17 |

## Virginia Lancers

|  | Games | G. | A. | Pts. | Pen. |
|---|---|---|---|---|---|
| Mike Chighisola | 59 | *45 | 38 | 83 | 122 |
| Steve Climo | 59 | 33 | 40 | 73 | 14 |
| Tim Schnobrich | 59 | 28 | 36 | 64 | 13 |
| Gabby McDuff | 33 | 27 | 25 | 52 | 25 |
| Bill Whitfield | 57 | 13 | 34 | 47 | 124 |
| Sam Farace | 60 | 18 | 28 | 46 | 138 |
| Bill Gutenberg | 59 | 11 | 29 | 40 | 37 |
| Greg Neish | 42 | 18 | 17 | 35 | 151 |
| Brad Courteau | 45 | 12 | 21 | 33 | 35 |
| Joe Mitchell | 35 | 15 | 14 | 29 | 58 |
| Don Rothgery, Knoxville | 36 | 8 | 14 | 22 | 38 |
| Virginia | 8 | 1 | 3 | 4 | 6 |
| Totals | 44 | 9 | 17 | 26 | 44 |
| Brian Clark, Carolina | 12 | 3 | 6 | 9 | 2 |
| Virginia | 17 | 5 | 12 | 17 | 27 |
| Totals | 29 | 8 | 18 | 26 | 29 |
| John Baker | 60 | 4 | 16 | 20 | 120 |
| Joel Burridge | 25 | 6 | 11 | 17 | 145 |
| Gary McColgan | 13 | 7 | 9 | 16 | 4 |
| Denis Fleming | 32 | 3 | 10 | 13 | 38 |
| Todd Morgan, Carolina | 4 | 0 | 1 | 1 | 8 |
| Johnstown | 27 | 2 | 9 | 11 | 91 |
| Virginia | 3 | 0 | 0 | 0 | 0 |
| Totals | 34 | 2 | 10 | 12 | 99 |
| Andy Akervick | 15 | 6 | 5 | 11 | 18 |
| David Schofield | 14 | 1 | 10 | 11 | 32 |
| Mark Issel | 16 | 1 | 10 | 11 | 12 |

|  | Games | G. | A. | Pts. | Pen. |
|---|---|---|---|---|---|
| Steve Cherrier, Knoxville | 4 | 0 | 0 | 0 | 0 |
| Carolina | 10 | 1 | 3 | 4 | 41 |
| Virginia | 6 | 2 | 4 | 6 | 9 |
| Totals | 20 | 3 | 7 | 10 | 50 |
| Tom Knowlton | 21 | 4 | 5 | 9 | 13 |
| Rock Derganc, Knoxville | 13 | 2 | 1 | 3 | 33 |
| Virginia | 6 | 4 | 1 | 5 | 7 |
| Totals | 19 | 6 | 2 | 8 | 40 |
| David Litz, Knoxville | 17 | 0 | 5 | 5 | 40 |
| Virginia | 6 | 0 | 3 | 3 | 8 |
| Totals | 23 | 0 | 8 | 8 | 48 |
| John Caraglino | 10 | 1 | 4 | 5 | 7 |
| Wally Creighton | 4 | 1 | 2 | 3 | 0 |
| John Blue (Goalie) | 10 | 0 | 2 | 2 | 9 |
| Steven Doll | 10 | 0 | 2 | 2 | 132 |
| Steve Averill, Johns. (G.) | 6 | 0 | 0 | 0 | 4 |
| Virginia (G.) | 25 | 0 | 2 | 2 | 51 |
| Totals | 31 | 0 | 2 | 2 | 55 |
| Greg Ware | 4 | 0 | 1 | 1 | 106 |
| Jim Flanigan (Goalie) | 31 | 0 | 1 | 1 | 26 |
| Bob Duff | 1 | 0 | 0 | 0 | 0 |
| Peter O'Shana (Goalie) | 1 | 0 | 0 | 0 | 0 |
| Al Vergilio | 1 | 0 | 0 | 0 | 0 |
| Steve Wallace | 1 | 0 | 0 | 0 | 0 |
| Bob Smith | 2 | 0 | 0 | 0 | 8 |
| Mike Sullivan | 2 | 0 | 0 | 0 | 0 |
| Mark Roof | 4 | 0 | 0 | 0 | 0 |

## Individual ECHL Goaltending

|  | Games | Mins. | Goals | SO. | Avg. |
|---|---|---|---|---|---|
| Kenton Rein | 4 | 222 | 15 | 0 | 4.05 |
| Nick Vitucci | 22 | 1238 | 96(1) | 1 | 4.65 |
| Gary Willett (a) | 17 | 810 | 68(1) | 0 | 5.03 |
| Mike Schwalb (b) | 17 | 835 | 79(1) | 0 | 5.68 |
| Dan Gatenby | 6 | 239 | 29 | 0 | 7.30 |
| Toby O'Brien | 3 | 130 | 17 | 0 | 7.89 |
| Shaun O'Sullivan | 4 | 132 | 19 | 0 | 8.66 |
| Scott Allen | 1 | 14 | 3 | 0 | 13.26 |
| Carolina Totals | 60 | 3620 | 329 | 1 | 5.45 |
| Paul Kenny | *34 | *1877 | 129(4) | 1 | 4.12 |
| Tony Mongillo | 31 | 1726 | 120(3) | *2 | 4.17 |
| Erie Totals | 60 | 3604 | 256 | 3 | 4.26 |
| Dana Heinze | 1 | 4 | 0 | 0 | 0.00 |
| Scott Gordon | 31 | 1839 | 117(2) | *2 | *3.82 |
| Lance Carlsen | 25 | 1447 | 102(2) | 1 | 4.23 |
| Steve Averill (c) | 6 | 339 | 27(1) | 0 | 4.77 |
| Johnstown Totals | 60 | 3630 | 251 | 3 | 4.15 |
| Gary Willett (a) | 6 | 247 | 18 | 0 | 4.38 |
| Peter Richards | 32 | 1557 | 116(1) | 1 | 4.47 |
| Al Loring | 32 | 1709 | 135(3) | 1 | 4.74 |
| Mike Schwalb (b) | 3 | 111 | 13 | 0 | 7.07 |
| Knoxville Totals | 60 | 3624 | 286 | 2 | 4.74 |
| John Blue | 10 | 570 | 38 | 0 | 4.00 |
| Steve Averill (c) | 25 | 1364 | 95(4) | 1 | 4.19 |
| Tim Flanigan | 31 | 1681 | *153(5) | 0 | 5.46 |
| Peter O'Shana | 1 | 14 | 3 | 0 | 12.68 |
| Virginia Totals | 60 | 3630 | 298 | 1 | 4.93 |

( )—Empty Net Goals. Do not count against a Goaltender's average.
(a)—Willett played for Carolina and Knoxville.
(b)—Schwalb played for Carolina and Knoxville.
(c)—Averill played for Johnstown and Virginia.

## Invididual 1988-89 Leaders

| | |
|---|---|
| Goals | Mike Chighisola, Virginia— 45 |
| Assists | Daryl Harpe, Erie— 84 |
| Points | Daryl Harpe, Erie— 122 |
| Penalty Minutes | Brock Kelly, Johnstown— 365 |
| Goaltending Average | Scott Gordon, Johnstown— 3.82 |
| Shutouts | Scott Gordon, Johnstown— 2 |
| | Tony Mongillo, Erie— 2 |

# 1988-89 ECHL Playoffs

(All Series best-of-seven)

## Semifinals

|  | W. | L. | Pts. | GF. | GA. |
|---|---|---|---|---|---|
| Carolina | 4 | 0 | 8 | 17 | 11 |
| Erie | 0 | 4 | 0 | 11 | 17 |

(Carolina wins series, 4 games to 0)

|  | W. | L. | Pts. | GF. | GA. |
|---|---|---|---|---|---|
| Johnstown | 4 | 0 | 8 | 28 | 7 |
| Knoxville | 0 | 4 | 0 | 7 | 28 |

(Johnstown wins series, 4 games to 0)

## Finals

|  | W. | L. | Pts. | GF. | GA. |
|---|---|---|---|---|---|
| Carolina | 4 | 3 | 8 | 32 | 33 |
| Johnstown | 3 | 4 | 6 | 33 | 32 |

(Carolina wins series and ECHL playoffs, 4 games to 3)

## Top 10 Playoff Scorers

|  | Games | G. | A. | Pts. | Pen. |
|---|---|---|---|---|---|
| 1. Tom Sasso, Johnstown | 11 | 5 | *19 | *24 | 2 |
| 2. Rob Hrytsak, Johnstown | 11 | *8 | 10 | 18 | 18 |
| 3. Scott Brown, Johnstown | 11 | *8 | 8 | 16 | 19 |
| 4. Mike Marcinkiewicz, Johnstown | 10 | *8 | 7 | 15 | 43 |
| Quintin Brickley, Johnstown | 11 | 7 | 8 | 15 | 15 |
| J.F. Nault, Johnstown | 11 | 4 | 11 | 15 | 22 |
| 7. John Devereaux, Carolina | 11 | 7 | 7 | 14 | 10 |
| 8. Randy Irving, Carolina | 11 | 4 | 9 | 13 | 35 |
| Bob Wensley, Carolina | 11 | 0 | 13 | 13 | 18 |
| 10. Joe Gurney, Johnstown | 11 | 7 | 5 | 12 | 32 |
| Rick McCarthy, Carolina | 11 | 6 | 6 | 12 | 13 |
| Scott Allen, Carolina | 11 | 5 | 7 | 12 | 28 |

## Team-by-Team Playoff Scoring

### Carolina Thunderbirds
(Winners of ECHL Playoffs)

|  | Games | G. | A. | Pts. | Pen. |
|---|---|---|---|---|---|
| John Devereaux | 11 | 7 | 7 | 14 | 10 |
| Randy Irving | 11 | 4 | 9 | 13 | 35 |
| Bob Wensley | 11 | 0 | 13 | 13 | 18 |
| Rick McCarthy | 11 | 6 | 6 | 12 | 13 |
| Scott Allen | 11 | 5 | 7 | 12 | 28 |
| E. J. Sauer | 11 | 6 | 5 | 11 | 15 |
| John Torchetti | 11 | 5 | 5 | 10 | 20 |
| Bill Huard | 10 | 7 | 2 | 9 | 70 |
| Scott Rettew | 11 | 3 | 4 | 7 | 50 |
| Blair McReynolds | 11 | 0 | 7 | 7 | 8 |
| Jay Fraser | 11 | 4 | 2 | 6 | 26 |
| Steve Plaskon | 8 | 0 | 5 | 5 | *132 |
| Michel Lanouette | 10 | 1 | 2 | 3 | 86 |
| Jeff Greene | 11 | 1 | 2 | 3 | 32 |
| Nick Vitucci (Goalie) | 10 | 0 | 1 | 1 | 4 |
| Gary Willett (Goalie) | 2 | 0 | 0 | 0 | 2 |

### Erie Panthers
(Lost semifinals to Carolina, 4 games to 0)

|  | Games | G. | A. | Pts. | Pen. |
|---|---|---|---|---|---|
| Harry Geary | 4 | 2 | 5 | 7 | 29 |
| Terry McCutcheon | 4 | 2 | 3 | 5 | 9 |
| Doug Marsden | 4 | 2 | 2 | 4 | 14 |
| Darryl Moise | 4 | 1 | 3 | 4 | 8 |
| Chris Walsh | 4 | 1 | 2 | 3 | 0 |
| Hank Banas | 4 | 1 | 1 | 2 | 15 |
| Daryl Harpe | 4 | 1 | 1 | 2 | 4 |
| Doug Stromback | 4 | 0 | 2 | 2 | 0 |
| Bob VanBiesbrouck | 4 | 0 | 2 | 2 | 2 |
| Grant Ottenbreit | 4 | 1 | 0 | 1 | 25 |
| Antti Autere | 4 | 0 | 1 | 1 | 6 |
| Paul Kenny (Goalie) | 1 | 0 | 0 | 0 | 2 |
| Tony Mongillo (Goalie) | 3 | 0 | 0 | 0 | 0 |
| Rick Lambert | 4 | 0 | 0 | 0 | 4 |
| Darren Miciak | 4 | 0 | 0 | 0 | 6 |
| Steve Wienke | 4 | 0 | 0 | 0 | 2 |

### Johnstown Chiefs
(Lost finals to Carolina, 4 games to 3)

|  | Games | G. | A. | Pts. | Pen. |
|---|---|---|---|---|---|
| Tom Sasso | 11 | 5 | *19 | *24 | 2 |
| Rob Hrytsak | 11 | *8 | 10 | 18 | 18 |
| Scott Brown | 11 | *8 | 8 | 16 | 19 |
| Mike Marcinkiewicz | 10 | *8 | 7 | 15 | 43 |
| Quintin Brickley | 11 | 7 | 8 | 15 | 15 |
| J. F. Nault | 11 | 4 | 11 | 15 | 22 |
| Joe Gurney | 11 | 7 | 5 | 12 | 32 |
| Darren Servatius | 11 | 5 | 3 | 8 | 22 |
| Ed Harding | 11 | 3 | 5 | 8 | 36 |
| Jeff Salzbrunn | 11 | 2 | 6 | 8 | 48 |
| Jamie Evans | 10 | 2 | 4 | 6 | 45 |
| Ron Servatius | 11 | 0 | 6 | 6 | 26 |
| Bob Kennedy | 11 | 2 | 3 | 5 | 12 |
| Brock Kelly | 10 | 0 | 2 | 2 | 47 |
| Scott Gordon (Goalie) | 11 | 0 | 1 | 1 | 8 |
| Lance Carlsen (Goalie) | 2 | 0 | 0 | 0 | 0 |

### Knoxville Cherokees
(Lost semifinals to Johnstown, 4 games to 0)

|  | Games | G. | A. | Pts. | Pen. |
|---|---|---|---|---|---|
| Bob Bennett | 4 | 1 | 4 | 5 | 9 |

| | Games | G. | A. | Pts. | Pen. | | Games | G. | A. | Pts. | Pen. |
|---|---|---|---|---|---|---|---|---|---|---|---|
| Patrick Noiseux | 4 | 3 | 0 | 3 | 0 | Mike Schwalb (Goalie) | 1 | 0 | 0 | 0 | 0 |
| Greg Batters | 4 | 1 | 1 | 2 | 69 | Peter Buckridge | 2 | 0 | 0 | 0 | 2 |
| Sean Dononue | 4 | 1 | 1 | 2 | 6 | Steve Farmer | 2 | 0 | 0 | 0 | 0 |
| Sean Mangan | 4 | 1 | 0 | 1 | 6 | Rob McDougal | 3 | 0 | 0 | 0 | 0 |
| Scott Johnson | 3 | 0 | 1 | 1 | 6 | Alex Daviault | 4 | 0 | 0 | 0 | 15 |
| Tom Benson | 4 | 0 | 1 | 1 | 23 | Frank O'Brien | 4 | 0 | 0 | 0 | 2 |
| Tim Brown | 4 | 0 | 1 | 1 | 0 | Dick Popiel | 4 | 0 | 0 | 0 | 11 |
| Al Loring (Goalie) | 4 | 0 | 1 | 1 | 0 | | | | | | |

## Complete ECHL Playoff Goaltending

| | Games | Mins. | Goals | SO. | Avg. |
|---|---|---|---|---|---|
| Scott Gordon, Johnstown | *11 | *647 | *36(2) | 0 | *3.34 |
| Nick Vitucci, Carolina | 10 | 592 | 35(1) | 0 | 3.55 |
| Tony Mongillo, Erie | 3 | 178 | 11(1) | 0 | 3.70 |
| Paul Kenny, Erie | 1 | 62 | 5 | 0 | 4.85 |
| Lance Carlsen, Johnstown | 2 | 10 | 1 | 0 | 6.25 |
| Al Loring, Knoxville | 4 | 234 | 25 | 0 | 6.41 |
| Gary Willett, Carolina | 2 | 70 | 8 | 0 | 6.90 |
| Mike Schwalb, Knoxville | 1 | 6 | 3 | 0 | 32.97 |

( )—Empty Net Goals. Do not count against a Goaltender's average.

## Individual ECHL Playoff Leaders

| | | |
|---|---|---|
| Goals | Rob Hrytsak, Johnstown— | 8 |
| | Scott Brown, Johnstown— | 8 |
| | Mike Marcinkiewicz, Johnstown— | 8 |
| Assists | Tom Sasso, Johnstown— | 19 |
| Points | Tom Sasso, Johnstown— | 24 |
| Penalty Minutes | Steve Plaskon, Carolina— | 132 |
| Goaltending Average | Scott Gordon, Johnstown— | 3.34 |
| Shutouts | — None | |

★★★★★★★★★★★★★★★★★★★★★★★★★★★★★★★★★★★★★★★★★★★

## ECHL 1988-89 All-Stars

| | |
|---|---|
| Goaltender | Scott Gordon, Johnston |
| Defense | Frank Lattuca, Carolina |
| | Kelly Szautner, Erie |
| | Bill Whitfield, Virginia |
| Center | Daryl Harpe, Erie |
| Right Wing | Doug Stromback, Erie |
| Left Wing | Rob Hrytsak, Johnstown |

★★★★★★★★★★★★★★★★★★★★★★★★★★★★★★★★★★★★★★★★★★★

## ECHL 1988-89 Trophy Winners

| | |
|---|---|
| Most Valuable Player | Daryl Harpe, Erie |
| Top Scorer | Daryl Harpe, Erie |
| Top Defenseman | Kelly Szautner, Erie |
| Rookie of the Year | Tom Sasso, Johnstown |
| Top Goaltender | Scott Gordon, Johnstown |
| Playoff MVP | Nick Vitucci, Carolina |
| Coach of the Year | Ron Hansis, Erie |

## ECHL Championship Teams

| Regular Season Champion | | Bob Payne Trophy Playoff Champion |
|---|---|---|
| Championship Team (Coach) | | Championship Team (Coach) |
| Salem Raiders (Pat Kelly) | 1981-82 | Mohawk Valley Stars (Bill Horton) |
| Carolina Thunderbirds (Rick Dudley) | 1982-83 | Carolina Thunderbirds (Rick Dudley) |
| Carolina Thunderbirds (Rick Dudley) | 1983-84 | Erie Golden Blades (Bill Horton) |
| Carolina Thunderbirds (Rick Dudley) | 1984-85 | Carolina Thunderbirds (Rick Dudley) |
| Carolina Thunderbirds (Rick Dudley) | 1985-86 | Carolina Thunderbirds (Rick Dudley) |
| Virginia Lancers (John Tortorella) | 1986-87 | Virginia Lancers (John Tortorella) |
| Virginia Lancers (John Tortorella) | 1987-88 | Virginia Lancers (John Tortorella) |
| Erie Panthers (Ron Hansis) | 1988-89 | Carolina Thunderbirds (Brendan Watson) |

## Most Valuable Player
1981-82—Dave MacQueen, Salem
1982-83—Rory Cava, Carolina
1983-84—Paul O'Neill, Virginia
1984-85—Barry Tabobondung, Erie
1985-86—Joe Curran, Carolina
1986-87—Peter DeArmas, Virginia
1987-88—John Torchetti, Carolina
1988-89—Daryl Harpe, Erie

## Top Scorer
1981-82—Dave MacQueen, Salem
1982-83—Dave Watson, Carolina
1983-84—Rob Clavette, Pinebridge-Erie
1984-85—Paul Mancini, Erie
1985-86—Dave Herbst, Erie
1986-87—Doug McCarthy, Carolina
1987-88—John Torchetti, Carolina
1988-89—Daryl Harpe, Erie

## Rookie of the Year
1984-85—Kurt Rugenius, Mohawk Valley
   Todd Bjorkstrand, Pinebridge (tie)
1985-86—Bobby Williams, New York
1986-87—Scott Knutson, Carolina
   Scott Curwin, Virginia (tie)
1987-88—Mike Sparago, Virginia
   Dean Dixon, Carolina (tie)
1988-89—Tom Sasso, Johnstown

## Top Goaltender
1981-82—Gilles Moffet, Salem
1982-83—Yves Dechene, Carolina
1983-84—Darrell May, Erie
1984-85—Dan Olson, Carolina
1985-86—Ray LeBlanc, Carolina
1986-87—Dana Demole, Virginia
1987-88—Tim Flanigan, Virginia
1988-89—Scott Gordon, Johnstown

## Playoff MVP
1984-85—Brian Carroll, Carolina
1985-86—Bob Dore, Carolina
1986-87—Peter DeArmas, Virginia
   Dana Demole, Virginia (tie)
1987-88—Tim Flanigan, Virginia
1988-89—Nick Vitucci, Carolina

## Coach of the Year
1981-82—Bill Horton, Mohawk Valley
1982-83—Jim Mikol, Erie
1983-84—Paul O'Neill, Virginia
1984-85—Frank Perkins, Pinebridge
1985-86—Rick Dudley, Carolina
1986-87—John Tortorella, Virginia
1987-88—John Tortorella, Virginia
1988-89—Ron Hansis, Erie

# MEMORIAL CUP WINNERS

| Season | Team |
|---|---|
| 1918-19— | University of Toronto Schools |
| 1919-20— | Toronto Canoe Club |
| 1920-21— | Winnipeg Falcons |
| 1921-22— | Fort William War Veterans |
| 1922-23— | Univ. of Manitoba-Winnipeg |
| 1923-24— | Owen Sound Greys |
| 1924-25— | Regina Pats |
| 1925-26— | Calgary Canadians |
| 1926-27— | Owen Sound Greys |
| 1927-28— | Regina Monarchs |
| 1928-29— | Toronto Marlboros |
| 1929-30— | Regina Pats |
| 1930-31— | Winnipeg Elmwoods |
| 1931-32— | Sudbury Wolves |
| 1932-33— | Newmarket |
| 1933-34— | Toronto St. Michael's |
| 1934-35— | Winnipeg Monarchs |
| 1935-36— | West Toronto Redmen |
| 1936-37— | Winnipeg Monarchs |
| 1937-38— | St. Boniface Seals |
| 1938-39— | Oshawa Generals |
| 1939-40— | Oshawa Generals |
| 1940-41— | Winnipeg Rangers |
| 1941-42— | Portage la Prairie |
| 1942-43— | Winnipeg Rangers |
| 1943-44— | Oshawa Generals |
| 1944-45— | Toronto St. Michael's |
| 1945-46— | Winnipeg Monarchs |
| 1946-47— | Toronto St. Michael's |
| 1947-48— | Port Arthur West End Bruins |
| 1948-49— | Montreal Royals |
| 1949-50— | Montreal Jr. Canadiens |
| 1950-51— | Barrie Flyers |
| 1951-52— | Guelph Biltmores |
| 1952-53— | Barrie Flyers |
| 1953-54— | St. Catharines Tee Pees |
| 1954-55— | Toronto Marlboros |
| 1955-56— | Toronto Marlboros |
| 1956-57— | Flin Flon Bombers |
| 1957-58— | Ottawa-Hull Jr. Canadiens |
| 1958-59— | Winnipeg Braves |
| 1959-60— | St. Catharines Tee Pees |
| 1960-61— | Toronto St. Michael's Majors |
| 1961-62— | Hamilton Red Wings |
| 1962-63— | Edmonton Oil Kings |
| 1963-64— | Toronto Marlboros |
| 1964-65— | Niagara Falls Flyers |
| 1965-66— | Edmonton Oil Kings |
| 1966-67— | Toronto Marlboros |
| 1967-68— | Niagara Falls Flyers |
| 1968-69— | Montreal Jr. Canadiens |
| 1969-70— | Montreal Jr. Canadiens |
| 1970-71— | Quebec Remparts |
| 1971-72— | Cornwall Royals |
| 1972-73— | Toronto Marlboros |
| 1973-74— | Regina Pats |
| 1974-75— | Toronto Marlboros |
| 1975-76— | Hamilton Fincups |
| 1976-77— | New Westminster Bruins |
| 1977-78— | New Westminster Bruins |
| 1978-79— | Peterborough Petes |
| 1979-80— | Cornwall Royals |
| 1980-81— | Cornwall Royals |
| 1981-82— | Kitchener Rangers |
| 1982-83— | Portland Winter Hawks |
| 1983-84— | Ottawa 67's |
| 1984-85— | Prince Albert Raiders |
| 1985-86— | Guelph Platers |
| 1986-87— | Medicine Hat Tigers |
| 1987-88— | Medicine Hat Tigers |
| 1988-89— | Swift Current Broncos |

# Ontario Hockey League

Commissioner—David E. Branch
Chairman of the Board—Dr. Robert Vaughan
305 Milner Avenue
Suite 208
Scarborough, Ontario M1B 3V4
Phone—(416) 299-8700

Director of Administration—Herb Morell
Director of Information—Ted Baker
Director of Officiating—Ken Bodendistel
Director of Central Scouting—To be announced

## 1988-89 Final OHL Standings

### Matt Leyden Division

|  | G. | W. | L. | T. | Pts. | GF. | GA. |
|---|---|---|---|---|---|---|---|
| Peterborough Petes | 66 | 42 | 22 | 2 | 86 | 302 | 235 |
| Oshawa Generals | 66 | 36 | 24 | 6 | 78 | 337 | 286 |
| Toronto Marlboros | 66 | 32 | 31 | 3 | 67 | 319 | 332 |
| Cornwall Royals | 66 | 31 | 30 | 5 | 67 | 350 | 308 |
| Ottawa 67's | 66 | 30 | 32 | 4 | 64 | 295 | 301 |
| Belleville Bulls | 66 | 27 | 35 | 4 | 58 | 292 | 322 |
| Kingston Raiders | 66 | 25 | 36 | 5 | 55 | 278 | 313 |

### Hap Emms Division

|  | G. | W. | L. | T. | Pts. | GF. | GA. |
|---|---|---|---|---|---|---|---|
| Kitchener Rangers | 66 | 41 | 19 | 6 | 88 | 318 | 251 |
| Niagara Falls Thunder | 66 | 41 | 23 | 2 | 84 | 410 | 319 |
| London Knights | 66 | 37 | 25 | 4 | 78 | 311 | 264 |
| Guelph Platers | 66 | 26 | 32 | 8 | 60 | 257 | 288 |
| Windsor Compuware Spitfires | 66 | 25 | 37 | 4 | 54 | 272 | 321 |
| North Bay Centennials | 66 | 24 | 36 | 6 | 54 | 282 | 334 |
| Sudbury Wolves | 66 | 23 | 36 | 7 | 53 | 262 | 334 |
| Sault Ste. Marie Greyhounds | 66 | 21 | 43 | 2 | 44 | 227 | 304 |

NOTE: Toronto awarded third place in Matt Leyden Division based on 6-2, won-lost record over Cornwall during regular season.
Windsor awarded fifth place in Hap Emms Division based on 3-2-1, won-lost-tied record over North Bay during regular season.

### Top 10 Scorers for the Eddie Powers Memorial Trophy

|  | Games | G. | A. | Pts. | Pen. |
|---|---|---|---|---|---|
| 1. Bryan Fogarty, Niagara Falls | 60 | 47 | *108 | *155 | 88 |
| 2. Stan Drulia, Niagara Falls | 47 | 52 | 93 | 145 | 59 |
| 3. Andrew Cassels, Ottawa | 56 | 37 | 97 | 134 | 66 |
| 4. Steve Maltais, Cornwall | 58 | 53 | 70 | 123 | 67 |
| 5. Kevin Miehm, Oshawa | 63 | 43 | 79 | 122 | 19 |
| 6. Tim Taylor, London | 61 | 34 | 80 | 114 | 93 |
| 7. Rob Zamuner, Guelph | 66 | 46 | 65 | 111 | 38 |
| 8. Keith Osborne, North Bay | 15 | 11 | 15 | 26 | 12 |
| Niagara Falls | 50 | 34 | 49 | 83 | 45 |
| Totals | 65 | 45 | 64 | 109 | 57 |
| 9. Jamie Leach, Niagara Falls | 58 | 45 | 62 | 107 | 47 |
| 10. Mike Ricci, Peterborough | 60 | 54 | 52 | 106 | 43 |

## Team-by-Team Breakdown of OHL Scoring

### Belleville Bulls

|  | Games | G. | A. | Pts. | Pen. |  | Games | G. | A. | Pts. | Pen. |
|---|---|---|---|---|---|---|---|---|---|---|---|
| Richard Fatrola, Corn. | 17 | 11 | 14 | 25 | 4 | Ken Rowbotham | 66 | 29 | 40 | 69 | 29 |
| Belleville | 49 | 31 | 29 | 60 | 47 | John Porco | 66 | 35 | 33 | 68 | 16 |
| Totals | 66 | 42 | 43 | 85 | 51 | Scott Thornton | 59 | 28 | 34 | 62 | 103 |
| Bob Berg | 66 | 33 | 51 | 84 | 88 | Kent Hulst | 45 | 21 | 41 | 62 | 43 |
|  |  |  |  |  |  | Jim Dean | 51 | 16 | 41 | 57 | 39 |

— 176 —

|  | Games | G. | A. | Pts. | Pen. |
|---|---|---|---|---|---|
| Bryan Marchment | 43 | 14 | 36 | 50 | 198 |
| Darryl Williams | 45 | 24 | 21 | 45 | 137 |
| Steve Bancroft | 66 | 7 | 30 | 37 | 99 |
| Greg Bignell | 54 | 6 | 27 | 33 | 180 |
| Scott Boston | 66 | 4 | 20 | 24 | 90 |
| Rob Pearson | 26 | 8 | 12 | 20 | 51 |
| Norm Batherson | 43 | 4 | 11 | 15 | 30 |
| Dan Poirier | 60 | 7 | 3 | 10 | 94 |
| Frank Melone, N. B. | 8 | 2 | 2 | 4 | 21 |
| Belleville | 5 | 4 | 1 | 5 | 18 |
| Totals | 13 | 6 | 3 | 9 | 39 |
| Scott Feasby | 41 | 2 | 6 | 8 | 58 |
| Gary Taylor | 60 | 0 | 8 | 8 | 85 |
| Jeff Cantlon | 50 | 4 | 2 | 6 | 139 |
| Dan White | 41 | 2 | 4 | 6 | 10 |
| Derek Morin | 64 | 0 | 5 | 5 | 63 |
| Troy Nelson (Goalie) | 35 | 0 | 4 | 4 | 11 |
| Jeff MacLeod | 25 | 0 | 3 | 3 | 2 |
| Jeff Fife (Goalie) | 41 | 0 | 2 | 2 | 4 |
| Kevin Doherty | 6 | 0 | 1 | 1 | 0 |
| Mark McDowell | 1 | 0 | 0 | 0 | 0 |
| Lyle Peel (Goalie) | 2 | 0 | 0 | 0 | 0 |
| Dean Hoskins | 3 | 0 | 0 | 0 | 0 |
| Robert McCleary | 4 | 0 | 0 | 0 | 0 |
| Mark Rupnow | 4 | 0 | 0 | 0 | 0 |
| Earle Wright | 6 | 0 | 0 | 0 | 0 |

## Cornwall Royals

|  | Games | G. | A. | Pts. | Pen. |
|---|---|---|---|---|---|
| Steve Maltais | 58 | 53 | 70 | 123 | 67 |
| Darren Colbourne | 62 | 51 | 46 | 97 | 49 |
| Darcy Cahill, Kingston | 17 | 11 | 21 | 32 | 33 |
| Cornwall | 49 | 24 | 36 | 60 | 16 |
| Totals | 66 | 35 | 57 | 92 | 49 |
| Jason Cirone | 64 | 39 | 44 | 83 | 67 |
| Mathieu Schneider | 59 | 16 | 57 | 73 | 96 |
| Paul Cain | 44 | 19 | 47 | 66 | 26 |
| Owen Nolan | 62 | 34 | 25 | 59 | 213 |
| John Slaney | 66 | 16 | 43 | 59 | 23 |
| Jason Hannigan | 54 | 32 | 23 | 55 | 165 |
| Derek Middleton | 29 | 10 | 19 | 29 | 29 |
| Tom Nemeth | 51 | 4 | 23 | 27 | 25 |
| Rich Stromback | 50 | 9 | 12 | 21 | 98 |
| Dean Pella, Windsor | 15 | 3 | 6 | 9 | 20 |
| Sudbury | 17 | 1 | 4 | 5 | 14 |
| Cornwall | 25 | 3 | 4 | 7 | 10 |
| Totals | 57 | 7 | 14 | 21 | 44 |
| Chris Cygan, Toronto | 12 | 0 | 1 | 1 | 10 |
| Cornwall | 47 | 1 | 17 | 18 | 15 |
| Totals | 59 | 1 | 18 | 19 | 25 |
| Denis Leger | 57 | 7 | 11 | 18 | 79 |
| Paul Lalande | 57 | 7 | 10 | 17 | 46 |
| Jeff Murray | 44 | 5 | 6 | 11 | 39 |
| Dan Haylow | 23 | 4 | 6 | 10 | 23 |
| Bob Babcock | 42 | 0 | 9 | 9 | 163 |
| Todd Mondor | 38 | 1 | 6 | 7 | 20 |
| Rick Tabaracci (Goalie) | 50 | 0 | 6 | 6 | 69 |
| Vern Ray, Ottawa | 16 | 0 | 0 | 0 | 14 |
| Cornwall | 29 | 1 | 4 | 5 | 30 |
| Totals | 45 | 1 | 4 | 5 | 44 |
| Kevin Meisner, Sudbury | 20 | 1 | 1 | 2 | 10 |
| Cornwall | 26 | 0 | 1 | 1 | 8 |
| Totals | 46 | 1 | 2 | 3 | 18 |
| Ron Jolie | 3 | 0 | 1 | 1 | 6 |
| Mike O'Rourke (Goalie) | 6 | 0 | 1 | 1 | 0 |
| Darryl Paquette (Goalie) | 13 | 0 | 1 | 1 | 4 |
| Dan Francoeur | 3 | 0 | 0 | 0 | 0 |

|  | Games | G. | A. | Pts. | Pen. |
|---|---|---|---|---|---|
| Scott Matthews | 7 | 0 | 0 | 0 | 0 |
| Allen Murphy | 7 | 0 | 0 | 0 | 15 |
| Richard St. Amand | 10 | 0 | 0 | 0 | 2 |
| Mike Mercier | 24 | 0 | 0 | 0 | 0 |

## Guelph Platers

|  | Games | G. | A. | Pts. | Pen. |
|---|---|---|---|---|---|
| Rob Zamuner | 66 | 46 | 65 | 111 | 38 |
| Rob Arabski | 61 | 18 | 51 | 69 | 51 |
| Sean Whyte | 53 | 20 | 44 | 64 | 57 |
| Owen Lessard | 63 | 29 | 31 | 60 | 93 |
| John McIntyre | 52 | 30 | 26 | 56 | 129 |
| Todd Hlushko | 66 | 28 | 18 | 46 | 71 |
| Mike Speer | 65 | 9 | 31 | 40 | 185 |
| Keith Whitmore | 66 | 13 | 22 | 35 | 102 |
| Kelly Bradley | 62 | 13 | 20 | 33 | 43 |
| Dave Noseworthy | 63 | 10 | 23 | 33 | 45 |
| Ray Edwards | 45 | 10 | 16 | 26 | 159 |
| Steve Perkovic | 41 | 1 | 23 | 24 | 63 |
| Dan Jensen, Peter | 22 | 3 | 6 | 9 | 12 |
| Guelph | 25 | 4 | 7 | 11 | 31 |
| Totals | 47 | 7 | 13 | 20 | 43 |
| Grayden Reid | 66 | 7 | 13 | 20 | 34 |
| Jeff Perry | 59 | 8 | 7 | 15 | 71 |
| Chris Driscoll | 61 | 7 | 6 | 13 | 15 |
| Craig Kitteringham, Tor. | 1 | 0 | 0 | 0 | 11 |
| Guelph | 30 | 2 | 10 | 12 | 73 |
| Totals | 31 | 2 | 10 | 12 | 84 |
| Mark Strohack | 65 | 0 | 9 | 9 | 65 |
| Mike Parson (Goalie) | 53 | 0 | 7 | 7 | 8 |
| Rob Thiel, Kitchener | 23 | 3 | 2 | 5 | 16 |
| Guelph | 14 | 1 | 0 | 1 | 8 |
| Totals | 37 | 4 | 2 | 6 | 24 |
| Bryan Drury | 63 | 0 | 6 | 6 | 85 |
| Kevin Mahony | 28 | 1 | 3 | 4 | 130 |
| Des Brown | 12 | 0 | 1 | 1 | 7 |
| Curtis Green (Goalie) | 2 | 0 | 0 | 0 | 0 |
| Emile DeRepentigny | 3 | 0 | 0 | 0 | 8 |
| Jay Evershed (Goalie) | 3 | 0 | 0 | 0 | 2 |
| Pat McGarry (Goalie) | 14 | 0 | 0 | 0 | 12 |
| Mike Seaton | 19 | 0 | 0 | 0 | 2 |

## Kingston Raiders

|  | Games | G. | A. | Pts. | Pen. |
|---|---|---|---|---|---|
| Jeff Waver, N. F. | 2 | 1 | 4 | 5 | 4 |
| Kingston | 53 | 29 | 39 | 68 | 91 |
| Totals | 55 | 30 | 43 | 73 | 95 |
| Wayne Doucet, N. F. | 22 | 11 | 20 | 31 | 20 |
| Kingston | 37 | 15 | 23 | 38 | 69 |
| Totals | 59 | 26 | 43 | 69 | 89 |
| Brad Gratton, Belleville | 17 | 12 | 10 | 22 | 8 |
| Kingston | 45 | 18 | 22 | 40 | 16 |
| Totals | 62 | 30 | 32 | 62 | 24 |
| Mike Bodnarchuk | 63 | 22 | 38 | 60 | 30 |
| Mark Major, North Bay | 11 | 3 | 2 | 5 | 58 |
| Kingston | 53 | 22 | 29 | 51 | 193 |
| Totals | 64 | 25 | 31 | 56 | 251 |
| Joey Simon, Sudbury | 6 | 0 | 2 | 2 | 0 |
| Kingston | 55 | 22 | 31 | 53 | 12 |
| Totals | 61 | 22 | 33 | 55 | 12 |
| Drake Berehowsky | 63 | 7 | 39 | 46 | 85 |
| Garth Joy | 50 | 10 | 33 | 43 | 37 |
| Jamie Allan, Windsor | 19 | 8 | 9 | 17 | 37 |
| Kingston | 43 | 8 | 16 | 24 | 82 |
| Totals | 62 | 16 | 25 | 41 | 119 |
| Bob McKillop, Windsor | 19 | 4 | 4 | 8 | 0 |
| Kingston | 49 | 12 | 21 | 33 | 12 |
| Totals | 68 | 16 | 25 | 41 | 12 |

|  | Games | G. | A. | Pts. | Pen. |
|---|---|---|---|---|---|
| Brock Shyiak | 66 | 4 | 28 | 32 | 87 |
| Matt Giesebrecht | 54 | 12 | 17 | 29 | 33 |
| Justin Morrison | 44 | 13 | 13 | 26 | 101 |
| Jason Snow | 53 | 9 | 17 | 26 | 44 |
| Jamie Vargo | 61 | 7 | 12 | 19 | 51 |
| Tony Iob | 49 | 7 | 11 | 18 | 78 |
| Mike Cavanagh | 48 | 8 | 8 | 16 | 42 |
| Tony Cimellaro, N. B. | 11 | 2 | 1 | 3 | 7 |
| Kingston | 47 | 6 | 7 | 13 | 12 |
| Totals | 58 | 8 | 8 | 16 | 19 |
| Geoff Schneider | 56 | 2 | 6 | 8 | 24 |
| Brock Woods | 52 | 1 | 5 | 6 | 41 |
| Jim Hulton | 13 | 1 | 4 | 5 | 21 |
| Marcus Schofield, N.B. | 10 | 1 | 1 | 2 | 5 |
| Kingston | 4 | 0 | 0 | 0 | 0 |
| Totals | 14 | 1 | 1 | 2 | 5 |
| Jeff Wilson (Goalie) | 47 | 0 | 2 | 2 | 33 |
| Ken Ristimaki | 2 | 0 | 1 | 1 | 0 |
| Stephane Finucan (G.) | 1 | 0 | 0 | 0 | 0 |
| Jeff Whittle | 1 | 0 | 0 | 0 | 0 |
| Chris Longo | 3 | 0 | 0 | 0 | 0 |
| Kevin Lune | 3 | 0 | 0 | 0 | 10 |
| Sean Gauthier (Goalie) | 37 | 0 | 0 | 0 | 8 |

## Kitchener Rangers

|  | Games | G. | A. | Pts. | Pen. |
|---|---|---|---|---|---|
| Mark Montanari | 64 | 33 | 69 | 102 | 172 |
| Shayne Stevenson | 56 | 25 | 51 | 76 | 86 |
| Steven Rice | 64 | 36 | 31 | 67 | 42 |
| Jason Firth | 56 | 31 | 36 | 67 | 21 |
| Joey St. Aubin | 60 | 18 | 45 | 63 | 26 |
| Kirk Tomlinson | 43 | 29 | 30 | 59 | 131 |
| Cory Keenan | 66 | 15 | 35 | 50 | 69 |
| Richard Borgo | 66 | 23 | 23 | 46 | 75 |
| Randy Pearce | 64 | 23 | 21 | 44 | 87 |
| Gilbert Dionne | 66 | 11 | 33 | 44 | 13 |
| Darren Rumble | 46 | 11 | 29 | 40 | 25 |
| Rival Fullum | 64 | 19 | 17 | 36 | 46 |
| Rob Sangster | 64 | 10 | 25 | 35 | *337 |
| John Uniac, Sudbury | 20 | 1 | 6 | 7 | 13 |
| Kitchener | 45 | 5 | 13 | 18 | 32 |
| Totals | 65 | 6 | 19 | 25 | 45 |
| Chris LiPuma | 59 | 7 | 13 | 20 | 101 |
| Steve Herniman | 61 | 3 | 16 | 19 | 112 |
| Rick Allain | 62 | 2 | 16 | 18 | 245 |
| Pierre Gagnon, Sudbury | 12 | 0 | 3 | 3 | 12 |
| Kitchener | 36 | 6 | 2 | 8 | 32 |
| Totals | 48 | 6 | 5 | 11 | 44 |
| Brad Barton | 60 | 2 | 4 | 6 | 61 |
| Phil Paquette, Guelph | 17 | 0 | 2 | 2 | 35 |
| Kitchener | 9 | 1 | 2 | 3 | 15 |
| Totals | 26 | 1 | 4 | 5 | 50 |
| Pat Gooley | 2 | 1 | 0 | 1 | 0 |
| Darrin Kinnear | 9 | 1 | 0 | 1 | 0 |
| Vince Oldford | 2 | 0 | 1 | 1 | 9 |
| Gus Morschauser (G.) | 41 | 0 | 1 | 1 | 6 |
| Duane Anderson (G.) | 1 | 0 | 0 | 0 | 7 |
| Chuck Dietrich | 1 | 0 | 0 | 0 | 5 |
| Kevin Doherty | 2 | 0 | 0 | 0 | 0 |
| Mike Torchia (Goalie) | 30 | 0 | 0 | 0 | 8 |

## London Knights

|  | Games | G. | A. | Pts. | Pen. |
|---|---|---|---|---|---|
| Tim Taylor | 61 | 34 | 80 | 114 | 93 |
| Dennis McEwen | 64 | 50 | 42 | 92 | 57 |
| Trevor Dam | 66 | 33 | 59 | 92 | 111 |
| Kelly Cain, S.S. Marie | 22 | 16 | 25 | 41 | 18 |
| London | 25 | 22 | 27 | 49 | 9 |
| Totals | 47 | 38 | 52 | 90 | 27 |
| Ron Jones, Windsor | 27 | 18 | 11 | 29 | 54 |
| London | 43 | 9 | 25 | 34 | 90 |
| Totals | 70 | 27 | 36 | 63 | 144 |
| Jeff Christian | 60 | 27 | 31 | 58 | 216 |
| Jim Sprott | 64 | 15 | 42 | 57 | 236 |
| Craig Booker | 24 | 9 | 25 | 34 | 84 |
| Paul Holden | 54 | 11 | 21 | 32 | 90 |
| Steve Boyd, Windsor | 7 | 0 | 1 | 1 | 8 |
| Sudbury | 17 | 3 | 2 | 5 | 24 |
| London | 46 | 7 | 17 | 24 | 46 |
| Totals | 70 | 10 | 20 | 30 | 78 |
| Jon Stos | 50 | 12 | 17 | 29 | 26 |
| Doug Synishin | 66 | 8 | 20 | 28 | 77 |
| Steve Martell | 65 | 9 | 17 | 26 | 59 |
| Gary Wenzel | 25 | 8 | 16 | 24 | 23 |
| John Battice, North Bay | 6 | 0 | 6 | 6 | 9 |
| London | 42 | 5 | 13 | 18 | 88 |
| Totals | 48 | 5 | 19 | 24 | 97 |
| Dan LeBlanc | 65 | 10 | 13 | 23 | 116 |
| Chris Taylor | 62 | 7 | 16 | 23 | 52 |
| Louie DeBrusk | 59 | 11 | 11 | 22 | 149 |
| Mark Guy | 65 | 6 | 11 | 17 | 83 |
| Rick Corriveau | 12 | 4 | 10 | 14 | 23 |
| Jerry Ribble, Windsor | 21 | 0 | 4 | 4 | 24 |
| London | 35 | 0 | 2 | 2 | 35 |
| Totals | 56 | 0 | 6 | 6 | 59 |
| Mike Christensen | 7 | 3 | 2 | 5 | 0 |
| Dennis Young | 9 | 1 | 2 | 3 | 13 |
| Gord Christian, Belleville | 7 | 1 | 0 | 1 | 10 |
| London | 6 | 1 | 0 | 1 | 4 |
| Totals | 13 | 2 | 0 | 2 | 14 |
| Peter Ing, Windsor (G.) | 19 | 0 | 1 | 1 | 4 |
| London (Goalie) | 32 | 0 | 1 | 1 | 11 |
| Totals | 51 | 0 | 2 | 2 | 15 |
| Gary Hickey | 2 | 1 | 0 | 1 | 2 |
| Mike Teeple | 4 | 1 | 0 | 1 | 0 |
| Jason Skellett | 5 | 0 | 1 | 1 | 0 |
| Pat Tenpenny, Tor. (G.) | 17 | 0 | 1 | 1 | 6 |
| London (Goalie) | 4 | 0 | 0 | 0 | 0 |
| Totals | 21 | 0 | 1 | 1 | 6 |
| Paolo Fiorin | 1 | 0 | 0 | 0 | 0 |
| Ian Witucki (Goalie) | 1 | 0 | 0 | 0 | 0 |
| Jeff Hauser | 2 | 0 | 0 | 0 | 4 |
| Oldrick Kuca | 2 | 0 | 0 | 0 | 7 |

## Niagara Falls Thunder

|  | Games | G. | A. | Pts. | Pen. |
|---|---|---|---|---|---|
| Bryan Fogarty | 60 | 47 | *108 | *155 | 88 |
| Stan Drulia | 47 | 52 | 93 | 145 | 59 |
| Keith Osborne, N.B. | 15 | 11 | 15 | 26 | 12 |
| Niagara Falls | 50 | 34 | 49 | 83 | 45 |
| Totals | 65 | 45 | 64 | 109 | 57 |
| Jamie Leach | 58 | 45 | 62 | 107 | 47 |
| Shawn McCosh | 56 | 41 | 62 | 103 | 75 |
| Colin Miller | 62 | 32 | 48 | 80 | 46 |
| Scott Pearson, Kingston | 13 | 9 | 8 | 17 | 34 |
| Niagara Falls | 32 | 26 | 34 | 60 | 90 |
| Totals | 45 | 35 | 42 | 77 | 124 |
| Steve Locke | 61 | 23 | 40 | 63 | 83 |
| Keith Primeau | 48 | 20 | 35 | 55 | 56 |
| Dennis Vial | 50 | 10 | 27 | 37 | 230 |
| Mark Lawrence | 63 | 9 | 27 | 36 | 142 |
| Greg Allen | 57 | 14 | 13 | 27 | 50 |
| Brad May | 65 | 8 | 14 | 22 | 304 |

|  | Games | G. | A. | Pts. | Pen. |
|---|---|---|---|---|---|
| Don Pancoe | 54 | 1 | 17 | 18 | 167 |
| Dave Carrie | 38 | 5 | 12 | 17 | 21 |
| Paul Wolanski | 61 | 7 | 9 | 16 | 63 |
| Alain Laforge | 48 | 4 | 11 | 15 | 89 |
| Jason Soules | 57 | 3 | 8 | 11 | 187 |
| Paul Laus | 49 | 1 | 10 | 11 | 225 |
| Brian Mueggler | 32 | 3 | 2 | 5 | 10 |
| Nick Zarafonitis | 14 | 2 | 1 | 3 | 33 |
| Rob Fournier, N.B. (G.) | 9 | 0 | 1 | 1 | 6 |
| Niagara Falls (G.) | 32 | 0 | 1 | 1 | 12 |
| Totals | 41 | 0 | 2 | 2 | 18 |
| Mike Rosati (Goalie) | 52 | 0 | 2 | 2 | 32 |
| Adrian VanderSloot | 22 | 0 | 1 | 1 | 45 |
| Rick Cormier | 2 | 0 | 0 | 0 | 0 |
| James Organ (Goalie) | 2 | 0 | 0 | 0 | 0 |
| Todd Reynolds (Goalie) | 4 | 0 | 0 | 0 | 2 |
| Mike Berlet | 5 | 0 | 0 | 0 | 12 |
| Bill Everson (Goalie) | 5 | 0 | 0 | 0 | 0 |

## North Bay Centennials

|  | Games | G. | A. | Pts. | Pen. |
|---|---|---|---|---|---|
| John Purves, N.F. | 5 | 5 | 11 | 16 | 2 |
| North Bay | 42 | 34 | 52 | 86 | 38 |
| Totals | 47 | 39 | 63 | 102 | 40 |
| Peter Bitonti | 61 | 34 | 31 | 65 | 20 |
| Derek Switzer | 60 | 20 | 42 | 62 | 14 |
| Tyler Ertel | 56 | 23 | 36 | 59 | 79 |
| Derek Langille | 60 | 20 | 38 | 58 | 128 |
| Shawn Roy | 61 | 15 | 23 | 38 | 50 |
| Joel Morin, Kingston | 9 | 3 | 4 | 7 | 7 |
| North Bay | 51 | 11 | 17 | 28 | 34 |
| Totals | 60 | 14 | 21 | 35 | 41 |
| John Spoltore | 57 | 16 | 18 | 34 | 9 |
| Jeff Gardiner, N. Falls | 13 | 4 | 7 | 11 | 5 |
| North Bay | 47 | 9 | 11 | 20 | 0 |
| Totals | 60 | 13 | 18 | 31 | 5 |
| Greg Capson, Kingston | 14 | 1 | 6 | 7 | 18 |
| North Bay | 50 | 7 | 17 | 24 | 86 |
| Totals | 64 | 8 | 23 | 31 | 104 |
| Shawn Antoski | 57 | 6 | 21 | 27 | 201 |
| Scott Shepherd | 63 | 8 | 18 | 26 | 79 |
| Mike Fiset, Kingston | 13 | 7 | 11 | 18 | 8 |
| North Bay | 9 | 3 | 3 | 6 | 6 |
| Totals | 22 | 10 | 14 | 24 | 14 |
| Steve Bisson, Cornwall | 2 | 0 | 0 | 0 | 6 |
| North Bay | 35 | 8 | 16 | 24 | 77 |
| Totals | 37 | 8 | 16 | 24 | 83 |
| Colin Austin, Niag. Falls | 8 | 0 | 0 | 0 | 27 |
| North Bay | 40 | 9 | 12 | 21 | 80 |
| Totals | 48 | 9 | 12 | 21 | 107 |
| John Van Kessel | 50 | 7 | 13 | 20 | 218 |
| Cory Pageau | 56 | 5 | 15 | 20 | 114 |
| Trevor Halverson | 52 | 8 | 10 | 18 | 77 |
| Adam Burt | 23 | 4 | 11 | 15 | 45 |
| Jason Corrigan | 23 | 7 | 2 | 9 | 6 |
| John Vary | 45 | 2 | 7 | 9 | 38 |
| Gary Miller | 59 | 2 | 6 | 8 | 57 |
| Richard Roesler, N. Falls | 9 | 1 | 2 | 3 | 9 |
| North Bay | 2 | 0 | 0 | 0 | 5 |
| Totals | 11 | 1 | 2 | 3 | 14 |
| Jason Houle (Goalie) | 28 | 1 | 0 | 1 | 14 |
| Dale Shannon, Oshawa | 2 | 0 | 0 | 0 | 0 |
| North Bay | 15 | 0 | 1 | 1 | 9 |
| Totals | 17 | 0 | 1 | 1 | 9 |
| John MacKinnon (G.) | 2 | 0 | 0 | 0 | 0 |
| Brad Traves | 4 | 0 | 0 | 0 | 2 |
| Mike Matuszek (Goalie) | 32 | 0 | 0 | 0 | 2 |

## Oshawa Generals

|  | Games | G. | A. | Pts. | Pen. |
|---|---|---|---|---|---|
| Kevin Miehm | 63 | 43 | 79 | 122 | 19 |
| Iain Fraser | 62 | 33 | 57 | 90 | 87 |
| Brian Hunt | 63 | 30 | 56 | 86 | 36 |
| Jarrod Skalde | 65 | 38 | 38 | 76 | 36 |
| Mike Craig | 63 | 36 | 36 | 72 | 34 |
| Brent Grieve | 49 | 34 | 33 | 67 | 105 |
| Craig Donaldson | 56 | 14 | 40 | 54 | 44 |
| Joe Busillo | 59 | 17 | 26 | 43 | 153 |
| Tony Joseph | 52 | 20 | 16 | 36 | 106 |
| Scott Mahoney | 56 | 14 | 22 | 36 | 207 |
| Jean Paul Davis | 55 | 2 | 28 | 30 | 20 |
| David Craievich | 62 | 2 | 23 | 25 | 78 |
| Dale Craigwell | 55 | 9 | 14 | 23 | 15 |
| Paul O'Hagan | 65 | 2 | 18 | 20 | 93 |
| Cory Banika | 57 | 11 | 8 | 19 | 100 |
| Trevor McIvor | 50 | 9 | 8 | 17 | 8 |
| Mike DeCoff | 38 | 6 | 9 | 15 | 58 |
| Mike Short | 47 | 4 | 11 | 15 | 127 |
| Jamie Lever | 36 | 3 | 7 | 10 | 60 |
| Jim Ritchie | 28 | 4 | 5 | 9 | 60 |
| Scott Taylor | 20 | 2 | 5 | 7 | 47 |
| Fred Goltz | 24 | 3 | 3 | 6 | 12 |
| Kevin Butt (Goalie) | 31 | 0 | 3 | 3 | 18 |
| Todd Blackman | 23 | 1 | 1 | 2 | 25 |
| Todd Coopman | 8 | 0 | 2 | 2 | 6 |
| Shawn Simpson (Goalie) | 33 | 0 | 1 | 1 | 10 |
| Derek Pifer | 5 | 0 | 0 | 0 | 16 |
| Dave Humphreys (G.) | 6 | 0 | 0 | 0 | 2 |
| Mike Lenarduzzi (G.) | 6 | 0 | 0 | 0 | 0 |

## Ottawa 67's

|  | Games | G. | A. | Pts. | Pen. |
|---|---|---|---|---|---|
| Andrew Cassels | 56 | 37 | 97 | 134 | 66 |
| Mike Griffin | 64 | 47 | 42 | 89 | 54 |
| Troy Binnie | 64 | 32 | 40 | 72 | 30 |
| Jerrett DeFazio | 65 | 35 | 36 | 71 | 21 |
| Chris Snell | 66 | 11 | 48 | 59 | 16 |
| Brett Seguin | 48 | 16 | 36 | 52 | 12 |
| Joni Lehto | 63 | 9 | 35 | 44 | 26 |
| Jamie Henckel, Belleville | 1 | 0 | 0 | 0 | 0 |
| Ottawa | 34 | 19 | 23 | 42 | 14 |
| Totals | 35 | 19 | 23 | 42 | 14 |
| Greg Walters | 28 | 17 | 21 | 38 | 20 |
| Joey McTamney, N. B. | 3 | 0 | 0 | 0 | 9 |
| Ottawa | 56 | 13 | 17 | 30 | 27 |
| Totals | 59 | 13 | 17 | 30 | 36 |
| Pat Howie | 64 | 14 | 13 | 27 | 54 |
| Steve Kluczkowski, N. B. | 28 | 4 | 3 | 7 | 4 |
| Ottawa | 26 | 8 | 10 | 18 | 7 |
| Totals | 54 | 12 | 13 | 25 | 11 |
| John East | 57 | 7 | 17 | 24 | 61 |
| Jeff Ballantyne | 61 | 3 | 21 | 24 | 155 |
| Peter Ambroziak | 50 | 8 | 15 | 23 | 11 |
| Scott McPherson | 63 | 7 | 15 | 22 | 6 |
| Jeff Ricciardi | 63 | 4 | 12 | 16 | 107 |
| Rob Boldon | 66 | 1 | 13 | 14 | 57 |
| Rob Papineau | 32 | 3 | 4 | 7 | 6 |
| Chris Simon | 36 | 4 | 2 | 6 | 31 |
| Dean Duggan | 6 | 0 | 2 | 2 | 0 |
| Wayne Verge | 7 | 0 | 2 | 2 | 11 |
| Scott Cumming (Goalie) | 46 | 0 | 2 | 2 | 24 |
| Mike Allen | 2 | 0 | 1 | 1 | 0 |
| Jeff Deavy | 11 | 0 | 1 | 1 | 7 |
| Todd Paterson, Oshawa | 4 | 0 | 1 | 1 | 6 |
| Ottawa | 40 | 0 | 0 | 0 | 56 |
| Totals | 44 | 0 | 1 | 1 | 62 |

|  | Games | G. | A. | Pts. | Pen. |
|---|---|---|---|---|---|
| Matt Smyth | 1 | 0 | 0 | 0 | 8 |
| Peter McGlynn (Goalie) | 4 | 0 | 0 | 0 | 2 |
| Jason Spencer | 8 | 0 | 0 | 0 | 0 |
| George Dourian (G.) | 29 | 0 | 0 | 0 | 2 |

## Peterborough Petes

|  | Games | G. | A. | Pts. | Pen. |
|---|---|---|---|---|---|
| Mike Ricci | 60 | 54 | 52 | 106 | 43 |
| Ross Wilson | 64 | 48 | 41 | 89 | 90 |
| Jamey Hicks | 58 | 18 | 39 | 57 | 38 |
| Dave Lorentz | 65 | 18 | 38 | 56 | 47 |
| Corey Foster | 55 | 14 | 42 | 56 | 42 |
| Andy MacVicar | 66 | 25 | 29 | 54 | 56 |
| Geoff Ingram | 64 | 15 | 32 | 47 | 121 |
| Joe Hawley | 49 | 13 | 30 | 43 | 61 |
| Mark Myles | 66 | 19 | 22 | 41 | 119 |
| Mike Dagenais | 62 | 14 | 24 | 38 | 122 |
| Brian Hayton | 43 | 6 | 30 | 36 | 102 |
| Troy Stephens | 63 | 17 | 18 | 35 | 32 |
| Jamie Pegg | 66 | 4 | 27 | 31 | 27 |
| Tie Domi | 43 | 14 | 16 | 30 | 175 |
| Rob Wilson | 63 | 4 | 14 | 18 | 146 |
| Steve DeGurse | 64 | 4 | 14 | 18 | 171 |
| Dan Brown | 51 | 3 | 15 | 18 | 29 |
| Paul Mitton | 59 | 6 | 4 | 10 | 224 |
| Mike Tomlinson | 28 | 1 | 4 | 5 | 27 |
| Jassen Cullimore | 20 | 2 | 1 | 3 | 6 |
| Scott Campbell | 29 | 0 | 1 | 1 | 16 |
| John Tanner (Goalie) | 34 | 0 | 1 | 1 | 32 |
| Todd Bojcun (Goalie) | 35 | 0 | 1 | 1 | 10 |
| Darren Cullimore | 1 | 0 | 0 | 0 | 0 |
| Greg Kains (Goalie) | 1 | 0 | 0 | 0 | 2 |
| Mike St. John | 5 | 0 | 0 | 0 | 0 |
| Tom Hopkins | 8 | 0 | 0 | 0 | 7 |

## Sault Ste. Marie Greyhounds

|  | Games | G. | A. | Pts. | Pen. |
|---|---|---|---|---|---|
| Troy Mallette | 64 | 39 | 37 | 76 | 172 |
| Mark Turner, Windsor | 15 | 7 | 12 | 19 | 16 |
| Sudbury | 9 | 5 | 1 | 6 | 8 |
| Sault Ste. Marie | 29 | 16 | 24 | 40 | 20 |
| Totals | 53 | 28 | 37 | 65 | 44 |
| Wayne Muir | 65 | 24 | 19 | 43 | 226 |
| Colin Ford | 50 | 11 | 29 | 40 | 93 |
| Don McConnell | 61 | 11 | 28 | 39 | 30 |
| Adam Foote | 66 | 7 | 31 | 38 | 120 |
| Dale Turnbull | 60 | 16 | 21 | 37 | 30 |
| Bob Jones | 60 | 13 | 21 | 34 | 136 |
| Denny Lambert | 61 | 14 | 15 | 29 | 203 |
| Glen Johnston | 52 | 11 | 18 | 29 | 53 |
| Peter Fiorentino | 55 | 5 | 24 | 29 | 220 |
| Bob Boughner | 64 | 6 | 15 | 21 | 182 |
| Gary Luther | 40 | 6 | 14 | 20 | 19 |
| Paul Silva | 45 | 5 | 12 | 17 | 121 |
| Brad Tiley | 50 | 4 | 11 | 15 | 31 |
| Derek Jefferson | 43 | 5 | 6 | 11 | 32 |
| Dan Ferguson | 62 | 3 | 5 | 8 | 199 |
| Bill Harrington | 23 | 2 | 4 | 6 | 9 |
| Shawn Simpson, King. | 5 | 0 | 0 | 0 | 4 |
| Sault Ste. Marie | 13 | 3 | 1 | 4 | 0 |
| Totals | 18 | 3 | 1 | 4 | 4 |
| Doug Minor | 36 | 1 | 2 | 3 | 66 |
| Brad Jones | 11 | 1 | 1 | 2 | 6 |
| Steve Udvari (Goalie) | 46 | 0 | 2 | 2 | 19 |
| Lenny DeVuono | 56 | 0 | 2 | 2 | 57 |
| Jason Duguay | 2 | 0 | 0 | 0 | 0 |

|  | Games | G. | A. | Pts. | Pen. |
|---|---|---|---|---|---|
| Bill Whistle | 3 | 0 | 0 | 0 | 5 |
| Graeme Harvey (Goalie) | 31 | 0 | 0 | 0 | 12 |

## Sudbury Wolves

|  | Games | G. | A. | Pts. | Pen. |
|---|---|---|---|---|---|
| Paul DiPietro | 57 | 31 | 48 | 79 | 27 |
| Todd Lalonde | 52 | 32 | 44 | 76 | 57 |
| Jordan Fois | 62 | 14 | 43 | 57 | 91 |
| Andy Paquette | 66 | 16 | 39 | 55 | 41 |
| Kevin Grant, Kitchener | 15 | 3 | 11 | 14 | 43 |
| Sudbury | 45 | 6 | 30 | 36 | 143 |
| Totals | 60 | 9 | 41 | 50 | 186 |
| Darren Bell | 66 | 22 | 22 | 44 | 59 |
| John Andersen, N.F. | 1 | 1 | 2 | 3 | 0 |
| Sudbury | 33 | 17 | 24 | 41 | 11 |
| Totals | 34 | 18 | 26 | 44 | 11 |
| Jim Smith | 39 | 14 | 28 | 42 | 68 |
| Jim Sonmez | 63 | 16 | 25 | 41 | 52 |
| Fred Pennell | 54 | 20 | 20 | 40 | 131 |
| Terry Chitaroni | 58 | 17 | 23 | 40 | 103 |
| Rob Knesaurek, Oshawa | 5 | 0 | 4 | 4 | 0 |
| Sudbury | 53 | 13 | 15 | 28 | 53 |
| Totals | 58 | 13 | 19 | 32 | 53 |
| Adam Bennett | 66 | 7 | 22 | 29 | 133 |
| Derek Booth, Cornwall | 24 | 3 | 13 | 16 | 42 |
| Sudbury | 31 | 0 | 11 | 11 | 47 |
| Totals | 55 | 3 | 24 | 27 | 89 |
| Trevor Smith, Kingston | 3 | 0 | 1 | 1 | 0 |
| Sault Ste. Marie | 29 | 7 | 3 | 10 | 23 |
| Sudbury | 23 | 4 | 3 | 7 | 6 |
| Totals | 55 | 11 | 7 | 18 | 29 |
| Alastair Still | 63 | 7 | 8 | 15 | 53 |
| Shannon Bolton | 58 | 4 | 11 | 15 | 138 |
| Shane Sargant, S.S.M. | 42 | 1 | 8 | 9 | 28 |
| Sudbury | 10 | 0 | 1 | 1 | 0 |
| Totals | 52 | 1 | 9 | 10 | 28 |
| Sean O'Donnell | 56 | 1 | 9 | 10 | 49 |
| Tyler Pella, Windsor | 14 | 2 | 2 | 4 | 26 |
| Sudbury | 39 | 3 | 1 | 4 | 24 |
| Totals | 53 | 5 | 3 | 8 | 50 |
| Sean Stansfield, Kit. | 8 | 0 | 0 | 0 | 2 |
| Sudbury | 29 | 3 | 5 | 8 | 10 |
| Totals | 37 | 3 | 5 | 8 | 12 |
| Danny Resko, Toronto | 5 | 2 | 2 | 4 | 13 |
| Sudbury | 8 | 1 | 0 | 1 | 9 |
| Totals | 13 | 3 | 2 | 5 | 22 |
| Derek Thompson | 7 | 1 | 1 | 2 | 9 |
| Brad Kutschke, Windsor | 8 | 1 | 0 | 1 | 4 |
| Sudbury | 1 | 0 | 0 | 0 | 0 |
| Totals | 9 | 1 | 0 | 1 | 4 |
| Dave Akey | 1 | 0 | 1 | 1 | 0 |
| Scott Herniman | 25 | 0 | 1 | 1 | 25 |
| D. Goverde, Wsr. (G.) | 5 | 0 | 0 | 0 | 2 |
| Sudbury (Goalie) | 39 | 0 | 1 | 1 | 25 |
| Totals | 44 | 0 | 1 | 1 | 27 |
| Rodney Lapointe | 1 | 0 | 0 | 0 | 0 |
| Tony MacAulay | 1 | 0 | 0 | 0 | 0 |
| Ken Resetar | 1 | 0 | 0 | 0 | 2 |
| Cory Lavigne (Goalie) | 3 | 0 | 0 | 0 | 0 |
| Dan Ryder (Goalie) | 5 | 0 | 0 | 0 | 0 |
| Ted Mielczarek (G.) | 32 | 0 | 0 | 0 | 2 |

## Toronto Marlboros

|  | Games | G. | A. | Pts. | Pen. |
|---|---|---|---|---|---|
| Rob Cimetta | 50 | *55 | 47 | 102 | 89 |
| Sean Davidson | 66 | 32 | 68 | 100 | 70 |
| John Nelson | 66 | 39 | 60 | 99 | 156 |

| | Games | G. | A. | Pts. | Pen. |
|---|---|---|---|---|---|
| Jason Winch | 66 | 33 | 50 | 83 | 8 |
| Chris Govedaris | 49 | 41 | 38 | 79 | 117 |
| Mike Jackson | 55 | 16 | 51 | 67 | 180 |
| Brian Collinson | 61 | 19 | 36 | 55 | 71 |
| Jeff Turcotte | 61 | 16 | 31 | 47 | 37 |
| Greg Suchan | 66 | 17 | 28 | 45 | 60 |
| Bill Kovacs | 66 | 12 | 21 | 33 | 60 |
| Mike Reier | 55 | 20 | 11 | 31 | 77 |
| Rob Leask | 64 | 4 | 21 | 25 | 63 |
| Jeff Sirkka, North Bay | 12 | 0 | 3 | 3 | 66 |
| Toronto | 29 | 1 | 14 | 15 | 71 |
| Totals | 41 | 1 | 17 | 18 | 137 |
| Bill Armstrong | 64 | 1 | 16 | 17 | 82 |
| Clayton Martin | 63 | 4 | 11 | 15 | 56 |
| Shawn Costello | 58 | 3 | 11 | 14 | 4 |
| Barry Young | 66 | 1 | 12 | 13 | 64 |
| George Radan | 62 | 1 | 6 | 7 | 44 |
| Shane Cretney | 19 | 2 | 1 | 3 | 0 |
| Steve Woods | 9 | 0 | 1 | 1 | 0 |
| John Batten | 1 | 0 | 0 | 0 | 0 |
| Dave Callan | 1 | 0 | 0 | 0 | 0 |
| Josh Foster | 2 | 0 | 0 | 0 | 0 |
| Don McCarthy | 2 | 0 | 0 | 0 | 2 |
| Dallas Mix (Goalie) | 2 | 0 | 0 | 0 | 0 |
| Jeff Bird (Goalie) | 32 | 0 | 0 | 0 | 4 |
| David Schill, Lon. (G.) | 30 | 0 | 0 | 0 | 12 |
| Toronto (Goalie) | 26 | 0 | 0 | 0 | 24 |
| Totals | 56 | 0 | 0 | 0 | 36 |

## Windsor Compuware Spitfires

| | Games | G. | A. | Pts. | Pen. |
|---|---|---|---|---|---|
| Peter DeBoer | 65 | 45 | 46 | 91 | 40 |
| Darrin Shannon | 54 | 33 | 48 | 81 | 47 |
| Jason York | 65 | 19 | 44 | 63 | 105 |
| Jason Simon, Kingston | 17 | 7 | 12 | 19 | 58 |
| Windsor | 45 | 16 | 27 | 43 | 135 |
| Totals | 62 | 23 | 39 | 62 | 193 |
| Mike Wolak | 35 | 19 | 38 | 57 | 56 |
| Ted Miskolczi, London | 23 | 6 | 2 | 8 | 26 |
| Windsor | 39 | 10 | 18 | 28 | 26 |
| Totals | 62 | 16 | 20 | 36 | 52 |
| Kevin White | 66 | 11 | 23 | 34 | 39 |
| Chris Lukey, Kingston | 16 | 5 | 9 | 14 | 24 |
| Windsor | 36 | 12 | 6 | 18 | 55 |
| Totals | 52 | 17 | 15 | 32 | 79 |
| Tom Purcell | 57 | 6 | 26 | 32 | 133 |
| Jim Revenberg | 58 | 9 | 15 | 24 | 292 |
| Karl Taylor | 66 | 8 | 15 | 23 | 28 |
| John Johnson | 53 | 10 | 10 | 20 | 13 |
| Chad Badawey, Sud. | 13 | 2 | 1 | 3 | 17 |
| Windsor | 41 | 11 | 5 | 16 | 10 |
| Totals | 54 | 13 | 6 | 19 | 27 |
| Kevin Falesy | 61 | 2 | 16 | 18 | 118 |
| Bob Leeming | 27 | 5 | 10 | 15 | 4 |
| Peter Liptrott, London | 20 | 1 | 2 | 3 | 39 |
| Windsor | 42 | 1 | 9 | 10 | 122 |
| Totals | 62 | 2 | 11 | 13 | 161 |
| Trent Gleason | 52 | 3 | 9 | 12 | 46 |
| Brian Forestell | 61 | 3 | 9 | 12 | 9 |
| Sean Burns | 56 | 4 | 7 | 11 | 94 |
| Jason Stos, London | 17 | 0 | 1 | 1 | 15 |
| Windsor | 37 | 2 | 7 | 9 | 63 |
| Totals | 54 | 2 | 8 | 10 | 78 |
| Trevor Walsh, London | 5 | 0 | 3 | 3 | 13 |
| Windsor | 2 | 0 | 1 | 1 | 0 |
| Totals | 7 | 0 | 4 | 4 | 13 |
| Troy Gleason | 7 | 0 | 2 | 2 | 2 |
| Sean O'Hagan (Goalie) | 27 | 0 | 2 | 2 | 8 |
| Dan Drouin | 14 | 0 | 1 | 1 | 9 |
| Dave Bonnar | 1 | 0 | 0 | 0 | 0 |
| Sam Haidy | 2 | 0 | 0 | 0 | 0 |
| K. McDougall, Lon. (G.) | 9 | 0 | 0 | 0 | 4 |
| Winsdor (Goalie) | 26 | 0 | 0 | 0 | 0 |
| Totals | 35 | 0 | 0 | 0 | 4 |

## Complete OHL Goaltending

| | Games | Mins. | Goals | SO. | Avg. |
|---|---|---|---|---|---|
| Lyle Peel | 2 | 80 | 6 | 0 | 4.50 |
| Jeff Fife | 41 | 2188 | 169(2) | 0 | 4.63 |
| Troy Nelson | 35 | 1714 | 143(2) | 1 | 5.01 |
| Belleville Totals | 66 | 3982 | 322 | 1 | 4.85 |
| Rick Tabaracci | 50 | 2974 | *210(2) | 1 | 4.24 |
| Mike O'Rourke | 6 | 329 | 30 | 0 | 5.47 |
| Darryl Paquette | 13 | 697 | 65(1) | 0 | 5.60 |
| Cornwall Totals | 66 | 4000 | 308 | 1 | 4.62 |
| Mike Parson | *53 | *3047 | 194(5) | 0 | 3.82 |
| Pat McGarry | 14 | 706 | 60(1) | 0 | 5.10 |
| Jay Evershed | 3 | 142 | 13 | 0 | 5.49 |
| Curtis Green | 2 | 120 | 14(1) | 0 | 7.00 |
| Guelph Totals | 66 | 4016 | 288 | 0 | 4.30 |
| Jeff Wilson | 47 | 2449 | 163(3) | 1 | 3.99 |
| Sean Gauthier | 37 | 1528 | 141(4) | 0 | 5.54 |
| Stephane Finucan | 1 | 20 | 2 | 0 | 6.00 |
| Kingston Totals | 66 | 3996 | 313 | 1 | 4.70 |
| Gus Morschauser | 41 | 2311 | 132(3) | *2 | 3.43 |
| Mike Torchia | 30 | 1672 | 112(2) | 0 | 4.02 |
| Duane Anderson | 1 | 16 | 2 | 0 | 7.50 |
| Kitchener Totals | 66 | 4000 | 251 | 2 | 3.76 |
| Ian Witucki | 1 | 9 | 0 | 0 | 0.00 |
| Peter Ing (a) | 32 | 1848 | 104(3) | *2 | 3.38 |
| Pat Tenpenny (b) | 4 | 200 | 12(1) | 0 | 3.60 |
| David Schill (c) | 30 | 1609 | 112(1) | 1 | 4.18 |
| Kevin McDougall (d) | 9 | 334 | 31 | 0 | 5.57 |
| London Totals | 66 | 4000 | 264 | 3 | 3.96 |

|  | Games | Mins. | Goals | SO. | Avg. |
|---|---|---|---|---|---|
| Mike Rosati | 52 | 2339 | 174 | 1 | 4.46 |
| Rob Fournier (e) | 32 | 1293 | 104(1) | 0 | 4.83 |
| James Organ | 2 | 28 | 3 | 0 | 6.43 |
| Todd Reynolds | 4 | 110 | 12 | 0 | 6.55 |
| Bill Everson | 5 | 208 | 24(1) | 0 | 6.92 |
| Niagara Falls Totals | 66 | 3977 | 319 | 1 | 4.81 |
| Mike Matuszek | 32 | 1879 | 132(2) | 0 | 4.22 |
| Jason Houle | 28 | 1530 | 136(2) | 0 | 5.33 |
| Rob Fournier (e) | 9 | 502 | 49(1) | 0 | 5.86 |
| John MacKinnon | 2 | 86 | 12 | 0 | 8.37 |
| North Bay Totals | 66 | 3997 | 334 | 0 | 5.01 |
| Mike Lenarduzzi | 6 | 166 | 9 | 0 | 3.25 |
| Dave Humphreys | 6 | 328 | 22 | 0 | 4.02 |
| Kevin Butt | 31 | 1687 | 120(3) | 0 | 4.27 |
| Shawn Simpson | 33 | 1818 | 131(1) | 0 | 4.32 |
| Oshawa Totals | 66 | 3999 | 286 | 0 | 4.29 |
| George Dourian | 29 | 1265 | 87 | 1 | 4.13 |
| Scott Cumming | 46 | 2491 | 185(3) | 0 | 4.46 |
| Peter McGlynn | 4 | 240 | 26 | 0 | 6.50 |
| Ottawa Totals | 66 | 3996 | 301 | 1 | 4.52 |
| John Tanner | 34 | 1923 | 107(2) | *2 | *3.34 |
| Todd Bojcun | 35 | 2054 | 123(1) | 1 | 3.59 |
| Greg Kains | 1 | 12 | 2 | 0 | 10.00 |
| Peterborough Totals | 66 | 3989 | 235 | 3 | 3.53 |
| Steve Udvari | 46 | 2476 | 178(5) | 1 | 4.31 |
| Graeme Harvey | 31 | 1509 | 121 | 0 | 4.81 |
| Sault Ste. Marie Totals | 66 | 3985 | 304 | 1 | 4.58 |
| David Goverde (f) | 39 | 2189 | 156(2) | 0 | 4.28 |
| Ted Mielczarek | 32 | 1565 | 139 | 0 | 5.33 |
| Cory Lavigne | 3 | 87 | 8 | 0 | 5.52 |
| Dan Ryder | 5 | 172 | 29 | 0 | 10.12 |
| Sudbury Totals | 66 | 4012 | 334 | 0 | 5.00 |
| David Schill (c) | 26 | 1475 | 113(1) | 0 | 4.60 |
| Jeff Bird | 32 | 1629 | 132(2) | 0 | 4.86 |
| Pat Tenpenny (b) | 17 | 836 | 78 | 0 | 5.60 |
| Dallas Mix | 2 | 47 | 6 | 0 | 7.66 |
| Toronto Totals | 66 | 3986 | 332 | 0 | 5.00 |
| Peter Ing (a) | 19 | 1043 | 76 | 1 | 4.37 |
| Kevin McDougall (d) | 26 | 1369 | 100(2) | 0 | 4.38 |
| Sean O'Hagan | 27 | 1361 | 115(3) | 0 | 5.07 |
| David Goverde (f) | 5 | 221 | 24(1) | 0 | 6.52 |
| Windsor Totals | 66 | 3994 | 321 | 1 | 4.82 |

( )—Empty Net Goals. Do not count against a Goaltender's average.
(a)—Ing played for London and Windsor.
(b)—Tenpenny played for London and Toronto.
(c)—Schill played for London and Toronto.
(d)—McDougall played for London and Winsdor.
(e)—Fournier played for Niagara Falls and North Bay.
(f)—Goverde played for Sudbury and Windsor.

## Individual 1988-89 Leaders

| | | |
|---|---|---|
| Goals | Rob Cimetta, Toronto— | 55 |
| Assists | Bryan Fogarty, Niagara Falls— | 108 |
| Points | Bryan Fogarty, Niagara Falls— | 155 |
| Penalty Minutes | Rob Sangster, Kitchener— | 337 |
| Goaltender's Average | John Tanner, Peterborough— | 3.34 |
| Shutouts | Peter Ing, London— | 2 |
| | Gus Morschauser, Kitchener— | 2 |
| | John Tanner, Peterborough— | 2 |

# 1989 J. Ross Robertson Cup Playoffs

(All series best-of-seven)

## Division Quarterfinals

### Leyden Division
**Series "A"**

|  | W. | L. | Pts. | GF. | GA. |
|---|---|---|---|---|---|
| Peterborough | 4 | 1 | 8 | 25 | 15 |
| Belleville | 1 | 4 | 2 | 15 | 25 |

(Peterborough wins series, 4 games to 1)

**Series "B"**

|  | W. | L. | Pts. | GF. | GA. |
|---|---|---|---|---|---|
| Ottawa | 4 | 2 | 8 | 23 | 23 |
| Oshawa | 2 | 4 | 4 | 23 | 23 |

(Ottawa wins series, 4 games to 2)

**Series "C"**

|  | W. | L. | Pts. | GF. | GA. |
|---|---|---|---|---|---|
| Cornwall | 4 | 2 | 8 | 38 | 24 |
| Toronto | 2 | 4 | 4 | 24 | 38 |

(Cornwall wins series, 4 games to 2)

### Emms Division
**Series "A"**

|  | W. | L. | Pts. | GF. | GA. |
|---|---|---|---|---|---|
| North Bay | 4 | 1 | 8 | 26 | 12 |
| Kitchener | 1 | 4 | 2 | 12 | 26 |

(North Bay wins series, 4 games to 1)

**Series "B"**

|  | W. | L. | Pts. | GF. | GA. |
|---|---|---|---|---|---|
| Niagara Falls | 4 | 0 | 8 | 30 | 17 |
| Windsor | 0 | 4 | 0 | 17 | 30 |

(Niagara Falls wins series, 4 games to 0)

**Series "C"**

|  | W. | L. | Pts. | GF. | GA. |
|---|---|---|---|---|---|
| London | 4 | 3 | 8 | 31 | 32 |
| Guelph | 3 | 4 | 6 | 32 | 31 |

(London wins series, 4 games to 3)

## Division Semifinals

**Series "D"**

|  | W. | L. | Pts. | GF. | GA. |
|---|---|---|---|---|---|
| Cornwall | 4 | 2 | 8 | 29 | 17 |
| Ottawa | 2 | 4 | 4 | 17 | 29 |

(Cornwall wins series, 4 games to 2)

**Series "D"**

|  | W. | L. | Pts. | GF. | GA. |
|---|---|---|---|---|---|
| London | 4 | 3 | 8 | 30 | 28 |
| North Bay | 3 | 4 | 6 | 28 | 30 |

(London wins series, 4 games to 3)

## Division Finals

**Series "E"**

|  | W. | L. | Pts. | GF. | GA. |
|---|---|---|---|---|---|
| Peterborough | 4 | 2 | 8 | 25 | 25 |
| Cornwall | 2 | 4 | 4 | 25 | 25 |

(Peterborough wins series, 4 games to 2)

**Series "E"**

|  | W. | L. | Pts. | GF. | GA. |
|---|---|---|---|---|---|
| Niagara Falls | 4 | 3 | 8 | 36 | 34 |
| London | 3 | 4 | 6 | 34 | 36 |

(Niagara Falls wins series, 4 games to 3)

# OHL Final Series for the J. Ross Robertson Cup

**Series "F"**

|  | W. | L. | Pts. | GF. | GA. |
|---|---|---|---|---|---|
| Peterborough | 4 | 2 | 8 | 33 | 19 |
| Niagara Falls | 2 | 4 | 4 | 19 | 33 |

(Peter. wins series, and Robertson Cup, 4 games to 2)

## Top 10 Playoff Scorers

|  | Games | G. | A. | Pts. | Pen. |
|---|---|---|---|---|---|
| 1. Tim Taylor, London | 21 | *21 | 25 | *46 | 58 |
| 2. Kelly Cain, London | 21 | 20 | 22 | 42 | 16 |
| 3. Stan Drulia, Niagara Falls | 17 | 11 | *26 | 37 | 18 |
| 4. Mike Ricci, Peterborough | 17 | 19 | 16 | 35 | 18 |
| 5. Bryan Fogarty, Niagara Falls | 17 | 10 | 22 | 32 | 36 |
| 6. Dennis McEwen, London | 20 | 15 | 16 | 31 | 44 |
| 7. Steve Maltais, Cornwall | 18 | 14 | 16 | 30 | 16 |
| 8. Jamey Hicks, Peterborough | 17 | 8 | 20 | 28 | 14 |
| 9. Jason Cirone, Cornwall | 17 | 19 | 8 | 27 | 14 |
| 10. John Purves, North Bay | 12 | 14 | 12 | 26 | 16 |
| Mathieu Schneider, Cornwall | 18 | 7 | 19 | 26 | 30 |

# Team-by-Team Playoff Scoring

## Belleville Bulls

(Lost division quarterfinals to Peterb'r'gh, 4 games to 1)

|  | Games | G. | A. | Pts. | Pen. |
|---|---|---|---|---|---|
| Richard Fatrola | 5 | 2 | 3 | 5 | 2 |
| Norm Batherson | 5 | 2 | 2 | 4 | 7 |
| Ken Rowbotham | 5 | 2 | 2 | 4 | 2 |
| Bob Berg | 5 | 1 | 3 | 4 | 8 |
| Kent Hulst | 5 | 1 | 3 | 4 | 4 |
| Dan Poirier | 5 | 2 | 0 | 2 | 6 |

|                       | Games | G. | A. | Pts. | Pen. |
|-----------------------|-------|----|----|------|------|
| Darryl Williams       | 5     | 2  | 0  | 2    | 17   |
| Scott Thornton        | 5     | 1  | 1  | 2    | 6    |
| Steve Bancroft        | 5     | 0  | 2  | 2    | 10   |
| Scott Feasby          | 5     | 0  | 2  | 2    | 21   |
| Scott Boston          | 5     | 1  | 0  | 1    | 8    |
| Jeff Cantlon          | 5     | 1  | 0  | 1    | 15   |
| Gary Taylor           | 4     | 0  | 1  | 1    | 2    |
| Greg Bignell          | 5     | 0  | 1  | 1    | 16   |
| Jim Dean              | 5     | 0  | 1  | 1    | 2    |
| Bryan Marchment       | 5     | 0  | 1  | 1    | 12   |
| Troy Nelson (Goalie)  | 1     | 0  | 0  | 0    | 0    |
| Mark Rupnow           | 1     | 0  | 0  | 0    | 0    |
| Jeff Fife (Goalie)    | 5     | 0  | 0  | 0    | 0    |
| Derek Morin           | 5     | 0  | 0  | 0    | 5    |
| John Porco            | 5     | 0  | 0  | 0    | 4    |

## Cornwall Royals
(Lost division finals to Peterborough, 4 games to 2)

|                         | Games | G. | A. | Pts. | Pen. |
|-------------------------|-------|----|----|------|------|
| Steve Maltais           | 18    | 14 | 16 | 30   | 16   |
| Jason Cirone            | 17    | 19 | 8  | 27   | 14   |
| Mathieu Schneider       | 18    | 7  | 20 | 27   | 30   |
| John Slaney             | 18    | 8  | 16 | 24   | 10   |
| Darren Colbourne        | 18    | 6  | 15 | 21   | 10   |
| Derek Middleton         | 18    | 5  | 15 | 20   | 24   |
| Darcy Cahill            | 13    | 9  | 8  | 17   | 4    |
| Owen Nolan              | 18    | 5  | 11 | 16   | 41   |
| Jason Hannigan          | 17    | 8  | 7  | 15   | 30   |
| Paul Cain               | 12    | 5  | 9  | 14   | 6    |
| Denis Leger             | 18    | 2  | 5  | 7    | 17   |
| Bob Babcock             | 18    | 1  | 3  | 4    | 29   |
| Rick Tabaracci (Goalie) | 18    | 0  | 3  | 3    | 16   |
| Tom Nemeth              | 18    | 1  | 1  | 2    | 2    |
| Chris Cygan             | 18    | 1  | 0  | 1    | 12   |
| Jeff Murray             | 18    | 1  | 0  | 1    | 0    |
| Rich Stromback          | 10    | 0  | 1  | 1    | 7    |
| Dean Pella              | 16    | 0  | 1  | 1    | 13   |
| Paul Lalande            | 18    | 0  | 1  | 1    | 17   |
| Kevin Meisner           | 1     | 0  | 0  | 0    | 0    |
| Todd Mondor             | 6     | 0  | 0  | 0    | 0    |
| Vern Ray                | 16    | 0  | 0  | 0    | 19   |

## Guelph Platers
(Lost division quarterfinals to London, 4 games to 3)

|                        | Games | G. | A. | Pts. | Pen. |
|------------------------|-------|----|----|------|------|
| Rob Arabski            | 7     | 6  | 9  | 15   | 8    |
| Owen Lessard           | 7     | 5  | 8  | 13   | 8    |
| Rob Zamuner            | 7     | 5  | 5  | 10   | 9    |
| John McIntyre          | 7     | 5  | 4  | 9    | 25   |
| Todd Hlushko           | 7     | 5  | 3  | 8    | 18   |
| Keith Whitmore         | 7     | 1  | 7  | 8    | 0    |
| Mike Speer             | 7     | 2  | 4  | 6    | 23   |
| Sean Whyte             | 7     | 1  | 3  | 4    | 8    |
| Steve Perkovic         | 6     | 0  | 3  | 3    | 6    |
| Craig Kitteringham     | 7     | 0  | 2  | 2    | 4    |
| Jeff Perry             | 6     | 1  | 0  | 1    | 15   |
| Grayden Reid           | 7     | 1  | 0  | 1    | 12   |
| Kelly Bradley          | 7     | 0  | 1  | 1    | 9    |
| Bryan Drury            | 7     | 0  | 1  | 1    | 16   |
| Dave Noseworthy        | 7     | 0  | 1  | 1    | 6    |
| Mark Strohack          | 7     | 0  | 1  | 1    | 2    |
| Ray Edwards            | 4     | 0  | 0  | 0    | 2    |
| Chris Driscoll         | 5     | 0  | 0  | 0    | 2    |
| Dan Jensen             | 7     | 0  | 0  | 0    | 13   |
| Mike Parson (Goalie)   | 7     | 0  | 0  | 0    | 2    |

## Kitchener Rangers
(Lost division quarterfinals to North Bay, 4 games to 1)

|                          | Games | G. | A. | Pts. | Pen. |
|--------------------------|-------|----|----|------|------|
| Kirk Tomlinson           | 5     | 2  | 4  | 6    | 2    |
| Shayne Stevenson         | 5     | 2  | 3  | 5    | 4    |
| Mark Montanari           | 5     | 2  | 2  | 4    | 13   |
| Jason Firth              | 5     | 0  | 4  | 4    | 2    |
| Steven Rice              | 5     | 2  | 1  | 3    | 8    |
| Gilbert Dionne           | 5     | 1  | 1  | 2    | 4    |
| John Uniac               | 5     | 0  | 2  | 2    | 0    |
| Darren Rumble            | 5     | 1  | 0  | 1    | 2    |
| Rob Sangster             | 5     | 1  | 0  | 1    | 12   |
| Joey St. Aubin           | 5     | 1  | 0  | 1    | 4    |
| Richard Borgo            | 5     | 0  | 1  | 1    | 4    |
| Cory Keenan              | 5     | 0  | 1  | 1    | 4    |
| Chris LiPuma             | 5     | 0  | 1  | 1    | 2    |
| Randy Pearce             | 5     | 0  | 1  | 1    | 6    |
| Duane Anderson (G.)      | 1     | 0  | 0  | 0    | 0    |
| Mike Torchia (Goalie)    | 2     | 0  | 0  | 0    | 0    |
| Gus Morschauser (G.)     | 3     | 0  | 0  | 0    | 0    |
| Rick Allain              | 5     | 0  | 0  | 0    | 10   |
| Rival Fullum             | 5     | 0  | 0  | 0    | 2    |
| Pierre Gagnon            | 5     | 0  | 0  | 0    | 2    |
| Steve Herniman           | 5     | 0  | 0  | 0    | 4    |

## London Knights
(Lost division finals to Niagara Falls, 4 games to 3)

|                        | Games | G.  | A. | Pts. | Pen. |
|------------------------|-------|-----|----|------|------|
| Tim Taylor             | 21    | *21 | 25 | *46  | 58   |
| Kelly Cain             | 21    | 20  | 22 | 42   | 16   |
| Dennis McEwen          | 20    | 15  | 16 | 31   | 44   |
| John Battice           | 21    | 8   | 13 | 21   | 54   |
| Jim Sprott             | 21    | 4   | 17 | 21   | 68   |
| Trevor Dam             | 21    | 9   | 11 | 20   | 39   |
| Steve Boyd             | 21    | 2   | 18 | 20   | 20   |
| Jeff Christian         | 20    | 3   | 4  | 7    | 56   |
| Ron Jones              | 21    | 2   | 5  | 7    | 50   |
| Steve Martell          | 21    | 2   | 5  | 7    | 18   |
| Dan LeBlanc            | 20    | 2   | 4  | 6    | 38   |
| Doug Synishin          | 21    | 1   | 4  | 5    | 29   |
| Mark Guy               | 21    | 2   | 2  | 4    | 25   |
| Paul Holden            | 20    | 1   | 3  | 4    | 17   |
| Mike Christensen       | 18    | 2   | 1  | 3    | 6    |
| Jon Stos               | 19    | 0   | 3  | 3    | 17   |
| Louie DeBrusk          | 19    | 1   | 1  | 2    | 43   |
| Chris Taylor           | 15    | 0   | 2  | 2    | 15   |
| Peter Ing (Goalie)     | 21    | 0   | 1  | 1    | 6    |
| Rick Corriveau         | 1     | 0   | 0  | 0    | 0    |
| Mike Teeple            | 1     | 0   | 0  | 0    | 0    |
| Pat Tenpenny (Goalie)  | 8     | 0   | 0  | 0    | 0    |
| Jerry Ribble           | 15    | 0   | 0  | 0    | 6    |

## Niagara Falls Thunder
(Lost league finals to Peterborough, 4 games to 2)

|                  | Games | G. | A.  | Pts. | Pen. |
|------------------|-------|----|-----|------|------|
| Stan Drulia      | 17    | 11 | *26 | 37   | 18   |
| Bryan Fogarty    | 17    | 10 | 22  | 32   | 36   |
| Keith Osborne    | 17    | 12 | 13  | 25   | 36   |
| Scott Pearson    | 17    | 14 | 10  | 24   | 53   |
| Jamie Leach      | 17    | 9  | 11  | 20   | 25   |
| Shawn McCosh     | 14    | 4  | 13  | 17   | 23   |
| Keith Primeau    | 17    | 9  | 6   | 15   | 12   |
| Steve Locke      | 17    | 5  | 5   | 10   | 24   |
| Mark Lawrence    | 17    | 3  | 5   | 8    | 23   |
| Dennis Vial      | 15    | 1  | 7   | 8    | 44   |
| Colin Miller     | 17    | 2  | 5   | 7    | 2    |

|  | Games | G. | A. | Pts. | Pen. |
|---|---|---|---|---|---|
| Paul Wolanski | 14 | 3 | 3 | 6 | 13 |
| Paul Laus | 15 | 0 | 5 | 5 | 56 |
| Dave Carrie | 12 | 1 | 2 | 3 | 12 |
| Mike Rosati (Goalie) | 16 | 0 | 3 | 3 | 19 |
| Alain Laforge | 14 | 0 | 2 | 2 | 25 |
| Don Pancoe | 15 | 0 | 2 | 2 | 38 |
| David Anderson | 2 | 1 | 0 | 1 | 0 |
| Greg Allen | 15 | 0 | 1 | 1 | 8 |
| Brad May | 17 | 0 | 1 | 1 | 55 |
| Todd Reynolds (Goalie) | 1 | 0 | 0 | 0 | 0 |
| Brian Mueggler | 4 | 0 | 0 | 0 | 2 |
| Jason Soules | 4 | 0 | 0 | 0 | 10 |
| Adrian VanderSloot | 4 | 0 | 0 | 0 | 23 |
| Mike Berlet | 7 | 0 | 0 | 0 | 14 |
| Rob Fournier (Goalie) | 7 | 0 | 0 | 0 | 2 |

### North Bay Centennials

(Lost division semifinals to London, 4 games to 3)

|  | Games | G. | A. | Pts. | Pen. |
|---|---|---|---|---|---|
| John Purves | 12 | 14 | 12 | 26 | 16 |
| Adam Burt | 12 | 2 | 12 | 14 | 12 |
| Derek Switzer | 12 | 7 | 5 | 12 | 6 |
| Steve Bisson | 11 | 5 | 7 | 12 | 10 |
| John Spoltore | 12 | 3 | 9 | 12 | 2 |
| Shawn Antoski | 9 | 5 | 3 | 8 | 24 |
| Tyler Ertel | 12 | 4 | 3 | 7 | 28 |
| Derek Langille | 12 | 1 | 6 | 7 | 22 |
| Peter Bitonti | 11 | 3 | 3 | 6 | 2 |
| John Van Kessel | 11 | 2 | 4 | 6 | 31 |
| Jason Corrigan | 12 | 0 | 5 | 5 | 16 |
| Shawn Roy | 12 | 2 | 2 | 4 | 10 |
| Cory Pageau | 9 | 1 | 3 | 4 | 10 |
| Joel Morin | 11 | 2 | 1 | 3 | 9 |
| Colin Austin | 10 | 1 | 2 | 3 | 19 |
| Jeff Gardiner | 7 | 1 | 1 | 2 | 0 |
| Scott Shepherd | 12 | 1 | 1 | 2 | 12 |
| Trevor Halverson | 4 | 0 | 1 | 1 | 0 |
| Gary Miller | 10 | 0 | 1 | 1 | 14 |
| Mike Matuszek (Goalie) | 12 | 0 | 1 | 1 | 0 |
| Jason Houle (Goalie) | 1 | 0 | 0 | 0 | 0 |
| John Vary | 3 | 0 | 0 | 0 | 0 |
| Greg Capson | 12 | 0 | 0 | 0 | 14 |

### Oshawa Generals

(Lost division quarterfinals to Ottawa, 4 games to 2)

|  | Games | G. | A. | Pts. | Pen. |
|---|---|---|---|---|---|
| Kevin Miehm | 6 | 6 | 6 | 12 | 0 |
| Iain Fraser | 6 | 2 | 8 | 10 | 12 |
| Brent Grieve | 6 | 4 | 3 | 7 | 4 |
| Tony Joseph | 6 | 4 | 2 | 6 | 22 |
| Jarrod Skalde | 6 | 1 | 5 | 6 | 2 |
| Scott Mahoney | 6 | 1 | 4 | 5 | 18 |
| Mike Craig | 6 | 3 | 1 | 4 | 6 |
| Brian Hunt | 6 | 2 | 2 | 4 | 0 |
| Joe Busillo | 6 | 0 | 3 | 3 | 7 |
| Scott Taylor | 4 | 0 | 2 | 2 | 2 |
| Paul O'Hagan | 6 | 0 | 2 | 2 | 10 |
| Jamie Lever | 3 | 0 | 1 | 1 | 7 |
| Mike Short | 6 | 0 | 1 | 1 | 14 |
| Shawn Simpson (Goalie) | 6 | 0 | 1 | 1 | 0 |
| Todd Coopman | 1 | 0 | 0 | 0 | 0 |
| Trevor McIvor | 1 | 0 | 0 | 0 | 0 |
| Cory Banika | 3 | 0 | 0 | 0 | 14 |
| David Craievich | 6 | 0 | 0 | 0 | 11 |
| Dale Craigwell | 6 | 0 | 0 | 0 | 0 |
| Jean Paul Davis | 6 | 0 | 0 | 0 | 0 |

|  | Games | G. | A. | Pts. | Pen. |
|---|---|---|---|---|---|
| Mike DeCoff | 6 | 0 | 0 | 0 | 2 |
| Craig Donaldson | 6 | 0 | 0 | 0 | 2 |

### Ottawa 67's

(Lost division semifinals to Cornwall, 4 games to 2)

|  | Games | G. | A. | Pts. | Pen. |
|---|---|---|---|---|---|
| Andrew Cassels | 12 | 5 | 10 | 15 | 10 |
| Troy Binnie | 12 | 9 | 3 | 12 | 0 |
| Chris Snell | 11 | 3 | 5 | 8 | 0 |
| Brett Seguin | 12 | 2 | 6 | 8 | 2 |
| Greg Walters | 12 | 3 | 4 | 7 | 20 |
| Jamie Henckel | 12 | 2 | 5 | 7 | 7 |
| Pat Howie | 12 | 2 | 5 | 7 | 21 |
| Joni Lehto | 12 | 0 | 7 | 7 | 4 |
| Steve Kluczkowski | 12 | 4 | 2 | 6 | 0 |
| Jerrett DeFazio | 12 | 3 | 2 | 5 | 2 |
| Mike Griffith | 12 | 2 | 3 | 5 | 12 |
| Jeff Ricciardi | 12 | 0 | 5 | 5 | 15 |
| John East | 12 | 1 | 3 | 4 | 26 |
| Peter Ambroziak | 12 | 1 | 2 | 3 | 2 |
| Joey McTamney | 12 | 1 | 2 | 3 | 0 |
| Scott McPherson | 12 | 1 | 1 | 2 | 0 |
| George Dourian (G.) | 2 | 0 | 0 | 0 | 0 |
| Todd Paterson | 4 | 0 | 0 | 0 | 0 |
| Jeff Ballantyne | 9 | 0 | 0 | 0 | 24 |
| Rob Boldon | 12 | 0 | 0 | 0 | 16 |
| Scott Cumming (Goalie) | 12 | 0 | 0 | 0 | 4 |

### Peterborough Petes

(Winners of 1989 J. Ross Robertson Cup Playoffs)

|  | Games | G. | A. | Pts. | Pen. |
|---|---|---|---|---|---|
| Mike Ricci | 17 | 19 | 16 | 35 | 18 |
| Jamey Hicks | 17 | 8 | 20 | 28 | 14 |
| Ross Wilson | 15 | 10 | 13 | 23 | 23 |
| Tie Domi | 17 | 10 | 9 | 19 | *70 |
| Corey Foster | 17 | 1 | 17 | 18 | 12 |
| Andy MacVicar | 17 | 5 | 6 | 11 | 30 |
| Geoff Ingram | 17 | 6 | 4 | 10 | 16 |
| Dave Lorentz | 17 | 2 | 8 | 10 | 16 |
| Joe Hawley | 17 | 3 | 6 | 9 | 4 |
| Rob Wilson | 17 | 2 | 7 | 9 | 29 |
| Jamie Pegg | 17 | 1 | 7 | 8 | 10 |
| Mike Dagenais | 13 | 3 | 3 | 6 | 12 |
| Mark Myles | 17 | 3 | 3 | 6 | 20 |
| Brian Hayton | 17 | 1 | 5 | 6 | 20 |
| Paul Mitton | 17 | 3 | 2 | 5 | 40 |
| Steve DeGurse | 17 | 0 | 5 | 5 | 45 |
| Troy Stephens | 12 | 3 | 0 | 3 | 9 |
| Mike Tomlinson | 6 | 1 | 2 | 3 | 0 |
| Dan Brown | 17 | 2 | 0 | 2 | 8 |
| Jassen Cullimore | 2 | 0 | 0 | 0 | 0 |
| Scott Campbell | 3 | 0 | 0 | 0 | 0 |
| John Tanner (Goalie) | 8 | 0 | 0 | 0 | 12 |
| Todd Bojcun (Goalie) | 12 | 0 | 0 | 0 | 4 |

### Toronto Marlboros

(Lost division quarterfinals to Cornwall, 4 games to 2)

|  | Games | G. | A. | Pts. | Pen. |
|---|---|---|---|---|---|
| Mike Jackson | 6 | 2 | 6 | 8 | 2 |
| Sean Davidson | 6 | 4 | 3 | 7 | 4 |
| Rob Cimetta | 6 | 3 | 3 | 6 | 0 |
| John Nelson | 6 | 3 | 3 | 6 | 15 |
| Jason Winch | 6 | 3 | 3 | 6 | 0 |
| Brian Collinson | 6 | 2 | 4 | 6 | 4 |
| Chris Govedaris | 6 | 2 | 3 | 5 | 0 |
| Greg Suchan | 6 | 2 | 3 | 5 | 6 |

| | Games | G. | A. | Pts. | Pen. |
|---|---|---|---|---|---|
| Jeff Turcotte | 6 | 1 | 4 | 5 | 0 |
| Jeff Sirkka | 6 | 1 | 3 | 4 | 10 |
| Mike Reier | 6 | 0 | 4 | 4 | 8 |
| Bill Kovacs | 6 | 1 | 1 | 2 | 0 |
| Bill Armstrong | 6 | 0 | 2 | 2 | 6 |
| Rob Leask | 6 | 0 | 1 | 1 | 4 |
| Barry Young | 6 | 0 | 1 | 1 | 6 |
| Jeff Bird (Goalie) | 2 | 0 | 0 | 0 | 0 |
| Shawn Costello | 6 | 0 | 0 | 0 | 0 |
| Clayton Martin | 6 | 0 | 0 | 0 | 7 |
| George Radan | 6 | 0 | 0 | 0 | 0 |
| David Schill (Goalie) | 6 | 0 | 0 | 0 | 2 |

### Windsor Compuware Spitfires

(Lost division quarterfinals to Niag. Falls, 4 games to 0)

| | Games | G. | A. | Pts. | Pen. |
|---|---|---|---|---|---|
| Mike Wolak | 4 | 5 | 4 | 9 | 4 |
| Darrin Shannon | 4 | 1 | 6 | 7 | 2 |

| | Games | G. | A. | Pts. | Pen. |
|---|---|---|---|---|---|
| Peter DeBoer | 4 | 2 | 3 | 5 | 0 |
| Jason Simon | 4 | 1 | 4 | 5 | 13 |
| Chris Lukey | 4 | 3 | 0 | 3 | 4 |
| Jason York | 4 | 2 | 1 | 3 | 8 |
| John Johnson | 4 | 1 | 2 | 3 | 4 |
| Jim Revenberg | 3 | 2 | 0 | 2 | 32 |
| Peter Liptrott | 4 | 0 | 2 | 2 | 8 |
| Jason Stos | 4 | 0 | 2 | 2 | 14 |
| Kevin Falesy | 4 | 0 | 1 | 1 | 0 |
| Kevin McDougall (G.) | 4 | 0 | 1 | 1 | 4 |
| Ted Miskolczi | 4 | 0 | 1 | 1 | 4 |
| Chad Badawey | 2 | 0 | 0 | 0 | 0 |
| Sean O'Hagan (Goalie) | 2 | 0 | 0 | 0 | 2 |
| Trevor Walsh | 3 | 0 | 0 | 0 | 0 |
| Sean Burns | 4 | 0 | 0 | 0 | 11 |
| Brian Forestell | 4 | 0 | 0 | 0 | 0 |
| Tom Purcell | 4 | 0 | 0 | 0 | 8 |
| Karl Taylor | 4 | 0 | 0 | 0 | 4 |
| Kevin White | 4 | 0 | 0 | 0 | 7 |

## Complete Robertson Cup Goaltending

| | Games | Mins. | Goals | SO. | Avg. |
|---|---|---|---|---|---|
| Jeff Fife | 5 | 260 | 20(1) | 0 | 4.62 |
| Troy Nelson | 1 | 40 | 4 | 0 | 6.00 |
| Belleville Totals | 5 | 300 | 25 | 0 | 5.00 |
| Rick Tabaracci | 18 | 1080 | 65(1) | *1 | 3.61 |
| Cornwall Totals | 18 | 1080 | 66 | 1 | 3.67 |
| Mike Parson | 7 | 421 | 29(2) | 0 | 4.13 |
| Guelph Totals | 7 | 421 | 31 | 0 | 4.42 |
| Mike Torchia | 2 | 126 | 8(1) | 0 | 3.81 |
| Gus Morschauser | 3 | 171 | 14 | 0 | 4.91 |
| Duane Anderson | 1 | 9 | 3 | 0 | 20.00 |
| Kitchener Totals | 5 | 306 | 26 | 0 | 5.10 |
| Pat Tenpenny | 8 | 168 | 12(2) | 0 | 4.29 |
| Peter Ing | *21 | *1093 | *82 | 0 | 4.50 |
| London Totals | 21 | 1261 | 96 | 0 | 4.57 |
| Mike Rosati | 16 | 861 | 62(1) | 0 | 4.32 |
| Rob Fournier | 7 | 154 | 20 | 0 | 7.79 |
| Todd Reynolds | 1 | 5 | 1 | 0 | 12.00 |
| Niagara Falls Totals | 17 | 1020 | 84 | 0 | 4.94 |
| Mike Matuszek | 12 | 688 | 38(1) | 0 | 3.31 |
| Jason Houle | 1 | 38 | 3 | 0 | 4.74 |
| North Bay Totals | 12 | 726 | 42 | 0 | 3.47 |
| Shawn Simpson | 6 | 368 | 23 | *1 | 3.75 |
| Oshawa Totals | 6 | 368 | 23 | 1 | 3.75 |
| George Dourian | 2 | 60 | 3 | 0 | 3.00 |
| Scott Cumming | 12 | 668 | 48(1) | 0 | 4.31 |
| Ottawa Totals | 12 | 728 | 52 | 0 | 4.29 |
| Todd Bojcun | 12 | 651 | 35(1) | 0 | *3.23 |
| John Tanner | 8 | 369 | 23 | 0 | 3.74 |
| Peterborough Totals | 17 | 1020 | 59 | 0 | 3.47 |
| David Schill | 6 | 343 | 34(1) | 0 | 5.95 |
| Jeff Bird | 2 | 17 | 3 | 0 | 10.59 |
| Toronto Totals | 6 | 360 | 38 | 0 | 6.33 |
| Sean O'Hagan | 2 | 40 | 4 | 0 | 6.00 |
| Kevin McDougall | 4 | 200 | 25(1) | 0 | 7.50 |
| Windsor Totals | 4 | 240 | 30 | 0 | 7.50 |

( )—Empty Net Goals. Do not count against a Goaltender's average.

# Individual OHL Playoff Leaders

| | | |
|---|---|---|
| Goals | Tim Taylor, London— | 21 |
| Assists | Stan Drulia, Niagara Falls— | 26 |
| Points | Tim Taylor, London— | 46 |
| Penalty Minutes | Tie Domi, Peterborough— | 70 |
| Goaltender's average | Todd Bojcun, Peterborough— | 3.23 |
| Shutouts | Shawn Simpson, Oshawa— | 1 |
| | Rick Tabaracci, Cornwall— | 1 |

★★★★★★★★★★★★★★★★★★★★★★★★★★★★★★★★★★★★★★★★★★★★★

## OHL 1988-89 All-Stars

| First Team | Position | Second Team |
|---|---|---|
| Gus Morschauser, Kitchener | Goal | Rick Tabaracci, Cornwall |
| Bryan Fogarty, Niagara Falls | Defense | Jim Sprott, London |
| Mathieu Schneider, Cornwall | Defense | Bryan Marchment, Belleville |
| Andrew Cassels, Ottawa | Center | Mike Ricci, Peterborough |
| Stan Drulia, Niagara Falls | Right Wing | John Purves, North Bay |
| Rob Cimetta, Toronto | Left Wing | Steve Maltais, Cornwall |

★★★★★★★★★★★★★★★★★★★★★★★★★★★★★★★★★★★★★★★★★★★★★

## OHL 1988-89 Trophy Winners

| | |
|---|---|
| Red Tilson Trophy (Outstanding Player) | Bryan Fogarty, Niagara Falls |
| Eddie Powers Memorial Trophy (Scoring Champion) | Bryan Fogarty, Niagara Falls |
| Dave Pinkney Trophy (Top Team Goaltending) | Todd Bojcun, Peterborough |
| | John Tanner, Peterborough |
| Max Kaminsky Trophy (Outstanding Defenseman) | Bryan Fogarty, Niagara Falls |
| William Hanley Trophy (Most Gentlemanly) | Kevin Miehm, Oshawa |
| Emms Family Award (Rookie of the Year) | Owen Nolan, Cornwall |
| Matt Leyden Trophy (Coach of the Year) | Joe McDonnell, Kitchener |
| Jim Mahon Memorial Trophy (Top scoring Right Wing) | Stan Drulia, Niagara Falls |
| F.W. Dinty Moore Trophy (Lowest average by a rookie goalie) | Jeff Wilson, Kingston |
| Leo Lalonde Memorial Trophy (Overage Player of Year) | Stan Drulia, Niagara Falls |

### Historical OHL Trophy Winners

**Red Tilson Trophy**
(Outstanding Player)

| Season | Player | Club |
|---|---|---|
| 1944-45 | Doug McMurdy, St. Catharines | |
| 1945-46 | Tod Sloan, St. Michael's | |
| 1946-47 | Ed Sanford, St. Michael's | |
| 1947-48 | George Armstrong, Stratford | |
| 1948-49 | Gil Mayer, Barrie | |
| 1949-50 | George Armstrong, Marlboros | |
| 1950-51 | Glenn Hall, Windsor | |
| 1951-52 | Bill Harrington, Kitchener | |
| 1952-53 | Bob Attersley, Oshawa | |
| 1953-54 | Brian Cullen, St. Catharines | |
| 1954-55 | Hank Ciesla, St. Catharines | |
| 1955-56 | Ron Howell, Guelph | |
| 1956-57 | Frank Mahovlich, St. Michael's | |
| 1957-58 | Murray Oliver, Hamilton | |
| 1958-59 | Stan Mikita, St. Catharines | |
| 1959-60 | Wayne Connelly, Peterborough | |
| 1960-61 | Rod Gilbert, Guelph | |
| 1961-62 | Pit Martin, Hamilton | |
| 1962-63 | Wayne Maxner, Niagara Falls | |
| 1963-64 | Yvan Cournoyer, Montreal | |
| 1964-65 | Andre Lacroix, Peterborough | |
| 1965-66 | Andre Lacroix, Peterborough | |
| 1966-67 | Mickey Redmond, Peterborough | |
| 1967-68 | Walt Tkaczuk, Kitchener | |
| 1968-69 | Rejean Houle, Montreal | |
| 1969-70 | Gilbert Perreault, Montreal | |
| 1970-71 | Dave Gardner, Marlboros | |
| 1971-72 | Don Lever, Niagara Falls | |
| 1972-73 | Rick Middleton, Oshawa | |
| 1973-74 | Jack Valiquette, Sault Ste. Marie | |
| 1974-75 | Dennis Maruk, London | |
| 1975-76 | Peter Lee, Ottawa | |
| 1976-77 | Dale McCourt, St. Catharines | |
| 1977-78 | Bobby Smith, Ottawa | |
| 1978-79 | Mike Foligno, Sudbury | |
| 1979-80 | Jim Fox, Ottawa | |
| 1980-81 | Ernie Godden, Windsor | |
| 1981-82 | Dave Simpson, London | |
| 1982-83 | Doug Gilmour, Cornwall | |
| 1983-84 | John Tucker, Kitchener | |
| 1984-85 | Wayne Groulx, Sault Ste. Marie | |
| 1985-86 | Ray Sheppard, Cornwall | |
| 1986-87 | Scott McCrory, Oshawa | |
| 1987-88 | Andrew Cassels, Ottawa | |
| 1988-89 | Bryan Fogarty, Niagara Falls | |

**Eddie Powers Memorial Trophy**
(Scoring Champion)

| Season | Player | Club |
|---|---|---|
| 1933-34 | J. Groboski, Oshawa | |
| 1934-35 | J. Good, Toronto Lions | |
| 1935-36 | John O'Flaherty, West Toronto | |

| Season | Player, Club |
|---|---|
| 1936-37 | Billy Taylor, Oshawa |
| 1937-38 | Hank Goldup, Tor. Marlboros |
| 1938-39 | Billy Taylor, Oshawa |
| 1939-40 | Jud McAtee, Oshawa |
| 1940-41 | Gaye Stewart, Tor. Marlboros |
| 1941-42 | Bob Wiest, Brantford |
| 1942-43 | Norman "Red" Tilson, Oshawa |
| 1943-44 | Ken Smith, Oshawa |
| 1944-45 | Leo Gravelle, St. Michael's |
| 1945-46 | Tod Sloan, St. Michael's |
| 1946-47 | Fleming Mackell, St. Michael's |
| 1947-48 | George Armstrong, Stratford |
| 1948-49 | Bert Giesebrecht, Windsor |
| 1949-50 | Earl Reibel, Windsor |
| 1950-51 | Lou Jankowski, Oshawa |
| 1951-52 | Ken Laufman, Guelph |
| 1952-53 | Jim McBurney, Galt |
| 1953-54 | Brian Cullen, St. Catharines |
| 1954-55 | Hank Ciesla, St. Catharines |
| 1955-56 | Stan Baliuk, Kitchener |
| 1956-57 | Bill Sweeney, Guelph |
| 1957-58 | John McKenzie, St. Catharines |
| 1958-59 | Stan Mikita, St. Catharines |
| 1959-60 | Chico Maki, St. Catharines |
| 1960-61 | Rod Gilbert, Guelph |
| 1961-62 | Andre Boudrias, Montreal |
| 1962-63 | Wayne Maxner, Niagara Falls |
| 1963-64 | Andre Boudrias, Montreal |
| 1964-65 | Ken Hodge, St. Catharines |
| 1965-66 | Andre Lacroix, Peterborough |
| 1966-67 | Derek Sanderson, Niagara Falls |
| 1967-68 | Tom Webster, Niagara Falls |
| 1968-69 | Rejean Houle, Montreal |
| 1969-70 | Marcel Dionne, St. Catharines |
| 1970-71 | Marcel Dionne, St. Catharines |
| 1971-72 | Bill Harris, Toronto |
| 1972-73 | Blake Dunlop, Ottawa |
| 1973-74 | Jack Valiquette, Sault Ste. Marie |
|  | Rick Adduono, St. Catharines |
| 1974-75 | Bruce Boudreau, Toronto |
| 1975-76 | Mike Kaszycki, Sault Ste. Marie |
| 1976-77 | Dwight Foster, Kitchener |
| 1977-78 | Bobby Smith, Ottawa |
| 1978-79 | Mike Foligno, Sudbury |
| 1979-80 | Jim Fox, Ottawa |
| 1980-81 | John Goodwin, Sault Ste. Marie |
| 1981-82 | Dave Simpson, London |
| 1982-83 | Doug Gilmour, Cornwall |
| 1983-84 | Tim Salmon, Kingston |
| 1984-85 | Dave MacLean, Belleville |
| 1985-86 | Ray Sheppard, Cornwall |
| 1986-87 | Scott McCrory, Oshawa |
| 1987-88 | Andrew Cassels, Ottawa |
| 1988-89 | Bryan Fogarty, Niagara Falls |

## Dave Pinkney Trophy
(Top Team Goaltending)

| Season | Player, Club |
|---|---|
| 1948-49 | Gil Mayer, Barrie |
| 1949-50 | Don Lockhart, Marlboros |
| 1950-51 | Don Lockhart, Marlboros |
|  | Lorne Howes, Barrie |
| 1951-52 | Don Head, Marlboros |
| 1952-53 | John Henderson, Marlboros |
| 1953-54 | Dennis Riggin, Hamilton |
| 1954-55 | John Albani, Marlboros |
| 1955-56 | Jim Crockett, Marlboros |
| 1956-57 | Len Broderick, Marlboros |
| 1957-58 | Len Broderick, Marlboros |
| 1958-59 | Jacques Caron, Peterborough |
| 1959-60 | Gerry Cheevers, St. Michael's |
| 1960-61 | Bud Blom, Hamilton |
| 1961-62 | George Holmes, Montreal |
| 1962-63 | Chuck Goddard, Peterborough |
| 1963-64 | Bernie Parent, Niagara Falls |
| 1964-65 | Bernie Parent, Niagara Falls |
| 1965-66 | Ted Quimet, Montreal |
| 1966-67 | Peter MacDuffe, St. Catharines |
| 1967-68 | Bruce Mullet, Montreal |
| 1968-69 | Wayne Wood, Montreal |
| 1969-70 | John Garrett, Peterborough |
| 1970-71 | John Garrett, Peterborough |
| 1971-72 | Michel Larocque, Ottawa |
| 1972-73 | Mike Palmateer, Toronto |
| 1973-74 | Don Edwards, Kitchener |
| 1974-75 | Greg Millen, Peterborough |
| 1975-76 | Jim Bedard, Sudbury |
| 1976-77 | Pat Riggin, London |
| 1977-78 | Al Jensen, Hamilton |
| 1978-79 | Nick Ricci, Niagara Falls |
| 1979-80 | Rick LaFerriere, Peterborough |
| 1980-81 | Jim Ralph, Ottawa |
| 1981-82 | Marc D'Amour, Sault Ste. Marie |
| 1982-83 | Peter Sidorkiewicz, Oshawa |
|  | Jeff Hogg, Oshawa |
| 1983-84 | Darren Pang, Ottawa |
|  | Greg Coram, Ottawa |
| 1984-85 | Scott Mosey, Sault Ste. Marie |
|  | Marty Abrams, Sault Ste. Marie |
| 1985-86 | Kay Whitmore, Peterborough |
|  | Ron Tugnutt, Peterborough |
| 1986-87 | Sean Evoy, Oshawa |
|  | Jeff Hackett, Oshawa |
| 1987-88 | Todd Bojcun, Peterborough |
|  | John Tanner, Peterborough |
| 1988-89 | Todd Bojcun, Peterborough |
|  | John Tanner, Peterborough |

## Max Kaminsky Trophy
(Outstanding Defenseman)

| Season | Player, Club |
|---|---|
| 1969-70 | Ron Plumb, Peterborough |
| 1970-71 | Jocelyn Guevremont, Montreal |
| 1971-72 | Denis Potvin, Ottawa |
| 1972-73 | Denis Potvin, Ottawa |
| 1973-74 | Jim Turkiewicz, Peterborough |
| 1974-75 | Mike O'Connell, Kingston |
| 1975-76 | Rick Green, London |
| 1976-77 | Craig Hartsburg, S. Ste. Marie |
| 1977-78 | Brad Marsh, London |
|  | Rob Ramage, London |
| 1978-79 | Greg Theberge, Peterborough |
| 1979-80 | Larry Murphy, Peterborough |
| 1980-81 | Steve Smith, Sault Ste. Marie |
| 1981-82 | Ron Meighan, Niagara Falls |
| 1982-83 | Allan MacInnis, Kitchener |
| 1983-84 | Brad Shaw, Ottawa |
| 1984-85 | Bob Halkidis, London |
| 1985-86 | Terry Carkner, Peterborough |
|  | Jeff Brown, Sudbury |
| 1986-87 | Kerry Huffman, Guelph |
| 1987-88 | Darryl Shannon, Windsor |
| 1988-89 | Bryan Fogarty, Niagara Falls |

## William Hanley Trophy
(Most Gentlemanly)

| Season | Player, Club |
|---|---|
| 1960-61 | Bruce Draper, St. Michael's |
| 1961-62 | Lowell MacDonald, Hamilton |
| 1962-63 | Paul Henderson, Hamilton |
| 1963-64 | Fred Stanfield, St. Catharines |
| 1964-65 | Jimmy Peters, Hamilton |
| 1965-66 | Andre Lacroix, Peterborough |
| 1966-67 | Mickey Redmond, Peterborough |

| Season | Player | Club |
|---|---|---|
| 1967-68 | Tom Webster, Niagara Falls | |
| 1968-69 | Rejean Houle, Montreal | |
| 1969-74 | No award presented | |
| 1974-75 | Doug Jarvis, Peterborough | |
| 1975-76 | Dale McCourt, Hamilton | |
| 1976-77 | Dale McCourt, St. Catharines | |
| 1977-78 | Wayne Gretzky, S.S. Marie | |
| 1978-79 | Sean Simpson, Ottawa | |
| 1979-80 | Sean Simpson, Ottawa | |
| 1980-81 | John Goodwin, Sault Ste. Marie | |
| 1981-82 | Dave Simpson, London | |
| 1982-83 | Kirk Muller, Guelph | |
| 1983-84 | Kevin Conway, Kingston | |
| 1984-85 | Scott Tottle, Peterborough | |
| 1985-86 | Jason Lafreniere, Belleville | |
| 1986-87 | Scott McCrory, Oshawa | |
|  | Keith Gretzky, Hamilton | |
| 1987-88 | Andrew Cassels, Ottawa | |
| 1988-89 | Kevin Miehm, Oshawa | |

## Emms Family Award
(Rookie of the Year)

| Season | Player | Club |
|---|---|---|
| 1972-73 | Dennis Maruk, London | |
| 1973-74 | Jack Valiquette, Sault Ste. Marie | |
| 1974-75 | Danny Shearer, Hamilton | |
| 1975-76 | John Travella, Sault Ste. Marie | |
| 1976-77 | Yvan Joly, Ottawa | |
| 1977-78 | Wayne Gretzky, S. S. Marie | |
| 1978-79 | John Goodwin, Sault Ste. Marie | |
| 1979-80 | Bruce Dowie, Toronto | |
| 1980-81 | Tony Tanti, Oshawa | |
| 1981-82 | Pat Verbeek, Sudbury | |
| 1982-83 | Bruce Cassidy, Ottawa | |
| 1983-84 | Shawn Burr, Kitchener | |
| 1984-85 | Derek King, Sault Ste. Marie | |
| 1985-86 | Lonnie Loach, Guelph | |
| 1986-87 | Andrew Cassels, Ottawa | |
| 1987-88 | Rick Corriveau, London | |
| 1988-89 | Owen Nolan, Cornwall | |

## Matt Leyden Trophy
(Coach of the Year)

| Season | Coach | Club |
|---|---|---|
| 1971-72 | Gus Bodnar, Oshawa | |
| 1972-73 | George Armstrong, Toronto | |
| 1973-74 | Jack Bownass, Kingston | |
| 1974-75 | Bert Templeton, Hamilton | |
| 1975-76 | Jerry Toppazzini, Sudbury | |
| 1976-77 | Bill Long, London | |
| 1977-78 | Bill White, Oshawa | |
| 1978-79 | Gary Green, Peterborough | |
| 1979-80 | Dave Chambers, Toronto | |
| 1980-81 | Brian Kilrea, Ottawa | |
| 1981-82 | Brian Kilrea, Ottawa | |
| 1982-83 | Terry Crisp, Sault Ste. Marie | |
| 1983-84 | Tom Barrett, Kitchener | |
| 1984-85 | Terry Crisp, Sault Ste. Marie | |
| 1985-86 | Jacques Martin, Guelph | |
| 1986-87 | Paul Theriault, Oshawa | |
| 1987-88 | Dick Todd, Peterborough | |
| 1988-89 | Joe McDonnell, Kitchener | |

## Jim Mahon Memorial Trophy
(Top Scoring Right Wing)

| Season | Player | Club |
|---|---|---|
| 1971-72 | Bill Harris, Toronto | |
| 1972-73 | Dennis Ververgaert, London | |
| 1973-74 | Dave Gorman, St. Catharines | |
| 1974-75 | Mark Napier, Toronto | |
| 1975-76 | Peter Lee, Ottawa | |
| 1976-77 | John Anderson, Toronto | |
| 1977-78 | Dino Ciccarelli, London | |
| 1978-79 | Mike Foligno, Sudbury | |
| 1979-80 | Jim Fox, Ottawa | |
| 1980-81 | Tony Tanti, Oshawa | |
| 1981-82 | Tony Tanti, Oshawa | |
| 1982-83 | Ian MacInnis, Cornwall | |
| 1983-84 | Wayne Presley, Kitchener | |
| 1984-85 | Dave MacLean, Belleville | |
| 1985-86 | Ray Sheppard, Cornwall | |
| 1986-87 | Ron Goodall, Kitchener | |
| 1987-88 | Sean Williams, Oshawa | |
| 1988-89 | Stan Drulia, Niagara Falls | |

## F.W. Dinty Moore Trophy
(Lowest Average by a Rookie Goalie)

| Season | Player | Club |
|---|---|---|
| 1975-76 | Mark Locken, Hamilton | |
| 1976-77 | Barry Heard, London | |
| 1977-78 | Ken Ellacott, Peterborough | |
| 1978-79 | Nick Ricci, Niagara Falls | |
| 1979-80 | Mike Vezina, Ottawa | |
| 1980-81 | John Vanbiesbrouck, Sault Ste. Marie | |
| 1981-82 | Shawn Kilroy, Peterborough | |
| 1982-83 | Dan Burrows, Belleville | |
| 1983-84 | Jerry Iuliano, Sault Ste. Marie | |
| 1984-85 | Ron Tugnutt, Peterborough | |
| 1985-86 | Paul Henriques, Belleville | |
| 1986-87 | Jeff Hackett, Oshawa | |
| 1987-88 | Todd Bojcun, Peterborough | |
| 1988-89 | Jeff Wilson, Kingston | |

## Leo Lalonde Memorial Trophy
(Overage Player of the Year)

| Season | Player | Club |
|---|---|---|
| 1983-84 | Don McLaren, Ottawa | |
| 1984-85 | Dunc MacIntyre, Belleville | |
| 1985-86 | Steve Guenette, Guelph | |
| 1986-87 | Mike Richard, Toronto | |
| 1987-88 | Len Soccio, North Bay | |
| 1988-89 | Stan Drulia, Niagara Falls | |

# Western Hockey League

(Known as Western Canada Hockey League prior to 1978-79)

President—Ed Chynoweth  
Vice-President—Richard Doerksen  
Executive Assistant—Norman Dueck  
Statistician—Randy Klassen  
616-5920 Macleod Trail S., Calgary, Alberta T2H 0K2  
Phone—(403) 253-8113

## Final 1988-89 WHL Standings

### East Division

|  | G. | W. | L. | T. | Pts. | GF. | GA. |
|---|---|---|---|---|---|---|---|
| Swift Current Broncos | 72 | 55 | 16 | 1 | 111 | 447 | 319 |
| Saskatoon Blades | 72 | 42 | 28 | 2 | 86 | 366 | 335 |
| Medicine Hat Tigers | 72 | 41 | 27 | 4 | 86 | 359 | 326 |
| Prince Albert Raiders | 72 | 37 | 33 | 2 | 76 | 302 | 286 |
| Lethbridge Hurricanes | 72 | 27 | 39 | 6 | 60 | 356 | 380 |
| Moose Jaw Warriors | 72 | 27 | 42 | 3 | 57 | 318 | 372 |
| Brandon Wheat Kings | 72 | 25 | 43 | 4 | 54 | 286 | 331 |
| Regina Pats | 72 | 23 | 43 | 6 | 52 | 306 | 358 |

### West Division

|  | G. | W. | L. | T. | Pts. | GF. | GA. |
|---|---|---|---|---|---|---|---|
| Portland Winter Hawks | 72 | 40 | 28 | 4 | 84 | 408 | 395 |
| Victoria Cougars | 72 | 36 | 32 | 4 | 76 | 341 | 351 |
| Kamloops Blazers | 72 | 34 | 33 | 5 | 73 | 326 | 309 |
| Tri-City Americans | 72 | 33 | 34 | 5 | 71 | 300 | 299 |
| Seattle Thunderbirds | 72 | 33 | 35 | 4 | 70 | 315 | 276 |
| Spokane Chiefs | 72 | 25 | 45 | 2 | 52 | 326 | 419 |

### Top 20 Scorers for the Bob Brownridge Memorial Trophy

|  | Games | G. | A. | Pts. | Pen. |
|---|---|---|---|---|---|
| 1. Dennis Holland, Portland | 69 | *82 | 85 | *167 | 120 |
| 2. Stu Barnes, Tri-City | 70 | 59 | 82 | 141 | 117 |
| 3. Tim Tisdale, Swift Current | 68 | 57 | 82 | 139 | 89 |
| 4. Blair Atcheynum, Moose Jaw | 71 | 70 | 68 | 138 | 70 |
| 5. Troy Mick, Portland | 66 | 49 | *87 | 136 | 70 |
| 6. Wayne Hynes, Medicine Hat | 72 | 54 | 81 | 135 | 66 |
| 7. Peter Kasowski, Swift Current | 72 | 58 | 73 | 131 | 46 |
| Michael Sillinger, Regina | 72 | 53 | 78 | 131 | 52 |
| 9 Sean Lebrun, Tri-City | 71 | 52 | 73 | 125 | 92 |
| 10. Kirby Lindal, Medicine Hat | 71 | 67 | 55 | 122 | 83 |
| Phil Huber, Kamloops | 72 | 54 | 68 | 122 | 103 |
| 12. Victor Gervais, Seattle | 72 | 54 | 65 | 119 | 158 |
| 13. Glen Goodall, Seattle | 70 | 52 | 62 | 114 | 58 |
| 14. Clayton Young, Victoria | 72 | 50 | 63 | 113 | 145 |
| 15. Cory Lyons, Lethbridge | 71 | 53 | 59 | 112 | 36 |
| 16. Gary Dickie, Regina | 59 | 48 | 60 | 108 | 113 |
| Mark Greig, Lethbridge | 71 | 36 | 72 | 108 | 113 |
| 18. Sheldon Kennedy, Swift Current | 51 | 58 | 48 | 106 | 92 |
| Jason Miller, Medicine Hat | 72 | 51 | 55 | 106 | 44 |
| Bryan Bosch, Lethbridge | 67 | 44 | 62 | 106 | 25 |

## Team-by-Team Breakdown of WHL Scoring

### Brandon Wheat Kings

|  | Games | G. | A. | Pts. | Pen. |
|---|---|---|---|---|---|
| Mark Bassen, Leth. | 7 | 1 | 4 | 5 | 12 |
| Brandon | 65 | 31 | 65 | 96 | 74 |
| Totals | 72 | 32 | 69 | 101 | 86 |
| Chris Robertson | 70 | 41 | 44 | 85 | 47 |
| Bob Woods | 68 | 26 | 50 | 76 | 100 |
| Jeff Odgers | 71 | 31 | 29 | 60 | 277 |
| Cam Brown | 72 | 17 | 42 | 59 | 225 |
| Troy Frederick | 72 | 26 | 30 | 56 | 72 |
| Paul Sutcliffe, Sask. | 36 | 11 | 6 | 17 | 17 |
| Brandon | 24 | 15 | 11 | 26 | 12 |
| Totals | 60 | 26 | 17 | 43 | 29 |
| Gary Audette | 71 | 18 | 15 | 33 | 40 |

|  | Games | G. | A. | Pts. | Pen. |
|---|---|---|---|---|---|
| Frank Melone, Tri-City | 16 | 4 | 9 | 13 | 23 |
| Brandon | 21 | 2 | 13 | 15 | 17 |
| Totals | 37 | 6 | 22 | 28 | 40 |
| Barry Dreger | 72 | 2 | 25 | 27 | 195 |
| Pryce Wood | 66 | 11 | 14 | 25 | 72 |
| Greg Hutchings | 54 | 9 | 16 | 25 | 46 |
| Kevin Chevaldayoff | 40 | 4 | 12 | 16 | 135 |
| Shane Kohl, P. Albert | 14 | 1 | 2 | 3 | 50 |
| Tri-City | 15 | 0 | 0 | 0 | 43 |
| Brandon | 28 | 2 | 9 | 11 | 81 |
| Totals | 57 | 3 | 11 | 14 | 174 |
| Don Laurin, Med. Hat | 15 | 1 | 0 | 1 | 6 |
| Brandon | 38 | 8 | 4 | 12 | 38 |
| Totals | 53 | 9 | 4 | 13 | 44 |
| Dwayne Newman | 72 | 2 | 11 | 13 | 143 |
| Mike Vandenberghe | 61 | 1 | 12 | 13 | 73 |
| Sheldon Kowalchuk | 67 | 6 | 6 | 12 | 59 |
| Martin Smith, Seattle | 1 | 0 | 0 | 0 | 0 |
| Saskatoon | 14 | 2 | 7 | 9 | 8 |
| Brandon | 1 | 0 | 0 | 0 | 0 |
| Totals | 16 | 2 | 7 | 9 | 8 |
| Brad Woods | 65 | 0 | 9 | 9 | 164 |
| Dave Hunter | 20 | 2 | 5 | 7 | 32 |
| Bill Whistle | 19 | 3 | 3 | 6 | 14 |
| Curtis Folkett | 48 | 2 | 3 | 5 | 138 |
| Glen Webster | 3 | 0 | 2 | 2 | 5 |
| Mike Sanderson | 6 | 0 | 2 | 2 | 2 |
| Kelly Hutchins (Goalie) | 54 | 0 | 2 | 2 | 30 |
| Trevor Kidd (Goalie) | 32 | 0 | 1 | 1 | 2 |
| Chad Berezniuk | 1 | 0 | 0 | 0 | 0 |
| Jason Sweeney | 1 | 0 | 0 | 0 | 0 |
| Brian Purdy | 2 | 0 | 0 | 0 | 0 |
| Rob Puchniak | 3 | 0 | 0 | 0 | 0 |

## Kamloops Blazers

|  | Games | G. | A. | Pts. | Pen. |
|---|---|---|---|---|---|
| Phil Huber | 72 | 54 | 68 | 122 | 103 |
| David Chyzowski | 68 | 56 | 48 | 104 | 139 |
| Brian Shantz | 62 | 33 | 53 | 86 | 47 |
| Cal McGowan | 72 | 21 | 31 | 52 | 44 |
| Mike Needham | 49 | 24 | 27 | 51 | 55 |
| Pat MacLeod | 37 | 11 | 34 | 45 | 14 |
| Darwin McLelland | 37 | 7 | 31 | 38 | 40 |
| Geoff Smith | 32 | 4 | 31 | 35 | 29 |
| Pat Bingham | 48 | 16 | 18 | 34 | 85 |
| Trevor Buchannan | 63 | 13 | 21 | 34 | 217 |
| Corey Andersen | 69 | 10 | 21 | 31 | 63 |
| Joel Dyck, S. Current | 29 | 5 | 7 | 12 | 20 |
| Regina | 15 | 0 | 3 | 3 | 20 |
| Kamloops | 20 | 1 | 13 | 14 | 26 |
| Totals | 64 | 6 | 23 | 29 | 66 |
| Ryan Harrison | 50 | 13 | 14 | 27 | 45 |
| Zac Boyer | 42 | 10 | 17 | 27 | 22 |
| Ed Bertuzzi | 63 | 13 | 13 | 26 | 134 |
| Daryl Sydor | 65 | 12 | 14 | 26 | 86 |
| Paul Kruse | 68 | 8 | 15 | 23 | 209 |
| Len Jorgenson | 42 | 5 | 10 | 15 | 17 |
| Don Schmidt | 35 | 5 | 9 | 14 | 135 |
| Steven Yule | 65 | 1 | 12 | 13 | 90 |
| Kim Deck | 41 | 0 | 11 | 11 | 24 |
| Dave Linford | 59 | 3 | 2 | 4 | 124 |
| Cory Crichton | 55 | 1 | 4 | 5 | 57 |
| Dean Cook (Goalie) | 53 | 0 | 5 | 5 | 4 |
| Brad Heschuk | 9 | 1 | 1 | 2 | 11 |
| Todd Esselmont | 13 | 1 | 1 | 2 | 0 |
| Bryan Dicken | 13 | 0 | 2 | 2 | 4 |

|  | Games | G. | A. | Pts. | Pen. |
|---|---|---|---|---|---|
| Craig Kalawsky, Spo. | 4 | 0 | 1 | 1 | 6 |
| Kamloops | 2 | 0 | 0 | 0 | 2 |
| Totals | 6 | 0 | 1 | 1 | 8 |
| Kevin Hoffman | 1 | 0 | 0 | 0 | 0 |
| Darryl Kruse | 1 | 0 | 0 | 0 | 2 |
| Willie McDonald (G.) | 1 | 0 | 0 | 0 | 2 |
| Craig Bonner | 2 | 0 | 0 | 0 | 0 |
| Corey Hirsch (Goalie) | 32 | 0 | 0 | 0 | 8 |

## Lethbridge Hurricanes

|  | Games | G. | A. | Pts. | Pen. |
|---|---|---|---|---|---|
| Cory Lyons | 71 | 53 | 59 | 112 | 36 |
| Mark Greig | 71 | 36 | 72 | 108 | 113 |
| Bryan Bosch | 67 | 44 | 62 | 106 | 25 |
| Wes Walz | 63 | 29 | 75 | 104 | 32 |
| Kelly Ens | 72 | 46 | 36 | 82 | 146 |
| Jason Ruff | 69 | 42 | 38 | 80 | 127 |
| Clarke Polglase | 57 | 8 | 36 | 44 | 78 |
| James Wheatcroft | 72 | 15 | 22 | 37 | 220 |
| Peter Berthelsen | 68 | 7 | 30 | 37 | 63 |
| Kevin St. Jacques, Spo. | 36 | 15 | 12 | 27 | 33 |
| Lethbridge | 28 | 5 | 4 | 9 | 8 |
| Totals | 64 | 20 | 16 | 36 | 41 |
| Brad Rubachuk | 66 | 19 | 13 | 32 | 161 |
| Mark Kuntz | 65 | 7 | 24 | 31 | 227 |
| Doug Barrault, Brandon | 6 | 1 | 1 | 2 | 4 |
| Lethbridge | 51 | 13 | 12 | 25 | 30 |
| Totals | 57 | 14 | 13 | 27 | 34 |
| Casey McMillan | 62 | 4 | 21 | 25 | 65 |
| Colin Gregor | 47 | 11 | 8 | 19 | 72 |
| Shane Mazutinec | 62 | 4 | 15 | 19 | 129 |
| Rob Hale | 64 | 7 | 3 | 10 | 211 |
| Pat Pylypuik | 49 | 2 | 6 | 8 | 161 |
| Chad Seibel | 58 | 1 | 7 | 8 | 52 |
| Ivan Jessey | 50 | 1 | 6 | 7 | 70 |
| Jeff Denham, S. Current | 5 | 1 | 1 | 2 | 2 |
| Lethbridge | 28 | 0 | 2 | 2 | 39 |
| Totals | 33 | 1 | 3 | 4 | 41 |
| Dusty Imoo (Goalie) | 47 | 0 | 3 | 3 | 12 |
| Ted Hutchings | 3 | 0 | 1 | 1 | 0 |
| Vance Wolsky | 1 | 0 | 0 | 0 | 0 |
| Scott Fukami | 2 | 0 | 0 | 0 | 0 |
| Jamie Pushor | 2 | 0 | 0 | 0 | 0 |
| Alan Lake | 3 | 0 | 0 | 0 | 26 |
| J. McLennan, Spo. (G.) | 11 | 0 | 0 | 0 | 0 |
| Lethbridge (Goalie) | 7 | 0 | 0 | 0 | 0 |
| Totals | 18 | 0 | 0 | 0 | 0 |

## Medicine Hat Tigers

|  | Games | G. | A. | Pts. | Pen. |
|---|---|---|---|---|---|
| Wayne Hynes | 72 | 54 | 81 | 135 | 66 |
| Kirby Lindal | 71 | 67 | 55 | 122 | 83 |
| Jason Miller | 72 | 51 | 55 | 106 | 44 |
| Mark Woolf | 65 | 27 | 54 | 81 | 89 |
| Ryan McGill | 57 | 26 | 45 | 71 | 172 |
| Kevin Riehl | 72 | 30 | 24 | 54 | 48 |
| Cal Zankowski | 54 | 24 | 27 | 51 | 56 |
| Vince Boe | 70 | 8 | 43 | 51 | 95 |
| Darren Stolk | 65 | 8 | 31 | 39 | 141 |
| Murray Garbutt | 64 | 14 | 24 | 38 | 145 |
| Jason Prosofsky | 67 | 7 | 16 | 23 | 170 |
| Clayton Gainer | 59 | 6 | 15 | 21 | 253 |
| Bart Cote | 70 | 4 | 16 | 20 | 142 |
| Lloyd Pellitier | 57 | 10 | 7 | 17 | 17 |
| Danny Kordic | 70 | 1 | 13 | 14 | 190 |
| Clayton Norris | 66 | 4 | 9 | 13 | 122 |

|  | Games | G. | A. | Pts. | Pen. |
|---|---|---|---|---|---|
| Brent Thompson | 72 | 3 | 10 | 13 | 160 |
| Chris Lafreniere, Spo. | 5 | 0 | 1 | 1 | 17 |
| Medicine Hat | 44 | 2 | 6 | 8 | 95 |
| Totals | 49 | 2 | 7 | 9 | 112 |
| Patrick Backland (G.) | 40 | 0 | 3 | 3 | 12 |
| Dwayne Brook | 41 | 1 | 1 | 2 | 29 |
| Alex Sheflo (Goalie) | 36 | 0 | 2 | 2 | 10 |
| Mick Majakovic | 21 | 0 | 1 | 1 | 0 |
| Rod Krushel | 1 | 0 | 0 | 0 | 0 |

## Moose Jaw Warriors

|  | Games | G. | A. | Pts. | Pen. |
|---|---|---|---|---|---|
| Blair Atcheynum | 71 | 70 | 68 | 138 | 70 |
| Rob Harvey | 71 | 37 | 48 | 85 | 33 |
| Jerome Bechard | 70 | 29 | 52 | 81 | 242 |
| Randy Keller, Kam. | 10 | 3 | 8 | 11 | 12 |
| Moose Jaw | 57 | 25 | 23 | 48 | 88 |
| Totals | 67 | 28 | 31 | 59 | 100 |
| Scott Humeniuk | 56 | 18 | 39 | 57 | 159 |
| Rob Reimer | 69 | 22 | 27 | 49 | 74 |
| Chris Bright | 71 | 18 | 27 | 45 | 61 |
| Devon Oleniuk | 68 | 6 | 32 | 38 | 151 |
| Steve Young | 72 | 20 | 17 | 37 | 224 |
| Scott Barnstable, P.A. | 34 | 5 | 7 | 12 | 58 |
| Moose Jaw | 37 | 7 | 10 | 17 | 41 |
| Totals | 71 | 12 | 17 | 29 | 99 |
| Scott Reid | 70 | 12 | 12 | 24 | 48 |
| Mike Zakowich | 59 | 16 | 7 | 23 | 36 |
| Corey Beaulieu, Seattle | 32 | 0 | 3 | 3 | 134 |
| Moose Jaw | 29 | 3 | 17 | 20 | 91 |
| Totals | 61 | 3 | 20 | 23 | 225 |
| Bob Loucks | 60 | 9 | 11 | 20 | 67 |
| Lyle Strom | 42 | 2 | 11 | 13 | 70 |
| Scott Thomas | 70 | 1 | 10 | 11 | 64 |
| Jason Peters | 38 | 0 | 7 | 7 | 9 |
| Jeff Rosner | 44 | 2 | 3 | 5 | 199 |
| Marty Loftsgard | 46 | 2 | 3 | 5 | 26 |
| Paul Giokas | 21 | 0 | 4 | 4 | 83 |
| Derry Menard | 12 | 1 | 2 | 3 | 8 |
| Kevin Masters | 32 | 1 | 2 | 3 | 4 |
| Derek Keltzel | 1 | 1 | 1 | 2 | 0 |
| Blaine Fomradas | 21 | 1 | 1 | 2 | 19 |
| Cal Fendelet, Brandson | 6 | 0 | 1 | 1 | 2 |
| Moose Jaw | 4 | 0 | 1 | 1 | 2 |
| Totals | 10 | 0 | 2 | 2 | 4 |
| Stan Reddick, P.A. (G.) | 19 | 0 | 0 | 0 | 6 |
| Moose Jaw (G.) | 33 | 0 | 2 | 2 | 2 |
| Totals | 52 | 0 | 2 | 2 | 8 |
| Wade Shutter | 4 | 1 | 0 | 1 | 22 |
| Scott Ironside (Goalie) | 25 | 0 | 1 | 1 | 11 |
| Derek Eberle | 1 | 0 | 0 | 0 | 2 |
| Scott Bailey (Goalie) | 2 | 0 | 0 | 0 | 0 |
| Dave McMillian | 3 | 0 | 0 | 0 | 0 |
| Byron Sheen | 3 | 0 | 0 | 0 | 0 |
| Tyler Wall (Goalie) | 4 | 0 | 0 | 0 | 2 |

## Portland Winter Hawks

|  | Games | G. | A. | Pts. | Pen. |
|---|---|---|---|---|---|
| Dennis Holland | 69 | *82 | 85 | *167 | 120 |
| Troy Mick | 66 | 49 | *87 | 136 | 70 |
| Terry Black | 72 | 34 | 70 | 104 | 62 |
| James Black | 71 | 45 | 51 | 96 | 57 |
| Shaun Clouston | 72 | 45 | 47 | 92 | 150 |
| Chad Biafore | 72 | 14 | 66 | 80 | 179 |
| Greg Leahy | 66 | 28 | 49 | 77 | 128 |
| Scott Myden | 63 | 33 | 27 | 60 | 54 |

|  | Games | G. | A. | Pts. | Pen. |
|---|---|---|---|---|---|
| Brent Fleetwood | 70 | 20 | 31 | 51 | 87 |
| Roy Mitchell | 72 | 9 | 34 | 43 | 177 |
| Mark Greyeyes | 69 | 15 | 24 | 39 | 28 |
| Mike Moore | 69 | 8 | 19 | 27 | 69 |
| Brian Gourlie | 70 | 10 | 14 | 24 | 34 |
| Joey Mittlelsteadt | 61 | 2 | 14 | 16 | 182 |
| Calvin Thudium | 68 | 6 | 9 | 15 | 24 |
| Kevin Jorgenson | 68 | 0 | 13 | 13 | 214 |
| Wayne Anchikoski | 32 | 6 | 5 | 11 | 8 |
| Rob Flintoft | 49 | 0 | 9 | 9 | 146 |
| Byron Dafoe (Goalie) | 59 | 0 | 6 | 6 | 18 |
| Rick Rehmann | 26 | 0 | 3 | 3 | 23 |
| Vince Cocciolo | 10 | 0 | 2 | 2 | 10 |
| Eric Badzgon (Goalie) | 25 | 0 | 2 | 2 | 10 |
| Jamie Linden | 1 | 0 | 1 | 1 | 0 |
| Graham Taylor | 3 | 0 | 1 | 1 | 12 |
| Jason Hicks | 19 | 1 | 0 | 1 | 2 |
| Jamie Graham | 21 | 1 | 0 | 1 | 8 |
| Jeff Resler | 1 | 0 | 0 | 0 | 0 |

## Prince Albert Raiders

|  | Games | G. | A. | Pts. | Pen. |
|---|---|---|---|---|---|
| Mike Modano | 41 | 39 | 66 | 105 | 74 |
| Jeff Nelson | 71 | 30 | 57 | 87 | 74 |
| Wayde Bucsis | 56 | 40 | 44 | 84 | 27 |
| Todd Nelson | 72 | 14 | 45 | 59 | 72 |
| Reid Simpson | 59 | 26 | 29 | 55 | 264 |
| Tracy Egeland, M. Hat | 42 | 11 | 12 | 23 | 64 |
| Prince Albert | 24 | 17 | 10 | 27 | 24 |
| Totals | 66 | 28 | 22 | 50 | 88 |
| Jeff Tomlinson | 55 | 13 | 29 | 42 | 49 |
| Brian Pellerin | 60 | 17 | 16 | 33 | 216 |
| Todd Kinniburgh | 67 | 17 | 16 | 33 | 48 |
| Gord Kruppke | 62 | 6 | 26 | 32 | 254 |
| Brad Harrison, M. Jaw | 31 | 4 | 6 | 10 | 51 |
| Prince Albert | 33 | 9 | 5 | 14 | 59 |
| Totals | 64 | 13 | 11 | 24 | 110 |
| Troy Neumeier | 72 | 7 | 17 | 24 | 89 |
| Graham Garden, Bran. | 27 | 10 | 10 | 20 | 36 |
| Prince Albert | 8 | 1 | 2 | 3 | 8 |
| Totals | 35 | 11 | 12 | 23 | 44 |
| Mark Stowe | 45 | 7 | 14 | 21 | 38 |
| Brad Boehm | 68 | 7 | 13 | 20 | 67 |
| Pat Odnokon | 51 | 11 | 8 | 19 | 20 |
| Terry Bendera | 62 | 10 | 9 | 19 | 64 |
| David Nielson | 63 | 6 | 13 | 19 | 114 |
| Scott Allison | 51 | 6 | 9 | 15 | 37 |
| Ron Gunville | 33 | 5 | 10 | 15 | 77 |
| Steven Tillmans | 51 | 2 | 8 | 10 | 93 |
| Trent Kachur, Tri-City | 21 | 1 | 7 | 8 | 45 |
| Prince Albert | 17 | 1 | 0 | 1 | 30 |
| Totals | 38 | 2 | 7 | 9 | 75 |
| Laurie Billeck | 60 | 2 | 4 | 6 | 65 |
| Curt Regnier | 15 | 2 | 1 | 3 | 2 |
| F. Chabot, M. J. (G.) | 26 | 0 | 3 | 3 | 22 |
| P. Albert (G.) | 28 | 0 | 0 | 0 | 6 |
| Totals | 54 | 0 | 3 | 3 | 28 |
| Dennis Sproxton (G.) | 33 | 0 | 1 | 1 | 4 |
| Corey Hastman | 1 | 0 | 0 | 0 | 0 |
| Scott Longstaff | 1 | 0 | 0 | 0 | 0 |
| Sandy Thaler | 1 | 0 | 0 | 0 | 4 |
| Troy Hjertaas | 2 | 0 | 0 | 0 | 0 |
| Cam Moon (Goalie) | 2 | 0 | 0 | 0 | 0 |

## Regina Pats

|  | Games | G. | A. | Pts. | Pen. |
|---|---|---|---|---|---|
| Michael Sillinger | 72 | 53 | 78 | 131 | 52 |

|  | Games | G. | A. | Pts | Pen. |
|---|---|---|---|---|---|
| Gary Dickie | 59 | 48 | 60 | 108 | 113 |
| Brad McGinnis | 68 | 32 | 36 | 68 | 57 |
| Jamie Heward | 52 | 31 | 28 | 59 | 29 |
| Chad Silver | 59 | 17 | 38 | 55 | 71 |
| Scott Daniels | 64 | 21 | 26 | 47 | 241 |
| Frank Kovacs | 70 | 16 | 27 | 43 | 90 |
| Kevin Haller | 72 | 10 | 31 | 41 | 99 |
| Corey Paterson | 72 | 18 | 17 | 35 | 36 |
| Terry Hollinger | 65 | 2 | 27 | 29 | 49 |
| Jim Mathieson | 62 | 5 | 22 | 27 | 151 |
| Brad Miller | 34 | 8 | 18 | 26 | 95 |
| Jeff Sebastian | 72 | 10 | 15 | 25 | 72 |
| Kelly Markwart | 70 | 12 | 10 | 22 | 49 |
| Darren Parsons | 49 | 6 | 15 | 21 | 47 |
| Mike Dyck | 53 | 3 | 18 | 21 | 115 |
| Jamie Splett | 28 | 6 | 4 | 10 | 14 |
| Cam Brauer | 49 | 0 | 9 | 9 | 59 |
| Shane Bogden | 19 | 2 | 1 | 3 | 22 |
| Dave Gerse | 27 | 1 | 2 | 3 | 48 |
| Curtis Nykyforuk | 37 | 1 | 1 | 2 | 40 |
| Rod Houk (Goalie) | 59 | 0 | 2 | 2 | 8 |
| Brad Treliving, Spo. | 3 | 0 | 0 | 0 | 8 |
| Regina | 10 | 0 | 1 | 1 | 26 |
| Totals | 13 | 0 | 1 | 1 | 34 |
| Dave Duquette | 17 | 0 | 1 | 1 | 42 |
| Mark Cipriano | 19 | 0 | 1 | 1 | 20 |
| Brian Leibel (Goalie) | 20 | 0 | 1 | 1 | 8 |
| Mike Kirby | 2 | 0 | 0 | 0 | 0 |
| Warren Joseph | 3 | 0 | 0 | 0 | 9 |
| John Badduke | 8 | 0 | 0 | 0 | 4 |
| Todd Leech | 12 | 0 | 0 | 0 | 14 |

## Saskatoon Blades

|  | Games | G. | A. | Pts | Pen. |
|---|---|---|---|---|---|
| Kory Kocur | 66 | 45 | 57 | 102 | 111 |
| Scott Scissons | 71 | 30 | 56 | 86 | 65 |
| Tracey Katelnikoff | 62 | 41 | 38 | 79 | 71 |
| Jason Christie | 72 | 33 | 46 | 79 | 98 |
| Collin Bauer | 61 | 17 | 62 | 79 | 71 |
| Kevin Kaminski | 52 | 25 | 43 | 68 | 199 |
| Brian Gerrits | 70 | 25 | 32 | 57 | 50 |
| Ken Sutton | 71 | 22 | 31 | 53 | 104 |
| Dean Holoein | 59 | 22 | 30 | 52 | 78 |
| David Struch | 66 | 20 | 31 | 51 | 18 |
| Kevin Yellowaga | 65 | 21 | 18 | 39 | 44 |
| Darin Bader | 66 | 19 | 14 | 33 | 214 |
| Jason Smart, P. Albert | 12 | 1 | 3 | 4 | 31 |
| Saskatoon | 36 | 6 | 17 | 23 | 33 |
| Totals | 48 | 7 | 20 | 27 | 64 |
| Shawn Snesar, Victoria | 28 | 3 | 10 | 13 | 49 |
| Saskatoon | 31 | 2 | 10 | 12 | 54 |
| Totals | 59 | 5 | 20 | 25 | 103 |
| Drew Sawtell | 57 | 8 | 14 | 22 | 146 |
| Darwin McPherson | 59 | 4 | 13 | 17 | 266 |
| Robert Lelacheur | 69 | 3 | 12 | 15 | 75 |
| Jody Praznik | 28 | 2 | 9 | 11 | 28 |
| Harri Leskinen | 29 | 1 | 5 | 6 | 6 |
| Shane Langager | 53 | 1 | 5 | 6 | 6 |
| Kirk Roworth, M. Jaw | 14 | 1 | 0 | 1 | 18 |
| Saskatoon | 37 | 1 | 2 | 3 | 49 |
| Totals | 51 | 2 | 2 | 4 | 67 |
| Dave Lipscombe | 10 | 1 | 3 | 4 | 5 |
| Dean Kuntz (Goalie) | 38 | 0 | 3 | 3 | 24 |
| Brad Murphy | 10 | 0 | 1 | 1 | 0 |
| Darin Baker (Goalie) | 19 | 0 | 1 | 1 | 2 |
| Mike Greenlay (Goalie) | 20 | 0 | 1 | 1 | 8 |
| Geoff McMaster | 1 | 0 | 0 | 0 | 0 |
| Dean Beattie | 2 | 0 | 0 | 0 | 7 |

|  | Games | G. | A. | Pts | Pen. |
|---|---|---|---|---|---|
| David Bell (Goalie) | 5 | 0 | 0 | 0 | 2 |
| Trent Hamm | 14 | 0 | 0 | 0 | 7 |

## Seattle Thunderbirds

|  | Games | G. | A. | Pts | Pen. |
|---|---|---|---|---|---|
| Victor Gervais | 72 | 54 | 65 | 119 | 158 |
| Glen Goodall | 70 | 52 | 62 | 114 | 58 |
| Lindsay Vallis | 63 | 21 | 32 | 53 | 48 |
| Dean Ewen, Spokane | 5 | 0 | 0 | 0 | 53 |
| Seattle | 56 | 22 | 30 | 52 | 254 |
| Totals | 61 | 22 | 30 | 52 | *307 |
| Stewart Malgunas | 72 | 11 | 41 | 52 | 51 |
| Ian McAmmond | 68 | 23 | 24 | 47 | 21 |
| Dean Hall | 33 | 18 | 19 | 37 | 8 |
| Rob Dumas | 70 | 10 | 27 | 37 | 161 |
| Andrew Schneider | 69 | 7 | 26 | 33 | 43 |
| Shannon Travis | 66 | 10 | 20 | 30 | 68 |
| Turner Stevenson | 69 | 15 | 12 | 27 | 84 |
| Greg Nicol | 55 | 15 | 11 | 26 | 131 |
| Brian Ilkuf, M. Jaw | 28 | 9 | 16 | 25 | 71 |
| Seattle | 4 | 0 | 0 | 0 | 0 |
| Totals | 32 | 9 | 16 | 25 | 71 |
| Kent Dochuk | 38 | 12 | 12 | 24 | 69 |
| Kevin Malgunas | 67 | 12 | 9 | 21 | 95 |
| Bradley Zavisha | 52 | 8 | 13 | 21 | 43 |
| Tom Sprague | 68 | 5 | 16 | 21 | 24 |
| Darcy Simon | 62 | 3 | 15 | 18 | 208 |
| Jason White, S. Current | 7 | 1 | 1 | 2 | 26 |
| Seattle | 62 | 6 | 8 | 14 | 63 |
| Totals | 69 | 7 | 9 | 16 | 89 |
| Jay Stark | 71 | 3 | 11 | 14 | 212 |
| Eddie Patterson | 46 | 4 | 6 | 10 | 55 |
| Danny Lorenz (Goalie) | 68 | 0 | 5 | 5 | 23 |
| Corey Schwab (Goalie) | 10 | 0 | 1 | 1 | 7 |
| Trevor Goertzen | 13 | 0 | 1 | 1 | 4 |
| Brian Arthur | 1 | 0 | 0 | 0 | 12 |

## Spokane Chiefs

|  | Games | G. | A. | Pts | Pen. |
|---|---|---|---|---|---|
| Travis Green | 72 | 51 | 51 | 102 | 79 |
| Pat Falloon | 72 | 22 | 56 | 78 | 41 |
| Rob Friesen | 71 | 34 | 42 | 76 | 51 |
| Mike Hawes, Tri-City | 5 | 2 | 1 | 3 | 6 |
| Spokane | 63 | 38 | 30 | 68 | 105 |
| Totals | 68 | 40 | 31 | 71 | 111 |
| Dean Sexsmith, Sask. | 11 | 4 | 2 | 6 | 17 |
| Spokane | 48 | 22 | 34 | 56 | 54 |
| Totals | 59 | 26 | 36 | 62 | 71 |
| Darcy Loewen | 60 | 31 | 27 | 58 | 194 |
| Ray Whitney | 71 | 17 | 33 | 50 | 16 |
| Marco Fuster, Seattle | 1 | 1 | 0 | 1 | 0 |
| Spokane | 61 | 18 | 23 | 41 | 170 |
| Totals | 62 | 19 | 23 | 42 | 170 |
| Scott Farrell | 67 | 10 | 32 | 42 | 221 |
| Jon Klemm, Seattle | 2 | 1 | 1 | 2 | 0 |
| Spokane | 66 | 6 | 34 | 40 | 42 |
| Totals | 68 | 7 | 35 | 42 | 42 |
| Steve Junker | 68 | 19 | 15 | 34 | 40 |
| Frank Evans | 70 | 6 | 27 | 33 | 130 |
| Chris Rowland | 57 | 13 | 17 | 30 | 95 |
| Milan Dragicevic, T.C. | 4 | 0 | 0 | 0 | 8 |
| Spokane | 63 | 8 | 21 | 29 | 272 |
| Totals | 67 | 8 | 21 | 29 | 280 |
| Korey Sundstrum | 22 | 7 | 9 | 16 | 24 |
| Dennis Saharchuk | 46 | 3 | 8 | 11 | 5 |
| Paul Checknita, Leth | 32 | 1 | 5 | 6 | 39 |
| Spokane | 22 | 0 | 3 | 3 | 36 |
| Totals | 54 | 1 | 8 | 9 | 75 |

|  | Games | G. | A. | Pts. | Pen. |
|---|---|---|---|---|---|
| Mike Barlage, M.H. | 6 | 0 | 1 | 1 | 22 |
| Spokane | 64 | 1 | 5 | 6 | 144 |
| Totals | 70 | 1 | 6 | 7 | 166 |
| Jeff Ferguson, Leth. (G) | 25 | 0 | 2 | 2 | 26 |
| Spokane (Goalie) | 27 | 0 | 5 | 5 | 16 |
| Totals | 52 | 0 | 7 | 7 | 42 |
| Gabe Giesick | 10 | 2 | 3 | 5 | 37 |
| Chad Larsen | 41 | 0 | 5 | 5 | 30 |
| Mike Chrun | 2 | 2 | 0 | 2 | 0 |
| L.D. McNabb | 21 | 1 | 1 | 2 | 23 |
| Jouni Loponen | 8 | 0 | 2 | 2 | 2 |
| Bill Harrington | 3 | 0 | 1 | 1 | 0 |
| Shane Massie | 6 | 0 | 1 | 1 | 19 |
| Trent Thibert | 21 | 0 | 1 | 1 | 65 |
| Shawn Dietrich (Goalie) | 1 | 0 | 0 | 0 | 0 |
| Bob Dever | 1 | 0 | 0 | 0 | 0 |
| Dave Thomas | 1 | 0 | 0 | 0 | 0 |
| Jason Dorey | 2 | 0 | 0 | 0 | 0 |
| Jeff Little (Goalie) | 4 | 0 | 0 | 0 | 20 |
| Bob Platzer | 21 | 0 | 0 | 0 | 81 |
| John Colvin, M.H. (G.) | 3 | 0 | 0 | 0 | 0 |
| Spokane (Goalie) | 37 | 0 | 0 | 0 | 28 |
| Totals | 40 | 0 | 0 | 0 | 28 |

## Swift Current Broncos

|  | Games | G. | A. | Pts. | Pen. |
|---|---|---|---|---|---|
| Tim Tisdale | 68 | 57 | 82 | 139 | 89 |
| Peter Kasowski | 72 | 58 | 73 | 131 | 46 |
| Sheldon Kennedy | 51 | 58 | 48 | 106 | 92 |
| Dan Lambert | 57 | 25 | 77 | 102 | 158 |
| Brian Sakic | 71 | 36 | 64 | 100 | 28 |
| Darren Kruger | 71 | 10 | *87 | 97 | 72 |
| Bob Wilkie | 62 | 18 | 67 | 85 | 89 |
| Kimbi Daniels | 68 | 30 | 31 | 61 | 48 |
| Peter Soberlak | 37 | 25 | 33 | 58 | 21 |
| Mark McFarlane | 58 | 28 | 23 | 51 | 278 |
| Trevor Sim, Regina | 21 | 4 | 8 | 12 | 48 |
| Swift Current | 42 | 16 | 19 | 35 | 69 |
| Totals | 63 | 20 | 27 | 47 | 117 |
| Kyle Reeves | 68 | 19 | 21 | 40 | 49 |
| Blake Knox | 70 | 13 | 17 | 30 | 116 |
| Geoff Sanderson | 58 | 17 | 11 | 28 | 16 |
| Kevin Knopp, Seattle | 6 | 2 | 1 | 3 | 16 |
| Swift Current | 64 | 5 | 17 | 22 | 75 |
| Totals | 70 | 7 | 18 | 25 | 91 |
| Matt Ripley | 40 | 9 | 14 | 23 | 25 |
| Jeff Knight | 65 | 4 | 12 | 16 | 74 |
| Wade Smith | 63 | 5 | 10 | 15 | 126 |
| Kevin Barrett | 63 | 4 | 6 | 10 | 184 |
| Chris Larkin | 41 | 3 | 3 | 6 | 37 |
| Trevor Kruger (Goalie) | 59 | 0 | 4 | 4 | 20 |
| Jason Yuzda | 17 | 0 | 3 | 3 | 6 |
| Evan Marble | 12 | 0 | 1 | 1 | 2 |
| Don Blishen (Goalie) | 24 | 0 | 1 | 1 | 14 |
| Greg Reid (Goalie) | 1 | 0 | 0 | 0 | 0 |
| Scott Albert | 2 | 0 | 0 | 0 | 0 |
| Trent McLeary | 3 | 0 | 0 | 0 | 0 |

## Tri-City Americans

|  | Games | G. | A. | Pts. | Pen. |
|---|---|---|---|---|---|
| Stu Barnes | 70 | 59 | 82 | 141 | 117 |
| Sean Lebrun | 71 | 52 | 73 | 125 | 92 |
| Troy Kennedy, Brandon | 42 | 16 | 23 | 39 | 23 |
| Tri-City | 35 | 30 | 21 | 51 | 44 |
| Totals | 77 | 46 | 44 | 90 | 67 |
| Greg Spenrath | 64 | 26 | 35 | 61 | 213 |

|  | Games | G. | A. | Pts. | Pen. |
|---|---|---|---|---|---|
| Steve Jaques | 61 | 18 | 34 | 52 | 233 |
| Steve Rennie | 72 | 14 | 38 | 52 | 28 |
| Gregg Delcourt, Spo. | 5 | 0 | 0 | 0 | 9 |
| Tri-City | 67 | 17 | 29 | 46 | 90 |
| Totals | 72 | 17 | 29 | 46 | 99 |
| Murray Duval, Spokane | 4 | 0 | 3 | 3 | 22 |
| Tri-City | 67 | 14 | 25 | 39 | 122 |
| Totals | 71 | 14 | 28 | 42 | 144 |
| Kalvin Knibbs | 65 | 14 | 21 | 35 | 43 |
| Rob Krauss | 66 | 4 | 23 | 27 | 257 |
| Darren Kwiatkowski | 62 | 14 | 10 | 24 | 144 |
| Steve McNutt | 62 | 8 | 11 | 19 | 50 |
| Kelly Chotowetz, Sask. | 3 | 0 | 2 | 2 | 18 |
| Tri-City | 67 | 3 | 12 | 15 | 126 |
| Totals | 70 | 3 | 14 | 17 | 144 |
| Devin Derksen | 70 | 6 | 10 | 16 | 120 |
| Rick Fry | 70 | 6 | 10 | 16 | 68 |
| Dan Sherstenka | 69 | 0 | 8 | 8 | 83 |
| Kevin Robertson | 60 | 4 | 3 | 7 | 36 |
| Trevor Senn | 29 | 3 | 3 | 6 | 43 |
| Paul Hampton | 4 | 0 | 3 | 3 | 8 |
| Olaf Kolzig (Goalie) | 30 | 0 | 2 | 2 | 24 |
| Colin Ruck | 46 | 1 | 0 | 1 | 59 |
| Frank Furlan (Goalie) | 46 | 0 | 1 | 1 | 12 |
| Marty Braithwaite (G.) | 1 | 0 | 0 | 0 | 0 |
| Steve Passmore (Goalie) | 1 | 0 | 0 | 0 | 0 |
| Jason Pronly | 1 | 0 | 0 | 0 | 2 |
| Steve Wienke | 1 | 0 | 0 | 0 | 0 |
| Terry Degner | 2 | 0 | 0 | 0 | 0 |
| Gerry St. Cyr | 2 | 0 | 0 | 0 | 6 |
| Calvin Wiltshire | 4 | 0 | 0 | 0 | 0 |
| Jay Dunham | 15 | 0 | 0 | 0 | 9 |
| Terran Sandwith | 31 | 0 | 0 | 0 | 29 |

## Victoria Cougars

|  | Games | G. | A. | Pts. | Pen. |
|---|---|---|---|---|---|
| Clayton Young | 72 | 50 | 63 | 113 | 145 |
| Micah Aivazoff | 70 | 35 | 65 | 100 | 136 |
| Jackson Penney | 63 | 41 | 49 | 90 | 78 |
| Len Barrie | 67 | 39 | 48 | 87 | 157 |
| Will Andersen | 69 | 23 | 50 | 73 | 102 |
| Darren Naylor | 63 | 27 | 31 | 58 | 80 |
| Mike Bertamini | 63 | 25 | 31 | 56 | 76 |
| Joel Savage | 60 | 17 | 30 | 47 | 95 |
| Jim McKenzie | 67 | 15 | 27 | 42 | 176 |
| Craig Gustafson | 65 | 13 | 25 | 38 | 44 |
| Grant Chorney | 64 | 9 | 18 | 27 | 174 |
| Rob Sumner | 66 | 2 | 15 | 17 | 228 |
| Geoff Kerr | 37 | 6 | 10 | 16 | 68 |
| Dave Shute | 69 | 5 | 11 | 16 | 26 |
| Andrew Wolf | 36 | 4 | 12 | 16 | 74 |
| Brent Thurston | 60 | 11 | 3 | 14 | 86 |
| Darin Feasy | 55 | 4 | 8 | 12 | 29 |
| Doneau Menard | 22 | 2 | 8 | 10 | 22 |
| Dwayne Keller | 36 | 2 | 6 | 8 | 99 |
| Shayne Green | 13 | 3 | 3 | 6 | 0 |
| Brad Hack | 28 | 1 | 4 | 5 | 37 |
| Jason Knox | 50 | 1 | 4 | 5 | 20 |
| Rob McCaig | 23 | 1 | 2 | 3 | 2 |
| Wade Flaherty (Goalie) | 42 | 0 | 3 | 3 | 14 |
| Terry Virtue | 8 | 1 | 1 | 2 | 13 |
| Mike Seaton | 22 | 1 | 1 | 2 | 6 |
| Jason Patterson | 6 | 0 | 1 | 1 | 0 |
| Jaret Burgoyne (Goalie) | 35 | 0 | 1 | 1 | 0 |
| Ernie Boudreault | 1 | 0 | 0 | 0 | 0 |
| Glen Nazaruk (Goalie) | 1 | 0 | 0 | 0 | 0 |
| Corey Jones (Goalie) | 2 | 0 | 0 | 0 | 0 |

# Complete WHL Goaltending

| | Games | Mins. | Goals | SO. | Avg. |
|---|---|---|---|---|---|
| Trevor Kidd | 32 | 1509 | 102(3) | 0 | 4.06 |
| Kelly Hitchins | 54 | 2877 | 224(2) | 0 | 4.67 |
| **Brandon Totals** | 72 | 4386 | 331 | 0 | 4.53 |
| Dean Cook | 53 | 2810 | 192(3) | 0 | 4.10 |
| Corey Hirsch | 32 | 1516 | 106(2) | 2 | 4.20 |
| Willy McDonald | 1 | 59 | 6 | 0 | 6.10 |
| **Kamloops Totals** | 72 | 4385 | 309 | 2 | 4.23 |
| Jamie McLennan (a) | 7 | 368 | 22(1) | 0 | 3.59 |
| Dusty Imoo | 47 | 2673 | 229(2) | 1 | 5.14 |
| Jeff Ferguson (b) | 25 | 1380 | 125(1) | 1 | 5.43 |
| **Lethbridge Totals** | 72 | 4421 | 380 | 2 | 5.16 |
| Patrick Backland | 40 | 2273 | 165(1) | 0 | 4.36 |
| Alex Sheflo | 36 | 1971 | 146(1) | 0 | 4.44 |
| John Colvin (c) | 3 | 160 | 13 | 0 | 4.88 |
| **Medicine Hat Totals** | 72 | 4404 | 326 | 0 | 4.44 |
| Stan Reddick (d) | 33 | 1881 | 121(1) | 1 | 3.86 |
| Frederic Chabot (e) | 26 | 1385 | 114(2) | 1 | 4.94 |
| Scott Ironside | 25 | 920 | 105 | 0 | 6.85 |
| Tyler Wall | 4 | 153 | 22 | 0 | 8.63 |
| Scott Bailey | 2 | 34 | 7 | 0 | 12.35 |
| **Moose Jaw Totals** | 72 | 4373 | 372 | 2 | 5.10 |
| Bryon Dafoe | 59 | 3279 | *291(3) | 1 | 5.32 |
| Eric Badzgon | 25 | 1119 | 100(1) | 1 | 5.36 |
| **Portland Totals** | 72 | 4398 | 395 | 2 | 5.39 |
| Frederic Chabot (e) | 28 | 1572 | 88(1) | 1 | 3.36 |
| Stan Reddick (d) | 19 | 994 | 67 | 0 | 4.04 |
| Dennis Sproxton | 33 | 1670 | 120 | 0 | 4.31 |
| Cam Moon | 2 | 120 | 9(1) | 0 | 4.50 |
| **Prince Albert Totals** | 72 | 4356 | 286 | 1 | 3.94 |
| Rod Houk | 59 | 3466 | 248(2) | 0 | 4.29 |
| Brian Leibel | 20 | 983 | 106(2) | 1 | 6.47 |
| **Regina Totals** | 72 | 4449 | 358 | 1 | 4.83 |
| Dean Kuntz | 38 | 2035 | 136(1) | 0 | 4.01 |
| Mike Greenlay | 20 | 1128 | 86(1) | 0 | 4.57 |
| Darin Baker | 19 | 959 | 83(2) | 0 | 5.19 |
| David Bell | 5 | 260 | 26 | 0 | 6.00 |
| **Saskatoon Totals** | 72 | 4382 | 335 | 0 | 4.59 |
| Danny Lorenz | *68 | *4003 | 240(5) | *3 | 3.60 |
| Corey Schwab | 10 | 386 | 31 | 0 | 4.82 |
| **Seattle Totals** | 72 | 4389 | 276 | 3 | 3.77 |
| Jeff Ferguson (b) | 27 | 1483 | 133(2) | 0 | 5.38 |
| John Colvin (c) | 37 | 2031 | 188(1) | 0 | 5.55 |
| Shawn Dietrich | 1 | 60 | 6 | 0 | 6.00 |
| Jamie McClennan (a) | 11 | 578 | 63 | 0 | 6.54 |
| Jeff Little | 4 | 199 | 26 | 0 | 7.84 |
| **Spokane Totals** | 72 | 4351 | 419 | 0 | 5.78 |
| Greg Reid | 1 | 2 | 0 | 0 | 0.00 |
| Trevor Kruger | 59 | 3246 | 217 | 1 | 4.01 |
| Don Blishen | 24 | 113 | 101(1) | 0 | 5.36 |
| **Swift Current Totals** | 72 | 4379 | 319 | 1 | 4.37 |
| Marty Braithwaite | 1 | 20 | 1 | 0 | 3.00 |
| Olaf Kolzig | 30 | 1671 | 97(1) | 1 | *3.48 |
| Frank Furlan | 46 | 2662 | 191(3) | 0 | 4.31 |
| Steve Passmore | 1 | 60 | 6 | 0 | 6.00 |
| **Tri-City Totals** | 72 | 4413 | 299 | 1 | 4.07 |
| Wade Flaherty | 42 | 2408 | 180(2) | 0 | 4.49 |
| Jaret Burgoyne | 35 | 1924 | 156 | 1 | 4.86 |
| Corey Jones | 2 | 73 | 11 | 0 | 9.04 |
| Glen Nazaruk | 1 | 9 | 2 | 0 | 13.33 |
| **Victoria Totals** | 72 | 4414 | 351 | 1 | 4.77 |

( )—Empty Net Goals. Do not count against a Goaltender's average.
(a)—McLennan played for Lethbridge and Spokane.
(b)—Ferguson played for Lethbridge and Spokane.

(c)—Colvin played for Medicine Hat and Spokane.
(d)—Reddick played for Moose Jaw and Prince Albert.
(e)—Chabot played for Moose Jaw and Prince Albert.

## Individual 1988-89 Leaders

| | | |
|---|---|---|
| Goals | Dennis Holland, Portland— | 82 |
| Assists | Darren Kruger, Swift Current— | 87 |
| | Troy Mick, Portland— | 87 |
| Points | Dennis Holland, Portland— | 167 |
| Penalty Minutes | Dean Ewen, Seattle— | 307 |
| Goaltender's Average | Olaf Kolzig, Tri-City— | 3.48 |
| Shutouts | Danny Lorenz, Seattle— | 3 |

## 1989 WHL Playoffs

### East Division Quarterfinals
(Best-of-five series)

| | W. | L. | Pts. | GF. | GA. | | W. | L. | Pts. | GF. | GA. |
|---|---|---|---|---|---|---|---|---|---|---|---|
| Moose Jaw | 3 | 0 | 6 | 16 | 9 | Lethbridge | 3 | 1 | 6 | 25 | 12 |
| Medicine Hat | 0 | 3 | 0 | 9 | 16 | Prince Albert | 1 | 3 | 2 | 12 | 25 |

(Moose Jaw wins series, 3 games to 0)    (Lethbridge wins series, 3 games to 1)

### East Division Semifinals
(Best-of-seven series)

| | W. | L. | Pts. | GF. | GA. | | W. | L. | Pts. | GF. | GA. |
|---|---|---|---|---|---|---|---|---|---|---|---|
| Swift Current | 4 | 0 | 8 | 28 | 8 | Saskatoon | 4 | 0 | 8 | 25 | 8 |
| Moose Jaw | 0 | 4 | 0 | 8 | 28 | Lethbridge | 0 | 4 | 0 | 8 | 25 |

(Swift Current wins series, 4 games to 0)    (Saskatoon wins series, 4 games to 0)

### West Division Semifinals
(Best-of-nine series)

| | W. | L. | Pts. | GF. | GA. | | W. | L. | Pts. | GF. | GA. |
|---|---|---|---|---|---|---|---|---|---|---|---|
| Portland | 5 | 2 | 10 | 37 | 25 | Kamloops | 5 | 3 | 10 | 35 | 32 |
| Tri-City | 2 | 5 | 4 | 25 | 37 | Victoria | 3 | 5 | 6 | 32 | 25 |

(Portland wins series, 5 games to 2)    (Kamloops wins series, 5 games to 3)

### East Division Finals
(Best-of-seven series)

| | W. | L. | Pts. | GF. | GA. | | W. | L. | Pts. | GF. | GA. |
|---|---|---|---|---|---|---|---|---|---|---|---|
| Swift Current | 4 | 0 | 8 | 32 | 20 | Portland | 5 | 3 | 10 | 45 | 38 |
| Saskatoon | 0 | 4 | 0 | 20 | 32 | Kamloops | 3 | 5 | 6 | 38 | 45 |

(Swift Current wins series, 4 games to 0)    (Portland wins series, 5 games to 3)

### West Division Finals
(Best-of-nine series)

## Western Hockey League Playoff Finals
(Best-of-seven series)

| | W. | L. | Pts. | GF. | GA. |
|---|---|---|---|---|---|
| Swift Current | 4 | 0 | 8 | 23 | 9 |
| Portland | 0 | 4 | 0 | 9 | 23 |

(Swift Current wins WHL Playoffs, 4 games to 0)

## Top 10 WHL Playoff Scorers

| | Games | G. | A. | Pts. | Pen. |
|---|---|---|---|---|---|
| 1. Dennis Holland, Portland | 19 | 15 | *22 | *37 | 18 |
| 2. Troy Mick, Portland | 19 | 15 | 19 | 34 | 17 |
| 3. Tim Tisdale, Swift Current | 12 | 17 | 15 | 32 | 22 |
| 4. Phil Huber, Kamloops | 16 | *18 | 13 | 31 | 48 |
| 5. Greg Leahy, Portland | 19 | 16 | 13 | 29 | 33 |
| 6. David Chyzowski, Kamloops | 16 | 15 | 13 | 28 | 32 |
| Dan Lambert, Swift Current | 12 | 9 | 19 | 28 | 12 |
| Pat MacLeod, Kamloops | 15 | 8 | 20 | 28 | 8 |
| 9. Sheldon Kennedy, Swift Current | 12 | 9 | 15 | 24 | 22 |
| 10. Chad Biafore, Portland | 19 | 3 | 19 | 22 | 48 |

# Team-by-Team Playoff Scoring

## Kamloops Blazers

(Lost West Division finals to Portland, 5 games to 3)

|  | Games | G. | A. | Pts. | Pen. |
|---|---|---|---|---|---|
| Phil Huber | 16 | *18 | 13 | 31 | 48 |
| David Chyzowski | 16 | 15 | 13 | 28 | 32 |
| Pat MacLeod | 15 | 8 | 20 | 28 | 8 |
| Zac Boyer | 16 | 9 | 8 | 17 | 10 |
| Mike Needham | 16 | 2 | 9 | 11 | 13 |
| Trevor Buchanan | 16 | 3 | 5 | 8 | 64 |
| Pat Bingham | 16 | 2 | 6 | 8 | 35 |
| Kim Deck | 16 | 0 | 8 | 8 | 14 |
| Ryan Harrison | 16 | 4 | 3 | 7 | 16 |
| Cal McGowan | 16 | 4 | 2 | 6 | 24 |
| Ed Bertuzzi | 16 | 3 | 2 | 5 | 27 |
| Daryl Sydor | 15 | 1 | 4 | 5 | 19 |
| Geoff Smith | 6 | 1 | 3 | 4 | 12 |
| Joel Dyck | 13 | 1 | 3 | 4 | 20 |
| Len Jorgenson | 2 | 1 | 0 | 1 | 0 |
| Corey Anderson | 16 | 1 | 0 | 1 | 16 |
| Tod Esselmont | 5 | 0 | 1 | 1 | 0 |
| Corey Hirsch (Goalie) | 5 | 0 | 1 | 1 | 0 |
| Cory Crichton | 9 | 0 | 1 | 1 | 0 |
| Dean Cook (Goalie) | 14 | 0 | 1 | 1 | 4 |
| David Linford | 16 | 0 | 1 | 1 | 14 |
| Steven Yule | 15 | 0 | 0 | 0 | 17 |
| Paul Kruse | 16 | 0 | 0 | 0 | 35 |

## Lethbridge Hurricanes

(Lost East Division semifinals to Saskatoon, 4 games to 0)

|  | Games | G. | A. | Pts. | Pen. |
|---|---|---|---|---|---|
| Corey Lyons | 8 | 4 | 9 | 13 | 7 |
| Bryan Bosch | 8 | 6 | 6 | 12 | 9 |
| Mark Greig | 8 | 5 | 5 | 10 | 16 |
| Kevin St. Jacques | 8 | 5 | 3 | 8 | 4 |
| Peter Berthelsen | 8 | 1 | 5 | 6 | 8 |
| Wes Walz | 8 | 1 | 5 | 6 | 6 |
| Jason Ruff | 7 | 2 | 3 | 5 | 28 |
| Kelly Ens | 8 | 4 | 1 | 5 | 15 |
| Brad Rubachuk | 6 | 3 | 1 | 4 | 25 |
| Mark Kuntz | 8 | 0 | 3 | 3 | 30 |
| Jim Wheatcroft | 7 | 1 | 1 | 2 | 24 |
| Clark Polglase | 8 | 1 | 1 | 2 | 12 |
| Casey McMillian | 8 | 0 | 2 | 2 | 9 |
| Dusty Imoo (Goalie) | 4 | 0 | 1 | 1 | 0 |
| Pat Pylypuik | 8 | 0 | 1 | 1 | 17 |
| Jeff Denham | 3 | 0 | 0 | 0 | 4 |
| Ivan Jessey | 4 | 0 | 0 | 0 | 7 |
| Shane Mazutinec | 4 | 0 | 0 | 0 | 0 |
| Chad Seibel | 5 | 0 | 0 | 0 | 5 |
| Doug Barrault | 6 | 0 | 0 | 0 | 7 |
| Colin Gregor | 6 | 0 | 0 | 0 | 11 |
| Jamie McLennan (G.) | 7 | 0 | 0 | 0 | 7 |
| Rob Hale | 8 | 0 | 0 | 0 | 24 |

## Medicine Hat Tigers

(Lost East Division quarterfinals to M. Jaw, 3 games to 0)

|  | Games | G. | A. | Pts. | Pen. |
|---|---|---|---|---|---|
| Kirby Lindal | 3 | 4 | 0 | 4 | 9 |
| Jason Miller | 3 | 1 | 2 | 3 | 2 |
| Bart Cote | 3 | 0 | 3 | 3 | 6 |
| Mark Woolf | 2 | 0 | 2 | 2 | 4 |
| Wayne Hynes | 3 | 0 | 2 | 2 | 6 |
| Ryan McGill | 3 | 0 | 2 | 2 | 15 |
| Dwayne Brook | 2 | 1 | 0 | 1 | 0 |
| Murray Garbutt | 3 | 1 | 0 | 1 | 6 |
| Jason Prosofsky | 3 | 1 | 0 | 1 | 6 |
| Kevin Riehl | 3 | 1 | 0 | 1 | 6 |
| Patrick Backlund (G.) | 2 | 0 | 1 | 1 | 0 |
| Cal Zankowski | 3 | 0 | 1 | 1 | 2 |
| Alec Sheflo (Goalie) | 1 | 0 | 0 | 0 | 0 |
| Lloyd Pelletier | 2 | 0 | 0 | 0 | 0 |
| Vince Boe | 3 | 0 | 0 | 0 | 4 |
| Clayton Gainer | 3 | 0 | 0 | 0 | 14 |
| Dan Kordic | 3 | 0 | 0 | 0 | 10 |
| Chris Lafreniere | 3 | 0 | 0 | 0 | 6 |
| Clayton Norris | 3 | 0 | 0 | 0 | 2 |
| Darren Stolk | 3 | 0 | 0 | 0 | 2 |
| Brent Thompson | 3 | 0 | 0 | 0 | 2 |

## Moose Jaw Warriors

(Lost E. Division semifinals to S. Current, 4 games to 0)

|  | Games | G. | A. | Pts. | Pen. |
|---|---|---|---|---|---|
| Jerome Bechard | 7 | 5 | 5 | 10 | 40 |
| Rob Harvey | 7 | 3 | 6 | 9 | 6 |
| Blair Atcheynum | 7 | 2 | 5 | 7 | 13 |
| Scott Humeniuk | 7 | 5 | 0 | 5 | 32 |
| Derek Kletzel | 7 | 3 | 1 | 4 | 0 |
| Cory Beaulieu | 7 | 1 | 2 | 3 | 16 |
| Rob Reimer | 7 | 1 | 2 | 3 | 8 |
| Mike Zakowich | 4 | 0 | 3 | 3 | 0 |
| Devon Oleniuk | 7 | 0 | 3 | 3 | 10 |
| Chris Bright | 7 | 2 | 0 | 2 | 6 |
| Randy Keller | 7 | 1 | 0 | 1 | 9 |
| Marty Loftsgard | 7 | 1 | 0 | 1 | 6 |
| Lyle Strom | 5 | 0 | 1 | 1 | 16 |
| Scott Barnstable | 7 | 0 | 1 | 1 | 25 |
| Bob Loucks | 7 | 0 | 1 | 1 | 13 |
| Stan Reddick (Goalie) | 7 | 0 | 1 | 1 | 2 |
| Scott Thomas | 7 | 0 | 1 | 1 | 2 |
| Scott Ironside (Goalie) | 2 | 0 | 0 | 0 | 0 |
| Kevin Masters | 3 | 0 | 0 | 0 | 7 |
| Scott Reid | 3 | 0 | 0 | 0 | 2 |
| Jeff Rosner | 6 | 0 | 0 | 0 | 33 |
| Steve Young | 7 | 0 | 0 | 0 | 26 |

## Portland Winter Hawks

(Lost WHL Finals to Swift Current, 4 games to 0)

|  | Games | G. | A. | Pts. | Pen. |
|---|---|---|---|---|---|
| Dennis Holland | 19 | 15 | *22 | *37 | 18 |
| Troy Mick | 19 | 15 | 19 | 34 | 17 |
| Greg Leahy | 19 | 16 | 13 | 29 | 33 |
| Chad Biafore | 19 | 3 | 19 | 22 | 48 |
| James Black | 19 | 13 | 6 | 19 | 28 |
| Terry Black | 19 | 3 | 16 | 19 | 28 |
| Shaun Clouston | 19 | 7 | 10 | 17 | 28 |
| Roy Mitchell | 19 | 1 | 8 | 9 | 38 |
| Wayne Anchikoski | 18 | 4 | 4 | 8 | 8 |
| Scott Mydan | 9 | 3 | 5 | 8 | 0 |
| Brent Fleetwood | 19 | 5 | 2 | 7 | 22 |
| Kevin Jorgenson | 19 | 0 | 7 | 7 | *78 |
| Bryan Gourlie | 17 | 3 | 3 | 6 | 10 |
| Joey Mittelsteadt | 19 | 0 | 6 | 6 | 68 |
| Mark Greyeyes | 17 | 1 | 4 | 5 | 2 |
| Jason Hicks | 17 | 0 | 5 | 5 | 2 |
| Mike Moore | 19 | 2 | 1 | 3 | 13 |
| Byron Dafoe (Goalie) | 18 | 0 | 3 | 3 | 4 |

— 197 —

|  | Games | G. | A. | Pts. | Pen. |
|---|---|---|---|---|---|
| Calvin Thudium | 17 | 0 | 1 | 1 | 2 |
| Eric Badzgon (Goalie) | 1 | 0 | 0 | 0 | 0 |
| Vince Cocciolo | 19 | 0 | 0 | 0 | 10 |

## Prince Albert Raiders
(Lost E. Division quarterfinals to Leth., 3 games to 1)

|  | Games | G. | A. | Pts. | Pen. |
|---|---|---|---|---|---|
| Jeff Tomlinson | 4 | 3 | 1 | 4 | 4 |
| Wayde Bucsis | 4 | 2 | 2 | 4 | 6 |
| Todd Nelson | 4 | 1 | 3 | 4 | 4 |
| Reid Simpson | 4 | 2 | 1 | 3 | 30 |
| Jeff Nelson | 4 | 0 | 3 | 3 | 4 |
| Pat Odnokon | 2 | 1 | 0 | 1 | 0 |
| Todd Kinniburgh | 3 | 1 | 0 | 1 | 0 |
| Laurie Billeck | 4 | 1 | 0 | 1 | 14 |
| Curt Regnier | 4 | 1 | 0 | 1 | 5 |
| Brian Pellerin | 3 | 0 | 1 | 1 | 27 |
| Tracey Egeland | 4 | 0 | 1 | 1 | 13 |
| Ron Gunville | 4 | 0 | 1 | 1 | 15 |
| Brad Boehm | 1 | 0 | 0 | 0 | 5 |
| Troy Hjertaas | 1 | 0 | 0 | 0 | 0 |
| David Neilson | 1 | 0 | 0 | 0 | 2 |
| Denis Sproxton (Goalie) | 2 | 0 | 0 | 0 | 7 |
| Scott Allison | 3 | 0 | 0 | 0 | 0 |
| Brad Harrison | 3 | 0 | 0 | 0 | 7 |
| Gord Kruppke | 3 | 0 | 0 | 0 | 11 |
| Terry Bendera | 4 | 0 | 0 | 0 | 11 |
| Fred Chabot (Goalie) | 4 | 0 | 0 | 0 | 2 |
| Troy Neumeier | 4 | 0 | 0 | 0 | 11 |
| Mark Stowe | 4 | 0 | 0 | 0 | 5 |
| Steve Tillmans | 4 | 0 | 0 | 0 | 5 |

## Saskatoon Blades
(Lost East Division finals to Swift Current, 4 games to 0)

|  | Games | G. | A. | Pts. | Pen. |
|---|---|---|---|---|---|
| Kory Kocur | 8 | 7 | 11 | 18 | 15 |
| Kevin Kaminski | 8 | 4 | 9 | 13 | 25 |
| Jason Christie | 8 | 6 | 5 | 11 | 13 |
| Darin Bader | 8 | 7 | 3 | 10 | 25 |
| Collin Bauer | 8 | 1 | 8 | 9 | 8 |
| Tracey Katelnikoff | 6 | 5 | 3 | 8 | 10 |
| Brian Gerrits | 8 | 4 | 4 | 8 | 4 |
| Dean Holoien | 8 | 3 | 4 | 7 | 7 |
| Ken Sutton | 8 | 2 | 5 | 7 | 12 |
| Jason Smart | 8 | 1 | 6 | 7 | 16 |
| David Struch | 8 | 2 | 3 | 5 | 6 |
| Scott Scissons | 7 | 0 | 4 | 4 | 16 |
| Shawn Snesar | 8 | 0 | 4 | 4 | 8 |
| Kevin Yellowaga | 8 | 2 | 0 | 2 | 4 |
| Shane Langager | 7 | 1 | 1 | 2 | 2 |
| Jody Praznik | 8 | 0 | 2 | 2 | 2 |
| Darwin McPherson | 8 | 0 | 1 | 1 | 27 |
| Drew Sawtell | 1 | 0 | 0 | 0 | 0 |
| Kirk Roworth | 3 | 0 | 0 | 0 | 0 |
| Mike Greenlay (Goalie) | 6 | 0 | 0 | 0 | 0 |
| Dean Kuntz (Goalie) | 6 | 0 | 0 | 0 | 0 |
| Rob Lelacheur | 8 | 0 | 0 | 0 | 2 |

## Swift Current Broncos
(Winners of 1989 WHL Playoffs)

|  | Games | G. | A. | Pts. | Pen. |
|---|---|---|---|---|---|
| Tim Tisdale | 12 | 17 | 15 | 32 | 22 |
| Dan Lambert | 12 | 9 | 19 | 28 | 12 |
| Sheldon Kennedy | 12 | 9 | 15 | 24 | 22 |
| Brian Sakic | 12 | 9 | 9 | 18 | 8 |
| Trevor Sim | 11 | 10 | 6 | 16 | 20 |
| Peter Soberlak | 12 | 5 | 11 | 16 | 11 |
| Kimbi Daniels | 12 | 6 | 6 | 12 | 12 |

|  | Games | G. | A. | Pts. | Pen. |
|---|---|---|---|---|---|
| Bob Wilkie | 12 | 1 | 11 | 12 | 47 |
| Darren Kruger | 12 | 0 | 10 | 10 | 17 |
| Kevin Knopp | 12 | 3 | 5 | 8 | 4 |
| Geoff Sanderson | 12 | 3 | 5 | 8 | 6 |
| Mark McFarlane | 7 | 4 | 3 | 7 | 39 |
| Peter Kasowski | 7 | 3 | 4 | 7 | 5 |
| Kyle Reeves | 9 | 2 | 1 | 3 | 15 |
| Blake Knox | 12 | 2 | 1 | 3 | 30 |
| Trevor Kruger (Goalie) | 12 | 0 | 3 | 3 | 2 |
| Matt Ripley | 4 | 0 | 1 | 1 | 12 |
| Jeff Knight | 12 | 0 | 1 | 1 | 12 |
| Don Blishen (Goalie) | 1 | 0 | 0 | 0 | 0 |
| Evan Marble | 5 | 0 | 0 | 0 | 0 |
| Chris Larkin | 6 | 0 | 0 | 0 | 0 |
| Wade Smith | 11 | 0 | 0 | 0 | 21 |
| Kevin Barrett | 12 | 0 | 0 | 0 | 4 |

## Tri-City Americans
(Lost West Division semifinals to Portland, 5 games to 2)

|  | Games | G. | A. | Pts. | Pen. |
|---|---|---|---|---|---|
| Stu Barnes | 7 | 6 | 5 | 11 | 10 |
| Troy Kennedy | 7 | 4 | 5 | 9 | 20 |
| Greg Spenrath | 7 | 4 | 2 | 6 | 23 |
| Gregg Delcourt | 7 | 1 | 5 | 6 | 6 |
| Kalvin Knibbs | 7 | 1 | 5 | 6 | 2 |
| Steve Rennie | 7 | 1 | 4 | 5 | 4 |
| Steve McNutt | 7 | 1 | 3 | 4 | 10 |
| Sean Lebrun | 5 | 0 | 4 | 4 | 13 |
| Rob Krauss | 7 | 1 | 2 | 3 | 19 |
| Murray Duval | 7 | 2 | 0 | 2 | 17 |
| Terry Degner | 7 | 1 | 1 | 2 | 0 |
| Darren Kwiatkowski | 7 | 1 | 1 | 2 | 14 |
| Kelly Chotowetz | 7 | 0 | 2 | 2 | 6 |
| Rick Fry | 6 | 1 | 0 | 1 | 2 |
| Devin Derksen | 7 | 1 | 0 | 1 | 16 |
| Steve Jaques | 2 | 0 | 0 | 0 | 9 |
| Frank Furlan (Goalie) | 3 | 0 | 0 | 0 | 0 |
| Colin Ruck | 3 | 0 | 0 | 0 | 0 |
| Olaf Kolzig (Goalie) | 6 | 0 | 0 | 0 | 2 |
| Kevin Robertson | 6 | 0 | 0 | 0 | 4 |
| Terran Sandwith | 6 | 0 | 0 | 0 | 4 |
| Dan Sherstenka | 7 | 0 | 0 | 0 | 11 |

## Victoria Cougars
(Lost W. Division semifinals to Kamloops, 5 games to 3)

|  | Games | G. | A. | Pts. | Pen. |
|---|---|---|---|---|---|
| Will Andersen | 8 | 2 | 11 | 13 | 20 |
| Clayton Young | 8 | 6 | 6 | 12 | 13 |
| Micah Aivazoff | 8 | 5 | 7 | 12 | 2 |
| Jackson Penney | 8 | 6 | 3 | 9 | 12 |
| Len Barrie | 7 | 5 | 2 | 7 | 23 |
| Mike Bertamini | 8 | 3 | 2 | 5 | 14 |
| Jim McKenzie | 8 | 1 | 4 | 5 | 30 |
| Andrew Wolf | 5 | 1 | 2 | 3 | 2 |
| Darren Naylor | 6 | 1 | 2 | 3 | 9 |
| Terry Virtue | 8 | 0 | 3 | 3 | 8 |
| Joel Savage | 6 | 1 | 1 | 2 | 8 |
| Brent Thurston | 6 | 0 | 2 | 2 | 8 |
| Dwayne Keller | 8 | 0 | 2 | 2 | 32 |
| Grant Chorney | 7 | 1 | 0 | 1 | 11 |
| Darin Feasey | 7 | 0 | 1 | 1 | 2 |
| Shayne Green | 8 | 0 | 1 | 1 | 4 |
| Dave Shute | 8 | 0 | 1 | 1 | 10 |
| Rob Sumner | 8 | 0 | 1 | 1 | 24 |
| Craig Gustafson | 1 | 0 | 0 | 0 | 0 |
| Jason Knox | 5 | 0 | 0 | 0 | 0 |
| Jeff Kerr | 6 | 0 | 0 | 0 | 6 |
| Wade Flaherty (Goalie) | 8 | 0 | 0 | 0 | 0 |

# Complete WHL Playoff Goaltending

| | Games | Mins. | Goals | SO. | Avg. |
|---|---|---|---|---|---|
| Corey Hirsch | 5 | 245 | 19 | 0 | 4.65 |
| Dean Cook | 14 | 717 | 57(1) | 0 | 4.77 |
| Kamloops Totals | 19 | 962 | 77 | 0 | 4.80 |
| Jamie McLennan | 7 | 388 | 24(1) | 0 | 3.71 |
| Dusty Imoo | 4 | 107 | 12 | 0 | 6.73 |
| Lethbridge Totals | 11 | 495 | 37 | 0 | 4.48 |
| Patrick Backlund | 2 | 121 | 9(1) | 0 | 4.46 |
| Alec Sheflo | 1 | 60 | 6 | 0 | 6.00 |
| Medicine Hat Totals | 3 | 181 | 16 | 0 | 5.30 |
| Stan Reddick | 7 | 349 | 26(2) | 0 | 4.47 |
| Scott Ironside | 2 | 51 | 9 | 0 | 10.59 |
| Moose Jaw Totals | 9 | 400 | 37 | 0 | 5.55 |
| Byron Dafoe | *18 | *1091 | *81 | *1 | 4.45 |
| Eric Badzgon | 1 | 63 | 5 | 0 | 4.76 |
| Portland Totals | 19 | 1154 | 86 | 1 | 4.47 |
| Fred Chabot | 4 | 199 | 16 | 0 | 4.82 |
| Denis Sproxton | 2 | 57 | 9 | 0 | 9.47 |
| Prince Albert Totals | 6 | 256 | 25 | 0 | 5.86 |
| Dean Kuntz | 6 | 306 | 24 | 0 | 4.71 |
| Mike Greenlay | 6 | 174 | 16 | 0 | 5.52 |
| Saskatoon Totals | 12 | 480 | 40 | 0 | 5.00 |
| Trevor Kruger | 12 | 713 | 35 | 0 | *2.95 |
| Don Blishen | 1 | 7 | 2 | 0 | 17.14 |
| Swift Current Totals | 13 | 720 | 37 | 0 | 3.08 |
| Olaf Kolzig | 6 | 363 | 29 | 0 | 4.79 |
| Frank Furlan | 3 | 67 | 7(1) | 0 | 6.27 |
| Tri-City Totals | 9 | 430 | 37 | 0 | 5.16 |
| Wade Flaherty | 8 | 480 | 35 | 0 | 4.38 |
| Victoria Totals | 8 | 480 | 35 | 0 | 4.38 |

( )—Empty Net Goals. Do not count against a goaltender's average.

# Individual WHL Playoff Leaders

| | | |
|---|---|---|
| Goals | Phil Huber, Kamloops— | 18 |
| Assists | Dennis Holland, Portland— | 22 |
| Points | Dennis Holland, Portland— | 37 |
| Penalty Minutes | Kevin Jorgenson, Portland— | 78 |
| Goaltender's Average (60 minutes) | Trevor Kruger, Swift Current— | 2.95 |
| Shutouts | Byron Dafoe, Portland— | 1 |

★★★★★★★★★★★★★★★★★★★★★★★★★★★★★★★★★★★★★★★★★★★★

# 1988-89 WHL All-Star Teams

| East Division | Position | West Division |
|---|---|---|
| Fred Chabot, Prince Albert | Goal | Danny Lorenz, Seattle |
| Dan Lambert, Swift Current | Defense | Steve Jaques, Tri City |
| Collin Bauer, Saskatoon | Defense | Chad Biafore, Portland |
| Mike Modano, Prince Albert | Center | Dennis Holland, Portland |
| Kirby Lindal, Medicine Hat | Left Wing | David Chyzowski, Kamloops |
| Blair Atcheynum, Moose Jaw | Right Wing | Jackson Penney, Victoria |

★★★★★★★★★★★★★★★★★★★★★★★★★★★★★★★★★★★★★★★★★★★★

# 1989 WHL Trophy Winners

Four Broncos Memorial Trophy (Most Valuable Player) ............................................ Stu Barnes, Tri-City
Bob Clarke Trophy (Top Scorer) ................................................................................ Dennis Holland, Portland
Jim Piggott Memorial Trophy (Rookie of the Year) ................................................. Wes Walz, Lethbridge
Brad Hornung Trophy (Most Sportsmanlike Player) ............................................... Blair Atcheynum, Moose Jaw
Bill Hunter Trophy (Top Defenseman) ...................................................................... Dan Lambert, Swift Current
Del Wilson Trophy (Top Goaltender) ........................................................................ Danny Lorenz, Seattle
Player of the Year ....................................................................................................... Dennis Holland, Portland
Dunc McCallum Memorial Trophy (Coach of the Year) ........................................ Ron Kennedy, Medicine Hat
Scott Munro Memorial Trophy (Regular Season Champion) ................................ Swift Current Broncos
Msgr. Athol Murray Memorial Trophy (Playoff Champion) .................................. Swift Current Broncos

## Historical WHL Trophy Winners

(Canadian Major Junior Hockey League in 1966-67, renamed the Western Canadian Hockey League from 1967-68 to 1976-77. Has been named the Western Hockey League since 1977-78 season).

### Four Broncos Memorial Trophy
(Most Valuable Player selected by coaches)

| | | |
|---|---|---|
| Gerry Pinder, Saskatoon | 1966-67 | |
| Jim Harrison Estevan | 1967-68 | |
| Bobby Clarke, Flin Flon | 1968-69 | |
| Reggie Leach, Flin Flon | 1969-70 | |
| Ed Dyck, Calgary | 1970-71 | |
| John Davidson, Calgary | 1971-72 | |
| Dennis Sobchuk, Regina | 1972-73 | |
| Ron Chipperfield, Brandon | 1973-74 | |
| Bryan Trottier, Lethbridge | 1974-75 | |
| Bernie Federko, Saskatoon | 1975-76 | |
| Barry Beck, New Westminster | 1976-77 | |
| Ryan Walter, Seattle | 1977-78 | |
| Perry Turnbull, Portland | 1978-79 | |
| Doug Wickenheiser, Regina | 1979-80 | |
| Steve Tsujiura, Medicine Hat | 1980-81 | |
| Mike Vernon, Calgary | 1981-82 | |
| Mike Vernon, Calgary | 1982-83 | |
| Ray Ferraro, Brandon | 1983-84 | |
| Cliff Ronning, New Westminster | 1984-85 | |
| Emanuel Viveiros, Prince Albert (East Division) Rob Brown, Kamloops (West Division) | 1985-86 | |
| Joe Sakic, Swift Current (East Division) Rob Brown, Kamloops (West Division) | 1986-87 | |
| Joe Sakic, Swift Current | 1987-88 | |
| Stu Barnes, Tri-City | 1988-89 | |

### Bob Clarke Trophy
(Originally called Bob Brownridge Memorial Trophy)
(Top Scorer)

Gerry Pinder, Saskatoon (140 pts)
Bobby Clarke, Flin Flon (168 pts)
Bobby Clarke, Flin Flon (137 pts)
Reggie Leach, Flin Flon (111 pts)
Chuck Arnason, Flin Flon (163 pts)
Tom Lysiak, Medicine Hat (143 pts)
Tom Lysiak, Medicine Hat (154 pts)
Ron Chipperfield, Brandon (162 pts)
Mel Bridgman, Victoria (157 pts)
Bernie Federko, Saskatoon (187 pts)
Bill Derlago, Brandon (178 pts)
Brian Propp, Brandon (182 pts)
Brian Propp, Brandon (194 pts)
Doug Wickenheiser, Regina (170 pts)
Brian Varga, Regina (187 pts)
Jock Callander, Regina (190 pts)
Dale Derkatch, Regina (179 pts)
Ray Ferraro, Brandon (192 pts)
Cliff Ronning, New Westminster (197 pts)
Rob Brown, Kamloops (173 pts)

Rob Brown, Kamloops (212 pts)

Joe Sakic, Swift Current (160 pts)
Theoren Fleury, Moose Jaw (160 pts)
Dennis Holland, Portland (167 pts)

### Jim Piggott Memorial Trophy
(Originally called Stewart "Butch" Paul Memorial Trophy)
(Rookie of the Year)

| | | |
|---|---|---|
| Ron Garwasiuk, Regina | 1966-67 | |
| Ron Fairbrother, Saskatoon | 1967-68 | |
| Ron Williams, Edmonton | 1968-69 | |
| Gene Carr, Flin Flon | 1969-70 | |
| Stan Weir, Medicine Hat | 1970-71 | |
| Dennis Sobchuk, Regina | 1971-72 | |
| Rick Blight, Brandon | 1972-73 | |
| Cam Connor, Flin Flon | 1973-74 | |
| Don Murdoch, Medicine Hat | 1974-75 | |
| Steve Tambellini, Lethbridge | 1975-76 | |
| Brian Propp, Brandon | 1976-77 | |
| John Ogrodnick, N.W.-Keith Brown, Port. | 1977-78 | |
| Kelly Kisio, Calgary | 1978-79 | |

### Brad Hornung Trophy
(Originally called Frank Boucher Memorial Trophy for Most Gentlemanly Player)
(Most Sportsmanlike Player)

Morris Stefaniw, Estevan
Bernie Blanchette, Saskatoon
Bob Liddington, Calgary
Randy Rota, Calgary
Lorne Henning, Estevan
Ron Chipperfield, Brandon
Ron Chipperfield, Brandon
Mike Rogers, Calgary
Danny Arndt, Saskatoon
Blair Chapman, Saskatoon
Steve Tambellini, Lethbridge
Steve Tambellini, Lethbridge
Errol Rausse, Seattle

| | | |
|---|---|---|
| Grant Fuhr, Victoria | 1979-80 | Steve Tsujiura, Medicine Hat |
| Dave Michayluk, Regina | 1980-81 | Steve Tsujiura, Medicine Hat |
| Dale Derkatch, Regina | 1981-82 | Mike Moller, Lethbridge |
| Dan Hodgson, Prince Albert | 1982-83 | Darren Boyko, Winnipeg |
| Cliff Ronning, New Westminster | 1983-84 | Mark Lamb, Medicine Hat |
| Mark Mackay, Moose Jaw | 1984-85 | Cliff Ronning, New Westminster |
| Neil Brady, Medicine Hat (East Division) | 1985-86 | Randy Smith, Saskatoon (East Division) |
| Ron Shudra, Kamloops (West Division) | | Ken Morrison, Kamloops (West Division) |
| Dave Waldie, Portland (West Division) | | |
| Joe Sakic, Swift Current (East Division) | 1986-87 | Len Nielsen, Regina (East Division) |
| Dennis Holland, Portland (West Division) | | Dave Archibald, Portland (West Division) |
| Stu Barnes, New Westminster | 1987-88 | Craig Endean, Regina |
| Wes Walz, Lethbridge | 1988-89 | Blair Atcheynum, Moose Jaw |

## Bill Hunter Trophy
### (Top Defenseman)

## Del Wilson Trophy
### (Top Goaltender)

| | | |
|---|---|---|
| Barry Gibbs, Estevan | 1966-67 | Ken Brown, Moose Jaw |
| Gerry Hart, Flin Flon | 1967-68 | Chris Worthy, Flin Flon |
| Dale Hoganson, Estevan | 1968-69 | Ray Martyniuk, Flin Flon |
| Jim Hargreaves, Winnipeg | 1969-70 | Ray Martyniuk, Flin Flon |
| Ron Jones, Edmonton | 1970-71 | Ed Dyck, Calgary |
| Jim Watson, Calgary | 1971-72 | John Davidson, Calgary |
| George Pesut, Saskatoon | 1972-73 | Ed Humphreys, Saskatoon |
| Pat Price, Saskatoon | 1973-74 | Garth Malarchuk, Calgary |
| Rick LaPointe, Victoria | 1974-75 | Bill Oleschuk, Saskatoon |
| Kevin McCarthy, Winnipeg | 1975-76 | Carey Walker, New Westminster |
| Barry Beck, New Westminster | 1976-77 | Glen Hanlon, Brandon |
| Brad McCrimmon, Brandon | 1977-78 | Bart Hunter, Portland |
| Keith Brown, Portland | 1978-79 | Rick Knickle, Brandon |
| David Babych, Portland | 1979-80 | Kevin Eastman, Victoria |
| Jim Benning, Portland | 1980-81 | Grant Fuhr, Victoria |
| Gary Nylund, Portland | 1981-82 | Mike Vernon, Calgary |
| Gary Leeman, Regina | 1982-83 | Mike Vernon, Calgary |
| Bob Rouse, Lethbridge | 1983-84 | Ken Wregget, Lethbridge |
| Wendel Clark, Saskatoon | 1984-85 | Troy Gamble, Medicine Hat |
| Emanuel Viveiros, Prince Albert (East Division) | 1985-86 | Mark Fitzpatrick, Medicine Hat |
| Glen Wesley, Portland (West Division) | | |
| Wayne McBean, Medicine Hat (East Division) | 1986-87 | Kenton Rein, Prince Albert (East Division) |
| Glen Wesley, Portland (West Division) | | Dean Cook, Kamloops (West Division) |
| Greg Hawgood, Kamloops | 1987-88 | Troy Gamble, Spokane |
| Dan Lambert, Swift Current | 1988-89 | Danny Lorenz, Seattle |

## Player Of The Year
### (Selected by fans and media)

## Dunc McCallum Memorial Trophy
### (Coach of the Year)

| | | |
|---|---|---|
| Dennis Holland, Portland | 1988-89 | Ron Kennedy, Medicine Hat |
| Joe Sakic, Swift Current | 1987-88 | Marcel Comeau, Saskatoon |
| Rob Brown, Kamloops | 1986-87 | Graham James, Swift Current (East Division) |
| | | Ken Hitchcock, Kamloops (West Division) |
| Emanuel Viveiros, Prince Albert | 1985-86 | Terry Simpson, Prince Albert |
| Dan Hodgson, Prince Albert | 1984-85 | Doug Sauter, Medicine Hat |
| Ray Ferraro, Brandon | 1983-84 | Terry Simpson, Prince Albert |
| Dean Evason, Kamloops | 1982-83 | Darryl Lubiniecki, Saskatoon |
| Mike Vernon, Calgary | 1981-82 | Jack Sangster, Seattle |
| Barry Pederson, Victoria | 1980-81 | Ken Hodge, Portland |
| Doug Wickenheiser, Regina | 1979-80 | Doug Sauter, Calgary |
| Brian Propp, Brandon | 1978-79 | Dunc McCallum, Brandon |
| Ryan Walter, Seattle | 1977-78 | Dave King, Billings |
| | | Jack Shupe, Victoria |
| Kevin McCarthy, Winnipeg | 1976-77 | Dunc McCallum, Brandon |
| Bernie Federko, Saskatoon | 1975-76 | Ernie McLean, New Westminster |
| Ed Staniowski, Regina | 1974-75 | Pat Ginnell, Victoria |
| No Award Given | 1973-74 | Stan Dunn, Swift Current |
| No Award Given | 1972-73 | Pat Ginnell, Flin Flon |
| No Award Given | 1971-72 | Earl Ingarfield, Regina |
| No Award Given | 1970-71 | Pat Ginnell, Flin Flon |
| No Award Given | 1969-70 | Pat Ginnell, Flin Flon |
| No Award Given | 1968-69 | Scotty Munro, Calgary |

| Scott Munro Memorial Trophy (Regular Season Champions) | | Msgr. Athol Murray Memorial Trophy (Playoff Champions) |
|---|---|---|
| Swift Current Broncos | 1988-89 | Swift Current Broncos |
| Saskatoon Blades | 1987-88 | Medicine Hat Tigers |
| Kamloops Blazers | 1986-87 | Medicine Hat Tigers |
| Medicine Hat Tigers | 1985-86 | Kamloops Blazers |
| Prince Albert Raiders | 1984-85 | Prince Albert Raiders |
| Kamloops Junior Oilers | 1983-84 | Kamloops Junior Oilers |
| Saskatoon Blades | 1982-83 | Lethbridge Broncos |
| Lethbridge Broncos | 1981-82 | Portland Winter Hawks |
| Victoria Cougars | 1980-81 | Victoria Cougars |
| Portland Winter Hawks | 1979-80 | Regina Pats |
| Brandon Wheat Kings | 1978-79 | Brandon Wheat Kings |
| Brandon Wheat Kings | 1977-78 | New Westminster Bruins |
| New Westminster Bruins | 1976-77 | New Westminster Bruins |
| New Westminster Bruins | 1975-76 | New Westminster Bruins |
| Victoria Cougars | 1974-75 | New Westminster Bruins |
| Regina Pats | 1973-74 | Regina Pats |
| Saskatoon Blades | 1972-73 | Medicine Hat Tigers |
| Calgary Centennials | 1971-72 | Edmonton Oil Kings |
| Edmonton Oil Kings | 1970-71 | Edmonton Oil Kings |
| Flin Flon Bombers | 1969-70 | Flin Flon Bombers |
| Flin Flon Bombers | 1968-69 | Flin Flon Bombers |
| Flin Flon Bombers | 1967-68 | Estevan Bruins |
| Edmonton Oil Kings | 1966-67 | Moose Jaw Canucks |

# Quebec Major Junior Hockey League

President and Executive Director—Gilles Courteau
Vice-President—Jacques Letellier
Statistician—Douglas Horman
110, rue de la Barre, bureau 210,
Longueuil, Quebec J4K 1A3
Phone—(514) 442-3590

## Final 1988-89 QMJHL Standings

|  | G. | W. | L. | T. | Pts. | GF. | GA. |
|---|---|---|---|---|---|---|---|
| Trois-Rivieres Draveurs | 70 | 43 | 25 | 2 | 88 | 378 | 314 |
| Laval Titans | 70 | 43 | 26 | 1 | 87 | 361 | 292 |
| Hull Olympiques | 70 | 40 | 25 | 5 | 85 | 329 | 264 |
| Victoriaville Tigres | 70 | 41 | 27 | 2 | 84 | 320 | 267 |
| Drummondville Voltigeurs | 70 | 37 | 28 | 5 | 79 | 358 | 303 |
| St. Jean Castors | 70 | 33 | 34 | 3 | 69 | 345 | 386 |
| Grandy Bisons | 70 | 32 | 35 | 3 | 67 | 286 | 327 |
| Shawinigan Cataractes | 70 | 31 | 35 | 4 | 66 | 318 | 321 |
| Chicoutimi Sagueneens | 70 | 32 | 37 | 1 | 65 | 335 | 348 |
| Longueuil College-Francais | 70 | 25 | 41 | 4 | 54 | 280 | 332 |
| Verdun Junior Canadiens | 70 | 12 | 56 | 2 | 26 | 231 | 387 |

### Top 10 Scorers for the Jean Beliveau Trophy

|  | Games | G. | A. | Pts. | Pen. |
|---|---|---|---|---|---|
| 1. Stephane Morin, Chicoutimi | 70 | 77 | *109 | *186 | 71 |
| 2. Steve Cadieux, Shawinigan | 70 | *80 | 86 | 166 | 22 |
| 3. Donald Audette, Laval | 70 | 76 | 85 | 161 | 123 |
| 4. Steve Chartrand, Drummondville | 70 | 74 | 83 | 157 | 46 |
| 5. Steve Larouche, Trois-Rivieres | 70 | 51 | 102 | 153 | 53 |
| 6. Jean Francois Quintin, Shawinigan | 69 | 52 | 100 | 152 | 105 |
| 7. Patrick Lebeau, St. Jean | 66 | 62 | 87 | 149 | 89 |
| 8. Jan Alston, St. Jean | 69 | 58 | 86 | 144 | 115 |
| 9. Michel Picard, Trois-Rivieres | 66 | 59 | 81 | 140 | 107 |
| 10. Patrice Tremblay, Chicoutimi | 70 | 67 | 70 | 137 | 100 |
| Denis Chalifoux, Laval | 70 | 46 | 91 | 137 | 38 |

## Team-by-Team Regular Season QMJHL Scoring

### Chicoutimi Sagueneens

|  | Games | G. | A. | Pts. | Pen. |
|---|---|---|---|---|---|
| Stephane Morin | 70 | 77 | *109 | *186 | 71 |
| Patrice Tremblay | 70 | 67 | 70 | 137 | 100 |
| Yves Gaucher | 69 | 35 | 58 | 93 | 208 |
| Brule Eric | 70 | 21 | 41 | 62 | 120 |
| Roger Larche | 65 | 18 | 30 | 48 | 160 |
| Francois Belanger | 63 | 25 | 16 | 41 | 33 |
| Carl Boudreau | 45 | 5 | 30 | 35 | 28 |
| Mika Soimakallio | 60 | 10 | 21 | 31 | 31 |
| Michel Bedard | 62 | 14 | 14 | 28 | 143 |
| Martin Lefebvre | 36 | 6 | 21 | 27 | 41 |
| Serge Vigneault | 67 | 9 | 17 | 26 | 212 |
| Eric Meloche | 62 | 10 | 13 | 23 | 48 |
| Laval Brassard | 41 | 3 | 19 | 22 | 69 |
| Eric Del Vecchio | 61 | 6 | 14 | 20 | 42 |
| Marc Boudreau | 63 | 5 | 10 | 15 | 62 |
| Guy Lehoux | 67 | 3 | 12 | 15 | 218 |
| Eric Rochette | 60 | 2 | 13 | 15 | 90 |
| Martin Gagne | 63 | 5 | 7 | 12 | 28 |
| Martin Beaupre | 49 | 1 | 10 | 11 | 58 |
| Ugo Bellante | 30 | 2 | 7 | 9 | 53 |
| Sebastien Lavalliere | 24 | 3 | 3 | 6 | 35 |
| Maxime Gagne | 35 | 2 | 4 | 6 | 40 |
| Luc Audet | 6 | 0 | 1 | 1 | 14 |
| Sylvain Chenard | 6 | 0 | 1 | 1 | 13 |
| Danny Hunter | 7 | 0 | 1 | 1 | 25 |
| Eric Richard | 1 | 0 | 0 | 0 | 0 |
| Eric Coulombe | 5 | 0 | 0 | 0 | 0 |
| Peter Dawe (Goalie) | 21 | 0 | .... | .... | 6 |
| Felix Potvin (Goalie) | 65 | 0 | .... | .... | 42 |

### Drummondville Voltigeurs

|  | Games | G. | A. | Pts. | Pen. |
|---|---|---|---|---|---|
| Steve Chartrand | 70 | 74 | 83 | 157 | 46 |
| Martin Bergeron | 68 | 55 | 81 | 136 | 95 |
| Daniel Maurice | 70 | 46 | 72 | 118 | 150 |
| Daniel Dore | 62 | 33 | 58 | 91 | 236 |
| Claude Boivin | 63 | 20 | 36 | 56 | 218 |
| Denis Chasse | 68 | 27 | 28 | 55 | 140 |
| Dany Duclos | 63 | 26 | 29 | 55 | 178 |
| Christian Ratthe | 69 | 8 | 34 | 42 | 72 |
| Rob Murphy | 26 | 13 | 25 | 38 | 16 |
| Eric Tremblay | 42 | 6 | 29 | 35 | 102 |
| Eric Dandenault | 66 | 5 | 24 | 29 | 64 |
| Pierre Paul Landry | 68 | 3 | 25 | 28 | 74 |
| Serge Anglehart | 39 | 6 | 15 | 21 | 89 |
| Daniel Montmarquette | 65 | 5 | 10 | 15 | 11 |
| Dave Paquette | 63 | 7 | 7 | 14 | 86 |
| Mathieu Bibeau | 57 | 4 | 9 | 13 | 96 |
| Michel Bergeron | 33 | 7 | 3 | 10 | 8 |

— 203 —

|  | Games | G. | A. | Pts. | Pen. |
|---|---|---|---|---|---|
| Alain Cote | 63 | 0 | 9 | 9 | 20 |
| Mario Mercier | 48 | 1 | 7 | 8 | 128 |
| Luc Theberge | 33 | 2 | 1 | 3 | 2 |
| Frederic Marion | 42 | 0 | 1 | 1 | 14 |
| Benoit Ducharme | 2 | 0 | 0 | 0 | 0 |
| Claude Galipeau | 3 | 0 | 0 | 0 | 2 |
| Frederic Brault (Goalie) | 1 | 0 | .... | .... | 0 |
| Bryan Paradis (Goalie) | 2 | 0 | .... | .... | 0 |
| Jocelyn Provost (Goalie) | 13 | 0 | .... | .... | 4 |
| Alain Harvey (Goalie) | 37 | 0 | .... | .... | 8 |
| Julien Cameron (Goalie) | 42 | 0 | .... | .... | 17 |

## Granby Bisons

|  | Games | G. | A. | Pts. | Pen. |
|---|---|---|---|---|---|
| Eddy Courtenay | 68 | 59 | 55 | 114 | 68 |
| Jesse Belanger | 67 | 40 | 63 | 103 | 26 |
| Benoit Groulx | 61 | 33 | 65 | 98 | 42 |
| Daniel Lacroix | 70 | 45 | 49 | 94 | 320 |
| Regis Tremblay | 67 | 31 | 30 | 61 | 101 |
| Claude Charles Sauriol | 57 | 16 | 32 | 48 | 152 |
| Eric Ricard | 68 | 5 | 31 | 36 | 213 |
| Marc Rodgers | 65 | 11 | 21 | 32 | 70 |
| Sylvain Thibault | 40 | 7 | 19 | 26 | 34 |
| Christian Tardif | 70 | 6 | 20 | 26 | 40 |
| Benoit Therrien | 60 | 4 | 19 | 23 | 76 |
| Carl Leblanc | 64 | 2 | 14 | 16 | 90 |
| Remi Belliveau | 60 | 4 | 11 | 15 | 132 |
| Simon Ouimette | 69 | 7 | 5 | 12 | 108 |
| Stephane Dubois | 43 | 4 | 8 | 12 | 85 |
| Guy Patenaude | 64 | 6 | 5 | 11 | 40 |
| Patrice Filiatrault | 63 | 2 | 9 | 11 | 125 |
| Sylvain Gourde | 59 | 1 | 10 | 11 | 74 |
| Sebastien Tremblay | 48 | 1 | 9 | 10 | 69 |
| Stephane Lapointe | 16 | 2 | 6 | 8 | 2 |
| Danny Judge | 3 | 0 | 1 | 1 | 2 |
| Stephane Chagnon | 5 | 0 | 1 | 1 | 0 |
| Benoit Raymond | 1 | 0 | 0 | 0 | 0 |
| Jocelyn Villeneuve | 3 | 0 | 0 | 0 | 0 |
| Sylvain Nadeau | 6 | 0 | 0 | 0 | 0 |
| Regis Tremblay (Goalie) | 1 | 0 | .... | .... | 0 |
| Patrick Taylor (Goalie) | 5 | 0 | .... | .... | 2 |
| Rock Chatel (Goalie) | 28 | 0 | .... | .... | 25 |
| Andre Racicot (Goalie) | 54 | 0 | .... | .... | 47 |

## Hull Olympiques

|  | Games | G. | A. | Pts. | Pen. |
|---|---|---|---|---|---|
| Stephane Matteau | 59 | 44 | 45 | 89 | 202 |
| Joe Suk | 69 | 35 | 54 | 89 | 40 |
| Martin Gelinas | 41 | 38 | 39 | 77 | 31 |
| Guy Dupuis | 70 | 15 | 56 | 71 | 89 |
| Jeremy Roenick | 28 | 34 | 36 | 70 | 14 |
| Kelly Nester | 49 | 24 | 40 | 64 | 50 |
| George Wilcox | 67 | 19 | 42 | 61 | 151 |
| Stephane Charbonneau | 64 | 23 | 29 | 52 | 142 |
| Todd Sparks | 69 | 15 | 31 | 46 | 47 |
| Craig Martin | 70 | 14 | 29 | 43 | 260 |
| Cam Russell | 66 | 8 | 32 | 40 | 109 |
| Kennie MacDermid | 68 | 17 | 20 | 37 | 76 |
| Andy Ross | 70 | 10 | 21 | 31 | 22 |
| Karl Dykhuis | 63 | 2 | 29 | 31 | 59 |
| Joel Blain | 64 | 14 | 16 | 30 | 105 |
| Bruno Villeneuve | 57 | 10 | 18 | 28 | 8 |
| Joe Aloi | 40 | 0 | 12 | 12 | 108 |
| Jim Moore | 47 | 3 | 7 | 10 | 226 |
| David Akey | 54 | 1 | 7 | 8 | 145 |
| Robert Melanson | 50 | 0 | 5 | 5 | 41 |

|  | Games | G. | A. | Pts. | Pen. |
|---|---|---|---|---|---|
| Benoit Poulin | 25 | 1 | 2 | 3 | 9 |
| Todd Kochler | 2 | 0 | 1 | 1 | 0 |
| Eric Fortin | 13 | 0 | 1 | 1 | 2 |
| Carlos Marjasin | 12 | 0 | 0 | 0 | 2 |
| Sylvain Marcotte (G.) | 11 | 0 | .... | .... | 0 |
| Johnny Lorenzo (Goalie) | 29 | 0 | .... | .... | 2 |
| Jason Glickman (Goalie) | 40 | 0 | .... | .... | 39 |

## Laval Titans

|  | Games | G. | A. | Pts. | Pen. |
|---|---|---|---|---|---|
| Donald Audette | 70 | 76 | 85 | 161 | 123 |
| Denis Chalifoux | 70 | 46 | 91 | 137 | 38 |
| Claude Lapointe | 63 | 32 | 72 | 104 | 158 |
| Patrick Caron | 69 | 29 | 47 | 76 | 149 |
| Sylvain Naud | 69 | 28 | 40 | 68 | 143 |
| Patrice Brisebois | 50 | 20 | 45 | 65 | 95 |
| Eric Dubois | 68 | 15 | 44 | 59 | 126 |
| Patrick Lemay | 69 | 30 | 23 | 53 | 171 |
| Steve Parent | 66 | 19 | 30 | 49 | 96 |
| Normand Demers | 47 | 14 | 23 | 37 | 22 |
| Carl Mantha | 70 | 11 | 26 | 37 | 70 |
| Patrice Martineau | 70 | 13 | 21 | 34 | 61 |
| Neil Carnes | 31 | 9 | 24 | 33 | 92 |
| Marc Picard | 56 | 5 | 27 | 32 | 18 |
| Michel Gingras | 60 | 7 | 19 | 26 | 136 |
| Christian Lariviere | 67 | 6 | 20 | 26 | 137 |
| Gino Odjick | 50 | 9 | 15 | 24 | 278 |
| Martin Fortin | 69 | 10 | 12 | 22 | 59 |
| Sylvain Beland | 60 | 3 | 11 | 14 | 104 |
| Keifer House | 32 | 3 | 10 | 13 | 31 |
| Marty Woodford | 16 | 2 | 2 | 4 | 14 |
| Stephane Renaud | 14 | 2 | 1 | 3 | 8 |
| Jason Brousseau | 23 | 1 | 1 | 2 | 19 |
| Dannick Courchesne | 23 | 1 | 1 | 2 | 2 |
| Richard Jolicoeur | 10 | 1 | 0 | 1 | 0 |
| Eric Bissonnette | 25 | 0 | 1 | 1 | 42 |
| Martin Lauzon | 2 | 0 | 0 | 0 | 0 |
| Raymond Martin | 6 | 0 | 0 | 0 | 0 |
| Alain Vezina | 19 | 0 | 0 | 0 | 41 |
| Boris Rousson (Goalie) | 22 | 0 | .... | .... | 10 |
| Ghislain Lefebvre (G.) | 53 | 0 | .... | .... | 20 |

## Longueuil College-Francais

|  | Games | G. | A. | Pts. | Pen. |
|---|---|---|---|---|---|
| Paul Willett | 60 | 45 | 67 | 112 | 89 |
| Sylvain Fleury | 69 | 47 | 54 | 101 | 59 |
| Patrick Sauriol | 54 | 37 | 51 | 88 | 18 |
| Norman Desjardins | 63 | 26 | 61 | 87 | 72 |
| David St. Pierre | 69 | 22 | 20 | 42 | 22 |
| Stephane Perron | 64 | 2 | 37 | 39 | 116 |
| Jeannot Ferland | 40 | 19 | 16 | 35 | 68 |
| Dave Chouinard | 66 | 13 | 18 | 31 | 44 |
| Serge Trepanier | 69 | 12 | 13 | 25 | 40 |
| Denis Cloutier | 66 | 4 | 18 | 22 | 69 |
| Christian Breton | 70 | 4 | 18 | 22 | 154 |
| Richard Ayotte | 57 | 7 | 14 | 21 | 66 |
| Mario Nobili | 61 | 8 | 6 | 14 | 32 |
| Serge Lirette | 52 | 7 | 7 | 14 | 93 |
| Dominic Turgeon | 34 | 4 | 9 | 13 | 55 |
| Dominic Emond | 30 | 2 | 9 | 11 | 2 |
| Francois Pelletier | 38 | 2 | 7 | 9 | 46 |
| Rico Smith | 54 | 2 | 6 | 8 | 120 |
| Marco Desmarais | 22 | 1 | 7 | 8 | 17 |
| Jerome Despard | 55 | 1 | 7 | 8 | 89 |
| Nichol Cloutier | 41 | 0 | 7 | 7 | 24 |
| Marco Lemay | 16 | 1 | 5 | 6 | 14 |

|  | Games | G. | A. | Pts. | Pen. |
|---|---|---|---|---|---|
| Serge Bilodeau | 52 | 1 | 5 | 6 | 37 |
| Martin Lajeunesse | 50 | 0 | 6 | 6 | 39 |
| Steve Letourneau | 2 | 0 | 0 | 0 | 0 |
| Martin Caron | 3 | 0 | 0 | 0 | 2 |
| Troy Ferreira | 9 | 0 | 0 | 0 | 15 |
| Eric Vachon (Goalie) | 3 | 0 | .... | .... | 2 |
| Patrick Jeanson (Goalie) | 4 | 0 | .... | .... | 0 |
| Pascal Mongrain (G.) | 14 | 0 | .... | .... | 2 |
| Francis Ouellette (G.) | 61 | 0 | .... | .... | 35 |

## Shawinigan Cataractes

|  | Games | G. | A. | Pts. | Pen. |
|---|---|---|---|---|---|
| Steve Cadieux | 70 | *80 | 86 | 166 | 22 |
| Jean Francois Quintin | 69 | 52 | 100 | 152 | 105 |
| Daniel Bock | 70 | 31 | 78 | 109 | 56 |
| Eric Nadeau | 69 | 27 | 50 | 77 | 138 |
| Yvan Bergeron | 69 | 35 | 38 | 73 | 130 |
| Stephane Groleau | 72 | 20 | 48 | 68 | 38 |
| Karlo Pavich | 71 | 17 | 49 | 66 | 94 |
| Richard Hamelin | 70 | 26 | 39 | 65 | 28 |
| Stephane Carrier | 69 | 5 | 31 | 36 | 352 |
| Patrick Hebert | 70 | 3 | 26 | 29 | 86 |
| Martin Venne | 69 | 5 | 18 | 23 | 50 |
| Francois Picard | 60 | 8 | 12 | 20 | 75 |
| Steve Dontigny | 68 | 6 | 13 | 19 | 27 |
| Dave Morissette | 66 | 4 | 11 | 15 | 298 |
| Alain Deeks | 69 | 4 | 11 | 15 | 71 |
| Aldo Decarolis | 35 | 5 | 9 | 14 | 75 |
| Pierre Cote | 68 | 1 | 8 | 9 | 67 |
| Patrice Gagnon | 68 | 3 | 4 | 7 | 78 |
| Sylvain Bedard | 4 | 0 | 0 | 0 | 0 |
| Patrick Damphousse | 9 | 0 | 0 | 0 | 0 |
| Steve Neron | 15 | 0 | 0 | 0 | 2 |
| Bruno Gagne (Goalie) | 8 | 0 | .... | .... | 4 |
| Andre Boulianne (G.) | 29 | 0 | .... | .... | 0 |
| Dominic Roussel (Goalie) | 46 | 0 | .... | .... | 62 |

## St. Jean Castors

|  | Games | G. | A. | Pts. | Pen. |
|---|---|---|---|---|---|
| Patrick Lebeau | 66 | 62 | 87 | 149 | 89 |
| Jan Alston | 69 | 58 | 86 | 144 | 115 |
| Stefan Figliuzzi | 59 | 46 | 62 | 108 | 59 |
| Pierre Millier | 60 | 39 | 47 | 86 | 118 |
| Eric Couvrette | 55 | 24 | 54 | 78 | 62 |
| Stephane Plante | 55 | 30 | 36 | 66 | *364 |
| Patrick Cloutier | 67 | 7 | 37 | 44 | 200 |
| Francois Leroux | 57 | 8 | 34 | 42 | 185 |
| Pascal Germain | 66 | 11 | 22 | 33 | 46 |
| Jean Blouin | 35 | 12 | 17 | 29 | 37 |
| David Bastille | 67 | 13 | 13 | 26 | 168 |
| Emile DeRepentigny | 61 | 6 | 18 | 24 | 149 |
| Francois Chaput | 44 | 5 | 16 | 21 | 127 |
| Serge Simard Jr. | 70 | 5 | 14 | 19 | 29 |
| Martin Thomas | 36 | 4 | 11 | 15 | 18 |
| Eric Marcoux | 70 | 3 | 12 | 15 | 219 |
| Jean Franco Cardinal | 37 | 3 | 9 | 12 | 6 |
| Marco Morin | 59 | 5 | 6 | 11 | 26 |
| Robert Ouellet | 8 | 3 | 5 | 8 | 4 |
| Carl Henri Exantus | 62 | 3 | 3 | 6 | 54 |
| Steve Armstrong | 63 | 2 | 1 | 3 | 49 |
| Martin Lavallee | 59 | 1 | 1 | 2 | 25 |
| Arnaud Briand | 1 | 0 | 0 | 0 | 0 |
| Joey Pirillo | 1 | 0 | 0 | 0 | 0 |
| Pascal Vincent | 48 | 0 | 0 | 0 | 0 |
| Patrick Labrecque (G.) | 30 | 0 | .... | .... | 4 |
| Eric Metivier (Goalie) | 36 | 0 | .... | .... | 22 |

## Trois-Rivieres Draveurs

|  | Games | G. | A. | Pts. | Pen. |
|---|---|---|---|---|---|
| Steve Larouche | 70 | 51 | 102 | 153 | 53 |
| Michel Picard | 66 | 59 | 81 | 140 | 107 |
| Yanic Perreault | 70 | 53 | 55 | 108 | 48 |
| Raymond Saumier | 65 | 30 | 62 | 92 | 307 |
| Serge Richard | 62 | 38 | 50 | 88 | 48 |
| Marco Pietroniro | 67 | 32 | 33 | 65 | 82 |
| Martin St. Amour | 54 | 27 | 38 | 65 | 156 |
| Christian Bertrand | 58 | 25 | 31 | 56 | 272 |
| Andre Brassard | 60 | 10 | 40 | 50 | 102 |
| Martin Cote | 56 | 9 | 32 | 41 | 80 |
| Eric St. Amant | 60 | 15 | 18 | 33 | 128 |
| Steve Veilleux | 49 | 5 | 28 | 33 | 149 |
| Sebastien Parent | 60 | 7 | 20 | 27 | 114 |
| Enrico Ciccone | 58 | 7 | 19 | 26 | 289 |
| Yannik Lemay | 51 | 5 | 20 | 25 | 69 |
| Pascal Dufault | 36 | 3 | 4 | 7 | 91 |
| Guy Lefebvre | 65 | 1 | 6 | 7 | 31 |
| Guy Lefebvre | 7 | 4 | 2 | 6 | 0 |
| Francis Couturier | 59 | 3 | 3 | 6 | 13 |
| Gilles Bouchard | 60 | 3 | 1 | 4 | 6 |
| Steve Richard | 10 | 3 | 0 | 3 | 0 |
| Louis Bellerive | 9 | 1 | 2 | 3 | 2 |
| Martin Lacombe | 35 | 0 | 1 | 1 | 61 |
| Eric Bouliane | 6 | 0 | 0 | 0 | 2 |
| Eric Bellerose | 10 | 0 | 0 | 0 | 4 |
| Patrice Rene | 11 | 0 | 0 | 0 | 0 |
| Marc Delorme (Goalie) | 28 | 0 | .... | .... | 6 |
| Alain Morissette (G.) | 46 | 0 | .... | .... | 6 |

## Verdun Junior Canadiens

|  | Games | G. | A. | Pts. | Pen. |
|---|---|---|---|---|---|
| Andrew McKim | 68 | 50 | 56 | 106 | 36 |
| Pierre Sevigny | 67 | 27 | 43 | 70 | 88 |
| Denis LeBlanc | 65 | 25 | 23 | 48 | 37 |
| Todd Gillingham | 67 | 16 | 25 | 41 | 253 |
| Eric Charron | 67 | 4 | 31 | 35 | 177 |
| Francois Dery | 59 | 14 | 15 | 29 | 29 |
| Mil Sukovic | 69 | 9 | 16 | 25 | 49 |
| Ronnie Bianchi | 56 | 13 | 9 | 22 | 30 |
| Sean Finn | 59 | 1 | 21 | 22 | 220 |
| Serge Renaud | 33 | 10 | 8 | 18 | 98 |
| Jim Bermingham | 69 | 7 | 9 | 16 | 118 |
| Patrick Ouimet | 27 | 1 | 14 | 15 | 28 |
| Trevor Boland | 35 | 5 | 9 | 14 | 17 |
| Paul Douglas | 56 | 2 | 10 | 12 | 79 |
| Ronald Kay | 69 | 1 | 10 | 11 | 66 |
| Guy Darveau | 25 | 1 | 9 | 10 | 38 |
| Jean Claude Mongrain | 31 | 0 | 10 | 10 | 23 |
| Dean Duggan | 25 | 1 | 7 | 8 | 12 |
| Martin Saurette | 10 | 4 | 3 | 7 | 10 |
| Jasmin Berube | 55 | 4 | 3 | 7 | 2 |
| Marc Talbot | 60 | 2 | 2 | 4 | 44 |
| Mark McLane | 25 | 1 | 3 | 4 | 14 |
| Mikko Auranen | 28 | 0 | 3 | 3 | 22 |
| Franz Demmel | 8 | 1 | 0 | 1 | 2 |
| Serge Lanthier | 2 | 0 | 0 | 0 | 0 |
| Eric Lussier | 5 | 0 | 0 | 0 | 18 |
| Eric Charron (Goalie) | 8 | 0 | .... | .... | 0 |
| Yannick Degrace (G.) | 24 | 0 | .... | .... | 18 |
| J. Claude Bergeron (G.) | 44 | 0 | .... | .... | 2 |

## Victoriaville Tigres

|  | Games | G. | A. | Pts. | Pen. |
|---|---|---|---|---|---|
| Daniel Gauthier | 64 | 41 | 75 | 116 | 84 |

| | Games | G. | A. | Pts. | Pen. | | Games | G. | A. | Pts. | Pen. |
|---|---|---|---|---|---|---|---|---|---|---|---|
| Reginald Savage | 54 | 58 | 55 | 113 | 178 | Martin Charrois | 33 | 1 | 12 | 13 | 109 |
| Yves Racine | 63 | 23 | 85 | 108 | 95 | Francois Michaud | 27 | 7 | 5 | 12 | 34 |
| Chris Bartolone | 68 | 14 | 56 | 70 | 40 | Daniel Lalande | 60 | 4 | 7 | 11 | 53 |
| Real Godin | 68 | 29 | 40 | 69 | 36 | Martin Tanguay | 54 | 6 | 4 | 10 | 12 |
| Alain Tardif | 57 | 27 | 40 | 67 | 139 | David Baird | 28 | 2 | 3 | 5 | 52 |
| Eric Pinard | 33 | 31 | 11 | 42 | 22 | Todd Meehan | 45 | 2 | 3 | 5 | 67 |
| Christian Campeau | 68 | 16 | 26 | 42 | 86 | Sylvain Bourgeois | 38 | 0 | 5 | 5 | 66 |
| Steven Paiement | 65 | 17 | 18 | 35 | 44 | Richard Cartier | 6 | 0 | 1 | 1 | 0 |
| Marc Labelle | 62 | 9 | 26 | 35 | 202 | Mathieu Lamothe | 1 | 0 | 0 | 0 | 0 |
| Alexandre Fortin | 55 | 5 | 20 | 25 | 217 | Mathieu Gagnon | 6 | 0 | 0 | 0 | 6 |
| David Chernis | 59 | 13 | 11 | 24 | 259 | Marc Cardinal | 7 | 0 | 0 | 0 | 5 |
| Dany Nolet | 49 | 3 | 16 | 19 | 14 | Martin Houle (Goalie) | 2 | 0 | .... | .... | 0 |
| Claude Barthe | 66 | 7 | 10 | 17 | 122 | Pierre Gagnon (Goalie) | 31 | 0 | .... | .... | 2 |
| Travor Duhaime | 67 | 5 | 12 | 17 | 176 | Stephane Fiset (Goalie) | 43 | 0 | .... | .... | 18 |

## Complete QMJHL Goaltending

| | Games | Mins. | Goals | SO. | Avg. |
|---|---|---|---|---|---|
| Martin Houle, Victoriaville | 2 | 70 | 4 | 0 | 3.43 |
| Stephane Fiset, Victoriaville | 43 | 2401 | 138 | 1 | *3.45 |
| Johnny Lorenzo, Hull | 29 | 1564 | 91 | 0 | 3.49 |
| Jason Glickman, Hull | 40 | 2116 | 131 | 1 | 3.71 |
| Alain Harvey, Drummondville | 37 | 2086 | 134 | *2 | 3.85 |
| Ghislain Lefebvre, Laval | 53 | 3045 | 198 | 0 | 3.90 |
| Sylvain Marcotte, Hull | 11 | 565 | 37 | 0 | 3.93 |
| Dominic Roussel, Shawinigan | 46 | 2555 | 171 | 0 | 4.02 |
| Pierre Gagnon, Victoriaville | 31 | 1761 | 118 | 0 | 4.02 |
| Andre Racicot, Granby | 54 | 2944 | 198 | 0 | 4.04 |
| Alain Morissette, Trois-Rivieres | 46 | 2360 | 167 | 1 | 4.25 |
| Francis Ouellette, Longueuil | 61 | 3296 | 235 | *2 | 4.28 |
| Andre Boulianne, Shawinigan | 29 | 1580 | 113 | 0 | 4.29 |
| Julien Cameron, Drummondville | 42 | 2143 | 156 | 1 | 4.37 |
| Boris Rousson, Laval | 22 | 1187 | 88 | 0 | 4.45 |
| Felix Potvin, Chicoutimi | *65 | *3489 | *271 | *2 | 4.66 |
| Bryan Paradis, Drummondville | 2 | 112 | 9 | 0 | 4.82 |
| Pascal Mongrain, Longueuil | 14 | 634 | 52 | 0 | 4.92 |
| Jean Claude Bergeron, Verdun | 44 | 2417 | 199 | 0 | 4.94 |
| Eric Metivier, St. Jean | 36 | 2025 | 172 | 1 | 5.10 |
| Patrick Daigneault, St. Jean | 15 | 656 | 56 | 0 | 5.12 |
| Marc Delorme, Trois-Rivieres | 28 | 1429 | 122 | 0 | 5.12 |
| Rock Chatel, Granby | 28 | 1159 | 100 | 0 | 5.18 |
| Jocelyn Provost, Drummondville | 13 | 450 | 40 | 0 | 5.33 |
| Patrick Blouin, St. Jean | 7 | 300 | 29 | 0 | 5.80 |
| Peter Dawe, Chicoutimi | 21 | 733 | 71 | 0 | 5.81 |
| Bruno Gagne, Shawinigan | 8 | 412 | 40 | 0 | 5.83 |
| Patrick Labrecque, St. Jean | 30 | 1417 | 140 | 0 | 5.93 |
| Patrick Taylor, Granby | 5 | 121 | 13 | 0 | 6.45 |
| Eric Vachon, Longueuil | 3 | 93 | 10 | 0 | 6.45 |
| Yannick Degrace, Verdun | 24 | 886 | 96 | 0 | 6.50 |
| Eric Charron, Verdun | 8 | 370 | 43 | 0 | 6.97 |
| Frederic Brault, Drummondville | 1 | 47 | 6 | 0 | 7.66 |
| Patrick Jeanson, Longueuil | 4 | 147 | 19 | 0 | 7.76 |
| Martin Lanoue, Longueuil | 2 | 81 | 11 | 0 | 8.15 |
| Regis Tremblay, Granby | 1 | 37 | 10 | 0 | 16.22 |

## Individual 1988-89 Leaders

| | | |
|---|---|---|
| Goals | Steve Cadieux, Shawinigan— | 80 |
| Assists | Stephane Morin, Chicoutimi— | 109 |
| Points | Stephane Morin, Chicoutimi— | 186 |
| Penalty Minutes | Stephane Plante, St. Jean— | 364 |
| Goaltending Average | Stephane Fiset, Victoriaville— | 3.45 |
| Shutouts | Alain Harvey, Drummondville— | 2 |
| | Francis Ouellette, Longueuil— | 2 |
| | Felix Potvin, Chicoutimi— | 2 |

# 1989 QMJHL President Cup Playoffs

## Quarterfinals
(Best-of-seven series)

### Series "A"

|  | W. | L. | Pts. | GF. | GA. |
|---|---|---|---|---|---|
| Shawinigan | 4 | 0 | 8 | 18 | 9 |
| Trois-Rivieres | 0 | 4 | 0 | 9 | 18 |

(Shawinigan wins series, 4 games to 0)

### Series "C"

|  | W. | L. | Pts. | GF. | GA. |
|---|---|---|---|---|---|
| Hull | 4 | 0 | 8 | 30 | 18 |
| St. Jean | 0 | 4 | 0 | 18 | 30 |

(Hull wins series, 4 games to 0)

### Series "B"

|  | W. | L. | Pts. | GF. | GA. |
|---|---|---|---|---|---|
| Laval | 4 | 0 | 8 | 18 | 9 |
| Granby | 0 | 4 | 0 | 9 | 18 |

(Laval wins series, 4 games to 0)

### Series "D"

|  | W. | L. | Pts. | GF. | GA. |
|---|---|---|---|---|---|
| Victoriaville | 4 | 0 | 8 | 31 | 10 |
| Drummondville | 0 | 4 | 0 | 10 | 31 |

(Victoriaville wins series, 4 games to 0)

## Semifinals
(Best-of-seven series)

### Series "E"

|  | W. | L. | Pts. | GF. | GA. |
|---|---|---|---|---|---|
| Laval | 4 | 2 | 8 | 27 | 23 |
| Shawinigan | 2 | 4 | 4 | 23 | 27 |

(Laval wins series, 4 games to 2)

### Series "F"

|  | W. | L. | Pts. | GF. | GA. |
|---|---|---|---|---|---|
| Victoriaville | 4 | 1 | 8 | 23 | 19 |
| Hull | 1 | 4 | 2 | 19 | 23 |

(Victoriaville wins series, 4 games to 1)

## Finals
(Best-of-seven series)

### Series "G"

|  | W. | L. | Pts. | GF. | GA. |
|---|---|---|---|---|---|
| Laval | 4 | 3 | 8 | 28 | 30 |
| Victoriaville | 3 | 4 | 6 | 30 | 28 |

(Laval wins series, and President Cup, 4 games to 3)

## Top 10 Playoff Scorers

|  | Games | G. | A. | Pts. | Pen. |
|---|---|---|---|---|---|
| 1. Yves Racine, Victoriaville | 16 | 3 | *30 | *33 | 41 |
| 2. Donald Audette, Laval | 17 | *17 | 12 | 29 | 43 |
| Daniel Gauthier, Victoriaville | 16 | 12 | 17 | 29 | 30 |
| 4. Reginald Savage, Victoriaville | 16 | 15 | 13 | 28 | 52 |
| 5. Eric Pinard, Victoriaville | 16 | 16 | 8 | 24 | 6 |
| Jean Francois Quintin, Shawinigan | 10 | 9 | 15 | 24 | 16 |
| 7. Real Godin, Victoriaville | 14 | 9 | 14 | 23 | 7 |
| 8. Patrice Brisebois, Laval | 17 | 8 | 14 | 22 | 45 |
| 9. Steve Cadieux, Shawinigan | 10 | 9 | 12 | 21 | 12 |
| 10. Jeremy Roenick, Hull | 9 | 7 | 12 | 19 | 6 |

# Team-by-Team Playoff Scoring

## Drummondville Voltigeurs
(Lost quarterfinals to Victoriaville, 4-0)

|  | Games | G. | A. | Pts. | Pen. |
|---|---|---|---|---|---|
| Steve Chartrand | 4 | 2 | 5 | 7 | 2 |
| Daniel Dore | 4 | 2 | 3 | 5 | 14 |
| Martin Bergeron | 4 | 3 | 1 | 4 | 4 |
| Rob Murphy | 4 | 1 | 3 | 4 | 20 |
| Eric Tremblay | 4 | 1 | 1 | 2 | 4 |
| Denis Chasse | 3 | 0 | 2 | 2 | 28 |
| Claude Boivin | 4 | 0 | 2 | 2 | 27 |
| Christian Ratthe | 4 | 1 | 0 | 1 | 16 |
| Eric Dandenault | 4 | 0 | 1 | 1 | 0 |
| Serge Anglehart | 3 | 0 | 0 | 0 | 37 |
| Daniel Maurice | 3 | 0 | 0 | 0 | 37 |
| Michel Bergeron | 4 | 0 | 0 | 0 | 0 |
| Mathieu Bibeau | 4 | 0 | 0 | 0 | 2 |
| Pierre Paul Landry | 4 | 0 | 0 | 0 | 2 |
| Frederic Marion | 4 | 0 | 0 | 0 | 7 |
| Mario Mercier | 4 | 0 | 0 | 0 | 8 |
| Daniel Montmarquette | 4 | 0 | 0 | 0 | 0 |
| Dave Paquette | 4 | 0 | 0 | 0 | 2 |
| Julien Cameron (Goalie) | 2 | 0 | ... | ... | 0 |
| Alain Harvey (Goalie) | 4 | 0 | ... | ... | 2 |

## Granby Bisons
(Lost quarterfinals to Laval, 4-0)

|  | Games | G. | A. | Pts. | Pen. |
|---|---|---|---|---|---|
| Jesse Belanger | 4 | 0 | 5 | 5 | 0 |
| Benoit Groulx | 4 | 2 | 2 | 4 | 6 |
| Christian Tardif | 4 | 2 | 0 | 2 | 0 |
| Eddy Courtenay | 4 | 1 | 1 | 2 | 22 |
| Daniel Lacroix | 4 | 1 | 1 | 2 | 57 |
| Eric Ricard | 4 | 1 | 1 | 2 | 21 |
| Regis Tremblay | 4 | 1 | 1 | 2 | 2 |
| Marc Rodgers | 4 | 0 | 2 | 2 | 44 |
| Simon Ouimette | 4 | 1 | 0 | 1 | 10 |
| Patrice Filiatrault | 4 | 0 | 1 | 1 | 10 |

|  | Games | G. | A. | Pts. | Pen. |
|---|---|---|---|---|---|
| Carl Leblanc | 4 | 0 | 1 | 1 | 11 |
| Benoit Therrien | 4 | 0 | 1 | 1 | 8 |
| Benoit Raymond | 2 | 0 | 0 | 0 | 0 |
| Claude Charles Sauriol | 3 | 0 | 0 | 0 | 12 |
| Remi Belliveau | 4 | 0 | 0 | 0 | 26 |
| Stephane Dubois | 4 | 0 | 0 | 0 | 7 |
| Sylvain Gourde | 4 | 0 | 0 | 0 | 0 |
| Guy Patenaude | 4 | 0 | 0 | 0 | 2 |
| Rock Chatel (Goalie) | 1 | 0 | .... | .... | 0 |
| Andre Racicot (Goalie) | 4 | 0 | .... | .... | 2 |

## Hull Olympiques

(Lost semifinals to Victoriaville, 4-1)

|  | Games | G. | A. | Pts. | Pen. |
|---|---|---|---|---|---|
| Jeremy Roenick | 9 | 7 | 12 | 19 | 6 |
| Kelly Nester | 9 | 3 | 14 | 17 | 18 |
| Stephane Matteau | 9 | 8 | 6 | 14 | 30 |
| Joe Suk | 9 | 2 | 11 | 13 | 6 |
| Karl Dykhuis | 9 | 1 | 9 | 10 | 6 |
| Martin Gelinas | 9 | 5 | 4 | 9 | 14 |
| Cam Russell | 9 | 2 | 6 | 8 | 6 |
| Kennie MacDermid | 9 | 3 | 4 | 7 | 8 |
| Joel Blain | 9 | 5 | 1 | 6 | 19 |
| Guy Dupuis | 9 | 3 | 3 | 6 | 8 |
| George Wilcox | 9 | 3 | 2 | 5 | 16 |
| Todd Sparks | 9 | 2 | 3 | 5 | 16 |
| Bruno Villeneuve | 5 | 2 | 2 | 4 | 2 |
| Stephane Charbonneau | 9 | 2 | 2 | 4 | 22 |
| David Akey | 9 | 1 | 2 | 3 | 26 |
| Andy Ross | 4 | 0 | 2 | 2 | 2 |
| Craig Martin | 9 | 0 | 1 | 1 | 10 |
| Jim Moore | 9 | 0 | 1 | 1 | 55 |
| Robert Melanson | 9 | 0 | 0 | 0 | 12 |
| Jason Glickman (Goalie) | 5 | 0 | .... | .... | 0 |
| Johnny Lorenzo (Goalie) | 5 | 0 | .... | .... | 4 |

## Laval Titans

(Winners of 1989 President Cup Playoffs)

|  | Games | G. | A. | Pts. | Pen. |
|---|---|---|---|---|---|
| Donald Audette | 17 | *17 | 12 | 29 | 43 |
| Patrice Brisebois | 17 | 8 | 14 | 22 | 45 |
| Claude Lapointe | 17 | 5 | 14 | 19 | 66 |
| Neil Carnes | 10 | 9 | 9 | 18 | 16 |
| Denis Chalifoux | 17 | 6 | 12 | 18 | 6 |
| Normand Demers | 17 | 6 | 9 | 15 | 4 |
| Steve Parent | 17 | 2 | 11 | 13 | 22 |
| Michel Gingras | 17 | 5 | 7 | 12 | 47 |
| Eric Dubois | 17 | 1 | 11 | 12 | 55 |
| Patrick Caron | 16 | 6 | 4 | 10 | 55 |
| Gino Odjick | 16 | 0 | 9 | 9 | *129 |
| Carl Mantha | 17 | 1 | 5 | 6 | 18 |
| Christian Lariviere | 17 | 3 | 2 | 5 | 41 |
| Sylvain Naud | 16 | 2 | 2 | 4 | 20 |
| Marc Picard | 13 | 0 | 4 | 4 | 8 |
| Patrick Lemay | 17 | 2 | 1 | 3 | 15 |
| Martin Fortin | 9 | 1 | 0 | 1 | 15 |
| Patrice Martineau | 12 | 1 | 0 | 1 | 2 |
| Eric Bissonnette | 5 | 0 | 0 | 0 | 21 |
| Alain Vezina | 7 | 0 | 0 | 0 | 9 |
| Sylvain Beland | 14 | 0 | 0 | 0 | 9 |
| Boris Rousson (Goalie) | 6 | 0 | .... | .... | 2 |
| Ghislain Lefebvre (G.) | 14 | 0 | .... | .... | 0 |

## Shawinigan Cataractes

(Lost semifinals to Laval, 4-2)

|  | Games | G. | A. | Pts. | Pen. |
|---|---|---|---|---|---|
| Jean Francois Quintin | 10 | 9 | 15 | 24 | 16 |
| Steve Cadieux | 10 | 9 | 12 | 21 | 12 |
| Yvan Bergeron | 10 | 5 | 8 | 13 | 33 |
| Daniel Bock | 10 | 4 | 7 | 11 | 4 |
| Karlo Pavich | 10 | 4 | 7 | 11 | 8 |
| Richard Hamelin | 10 | 5 | 3 | 8 | 6 |
| Stephane Groleau | 10 | 2 | 6 | 8 | 29 |
| Eric Nadeau | 10 | 2 | 6 | 8 | 32 |
| Stephane Carrier | 10 | 2 | 3 | 5 | 42 |
| Steve Dontigny | 10 | 0 | 4 | 4 | 11 |
| Francois Picard | 10 | 2 | 1 | 3 | 28 |
| Alain Deeks | 10 | 0 | 3 | 3 | 17 |
| Dave Morissette | 9 | 0 | 1 | 1 | 43 |
| Pierre Cote | 10 | 0 | 1 | 1 | 8 |
| Patrick Hebert | 10 | 0 | 1 | 1 | 21 |
| Martin Venne | 10 | 0 | 1 | 1 | 2 |
| Patrice Gagnon | 3 | 0 | 0 | 0 | 0 |
| Sylvain Bedard | 5 | 0 | 0 | 0 | 0 |
| Steve Neron | 10 | 0 | 0 | 0 | 0 |
| Dominic Roussel (Goalie) | 10 | 0 | .... | .... | 4 |

## St. Jean Castors

(Lost quarterfinals to Hull, 4-0)

|  | Games | G. | A. | Pts. | Pen. |
|---|---|---|---|---|---|
| Jan Alston | 4 | 6 | 9 | 15 | 0 |
| Patrick Lebeau | 4 | 4 | 3 | 7 | 6 |
| Pierre Millier | 4 | 2 | 5 | 7 | 11 |
| Stefan Figliuzzi | 4 | 3 | 3 | 6 | 6 |
| Emile DeRepentigny | 4 | 0 | 5 | 5 | 8 |
| Francois Chaput | 4 | 0 | 2 | 2 | 24 |
| Marco Morin | 4 | 1 | 0 | 1 | 0 |
| Stephane Plante | 4 | 1 | 0 | 1 | 20 |
| Martin Thomas | 4 | 1 | 0 | 1 | 2 |
| Patrick Cloutier | 4 | 0 | 1 | 1 | 27 |
| Eric Marcoux | 4 | 0 | 1 | 1 | 4 |
| Steve Armstrong | 4 | 0 | 0 | 0 | 13 |
| David Bastille | 4 | 0 | 0 | 0 | 9 |
| Eric Couvrette | 4 | 0 | 0 | 0 | 0 |
| Carlo Henri Exantus | 4 | 0 | 0 | 0 | 17 |
| Pascal Germain | 4 | 0 | 0 | 0 | 2 |
| Martin Lavallee | 4 | 0 | 0 | 0 | 0 |
| Serge Simard Jr. | 4 | 0 | 0 | 0 | 0 |
| Eric Metivier (Goalie) | 2 | 0 | .... | .... | 2 |
| Patrick Labrecque (G.) | 4 | 0 | .... | .... | 0 |

## Trois-Rivieres Draveurs

(Lost quarterfinals to Shawinigan, 4-0)

|  | Games | G. | A. | Pts. | Pen. |
|---|---|---|---|---|---|
| Steve Larouche | 4 | 4 | 2 | 6 | 6 |
| Michel Picard | 4 | 1 | 3 | 4 | 2 |
| Martin St. Amour | 4 | 1 | 2 | 3 | 0 |
| Andre Brassard | 4 | 0 | 3 | 3 | 6 |
| Raymond Saumier | 2 | 1 | 1 | 2 | 12 |
| Martin Cote | 4 | 1 | 1 | 2 | 4 |
| Serge Richard | 4 | 0 | 2 | 2 | 2 |
| Eric St. Amant | 4 | 1 | 0 | 1 | 10 |
| Sebastien Parent | 4 | 0 | 1 | 1 | 12 |
| Louis Bellerive | 2 | 0 | 0 | 0 | 0 |
| Enrico Ciccone | 2 | 0 | 0 | 0 | 4 |
| Francis Couturier | 2 | 0 | 0 | 0 | 0 |
| Patrice Rene | 2 | 0 | 0 | 0 | 0 |
| Christian Bertrand | 4 | 0 | 0 | 0 | 8 |
| Gilles Bouchard | 4 | 0 | 0 | 0 | 0 |
| Martin Lacombe | 4 | 0 | 0 | 0 | 4 |
| Guy Lefebvre | 4 | 0 | 0 | 0 | 2 |
| Yanic Perreault | 4 | 0 | 0 | 0 | 7 |
| Marco Pietroniro | 4 | 0 | 0 | 0 | 13 |
| Steve Veilleux | 4 | 0 | 0 | 0 | 10 |
| Marc Delorme (Goalie) | 1 | 0 | .... | .... | 0 |
| Alain Morissette (Goalie) | 4 | 0 | .... | .... | 0 |

## Victoriaville Tigres
(Lost finals to Laval, 4-3)

| | Games | G. | A. | Pts. | Pen. |
|---|---|---|---|---|---|
| Yves Racine | 16 | 3 | *30 | *33 | 41 |
| Daniel Gauthier | 16 | 12 | 17 | 29 | 30 |
| Reginald Savage | 16 | 15 | 13 | 28 | 52 |
| Eric Pinard | 16 | 16 | 8 | 24 | 6 |
| Real Godin | 14 | 9 | 14 | 23 | 7 |
| Chris Bartolone | 16 | 2 | 16 | 18 | 4 |
| Alain Tardif | 16 | 7 | 9 | 16 | 36 |
| Marc Labelle | 15 | 6 | 3 | 9 | 30 |
| Dany Nolet | 16 | 5 | 4 | 9 | 17 |
| Claude Barthe | 16 | 2 | 7 | 9 | 40 |
| Christian Campeau | 16 | 2 | 6 | 8 | 34 |
| Travor Duhaime | 14 | 4 | 3 | 7 | 18 |
| Steven Paiement | 15 | 1 | 5 | 6 | 16 |
| Mathieu Lamothe | 16 | 0 | 4 | 4 | 14 |
| Martin Charrois | 6 | 1 | 1 | 2 | 6 |
| Alexandre Fortin | 10 | 0 | 2 | 2 | 12 |
| Sylvain Bourgeois | 11 | 0 | 1 | 1 | 30 |
| Daniel Lalande | 16 | 0 | 1 | 1 | 15 |
| Martin Tanguay | 7 | 0 | 0 | 0 | 0 |
| Todd Meehan | 9 | 0 | 0 | 0 | 7 |
| Richard Cartier | 11 | 0 | 0 | 0 | 0 |
| Pierre Gagnon (Goalie) | 5 | 0 | .... | .... | 2 |
| Stephane Fiset (Goalie) | 12 | 0 | .... | .... | 10 |

## Complete 1989 President Cup Goaltending

| | Games | Mins. | Goals | SO. | Avg. |
|---|---|---|---|---|---|
| Stephane Fiset, Victoriaville | 12 | 711 | 33 | 0 | *2.78 |
| Rock Chatel, Granby | 1 | 20 | 1 | 0 | 3.00 |
| Boris Rousson, Laval | 6 | 295 | 15 | 0 | 3.05 |
| Dominic Roussel, Shawinigan | 10 | 638 | 36 | 0 | 3.39 |
| Ghislain Lefebvre, Laval | *14 | *769 | *47 | 0 | 3.67 |
| Johnny Lorenzo, Hull | 5 | 307 | 20 | 0 | 3.91 |
| Alain Morissette, Trois-Rivieres | 4 | 243 | 18 | 0 | 4.44 |
| Jason Glickman, Hull | 5 | 274 | 21 | 0 | 4.60 |
| Pierre Gagnon, Victoriaville | 5 | 311 | 24 | 0 | 4.63 |
| Andre Racicot, Granby | 4 | 218 | 18 | 0 | 4.95 |
| Patrick Labrecque, St. Jean | 4 | 194 | 17 | 0 | 5.26 |
| Julien Cameron, Drummondville | 2 | 70 | 7 | 0 | 6.00 |
| Alain Harvey, Drummondville | 4 | 170 | 24 | 0 | 8.47 |
| Marc Delorme, Trois-Rivieres | 1 | 20 | 3 | 0 | 9.00 |
| Eric Metivier, St. Jean | 2 | 60 | 13 | 0 | 13.00 |

## Individual President Cup Playoff Leaders

| | | |
|---|---|---|
| Goals | Donald Audette, Laval — | 17 |
| Assists | Yves Racine, Victoriaville — | 30 |
| Points | Yves Racine, Victoriaville — | 33 |
| Penalty Minutes | Gino Odjick, Laval — | 129 |
| Goaltender's Average | Stephane Fiset, Victoriaville — | 2.78 |
| Shutouts | | — None |

★★★★★★★★★★★★★★★★★★★★★★★★★★★★★★★★★★★★★★★★★★★★★

## 1988-89 QMJHL All-Star Teams

| First Team | Position | Second Team |
|---|---|---|
| Stephane Fiset, Victoriaville | Goalie | Andre Racicot, Granby |
| Yves Racine, Victoriaville | Defense | Steve Veilleux, Trois-Rivieres |
| Eric Dubois, Laval | Defense | Guy Dupuis, Hull |
| Stephane Morin, Chicoutimi | Center | Jeremy Roenick, Hull |
| Donald Audette, Laval | Right Wing | Jean Francois Quintin, Shaw. |
| | | Eddy Courtenay, Granby |
| Steve Chartrand, Drummondville | Left Wing | Michel Picard, Trois-Rivieres |

★★★★★★★★★★★★★★★★★★★★★★★★★★★★★★★★★★★★★★★★★★★★★

# 1988-89 QMJHL Trophy Winners

Frank Selke Trophy (Most Gentlemanly Player).................................................Steve Cadieux, Shawinigan
Michel Bergeron Trophy (Top Rookie Forward)..............................................Yanick Perreault, Trois-Rivieres
Raymond Lagace Trophy (Top Rookie Defenseman or Goaltender) .......................Karl Dykhuis, Hull
Jean Beliveau Trophy (Leading Point Scorer) ...............................................Stephane Morin, Chicoutimi
Michel Briere Trophy (Regular Season MVP)................................................Stephane Morin, Chicoutimi
Marcel Robert Trophy (Top Scholastic/Athletic Performer) .............................Daniel Lacroix, Granby
Mike Bossy Trophy (Top Pro Prospect)........................................................Patrice Brisebois, Laval
Emile "Butch" Bouchard Trophy (Top Defenseman) ....................................Yves Racine, Victoriaville
Jacques Plante Trophy (Best Goalie).........................................................Stephane Fiset, Victoriaville
Guy Lafleur Trophy (Playoff MVP).............................................................Donald Audette, Laval
Robert LeBel Trophy (Best Team Defensive Average)....................................Hull Olympiques
John Rougeau Trophy (Regular Season Champion) ....................................Trois-Rivieres Draveurs
President Cup (Playoff Champion).............................................................Laval Titans

## Historical QMJHL Trophy Winners

### Frank Selke Trophy
### (Most Gentlemanly Player)
1970-71—Norm Dube, Sherbrooke
1971-72—Gerry Teeple, Cornwall
1972-73—Claude Larose, Drummondville
1973-74—Gary MacGregor, Cornwall
1974-75—Jean-Luc Phaneuf, Montreal
1975-76—Norm Dupont, Montreal
1976-77—Mike Bossy, Laval
1977-78—Kevin Reeves, Montreal
1978-79—Ray Bourque, Verdun
           Jean-Francois Sauve, Trois-Rivieres
1979-80—Jean-Francois Sauve, Trois-Rivieres
1980-81—Claude Verret, Trois-Rivieres
1981-82—Claude Verret, Trois-Rivieres
1982-83—Pat LaFontaine, Verdun
1983-84—Jerome Carrier, Verdun
1984-85—Patrick Emond, Chicoutimi
1985-86—Jimmy Carson, Verdun
1986-87—Luc Beausoleil, Laval
1987-88—Stephan Lebeau, Shawinigan
1988-89—Steve Cadieux, Shawinigan

### Michel Bergeron Trophy
### (Top Rookie Forward)
(Prior to 1980-81 season, award was given to QMJHL Rookie-of-the-Year.)
1969-70—Serge Martel, Verdun
1970-71—Bob Murphy, Cornwall
1971-72—Bob Murray, Cornwall
1972-73—Pierre Larouche, Sorel
1973-74—Mike Bossy, Laval
1974-75—Dennis Pomerleau, Hull
1975-76—Jean-Marc Bonamie, Shawinigan
1976-77—Rick Vaive, Sherbrooke
1977-78—Norm Rochefort, Trois-Rivieres
           Denis Savard, Montreal
1978-79—Alan Grenier, Laval
1979-80—Dale Hawerchuk, Cornwall
1980-81—Claude Verret, Trois-Rivieres
1981-82—Sylvain Turgeon, Hull
1982-83—Pat LaFontaine, Verdun
1983-84—Stephane Richer, Granby
1984-85—Jimmy Carson, Verdun
1985-86—Pierre Turgeon, Granby
1986-87—Rob Murphy, Laval
1987-88—Martin Gelinas, Hull
1988-89—Yanick Perreault, Trois-Rivieres

### Raymond Lagace Trophy
### (Top Rookie Defenseman or Goaltender)
1980-81—Billy Campbell, Montreal
1981-82—Michel Petit, Sherbrooke
1982-83—Bobby Dollas, Laval
1983-84—James Gasseau, Drummondville
1984-85—Robert Desjardins, Shawinigan
1985-86—Stephane Guerard, Shawinigan
1986-87—Jimmy Waite, Chicoutimi
1987-88—Stephane Beauregard, St. Jean
1988-89—Karl Dykhuis, Hull

### Jean Beliveau Trophy
### (Leading Point Scorer)
1969-70—Luc Simard, Trois-Rivieries
1970-71—Guy Lafleur, Quebec
1971-72—Jacques Richard, Quebec
1972-73—Andre Savard, Quebec
1973-74—Pierre Larouche, Sorel
1974-75—Norm Dupont, Montreal
1975-76—Richard Dalpe, Trois-Rivieres
           Sylvain Locas, Chicoutimi
1976-77—Jean Savard, Quebec
1977-78—Ron Carter, Sherbrooke
1978-79—Jean-Francois Sauve, Trois-Rivieres
1979-80—Jean-Francois Sauve, Trois-Rivieres
1980-81—Dale Hawerchuk, Cornwall
1981-82—Claude Verret, Trois-Rivieres
1982-83—Pat LaFontaine, Verdun
1983-84—Mario Lemieux, Laval
1984-85—Guy Rouleau, Longueuil
1985-86—Guy Rouleau, Hull
1986-87—Marc Fortier, Chicoutimi
1987-88—Patrice Lefebvre, Shawinigan
1988-89—Stephane Morin, Chicoutimi

### Michael Briere Trophy
### (Regular Season Most Valuable Player)
1972-73—Andre Savard, Quebec
1973-74—Gary MacGregor, Cornwall
1974-75—Mario Viens, Cornwall
1975-76—Peter Marsh, Sherbrooke
1976-77—Lucien DeBlois, Sorel
1977-78—Kevin Reeves, Montreal
1978-79—Pierre Lacroix, Trois-Rivieres
1979-80—Denis Savard, Montreal
1980-81—Dale Hawerchuk, Cornwall
1981-82—John Chabot, Sherbrooke
1982-83—Pat LaFontaine, Verdun
1983-84—Mario Lemieux, Laval
1984-85—Daniel Berthiaune, Chicoutimi
1985-86—Guy Rouleau, Hull
1986-87—Robert Desjardins, Longueuil
1987-88—Marc Saumier, Hull
1988-89—Stephane Morin, Chicoutimi

## Marcel Robert Trophy
### (Top Scholastic/Athletic Performer)
1981-82—Jacques Sylvestre, Granby
1982-83—Claude Gosselin, Quebec
1983-84—Gilbert Paiement, Chicoutimi
1984-85—Claude Gosselin, Longueuil
1985-86—Bernard Morin, Laval
1986-87—Patrice Tremblay, Chicoutimi
1987-88—Stephane Beauregard, St. Jean
1988-89—Daniel Lacroix, Granby

## Mike Bossy Trophy
### (Top Pro Prospect)
(Originally called Association of Journalism of Hockey Trophy from 1980-81 through 1982-83.)
1980-81—Dale Hawerchuk, Cornwall
1981-82—Michel Petit, Sherbrooke
1982-83—Pat LaFontaine, Verdun
Sylvain Turgeon, Hull (tie)
1983-84—Mario Lemieux, Laval
1984-85—Jose Charbonneau, Drummondville
1985-86—Jimmy Carson, Verdun
1986-87—Pierre Turgeon, Granby
1987-88—Daniel Dore, Drummondville
1988-89—Patrice Brisebois, Laval

## Emile "Butch" Bouchard Trophy
### (Top Defenseman)
1975-76—Jean Gagnon, Quebec
1976-77—Robert Picard, Montreal
1977-78—Mark Hardy, Montreal
1978-79—Ray Bourque, Verdun
1979-80—Gaston Therrien, Quebec
1980-81—Fred Boimistruck, Cornwall
1981-82—Paul Andre Boutilier, Sherbrooke
1982-83—Jean-Jacques Daigneault, Longueuil
1983-84—Billy Campbell, Verdun
1984-85—Yves Beaudoin, Shawinigan
1985-86—Sylvain Cote, Hull
1986-87—Jean Marc Richard, Chicoutimi
1987-88—Eric Desjardins, Granby
1988-89—Yves Racine, Victoriaville

## Jacques Plante Trophy
### (Best Goalie)
1969-70—Michael Deguise, Sorel
1970-71—Reynald Fortier, Quebec
1971-72—Richard Brodeur, Cornwall
1972-73—Pierre Perusse, Quebec
1973-74—Claude Legris, Sorel
1974-75—Nick Sanza, Sherbrooke
1975-76—Tim Bernhardt, Cornwall
1976-77—Tim Bernhardt, Cornwall
1977-78—Tim Bernhardt, Cornwall
1978-79—Jacques Cloutier, Trois-Rivieres
1979-80—Corrado Micalef, Sherbrooke
1980-81—Michel Dufour, Sorel
1981-82—Jeff Barratt, Montreal
1982-83—Tony Haladuick, Laval
1983-84—Tony Haladuick, Laval
1984-85—Daniel Berthiaume, Chicoutimi
1985-86—Robert Desjardins, Hull
1986-87—Robert Desjardins, Longueuil
1987-88—Stephane Beauregard, St. Jean
1988-89—Stephane Fiset, Victoriaville

## Guy Lafleur Trophy
### (Most Valuable Player During Playoffs)
1977-78—Richard David, Trois-Rivieres
1978-79—Jean-Francois Sauve, Trois-Rivieres
1979-80—Dale Hawerchuk, Cornwall
1980-81—Alain Lemieux, Trois-Rivieres
1981-82—Michel Morissette, Sherbrooke
1982-83—Pat LaFontaine, Verdun
1983-84—Mario Lemieux, Laval
1984-85—Claude Lemieux, Verdun
1985-86—Sylvain Cote, Hull
Luc Robitaille, Hull (tie)
1986-87—Marc Saumier, Longueuil
1987-88—Marc Saumier, Hull
1988-89—Donald Audette, Laval

## Robert LeBel Trophy
### (Best Team Defensive Average)
1977-78—Trois-Rivieres Draveurs
1978-79—Trois-Rivieres Draveurs
1979-80—Sherbrooke Beavers
1980-81—Sorel Black Hawks
1981-82—Montreal Juniors
1982-83—Shawinigan Cataracts
1983-84—Shawinigan Cataracts
1984-85—Shawinigan Cataracts
1985-86—Hull Olympiques
1986-87—Longueuil Chevaliers
1987-88—St. Jean Castors
1988-89—Hull Olympiques

## John Rougeau Trophy
### (Regular Season Champions)
(Originally called Governors Trophy from 1969-70 through 1982-83.)
1969-70—Quebec Remparts
1970-71—Quebec Remparts
1971-72—Cornwall Royals
1972-73—Quebec Remparts
1973-74—Sorel Black Hawks
1974-75—Sherbrooke Beavers
1975-76—Sherbrooke Beavers
1976-77—Quebec Remparts
1977-78—Trois-Rivieres Draveurs
1978-79—Trois-Rivieres Draveurs
1979-80—Sherbrooke Beavers
1980-81—Cornwall Royals
1981-82—Sherbrooke Beavers
1982-83—Laval Voisins
1983-84—Laval Voisins
1984-85—Shawinigan Cataracts
1985-86—Hull Olympiques
1986-87—Granby Bisons
1987-88—Hull Olympiques
1988-89—Trois-Rivieres Draveurs

## President Cup
### (Playoff Champions)
1969-70—Quebec Remparts
1970-71—Quebec Remparts
1971-72—Cornwall Royals
1972-73—Quebec Remparts
1973-74—Quebec Remparts
1974-75—Sherbrooke Beavers
1975-76—Quebec Remparts
1976-77—Sherbrooke Beavers
1977-78—Trois-Rivieres Draveurs
1978-79—Trois-Rivieres Draveurs
1979-80—Cornwall Royals
1980-81—Cornwall Royals
1981-82—Sherbrooke Beavers
1982-83—Verdun Juniors
1983-84—Laval Voisins
1984-85—Verdun Junior Canadiens
1985-86—Hull Olympiques
1986-87—Longueuil Chevaliers
1987-88—Hull Olympiques
1988-89—Laval Titans

## National Collegiate Athletic Association

| Year | Champion | Coach | Runner-Up |
|---|---|---|---|
| 1948 | Michigan | Vic Heyliger | Dartmouth |
| 1949 | Boston College | John Kelley | Dartmouth |
| 1950 | Colorado College | Cheddy Thompson | Boston University |
| 1951 | Michigan | Vic Heyliger | Brown |
| 1952 | Michigan | Vic Heyliger | Colorado College |
| 1953 | Michigan | Vic Heyliger | Minnesota |
| 1954 | Rensselaer Poly | Ned Harkness | Minnesota |
| 1955 | Michigan | Vic Heyliger | Colorado College |
| 1956 | Michigan | Vic Heyliger | Michigan Tech |
| 1957 | Colorado College | Thomas Bedecki | Michigan |
| 1958 | Denver | Murray Armstrong | North Dakota |
| 1959 | North Dakota | Bob May | Michigan State |
| 1960 | Denver | Murray Armstrong | Michigan Tech |
| 1961 | Denver | Murray Armstrong | St. Lawrence |
| 1962 | Michigan Tech | John MacInnes | Clarkson |
| 1963 | North Dakota | Barry Thorndycraft | Denver |
| 1964 | Michigan | Al Renfrew | Denver |
| 1965 | Michigan Tech | John MacInnes | Boston College |
| 1966 | Michigan State | Amo Bessone | Clarkson |
| 1967 | Cornell | Ned Harkness | Boston University |
| 1968 | Denver | Murray Armstrong | North Dakota |
| 1969 | Denver | Murray Armstrong | Cornell |
| 1970 | Cornell | Ned Harkness | Clarkson |
| 1971 | Boston University | Jack Kelley | Minnesota |
| 1972 | Boston University | Jack Kelley | Cornell |
| 1973 | Wisconsin | Bob Johnson | Denver |
| 1974 | Minnesota | Herb Brooks | Michigan Tech |
| 1975 | Michigan Tech | John MacInnes | Minnesota |
| 1976 | Minnesota | Herb Brooks | Michigan Tech |
| 1977 | Wisconsin | Bob Johnson | Michigan |
| 1978 | Boston University | Jack Parker | Boston College |
| 1979 | Minnesota | Herb Brooks | North Dakota |
| 1980 | North Dakota | Gino Gasparini | Northern Michigan |
| 1981 | Wisconsin | Bob Johnson | Minnesota |
| 1982 | North Dakota | Gino Gasparini | Wisconsin |
| 1983 | Wisconsin | Jeff Sauer | Harvard |
| 1984 | Bowling Green | Jerry York | Minnesota-Duluth |
| 1985 | Rensselaer Polytechnic Inst. | Mike Addesa | Providence College |
| 1986 | Michigan State | Ron Mason | Harvard |
| 1987 | North Dakota | Gino Gasparini | Michigan State |
| 1988 | Lake Superior | Frank Anzalone | St. Lawrence |
| 1989 | Harvard | Bill Cleary | Minnesota |

## WESTERN COLLEGIATE HOCKEY ASSOCIATION

|  | W. | L. | T. | GF. | GA. | Pct. |
|---|---|---|---|---|---|---|
| Minnesota (34-11-3) | 27 | 6 | 2 | 157 | 91 | .800 |
| Northern Michigan (26-17-2) | 20 | 13 | 2 | 163 | 110 | .600 |
| North Dakota (22-18-1) | 19 | 15 | 1 | 131 | 119 | .557 |
| Wisconsin (25-16-5) | 17 | 13 | 5 | 126 | 108 | .557 |
| Denver (22-19-2) | 16 | 17 | 2 | 143 | 144 | .486 |
| Michigan Tech (15-25-2) | 15 | 19 | 1 | 128 | 150 | .443 |
| Minnesota-Duluth (15-23-2) | 12 | 21 | 2 | 106 | 135 | .371 |
| Colorado College (11-26-3) | 9 | 23 | 3 | 115 | 157 | .300 |

Overall record in parentheses.

### 1988-89 WCHA All-Stars

| First Team | Position | Second Team |
|---|---|---|
| Curtis Joseph, Wisconsin | Goalie | Robb Stauber, Minnesota |
| Darryl Olsen, Northern Michigan | Defenseman | Russ Parent, North Dakota |
| Paul Stanton, Wisconsin | Defenseman | Todd Richards, Minnesota |
| Tom Chorske, Minnesota | Forward | Phil Berger, Northern Michigan |
| Shawn Harrison, Michigan Tech | Forward | John Byce, Wisconsin |
| Daryn McBride, Denver | Forward | Dave Snuggerud, Minnesota |

WCHA Player of the Year: Curtis Joseph, Wisconsin
WCHA Freshman of the Year: Curtis Joseph, Wisconsin
WCHA Coach of the Year: Rick Comley, Northern Michigan

### WCHA PLAYOFFS
#### Quarterfinals
(Best-of-three-series)

Minnesota 5, Colorado College 4
Minnesota 7, Colorado College 1
   (Minnesota wins series, 2 games to 0)

Northern Michigan 7, Minnesota-Duluth 2
Northern Michigan 6, Minnesota-Duluth 3
   (Northern Michigan wins series, 2 games to 0)

Wisconsin 5, Michigan Tech 2
Wisconsin 5, Michigan Tech 3
   (Wisconsin wins series, 2 games to 0)

North Dakota 7, Denver 1
Denver 5, North Dakota 4 (OT)
Denver 3, North Dakota 2
   (Denver wins series, 2 games to 1)

#### Semifinals
Northern Michigan 4, Wisconsin 2
Denver 2, Minnesota 1

#### Third Place
Wisconsin 4, Minnesota 3

#### Championship Game
Northern Michigan 9, Denver 4

# CENTRAL COLLEGIATE HOCKEY ASSOCIATION

|  | W. | L. | T. | GF. | GA. | Pct. |
|---|---|---|---|---|---|---|
| Michigan State (37-9-1) | 25 | 6 | 1 | 188 | 95 | .797 |
| Lake Superior State (29-11-6) | 19 | 7 | 6 | 128 | 90 | .688 |
| Illinois-Chicago (23-14-5) | 18 | 10 | 4 | 132 | 120 | .625 |
| Michigan (22-15-4) | 17 | 11 | 4 | 137 | 118 | .594 |
| Bowling Green State (26-18-3) | 15 | 14 | 3 | 131 | 125 | .516 |
| Western Michigan (14-23-6) | 9 | 17 | 6 | 121 | 145 | .375 |
| Ferris State (12-22-6) | 9 | 18 | 5 | 99 | 144 | .359 |
| Ohio State (9-26-5) | 7 | 20 | 5 | 106 | 160 | .297 |
| Miami (O.) (11-27-0) | 8 | 24 | 0 | 125 | 170 | .250 |

Overall record in parentheses.

### 1988-89 CCHA All-Stars

| First Team | Position | Second Team |
|---|---|---|
| Bruce Hoffort, Lake Superior State | Goalie | Dave DePinto, Illinois-Chicago |
| Kord Cernich, Lake Superior State | Defenseman | Rob Blake, Bowling Green St. |
| Myles O'Connor, Michigan | Defenseman | Chris Luongo, Michigan State |
| Greg Parks, Bowling Green State | Forward | Bob Reynolds, Michigan State |
| Kip Miller, Michigan State | Forward | Nelson Emerson, Bowl. Green |
| Sheldon Gorski, Illinois-Chicago | Forward | Todd Brost, Michigan |

CCHA Player of the Year: Bruce Hoffort, Lake Superior State
CCHA Freshman of the Year: Rod Brind'Amour, Michigan State
CCHA Coach of the Year: Ron Mason, Michigan State

### CCHA PLAYOFFS
#### Quarterfinals
(Best-of-three series)

Illinois-Chicago 8, Western Michigan 4
Western Michigan 6, Illinois-Chicago 4
Illinois-Chicago 6, Western Michigan 2
   (Illinois-Chicago wins series, 2-1)

Lake Superior State 5, Ferris State 0
Lake Superior State 3, Ferris State 0
   (Lake Superior State wins series, 2-0)

Michigan State 9, Ohio State 5
Michigan State 11, Ohio State 4
   (Michigan State wins series, 2-0)

Bowling Green State 6, Michigan 4
Michigan 4, Bowling Green State 1
Bowling Green State 3, Michigan 2 (OT)
   (Bowling Green State wins series, 2-1)

### Semifinals
Lake Superior State 6, Illinois-Chicago 3
Michigan State 3, Bowling Green State 2

### Consolation Game
Bowling Green State 5, Illinois-Chicago 3

### Championship Game
Michigan State 4, Lake Superior State 1

# EASTERN COLLEGIATE ATHLETIC CONFERENCE

|  | W. | L. | T. | GF. | GA. | Pct. |
|---|---|---|---|---|---|---|
| Harvard (31-3-0) | 20 | 2 | 0 | 130 | 49 | .909 |
| St. Lawrence (29-7-0) | 18 | 4 | 0 | 99 | 56 | .818 |
| Colgate (19-10-2) | 15 | 6 | 1 | 108 | 82 | .705 |
| Clarkson (16-13-3) | 13 | 7 | 2 | 104 | 87 | .636 |
| Cornell (16-13-1) | 13 | 9 | 0 | 87 | 74 | .591 |
| Vermont (20-13-1) | 13 | 9 | 0 | 108 | 74 | .591 |
| Yale (11-19-1) | 10 | 12 | 0 | 72 | 84 | .455 |
| RPI (12-17-3) | 8 | 12 | 2 | 72 | 78 | .409 |
| Dartmouth (8-17-1) | 7 | 14 | 1 | 70 | 96 | .341 |
| Army (13-16-1) | 6 | 15 | 1 | 62 | 110 | .295 |
| Princeton (6-19-1) | 4 | 17 | 1 | 73 | 113 | .205 |
| Brown (1-25-0) | 1 | 21 | 0 | 51 | 132 | .045 |

Overall record in parentheses.

## 1988-89 ECAC All-Stars

| First Team | Position | Second Team |
|---|---|---|
| Michael O'Neill, Yale | Goalie | Paul Cohen, St. Lawrence |
| Dave Williams, Dartmouth | Defenseman | Dave Basseggio, Yale |
| Mike Hurlbut, St. Lawrence | Defenseman | Mike Bishop, Colgate |
| Scott Young, Colgate | | |
| Lane MacDonald, Harvard | Forward | C.J. Young, Harvard |
| Kyle McDonough, Vermont | Forward | Allen Bourbeau, Harvard |
| Jarmo Kekalainen, Clarkson | Forward | Peter Ciavaglia, Harvard |

ECAC Player of the Year: Lane MacDonald, Harvard
ECAC Rookie of the Year: Andre Faust, Princeton
ECAC Coach of the Year: Joe Marsh, St. Lawrence

## ECAC PLAYOFFS
### Quarterfinals
(Two-game, Total Goal Series)

Colgate 2, Vermont 2
Vermont 8, Colgate 4
    (Vermont wins series, 10-6)

Cornell 5, Clarkson 3
Clarkson 0, Cornell 0
    (Cornell wins series, 5-3)

St. Lawrence 2, Yale 1
St. Lawrence 9, Yale 2
    (St. Lawrence wins series, 11-3)

Harvard 7, RPI 3
Harvard 5, RPI 4
    (Harvard wins series, 12-7)

### Semifinals
St. Lawrence 6, Cornell 1
Vermont 3, Harvard 2 (OT)

### Consolation Game
Harvard 6, Cornell 3

### Championship Game
St. Lawrence 4, Vermont 1

# HOCKEY EAST

|  | W. | L. | T. | GF. | GA. | Pct. |
|---|---|---|---|---|---|---|
| Boston College (25-11-4) | 16 | 6 | 4 | 122 | 84 | .692 |
| Maine (31-14-0) | 17 | 9 | 0 | 127 | 97 | .654 |
| Northeastern (18-16-2) | 13 | 11 | 2 | 126 | 120 | .538 |
| Providence (22-18-2) | 13 | 11 | 2 | 106 | 112 | .538 |
| Boston University (14-21-1) | 10 | 15 | 1 | 114 | 116 | .404 |
| New Hampshire (12-22-0) | 9 | 17 | 0 | 75 | 120 | .346 |
| Lowell (8-24-2) | 4 | 21 | 1 | 82 | 156 | .173 |

Overall record in parentheses.

## 1988-89 Hockey East All-Stars

| First Team | Position | Second Team |
|---|---|---|
| David Littman, Boston College | Goalie | Scott King, Maine |
| Jim Hughes, Providence | Defenseman | Bob Beers, Maine |
| Greg Brown, Boston College | Defenseman | Rob Cowie, Northeastern |
| David Capuano, Maine | Forward | David Emma, Boston College |
| Tim Sweeney, Boston College | Forward | Mike Kelfer, Boston Univ. |
| Dave Buda, Northeastern | Forward | Harry Mews, Northeastern |

Hockey East Player of the Year: Greg Brown, Boston College

Hockey East Rookie of the Year: Scott Pellerin, Maine,
    Rob Gaudreau, Providence

Hockey East Coach of the Year: Fern Flaman, Northeastern

## HOCKEY EAST PLAYOFFS

### Quarterfinals
Providence 3, Boston University 2
Northeastern 5, New Hampshire 4 (OT)

### Consolation Game
Providence 3, Northeastern 2

### Semifinals
Boston College 6, Providence 5 (2 OT)
Maine 3, Northeastern 2 (OT)

### Championship Game
Maine 5, Boston College 4

# 1989 NCAA Tournament

## First Round Series
(Best-of-three series)

Lake Superior State 6, St. Cloud State 3
Lake Superior State 4, St. Cloud State 2
(Lake Superior State wins series, 2-0)

Northern Michigan 9, Providence 5
Providence 4, Northern Michigan 2
Providence 2, Northern Michigan 0
(Providence wins series, 2-1)

Boston College 8, Bowling Green State 5
Boston College 4, Bowling Green State 2
(Boston College wins series, 2-0)

Wisconsin 3, St. Lawrence 1
Wisconsin 4, St. Lawrence 2
(Wisconsin wins series, 2-0)

## Quarterfinal Series
(Best-of-three series)

Boston College 6, Michigan State 3
Michigan State 7, Boston College 2
Michigan State 5, Boston College 4 (OT)
(Michigan State wins series, 2-1)

Providence 8, Maine 6
Maine 3, Providence 2
Maine 4, Providence 3 (OT)
(Maine wins series, 2-1)

Harvard 4, Lake Superior State 2
Harvard 5, Lake Superior State 2
(Harvard wins series, 2-0)

Minnesota 4, Wisconsin 2
Minnesota 4, Wisconsin 2
(Minnesota wins series, 2-0)

### Semifinal Series
Played at St. Paul, Minn.
Harvard 6, Michigan State 3
Minnesota 7, Maine 4

### Consolation Game
Michigan State 7, Maine 4

### Championship Game
Harvard 4, Minnesota 3 (OT)
1989 NCAA Champion: Harvard

## 1989 NCAA All-Tournament Team

| Position | Player | College |
|---|---|---|
| Goalie | Allain Roy | Harvard |
| Defenseman | Kevin Sneddon | Harvard |
| Defenseman | Todd Richards | Minnesota |
| Forward | Lane MacDonald | Harvard |
| Forward | Jon Anderson | Minnesota |
| Forward | Ted Donato | Harvard |

NCAA Tournament MVP: Ted Donato, Harvard

## 1988-89 College Hockey All-America Teams

### WEST
#### FIRST TEAM

| Position | Player | College |
|---|---|---|
| Goalie | Bruce Hoffort | Lake Superior State |
| Defenseman | Kord Cernich | Lake Superior State |
| Defenseman | Myles O'Connor | Michigan |
| Forward | Greg Parks | Bowling Green State |
| Forward | Kip Miller | Michigan State |
| Forward | Bobby Reynolds | Michigan State |

#### SECOND TEAM

| Position | Player | College |
|---|---|---|
| Goalie | Curtis Joseph | Wisconsin |
| Defenseman | Darryl Olsen | Northern Michigan |
| Defenseman | Todd Richards | Minnesota |
| Forward | Sheldon Gorski | Illinois-Chicago |
| Forward | Daren McBride | Denver |
| Forward | Dave Snuggerud | Minnesota |

### EAST
#### FIRST TEAM

| Position | Player | College |
|---|---|---|
| Goalie | Mike O'Neill | Yale |
| Defenseman | Mike Hurlbut | St. Lawrence |
| Defenseman | Greg Brown | Boston College |
| Forward | David Capuano | Maine |
| Forward | Lane MacDonald | Harvard |
| Forward | Kyle McDonough | Vermont |

## SECOND TEAM

| Position | Player | College |
|---|---|---|
| Goalie | David Littman | Boston College |
| Defenseman | Bob Beers | Maine |
| Defenseman | Dave Williams | Dartmouth |
| Forward | Rick Bennett | Providence |
| Forward | C. J. Young | Harvard |
| Forward | Tim Sweeney | Boston College |

## All-Time NCAA Tournament Records and Finishes

|  | Visits | Tournament W. | L. | GF | GA | Pct. | Finished 1st | 2nd |
|---|---|---|---|---|---|---|---|---|
| Michigan | 13 | 21 | 6 | 173 | 91 | .778 | 7 | 2 |
| ‡Wisconsin | 10 | 19 | 8 | 116 | 78 | .704 | 4 | 1 |
| North Dakota | 12 | 21 | 9 | 121 | 87 | .700 | 5 | 3 |
| Denver | 11 | 17 | 9 | 121 | 73 | .654 | 5 | 2 |
| *Northeastern | 2 | 3 | 2 | 25 | 24 | .600 | 0 | 0 |
| †Michigan State | 11 | 19 | 13 | 141 | 119 | .594 | 2 | 2 |
| Michigan Tech | 10 | 13 | 9 | 118 | 85 | .591 | 3 | 4 |
| Minnesota | 14 | 17 | 13 | 183 | 152 | .567 | 3 | 6 |
| #RPI | 6 | 8 | 6 | 52 | 50 | .567 | 2 | 0 |
| #Lake Superior State | 3 | 5 | 4 | 38 | 34 | .556 | 1 | 0 |
| Boston University | 15 | 16 | 16 | 136 | 151 | .500 | 3 | 2 |
| Cornell | 8 | 8 | 8 | 54 | 52 | .500 | 2 | 2 |
| Merrimack | 1 | 2 | 2 | 14 | 16 | .500 | 0 | 0 |
| Yale | 1 | 1 | 1 | 7 | 5 | .500 | 0 | 0 |
| Providence | 5 | 8 | 9 | 55 | 54 | .471 | 0 | 1 |
| Maine | 3 | 5 | 6 | 43 | 50 | .455 | 0 | 0 |
| *Bowling Green State | 8 | 8 | 10 | 60 | 75 | .444 | 1 | 0 |
| Dartmouth | 5 | 4 | 5 | 38 | 37 | .444 | 0 | 2 |
| Minnesota-Duluth | 3 | 4 | 5 | 33 | 34 | .444 | 0 | 1 |
| Clarkson | 8 | 7 | 9 | 48 | 67 | .438 | 0 | 3 |
| Colorado College | 9 | 6 | 10 | 76 | 84 | .375 | 2 | 2 |
| †Harvard | 14 | 13 | 22 | 132 | 159 | .371 | 1 | 2 |
| Brown | 3 | 2 | 4 | 28 | 38 | .333 | 0 | 1 |
| Boston College | 17 | 11 | 25 | 129 | 98 | .306 | 1 | 2 |
| Northern Michigan | 3 | 2 | 5 | 21 | 30 | .286 | 0 | 1 |
| St. Lawrence | 11 | 5 | 20 | 74 | 118 | .200 | 0 | 2 |
| New Hampshire | 4 | 2 | 8 | 35 | 56 | .200 | 0 | 0 |
| ‡Lowell | 1 | 0 | 1 | 5 | 11 | .000 | 0 | 0 |
| St. Cloud State | 1 | 0 | 2 | 5 | 10 | .000 | 0 | 0 |
| Vermont | 1 | 0 | 2 | 2 | 10 | .000 | 0 | 0 |
| Western Michigan | 1 | 0 | 2 | 4 | 11 | .000 | 0 | 0 |

(Denver also participated in 1973 tournament but its record was voided by the NCAA in 1977 upon discovery of violations by the University. The team had finished second in '73.)
*Bowling Green and Northeastern played to a 2-2 tie in 1981-82.
†Harvard and Michigan State played to a 3-3 tie in 1982-83.
#Lake Superior State and RPI played to a 3-3 tie in 1984-85.
‡Wisconsin and Lowell played to a 4-4 tie in 1987-88.
HOBEY BAKER MEMORIAL TROPHY (Top College hockey player in U.S.): Lane MacDonald, Harvard.

## Air Force Academy
Overall: 14-12-3

|  | Pos. | Class | Games | G. | A. | Pts. | Pen. |
|---|---|---|---|---|---|---|---|
| Joe Doyle | F | Sr. | 28 | 24 | 24 | 48 | 10 |
| Joe Delich | F | Sr. | 28 | 13 | 31 | 44 | 47 |
| Jim Jirele | F | Sr. | 29 | 19 | 13 | 32 | 10 |
| Greg Gutterman | F | Sr. | 29 | 11 | 18 | 29 | 26 |
| John Anzelc | D | Sr. | 28 | 11 | 17 | 28 | 19 |
| Jason Beckman | F | Fr. | 29 | 10 | 17 | 27 | 2 |
| Jason Mantaro | F | Fr. | 28 | 11 | 15 | 26 | 14 |
| Matt Watson | D | Jr. | 29 | 8 | 15 | 23 | 38 |
| Kevin McManaman | D | Sr. | 28 | 3 | 19 | 22 | 59 |
| Kurt Rohloff | F | Jr. | 24 | 7 | 9 | 16 | 18 |
| Jeff Banks | F | Sr. | 29 | 9 | 5 | 14 | 12 |
| Mike Veneri | D | So. | 25 | 2 | 11 | 13 | 16 |

| | Pos. | Class | Games | G. | A. | Pts. | Pen. |
|---|---|---|---|---|---|---|---|
| Mike Travalent | F | Sr. | 28 | 4 | 8 | 12 | 12 |
| Rob Haataja | F | So. | 22 | 6 | 5 | 11 | 4 |
| Mark Skibinski | F | So. | 25 | 3 | 8 | 11 | 14 |
| Kent Landreth | F | So. | 28 | 3 | 5 | 8 | 26 |
| Dan Greene | D | So. | 26 | 2 | 6 | 8 | 8 |
| Mike Parent | D | So. | 28 | 2 | 4 | 6 | 22 |
| Noel Nistler | F | Jr. | 8 | 1 | 2 | 3 | 2 |
| Eric Nelson | D | So. | 4 | 0 | 2 | 2 | 2 |
| Mark Majewski | F | Fr. | 6 | 1 | 0 | 1 | 0 |
| Geno Ranaldi | D | Jr. | 4 | 0 | 1 | 1 | 0 |
| Jeff Seminaro | F | So. | 7 | 0 | 1 | 1 | 0 |
| Matt Snyder | F | Fr. | 1 | 0 | 0 | 0 | 0 |
| Tony Roe | F | Fr. | 2 | 0 | 0 | 0 | 0 |
| Mike Blank | G | So. | 15 | 0 | 0 | 0 | 0 |
| Mark Liebich | G | Fr. | 17 | 0 | 0 | 0 | 0 |

## U.S. Military Academy (Army)
Overall: 13-16-1; ECAC: 6-15-1

| | Pos. | Class | Games | G. | A. | Pts. | Pen. |
|---|---|---|---|---|---|---|---|
| Rich Sheridan | F | Jr. | 30 | 13 | 28 | 41 | 36 |
| Rob Tobin | F | So. | 30 | 15 | 15 | 30 | 58 |
| Scott Schulze | D | Jr. | 30 | 4 | 18 | 22 | 24 |
| Brian Cox | F | Sr. | 27 | 10 | 10 | 20 | 20 |
| Todd Tamburino | D | So. | 30 | 1 | 12 | 13 | 46 |
| Mark Hudak | D | Sr. | 29 | 5 | 6 | 11 | 64 |
| Todd Traczyk | F | Jr. | 24 | 4 | 6 | 10 | 20 |
| Brad Hamacher | D | So. | 20 | 3 | 7 | 10 | 20 |
| Al Brenner | F | So. | 25 | 7 | 2 | 9 | 8 |
| Paul Haggerty | F | So. | 27 | 6 | 2 | 8 | 22 |
| Tim McWain | F | Sr. | 30 | 5 | 3 | 8 | 10 |
| Chris Kindgren | F | So. | 30 | 6 | 1 | 7 | 32 |
| Mike Kennedy | F | So. | 25 | 4 | 3 | 7 | 20 |
| Scott Williams | D | So. | 30 | 0 | 7 | 7 | 32 |
| Mike Gengler | F | Jr. | 30 | 3 | 3 | 6 | 22 |
| John Griffin | F | So. | 17 | 3 | 2 | 5 | 25 |
| Kevin Darby | F | Fr. | 19 | 2 | 3 | 5 | 4 |
| Scott Tardif | F | Fr. | 11 | 0 | 5 | 5 | 2 |
| Ross Erzar | F | Fr. | 5 | 2 | 2 | 4 | 6 |
| Mike Kelsey | F | Fr. | 8 | 0 | 3 | 3 | 4 |
| Neil Minihane | D | Jr. | 29 | 0 | 3 | 3 | 53 |
| Chris Mead | D | Fr. | 18 | 0 | 1 | 1 | 16 |
| Brandon Hayes | G | Fr. | 5 | 0 | 0 | 0 | 0 |
| Mike Houmiel | F | So. | 7 | 0 | 0 | 0 | 9 |
| Fi DeCosty | F | Jr. | 9 | 0 | 0 | 0 | 2 |
| Corey Averill | G | Jr. | 10 | 0 | 0 | 0 | 4 |
| Brooks Chretien | G | So. | 20 | 0 | 0 | 0 | 12 |

## Boston College
Overall: 25-11-4; Hockey East: 16-6-4

| | Pos. | Class | Games | G. | A. | Pts. | Pen. |
|---|---|---|---|---|---|---|---|
| Tim Sweeney | F | Sr. | 39 | 29 | 44 | 73 | 26 |
| David Emma | F | So. | 36 | 20 | 31 | 51 | 36 |
| Steve Heinze | F | Fr. | 36 | 26 | 23 | 49 | 26 |
| Greg Brown | D | So. | 40 | 9 | 34 | 43 | 24 |
| Steve Scheifele | F | Jr. | 40 | 24 | 14 | 38 | 30 |
| Marty McInnis | F | Fr. | 39 | 13 | 19 | 32 | 8 |
| Jeff O'Neill | F | So. | 40 | 10 | 15 | 25 | 30 |
| Shawn Kennedy | F | Sr. | 40 | 12 | 12 | 24 | 20 |
| Paul Marshall | D | Sr. | 40 | 4 | 18 | 22 | 36 |
| Dave Pergola | F | So. | 39 | 12 | 9 | 21 | 16 |
| Bill Nolan | F | Jr. | 32 | 5 | 9 | 14 | 12 |
| Joe Cleary | D | Fr. | 38 | 5 | 7 | 12 | 36 |
| Mark Dennehy | D | So. | 37 | 3 | 8 | 11 | 12 |
| Richard Braccia | F | Sr. | 36 | 3 | 7 | 10 | 78 |
| David Buckley | D | Sr. | 40 | 3 | 7 | 10 | 48 |
| Mike Mullowney | D | Sr. | 39 | 2 | 7 | 9 | 64 |
| David Franzosa | F | Fr. | 23 | 2 | 5 | 7 | 4 |
| Matt Glennon | F | So. | 16 | 1 | 6 | 7 | 4 |
| Tim Delay | F | Jr. | 5 | 4 | 1 | 5 | 2 |
| Sean Farley | F | So. | 25 | 3 | 2 | 5 | 18 |
| Jason Rathbone | F | Fr. | 21 | 0 | 3 | 3 | 10 |

|  | Pos. | Class | Games | G. | A. | Pts. | Pen. |
|---|---|---|---|---|---|---|---|
| David Littman | G | Sr. | 32 | 0 | 2 | 2 | 4 |
| Mike Delay | F | Fr. | 1 | 1 | 0 | 1 | 0 |
| Darren Emery | D | So. | 1 | 0 | 0 | 0 | 0 |
| Sean Delaney | F | Jr. | 2 | 0 | 0 | 0 | 0 |
| Jeff Walker | G | Sr. | 2 | 0 | 0 | 0 | 0 |
| Rob Cheevers | F | Jr. | 4 | 0 | 0 | 0 | 0 |
| Brian Looney | F | Fr. | 5 | 0 | 0 | 0 | 2 |
| Tim Shenk | D | Jr. | 7 | 0 | 0 | 0 | 2 |
| Sandy Galuppo | G | So. | 12 | 0 | 0 | 0 | 0 |

## Boston University
Overall: 14-21-1; Hockey East: 10-15-1

|  | Pos. | Class | Games | G. | A. | Pts. | Pen. |
|---|---|---|---|---|---|---|---|
| Mike Kelfer | F | Sr. | 33 | 23 | 29 | 52 | 22 |
| Shawn McEachern | F | Fr. | 36 | 20 | 28 | 48 | 32 |
| David Tomlinson | F | So. | 34 | 16 | 30 | 46 | 28 |
| David Sacco | F | Fr. | 35 | 14 | 29 | 43 | 40 |
| Joe Sacco | F | So. | 33 | 21 | 19 | 40 | 66 |
| Mike Sullivan | F | Jr. | 36 | 19 | 17 | 36 | 30 |
| Mike Lappin | F | So. | 27 | 11 | 16 | 27 | 43 |
| Tom Dion | D | So. | 33 | 3 | 15 | 18 | 40 |
| Edward Ronan | F | So. | 36 | 4 | 11 | 15 | 34 |
| Darin MacDonald | F | So. | 35 | 6 | 6 | 12 | 20 |
| Ville Kentala | F | Jr. | 34 | 5 | 7 | 12 | 46 |
| Matt Pesklewis | F | Jr. | 12 | 2 | 7 | 9 | 31 |
| Ian Wood | F | Sr. | 32 | 3 | 5 | 8 | 12 |
| Chris Lappin | D | So. | 27 | 2 | 6 | 8 | 26 |
| Phil Von Stefenelli | D | So. | 33 | 2 | 6 | 8 | 34 |
| Mark Brownschidle | D | Fr. | 35 | 0 | 7 | 7 | 12 |
| Mark Krys | D | So. | 35 | 0 | 7 | 7 | 54 |
| John MacDougall | F | Fr. | 24 | 1 | 3 | 4 | 4 |
| Peter Headon | F | Sr. | 13 | 1 | 2 | 3 | 8 |
| Charles Beauchain | F | Fr. | 6 | 1 | 1 | 2 | 2 |
| Ron Trentini | F | Jr. | 10 | 1 | 1 | 2 | 0 |
| Chris McCann | F | So. | 12 | 1 | 1 | 2 | 2 |
| Robert Regan | F | Jr. | 22 | 1 | 1 | 2 | 29 |
| Steve Shaunessy | D | Jr. | 11 | 0 | 2 | 2 | 36 |
| Peter Fish | G | Sr. | 17 | 0 | 1 | 1 | 8 |
| John Bradley | G | So. | 11 | 0 | 0 | 0 | 4 |
| Bryan LaFort | G | Fr. | 11 | 0 | 0 | 0 | 0 |

## Bowling Green State University
Overall: 26-18-3; CCHA: 15-14-3

|  | Pos. | Class | Games | G. | A. | Pts. | Pen. |
|---|---|---|---|---|---|---|---|
| Greg Parks | F | Sr. | 47 | 32 | 42 | 74 | 96 |
| Nelson Emerson | F | Jr. | 44 | 22 | 46 | 68 | 46 |
| Joe Quinn | F | Jr. | 47 | 21 | 20 | 41 | 36 |
| Pierrick Maia | F | So. | 43 | 15 | 21 | 36 | 32 |
| Marc Potvin | F | Jr. | 46 | 23 | 12 | 35 | 63 |
| Kevin Dahl | D | Jr. | 46 | 9 | 26 | 35 | 51 |
| Matt Ruchty | F | So. | 43 | 11 | 21 | 32 | 110 |
| Rob Blake | D | So. | 46 | 11 | 21 | 32 | 140 |
| Peter Holmes | F | Fr. | 46 | 14 | 14 | 28 | 16 |
| Martin Jiranek | F | Fr. | 41 | 9 | 18 | 27 | 36 |
| Thad Rusiecki | D | Sr. | 47 | 6 | 11 | 17 | 66 |
| Chad Arthur | F | Sr. | 46 | 4 | 13 | 17 | 57 |
| Alan Leggett | D | Sr. | 47 | 1 | 15 | 16 | 30 |
| Jim Solly | F | Fr. | 40 | 4 | 9 | 13 | 14 |
| Braden Shavchook | F | So. | 40 | 7 | 5 | 12 | 26 |
| Otis Plageman | D | Fr. | 45 | 3 | 9 | 12 | 26 |
| Steve Dickinson | F | Sr. | 26 | 5 | 6 | 11 | 15 |
| Dan Bylsma | F | Fr. | 39 | 4 | 7 | 11 | 16 |
| Derek Hopko | D | Fr. | 39 | 0 | 5 | 5 | 26 |
| Paul Connell | G | Jr. | 41 | 0 | 3 | 3 | 14 |
| Llew Ncwana | D | Fr. | 16 | 0 | 2 | 2 | 12 |
| Ty Eigner | F | Fr. | 5 | 1 | 0 | 1 | 0 |
| Christian Albitz | G | So. | 2 | 0 | 0 | 0 | 0 |
| Matt Weir | F | Fr. | 2 | 0 | 0 | 0 | 0 |
| John Burke | G | So. | 10 | 0 | 0 | 0 | 4 |

## Brown University

Overall: 1-25; ECAC: 1-21

| | Pos. | Class | Games | G. | A. | Pts. | Pen. |
|---|---|---|---|---|---|---|---|
| Gordie Ernst | F | Sr. | 25 | 10 | 9 | 19 | 24 |
| Steve King | F | So. | 26 | 8 | 5 | 13 | 73 |
| Mike Brewer | F | Fr. | 23 | 5 | 8 | 13 | 10 |
| Jim Lombardi | D | Sr. | 21 | 1 | 10 | 11 | 47 |
| Mike Langton | F | Sr. | 23 | 6 | 4 | 10 | 63 |
| Bob Kenneally | F | Jr. | 26 | 3 | 7 | 10 | 46 |
| Brad Kreick | D | So. | 26 | 1 | 9 | 10 | 28 |
| Darrin MacKay | F | Fr. | 22 | 8 | 1 | 9 | 24 |
| Joe Verderber | F | Fr. | 26 | 6 | 3 | 9 | 16 |
| Mark LaChance | D | Sr. | 23 | 2 | 7 | 9 | 61 |
| Rob Hardy | F | Sr. | 26 | 2 | 6 | 8 | 59 |
| Rick Olczyk | D | Fr. | 26 | 0 | 5 | 5 | 30 |
| Eric Bommer | F | So. | 21 | 3 | 1 | 4 | 2 |
| Rod Pritchard | F | Sr. | 12 | 1 | 2 | 3 | 12 |
| Bob Ernst | F | Sr. | 17 | 1 | 1 | 2 | 6 |
| Jeff Schmitz | F | Fr. | 26 | 1 | 1 | 2 | 18 |
| Kevin Burke | F | Fr. | 11 | 0 | 2 | 2 | 8 |
| Todd MacCallum | D | So. | 14 | 0 | 2 | 2 | 10 |
| Chris Mills | D | Fr. | 16 | 0 | 2 | 2 | 15 |
| Craig Pho | D | Fr. | 24 | 0 | 1 | 1 | 70 |
| David Bolduc | F | So. | 1 | 0 | 0 | 0 | 0 |
| Brian Day | F | So. | 1 | 0 | 0 | 0 | 2 |
| Jamie Sullivan | G | Fr. | 1 | 0 | 0 | 0 | 0 |
| Rick Bonine | F | Sr. | 6 | 0 | 0 | 0 | 2 |
| Dan Quinn | G | Jr. | 6 | 0 | 0 | 0 | 0 |
| Brad Hendrikson | D | Fr. | 7 | 0 | 0 | 0 | 8 |
| Grant Swenson | F | Fr. | 18 | 0 | 0 | 0 | 15 |
| Chris Harvey | G | Jr. | 23 | 0 | 0 | 0 | 34 |

## Clarkson University

Overall: 16-13-3; ECAC: 13-7-2

| | Pos. | Class | Games | G. | A. | Pts. | Pen. |
|---|---|---|---|---|---|---|---|
| Jarmo Kekalainen | F | Jr. | 31 | 19 | 25 | 44 | 47 |
| Dave Trombley | F | So. | 32 | 10 | 29 | 39 | 28 |
| Shawn LaVoy | F | Sr. | 32 | 20 | 16 | 36 | 56 |
| Mike Morrison | F | Sr. | 26 | 10 | 20 | 30 | 52 |
| Mark Tretowicz | F | Jr. | 32 | 7 | 22 | 29 | 18 |
| Mark Green | F | So. | 30 | 16 | 11 | 27 | 42 |
| Dan O'Brien | F | Sr. | 32 | 13 | 13 | 26 | 48 |
| Dave Tretowicz | D | So. | 32 | 6 | 17 | 23 | 22 |
| Mike Kozak | F | So. | 27 | 10 | 9 | 19 | 24 |
| Mike Casselman | F | So. | 31 | 3 | 14 | 17 | 36 |
| Pierre Morin | D | Jr. | 18 | 3 | 12 | 15 | 24 |
| Jeff Torrey | F | Fr. | 32 | 6 | 6 | 12 | 20 |
| Mike Ashe | D | Sr. | 32 | 5 | 4 | 9 | 32 |
| Todd Tyo | F | Jr. | 28 | 1 | 8 | 9 | 22 |
| Steve Brennan | F | Jr. | 25 | 3 | 4 | 7 | 42 |
| Dave Mellen | D | Sr. | 31 | 0 | 5 | 5 | 44 |
| Ron Reagan | F | Jr. | 26 | 2 | 2 | 4 | 10 |
| Rich Denicourt | F | Fr. | 21 | 0 | 3 | 3 | 16 |
| Tony Calandra | D | Fr. | 6 | 0 | 2 | 2 | 4 |
| John Fletcher | G | Jr. | 23 | 0 | 2 | 2 | 0 |
| Paul Donovan | F | Jr. | 9 | 1 | 0 | 1 | 10 |
| Ed Sabo | F | Fr. | 1 | 0 | 0 | 0 | 8 |
| Scott Denicourt | D | Jr. | 2 | 0 | 0 | 0 | 0 |
| Jason Poirier | G | Sr. | 16 | 0 | 0 | 0 | 0 |
| Kent Anderson | D | Fr. | 17 | 0 | 0 | 0 | 6 |
| John Bolton | D | Jr. | 22 | 0 | 0 | 0 | 4 |

## Colgate University

Overall: 19-10-2; ECAC: 15-6-1

| | Pos. | Class | Games | G. | A. | Pts. | Pen. |
|---|---|---|---|---|---|---|---|
| Shawn Lillie | F | Jr. | 31 | 16 | 38 | 54 | 12 |
| Craig Woodcroft | F | So. | 29 | 20 | 29 | 49 | 62 |
| Joel Gardner | F | Jr. | 30 | 21 | 25 | 46 | 38 |

| | Pos. | Class | Games | G. | A. | Pts. | Pen. |
|---|---|---|---|---|---|---|---|
| Marc Dupere | F | Jr. | 29 | 18 | 19 | 37 | 25 |
| Scott Young | D | Sr. | 31 | 15 | 22 | 37 | 150 |
| Steve Spott | F | Jr. | 29 | 20 | 15 | 35 | 58 |
| Dale Band | F | Fr. | 31 | 9 | 21 | 30 | 20 |
| Jamie Cooke | F | Fr. | 28 | 13 | 11 | 24 | 26 |
| Mike Bishop | D | Sr. | 31 | 8 | 13 | 21 | 92 |
| Jason Greyerbiehl | F | Fr. | 31 | 6 | 9 | 15 | 14 |
| Hugues Rivard | F | So. | 30 | 4 | 10 | 14 | 58 |
| Todd Wolf | D | So. | 29 | 1 | 13 | 14 | 58 |
| Grant Slater | F | Jr. | 20 | 3 | 3 | 6 | 6 |
| Brett Lawrence | F | Jr. | 26 | 2 | 4 | 6 | 10 |
| Karl Clauss | D | Sr. | 31 | 1 | 5 | 6 | 38 |
| Scott Gordon | D | So. | 19 | 0 | 6 | 6 | 12 |
| Steve Poapst | D | So. | 30 | 0 | 5 | 5 | 38 |
| Gregg Wolf | D | So. | 13 | 1 | 3 | 4 | 20 |
| Dave Gagnon | G | So. | 28 | 0 | 4 | 4 | 24 |
| Jim White | F | So. | 17 | 2 | 1 | 3 | 34 |
| Dave Doherty | F | Fr. | 15 | 1 | 2 | 3 | 2 |
| Jeff Weber | F | Jr. | 26 | 0 | 2 | 2 | 30 |
| Greg Menges | G | So. | 6 | 0 | 0 | 0 | 0 |

## Colorado College
Overall: 11-26-3; WCHA: 9-23-3

| | Pos. | Class | Games | G. | A. | Pts. | Pen. |
|---|---|---|---|---|---|---|---|
| Tim Budy | F | Sr. | 40 | 23 | 23 | 46 | 54 |
| Steve Strunk | F | Fr. | 39 | 22 | 22 | 44 | 43 |
| Chris Anderson | F | Jr. | 38 | 18 | 12 | 30 | 14 |
| Cal Brown | D | Jr. | 37 | 2 | 27 | 29 | 63 |
| Brent Mowery | F | Jr. | 40 | 11 | 16 | 27 | 54 |
| Doug Kirton | F | Jr. | 38 | 8 | 16 | 24 | 33 |
| Matt Shaw | D | Sr. | 37 | 9 | 14 | 23 | 59 |
| Grant Block | F | Fr. | 40 | 5 | 13 | 18 | 22 |
| Ed Zawatsky | F | So. | 40 | 4 | 14 | 18 | 35 |
| Joe Schwartz | F | Jr. | 29 | 5 | 9 | 14 | 46 |
| Trevor Pochpnski | D | So. | 40 | 4 | 10 | 14 | 74 |
| Mark Olsen | D | Sr. | 21 | 5 | 5 | 10 | 28 |
| Sean Foley | F | Fr. | 34 | 5 | 4 | 9 | 36 |
| Alan Schuler | D | Fr. | 40 | 1 | 9 | 9 | 22 |
| Jon Manthey | F | So. | 35 | 2 | 6 | 8 | 20 |
| Guy Gadowsky | F | Sr. | 31 | 3 | 4 | 7 | 16 |
| Chic Pojar | F | Fr. | 40 | 2 | 3 | 5 | 32 |
| Rik Duryea | D | Fr. | 30 | 1 | 2 | 3 | 14 |
| Brian Bruininks | D | Fr. | 31 | 1 | 2 | 3 | 35 |
| Kevin Lee | F | So. | 5 | 1 | 1 | 2 | 2 |
| Colin Aymond | F | Fr. | 12 | 1 | 0 | 1 | 10 |
| Jim Wilharm | D | Jr. | 12 | 0 | 1 | 1 | 16 |
| Derek Pizzey | G | Sr. | 30 | 0 | 1 | 1 | 2 |
| James MacDougall | G | So. | 2 | 0 | 0 | 0 | 0 |
| Tom Crum | F | So. | 5 | 0 | 0 | 0 | 0 |
| Jody Praznik | D | So. | 8 | 0 | 0 | 0 | 20 |
| Jon Gustafson | G | So. | 14 | 0 | 0 | 0 | 2 |

## Cornell University
Overall: 16-13-1; ECAC: 13-9

| | Pos. | Class | Games | G. | A. | Pts. | Pen. |
|---|---|---|---|---|---|---|---|
| Rob Levasseur | F | Sr. | 30 | 26 | 12 | 38 | 41 |
| Casey Jones | F | Jr. | 29 | 8 | 27 | 35 | 22 |
| Trent Andison | F | So. | 28 | 17 | 16 | 33 | 28 |
| Chris Grenier | F | Sr. | 30 | 7 | 22 | 29 | 22 |
| Doug Derraugh | F | So. | 30 | 9 | 17 | 26 | 20 |
| Ross Lemon | F | Jr. | 26 | 7 | 11 | 18 | 12 |
| Tim Vanini | D-F | So. | 30 | 4 | 14 | 18 | 20 |
| Bruce Frauley | D | So. | 30 | 3 | 13 | 16 | 6 |
| Dan Ratushny | D | Fr. | 28 | 2 | 13 | 15 | 50 |
| Jim Goerz | F | Jr. | 28 | 8 | 6 | 14 | 6 |
| Phil Nobel | F | Fr. | 29 | 7 | 5 | 12 | 10 |
| Karl Williams | F | Fr. | 30 | 2 | 8 | 10 | 24 |
| Stewart Smith | F | Sr. | 22 | 5 | 3 | 8 | 20 |
| Alan Tigert | D | Sr. | 27 | 2 | 6 | 8 | 16 |

| | Pos. | Class | Games | G. | A. | Pts. | Pen. |
|---|---|---|---|---|---|---|---|
| Marc Deschamps | D | Fr. | 30 | 0 | 8 | 8 | 30 |
| Stephane Gauvin | F | Fr. | 30 | 2 | 5 | 7 | 24 |
| Paul Dukovac | D | Fr. | 14 | 1 | 4 | 5 | 8 |
| Neil Paterson | F | Jr. | 12 | 1 | 2 | 3 | 0 |
| Alex Nikolic | F | Fr. | 13 | 0 | 3 | 3 | 31 |
| Dave Burke | D | Fr. | 30 | 0 | 3 | 3 | 24 |
| Joe Dragon | F | Fr. | 3 | 1 | 1 | 2 | 2 |
| Mike Tallman | F | Jr. | 3 | 1 | 1 | 2 | 0 |
| Jim Crozier | G | So. | 5 | 0 | 0 | 0 | 2 |
| Devin Mintz | F | Fr. | 7 | 0 | 0 | 0 | 6 |
| Corrie D'Alessio | G | So. | 29 | 0 | 0 | 0 | 0 |

## Dartmouth College
Overall: 8-17-1; ECAC: 7-14-1

| | Pos. | Class | Games | G. | A. | Pts. | Pen. |
|---|---|---|---|---|---|---|---|
| Jamie Hanlon | F | Jr. | 26 | 6 | 18 | 24 | 40 |
| Derek Tweddell | F | Sr. | 20 | 9 | 13 | 22 | 20 |
| Sean Tomalty | F | So. | 26 | 12 | 9 | 21 | 62 |
| Tom Finks | F | Sr. | 26 | 10 | 11 | 21 | 16 |
| Tom Nieman | F | Fr. | 26 | 7 | 11 | 18 | 38 |
| Jeff Miller | D | Jr. | 26 | 8 | 8 | 16 | 32 |
| Dave Williams | D | Jr. | 25 | 4 | 11 | 15 | 28 |
| Joe Gualtieri | D | Jr. | 24 | 5 | 8 | 13 | 18 |
| Mike Daly | F | So. | 22 | 6 | 4 | 10 | 26 |
| Rob Goulet | D | Sr. | 26 | 1 | 9 | 10 | 32 |
| Cam McKennitt | F | So. | 11 | 4 | 2 | 6 | 10 |
| Pat Wildman | D | So. | 21 | 3 | 2 | 5 | 4 |
| Peter Lardner | F | So. | 18 | 2 | 2 | 4 | 10 |
| Shane Feeney | F | Fr. | 25 | 2 | 2 | 4 | 4 |
| Roger Chiasson | F | Jr. | 15 | 1 | 3 | 4 | 4 |
| Paul Kinnaly | F | So. | 20 | 1 | 3 | 4 | 6 |
| Ned Desmond | D | Sr. | 17 | 0 | 4 | 4 | 10 |
| Mike Freedman | F | Sr. | 23 | 0 | 4 | 4 | 22 |
| Bill Fitzpatrick | F | So. | 11 | 0 | 3 | 3 | 2 |
| Butch Coughlin | D | Sr. | 18 | 0 | 3 | 3 | 24 |
| Kyle Flik | F | So. | 9 | 1 | 1 | 2 | 0 |
| Nate Dudley | D | So. | 3 | 0 | 1 | 1 | 0 |
| Matt Ocken | F | Fr. | 7 | 0 | 1 | 1 | 6 |
| Tim Osby | G | Sr. | 14 | 0 | 0 | 0 | 0 |
| Steve Laurin | G | Jr. | 13 | 0 | 0 | 0 | 0 |
| Chris Driscoll | F | So. | 15 | 0 | 0 | 0 | 4 |

## University of Denver
Overall: 22-19-2; WCHA: 16-17-2

| | Pos. | Class | Games | G. | A. | Pts. | Pen. |
|---|---|---|---|---|---|---|---|
| Daryn McBride | F | Jr. | 42 | 19 | 32 | 51 | 74 |
| Jay Moore | F | So. | 42 | 18 | 30 | 48 | 70 |
| Dave Shields | F | Jr. | 43 | 12 | 28 | 40 | 12 |
| Ed Cristofoli | F | Sr. | 43 | 20 | 19 | 39 | 50 |
| Rick Berens | F | So. | 40 | 19 | 19 | 38 | 52 |
| Ken MacArthur | D | So. | 42 | 11 | 19 | 30 | 77 |
| Eric Murano | F | Jr. | 42 | 13 | 16 | 29 | 52 |
| Marc Rousseau | D | Jr. | 43 | 10 | 18 | 28 | 68 |
| Glen Engevik | F | Sr. | 42 | 12 | 12 | 24 | 33 |
| Rod Summers | D | Jr. | 43 | 7 | 17 | 24 | 32 |
| Scott Mathias | F | Sr. | 39 | 8 | 12 | 20 | 38 |
| Jim Hau | F | Jr. | 41 | 8 | 10 | 18 | 22 |
| Mike Markovich | D | Fr. | 43 | 5 | 13 | 18 | 38 |
| Lance Momotani | F | Fr. | 43 | 5 | 11 | 16 | 22 |
| Darren Biggs | F | Fr. | 43 | 8 | 6 | 14 | 8 |
| Bruce Robinson | F | So. | 35 | 3 | 5 | 8 | 8 |
| Dan Brooks | D | Jr. | 41 | 0 | 6 | 6 | 36 |
| Don McLennan | D | Jr. | 26 | 1 | 3 | 4 | 28 |
| Brett Petersen | D | Fr. | 19 | 0 | 3 | 3 | 4 |
| Greg Moore | D | So. | 5 | 0 | 1 | 1 | 4 |
| Chris Teufel | D | Fr. | 10 | 0 | 1 | 1 | 6 |
| Chris Gillies | G | Sr. | 16 | 0 | 1 | 1 | 4 |
| Lucien Carignan | G | So. | 29 | 0 | 1 | 1 | 4 |
| Rolf Beutel | F | Fr. | 3 | 0 | 0 | 0 | 0 |
| Greg Stocklan | F | So. | 3 | 0 | 0 | 0 | 0 |

## Ferris State University
Overall: 12-22-6; CCHA: 9-18-5

| | Pos. | Class | Games | G. | A. | Pts. | Pen. |
|---|---|---|---|---|---|---|---|
| Rod Schluter | F | Sr. | 40 | 23 | 20 | 43 | 56 |
| Dean Cowling | F | Sr. | 38 | 14 | 23 | 37 | 26 |
| Rod Thomas | F | Jr. | 40 | 11 | 18 | 29 | 64 |
| John dePourcq | F | So. | 23 | 9 | 19 | 28 | 4 |
| Randy Robertson | D | Sr. | 36 | 5 | 15 | 20 | 67 |
| Greg Cyr | D | Jr. | 34 | 4 | 16 | 20 | 44 |
| Andy Black | F | Sr. | 19 | 10 | 9 | 19 | 18 |
| Mike Jorgensen | F | So. | 36 | 9 | 6 | 15 | 32 |
| Clark Davies | D | Jr. | 32 | 3 | 10 | 13 | 59 |
| Norm Krumpschmid | F | Fr. | 35 | 5 | 7 | 12 | 40 |
| Dean Davies | D | Sr. | 39 | 3 | 9 | 12 | 37 |
| Bob Nardella | F | So. | 28 | 6 | 4 | 10 | 18 |
| Chuck Wiegand | F | Fr. | 36 | 5 | 5 | 10 | 44 |
| John Bergeron | D | Jr. | 39 | 2 | 7 | 9 | 69 |
| Matt Evo | F | So. | 26 | 3 | 4 | 7 | 38 |
| Derek Frenette | F | Fr. | 27 | 3 | 4 | 7 | 17 |
| Justin LaFayette | F | So. | 36 | 3 | 4 | 7 | 59 |
| Tim Corkery | D | So. | 23 | 2 | 5 | 7 | 53 |
| Tom O'Rourke | F | Fr. | 31 | 2 | 5 | 7 | 16 |
| Kelly Sorensen | F | Fr. | 29 | 1 | 3 | 4 | 25 |
| Rod Taylor | F | Jr. | 13 | 3 | 0 | 3 | 6 |
| Mike LaLonde | F | Jr. | 19 | 0 | 2 | 2 | 8 |
| Dan Rolfe | D | So. | 26 | 0 | 2 | 2 | 54 |
| Marc Felicio | G | So. | 19 | 0 | 1 | 1 | 2 |
| Monte French | F | Jr. | 2 | 0 | 0 | 0 | 0 |
| Doug Miller | D | Jr. | 10 | 0 | 0 | 0 | 18 |
| Mike Williams | G | Jr. | 25 | 0 | 0 | 0 | 10 |

## Harvard University
Overall: 31-3-0; ECAC: 20-2-0

| | Pos. | Class | Games | G. | A. | Pts. | Pen. |
|---|---|---|---|---|---|---|---|
| Peter Ciavaglia | F | So. | 34 | 15 | 48 | 63 | 36 |
| Lane MacDonald | F | Sr. | 32 | 31 | 29 | 60 | 42 |
| C.J. Young | F | Jr. | 34 | 33 | 22 | 55 | 24 |
| Allen Bourbeau | F | Sr. | 33 | 11 | 43 | 54 | 48 |
| Ted Donato | F | So. | 34 | 14 | 37 | 51 | 30 |
| John Weisbrod | F | So. | 31 | 22 | 13 | 35 | 61 |
| Ed Krayer | F | Jr. | 34 | 12 | 14 | 26 | 4 |
| John Murphy | F | Jr. | 33 | 9 | 13 | 22 | 12 |
| Nick Carone | D | Sr. | 33 | 8 | 14 | 22 | 36 |
| Tod Hartje | F | Jr. | 33 | 4 | 17 | 21 | 40 |
| Mike Vukonich | F | So. | 27 | 11 | 8 | 19 | 12 |
| Ed Presz | F | Sr. | 34 | 9 | 7 | 16 | 28 |
| Kevan Melrose | D | Jr. | 32 | 2 | 13 | 15 | 126 |
| Paul Howley | F | Sr. | 34 | 6 | 6 | 12 | 28 |
| Josh Caplan | D | Sr. | 33 | 0 | 11 | 11 | 34 |
| Craig Taucher | F | Sr. | 13 | 2 | 7 | 9 | 2 |
| Scott McCormack | D | Jr. | 19 | 1 | 8 | 9 | 10 |
| Brian McCormack | D | Fr. | 31 | 0 | 8 | 8 | 16 |
| Kevin Sneddon | D | Fr. | 32 | 0 | 6 | 6 | 22 |
| Brian Popiel | D | Jr. | 15 | 0 | 3 | 3 | 2 |
| Scott Farden | D | Sr. | 4 | 0 | 2 | 2 | 2 |
| Rich DeFreitas | D | Fr. | 5 | 0 | 2 | 2 | 6 |
| Chuckie Hughes | G | Fr. | 17 | 0 | 2 | 2 | 2 |
| Timmy Burke | F | Fr. | 2 | 1 | 0 | 1 | 2 |
| Allain Roy | G | Fr. | 16 | 0 | 1 | 1 | 2 |
| Michael Francis | G | So. | 3 | 0 | 0 | 0 | 0 |

## University of Illinois-Chicago
Overall: 23-14-5; CCHA: 18-10-4

| | Pos. | Class | Games | G. | A. | Pts. | Pen. |
|---|---|---|---|---|---|---|---|
| Sheldon Gorski | F | Sr. | 41 | 38 | 22 | 60 | 68 |
| Bob Melton | F | So. | 42 | 19 | 40 | 59 | 24 |
| Rick Judson | F | Fr. | 42 | 14 | 20 | 34 | 20 |
| Darryl Noren | F | So. | 38 | 16 | 17 | 33 | 54 |
| Kurt Kabat | F | Jr. | 42 | 13 | 20 | 33 | 58 |
| Darin Banister | D | Jr. | 41 | 7 | 26 | 33 | 88 |

| | Pos. | Class | Games | G. | A. | Pts. | Pen. |
|---|---|---|---|---|---|---|---|
| Dominic Dunlap | F | So. | 41 | 18 | 11 | 29 | 40 |
| Todd Beyer | F | Sr. | 37 | 7 | 19 | 26 | 68 |
| Randy Zulinick | F | Fr. | 34 | 8 | 17 | 25 | 14 |
| Kevin Alexander | F | Jr. | 35 | 7 | 14 | 21 | 20 |
| Brad Smiley | F | Fr. | 38 | 6 | 11 | 17 | 14 |
| Trent Rees | F | Sr. | 41 | 4 | 11 | 15 | 16 |
| Jim Marchi | D | So. | 39 | 5 | 9 | 14 | 62 |
| Paul Tory | F | Sr. | 21 | 5 | 8 | 13 | 33 |
| Scott Wolter | F | Jr. | 29 | 6 | 4 | 10 | 6 |
| Chris Wolanin | D | So. | 30 | 1 | 9 | 10 | 33 |
| Trevor Wallace | D | So. | 25 | 0 | 9 | 9 | 22 |
| Eric Schneider | D | Fr. | 42 | 2 | 6 | 8 | 50 |
| Jim Maher | D | Fr. | 41 | 1 | 5 | 6 | 40 |
| Henry Reimer | F | Sr. | 11 | 1 | 4 | 5 | 16 |
| Dan Marquardt | D | Fr. | 29 | 0 | 3 | 3 | 24 |
| Dave DePinto | G | Jr. | 38 | 0 | 3 | 3 | 17 |
| Dan Perry | F | Sr. | 7 | 0 | 2 | 2 | 19 |
| Eric Klutke | F | So. | 4 | 0 | 1 | 1 | 0 |
| Damion Holland | G | Fr. | 1 | 0 | 0 | 0 | 0 |
| Erik Magsamen | D | Fr. | 2 | 0 | 0 | 0 | 0 |
| Brent Polischuk | D | Fr. | 4 | 0 | 0 | 0 | 4 |
| Gary Mangino | G | So. | 7 | 0 | 0 | 0 | 0 |

### Lake Superior State University
Overall: 29-11-6; CCHA: 19-7-6

| | Pos. | Class | Games | G. | A. | Pts. | Pen. |
|---|---|---|---|---|---|---|---|
| Anthony Palumbo | F | Sr. | 46 | 22 | 44 | 66 | 38 |
| Jim Dowd | F | So. | 46 | 24 | 35 | 59 | 40 |
| Mike de Carle | F | Sr. | 38 | 20 | 24 | 44 | 86 |
| Pete Stauber | F | Jr. | 46 | 25 | 13 | 38 | 115 |
| Kord Cernich | D | Jr. | 46 | 7 | 31 | 38 | 74 |
| Dan Keczmer | D | Jr. | 46 | 3 | 26 | 29 | 70 |
| Jeff Napierala | F | So. | 43 | 17 | 9 | 26 | 22 |
| Brett Barnett | F | So. | 30 | 15 | 11 | 26 | 104 |
| Karl Johnston | D | So. | 43 | 7 | 19 | 26 | 38 |
| Jeff Jablonski | F | Jr. | 45 | 11 | 12 | 23 | 50 |
| Tim Breslin | F | So. | 42 | 7 | 13 | 20 | 34 |
| Dean Dyer | F | So. | 41 | 4 | 11 | 15 | 52 |
| Mark Astley | D | Fr. | 42 | 3 | 12 | 15 | 26 |
| Rene Chapdelaine | D | Sr. | 46 | 4 | 9 | 13 | 52 |
| Paul Constantin | F | Fr. | 28 | 5 | 5 | 10 | 0 |
| Sandy Moger | F | Fr. | 31 | 4 | 6 | 10 | 28 |
| Doug Laprade | F | So. | 45 | 4 | 6 | 10 | 48 |
| Ken Martel | D | Sr. | 40 | 1 | 7 | 8 | 30 |
| Tim Harris | F | So. | 29 | 1 | 5 | 6 | 78 |
| Vince Faucher | F | Fr. | 27 | 2 | 3 | 5 | 18 |
| David DiVita | D | So. | 25 | 1 | 4 | 5 | 28 |
| Bruce Hoffort | G | So. | 44 | 0 | 2 | 2 | 6 |
| Mike Bachusz | D | Fr. | 1 | 0 | 0 | 0 | 0 |
| Mike Greenlay | G | Jr. | 2 | 0 | 0 | 0 | 0 |
| Brandon Reed | G | So. | 3 | 0 | 0 | 0 | 0 |

### University of Lowell
Overall: 8-24-2; Hockey East: 4-21-1

| | Pos. | Class | Games | G. | A. | Pts. | Pen. |
|---|---|---|---|---|---|---|---|
| Scott MacPherson | F | Jr. | 34 | 19 | 19 | 38 | 14 |
| Craig Charron | F | Jr. | 32 | 14 | 21 | 35 | 32 |
| Randy LeBrasseur | F | Jr. | 31 | 16 | 13 | 29 | 32 |
| Peter Sentner | D | So. | 34 | 6 | 20 | 26 | 46 |
| Jeff Flaherty | F | Jr. | 22 | 12 | 11 | 23 | 77 |
| Brendan Flynn | F | So. | 31 | 4 | 15 | 19 | 20 |
| Pascal Labrecque | F | So. | 32 | 6 | 11 | 17 | 18 |
| John Borrell | F | Sr. | 29 | 8 | 8 | 16 | 24 |
| Steve Ablitt | F | So. | 30 | 4 | 11 | 15 | 83 |
| Greg Carter | F | Fr. | 28 | 6 | 7 | 13 | 17 |
| Gary Murphy | D | Sr. | 28 | 4 | 7 | 11 | 51 |
| Conrade Thomas | F | Jr. | 30 | 2 | 9 | 11 | 59 |
| Eric Richard | F | So. | 29 | 4 | 5 | 9 | 14 |
| Jyrki Maki | D | Sr. | 31 | 3 | 6 | 9 | 18 |
| Dave Gatti | F | .... | 14 | 4 | 4 | 8 | 10 |
| Mike Erickson | D | So. | 33 | 4 | 2 | 6 | 50 |

| | Pos. | Class | Games | G. | A. | Pts. | Pen. |
|---|---|---|---|---|---|---|---|
| Dan Geary | F | So. | 11 | 3 | 2 | 5 | 4 |
| Rocco Amonte | F | So. | 21 | 1 | 3 | 4 | 8 |
| Matt Hayes | D | Fr. | 30 | 0 | 4 | 4 | 30 |
| Don Parsons | F-D | Fr. | 18 | 2 | 1 | 3 | 14 |
| Garrett Burke | D | Fr. | 7 | 0 | 3 | 3 | 17 |
| Jim Geary | F | Fr. | 3 | 0 | 2 | 2 | 6 |
| Kyle Favreau | D | So. | 17 | 0 | 2 | 2 | 6 |
| Tomi Maarni | D | So. | 20 | 0 | 2 | 2 | 12 |
| Craig Daly | D | Fr. | 2 | 0 | 1 | 1 | 2 |
| Sean Boudreault | F | So. | 14 | 0 | 1 | 1 | 12 |
| Peter Harris | G | Jr. | 9 | 0 | 0 | 0 | 0 |
| Ken Stein | G | Sr. | 14 | 0 | 0 | 0 | 8 |
| Mark Richards | G | Fr. | 18 | 0 | 0 | 0 | 6 |

### University of Maine
**Overall: 31-14; Hockey East: 17-9**

| | Pos. | Class | Games | G. | A. | Pts. | Pen. |
|---|---|---|---|---|---|---|---|
| David Capuano | F | Jr. | 41 | 37 | 30 | 67 | 38 |
| Scott Pellerin | F | Fr. | 45 | 29 | 33 | 62 | 92 |
| Guy Perron | F | Jr. | 34 | 22 | 27 | 49 | 14 |
| Bob Corkum | F | Sr. | 45 | 17 | 31 | 48 | 64 |
| Martin Robitaille | F | Fr. | 45 | 17 | 31 | 48 | 10 |
| Christian Lalonde | F | Sr. | 39 | 10 | 29 | 39 | 41 |
| Bob Beers | D | Sr. | 44 | 10 | 27 | 37 | 53 |
| Vince Guidotti | D | Sr. | 42 | 7 | 23 | 30 | 76 |
| Claudio Scremin | D | Jr. | 45 | 5 | 24 | 29 | 42 |
| Mike Barkley | F | Fr. | 41 | 12 | 16 | 28 | 16 |
| Keith Carney | D | Fr. | 40 | 4 | 22 | 26 | 24 |
| Bruce Major | F | Sr. | 42 | 13 | 11 | 24 | 22 |
| Chris Cambio | F | Sr. | 30 | 7 | 11 | 18 | 15 |
| Todd Jenkins | F | Sr. | 25 | 8 | 9 | 17 | 20 |
| Mario Thyer | F | So. | 9 | 9 | 7 | 16 | 0 |
| Brian Bellefeuille | F | Jr. | 36 | 5 | 10 | 15 | 32 |
| Steve Tepper | F | Fr. | 26 | 3 | 9 | 12 | 32 |
| Joakim Wahlstrom | F | So. | 24 | 5 | 6 | 11 | 6 |
| Luke Vitale | F | Sr. | 25 | 5 | 6 | 11 | 12 |
| Campbell Blair | D | So. | 36 | 2 | 9 | 11 | 20 |
| Jim Burke | D | Jr. | 41 | 1 | 7 | 8 | 56 |
| John Massara | F | Jr. | 32 | 5 | 2 | 7 | 18 |
| Tony Link | D | Fr. | 22 | 0 | 3 | 3 | 12 |
| Garth Snow | G | Fr. | 5 | 0 | 1 | 1 | 0 |
| Matt DelGuidice | G | So. | 20 | 0 | 1 | 1 | 4 |
| Brendan Macauley | G | So. | 1 | 0 | 0 | 0 | 0 |
| Scott King | G | Jr. | 27 | 0 | 0 | 0 | 14 |

### Merrimack College
**Overall: 27-7; ECAC East-West: 16-2**

| | Pos. | Class | Games | G. | A. | Pts. | Pen. |
|---|---|---|---|---|---|---|---|
| Richard Pion | F | Sr. | 34 | 28 | 42 | 70 | 34 |
| Andy Heinze | F | Jr. | 33 | 28 | 25 | 53 | 36 |
| Jim Alcott | F | Sr. | 34 | 22 | 26 | 48 | 22 |
| Mark Ziliotto | F | Sr. | 30 | 21 | 17 | 38 | 72 |
| Ben Lebeau | F | So. | 32 | 18 | 20 | 38 | 46 |
| Frank Schofield | F | Jr. | 33 | 13 | 20 | 33 | 28 |
| Chris Kiene | D | Sr. | 32 | 3 | 25 | 28 | 76 |
| Claude Maillet | D | Fr. | 30 | 1 | 27 | 28 | 30 |
| Agostino Casale | F | Fr. | 31 | 12 | 15 | 27 | 20 |
| Dave Vater | F | Sr. | 34 | 14 | 12 | 26 | 12 |
| Brad Atol | F | Sr. | 25 | 7 | 19 | 26 | 42 |
| Doug Greschuk | D | So. | 34 | 2 | 23 | 25 | 38 |
| Brian Hayward | F | Jr. | 29 | 6 | 16 | 22 | 6 |
| Marc Vachon | F | Sr. | 30 | 6 | 15 | 21 | 40 |
| Ed Locke | F | Jr. | 34 | 9 | 11 | 20 | 38 |
| Matt Hentges | D | Fr. | 33 | 0 | 16 | 16 | 22 |
| Tim Doyle | D | So. | 32 | 0 | 12 | 12 | 10 |
| Sean Dooley | D | So. | 19 | 2 | 8 | 10 | 10 |
| Jamie Sullivan | D | So. | 28 | 2 | 5 | 7 | 6 |
| Jamie Baker | D | Fr. | 8 | 0 | 7 | 7 | 6 |
| Jeff Massey | F | Fr. | 1 | 3 | 0 | 3 | 0 |
| Howie Rosenblatt | F | So. | 7 | 1 | 1 | 2 | 8 |
| Jim Hrivnak | G | Sr. | 22 | 0 | 1 | 1 | 0 |

| | Pos. | Class | Games | G. | A. | Pts. | Pen. |
|---|---|---|---|---|---|---|---|
| Steve Cardosi | F | So. | 1 | 0 | 0 | 0 | 0 |
| Brendan Locke | F | Fr. | 2 | 0 | 0 | 0 | 0 |
| Mike Marchese | F | So. | 5 | 0 | 0 | 0 | 0 |
| Craig DalFarra | G | Jr. | 8 | 0 | 0 | 0 | 0 |
| John Moltenbrey | G | Jr. | 11 | 0 | 0 | 0 | 0 |

## Miami (O.) University
Overall: 11-27; CCHA: 8-24

| | Pos. | Class | Games | G. | A. | Pts. | Pen. |
|---|---|---|---|---|---|---|---|
| Craig Fisher | F | Fr. | 37 | 22 | 20 | 42 | 37 |
| Boyd Sutton | F | Sr. | 37 | 16 | 23 | 39 | 24 |
| Jeff Sisto | F | Sr. | 37 | 15 | 22 | 37 | 16 |
| Ken House | F | Fr. | 38 | 19 | 14 | 33 | 18 |
| Rob Vanderydt | F | So. | 38 | 12 | 18 | 30 | 26 |
| Scott Luik | F | So. | 36 | 13 | 13 | 26 | 92 |
| Jim Bodden | F | So. | 33 | 11 | 10 | 21 | 15 |
| Steve McGrinder | D | Jr. | 34 | 6 | 14 | 20 | 24 |
| Dan Beaudette | F | Jr. | 34 | 5 | 13 | 18 | 32 |
| Scott Mazi | F | So. | 36 | 4 | 12 | 16 | 54 |
| Todd Harkins | F | So. | 36 | 8 | 7 | 15 | 77 |
| Rhys Hollyman | D | Fr. | 33 | 8 | 5 | 13 | 60 |
| Chris Archer | F | Sr. | 38 | 6 | 6 | 12 | 44 |
| Joe Tonello | D | Jr. | 29 | 2 | 9 | 11 | 4 |
| Greg Island | D | Jr. | 19 | 0 | 11 | 11 | 14 |
| Tom Neziol | F | Jr. | 12 | 5 | 4 | 9 | 14 |
| Bob Wallwork | F-D | So. | 19 | 1 | 8 | 9 | 30 |
| Jaan Luik | D | So. | 33 | 1 | 8 | 9 | 43 |
| Rob Robinson | D | Sr. | 30 | 3 | 4 | 7 | 42 |
| Steve Wilson | D | Fr. | 30 | 1 | 3 | 4 | 20 |
| Robert Fischer | D | Fr. | 26 | 0 | 3 | 3 | 36 |
| Lee Cannon | G | Fr. | 1 | 0 | 0 | 0 | 0 |
| Ryan Schiff | F | Sr. | 4 | 0 | 0 | 0 | 0 |
| Paul Swift | F | Jr. | 7 | 0 | 0 | 0 | 18 |
| Steve McKichan | G | Jr. | 21 | 0 | 0 | 0 | 2 |
| Mark Michaud | G | Fr. | 24 | 0 | 0 | 0 | 0 |

## University of Michigan
Overall: 22-15-4; CCHA: 17-11-4

| | Pos. | Class | Games | G. | A. | Pts. | Pen. |
|---|---|---|---|---|---|---|---|
| Todd Brost | F | Sr. | 40 | 20 | 30 | 50 | 43 |
| Denny Felsner | F | Fr. | 39 | 30 | 19 | 49 | 22 |
| Don Stone | F | So. | 40 | 24 | 17 | 41 | 19 |
| Mike Moes | F | Jr. | 41 | 14 | 24 | 38 | 22 |
| Myles O'Connor | D | Sr. | 40 | 3 | 31 | 34 | 91 |
| Ted Kramer | F | Fr. | 40 | 17 | 15 | 32 | 78 |
| Rob Brown | F | Jr. | 41 | 10 | 18 | 28 | 26 |
| Alex Roberts | D | Jr. | 41 | 5 | 19 | 24 | 116 |
| Jim Ballantine | F | So. | 37 | 9 | 14 | 23 | 27 |
| Todd Copeland | D | Jr. | 39 | 5 | 14 | 19 | 102 |
| Mike Helber | F | Fr. | 35 | 8 | 10 | 18 | 15 |
| Ryan Pardoski | F | Jr. | 38 | 11 | 3 | 14 | 36 |
| Kent Brothers | F | So. | 36 | 7 | 5 | 12 | 24 |
| Brad Turner | D | Jr. | 33 | 3 | 8 | 11 | 38 |
| Jeff Urban | F | Sr. | 31 | 4 | 6 | 10 | 20 |
| Tim Helber | F | Fr. | 37 | 4 | 5 | 9 | 18 |
| Doug Evans | D | Fr. | 38 | 0 | 8 | 8 | 41 |
| Randy Kwong | D | Jr. | 31 | 1 | 5 | 6 | 10 |
| Mark Sorensen | D | So. | 33 | 1 | 5 | 6 | 33 |
| Billy Jaffe | F | So. | 11 | 1 | 1 | 2 | 4 |
| Franz Herbert | F | Fr. | 3 | 0 | 2 | 2 | 2 |
| Warren Sharples | G | Jr. | 33 | 0 | 1 | 1 | 4 |
| Vaclav Nedomansky | F | Fr. | 5 | 0 | 0 | 0 | 2 |
| Tim Keough | G | Fr. | 13 | 0 | 0 | 0 | 4 |

## Michigan State University
Overall: 37-9-1; CCHA: 25-6-1

| | Pos. | Class | Games | G. | A. | Pts. | Pen. |
|---|---|---|---|---|---|---|---|
| Bobby Reynolds | F | Sr. | 47 | 36 | 41 | 77 | 78 |
| Kip Miller | F | Jr. | 47 | 32 | 45 | 77 | 94 |
| Danton Cole | F | Sr. | 47 | 29 | 33 | 62 | 46 |
| Pat Murray | F | So. | 46 | 21 | 41 | 62 | 65 |

|  | Pos. | Class | Games | G. | A. | Pts. | Pen. |
|---|---|---|---|---|---|---|---|
| Rod Brind'Amour | F | Fr. | 42 | 27 | 32 | 59 | 63 |
| Steve Beadle | D | Jr. | 46 | 14 | 40 | 54 | 35 |
| Peter White | F | Fr. | 46 | 20 | 33 | 53 | 17 |
| Shawn Heaphy | F | So. | 47 | 26 | 17 | 43 | 80 |
| Dwayne Norris | F | Fr. | 47 | 16 | 23 | 39 | 40 |
| Jason Woolley | D | Fr. | 47 | 12 | 25 | 37 | 26 |
| Brad Hamilton | D | Sr. | 47 | 9 | 20 | 29 | 86 |
| Kerry Russell | F | So. | 46 | 5 | 23 | 28 | 50 |
| Chris Luongo | D | Sr. | 47 | 4 | 21 | 25 | 42 |
| Don Gibson | D | Jr. | 39 | 7 | 10 | 17 | 107 |
| Walt Bartels | F | So. | 45 | 5 | 9 | 14 | 12 |
| Jim Cummins | F | Fr. | 36 | 3 | 9 | 12 | 100 |
| Joby Messier | D | Fr. | 46 | 2 | 10 | 12 | 70 |
| Mark Hirth | F | Fr. | 40 | 6 | 1 | 7 | 8 |
| Mike O'Toole | F | Jr. | 24 | 3 | 1 | 4 | 28 |
| Jason Muzzatti | G | So. | 42 | 0 | 3 | 3 | 35 |
| Mike Gilmore | G | Fr. | 3 | 0 | 1 | 1 | 2 |
| Chris Marshall | F | So. | 7 | 0 | 1 | 1 | 11 |
| Doug Collins | D | Fr. | 5 | 0 | 0 | 0 | 0 |
| Jamie Stewart | G | So. | 5 | 0 | 0 | 0 | 0 |

## Michigan Technological University
Overall: 15-25-2; WCHA: 15-19-1

|  | Pos. | Class | Games | G. | A. | Pts. | Pen. |
|---|---|---|---|---|---|---|---|
| Shawn Harrison | F | Jr. | 42 | 17 | 33 | 50 | 58 |
| Tom Bissett | F | Sr. | 42 | 19 | 28 | 47 | 16 |
| Kelly Hurd | F | So. | 42 | 18 | 14 | 32 | 36 |
| Kip Noble | D | Jr. | 42 | 8 | 22 | 30 | 38 |
| Jamie Steer | F | Fr. | 42 | 13 | 16 | 29 | 22 |
| Ron Rolston | F | Jr. | 32 | 14 | 11 | 25 | 50 |
| Scott White | D | Sr. | 38 | 6 | 18 | 24 | 38 |
| Jim Carroll | F | Jr. | 29 | 10 | 13 | 23 | 37 |
| Richard Novak | F | Sr. | 40 | 10 | 11 | 21 | 26 |
| Jay Luknowsky | F | So. | 30 | 8 | 12 | 20 | 40 |
| Jamie Russell | D | Sr. | 40 | 4 | 10 | 14 | 57 |
| Davis Payne | F | Fr. | 35 | 5 | 3 | 8 | 39 |
| Greg Parnell | F | Fr. | 36 | 3 | 4 | 7 | 8 |
| Rob Cederberg | F | Sr. | 38 | 3 | 4 | 7 | 36 |
| Steve Wendorf | D | Sr. | 42 | 1 | 6 | 7 | 36 |
| Jeff St. Cyr | D | Jr. | 41 | 0 | 7 | 7 | 79 |
| Damian Rhodes | G | So. | 37 | 1 | 3 | 4 | 0 |
| Darcy Martini | D | Fr. | 37 | 1 | 2 | 3 | 107 |
| Rob Tustian | F | So. | 37 | 0 | 3 | 3 | 51 |
| Jay Boxer | F | Fr. | 12 | 1 | 0 | 1 | 9 |
| Brent Ketzenberger | F | Fr. | 5 | 0 | 0 | 0 | 0 |
| Rob Pallante | D | Fr. | 6 | 0 | 0 | 0 | 0 |
| Geoff Sarjeant | G | Fr. | 6 | 0 | 0 | 0 | 2 |
| Dennis Young | F | Fr. | 7 | 0 | 0 | 0 | 12 |
| Tim Hartnett | F | Fr. | 12 | 0 | 0 | 0 | 0 |
| Reid McDonald | F | Fr. | 18 | 0 | 0 | 0 | 12 |

## University of Minnesota
Overall: 34-11-3; WCHA: 27-6-2

|  | Pos. | Class | Games | G. | A. | Pts. | Pen. |
|---|---|---|---|---|---|---|---|
| Tom Chorske | F | Jr. | 37 | 25 | 24 | 49 | 28 |
| Dave Snuggerud | F | Jr. | 45 | 29 | 20 | 49 | 39 |
| Jason Miller | F | So. | 47 | 16 | 29 | 45 | 8 |
| Peter Hankinson | F | Jr. | 48 | 16 | 27 | 43 | 42 |
| Larry Olimb | F | Fr. | 47 | 10 | 29 | 39 | 50 |
| Todd Richards | D | Sr. | 46 | 6 | 32 | 38 | 60 |
| Grant Bischoff | F | So. | 47 | 21 | 16 | 37 | 14 |
| Jon Anderson | F | Jr. | 47 | 20 | 16 | 36 | 52 |
| Randy Skarda | D | Jr. | 43 | 6 | 24 | 30 | 91 |
| Tom Pederson | D | Fr. | 42 | 5 | 24 | 29 | 46 |
| Cory Laylin | F | Fr. | 47 | 14 | 10 | 24 | 24 |
| Ken Gernander | F | So. | 44 | 9 | 11 | 20 | 2 |
| Dean Williamson | F | Jr. | 38 | 11 | 9 | 20 | 38 |
| Ben Hankinson | F | So. | 43 | 7 | 11 | 18 | 115 |
| Brett Strot | F | Jr. | 35 | 6 | 11 | 17 | 16 |
| Lance Pitlick | D | Jr. | 47 | 4 | 9 | 13 | 95 |
| David Espe | D | Sr. | 47 | 0 | 11 | 11 | 61 |

| | Pos. | Class | Games | G. | A. | Pts. | Pen. |
|---|---|---|---|---|---|---|---|
| Brett Nelson | D | Sr. | 38 | 1 | 8 | 9 | 27 |
| Luke Johnson | D | So. | 21 | 2 | 6 | 8 | 12 |
| Scott Bloom | F | Jr. | 19 | 2 | 5 | 7 | 22 |
| Robb Stauber | G | Jr. | 34 | 0 | 7 | 7 | 10 |
| Lance Werness | F | So. | 13 | 2 | 4 | 6 | 12 |
| Jake Enebak | F | So. | 15 | 1 | 2 | 3 | 26 |
| Jeff Stolp | G | Fr. | 16 | 0 | 1 | 1 | 0 |
| Jeff Pauletti | D | Jr. | 1 | 0 | 0 | 0 | 0 |
| Al Fritsinger | G | So. | 5 | 0 | 0 | 0 | 0 |
| Jeff Johnson | F | Jr. | 2 | 0 | 0 | 0 | 2 |
| Rob Potter | F | So. | 1 | 0 | 0 | 0 | 0 |

## University of Minnesota-Duluth
Overall: 15-23-2; WCHA: 12-21-2

| | Pos. | Class | Games | G. | A. | Pts. | Pen. |
|---|---|---|---|---|---|---|---|
| Dale Jago | D | Jr. | 40 | 12 | 24 | 36 | 52 |
| Jerry Chumola | F | So. | 40 | 18 | 17 | 35 | 16 |
| Chris Lindberg | F | So. | 36 | 15 | 18 | 33 | 51 |
| Dennis Vaske | D | Jr. | 37 | 9 | 19 | 28 | 86 |
| Scott Keller | F | So. | 40 | 9 | 18 | 27 | 34 |
| Sandy Smith | F | Jr. | 40 | 6 | 16 | 22 | 75 |
| Shawn Howard | F | So. | 39 | 7 | 9 | 16 | 31 |
| Darrin Amundson | F | So. | 37 | 5 | 11 | 16 | 23 |
| Darren Nauss | F | So. | 40 | 10 | 4 | 14 | 40 |
| Stu Plante | F | Jr. | 38 | 7 | 6 | 13 | 34 |
| Wane Sager | F | Fr. | 37 | 6 | 7 | 13 | 6 |
| Shjon Podein | F | Jr. | 36 | 7 | 5 | 12 | 46 |
| Greg Andrusak | D | So. | 35 | 4 | 8 | 12 | 74 |
| Kris Miller | D | So. | 39 | 2 | 10 | 12 | 37 |
| Doug Torrel | F | Fr. | 40 | 4 | 6 | 10 | 36 |
| Kevin Kaiser | F | Fr. | 40 | 2 | 5 | 7 | 26 |
| Pat Janostin | D | Sr. | 40 | 1 | 6 | 7 | 36 |
| Jon Rohloff | D | Fr. | 39 | 1 | 2 | 3 | 44 |
| Glen Lang | F | Fr. | 7 | 0 | 3 | 3 | 0 |
| Kevin Starren | D | Fr. | 7 | 1 | 0 | 1 | 2 |
| Terry Shold | F | Sr. | 2 | 0 | 1 | 1 | 0 |
| Steve Cronkhite | F | Fr. | 6 | 0 | 1 | 1 | 0 |
| John Hyduke | G | Sr. | 28 | 0 | 1 | 1 | 0 |
| Tom Hanson | D | Sr. | 3 | 0 | 0 | 0 | 4 |
| Chad Erickson | G | Fr. | 15 | 0 | 0 | 0 | 4 |

## University of New Hampshire
Overall: 12-22-0; Hockey East: 9-17-0

| | Pos. | Class | Games | G. | A. | Pts. | Pen. |
|---|---|---|---|---|---|---|---|
| Joe Flanagan | F | Fr. | 34 | 23 | 11 | 34 | 4 |
| David Aiken | F | Jr. | 34 | 14 | 17 | 31 | 30 |
| Chris Winnes | F | So. | 30 | 11 | 20 | 31 | 22 |
| Steve Horner | F | Sr. | 32 | 15 | 13 | 28 | 14 |
| Tim Shields | F | Sr. | 30 | 9 | 18 | 27 | 34 |
| Jeff Lazaro | D | Jr. | 31 | 8 | 14 | 22 | 38 |
| Dominic Amodeo | F | Fr. | 32 | 6 | 12 | 18 | 10 |
| Chris Grassie | D | Jr. | 32 | 4 | 12 | 16 | 22 |
| Scott Morrow | F | Fr. | 19 | 6 | 7 | 13 | 14 |
| Kevin Dean | D | So. | 34 | 1 | 12 | 13 | 28 |
| Mark McGinn | F | Fr. | 23 | 3 | 7 | 10 | 18 |
| Savo Mitrovic | F | Fr. | 34 | 2 | 8 | 10 | 22 |
| Mark Johnson | F | Jr. | 28 | 3 | 5 | 8 | 2 |
| Greg Boudreau | D | Sr. | 16 | 1 | 4 | 5 | 8 |
| Burce MacDonald | F | So. | 21 | 1 | 3 | 4 | 8 |
| David MacIntyre | D | So. | 33 | 0 | 4 | 4 | 24 |
| Adam Hayes | F | Fr. | 10 | 1 | 1 | 2 | 4 |
| Dan Prachar | F | Sr. | 33 | 1 | 1 | 2 | 4 |
| Pat Morrison | G | So. | 25 | 0 | 2 | 2 | 4 |
| Bill LaCouture | F | So. | 20 | 1 | 0 | 1 | 2 |
| Frank Messina | D | So. | 24 | 1 | 0 | 1 | 12 |
| Matt Trenovich | D | So. | 10 | 0 | 1 | 1 | 10 |
| Riel Bellegard | F | So. | 24 | 0 | 1 | 1 | 14 |
| Pat Szturm | G | Jr. | 11 | 0 | 0 | 0 | 8 |
| Steve Morrow | D | Fr. | 30 | 0 | 0 | 0 | 28 |

## University of North Dakota
Overall: 22-18-1; WCHA: 19-15-1

|  | Pos. | Class | Games | G. | A. | Pts. | Pen. |
|---|---|---|---|---|---|---|---|
| Lee Davidson | F | Jr. | 41 | 16 | 37 | 53 | 60 |
| Scott Koberinski | F | Sr. | 40 | 15 | 26 | 41 | 48 |
| Neil Eisenhut | F | So. | 41 | 22 | 16 | 38 | 20 |
| Russ Parent | D | Jr. | 40 | 9 | 28 | 37 | 51 |
| Jason Herter | D | Fr. | 41 | 8 | 24 | 32 | 62 |
| Russ Romaniuk | F | Fr. | 39 | 17 | 14 | 31 | 32 |
| Garry Valk | F | So. | 40 | 14 | 17 | 31 | 71 |
| Grant Paranica | F | Sr. | 39 | 14 | 13 | 27 | 63 |
| Brent Bobyck | F | Jr. | 28 | 11 | 8 | 19 | 16 |
| Dixon Ward | F | Fr. | 37 | 8 | 9 | 17 | 26 |
| Mike LaMoine | D | Sr. | 40 | 3 | 12 | 15 | 51 |
| Ross Johnson | F | So. | 19 | 5 | 7 | 12 | 6 |
| David Marvin | D | So. | 38 | 4 | 6 | 10 | 24 |
| Dane Jackson | F | Fr. | 30 | 4 | 5 | 9 | 33 |
| Murray Baron | D | Jr. | 40 | 2 | 6 | 8 | 92 |
| John Hanson | F | Fr. | 23 | 2 | 4 | 6 | 18 |
| Matt Morelli | F | So. | 20 | 4 | 1 | 5 | 2 |
| Justin Duberman | F | Fr. | 36 | 3 | 2 | 5 | 36 |
| Mike McCormick | F | So. | 29 | 1 | 4 | 5 | 22 |
| Shane McFarlane | F | So. | 30 | 1 | 4 | 5 | 8 |
| Wade Bartley | D | Fr. | 32 | 1 | 1 | 2 | 8 |
| Jeoff Smith | D | So. | 9 | 0 | 1 | 1 | 14 |
| Greg Geldart | D | Fr. | 1 | 0 | 0 | 0 | 0 |
| Brad Pascall | D | Fr. | 3 | 0 | 0 | 0 | 0 |
| Tony Couture | G | So. | 7 | 0 | 0 | 0 | 4 |
| Steve Peters | G | So. | 9 | 0 | 0 | 0 | 2 |
| Chris Dickson | G | So. | 29 | 0 | 0 | 0 | 10 |

## Northeastern University
Overall: 18-16-2; Hockey East: 13-11-2

|  | Pos. | Class | Games | G. | A. | Pts. | Pen. |
|---|---|---|---|---|---|---|---|
| Dave Buda | F | Sr. | 35 | 23 | 23 | 46 | 45 |
| Harry Mews | F | Jr. | 31 | 18 | 24 | 42 | 103 |
| Rob Cowie | D | So. | 36 | 7 | 34 | 41 | 60 |
| Rico Rossi | F | Sr. | 29 | 12 | 18 | 30 | 102 |
| Brian Sullivan | F | So. | 34 | 13 | 14 | 27 | 65 |
| Andy May | F | Jr. | 30 | 12 | 14 | 26 | 43 |
| Keith Cyr | F | Fr. | 34 | 14 | 11 | 25 | 22 |
| Jay Schiavo | F | Fr. | 36 | 11 | 13 | 24 | 10 |
| Will Averill | D | So. | 36 | 4 | 16 | 20 | 40 |
| Robbie Grant | F | So. | 28 | 5 | 12 | 17 | 16 |
| Tom Bivona | F | Jr. | 33 | 10 | 6 | 16 | 31 |
| Matt Saunders | F | Fr. | 27 | 8 | 8 | 16 | 17 |
| Paul Sacco | D | Fr. | 35 | 3 | 12 | 15 | 10 |
| Marty Raus | D | Sr. | 34 | 4 | 10 | 14 | 51 |
| Peter Schure | F | So. | 26 | 7 | 6 | 13 | 33 |
| Mike Jankowski | F | So. | 29 | 5 | 7 | 12 | 18 |
| Sean Curtin | F | So. | 25 | 4 | 6 | 10 | 10 |
| Mike Roberts | D | Jr. | 32 | 2 | 6 | 8 | 10 |
| Matt Sweeney | F | So. | 20 | 3 | 4 | 7 | 4 |
| Paul Flanagan | D | Fr. | 25 | 1 | 4 | 5 | 24 |
| Steve Schofield | D | Sr. | 18 | 0 | 4 | 4 | 12 |
| Rich Burchill | G | Sr. | 30 | 0 | 1 | 1 | 6 |
| Keith Slifstein | F | Fr. | 1 | 0 | 0 | 0 | 0 |
| Jim Abban | F | Fr. | 2 | 0 | 0 | 0 | 0 |
| Greg McGlame | F | Fr. | 2 | 0 | 0 | 0 | 0 |
| Paul Russo | F | So. | 2 | 0 | 0 | 0 | 0 |
| John Schultz | F | Fr. | 3 | 0 | 0 | 0 | 2 |
| Tom Cole | G | Fr. | 6 | 0 | 0 | 0 | 0 |

## Northern Michigan University
Overall: 26-17-2; WCHA: 20-13-2

|  | Pos. | Class | Games | G. | A. | Pts. | Pen. |
|---|---|---|---|---|---|---|---|
| Phil Berger | F | Sr. | 44 | 30 | 33 | 63 | 24 |
| Dean Antos | F | So. | 45 | 25 | 24 | 49 | 28 |
| Dallas Drake | F | Fr. | 45 | 18 | 24 | 42 | 26 |
| Darryl Olsen | F | Fr. | 45 | 16 | 26 | 42 | 88 |
| Troy Jacobsen | F | Sr. | 45 | 11 | 28 | 39 | 50 |

| | Pos. | Class | Games | G. | A. | Pts. | Pen. |
|---|---|---|---|---|---|---|---|
| Eric LeMarque | F | Jr. | 43 | 20 | 17 | 37 | 40 |
| Pete Podrasky | D | Jr. | 43 | 5 | 31 | 36 | 28 |
| Darryl Plandowski | F | So. | 44 | 9 | 22 | 31 | 52 |
| Jeff Gawlicki | F | Jr. | 45 | 16 | 11 | 27 | 99 |
| Phil Soukoroff | D | Fr. | 45 | 5 | 22 | 27 | 26 |
| Kevin Scott | F | So. | 40 | 11 | 14 | 25 | 36 |
| Doug Garrow | F | Jr. | 44 | 11 | 11 | 22 | 72 |
| John Goode | D | Sr. | 41 | 5 | 17 | 22 | 60 |
| Brad Werenka | D | Jr. | 28 | 7 | 13 | 20 | 16 |
| Phil Brown | F | Jr. | 43 | 6 | 14 | 20 | 28 |
| Ed Ward | F | So. | 42 | 5 | 15 | 20 | 36 |
| Dave Porter | F | Jr. | 31 | 5 | 9 | 14 | 16 |
| Dave Shyiak | F | So. | 24 | 2 | 5 | 7 | 22 |
| Lou Melone | D | Fr. | 24 | 3 | 2 | 5 | 8 |
| Perry Florio | D | Jr. | 10 | 0 | 4 | 4 | 8 |
| Mark Beaufait | F | Fr. | 11 | 2 | 1 | 3 | 2 |
| Bill Pye | G | So. | 43 | 0 | 2 | 2 | 8 |
| Phil Neururer | D | Fr. | 23 | 0 | 1 | 1 | 12 |
| Dean Hall | F | Jr. | 2 | 0 | 0 | 0 | 0 |
| Mark Olson | F | Fr. | 3 | 0 | 0 | 0 | 0 |
| Willie Mitchell | G | Fr. | 8 | 0 | 0 | 0 | 0 |

## Ohio State University
Overall: 9-26-5; CCHA: 7-20-5

| | Pos. | Class | Games | G. | A. | Pts. | Pen. |
|---|---|---|---|---|---|---|---|
| Andy Forcey | F | Sr. | 39 | 15 | 33 | 48 | 57 |
| Paul Rutherford | F | So. | 39 | 16 | 27 | 43 | 52 |
| Derek Higdon | F | Jr. | 38 | 19 | 15 | 34 | 82 |
| Scott Rex | D | Jr. | 40 | 6 | 24 | 30 | 86 |
| Don Oliver | F | So. | 39 | 15 | 14 | 29 | 29 |
| Daryn Fersovich | F | Sr. | 39 | 10 | 17 | 27 | 4 |
| Dan Wilhelm | F | Sr. | 40 | 7 | 12 | 19 | 38 |
| Stacey Hartnell | F | So. | 39 | 12 | 6 | 18 | 36 |
| Rob Schriner | F | Fr. | 35 | 6 | 7 | 13 | 37 |
| Greg Beaucage | F | Fr. | 37 | 5 | 8 | 13 | 85 |
| David Smith | F | Fr. | 21 | 5 | 7 | 12 | 26 |
| Sean Hartnell | D | So. | 40 | 1 | 11 | 12 | 89 |
| Greg Burke | F | Fr. | 40 | 3 | 8 | 11 | 44 |
| Eric Reisman | D | So. | 38 | 4 | 6 | 10 | 56 |
| Brian Baldrica | D | Fr. | 38 | 5 | 4 | 9 | 31 |
| Scott Walsh | F | Fr. | 37 | 7 | 1 | 8 | 6 |
| Sean Clifford | D | Sr. | 17 | 1 | 7 | 8 | 18 |
| Marko Kreus | D | Fr. | 24 | 2 | 3 | 5 | 10 |
| Butch Kowalka | D | Fr. | 9 | 1 | 2 | 3 | 0 |
| Paul Forfia | F | Fr. | 15 | 1 | 2 | 3 | 8 |
| Jeff Ladrow | F | Jr. | 19 | 0 | 2 | 2 | 20 |
| Al Novakowski | D | So. | 2 | 0 | 1 | 1 | 6 |
| Todd Fanning | G | Jr. | 33 | 0 | 1 | 1 | 6 |
| Hank Horn | G | Sr. | 1 | 0 | 0 | 0 | 0 |
| Rick Faull | F | Fr. | 11 | 0 | 0 | 0 | 2 |
| Roger Beedon | G | Sr. | 12 | 0 | 0 | 0 | 0 |

## Princeton University
Overall: 6-19-1; ECAC: 4-17-1

| | Pos. | Class | Games | G. | A. | Pts. | Pen. |
|---|---|---|---|---|---|---|---|
| John Messuri | F | Sr. | 26 | 12 | 38 | 50 | 32 |
| Andre Faust | F | Fr. | 26 | 18 | 16 | 34 | 34 |
| Bart Blaeser | F | Jr. | 26 | 11 | 19 | 30 | 26 |
| Greg Polaski | F | Jr. | 17 | 9 | 14 | 23 | 26 |
| Mark Khozozian | F | Jr. | 13 | 9 | 8 | 17 | 16 |
| Andy Cesarski | D | So. | 26 | 6 | 10 | 16 | 34 |
| Kevin Sullivan | F | Jr. | 26 | 7 | 7 | 14 | 58 |
| Sean Murphy | F | So. | 26 | 5 | 8 | 13 | 16 |
| Chris Hughes | F | Sr. | 19 | 3 | 7 | 10 | 26 |
| Mike McKee | D | Fr. | 23 | 4 | 4 | 8 | 25 |
| Chris Tatum | F | Jr. | 26 | 2 | 6 | 8 | 24 |
| Danny Maze | F | Jr. | 24 | 3 | 4 | 7 | 20 |
| Mike Cole | F | So. | 22 | 2 | 4 | 6 | 6 |
| Nate Smith | D | Jr. | 24 | 1 | 5 | 6 | 12 |
| Tom Shimabukuro | F | So. | 25 | 3 | 2 | 5 | 2 |
| Dan Slattalla | F | Fr. | 11 | 0 | 5 | 5 | 10 |

| | Pos. | Class | Games | G. | A. | Pts. | Pen. |
|---|---|---|---|---|---|---|---|
| Christian DeFazio | D | Jr. | 22 | 0 | 4 | 4 | 6 |
| Jeff Kampersal | D | Fr. | 26 | 0 | 3 | 3 | 32 |
| Joel Gaustad | F | So. | 8 | 1 | 1 | 2 | 2 |
| Sean Gorman | D | So. | 17 | 0 | 2 | 2 | 20 |
| Ward Welles | F | Jr. | 4 | 1 | 0 | 1 | 0 |
| Jim Sourges | F | Jr. | 12 | 0 | 1 | 1 | 4 |
| Jack Craig | D | Fr. | 15 | 0 | 1 | 1 | 14 |
| Brent Johnston | D | Fr. | 1 | 0 | 0 | 0 | 0 |
| Chris Stewart | F | Fr. | 3 | 0 | 0 | 0 | 2 |
| Ron High | G | So. | 12 | 0 | 0 | 0 | 0 |
| Mark Salsbury | G | So. | 23 | 0 | 0 | 0 | 0 |

## Providence College
Overall: 22-18-2; Hockey East: 13-11-2

| | Pos. | Class | Games | G. | A. | Pts. | Pen. |
|---|---|---|---|---|---|---|---|
| Rob Gaudreau | F | Fr. | 42 | 28 | 29 | 57 | 32 |
| Mike Boback | F | Fr. | 38 | 21 | 27 | 48 | 26 |
| Rick Bennett | F | Jr. | 32 | 14 | 32 | 46 | 74 |
| Mario Aube | F | So. | 42 | 22 | 23 | 45 | 40 |
| Jim Hughes | D | Sr. | 39 | 10 | 20 | 30 | 43 |
| John Ferguson | F | Sr. | 40 | 14 | 15 | 29 | 66 |
| Lyle Wildgoose | F | So. | 32 | 11 | 17 | 28 | 34 |
| Pat Becker | F | Jr. | 42 | 7 | 11 | 18 | 22 |
| Jeff Serowik | D | Jr. | 35 | 3 | 14 | 17 | 48 |
| Paul Saundercook | D | Jr. | 42 | 1 | 13 | 14 | 70 |
| Pat Madigan | F | So. | 39 | 4 | 8 | 12 | 36 |
| John Butterworth | F | Sr. | 34 | 4 | 7 | 11 | 29 |
| Shaun Kane | D | Fr. | 37 | 2 | 9 | 11 | 54 |
| Mike Dempsey | F | So. | 22 | 6 | 4 | 10 | 26 |
| Bob Creamer | F | Fr. | 40 | 5 | 4 | 9 | 30 |
| Todd Whittemore | F | Jr. | 29 | 7 | 1 | 8 | 28 |
| Dave Guden | F | Jr. | 31 | 2 | 6 | 8 | 14 |
| Paul Flaherty | F | So. | 19 | 3 | 2 | 5 | 30 |
| Jeff Robison | D | Fr. | 41 | 0 | 5 | 5 | 36 |
| Larry Rooney | D | So. | 10 | 0 | 4 | 4 | 18 |
| Steve Higgins | D | Jr. | 36 | 1 | 2 | 3 | 16 |
| Joe DiGiacomo | D | Jr. | 18 | 1 | 1 | 2 | 23 |
| Mark Romaine | G | Jr. | 29 | 0 | 1 | 1 | 2 |
| Mark Doshan | F | Fr. | 2 | 0 | 0 | 0 | 0 |
| Rich Newar | F | Sr. | 7 | 0 | 0 | 0 | 0 |
| Ken Sweezey | F | Jr. | 7 | 0 | 0 | 0 | 0 |
| Matt Merten | G | Jr. | 20 | 0 | 0 | 0 | 0 |

## Rensselaer Polytechnic Institute
Overall: 12-17-3; ECAC: 8-12-2

| | Pos. | Class | Games | G. | A. | Pts. | Pen. |
|---|---|---|---|---|---|---|---|
| Joey Juneau | F | So. | 30 | 12 | 23 | 35 | 40 |
| Kevin Mazzella | F | Jr. | 31 | 16 | 16 | 32 | 34 |
| Bruce Coles | F | So. | 27 | 8 | 14 | 22 | 66 |
| Denis Poissant | F | Jr. | 29 | 8 | 14 | 22 | 14 |
| Graeme Townshend | F | Sr. | 31 | 6 | 16 | 22 | 50 |
| Tony Hejna | F | Jr. | 29 | 12 | 9 | 21 | 14 |
| Gary Woolford | F | So. | 29 | 8 | 9 | 17 | 20 |
| Brian Ferreira | F-D | Jr. | 15 | 3 | 13 | 16 | 28 |
| Bill Flanagan | F | Jr. | 24 | 8 | 7 | 15 | 14 |
| Mickey LeBlanc | F | So. | 27 | 8 | 7 | 15 | 14 |
| Tim Roberts | F | So. | 27 | 4 | 11 | 15 | 50 |
| Rob Schena | D | Sr. | 32 | 7 | 5 | 12 | 64 |
| Steve Moore | D | Sr. | 32 | 2 | 10 | 12 | 61 |
| Stephane Robitaille | D | Fr. | 22 | 3 | 8 | 11 | 4 |
| Dave Casalena | F | So. | 22 | 5 | 5 | 10 | 33 |
| Rick Borina | F | Fr. | 26 | 2 | 8 | 10 | 22 |
| Ryan Kummu | D | Sr. | 29 | 2 | 5 | 7 | 28 |
| Ivan Moore | F | Fr. | 27 | 0 | 6 | 6 | 24 |
| Phil Kenner | F | So. | 10 | 2 | 2 | 4 | 2 |
| Zachary Dargaty | D | Fr. | 25 | 1 | 1 | 2 | 16 |
| Todd Hilditch | D | Fr. | 29 | 1 | 1 | 2 | 56 |
| Sean Sarbacker | G | Jr. | 1 | 0 | 0 | 0 | 0 |
| Jamie Bellanca | G | So. | 4 | 0 | 0 | 0 | 0 |
| Sean Kennedy | G | Fr. | 15 | 0 | 0 | 0 | 0 |
| Dan Vaillant | D | Fr. | 16 | 0 | 0 | 0 | 10 |
| Steve Duncan | G | Sr. | 22 | 0 | 0 | 0 | 2 |

## St. Lawrence University
Overall: 29-7-0; ECAC: 18-4-0

| | Pos. | Class | Games | G. | A. | Pts. | Pen. |
|---|---|---|---|---|---|---|---|
| Andy Pritchard | F | So. | 35 | 27 | 23 | 50 | 43 |
| Joe Day | F | Jr. | 36 | 21 | 27 | 48 | 44 |
| Doug Murray | F | Jr. | 36 | 13 | 35 | 48 | 32 |
| Mike Hurlbut | D | Sr. | 36 | 8 | 25 | 33 | 30 |
| Dave Witherell | F | Sr. | 36 | 15 | 16 | 31 | 11 |
| Gary Robertson | F | Sr. | 35 | 16 | 12 | 28 | 66 |
| Jamie Baker | F | Sr. | 13 | 11 | 16 | 27 | 16 |
| Marty Ball | F | Jr. | 36 | 11 | 15 | 26 | 40 |
| Shawn Rivers | D | Fr. | 36 | 3 | 23 | 26 | 20 |
| Chris Consorte | F | Jr. | 35 | 15 | 9 | 24 | 70 |
| Rob White | D | Jr. | 35 | 5 | 19 | 24 | 64 |
| Russ Mann | D | Sr. | 35 | 7 | 12 | 19 | 44 |
| Bill MacCuaig | F | So. | 34 | 5 | 8 | 13 | 10 |
| Kevin Wright | F | Jr. | 30 | 6 | 6 | 12 | 38 |
| Dan Laperriere | D | Fr. | 34 | 1 | 11 | 12 | 14 |
| Brad James | D | Jr. | 36 | 2 | 9 | 11 | 48 |
| Martin LaCroix | F | Fr. | 19 | 1 | 5 | 6 | 23 |
| Mike Polomsky | F | Fr. | 19 | 2 | 1 | 3 | 8 |
| Sean Lundin | D | Fr. | 29 | 0 | 3 | 3 | 14 |
| Teddy Dent | F | Fr. | 13 | 0 | 2 | 2 | 12 |
| Paul Cohen | G | Sr. | 25 | 0 | 2 | 2 | 4 |
| Phil Polomsky | F | Fr. | 13 | 0 | 1 | 1 | 2 |
| Rich Stewart | D | Sr. | 1 | 0 | 0 | 0 | 2 |
| Steve Torkos | D | Jr. | 2 | 0 | 0 | 0 | 4 |
| Mike Mudd | G | Jr. | 4 | 0 | 0 | 0 | 0 |
| Chris Wells | F | Fr. | 13 | 0 | 0 | 0 | 6 |
| Les Kuntar | G | So. | 14 | 0 | 0 | 0 | 4 |

## University of Vermont
Overall: 20-13-1; ECAC: 13-9-0

| | Pos. | Class | Games | G. | A. | Pts. | Pen. |
|---|---|---|---|---|---|---|---|
| Kyle McDonough | F | Sr. | 34 | 27 | 28 | 55 | 60 |
| Ian Boyce | F | Sr. | 31 | 15 | 27 | 42 | 28 |
| Jim Larkin | F | Fr. | 34 | 16 | 19 | 35 | 8 |
| Jim Walsh | F | Sr. | 34 | 14 | 19 | 33 | 40 |
| Ricker Love | F | So. | 32 | 9 | 20 | 29 | 20 |
| Duke Stump | F | Sr. | 26 | 12 | 16 | 28 | 28 |
| Jerry Tarrant | D | Sr. | 34 | 3 | 19 | 22 | 54 |
| Dan Lambert | F | Sr. | 34 | 11 | 10 | 21 | 10 |
| John LeClair | F | So. | 18 | 9 | 12 | 21 | 40 |
| Marc Lebreux | D | Sr. | 34 | 8 | 10 | 18 | 36 |
| David Browne | F | So. | 32 | 5 | 10 | 15 | 22 |
| Jim Fernholz | F | So. | 28 | 3 | 11 | 14 | 16 |
| Dennis Miller | D | Sr. | 34 | 3 | 9 | 12 | 12 |
| Mike McLaughlin | F | Fr. | 32 | 5 | 6 | 11 | 12 |
| Stephane Venne | D | So. | 19 | 4 | 5 | 9 | 35 |
| Dave Weber | F-D | Jr. | 33 | 4 | 3 | 7 | 40 |
| Jeff Schulman | D | Sr. | 34 | 3 | 4 | 7 | 22 |
| Bill Butler | F | Jr. | 10 | 1 | 6 | 7 | 8 |
| Jeremy Benoit | D | Fr. | 17 | 0 | 6 | 6 | 4 |
| Scott Jagod | F | So. | 17 | 2 | 3 | 5 | 2 |
| Rob Bateman | D | So. | 32 | 1 | 4 | 5 | 38 |
| Leif Selstad | F | Fr. | 13 | 3 | 1 | 4 | 12 |
| Mike Millham | G | So. | 28 | 0 | 1 | 1 | 2 |
| Elias Delany | G | Sr. | 4 | 0 | 0 | 0 | 0 |
| Phil Marrandette | G | Sr. | 4 | 0 | 0 | 0 | 4 |

## Western Michigan University
Overall: 14-23-6; CCHA: 9-17-6

| | Pos. | Class | Games | G. | A. | Pts. | Pen. |
|---|---|---|---|---|---|---|---|
| Paul Polillo | F | Jr. | 41 | 20 | 46 | 66 | 32 |
| Ron Hoover | F | Sr. | 42 | 32 | 27 | 59 | 66 |
| Jeff Green | F | Jr. | 35 | 23 | 29 | 52 | 68 |
| Bill Armstrong | F | Jr. | 40 | 23 | 19 | 42 | 97 |
| Mike Posma | D | Jr. | 43 | 7 | 34 | 41 | 58 |
| Shane Redshaw | F | Jr. | 31 | 10 | 19 | 29 | 77 |
| Chris Clarke | D | So. | 38 | 3 | 21 | 24 | 51 |
| Mike Eastwood | F | So. | 40 | 10 | 13 | 23 | 87 |
| Keith Jones | F | Fr. | 37 | 9 | 12 | 21 | 65 |

|  | Pos. | Class | Games | G. | A. | Pts. | Pen. |
|---|---|---|---|---|---|---|---|
| Tom Auge | F | So. | 43 | 9 | 10 | 19 | 36 |
| Scott Garrow | F | Fr. | 43 | 7 | 7 | 14 | 30 |
| Mike Ross | D | So. | 30 | 5 | 8 | 13 | 24 |
| Chris Venkus | F | So. | 42 | 2 | 11 | 13 | 66 |
| Brian Tulik | D | So. | 43 | 7 | 5 | 12 | 62 |
| Rich Whitten | F-D | So. | 40 | 5 | 4 | 9 | 14 |
| Andy Rymsha | F | Jr. | 35 | 3 | 4 | 7 | 139 |
| Rob Pallin | F-D | Jr. | 36 | 3 | 4 | 7 | 18 |
| Doug Melnyk | D | Jr. | 30 | 2 | 4 | 6 | 28 |
| Andy Suhy | D | Fr. | 42 | 0 | 4 | 4 | 74 |
| Brad Dawson | F | Fr. | 23 | 2 | 0 | 2 | 6 |
| Bill Horn | G | Sr. | 37 | 0 | 1 | 1 | 13 |
| Todd Halloran | F | Fr. | 1 | 0 | 0 | 0 | 0 |
| Al Lariviere | G | So. | 1 | 0 | 0 | 0 | 0 |
| Todd Lawson | F | Sr. | 7 | 0 | 0 | 0 | 2 |
| Rob Laurie | G | Fr. | 9 | 0 | 0 | 0 | 0 |

## University of Wisconsin
Overall: 25-16-5; WCHA: 17-13-5

|  | Pos. | Class | Games | G. | A. | Pts. | Pen. |
|---|---|---|---|---|---|---|---|
| John Byce | F | Jr. | 42 | 27 | 28 | 55 | 16 |
| Doug MacDonald | F | Fr. | 44 | 23 | 25 | 48 | 50 |
| Chris Tancill | F | Jr. | 44 | 20 | 23 | 43 | 50 |
| Gary Shuchuk | F | Jr. | 46 | 18 | 19 | 37 | 102 |
| Paul Stanton | D | Sr. | 45 | 7 | 29 | 36 | 126 |
| Steve Rohlik | F | Jr. | 45 | 11 | 14 | 25 | 44 |
| Sean Hill | D | Fr. | 45 | 2 | 23 | 25 | 69 |
| Rob Andringa | D | So. | 45 | 2 | 19 | 21 | 52 |
| Don Granato | F | So. | 39 | 9 | 10 | 19 | 50 |
| Tom Sagissor | F | Jr. | 40 | 7 | 11 | 18 | 119 |
| Dennis Snedden | F | So. | 40 | 12 | 5 | 17 | 44 |
| Kurt Semandel | F | Sr. | 39 | 7 | 10 | 17 | 34 |
| Rob Mendel | D | Jr. | 44 | 1 | 14 | 15 | 37 |
| Brett Kurtz | F | Fr. | 44 | 4 | 9 | 13 | 22 |
| Greg Poss | F | Sr. | 38 | 5 | 4 | 9 | 32 |
| Jon Helgeson | F | So. | 36 | 7 | 1 | 8 | 28 |
| John Parker | F | Jr. | 20 | 1 | 7 | 8 | 16 |
| Joe Decker | F | So. | 35 | 2 | 5 | 7 | 6 |
| Chris Nelson | D | Fr. | 21 | 1 | 4 | 5 | 24 |
| Mark Osiecki | D | Jr. | 44 | 1 | 3 | 4 | 56 |
| Chris Jensen | D | So. | 2 | 1 | 0 | 1 | 0 |
| Rodger Sykes | D | So. | 27 | 0 | 1 | 1 | 24 |
| Chris Joseph | G | Fr. | 38 | 0 | 1 | 1 | 15 |
| Kurt Gonce | C | Jr. | 1 | 0 | 0 | 0 | 2 |
| John Lambie | G | Sr. | 1 | 0 | 0 | 0 | 0 |
| Duane Derksen | G | Fr. | 11 | 0 | 0 | 0 | 4 |

## Yale University
Overall: 11-19-1; ECAC: 10-12

|  | Pos. | Class | Games | G. | A. | Pts. | Pen. |
|---|---|---|---|---|---|---|---|
| Dave Baseggio | D | Sr. | 28 | 10 | 23 | 33 | 41 |
| Jeff Blaeser | F | Fr. | 31 | 8 | 19 | 27 | 12 |
| Julian Binavince | F | Sr. | 31 | 10 | 15 | 25 | 54 |
| Craig Ferguson | F | Fr. | 24 | 11 | 6 | 17 | 20 |
| Robert Bowse | F | So. | 30 | 12 | 4 | 16 | 4 |
| Chris Gruber | F | So. | 29 | 7 | 9 | 16 | 33 |
| Scott D'Orsi | F | Jr. | 26 | 5 | 10 | 15 | 28 |
| Scott Matusovich | D | Fr. | 25 | 3 | 11 | 14 | 40 |
| Tom Walsh | F | Sr. | 16 | 5 | 8 | 13 | 20 |
| Greg Harrison | D | Jr. | 30 | 3 | 9 | 12 | 51 |
| Billy Matthews | D | Jr. | 29 | 1 | 9 | 10 | 24 |
| Jason O'Neill | F | Jr. | 15 | 4 | 4 | 8 | 6 |
| Mike Miller | F | So. | 19 | 4 | 3 | 7 | 10 |
| Tom Bachner | F | Sr. | 29 | 3 | 4 | 7 | 22 |
| Greg Seitz | F | Jr. | 13 | 3 | 3 | 6 | 4 |
| John Sather | F | Fr. | 20 | 3 | 3 | 6 | 10 |
| John Moore | F | Sr. | 24 | 3 | 3 | 6 | 38 |
| Eric Thieringer | D | Sr. | 28 | 1 | 5 | 6 | 24 |
| Mike Abraham | F | Jr. | 11 | 2 | 3 | 5 | 19 |
| Marc Cridge | F | Sr. | 18 | 0 | 2 | 2 | 0 |
| Lance Marciano | D | So. | 24 | 1 | 0 | 1 | 26 |

| | Pos. | Class | Games | G. | A. | Pts. | Pen. |
|---|---|---|---|---|---|---|---|
| Ray Letourneau | G | So. | 7 | 0 | 1 | 1 | 0 |
| Erik O'Borsky | F | Jr. | 15 | 0 | 1 | 1 | 27 |
| Mike Dora | F | Sr. | 17 | 0 | 1 | 1 | 0 |
| Bruce Wolanin | D | So. | 19 | 0 | 1 | 1 | 28 |
| Mike O'Neill | G | Sr. | 25 | 0 | 0 | 0 | 4 |

## Collegiate Goaltending Records

| | G. | W. | L. | T. | Min. | Goals | Avg. |
|---|---|---|---|---|---|---|---|
| **AIR FORCE ACADEMY** | | | | | | | |
| Mark Liebich | 17 | 8 | 5 | 1 | 928 | 66 | 4.27 |
| Mike Blank | 15 | 6 | 7 | 2 | 840 | 61 | 4.36 |
| **(ARMY) U.S. MILITARY** | | | | | | | |
| Corey Averill | 10 | 5 | 4 | 0 | 527 | 32 | 3.64 |
| Brooks Chretien | 20 | 8 | 11 | 1 | 1176 | 75 | 3.83 |
| Brandon Hayes | 5 | 0 | 1 | 0 | 160 | 20 | 7.49 |
| **BOSTON COLLEGE** | | | | | | | |
| Sandy Galuppo | 12 | 6 | 2 | 0 | 525 | 28 | 3.20 |
| David Littman | 32 | 19 | 9 | 4 | 1945 | 107 | 3.30 |
| Jeff Walker | 2 | 0 | 0 | 0 | 10 | 1 | 6.00 |
| **BOSTON UNIVERSITY** | | | | | | | |
| Peter Fish | 17 | 6 | 10 | 0 | 1005 | 64 | 3.82 |
| Bryan LaFort | 11 | 3 | 7 | 0 | 584 | 48 | 4.93 |
| John Bradley | 11 | 5 | 4 | 1 | 583 | 53 | 5.45 |
| **BOWLING GREEN STATE UNIVERSITY** | | | | | | | |
| Christian Albitz | 2 | 0 | 0 | 0 | 3 | 0 | 0.00 |
| Paul Connell | 41 | 21 | 16 | 3 | 2439 | 140 | 3.44 |
| John Burke | 10 | 5 | 2 | 0 | 415 | 25 | 3.61 |
| **BROWN UNIVERSITY** | | | | | | | |
| Jamie Sullivan | 1 | 0 | 0 | 0 | 40 | 3 | 4.50 |
| Dan Quinn | 6 | 0 | 3 | 0 | 187 | 18 | 5.78 |
| Chris Harvey | 23 | 1 | 22 | 0 | 1327 | 131 | 5.92 |
| **CLARKSON UNIVERSITY** | | | | | | | |
| Jason Poirier | 16 | 7 | 5 | 1 | 789 | 46 | 3.50 |
| John Fletcher | 23 | 9 | 8 | 2 | 1147 | 79 | 4.14 |
| **COLGATE UNIVERSITY** | | | | | | | |
| Greg Menges | 6 | 2 | 1 | 0 | 260 | 16 | 3.70 |
| Dave Gagnon | 28 | 17 | 9 | 2 | 1622 | 102 | 3.77 |
| **COLORADO COLLEGE** | | | | | | | |
| Jon Gustafson | 14 | 5 | 5 | 0 | 673 | 48 | 4.28 |
| Derek Pizzey | 30 | 6 | 20 | 3 | 1703 | 122 | 4.30 |
| James MacDougall | 2 | 0 | 1 | 0 | 66 | 5 | 4.56 |
| **CORNELL UNIVERSITY** | | | | | | | |
| Jim Crozier | 5 | 1 | 0 | 0 | 127 | 2 | 0.94 |
| Corrie D'Alessio | 29 | 15 | 13 | 1 | 1684 | 96 | 3.42 |
| **DARTMOUTH COLLEGE** | | | | | | | |
| Tim Osby | 14 | 6 | 8 | 0 | 829 | 55 | 3.98 |
| Steve Laurin | 13 | 2 | 9 | 1 | 747 | 57 | 4.57 |
| **UNIVERSITY OF DENVER** | | | | | | | |
| Chris Gillies | 16 | 7 | 9 | 0 | 895 | 60 | 4.02 |
| Lucien Carignan | 29 | 15 | 10 | 2 | 1712 | 117 | 4.10 |
| **FERRIS STATE UNIVERSITY** | | | | | | | |
| Mike Williams | 25 | 6 | 13 | 5 | 1394 | 84 | 3.62 |
| Marc Felicio | 19 | 6 | 9 | 1 | 1045 | 85 | 4.88 |
| **HARVARD UNIVERSITY** | | | | | | | |
| Michael Francis | 3 | 2 | 0 | 0 | 140 | 2 | 0.86 |
| Allain Roy | 16 | 14 | 2 | 0 | 952 | 40 | 2.46 |
| Chuckie Hughes | 17 | 15 | 1 | 0 | 990 | 46 | 2.79 |
| **UNIVERSITY OF ILLINOIS-CHICAGO** | | | | | | | |
| Gary Mangino | 7 | 2 | 2 | 0 | 250 | 9 | 2.16 |
| Dave DePinto | 38 | 21 | 12 | 4 | 2266 | 137 | 3.63 |
| Damion Holland | 1 | 0 | 0 | 1 | 40 | 4 | 6.00 |
| **LAKE SUPERIOR STATE UNIVERSITY** | | | | | | | |
| Brandon Reed | 3 | 1 | 0 | 1 | 111 | 3 | 1.63 |
| Bruce Hoffort | 44 | 27 | 10 | 5 | 2595 | 117 | 2.71 |
| Mike Greenlay | 2 | 1 | 1 | 0 | 85 | 6 | 4.26 |

| | G. | W. | L. | T. | Min. | Goals | Avg. |
|---|---|---|---|---|---|---|---|
| **UNIVERSITY OF LOWELL** | | | | | | | |
| Peter Harris | 9 | 3 | 3 | 0 | 401 | 29 | 4.34 |
| Mark Richards | 18 | 1 | 12 | 1 | 919 | 83 | 5.42 |
| Ken Stein | 14 | 4 | 9 | 1 | 741 | 74 | 5.99 |
| **UNIVERSITY OF MAINE** | | | | | | | |
| Brendan Macauley | 1 | 0 | 0 | 0 | 1 | 0 | 0.00 |
| Matt Del Guidice | 20 | 16 | 4 | 0 | 1090 | 57 | 3.14 |
| Garth Snow | 5 | 2 | 2 | 0 | 241 | 14 | 3.49 |
| Scott King | 27 | 13 | 8 | 0 | 1394 | 83 | 3.57 |
| **MERRIMACK COLLEGE** | | | | | | | |
| Craig Dal Farra | 8 | 3 | 1 | 0 | 300 | 11 | 2.20 |
| Jim Hrivnak | 22 | 18 | 4 | 0 | 1295 | 52 | 2.41 |
| John Moltenbrey | 11 | 6 | 2 | 0 | 447 | 21 | 2.82 |
| **MIAMI (O.) UNIVERSITY** | | | | | | | |
| Steve McKichan | 21 | 4 | 15 | 0 | 1014 | 85 | 5.02 |
| Mark Michaud | 24 | 7 | 12 | 0 | 1241 | 105 | 5.07 |
| Lee Cannon | 1 | 0 | 0 | 0 | 20 | 4 | 12.00 |
| **UNIVERSITY OF MICHIGAN** | | | | | | | |
| Tim Keough | 13 | 5 | 4 | 2 | 633 | 37 | 3.51 |
| Warren Sharples | 33 | 17 | 11 | 2 | 1887 | 116 | 3.69 |
| **MICHIGAN STATE UNIVERSITY** | | | | | | | |
| Jason Muzzatti | 42 | 32 | 9 | 1 | 2515 | 127 | 3.03 |
| Mike Gilmour | 3 | 1 | 0 | 0 | 74 | 5 | 4.04 |
| Jamie Stewart | 5 | 4 | 0 | 0 | 247 | 17 | 4.13 |
| **MICHIGAN TECHNOLOGICAL UNIV.** | | | | | | | |
| Geoff Sarjeant | 6 | 0 | 3 | 2 | 329 | 22 | 4.01 |
| Damian Rhodes | 37 | 15 | 22 | 0 | 2216 | 163 | 4.41 |
| **UNIVERSITY OF MINNESOTA** | | | | | | | |
| Robb Stauber | 34 | 26 | 8 | 0 | 2024 | 82 | 2.43 |
| Jeff Stolp | 16 | 7 | 2 | 3 | 742 | 45 | 3.64 |
| Al Fritsinger | 5 | 1 | 1 | 0 | 147 | 11 | 4.48 |
| **UNIVERSITY OF MINNESOTA-DULUTH** | | | | | | | |
| Chad Erickson | 15 | 5 | 7 | 1 | 821 | 49 | 3.58 |
| John Hyduke | 28 | 10 | 16 | 1 | 1622 | 103 | 3.81 |
| **UNIVERSITY OF NEW HAMPSHIRE** | | | | | | | |
| Pat Szturm | 12 | 3 | 6 | 0 | 594 | 49 | 4.95 |
| Pat Morrison | 25 | 9 | 16 | 0 | 1456 | 101 | 4.16 |
| **UNIVERSITY OF NORTH DAKOTA** | | | | | | | |
| Tony Couture | 7 | 3 | 2 | 0 | 360 | 19 | 3.17 |
| Chris Dickson | 29 | 15 | 13 | 1 | 1670 | 89 | 3.19 |
| Steve Peters | 9 | 4 | 3 | 0 | 468 | 26 | 3.34 |
| **NORTHEASTERN UNIVERSITY** | | | | | | | |
| Rich Burchill | 30 | 16 | 12 | 2 | 1816 | 118 | 3.90 |
| Tom Cole | 6 | 2 | 4 | 0 | 319 | 30 | 5.64 |
| **NORTHERN MICHIGAN UNIVERSITY** | | | | | | | |
| Willie Mitchell | 8 | 0 | 2 | 0 | 214 | 10 | 2.80 |
| Bill Pye | 43 | 26 | 15 | 2 | 2533 | 133 | 3.15 |
| **OHIO STATE UNIVERSITY** | | | | | | | |
| Hank Horn | 1 | 0 | 0 | 0 | 30 | 2 | 4.03 |
| Todd Fanning | 33 | 9 | 19 | 4 | 1894 | 154 | 4.88 |
| Roger Beedon | 12 | 0 | 7 | 1 | 496 | 54 | 6.54 |
| **PRINCETON UNIVERSITY** | | | | | | | |
| Ron High | 12 | 2 | 5 | 0 | 477 | 34 | 4.27 |
| Mark Salsbury | 23 | 4 | 14 | 1 | 1097 | 98 | 5.38 |
| **PROVIDENCE COLLEGE** | | | | | | | |
| Mark Romaine | 29 | 15 | 10 | 1 | 1536 | 96 | 3.75 |
| Matt Merten | 20 | 7 | 8 | 1 | 1047 | 69 | 3.95 |
| **RENSSELAER POLYTECHNIC INSTITUTE** | | | | | | | |
| Sean Sarbacker | 1 | 0 | 0 | 0 | 5 | 0 | 0.00 |
| Sean Kennedy | 15 | 4 | 8 | 1 | 709 | 41 | 3.47 |
| Steve Duncan | 22 | 8 | 9 | 2 | 1210 | 72 | 3.57 |
| Jamie Bellanca | 4 | 0 | 0 | 0 | 59 | 7 | 7.10 |

| | G. | W. | L. | T. | Min. | Goals | Avg. |
|---|---|---|---|---|---|---|---|
| **ST. LAWRENCE UNIVERSITY** | | | | | | | |
| Les Kuntar | 14 | 11 | 2 | 0 | 786 | 31 | 2.37 |
| Paul Cohen | 25 | 17 | 5 | 0 | 1305 | 60 | 2.76 |
| Mike Mudd | 4 | 1 | 0 | 0 | 73 | 4 | 3.29 |
| **UNIVERSITY OF VERMONT** | G. | W. | L. | T. | Min. | Goals | Avg. |
| Elias Delany | 4 | 2 | 1 | 0 | 203 | 10 | 2.96 |
| Mike Millham | 28 | 16 | 11 | 1 | 1657 | 91 | 3.30 |
| Phil Marrandette | 4 | 2 | 1 | 0 | 179 | 12 | 4.02 |
| **WESTERN MICHIGAN UNIVERSITY** | G. | W. | L. | T. | Min. | Goals | Avg. |
| Al Lariviere | 1 | 0 | 0 | 0 | 15 | 0 | 0.00 |
| Bill Horn | 37 | 12 | 19 | 6 | 2181 | 153 | 4.21 |
| Rob Laurie | 9 | 2 | 4 | 0 | 419 | 41 | 5.87 |
| **UNIVERSITY OF WISCONSIN** | G. | W. | L. | T. | Min. | Goals | Avg. |
| John Lambie | 1 | 0 | 0 | 0 | 2 | 0 | 0.00 |
| Chris Joseph | 38 | 21 | 11 | 5 | 2267 | 94 | 2.49 |
| Duane Derksen | 11 | 4 | 5 | 0 | 561 | 37 | 3.96 |
| **YALE UNIVERSITY** | G. | W. | L. | T. | Min. | Goals | Avg. |
| Mike O'Neill | 25 | 10 | 14 | 1 | 1490 | 93 | 3.74 |
| Ray Letourneau | 7 | 1 | 5 | 0 | 378 | 42 | 6.66 |

# National Hockey League Schedule 1989-90

*Denotes afternoon game.

**THURSDAY, OCTOBER 5**
Pittsburgh at Boston
Montreal at Hartford
Quebec at Buffalo
New York Islanders at Minnesota
New Jersey at Philadelphia
Toronto at Los Angeles
Detroit at Calgary
St. Louis at Chicago
Edmonton at Vancouver

**FRIDAY, OCTOBER 6**
New York Rangers at Winnipeg
Philadelphia at Washington

**SATURDAY, OCTOBER 7**
Boston at Quebec
Minnesota at Hartford
Buffalo at Montreal
New York Islanders at Calgary
Pittsburgh at New Jersey
Chicago at Washington
Toronto at St. Louis
Detroit at Vancouver
Edmonton at Los Angeles

**SUNDAY, OCTOBER 8**
Hartford at Quebec
Minnesota at Buffalo
New York Rangers at Chicago
Philadelphia at Winnipeg
Detroit at Los Angeles

**MONDAY, OCTOBER 9**
Montreal at Boston
*New York Islanders at Vancouver

**TUESDAY, OCTOBER 10**
Calgary at New Jersey
Winnipeg at Pittsburgh

**WEDNESDAY, OCTOBER 11**
Boston at Montreal
Washington at Hartford
Buffalo at Toronto
New York Islanders at Los Angeles
Calgary at New York Rangers
Vancouver at Edmonton

**THURSDAY, OCTOBER 12**
Quebec at Philadelphia
Toronto at Chicago
Winnipeg at Detroit
St. Louis at Minnesota

**FRIDAY, OCTOBER 13**
Boston at Edmonton
Hartford at Buffalo
Montreal at New Jersey
New York Rangers at Washington
Los Angeles at Vancouver

**SATURDAY, OCTOBER 14**
New Jersey at Hartford
Buffalo at Detroit
Montreal at Pittsburgh
Quebec at Minnesota
Philadelphia at New York Islanders
Calgary at Washington
Winnipeg at Toronto
Chicago at St. Louis

**SUNDAY, OCTOBER 15**
*Boston at Vancouver
Pittsburgh at New York Rangers
Calgary at Philadelphia
Detroit at Chicago
Los Angeles at Edmonton

**MONDAY, OCTOBER 16**
Washington at Montreal

**TUESDAY, OCTOBER 17**
Boston at Los Angeles
Calgary at Quebec
Minnesota at New York Islanders
Chicago at New York Rangers
Toronto at Pittsburgh

**WEDNESDAY, OCTOBER 18**
Buffalo at Hartford
Calgary at Montreal
Philadelphia at New Jersey
St. Louis at Pittsburgh
Vancouver at Toronto
Minnesota at Detroit
Winnipeg at Edmonton

**THURSDAY, OCTOBER 19**
Hartford at New York Rangers
Quebec at Chicago
Detroit at St. Louis

**FRIDAY, OCTOBER 20**
Boston at Edmonton
Montreal at Buffalo
New York Islanders at Washington
Vancouver at New Jersey
Chicago at Winnipeg

**SATURDAY, OCTOBER 21**
Boston at Calgary
Detroit at Hartford
Buffalo at Pittsburgh
New Jersey at Montreal
Minnesota at Quebec
Vancouver at New York Islanders
New York Rangers at Philadelphia
Washington at Toronto
Los Angeles at St. Louis

**SUNDAY, OCTOBER 22**
Los Angeles at Chicago
Edmonton at Winnipeg

**MONDAY, OCTOBER 23**
Hartford at Montreal
Vancouver at New York Rangers
New Jersey at Toronto
Washington at Calgary

**TUESDAY, OCTOBER 24**
Edmonton at New York Islanders
St. Louis at Philadelphia
Chicago at Detroit

**WEDNESDAY, OCTOBER 25**
Quebec at Hartford

Buffalo at Minnesota
Edmonton at New York Rangers
Toronto at Pittsburgh
Washington at Winnipeg
Calgary at Los Angeles

**THURSDAY, OCTOBER 26**
Quebec at Boston
Hartford at New Jersey
Montreal at Chicago
Pittsburgh at Detroit
Minnesota at St. Louis

**FRIDAY, OCTOBER 27**
Toronto at Buffalo
N. York Islanders at N. York Rangers
Los Angeles at Winnipeg
Vancouver at Calgary

**SATURDAY, OCTOBER 28**
Hartford at Boston
Pittsburgh at Montreal
Edmonton at Quebec
N. York Rangers at N. York Islanders
Chicago at New Jersey
Philadelphia at Minnesota
Washington at St. Louis
Detroit at Toronto
Calgary at Vancouver

**SUNDAY, OCTOBER 29**
Boston at Buffalo
Edmonton at Montreal
Washington at Chicago
Los Angeles at Winnipeg

**MONDAY, OCTOBER 30**
Philadelphia at New York Rangers

**TUESDAY, OCTOBER 31**
Montreal at New York Islanders
Chicago at Quebec
New Jersey at Vancouver
Los Angeles at Pittsburgh
St. Louis at Washington
Toronto at Minnesota

**WEDNESDAY, NOVEMBER 1**
St. Louis at Hartford
New Jersey at Edmonton
Philadelphia at Detroit
Winnipeg at Calgary

**THURSDAY, NOVEMBER 2**
Los Angeles at Boston
Buffalo at Montreal
Quebec at New York Rangers
New York Islanders at Pittsburgh
Minnesota at Chicago

**FRIDAY, NOVEMBER 3**
Hartford at Detroit
Toronto at Washington
Winnipeg at Vancouver
Calgary at Edmonton

**SATURDAY, NOVEMBER 4**
Buffalo at Boston
Los Angeles at Hartford
New York Rangers at Montreal
*St. Louis at Quebec
Detroit at New York Islanders
New Jersey at Calgary
Philadelphia at Toronto
Pittsburgh at Edmonton
Chicago at Minnesota

**SUNDAY, NOVEMBER 5**
Los Angeles at Buffalo
*Washington at Quebec
New York Islanders at Philadelphia
Pittsburgh at Vancouver
Winnipeg at Chicago

**MONDAY, NOVEMBER 6**
St. Louis at Montreal

Detroit at New York Rangers
Minnesota at Toronto
Edmonton at Calgary

**TUESDAY, NOVEMBER 7**
Washington at New York Islanders

**WEDNESDAY, NOVEMBER 8**
Buffalo at Hartford
Montreal at New York Rangers
Quebec at New Jersey
Vancouver at Winnipeg
Calgary at Los Angeles

**THURSDAY, NOVEMBER 9**
Edmonton at Boston
Montreal at St. Louis
Quebec at New York Islanders
Toronto at Philadelphia
Pittsburgh at Chicago
Detroit at Minnesota

**FRIDAY, NOVEMBER 10**
Boston at Washington
Hartford at Winnipeg
Vancouver at Buffalo

**SATURDAY, NOVEMBER 11**
Montreal at Los Angeles
Vancouver at Quebec
Chicago at New York Islanders
*Philadelphia at New Jersey
Pittsburgh at St. Louis
Edmonton at Washington
Detroit at Toronto
Calgary at Minnesota

**SUNDAY, NOVEMBER 12**
Hartford at Chicago
Edmonton at Buffalo
N. York Islanders at N. York Rangers
New Jersey at Philadelphia
Toronto at Minnesota
Calgary at Winnipeg

**TUESDAY, NOVEMBER 14**
Hartford at Detroit
Winnipeg at Quebec
Philadelphia at New York Islanders
New York Rangers at Pittsburgh
Washington at Vancouver
Los Angeles at Calgary

**WEDNESDAY, NOVEMBER 15**
Boston at Hartford
Winnipeg at Montreal
Minnesota at New Jersey
St. Louis at Toronto
Los Angeles at Edmonton

**THURSDAY, NOVEMBER 16**
Montreal at Boston
Buffalo at Calgary
Quebec at Pittsburgh
Toronto at New York Islanders
Minnesota at Philadelphia
St. Louis at Detroit
Chicago at Vancouver

**FRIDAY, NOVEMBER 17**
Buffalo at Edmonton
New York Rangers at New Jersey

**SATURDAY, NOVEMBER 18**
New Jersey at Boston
New York Rangers at Hartford
Toronto at Montreal
Detroit at Quebec
New York Islanders at Pittsburgh
*Winnipeg at Philadelphia
Washington at Los Angeles
Chicago at Calgary
St. Louis at Minnesota

**SUNDAY, NOVEMBER 19**
Buffalo at Vancouver
Chicago at Edmonton

**MONDAY, NOVEMBER 20**
Calgary at Montreal
Winnipeg at New York Rangers

**TUESDAY, NOVEMBER 21**
Boston at Detroit
Calgary at Quebec
Winnipeg at New York Islanders
Minnesota at St. Louis
Vancouver at Edmonton

**WEDNESDAY, NOVEMBER 22**
Quebec at Hartford
New York Rangers at Buffalo
Montreal at Philadelphia
New York Islanders at Washington
New Jersey at Pittsburgh
Toronto at Minnesota
Chicago at Los Angeles

**THURSDAY, NOVEMBER 23**
Toronto at Boston
St. Louis at Winnipeg

**FRIDAY, NOVEMBER 24**
New Jersey at Minnesota
*Edmonton at Philadelphia
Pittsburgh at Washington
Calgary at Detroit

**SATURDAY, NOVEMBER 25**
Boston at Montreal
Philadelphia at Hartford
Buffalo at Quebec
Edmonton at New York Islanders
New York Rangers at Toronto
New Jersey at Winnipeg
Washington at Pittsburgh
Calgary at St. Louis
Vancouver at Los Angeles

**SUNDAY, NOVEMBER 26**
Hartford at Buffalo
Quebec at New York Rangers
Chicago at Minnesota
Los Angeles at Vancouver

**MONDAY, NOVEMBER 27**
Edmonton at Detroit

**TUESDAY, NOVEMBER 28**
Boston at St. Louis
Buffalo at Hartford
New York Islanders at New Jersey
Philadelphia at Pittsburgh

**WEDNESDAY, NOVEMBER 29**
Quebec at Montreal
New York Rangers at Winnipeg
Washington at Detroit
Toronto at Vancouver

**THURSDAY, NOVEMBER 30**
Buffalo at Boston
Hartford at St. Louis
Montreal at Quebec
New York Islanders at Chicago
Pittsburgh at Philadelphia
Minnesota at Calgary
Edmonton at Los Angeles

**FRIDAY, DECEMBER 1**
New Jersey at Buffalo
New York Rangers at Vancouver
Philadelphia at Washington
Detroit at Winnipeg

**SATURDAY, DECEMBER 2**
St. Louis at Boston
Hartford at Montreal
Pittsburgh at Quebec
New York Islanders at Winnipeg
New York Rangers at Los Angeles
Washington at New Jersey
Toronto at Calgary
Minnesota at Edmonton

**SUNDAY, DECEMBER 3**
Boston at Philadelphia
St. Louis at Buffalo
Toronto at Edmonton
Detroit at Chicago
Minnesota at Vancouver

**TUESDAY, DECEMBER 5**
Boston at Quebec
Buffalo at New York Islanders
Washington at Philadelphia
St. Louis at Detroit

**WEDNESDAY, DECEMBER 6**
New York Islanders at Hartford
Montreal at Minnesota
New Jersey at New York Rangers
Washington at Pittsburgh
Toronto at Chicago
Winnipeg at Calgary
Vancouver at Los Angeles

**THURSDAY, DECEMBER 7**
Hartford at Boston
Buffalo at Philadelphia
Toronto at St. Louis

**FRIDAY, DECEMBER 8**
Montreal at Winnipeg
Pittsburgh at New Jersey
Minnesota at Detroit
Los Angeles at Edmonton

**SATURDAY, DECEMBER 9**
*Washington at Boston
New Jersey at Hartford
Montreal at Toronto
*Philadelphia at Quebec
N. York Rangers at N. York Islanders
Chicago at Pittsburgh
Detroit at Minnesota
Vancouver at St. Louis

**SUNDAY, DECEMBER 10**
Washington at Buffalo
*Los Angeles at Quebec
Philadelphia at New York Rangers
Vancouver at Chicago
*Calgary at Winnipeg

**MONDAY, DECEMBER 11**
Los Angeles at Montreal
St. Louis at Toronto
Calgary at Edmonton

**TUESDAY, DECEMBER 12**
Boston at Pittsburgh
New Jersey at New York Islanders
Vancouver at Minnesota

**WEDNESDAY, DECEMBER 13**
Boston at Buffalo
Los Angeles at Hartford
Chicago at Montreal
Quebec at Edmonton
New York Islanders at New Jersey
St. Louis at New York Rangers
Toronto at Detroit
Vancouver at Winnipeg

**THURSDAY, DECEMBER 14**
Hartford at Philadelphia
Quebec at Calgary
Pittsburgh at Minnesota

**FRIDAY, DECEMBER 15**
New York Islanders at Washington
Los Angeles at New Jersey
Chicago at Detroit
Winnipeg at Vancouver

**SATURDAY, DECEMBER 16**
*Buffalo at Boston
Washington at Hartford
Detroit at Montreal
N. York Rangers at N. York Islanders

Los Angeles at Philadelphia
Pittsburgh at Calgary
Minnesota at Toronto
Edmonton at St. Louis

**SUNDAY, DECEMBER 17**
Boston at New Jersey
Philadelphia at Buffalo
Montreal at New York Rangers
Quebec at Vancouver
Edmonton at Chicago

**MONDAY, DECEMBER 18**
St. Louis at Toronto

**TUESDAY, DECEMBER 19**
Hartford at Pittsburgh
New Jersey at New York Islanders
Washington at Philadelphia
Edmonton at Minnesota
Winnipeg at Los Angeles
Calgary at Vancouver

**WEDNESDAY, DECEMBER 20**
Boston at Hartford
Buffalo at New York Rangers
Toronto at Detroit
St. Louis at Chicago
Vancouver at Calgary

**THURSDAY, DECEMBER 21**
Minnesota at Boston
Quebec at Los Angeles
Washington at Pittsburgh
Winnipeg at Edmonton

**FRIDAY, DECEMBER 22**
Montreal at Buffalo
New Jersey at Philadelphia
Toronto at Chicago

**SATURDAY, DECEMBER 23**
*Detroit at Boston
Minnesota at Hartford
Buffalo at Quebec
Philadelphia at Montreal
*Pittsburgh at New York Islanders
New York Rangers at Washington
St. Louis at New Jersey
Chicago at Toronto
Calgary at Edmonton
Vancouver at Los Angeles

**TUESDAY, DECEMBER 26**
Toronto at Boston
Hartford at Quebec
Detroit at Buffalo
New Jersey at New York Rangers
Pittsburgh at Washington
Chicago at St. Louis
Minnesota at Winnipeg

**WEDNESDAY, DECEMBER 27**
Montreal at Vancouver
New York Rangers at Pittsburgh
Washington at New Jersey
Philadelphia at Edmonton
Detroit at Toronto
Calgary at Los Angeles

**THURSDAY, DECEMBER 28**
St. Louis at New York Islanders
Minnesota at Chicago

**FRIDAY, DECEMBER 29**
Boston at Buffalo
Montreal at Edmonton
New York Rangers at New Jersey
Detroit at Washington
Winnipeg at Calgary

**SATURDAY, DECEMBER 30**
Boston at Toronto
Hartford at Chicago
Montreal at Calgary
New York Islanders at Quebec
Philadelphia at Los Angeles

Minnesota at St. Louis

**SUNDAY, DECEMBER 31**
New York Islanders at Buffalo
*Pittsburgh at New York Rangers
New Jersey at Detroit
Philadelphia at Vancouver
St. Louis at Minnesota
*Edmonton at Winnipeg

**MONDAY, JANUARY 1**
*Los Angeles at Washington

**TUESDAY, JANUARY 2**
Boston at Pittsburgh
Buffalo at New Jersey
Los Angeles at New York Islanders
Philadelphia at Calgary
Vancouver at Detroit
Edmonton at St. Louis

**WEDNESDAY, JANUARY 3**
Winnipeg at Hartford
Quebec at Toronto
Washington at New York Rangers
Edmonton at Chicago

**THURSDAY, JANUARY 4**
Winnipeg at Boston
Quebec at Detroit
New York Rangers at Minnesota
Los Angeles at New Jersey
Philadelphia at St. Louis
Vancouver at Pittsburgh

**FRIDAY, JANUARY 5**
Hartford at Calgary
Vancouver at Washington

**SATURDAY, JANUARY 6**
Washington at Boston
Hartford at Edmonton
Buffalo at Montreal
Quebec at New York Islanders
New York Rangers at St. Louis
Philadelphia at Chicago
Winnipeg at Pittsburgh
Los Angeles at Toronto
Detroit at Minnesota

**SUNDAY, JANUARY 7**
Boston at Buffalo
Vancouver at Montreal
Calgary at Edmonton

**MONDAY, JANUARY 8**
Pittsburgh at New York Rangers
Winnipeg at New Jersey
Washington at Toronto

**TUESDAY, JANUARY 9**
Montreal at Quebec
Minnesota at Detroit
St. Louis at Los Angeles
Edmonton at Calgary

**WEDNESDAY, JANUARY 10**
Hartford at Vancouver
New York Islanders at Toronto
Chicago at New York Rangers
Pittsburgh at New Jersey
Washington at Winnipeg

**THURSDAY, JANUARY 11**
Quebec at Boston
Buffalo at Calgary
New York Islanders at Minnesota
Chicago at Philadelphia
Edmonton at Los Angeles

**FRIDAY, JANUARY 12**
Montreal at New Jersey
Pittsburgh at Washington
Detroit at Winnipeg
St. Louis at Vancouver

**SATURDAY, JANUARY 13**
*New York Rangers at Boston

Hartford at Los Angeles
Buffalo at Vancouver
Philadelphia at Montreal
New Jersey at Quebec
Washington at New York Islanders
Calgary at Toronto
Detroit at Minnesota

**SUNDAY, JANUARY 14**
Philadelphia at New York Rangers
Calgary at Chicago
St. Louis at Winnipeg

**MONDAY, JANUARY 15**
Hartford at Boston
Minnesota at Montreal
Chicago at Toronto

**TUESDAY, JANUARY 16**
Buffalo at Los Angeles
Quebec at Winnipeg
Vancouver at New York Islanders
New Jersey at Washington
Philadelphia at Pittsburgh
Detroit at Edmonton
Calgary at St. Louis

**WEDNESDAY, JANUARY 17**
Boston at Hartford
New York Islanders at Montreal
Minnesota at Chicago
Winnipeg at Edmonton

**THURSDAY, JANUARY 18**
Calgary at Boston
Quebec at Minnesota
New York Rangers at Pittsburgh
Vancouver at Philadelphia
Toronto at St. Louis
Detroit at Los Angeles

**FRIDAY, JANUARY 19**
Calgary at Hartford
Washington at Buffalo
New York Islanders at Winnipeg
Vancouver at Chicago

**SUNDAY, JANUARY 21**
All-Star Game at Pittsburgh

**TUESDAY, JANUARY 23**
Boston at Quebec
New York Islanders at Hartford
Buffalo at Philadelphia
New York Rangers at Edmonton
New Jersey at Pittsburgh
Winnipeg at Washington
St. Louis at Detroit
Los Angeles at Vancouver

**WEDNESDAY, JANUARY 24**
Buffalo at Chicago
Quebec at Montreal
Washington at New Jersey
Minnesota at Toronto

**THURSDAY, JANUARY 25**
New York Islanders at Boston
Hartford at St. Louis
New York Rangers at Calgary
Winnipeg at Philadelphia
Pittsburgh at Detroit
Los Angeles at Edmonton

**FRIDAY, JANUARY 26**
Chicago at Buffalo
Montreal at Washington
Toronto at New Jersey
Minnesota at Vancouver

**SATURDAY, JANUARY 27**
*Philadelphia at Boston
Chicago at Hartford
Montreal at Toronto
Detroit at Quebec
*Pittsburgh at New York Islanders

New York Rangers at Los Angeles
Winnipeg at St. Louis
Minnesota at Calgary
Vancouver at Edmonton

**SUNDAY, JANUARY 28**
*Pittsburgh at Buffalo
*New Jersey at New York Islanders
*Philadelphia at Washington

**MONDAY, JANUARY 29**
Boston at Montreal
Winnipeg at Minnesota

**TUESDAY, JANUARY 30**
Edmonton at Hartford
Buffalo at Quebec
St. Louis at New York Islanders
New Jersey at Los Angeles
Philadelphia at Pittsburgh
Calgary at Vancouver

**WEDNESDAY, JANUARY 31**
Quebec at Buffalo
St. Louis at New York Rangers
Washington at Minnesota
Toronto at Winnipeg
Edmonton at Detroit

**THURSDAY, FEBRUARY 1**
Montreal at Boston
Hartford at Philadelphia
Chicago at Los Angeles
Vancouver at Calgary

**FRIDAY, FEBRUARY 2**
Washington at New York Islanders
Edmonton at Pittsburgh
Toronto at Detroit
Vancouver at Winnipeg

**SATURDAY, FEBRUARY 3**
*New York Rangers at Boston
*Hartford at Quebec
Buffalo at Montreal
*Minnesota at Philadelphia
Pittsburgh at Toronto
Detroit at St. Louis
Calgary at Los Angeles

**SUNDAY, FEBRUARY 4**
*Boston at Quebec
Hartford at Montreal
New York Islanders at Buffalo
*Minnesota at New York Rangers
New Jersey at Vancouver
*Edmonton at Washington
Chicago at Winnipeg

**TUESDAY, FEBRUARY 6**
Boston at Detroit
Quebec at Washington
New York Islanders at Pittsburgh
Edmonton at New Jersey
Toronto at St. Louis
Winnipeg at Vancouver
Los Angeles at Calgary

**WEDNESDAY, FEBRUARY 7**
Hartford at Minnesota
Montreal at Buffalo
Edmonton at New York Rangers
St. Louis at Toronto

**THURSDAY, FEBRUARY 8**
Quebec at Boston
New York Islanders at Philadelphia
Washington at Pittsburgh
Chicago at Detroit
Winnipeg at Los Angeles

**FRIDAY, FEBRUARY 9**
Vancouver at Hartford
New York Rangers at Buffalo
New Jersey at Washington

**SATURDAY, FEBRUARY 10**
*New York Islanders at Boston

Toronto at Hartford
Quebec at Montreal
New Jersey at St. Louis
Los Angeles at Pittsburgh
*Calgary at Detroit
*Chicago at Minnesota

**SUNDAY, FEBRUARY 11**
*Vancouver at Boston
Buffalo at St. Louis
*Calgary at New York Rangers
Pittsburgh at Philadelphia
*Minnesota at Washington
Winnipeg at Edmonton

**MONDAY, FEBRUARY 12**
Detroit at New Jersey
Los Angeles at Toronto

**TUESDAY, FEBRUARY 13**
Buffalo at Chicago
Vancouver at Quebec
Calgary at New York Islanders
New York Rangers at Philadelphia
St. Louis at Minnesota

**WEDNESDAY, FEBRUARY 14**
Boston at Winnipeg
Hartford at Toronto
Vancouver at Montreal
Pittsburgh at New York Rangers
Washington at Edmonton
Los Angeles at Detroit

**THURSDAY, FEBRUARY 15**
Quebec at St. Louis
Toronto at Philadelphia
Calgary at Chicago
Los Angeles at Minnesota

**FRIDAY, FEBRUARY 16**
Montreal at Buffalo
New York Rangers at New Jersey
Philadelphia at Detroit
Pittsburgh at Winnipeg
Edmonton at Vancouver

**SATURDAY, FEBRUARY 17**
Hartford at Montreal
Quebec at Los Angeles
*Chicago at New York Islanders
New Jersey at Toronto
Detroit at St. Louis

**SUNDAY, FEBRUARY 18**
Boston at Vancouver
Hartford at Buffalo
*New York Islanders at Philadelphia
*Pittsburgh at Chicago
Minnesota at Edmonton
*Calgary at Winnipeg

**MONDAY, FEBRUARY 19**
Montreal at Detroit
*New Jersey at New York Rangers
*Washington at Los Angeles

**TUESDAY, FEBRUARY 20**
Boston at Calgary
Buffalo at Winnipeg
Philadelphia at Pittsburgh
Chicago at St. Louis
Edmonton at Vancouver

**WEDNESDAY, FEBRUARY 21**
Quebec at Hartford
Buffalo at Edmonton
New York Rangers at Detroit
Minnesota at Los Angeles

**THURSDAY, FEBRUARY 22**
Boston at Chicago
Montreal at Quebec
New York Islanders at Pittsburgh
Winnipeg at New Jersey
Philadelphia at St. Louis
Toronto at Calgary

**FRIDAY, FEBRUARY 23**
Hartford at Buffalo
New York Rangers at Washington
Toronto at Edmonton

**SATURDAY, FEBRUARY 24**
Boston at Minnesota
Winnipeg at Hartford
Pittsburgh at Montreal
St. Louis at Quebec
*Detroit at New York Islanders
*Chicago at New Jersey
Vancouver at Los Angeles

**SUNDAY, FEBRUARY 25**
Winnipeg at Buffalo
St. Louis at Montreal
*New Jersey at New York Islanders
*Philadelphia at Chicago
*Detroit at Washington
Edmonton at Calgary

**MONDAY, FEBRUARY 26**
Boston at New York Rangers
Pittsburgh at Quebec
Toronto at Vancouver

**TUESDAY, FEBRUARY 27**
Buffalo at St. Louis
Chicago at Washington
Winnipeg at Minnesota

**WEDNESDAY, FEBRUARY 28**
Montreal at Hartford
Quebec at Toronto
New York Islanders at Detroit
Washington at New York Rangers
New Jersey at Pittsburgh
Philadelphia at Vancouver
Edmonton at Los Angeles

**THURSDAY, MARCH 1**
Montreal at Boston
Philadelphia at Calgary
St. Louis at Chicago

**FRIDAY, MARCH 2**
Hartford at Washington
N. York Islanders at N. York Rangers
Pittsburgh at New Jersey
Toronto at Detroit
Los Angeles at Winnipeg

**SATURDAY, MARCH 3**
*Chicago at Boston
New York Rangers at Hartford
Buffalo at Quebec
Montreal at Minnesota
New York Islanders at St. Louis
Philadelphia at Edmonton
Detroit at Toronto
Vancouver at Calgary

**SUNDAY, MARCH 4**
*Boston at Chicago
Quebec at Buffalo
*New Jersey at Washington
Minnesota at Pittsburgh
*Los Angeles at Winnipeg
Vancouver at Edmonton

**MONDAY, MARCH 5**
Detroit at New York Rangers
Los Angeles at Calgary

**TUESDAY, MARCH 6**
Boston at Philadelphia
Hartford at New York Islanders
Buffalo at Washington
St. Louis at New Jersey
Pittsburgh at Edmonton

**WEDNESDAY, MARCH 7**
Montreal at Los Angeles
Quebec at Winnipeg
Pittsburgh at Calgary
Chicago at Minnesota

**THURSDAY, MARCH 8**
Buffalo at Boston
Toronto at Hartford
New York Islanders at New Jersey
New York Rangers at Philadelphia
St. Louis at Detroit

**FRIDAY, MARCH 9**
Quebec at Washington
Edmonton at Winnipeg
Calgary at Vancouver

**SATURDAY, MARCH 10**
Boston at New York Islanders
Buffalo at Hartford
Detroit at Montreal
Quebec at New Jersey
*New York Rangers at Minnesota
Washington at Philadelphia
*Pittsburgh at Los Angeles
Edmonton at Toronto
Chicago at St. Louis

**SUNDAY, MARCH 11**
Boston at Hartford
*Pittsburgh at Vancouver
St. Louis at Chicago
*Calgary at Winnipeg

**MONDAY, MARCH 12**
Los Angeles at New York Rangers
Minnesota at Toronto
Winnipeg at Calgary

**TUESDAY, MARCH 13**
Hartford at Vancouver
Montreal at New York Islanders
Edmonton at Quebec
New Jersey at Minnesota
St. Louis at Washington
Detroit at Chicago

**WEDNESDAY, MARCH 14**
Los Angeles at Buffalo
Edmonton at Montreal
New York Rangers at Toronto

**THURSDAY, MARCH 15**
Winnipeg at Boston
Chicago at Quebec
New York Islanders at Philadelphia
New Jersey at Calgary
Detroit at Pittsburgh
Vancouver at St. Louis

**FRIDAY, MARCH 16**
Toronto at Buffalo

**SATURDAY, MARCH 17**
*Los Angeles at Boston
Hartford at Calgary
Chicago at Montreal
Philadelphia at Quebec
*N. York Rangers at N. York Islanders
New Jersey at Edmonton
*Minnesota at Pittsburgh
Vancouver at Washington
Winnipeg at Toronto
Detroit at St. Louis

**SUNDAY, MARCH 18**
Hartford at Edmonton
Winnipeg at Buffalo
Quebec at Montreal
*Pittsburgh at New York Islanders
Vancouver at New York Rangers
Los Angeles at Philadelphia
Washington at Minnesota

**MONDAY, MARCH 19**
Chicago at Toronto
St. Louis at Calgary

**TUESDAY, MARCH 20**
New York Islanders at Washington
Philadelphia at New Jersey
Vancouver at Detroit

Los Angeles at Minnesota

**WEDNESDAY, MARCH 21**
Quebec at Hartford
Calgary at Buffalo
Montreal at Winnipeg
Toronto at New York Rangers
St. Louis at Edmonton

**THURSDAY, MARCH 22**
Quebec at Boston
New York Islanders at Los Angeles
New Jersey at Chicago
Pittsburgh at Philadelphia
Minnesota at Detroit

**FRIDAY, MARCH 23**
Montreal at Washington
Vancouver at Winnipeg

**SATURDAY, MARCH 24**
*Minnesota at Boston
Montreal at Hartford
Toronto at Quebec
New York Islanders at Edmonton
*New Jersey at Philadelphia
*Calgary at Pittsburgh
*Chicago at Detroit
St. Louis at Los Angeles

**SUNDAY, MARCH 25**
Pittsburgh at Hartford
*New Jersey at Buffalo
*Philadelphia at New York Rangers
*Calgary at Washington
*Detroit at Chicago
Winnipeg at Vancouver

**MONDAY, MARCH 26**
Toronto at Minnesota

**TUESDAY, MARCH 27**
Boston at St. Louis
Hartford at Pittsburgh
Buffalo at Detroit
New York Rangers at Quebec
Calgary at New York Islanders
Washington at New Jersey
Winnipeg at Los Angeles
Edmonton at Vancouver

**WEDNESDAY, MARCH 28**
New York Islanders at Toronto

**THURSDAY, MARCH 29**
Hartford at Boston
Minnesota at Buffalo
Montreal at Quebec
New York Rangers at New Jersey
Washington at Philadelphia
Pittsburgh at St. Louis
Toronto at Chicago
Winnipeg at Los Angeles

**FRIDAY, MARCH 30**
Edmonton at Calgary

**SATURDAY, MARCH 31**
Boston at Montreal
Hartford at Quebec
Buffalo at Pittsburgh
Philadelphia at New York Islanders
New York Rangers at Washington
*Detroit at New Jersey
Chicago at Toronto
Minnesota at St. Louis
Los Angeles at Vancouver

**SUNDAY, APRIL 1**
New Jersey at Boston
Montreal at Hartford
Quebec at Buffalo
Washington at New York Rangers
Detroit at Philadelphia
Minnesota at Chicago
*Edmonton at Winnipeg
Los Angeles at Calgary